Here's What You Get on the C

The CD included with the *CCNP: Advanced Cisco Router Configu...*   ...ble
programs and information to help you prepare for the ACRC exam. You ...   ...ugh
a user-friendly graphical interface by running the CLICKME.EXE file located in the root directory of the CD.

Edge Test ACRC Exam Prep Program

Test your knowledge with the Edge Test ACRC Exam Preparation program.
The version included on the CD was produced exclusively for Sybex by EdgeTek.
Click on the Instructions button on the opening screen for a detailed explanation of
how to navigate this advanced testing program.

Visio Network Professional 5 & Network Equipment

Visio® Professional and Visio Network Equipment allow you to tap into a library of
more than 13,000 exact-replica, vendor-specific network device shapes. Create proposals, design and document LANs, WANs, wiring closets, whatever you need. Link
diagrams with databases to keep your graphics and data in synch.

EtherPeek & TokenPeek

Produced by The AG Group, Inc., EtherPeek and TokenPeek are network
and protocol analysis tools designed to help you troubleshoot, optimize,
plan and configure networks. Also from The AG Group, we've included
AG NetTools and NetSense. NetTools is a shareware IP utility suite available
for Macintosh, Windows 95/98 and NT 4. NetSense is a powerful software
application that performs peer-to-peer packet transaction analysis of network
protocols on Ethernet or Token Ring trace files.

When installing EtherPeek and TokenPeek, you will be asked to enter a serial number.
The serial number for EtherPeek is 2B000-AB13G-021LZ. The serial number for
TokenPeek is 2B000-A41AG-Z41L2.

IPCalc 2

IPCalc 2 is a TCP/IP address calculator designed to help you better understand the concepts behind IP addressing. It visually illustrates the bit patterns of an IP address and their
behavior as you move from one addressing scheme to another. IPCalc 2 will run on
Windows 95/98 or NT. The copy of IPCalc on the CD is an evaluation copy; it is designed
to run for ten days after installation or 30 times.

The files included on this CD were created and tested for Windows 95/98 and
Windows NT 4 systems. You may encounter difficulties if you try to run them on
other operating systems.

CCNP: Advanced Cisco Router Configuration Study Guide

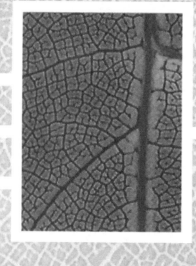

CCNP: Advanced Cisco® Router Configuration Study Guide

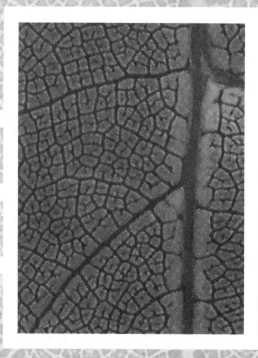

Todd Lammle
Kevin Hales
Donald Porter

San Francisco • Paris • Düsseldorf • Soest

Associate Publisher: Guy Hart-Davis
Contracts and Licensing Manager: Kristine O'Callaghan
Acquisitions & Developmental Editor: Neil Edde
Editor: Ronn Jost
Project Editor: Jeremy Crawford
Technical Editors: John Chong, Brian Horakh
Book Designer: Bill Gibson
Graphic Illustrator: Tony Jonick
Electronic Publishing Specialists: Nila Nichols, Robin Kibby
Production Coordinator: Susan Berge
Indexer: Ted Laux
Companion CD: Ginger Warner
Cover Designer: Archer Design
Cover Photographer: The Image Bank

Library of Congress Card Number: 98-88911
ISBN: 0-7821-2403-8

Manufactured in the United States of America

10 9 8 7 6 5 4 3 2 1

To my son, Joshua, who helps me remember what is really important in life:
That you must take time out each day for playtime.
—Todd Lammle

For Claudia and Christopher:

    My inspiration and sanctuary.

    La fuerza del amor.

—Kevin Hales

For my grandfather, Max Willis, who taught me patience and perseverance in
woodworking and everything else…

—Donald Porter

Acknowledgments

I would personally like to acknowledge the great support I received from Neil Edde and James Chellis. Without their constant guidance and wisdom, these books would have never been written. I also would like to thank Don Porter for helping me put everything together, and for introducing me to Kevin Hales and Scott Richardson.

—Todd Lammle

First of all, I would like to thank Don Porter, the wearer of the "Blue Robe," for recruiting me for this project.

I would also like to thank Todd and Monica Lammle for this opportunity and for working with me to make sure this book would be useful and effective for the reader.

Thanks should also go to my managers, Mike Cleary and Bill Kelleher. They were very supportive and accommodating in allowing me to work on this project. Thanks to Ross Nakamura for being my sounding board.

—Kevin Hales

Thanks to my coauthors, Todd and Kevin, for their help and patience. It always seemed that my work was the last finished. My thanks also to my coworkers at the university: Mike, Bill, and Ross. They truly set the standard in this field. Thanks to Travis, Scott, Jeff, Shawn, Steve, Andy, Rick, Ralph, and everyone else who has gone out of their way to put information into my head. Finally, thanks to Brian for introducing me to the Internet.

—Donald Porter

Let us not forget all the wonderful editors: Ronn Jost, the copy editor; Jeremy Crawford, the project editor; and John Chong, the technical editor, who went tirelessly over and over the material.

Last in the editorial chain, but certainly not the least, is Brian Horakh. He did a last editorial review not only to check for technical errors, but also to ensure that this book meets the CCNP test objectives so that you, the reader, can pass the exam the first time. Be sure to check out his Web site, www .networkstudyguides.com, for the latest in Cisco certification news and updates.

We gratefully acknowledge the hard work of the Sybex production team: Nila Nichols and Robin Kibby, electronic publishing specialists, and Susan Berge, production coordinator.

We'd also like to thank the many terrific people who helped put the CD together:

Jerry Camel for writing and providing the best IP calculator program you can find. More information can be found at www.progression-inc.com.

James Chellis and Matt for creating and letting us use the EdgeTest engine. There are more CCNA/CCNP testing questions available. Check www.lammle.com for updates on Cisco videos and testing questions regarding the Cisco certifications. You can also call 1-800-800-1NET (1638) for more information.

Janice Spampinato from AG Group. Thanks to AG Group, we were able to include network traces throughout this book with one of the best network analyzers on the market: EtherPeek.

Christy Delger from Visio Corporation provided an awesome product for the CD that can easily help you document your network plus more. Most of the figures in this book were produced in full or in part from Visio.

—The Authors

Contents at a Glance

Table of Contents

Introduction

This book is intended to help you continue on your exciting new path toward obtaining your CCNP and CCIE certification. Before reading this book, it is important to have at least read the Sybex *CCNA Study Guide*. You can take the tests in any order, but the CCNA exam should probably be your first test.

The new Cisco certifications reach beyond the popular certifications, such as the MCSE and CNE, to provide you with an indispensable factor in understanding today's network—insight into the Cisco world of internetworking.

Cisco—A Brief History

A lot of readers may already be familiar with Cisco and what they do. However, those of you who are new to the field, just coming in fresh from your MCSE, or maybe even with 10 or more years in the field wishing to brush up on the new technology may appreciate a little background on Cisco.

In the early 1980s, a married couple that worked in different computer departments at Stanford University started up cisco Systems (notice the small *c*). Their names are Len and Sandy Bosack. They were having trouble getting their individual systems to communicate (like many married people), so in their living room they created a gateway server to make it easier for their disparate computers in two different departments to communicate using the IP protocol.

In 1984, cisco Systems was founded with a small commercial gateway server product that changed networking forever. Some people think the name was intended to be San Francisco Systems, but the paper got ripped on the way to the incorporation lawyers—who knows?—but in 1992, the company name was changed to Cisco Systems, Inc.

The first product they marketed was called the Advanced Gateway Server (AGS). Then came the Mid-Range Gateway Server (MGS), the Compact Gateway Server (CGS), the Integrated Gateway Server (IGS), and the AGS+. Cisco calls these "the old alphabet soup products."

Then, in 1993, Cisco came out with the amazing 4000 router, and then the even more amazing 7000, 2000, and 3000 series routers. These are still around and evolving (almost daily it seems).

Cisco Systems has since become an unrivaled worldwide leader in networking for the Internet. Its networking solutions can easily connect users working from diverse devices on disparate networks. Cisco products make it simple for people to access and transfer information without regard to differences in time, place, or platform.

Cisco Systems' big picture is that it provides end-to-end networking solutions that customers can use to build an efficient, unified information infrastructure of their own or to connect to someone else's—an important piece in the Internet/networking-industry puzzle, because a common architecture that delivers consistent network services to all users is now a functional imperative. Because Cisco Systems offers such a broad range of networking and Internet services and capabilities, users needing regular access to their local network or the Internet can do so unhindered, making Cisco's wares indispensable.

Cisco answers this need with a wide range of hardware products used to form information networks using the Cisco Internetworking Operating System (IOS) software. This software provides network services, paving the way for networked technical support and professional services for maintaining and optimizing all network operations.

Along with the Cisco IOS, one of the services Cisco has created to help support the vast amount of hardware they have engineered is the Cisco Certified Internetworking Expert (CCIE) program, designed specifically to equip people to effectively manage the vast quantity of installed Cisco networks. Their business plan is simple: If you want sell more Cisco equipment and have more Cisco networks installed, ensure that the networks you've installed run properly.

However, having a fabulous product line isn't all it takes to guarantee the huge success that Cisco enjoys—lots of companies with great products are now defunct. If you have complicated products designed to solve complicated problems, you need knowledgeable people who are fully capable of installing, managing, and troubleshooting them. That part isn't easy, so Cisco began the CCIE program to equip people in supporting these complicated networks. This program, known colloquially as the Doctorate of Networking, has also been very successful, primarily due to its extreme difficulty. Cisco continuously monitors the program, changing it as they see fit to make sure it remains pertinent and accurately reflects the demands of today's internetworking business environments.

Building upon the highly successful CCIE program, Cisco Career Certifications permit you to become certified at various levels of technical proficiency, spanning the disciplines of network design and support. So whether you're beginning a career, changing careers, securing your present position, or seeking to refine and promote your position, this is the book for you!

Cisco's Network Support Certifications

Cisco has created new certifications that will help you get the coveted CCIE as well as aid prospective employers in measuring skill levels. Before these new certifications, you took only one test and were then faced with the lab, which made it difficult to succeed. With these new certifications that add a better approach to preparing for that almighty lab, Cisco has opened doors that few were allowed through before. So what are these new certifications, and how do they help you get your CCIE?

Cisco Certified Network Associate (CCNA)

The CCNA certification is the first certification in the new line of Cisco certifications and is a precursor to all current Cisco certifications. With the new certification programs, Cisco has created a type of stepping-stone approach to CCIE certification. Now you can become a Cisco Certified Network Associate for the meager cost of the Sybex *CCNA Study Guide* book plus $100 for the test. And you don't have to stop there—you can choose to continue with your studies and achieve a higher certification called the Cisco Certified Network Professional (CCNP). Someone with a CCNP has all the skills and knowledge they need to attempt the CCIE lab. However, since no textbook can take the place of practical experience, we'll discuss what else you need to be ready for the CCIE lab shortly.

Why Become a CCNA?   Cisco has created the certification process, not unlike Microsoft or Novell, to give administrators a set of skills, and to equip prospective employers with a way to measure skills or match certain criteria. Becoming a CCNA can be the initial step of a successful journey toward a new, highly rewarding, and sustainable career.

The CCNA program was not only created to provide a solid introduction to the Cisco Internetworking Operating System (IOS) and Cisco hardware, but to internetworking in general, making it helpful to you in areas not exclusively Cisco's. At this point in the certification process, it's not unrealistic to imagine that future network managers—even those without Cisco equipment—could easily require Cisco certifications of their job applicants.

If you make it through the CCNA still interested in Cisco and internetworking, you're headed down a certain path to success.

To meet the CCNA certification skill level, you must be able to understand or do the following:

- Install, configure, and operate simple-routed LAN, routed WAN, and switched LAN and LANE networks

- Understand and be able to configure IP, IGRP, IPX, Serial, AppleTalk, Frame Relay, IP RIP, VLANs, IPX RIP, Ethernet, and access lists

- Install and/or configure a network

- Optimize WAN through Internet-access solutions that reduce bandwidth and WAN costs using features such as filtering with access lists, bandwidth on demand (BOD), and dial-on-demand routing (DDR)

- Provide remote access by integrating dial-up connectivity with traditional, remote LAN-to-LAN access as well as supporting the higher levels of performance required for new applications such as Internet commerce, multimedia, etc.

How Do You Become a CCNA?   The first step is to pass one "little" test, and poof—you're a CCNA! (Don't you wish it were that easy?) True, it's just one test, but you still have to possess enough knowledge to understand (and read between the lines—trust us) what the test writers are saying.

We can't say this enough—it's critical that you have some hands-on experience with Cisco routers. If you can get your hands on some 2500 routers, you're set. But if you can't, we've worked hard to provide hundreds of configuration examples throughout the Sybex *CCNA Study Guide* book to help network administrators (or people who want to become network administrators) learn what they need to know to pass the CCNA exam.

One way to get the hands-on router experience you'll need in the real world is to attend one of the seminars offered by Globalnet System Solutions, Inc. (www.lammle.com). Cyberstate University also is providing hands-on Cisco router courses over the Internet using the Sybex *Cisco Certification* series books. Go to www.cyberstateu.com for more information. Keystone Learning Systems (www.klscorp.com) also offers the popular Cisco video certification series featuring Todd Lammle.

It can also be helpful to take an Introduction to Cisco Router Configuration (ICRC) course at an authorized Cisco Education Center, but you should understand that this class doesn't meet all of the test objectives. If you decide to do that, reading the Sybex *CCNA Study Guide* book in conjunction with the hands-on course will give you the knowledge you need for certification. We've heard that Cisco Authorized Training Centers will offer the CCNA and other certification courses sometime in 1999, but check the Cisco Web page (www.cisco.com) for updated information. There are hundreds of Cisco Authorized Training Centers around the world—see the Cisco Web page for a location nearest you.

In addition to the Sybex *CCNA: Cisco Certified Network Associate Study Guide*, there are other useful ways to supplement your studies for the CCNA exam. CiscoTests (http://www.networkstudyguides.com) offers an online study guide with sample questions and information about the most current release of the CCNA, CCNP, and CCIE exams. CiscoTests also provides a discount for owners of the Sybex *CCNP: Advanced Cisco Router Configuration Study Guide*. To get instant access and the discount, you should visit the URL http://www.networkstudyguides.com/sybex.html.

Cisco Certified Network Professional (CCNP)

This new Cisco certification has opened up many opportunities for the individual wishing to become Cisco certified, but who is lacking the training, expertise, or the bucks to pass the notorious and often failed two-day Cisco-torture lab. The new Cisco certifications will truly provide exciting new opportunities for the CNE and MCSE who just didn't know how to advance to a higher level.

So you're thinking, "Great, what do I do after I pass the CCNA exam?" Well, if you want to become a CCIE in Routing and Switching (the most popular certification), understand that there's more than one path to that much-coveted CCIE certification. The first way is to continue studying and become a Cisco Certified Network Professional (CCNP). That means four more tests, and the CCNA certification, to you.

The CCNP program will prepare you to understand and comprehensively tackle the internetworking issues of today and beyond—not limited to the Cisco world. You will undergo an immense metamorphosis, vastly increasing your knowledge and skills through the process of obtaining these certifications.

Remember that you don't need to be a CCNP or even a CCNA to take the CCIE lab, but to accomplish that, it's extremely helpful if you already have these certifications.

What Are the CCNP Certification Skills?   Cisco is demanding a certain level of proficiency for their CCNP certification. In addition to those required for the CCNA, these skills include:

- Installing, configuring, operating, and troubleshooting complex routed LAN, routed WAN, and switched LAN networks, and Dial Access Services

- Understanding complex networks, such as IP, IGRP, IPX, Async Routing, AppleTalk, extended access lists, IP RIP, route redistribution, IPX RIP, route summarization, OSPF, VLSM, BGP, Serial, IGRP, Frame Relay, ISDN, ISL, X.25, DDR, PSTN, PPP, VLANs, Ethernet, ATM LAN-emulation, access lists, 802.10, FDDI, and transparent and translational bridging

To meet the Cisco Certified Network Professional requirements, you must be able to perform the following:

- Install and/or configure a network to increase bandwidth, quicken network response times, and improve reliability and quality of service

- Maximize performance through campus LANs, routed WANs, and remote access

- Improve network security

- Create a global intranet

- Provide access security to campus switches and routers

- Provide increased switching and routing bandwidth—end-to-end resiliency services

- Provide custom queuing and routed priority services

How Do You Become a CCNP?   After becoming a CCNA, the four exams you must take to get your CCNP are as follows:

- Exam 640-403: Advanced Cisco Router Configuration (ACRC) continues to build on the fundamentals learned in the ICRC course. It focuses on large multiprotocol internetworks and how to manage them with access lists, queuing, tunneling, route distribution, route summarization, and dial-on-demand.

- Exam 640-404: Cisco Lan Switch Configuration (CLSC) tests your understanding of configuring, monitoring, and troubleshooting Cisco switching products.

- Exam 640-406: Cisco Internetwork Troubleshooting (CIT) tests you on the troubleshooting information you learned in the other Cisco courses.

- Exam 640-405: Configuring, Monitoring, and Troubleshooting Dial-up Services (CMTD) tests your knowledge of installing, configuring, monitoring, and troubleshooting Cisco ISDN and dial-up access products.

If you hate tests, you can take fewer of them by signing up for the CCNA exam and the CIT exam, and then take just one more long exam called the Foundation R/S exam (640-409). Doing this will also give you your CCNP— but beware, it's a really long test that fuses all the material listed above into one exam. Good luck! However, by taking this exam, you get three tests for the price of two, which saves you $100 (if you pass). Some people think it's easier to take the Foundation R/S exam because you can leverage the areas you would score higher in against the areas in which you wouldn't.

Remember that test objectives and tests can change at any time without notice. Always check the Cisco Web site for the most up-to-date information: http://www.cisco.com.

Cisco Certified Internetworking Expert (CCIE)

You've become a CCNP, and now you've fixed your sights on getting your CCIE in Routing and Switching—what do you do next? Cisco recommends that before you take the lab, you take test 640-025: Cisco Internetwork Design (CID) and the Cisco authorized course Installing and Maintaining Cisco Routers (IMCR). By the way, no Prometric test for IMCR exists at the time of this writing, and Cisco recommends a *minimum* of two years on-the-job experience before taking the CCIE lab. After jumping those hurdles, you then have to pass the CCIE-R/S Exam Qualification (exam 350-001) before taking the actual lab.

To become a CCIE, Cisco recommends the following:

1. Attend all the recommended courses at an authorized Cisco training center and pony up around $15,000–$20,000, depending on your corporate discount.

2. Pass the Drake/Prometric exam ($200 per exam—so hopefully, you'll pass it the first time).

3. Pass the two-day hands-on lab at Cisco. This costs $1,000 per lab, which many people fail two or more times. (Some never make it through!) Also, because you can take the exam only in San Jose, California; Research Triangle Park, North Carolina; Sydney, Australia; Halifax, Nova Scotia; Tokyo, Japan; and Brussels, Belgium, you might just need to add travel costs to those 1,000 big dogs.

The CCIE Skills   The CCIE Router and Switching exam will include advanced technical skills required to maintain optimum network performance and reliability as well as advanced skills in supporting diverse networks that use disparate technologies. CCIEs just don't have problems getting a job. These experts are basically inundated with offers to work for six-figure salaries! But that's because it isn't easy to attain the level of capability mandatory for Cisco's CCIE. For example, a CCIE will have the following skills down pat:

- Installing, configuring, operating, and troubleshooting complex routed LAN, routed WAN, switched LAN, and ATM LANE networks, and Dial-Access Services

- Diagnosing and resolving network faults

- Using packet/frame analysis and Cisco debugging tools

- Documenting and reporting the problem-solving processes used

- Having general LAN/WAN knowledge, including data encapsulation and layering; windowing and flow control, and their relation to delay; error detection and recovery; link-state, distance vector, and switching algorithms; management, monitoring, and fault isolation

- Having knowledge of a variety of corporate technologies—including major services provided by Desktop, WAN, and Internet groups—as well as the functions, addressing structures, and routing, switching, and bridging implications of each of their protocols

- Having knowledge of Cisco-specific technologies, including router/switch platforms, architectures, and applications; communication servers; protocol translation and applications; configuration commands and system/network impact; and LAN/WAN interfaces, capabilities, and applications

Cisco's Network Design Certifications

In addition to the Network Support certifications, Cisco has created another certification track for network designers. The two certifications within this track are the Cisco Certified Design Associate and Cisco Certified Design Professional certifications. If you're reaching for the CCIE stars, we'd highly recommend the CCNP and CCDP certifications before attempting the lab (or attempting to advance your career).

This certification will give you the knowledge to design routed LAN, routed WAN, and switched LAN and ATM LANE networks.

Cisco Certified Design Associate (CCDA)

To become a CCDA, you must pass the CDS (Cisco Design Specialist) test (9E0-004). To pass this test, you must understand how to do the following:

- Design simple routed LAN, routed WAN, and switched LAN and ATM LANE networks

- Use Network-layer addressing

- Filter with access lists

- Use and propagate VLAN

- Size networks

Cisco Certified Design Professional (CCDP)

If you're already a CCNP and want to get your CCDP, you can simply take the CID 640-025 test. But if you're not yet a CCNP, you must take the ACRC, CLSC, CIT, and CMTD exams.

CCDP certification skills include:

- Designing complex routed LAN, routed WAN, and switched LAN and ATM LANE networks, building upon the base level of the CCDA technical knowledge

CCDPs must also demonstrate proficiency in:

- Network-layer addressing in a hierarchical environment

- Traffic management with access lists

- Hierarchical network design

- VLAN use and propagation

- Performance considerations: required hardware and software; switching engines; memory, cost, and minimization

What Does This Book Cover?

This book covers everything you need to pass the CCNP: Advanced Cisco Router Configuration exam. It will teach you how to perform advanced configurations on Cisco routers using multiple protocols. Each chapter begins with a list of the CCNP: ACRC test objectives covered, so make sure to read over them before working through the chapter.

The *CCNP Study Guide* begins where the CCNA Study Guide left off. You will learn how to performance-tune your internetwork using various Cisco IOS features. You'll also learn more about IP and IPX filtering using access lists. We'll also talk about high-end router architecture such as Netflow-switching and how to control router traffic using queuing. IP routing protocols such as IGRP, EIGRP, OSPF, and BGP are discussed in detail, along with IPX routing protocols such as NLSP and EIGRP. We finish the book with an advanced discussion and configuration tips for AppleTalk, bridging protocols, and WAN encapsulation methods for Frame Relay, ISDN, and DDR.

Each chapter ends with review questions that have been specifically designed to help retain the knowledge presented. To really nail down your skills, read each question carefully, and if possible, work through the hands-on labs at the end of most chapters.

The ACRC (640-403) exam consists of a combination of the following objectives:

1. Describe the key requirements of a scalable internetwork.

2. Select a Cisco IOS feature as a solution for a given internetwork requirement.

3. Describe causes of network congestion.

4. List solutions for controlling network congestion.

5. Introduction to Managing Traffic and Access.

6. Configure IP standard access lists.

7. Limit virtual terminal access.

8. Configure IP extended access lists.

9. Verify access list operation.

10. Configure an alternative to using access lists.

11. Configure an IP helper address to manage broadcasts.

12. Describe IPX/SPX traffic management issues.

13. Filter IPX traffic using IPX access lists.

14. Manage IPX/SPX traffic over WAN.

15. Verify IPX/SPX filter operation.

16. Describe the need for queuing in a large network.

17. Describe weighted fair queuing operation.

18. Configure priority.

19. Configure custom queuing.

20. Verify queuing operation.

21. List the key information routers needed to route data.

22. Compare distance vector and link-state protocol operation.

23. Given an IP address, use VLSMs to extend the use of the IP address.

24. Given a network plan that includes IP addressing, explain if route summarization is or is not possible.

25. Define private addressing and determine when it can be used.

26. Define network address translation and determine when it can be used.

27. Explain why OSPF is better than RIP in a large internetwork.

28. Explain how OSPF discovers, chooses, and maintains routes.

29. Configure OSPF for proper operation.

30. Verify OSPF operation.

31. Describe the issues with interconnecting multiple areas and how OSPF addresses.

32. Explain the differences between the possible types of areas, routers, and LSAs.

33. Configure a multiarea OSPF network.

34. Verify OSPF operation.

35. Describe Enhanced IGRP features and operation.

36. Configure Enhanced IGRP.

37. Verify Enhanced IGRP operation.

38. Select and configure the different ways to control route update traffic.

39. Configure route redistribution in a network that does not have redundant paths between dissimilar routing processes.

40. Configure route redistribution in a network that has redundant paths between dissimilar routing processes.

41. Resolve path selection problems that result in a redistributed network.

42. Verify route redistribution.

43. Describe when to use BGP to connect to an ISP.

44. Describe methods to connect to an ISP using static and default routes, and BGP.

45. Compare the differences between WAN connection types: dedicated, asynchronous dial-in, dial-on-demand, and packet switched services.

46. Determine when to use PPP, HDLC, LAPB, and IETF encapsulation types.

47. List at least four common issues to be considered when evaluating WAN services.

48. Describe the components that make up ISDN connectivity.

49. Configure ISDN BRI.

50. Configure Legacy dial-on-demand routing (DDR).

51. Configure dialer profiles.

52. Verify DDR operation.

53. Configure dial backup.

54. Verify dial backup operation.

55. Configure MultiLink PPP.

56. Verify MultiLink PPP operation.

57. Configure snapshot routing.

58. Configure IPX spoofing.

59. Define routable and nonroutable protocols and give an example of each.

60. Define various bridging types and describe when to use each type.

61. Configure transparent bridging.

62. Configure integrated Routing and Bridging (IRB).

63. Describe the basic functions of source-route bridging (SRB).

64. Configure SRB.

65. Configure source-route transparent bridging (SRT).

66. Configure source-route translational bridging (SR/TLB).

67. Verify SRB operation.

68. Identify potential sources of congestion in an AppleTalk network.

69. Configure zone filters.

70. Configure RTMP filters.

71. Configure NBP filters.

72. Identify channelized T1 and E1 configurations.

73. Identify ISDN PRI configuration commands.

 We've included an objective map on the inside back cover of this book that will help you find all the information relevant to each objective in this book. Keep in mind that at the beginning of each chapter, we've listed all actual exam objectives covered in that particular chapter.

Where Do You Take the Exam?

You may take the exams at any one of the more than 800 Sylvan Prometric Authorized Testing Centers around the world. For the location of a testing center near you, call (800) 204-3926. Outside the United States and Canada, contact your local Sylvan Prometric Registration Center.

To register for a Cisco Certified Network Professional exam:

1. Determine the number of the exam you want to take. (The ACRC exam number is 640-403.)

2. Register with the nearest Sylvan Prometric Registration Center. At this point, you will be asked to pay in advance for the exam. At the time of this writing, the exams are $100 each and must be taken within one year of payment. You can schedule exams up to six weeks in advance or as soon as one working day prior to the day you wish to take it. If something comes up and you need to cancel or reschedule your exam appointment, contact Sylvan Prometric at least 24 hours in advance. Same-day registration isn't available for the Cisco tests.

3. When you schedule the exam, you'll be provided with instructions regarding all appointment and cancellation procedures, the ID requirements, and information about the testing-center location.

Tips for Taking Your CCNP Exam

The CCNP ACRC test contains around 70 questions to be completed in 90 minutes. You must schedule a test at least 24 hours in advance (unlike the Novell or Microsoft exams), and you aren't allowed to take more than one Cisco exam per day.

Many questions on the exam will have answer choices that at first glance look identical—especially the syntax questions! Remember to read through the choices carefully because close won't cut it. If you get commands in the wrong order or forget one measly character, you'll get the question wrong. So to practice, do the hands-on exercises at the end of the chapters over and over again until they feel natural to you.

Unlike Microsoft or Novell tests, the exam has answer choices that are really similar in syntax—some syntax will be dead wrong, but more than likely, it will just be *subtly* wrong. Some other syntax choices may be right, but they're shown in the wrong order. Cisco does split hairs, and they're not at all above giving you classic trick questions. Here's an example:

- `access-list 101 deny ip any eq 23` denies Telnet access to all systems.

This question looks right since most people will refer to the port number (23) and think, "Yes, that's the port used for Telnet." The catch is that you can't filter IP on port numbers (only TCP and UDP).

Also, never forget that the right answer is the Cisco answer. In many cases, they'll present more than one appropriate answer, but the *correct* answer is the one Cisco recommends.

Here are some general tips for exam success:

- Arrive early at the exam center so you can relax and review your study materials.

- Read the questions *carefully*. Just don't jump to conclusions. Make sure you're clear on *exactly* what the question is asking.

- Don't leave any unanswered questions. They count against you.

- When answering multiple-choice questions you're not sure about, use a process of elimination to get rid of the obviously incorrect answers first. Doing this will greatly improve your odds if you need to make an educated guess.

- Because the hard questions will eat up the most time, save them for last. You can move forward and backward through the exam.

- If you are unsure of the answer to a question, choose one of the answers and mark the question so that if you have time you can go back to it, and then go on. Remember that an unanswered question is as bad as a wrong one, so answer it because you may run out of time or forget to go back to it.

Once you have completed an exam, you'll be given immediate, online notification of your pass or fail status, a printed Examination Score Report indicating your pass or fail status, and your exam results by section. (The test administrator will give you the printed score report.) Test scores are automatically forwarded to Cisco within five working days after you take the test, so you don't need to send your score to them. If you pass the exam, you'll receive confirmation from Cisco, typically within two to four weeks.

Here's one more thing you can do: Go to Brian Horakh's Web site at www.networkstudyguides.com, and go through the exercise and practice test questions he has available. These will really help you keep abreast of any changes made to the test.

How to Use This Book

This book can provide a solid foundation for the serious effort of preparing for the Cisco Certified Network Professional ACRC (Advanced Cisco Router Configuration) exam. To best benefit from this book, use the following study method:

1. Study each chapter carefully, making sure you fully understand the information and the test objectives listed at the beginning of each chapter.

2. Complete all hands-on exercises in the chapter, referring to the chapter so that you understand the reason for each step you take. If you do not have Cisco equipment available, make sure to study the examples carefully.

3. Answer the review questions related to that chapter. (The answers are in Appendix A.)

4. Note which questions confuse you, and study those sections of the book again.

5. Before taking the exam, try your hand on the practice exams included on the CD that comes with this book. They'll give you a complete overview of what you can expect to see on the real thing.

6. Remember to use the products on the CD included with this book. Visio, EtherPeek, and the EdgeTest test preparation software have all been specifically picked to help you study for and pass your exam.

To learn all the material covered in this book, you'll have to apply yourself regularly and with discipline. Try to set aside the same time period every day to study, and select a comfortable and quiet place to do so. If you work hard, you will be surprised at how quickly you learn this material. All the best!

What's on the CD?

We've worked hard to provide some really great tools to help you with your certification process. All of these should be loaded on your workstation when studying for the test.

The EdgeTest for Cisco CCNP Test Preparation Software

Provided by EdgeTek Learning Systems, this test preparation software prepares you for successfully passing the Cisco Certified Network Professional exam. To find more test simulation software for all Cisco and NT exams, look for the exam link on www.lammle.com. You can also call 1-800-800-1NET (1638) for more information.

IPCalc

Produced by Jerry Camel, this is one of the best IP calculator programs we have ever seen. The program on this CD is an evaluation program that can easily be upgraded to the full version by contacting www.progression-inc.com.

IPCalc 2 is a TCP/IP address calculator designed to help you better understand the concepts behind IP addressing. It visually illustrates the bit patterns of an IP address and their behavior as you move from one addressing scheme to another. IPCalc 2 is a 32-bit application and will run on Windows 95 or NT.

Visio

Visio Professional, combined with Visio Network Equipment, offers the most complete network documentation solution. Work with over 14,000 exact-replica manufacturer-specific network hardware and telecom shapes to create proposals, implementation plans, and any other documents your company uses to represent and manage its networks. Install the Visio Professional 5 30-day test drive and the sampling of over 100 Visio Network Equipment shapes included on the CD. To order a Visio product, obtain more information, or locate your nearest reseller, call (800) 248-4746 or visit Visio's Web site at www.visio.com for more information.

AG Group NetTools and EtherPeek

Two AG Group products appear on the CD: EtherPeek™ for Windows demonstration software, requiring a serial number, and the freeware version of AG NetTools™. EtherPeek is a full-featured, affordable packet and network analyzer. AG NetTools is an interface- and menu-driven IP tool compilation.

The serial numbers are included in the readme file located on the CD. You can find out more information about AG Group and purchase the license for EtherPeek and other products at www.aggroup.com.

How to Contact the Authors

You can reach Todd Lammle through Globalnet System Solutions, Inc. (www.lammle.com)—his Training and Systems Integration Company in Colorado—or e-mail him at info@lammle.com.

To contact Kevin Hales, you can e-mail him at khales@uen.org.

To reach Donald Porter, send him e-mail at don@uen.org.

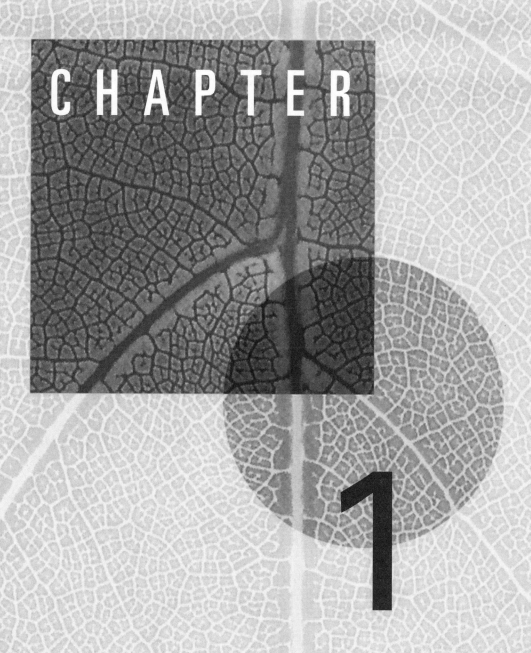

CHAPTER

1

Scaling Large Internetworks

We'll begin this book with a review of internetworks and a discussion of the typical business requirements for their implementation in today's marketplace. This discussion will lead naturally into exploring the ubiquitous but avoidable problem of network congestion. Examining both its causes and the solutions for controlling it, we'll describe the key requirements for a scalable internetwork. We'll also look to the Cisco three-layer model for the inherent solutions it provides, and unveil helpful Cisco IOS features that will aid us in scaling large internetworks.

All this will provide an important backdrop for Chapter 2's tableau of design considerations, network availability issues, and the problems and solutions centered around the goal of keeping a large internetwork up and running 365 days a year. Also, because it's not enough to have a network that's merely running, we'll probe further to uncover techniques to make a network run *most efficiently* through minimizing delay and maximizing protocol responsiveness.

The ACRC exam objectives covered in this chapter are as follows:

- Describe causes of network congestion
- List solutions for controlling network congestion
- Describe the key requirements of a scalable internetwork
- Select a Cisco IOS feature as a solution for a given internetwork requirement

Internetworks

An *internetwork* is the communication structure that works to tie LANs and WANs together. Its primary goal is to efficiently move information anywhere within a corporation quickly, upon demand, and with complete integrity. Today's users have become increasingly dependent on their networks—just make a group of users' server or hub go offline and watch the chaos that results around the office.

Where this has led—and what this means for corporations that want to remain capable of competing in today's global market—is that the networks they depend on today have to efficiently manage, on a daily basis, some or all of the following:

- Graphics and imaging

- Files in the gigabyte range

- Client-server computing

- High network traffic loads

To be able to amply meet these needs, the IS department must provide the following to users:

- More bandwidth

- Bandwidth on demand

- Low delays

- Data, voice, and video capabilities on the same media

Also, the network of today must be adaptable in that it must be ready to suit the applications of tomorrow. In the not-too-distant future, networks will need to be equipped to handle:

- High-definition imaging

- Full motion video

- Digitized audio

In short, for an internetwork to realize its purpose, it must be able to efficiently connect many different networks together to serve the organizations that depend on it. This connectivity must happen regardless of the type of physical media involved. Companies expanding their networks must overcome the limitations of physical and geographic boundaries. The Internet has served as a model to facilitate this growth.

Clearing Up Network Congestion

With a combination of powerful workstations, audio and video to the desktop, and network-intensive applications, 10Mbps Ethernet networks no longer offer enough bandwidth to fulfill the business requirements of the typical large business today.

As more and more users are connected to the network, an Ethernet network's performance begins to wane as users fight for more bandwidth. Like when too many cars try to get onto a freeway at rush hour, this increased utilization causes an increase in network congestion as more users try to access the existing network resources. Congestion causes users to scream for more bandwidth. However, simply increasing bandwidth can't always solve the problem. A slow server CPU or insufficient memory on the workstations and servers can also be culprits, and need to be considered as well.

One way to solve congestion problems and increase the networking performance of your LAN is to divide a single Ethernet segment into multiple network segments. This maximizes the available bandwidth. Some of the ways to do that are as follows:

Physical segmentation   You can segment the network with bridges and routers, thereby breaking up the collision domains. This minimizes packet collisions by decreasing the number of workstations on the same physical network.

Network switching technology (microsegmenting)   Like a bridge or router, switches can also provide LAN segmentation capabilities. LAN switches (for example, the Cisco Catalyst 5000) provide dedicated, point-to-point, packet switched connections between their ports. Since this provides simultaneous switching of packets between the ports in the switch, it increases the amount of bandwidth open to each workstation.

Using full-duplex Ethernet devices   Full-duplex Ethernet can provide almost twice the bandwidth of traditional Ethernet networks. However, for this to work, the network interface cards (NICs) must be able to run in Full Duplex mode.

Using Fast Ethernet   Using Fast Ethernet switches can provide 10 times the amount of bandwidth available from 10BaseT.

Using FDDI   FDDI is an older, solid technology that can provide 100Mbps bandwidth. By running dual rings, it has the capability of up to 200Mbps. It's typically used between closets and floors, or in a campus environment.

It's no surprise—reducing the number of users per collision domain increases the bandwidth on your network segment. By keeping the traffic local to the network segment, users have more bandwidth available to them, and enjoy a noticeably better response time than if there was simply one large backbone in place.

OK, now let's explore some different ways to clear up nasty network congestion problems:

- Segmentation with bridges

- Segmentation with routers

- Segmentation with switches

Segmentation with a Bridge

A bridge can segment or break up your network into smaller, more manageable pieces. However, if it's placed incorrectly in your network, it can be a bad thing that causes more harm than good.

Bridges perform at the MAC sublayer of the Data Link layer. They create both physical and logical separate network segments to reduce the traffic load. There are solid advantages to bridging—by segmenting a logical network into multiple physical pieces, it secures network reliability, availability, scalability, and manageability.

As Figure 1.1 shows, bridges work by examining the MAC or hardware addresses in each frame and forwarding the frame to the other physical segments—only if necessary. These devices dynamically build a forwarding table of information comprised of each MAC address and which segment that address is located on.

Now for the bad news... A drawback to using bridges is that if the destination MAC address is unknown to the bridge, it will forward the frame to all segments except the port from which it received the frame. Also, a 20–30% latency period can occur for the processing of frames. This delay can increase significantly if the frame cannot be immediately forwarded due to current activity on the destination segment.

Bridges will forward packets and multicast packets to all other segments to which they're attached. Because, by default, the addresses from these broadcasts are never seen by the bridge, and hence are not filtered, broadcast storms can result. The same problem can happen with switches, because theoretically, switch ports are bridge ports. A Cisco switch is really a multiport bridge that runs the Cisco IOS and performs the same functions as a bridge.

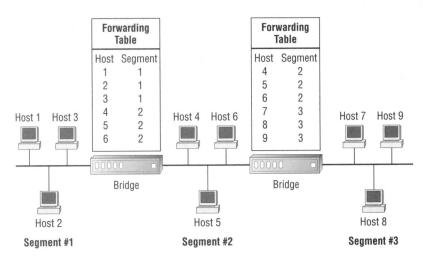

FIGURE 1.1

Segmentation with
a bridge

Segmentation with a Router

As you know, routers work at the Network layer and are used to route packets to destination networks. Routers, like bridges, use tables to make routing decisions. However, routers keep information on how to get to only remote networks in their tables, not to hosts, using that information to route packets through an internetwork. Routers use IP addresses instead of hardware addresses when making their routing decisions. They maintain a routing table for each protocol on the network—a Cisco router will keep a routing table for AppleTalk, a different one for IPX, and still another for IP, as shown in Figure 1.2.

Here are the pros regarding routers:

Manageability Multiple routing protocols give the network manager who's creating an internetwork a lot of flexibility.

Increased functionality Cisco routers provide features that address the issues of flow, error and congestion control, fragmentation, reassembly, and control over a packet's lifetime.

Multiple active paths Using the protocol, DSAPs, SSAPs, and path metrics, routers can make informed routing decisions and interpret the next layer protocol. This allows routers to have more than one active path between networks.

FIGURE 1.2

Routing tables are kept for each Network layer routing protocol.

IP ROUTING TABLE

Subnet	Interface
172.16.10.0	E0
172.16.20.0	S0

IP ROUTING TABLE

Subnet	Interface
172.16.30.0	E0
172.16.20.0	S0

IPX ROUTING TABLE

Subnet	Interface
117	S0
108	E0

IPX ROUTING TABLE

Subnet	Interface
117	S0
109	E0

AppleTalk ROUTING TABLE

Subnet	Interface
2-2	E0
10-10	S0

AppleTalk ROUTING TABLE

Subnet	Interface
1-1	E0
10-10	S0

To provide these advantages, routers must be more complex and more software intensive than bridges. Routers provide a lower level of performance in terms of the number of frames or packets that can be processed per unit. A router must examine more fields in a packet than a bridge, resulting in a 30–40% loss of throughput for acknowledgment-oriented protocols, and a 20–30% loss for sliding-window protocols.

Segmentation with LAN Switches

LAN switching is a great strategy for LAN segmentation. LAN switches improve performance by employing frame switching, which permits high-speed data exchanges.

Just like bridges, switches use the destination MAC address to ensure that the packet is forwarded to the right outgoing port. Cut-through switches begin forwarding the packet before reception is complete, keeping latency to a minimum. Store-and-forward-switching receives the entire frame onto its onboard buffers, runs a CRC, and then forwards the frame out the destination port.

There are three different switching-method terms:

Port configuration–switching Allows a port to be assigned to a physical network segment under software control. It's the simplest form of switching.

Frame-switching Used to increase available bandwidth on the network. Frame-switching allows multiple transmissions to occur in parallel. This is the type of switching performed by all Catalyst switches.

Cell-switching (ATM) Similar to frame-switching, ATM uses small, fixed-length cells that are switched on the network. It's the switching method used by all Cisco Lightstream switches.

A LAN switch supplies you with considerably higher port density at a lower cost than standard bridges. Since LAN switches permit fewer users per segment, the average available bandwidth per user increases. This fewer-users-per-segment trend is known as microsegmentation, which lets you create dedicated segments. When you have one user per segment, each one enjoys instant access to the full lot of available bandwidth instead of competing for it with other users. Because of this, the collisions so common with shared, medium-sized networks that use hubs just don't happen.

A LAN switch bases the forwarding of frames on the frame's Layer 2 address (Layer 2 LAN switch), or on the frame's Layer 3 address (multilayer LAN switch). LAN switches are sometimes referred to as frame switches because they generally forward Layer 2 frames in contrast to an ATM switch, which forwards cells.

As network usage increases, we're seeing more Token Ring and FDDI LAN switches, but Ethernet LAN switches are still the most common type.

LAN switches uniquely support some very cool new features, including the following:

- Numerous, simultaneous conversations
- High-speed data exchanges
- Low latency and high frame-forwarding rates
- Dedicated communication between devices
- Full-duplex communication
- Media rate adaptation (both 10 and 100Mbps hosts can work on the same network)
- The ability to work with existing 802.3-compliant network interface cards and cabling

Thanks to dedicated, collision-free communication between network devices, file-transfer throughput is increased. Many conversations can occur simultaneously by forwarding or switching several packets at the same time, which expands the network capacity by the amount of supported conversations.

Full-duplex communication fully doubles throughput, and media rate adaptation allows the LAN switch to translate between 10 and 100Mbps to allocate bandwidth on an as-needed basis. Another benefit is that changing over to LAN switches doesn't require changing the existing hubs, network interface cards, or cabling.

The Cisco Three-Layer Model

Cisco has created their own three-layer hierarchical model, which you can follow when building or designing a scalable internetwork. The three layers are as follows:

- Core

- Distribution

- Access

Figure 1.3 shows the Cisco three-layer model.

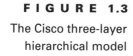

FIGURE 1.3

The Cisco three-layer hierarchical model

This hierarchical model makes addressing and device management easier, because mapping network addresses to the hierarchy reduces the odds that you'll have to reconfigure them as the network grows. Plus, if you know where all devices that do similar things are placed within the hierarchy, consistently configuring all routers within a particular layer is much simpler.

Core-Layer Functions

The primary function of the Core layer is to provide an optimized and reliable transport structure. This is essential for the entire enterprise internetwork, and may include LAN and WAN backbones.

Figure 1.4 shows the Core routers in a hierarchy.

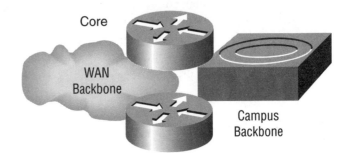

Services that enhance communication between routes in a different logical group, or that are located at different sites, function at the Core layer. Its routers provide maximum reliability and availability, and if a LAN or WAN circuit falters here, Core routers can usually maintain connectivity nevertheless.

Distribution-Layer Functions

The Distribution layer's *raison d'être* is to provide access to various parts of the internetwork, as well as to services. This represents the campus backbone.
Figure 1.5 shows Distribution routers in a hierarchy.

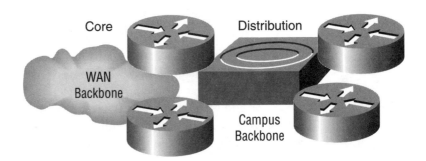

Distribution-layer routers govern access to Core-layer resources, and it's vital for Distribution-layer routers to utilize bandwidth efficiently. They must also fulfill the quality-of-service (QOS) requirements of various protocols by exerting a policy-based form of traffic control that sequesters local and backbone environments.

Access-Layer Functions

The Access layer provides access to corporate resources for a workgroup or users on a local segment.

Figure 1.6 shows Access routers in a hierarchy.

F I G U R E 1.6

Access routers in
a hierarchy

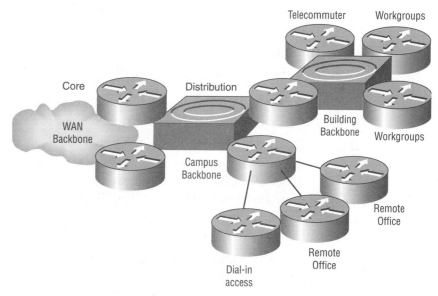

Routers at the Access layer manage traffic by restricting all service requests and broadcasts to the access media, and must provide connectivity while sustaining the network's integrity. The routers situated at the point of access must determine the legitimacy of users dialing in while requiring only minimal authentication steps from them.

Requirements of the Scalable Internetwork

Today's internetworks are experiencing extraordinary growth due to increasing demands for connectivity both in businesses and at home. Therefore, it's very important for them to be scalable. It's now vital for administrators to understand what a scalable network is, as well as what is required to effectively manage its incessant growth.

Since a scalable internetwork undergoes continual growth, it has to be both flexible and easily appended. An ideal design is based on the hierarchical model to simplify management and permit well-planned growth that honors the network's requirements. Here are the mandatory requirements of a scalable internetwork:

It must be reliable and available   The Cisco IOS provides features for implementing redundancy, load balancing, and reachability with protocols such as EIGRP and OSPF (which we'll thoroughly analyze in Chapters 5 and 6). Strategies such as tunneling and dial backups can also help keep an internetwork up and running (we'll cover IPX tunneling in Chapter 7 and dial backups in Chapter 13).

It must be responsive   Because network growth often occurs on a daily basis, the administrator's duty to maintain the network's responsiveness can become overwhelming. The Cisco IOS provides solutions such as queuing that's configured by an administrator to keep latency to a minimum. (Queuing will be covered in detail in Chapter 4.)

It must be efficient   Efficiency in a nutshell is keeping the bandwidth from becoming saturated. A central goal of this book is to arm you with information on fine-tuning your router to optimize the existing bandwidth on your internetwork. You'll learn how to achieve that objective through innovative techniques such as snapshot routing (presented in Chapter 2), access lists (covered in Chapters 3 and 7), and dialup routing (covered in Chapter 13).

It must be adaptable   The internetwork designed to respond masterfully to change, and manage both routed and nonroutable protocols, is a true prize—the Cisco IOS provides valuable bridging features (which we'll detail in Chapter 10) to help you win that prize.

It must be easily accessible while being secure   It is a network administrator's foremost obligation (obsession?) to meet business requirements by ensuring that network resources remain available to users at all times, while managing to keep any and all hackers out. The Cisco IOS provides dedicated and switched WAN support such as Frame Relay, SMDS, X.25, and ATM to equip networking professionals with options to meet cost, location, security, and traffic requirements. The Cisco IOS also provides exterior routing support with the Exterior Gateway Protocol (EGP) and Border Gateway Protocol (BGP) to permit routing on the Internet with maximum security.

WAN topics are covered in Chapters 11 through 13, while exterior routing protocols are thoroughly discussed in Chapter 4.

Reliability and Availability

Because a network is depended upon so heavily—ideally, it's up and running 24 hours a day, 365 days a year—failures and downtime must be kept to a minimum. It's also vital that when a failure does occur, it's easy to isolate, reducing the time needed for troubleshooting.

When it comes to reliability, the internetwork's Core layer is the most critical. Cisco's definition of *reliable* is an internetwork that can respond quickly to changes in the network topology and accommodate failures by rerouting traffic.

Some Cisco IOS features that serve to provide stability and availability are as follows:

Reachability OSPF, EIGRP, and NLSP use expanded metrics that can go beyond the hop count limitations of distance vector routing algorithms. These routing protocols analyze a combination of factors to establish the real cost of a path to a network, making Cisco routers able to support very large internetworks.

Convergence Scalable routing protocols can converge quickly because of each router's complete understanding of the internetwork and ability to detect problems.

Alternate paths routing Because OSPF and EIGRP build a complete map of the internetwork, a router can easily reroute traffic to an alternate path if a problem occurs.

Load balancing Through the EIGRP and OSPF routing algorithms, the Cisco IOS is able to perform load balancing. This allows for redundant links, and for more bandwidth to be available to locations needing more than just one link. For example, if two T1 WAN links were installed between buildings, the actual bandwidth between them would reach approximately 3Mbps.

Tunneling Running a tunneling protocol affords the ability to communicate across WAN links that were previously unreachable. For example, if you have a WAN link that supports only TCP/IP and you want to manage a Novell NetWare server that supports only IPX, you could tunnel IPX packets inside of IP packets to achieve your goal.

Dial backup You can configure dial-backup links for redundancy on your WAN links and to add extra bandwidth whenever it becomes saturated, enhancing the link's reliability and availability.

Responsiveness

Since it's the network administrator's responsibility to make sure users don't experience delays in responsiveness as the internetwork grows, he or she must be keenly aware of the latency factor that each piece of equipment (routers, switches, and bridges) contributes to the internetwork. The Cisco IOS provides mitigation for the latency needs of each protocol running on your internetwork with features such as:

Weighted fair queuing Prevents a single user or network device from monopolizing the internetwork's bandwidth and causing delays for the others. It fairly allots bandwidth to all users.

Priority queuing Used to tag a particular traffic type as a priority, ensuring that important information reaches its destination in a timely fashion. However, when using it, nonpriority traffic may not make it to its destination on time.

Custom queuing Allows bandwidth to be divided up into slots (large or small), according to the business requirements of various types of traffic.

Efficiency

The task of creating smoothly running, efficient LANs and internetworks is obviously very important, but optimizing the bandwidth on a WAN can be very difficult—that's the focus of this book. The best way to reduce the bandwidth usage is to reduce the amount of update traffic on the LAN that will be sent over your WAN. The Cisco IOS features available to help reduce bandwidth usage are as follows:

Access lists Used to permit or deny certain types of traffic from entering or exiting a specific router interface. They can stop basic traffic, broadcasts, and protocol updates from saturating a particular link. TCP/IP, IPX, and AppleTalk can all be filtered extensively.

Snapshot routing Commonly used for ISDN connections when running distance vector protocols, it allows routers to exchange full distance vector routing information at an interval defined by the administrator.

Compression over WANs The Cisco IOS supports TCP/IP header and data compression to reduce the amount of traffic crossing a WAN link. Link compression can be configured, which compresses header and data information into packets. This is accomplished by the Cisco IOS prior to sending the frame across the WAN.

DDR (Dial-on-demand routing) Allows wide area links to be used selectively. With it, the administrator can define "interesting" traffic on the router and initiate point-to-point WAN links based upon that traffic. What denotes interesting traffic is defined by access lists, so a great deal of flexibility is afforded to the administrator. For instance, an expensive ISDN connection to the Internet could be initiated to retrieve e-mail, but not for a WWW request. DDR is an effective tool in situations where WAN access is charged according to a quantified time interval—it's best to use it in situations where WAN access is infrequent.

Reduction in routing table entries By using route summarization and incremental updates, you can reduce the number of router processing cycles by reducing the entries in a routing table. Route summarization occurs at major network boundaries, which summarize all the routes advertised into one entry. Incremental updates save bandwidth by sending only topology changes instead of the entire routing table when transmitting updates.

Adaptability

Another important goal for an administrator is to design an internetwork that responds well to change. To achieve this goal, internetworks need to be able to:

Pass both routable and nonroutable network protocols Examples would be TCP/IP, which is routable, and Microsoft's NetBEUI (NetBIOS Extended User Interface), which is not routable, only bridgeable.

Create islands of networks using different protocols This allows you to add protocols used by the network islands to Core-layer routers, or use tunneling in the backbone to connect the islands, which keeps you from having to add unwanted protocols to the core backbone.

Balance between multiple protocols in a network Each protocol has different requirements, and the internetwork must be able to accommodate the specific issues of each one.

The Cisco IOS also has many different features that contribute to network adaptability:

EIGRP Cisco's proprietary EIGRP allows you to use multiple protocols within one routing algorithm. EIGRP supports IP, IPX, and AppleTalk.

Redistribution Allows you to exchange routing information between networks that use different routing protocols. For example, you can update a routing table from a network running IGRP on a router participating in a RIP network.

Bridging By using source-route bridging and integrated routing and bridging, you can integrate your older networks and protocols that do not support routing into the new internetwork.

Accessibility and Security

Access routers must be both accessed and used to access a variety of WAN services, while maintaining security to keep hackers out.

The Cisco IOS features that support these requirements are as follows:

Dedicated and switched WAN support You can create a direct connection with Cisco routers using basic or digital services (a T1, for example). Cisco routers also support many different switched services, such as Frame Relay, SMDS, X.25, and ATM, to give you options to meet cost, location, and traffic requirements.

Exterior protocol support Both Exterior Gateway Protocol (EGP) and Border Gateway Protocol (BGP) are supported by the Cisco IOS. BGP (discussed in detail later in this book) is used mostly by Internet service providers (ISPs), and has mostly replaced EGP.

Access lists Used to filter specific kinds of traffic from either entering or leaving a Cisco router.

Authentication protocols Cisco supports both Password Authentication Protocol (PAP) and Challenge Handshake Authentication Protocol (CHAP) for providing authentication on WAN connections using PPP.

Summary

This chapter covered the following points:

- For an internetwork to realize its purpose, it must be able to efficiently connect many different networks together to serve the organizations depending on it. However, the more users and networks that you tie together, the more network congestion is caused. The causes of network congestion are typically too many hosts on a network or internetworks that all compete for the available bandwidth.

- A way to solve congestion problems and increase the networking performance of your LAN is to divide a single Ethernet segment into multiple network segments. Some of the ways to do that are as follows: physical segmentation, network switching technology (microsegmenting), full-duplex Ethernet devices, Fast Ethernet, and FDDI. Solutions discussed in this chapter for controlling network congestion were bridges, routers, and switches.

- The key requirements of a scalable internetwork are based on an ideal design using the Cisco hierarchical model to simplify management, which permits well-planned growth that honors the network's requirements. The following issues were discussed as mandatory requirements of a scalable internetwork: reliability and availability, responsiveness, efficiency, adaptability, and easy accessibility while maintaining security.

- When discussing the key requirements of a scalable internetwork using the Cisco hierarchical model, features found in the Cisco IOS were compared with the mandatory requirements of a scalable internetwork. The Cisco IOS features for implementing redundancy, load balancing, and reachability with protocols fall within the reliable and available parameters. Queuing was discussed for the responsive requirements. Snapshot routing, access-list strategies, and dial-up routing were covered under the features used for efficient internetworks. We also discussed adaptable features, and both routing and bridging within the Cisco IOS. To make the internetwork accessible while being secure, the Cisco IOS provides dedicated and switched WAN support.

Review Questions

1. Which of the following can you use to alleviate congestion in an internetwork (if used correctly)?

   A. Repeaters

   B. Routers

   C. DLC

   D. Switches

   E. Bridges

2. Choose the three layers Cisco uses for building its hierarchical internetwork model.

   A. Fundamental

   B. Distribution

   C. IGRP

   D. Core

   E. Backbone

   F. Access

3. Identify the characteristics of a scalable internetwork.

   A. Reliability

   B. Responsiveness

   C. Efficiency

   D. Adaptability

   E. Accessibility

   F. All of the above

4. What is the primary function of the Core layer?

   A. To distribute client-server router information

   B. To provide an optimized and reliable transport structure

   C. To provide access to various parts of the internetwork, as well as to services

   D. To provide access to corporate resources for a workgroup or users on a local segment

5. What is the primary function of the Distribution layer?

   A. To distribute client-server router information

   B. To provide an optimized and reliable transport structure

   C. To provide access to various parts of the internetwork, as well as to services

   D. To provide access to corporate resources for a workgroup or users on a local segment

6. What is the purpose of the Access-layer functions?

   A. To distribute client-server router information

   B. To provide an optimized and reliable transport structure

   C. To provide access to various parts of the internetwork, as well as to services

   D. To provide access to corporate resources for a workgroup or users on a local segment

7. How do LAN switches improve performance on a LAN?

   A. By filtering via logical address

   B. By regenerating the digital signal

   C. By employing packet-switching that permits high-speed data exchanges

   D. By employing frame-switching that permits high-speed data exchanges

8. What is a benefit of bridge segmentation?

   A. Regeneration and propagation

   B. Segmenting or breaking up your network into smaller, more manageable pieces

   C. LAN queuing

   D. Bridges begin forwarding the frame before reception is complete

9. How does cut-through switching provide better performance than other switching methods?

   A. LAN queuing

   B. Microsegmentation

   C. Receiving the entire frame onto onboard buffers, running a CRC, and then forwarding the frames out the destination port

   D. Forwarding the frame before reception is complete

10. LAN segmentation with switches is also called what?

   A. Filtering

   B. Microsegmenting

   C. Bridging

   D. Routing

11. Which router layers govern access to Core-layer resources?

   A. Distribution

   B. Core

   C. Backbone

   D. Access

12. Which layer has services that enhance communication between routes in different logical groups?

   A. Backbone

   B. Core

   C. Distribution

   D. Access

13. How do bridges filter a network?

   A. By logical address

   B. By IP address

   C. By hardware address

   D. By digital signaling

14. How do routers filter a network? (Choose all that apply.)

   A. By logical address

   B. By IP address

   C. By digital signaling

   D. By hardware address

   E. By IPX address

15. How do switches segment a network?

   A. By logical address

   B. By IP address

   C. By hardware address

   D. By IPX address

16. What is a drawback of filtering a network with bridges?

   A. It segments the network

   B. It creates internetworks

   C. It passes datagram broadcasts

   D. It filters frames

17. How can you reduce route table entries?

   A. Route summarization

   B. Incremental updates

   C. Filtering

   D. VLANs

18. Which Cisco IOS features are available to help reduce bandwidth usage? (Choose all that apply.)

A. Access lists

B. Snapshot routing

C. Compression of WANs

D. TTL

E. DDR

F. Incremental updates

19. Which Cisco IOS features serve to provide stability and availability? (Choose all that apply.)

A. Reachability

B. Convergence

C. Alternative path routing

D. Snapshot routing

E. Tunneling

F. Dial backup

G. Load balancing

20. The Cisco IOS provides mitigation for the latency needs of each protocol running on your internetwork with which features? (Choose all that apply.)

A. Snapshot routing

B. Weighted fair queuing

C. Priority queuing

D. Custom queuing

CHAPTER

2

Other Design Considerations

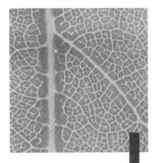

It should be painfully obvious that it's really important to design a network that will effectively meet the demands of the users who access it. This is crucial—it's the whole point, right? Well, availability is becoming much more important as the demand for network access increases. However, it's not *just* availability that's crucial—it's also how well that network performs once it's been accessed. That last issue is absolutely pivotal. To these ends, this chapter will be devoted to exploring the available options used to improve both network availability and the network's performance.

We'll begin by looking at some different levels of redundancy and then discuss how they can be implemented. We'll also discuss the concept of alternate path routing and even some design options for creating an adaptable network.

After we cover how to increase network availability, we'll move on to improving network performance. You'll learn ways to create an efficient network by fine-tuning its various components. We'll also go over minimizing network delay, as well as looking into the responsiveness of routing protocols.

The exam objectives covered in this chapter are as follows:

- Describe the key requirements of a scalable network

- Describe causes of network congestion

- List solutions for controlling network congestion

Increasing Network Availability

You can approach the network availability issue in three different ways, which can be separated into two implementations. The three ways of increasing network availability are as follows:

- Increasing bandwidth

- Using dynamic routing protocols
- Implementing redundant or backup connectivity

The two implementations are hardware and software. For a network to fulfill its maximum availability potential, all three methods should be implemented simultaneously.

Most of the time, people think about hardware when trying to achieve availability. Similarly, when the network becomes unavailable, they often chalk it up to hardware failure. This tendency explains why the most popular form of increasing network availability is to grab for additional hardware or circuits to provide redundancy or backup for the production equipment. Though doing that is sometimes unavoidable, fancy hardware is pricey stuff—this solution can quickly become costly for a large enterprise network. That's why it's so important to utilize the other methods of increasing network availability in concert with the acquisition of additional hardware.

In many cases, it's not a hardware failure that causes network downtime. Many times, routing problems can be responsible for the production network's sudden, even chronic, unavailability. For this reason, it's imperative to use routing protocols that are dynamic enough to be able to keep a topology database of the network. That topology database stores all of the paths by which a given network is learned, and the router relies on it to make its packet routing decisions.

Even with hardware/software redundancy in place, outages will still occur, causing minimal downtime. The ability to minimize that outage period correlates directly to how adaptable a network is to change. Network adaptability can be achieved by using scalable protocols that utilize the topology database. This way, the network can dynamically adjust to changes occurring within it.

Redundancy vs. Backup

OK, so what's better, making a network redundant, or just providing backup connectivity when the inevitable network outage occurs? Before you can make this decision, redundant and backup connectivity must be defined. *Redundant connectivity* provides a continuous alternate path for traffic to transit in the case of an outage or extreme interface congestion. Network convergence time is relatively low when using redundant connectivity. *Backup connectivity* remains in a nonactive state until the primary link fails. When a failure occurs, the backup link is established to provide connectivity. This process takes time and slows network convergence. These terms apply not only to physical media, but also to power systems.

Now that these terms have been explained, it's easy to see that there's not a simple answer—there are many design considerations to sift through when making a decision. And to complicate matters, several different levels of redundancy are possible. What do we mean by "different levels of redundancy"? Well, in case of circuit failure, one design may simply require redundant links between campuses, while another design may need redundant routers and other equipment, in addition to redundant links.

Redundancy

In accordance with Cisco's three-layer model, redundancy can be designed and implemented in any one, or even all, of the layers. Since the associated equipment isn't often found at garage sales, cost is a major factor in deciding just how much redundancy and backup equipment can be designed in a given network. Therefore, it's highly important to first assess both the needs of the end users and the applications that your network will be providing. Armed with an accurate analysis of the particular demands and required availability of your network, you can make a sound decision regarding the type of redundancy or backup necessary.

It sounds complicated because it is complicated, but a good (and in many cases, the most cost-effective) strategy for approaching this is to start by creating redundancy at the core of the network. That's the most critical layer, so it's wise to implement your redundancy there first.

But again, you have choices. You can implement several types of physical redundancy. Physical elements of a redundant network design include:

- Multiple links

- Meshed links

- Redundant power systems

Multiple Links   In Figure 2.1, you can see that dual or multiple links can be implemented in two ways: between the *edge* and *distribution* devices, or between the *distribution* and *core* devices. The benefits are twofold: The dual links provide redundancy in case of a failure and can increase the available bandwidth between the two devices. Increased bandwidth decreases delay while simultaneously increasing network availability. How's that for results!

Routing protocols provide several services on routers that have multiple links connecting them to other routers, which means load balancing can be accomplished through either packet or session balancing. Routing protocols also provide quick route convergence when a failure occurs.

FIGURE 2.1

Star networks with
multiple links

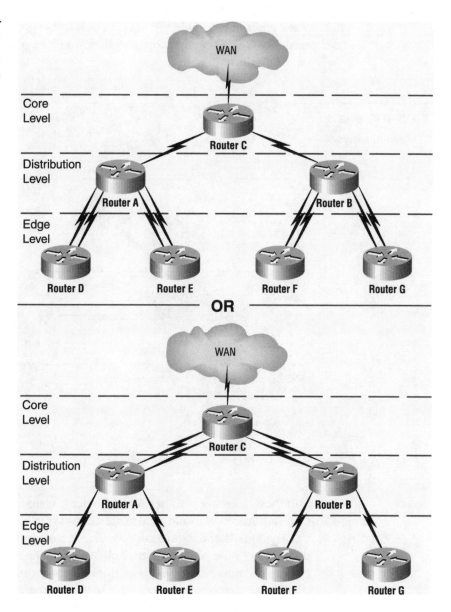

Meshed Networks   Meshed networks are also a cost-effective solution for creating a redundant network. This type of network differs from multiple-linked networks in that fewer circuits are needed, which in turn provides direct communication between two routers on the same hierarchical level.

Figure 2.2 details how multiple links can be used to connect two *distribution* devices and a single *core*-level device. It shows that one less circuit is needed to create a meshed topology than would be required to create a dual-linked network.

FIGURE 2.2

Meshed network

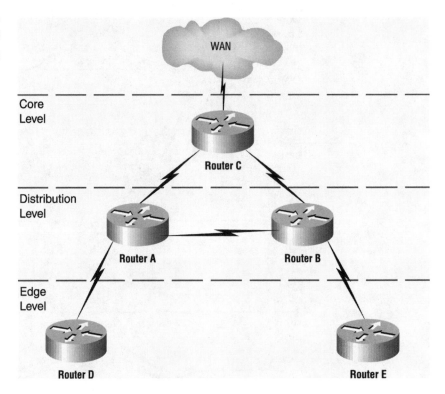

If the link between Router A and Router C were to fail, the IGP (Interior Gateway Protocol) would recalculate the route table using the new topology information. After the route table converges, Router A will then send packets destined to Router C through the link between Router A and Router B. Packets will then be forwarded by Router B to Router C. Moreover, if both of the links connecting the two *edge* routers to the *distribution* router fail, the two *edge* routers will still be able to communicate with each other. You just don't get that kind of flexibility with a dual-linked architecture

The following list compares dual-linked topology and meshed topology.

Dual-Linked	**Meshed** .
Load balancing	Slightly lower cost
Increased bandwidth	Direct communication with peers
Great when applications are delay sensitive	Allows direct access to applications and servers that are distributed among different locations

Backup Power Systems   In addition to multiple links and meshed topologies, the third element of redundancy consists of backup power systems. Power outages come in different sizes, from local to widespread, with the local variety being the easiest to fortify your network against through redundancy. Cisco provides space for a second power supply to be installed for core devices. This works really well if the outage is isolated to a certain machine. UPS (uninterruptable power supply) units should be used to provide redundancy on a larger scale for all network equipment. Other forms of redundant power systems consist of additional and disparate power grids within the building—ideally, equipment should be powered across different power grids.

Additionally, software can provide a good redundancy solution in conjunction with hardware solutions. Some examples of software used for redundancy are dynamic routing protocols such as:

- Interior Gateway Routing Protocol (IGRP)

- Enhanced Interior Gateway Routing Protocol (EIGRP)

- Open Shortest Path First (OSPF)

Although these dynamic protocols can converge and find alternate paths to route packets on, any established connections or sessions will be terminated during the convergence period. Only when convergence is complete can connections be reestablished and sessions restarted. Sometimes the resulting unavailability of the network is acceptable, but in mission-critical situations, this downtime can be costly in a variety of ways. And again, cost will drive the network design—if reliability and availability must be present at all costs, other design solutions should be considered.

The solution to the aforementioned problem, and an example of teaming up software with hardware, is found in Hot Standby Routing Protocol (HSRP). It works by using physical redundancy in combination with software solutions by providing redundancy for the Internet Protocol (IP)—it does this by fooling with the unique addressing rule. To get an idea of how HSRP works, refer to Figure 2.3. This figure shows how the two physical routers simulate a virtual router and link. With HSRP, you can make two physically redundant routers share both IP addresses and MAC (Media Access Control) addresses—well, sort of.

How can this be? HSRP creates *virtual* MAC and IP addresses, and makes two routers (or however many devices belong to a specified group) share them. These virtual addresses are similar to a loopback interface that can be configured on a router. The interface is just a virtual one, but has an actual IP address that can be advertised to other networks. In this manner, a virtual router is created by HSRP, so routers are configured to be part of a specific HSRP group. At start-up, one of the two devices is assigned the role of active router, and the other, by default, is assigned the role of backup router. With this arrangement in place, the active router will listen for packets destined for the virtual MAC or IP address as well as traffic destined for real, physical MAC and IP addresses.

Routers that participate in a given group communicate via User Datagram Protocol (UDP) by sending HSRP hello packets. So, if communication between the routers fails—if the backup router doesn't receive the hello packet from the active router—the backup router kicks in and takes over for the active router. Control of the MAC and IP addresses is given over to the backup router—the new active router.

For the network and HSRP to work properly, connectivity between HSRP group routers must be guaranteed. If the connection between the two HSRP-speaking routers fails, both routers will advertise the primary IP address to the rest of the network. Cisco introduced HSRP into the version 10 release of Cisco IOS™.

In Figure 2.3, HSRP has created what appears to be a virtual router and path. With HSRP enabled, Router A and Router B continue to function normally. Host X is trying to reach Host Y. For HSRP to work properly, the host must have the virtual MAC and IP address configured locally as the gateway. The active router—in this case, Router A—listens for virtual addresses. Router A forwards all packets to the WAN via its own link. Router B continues to function normally while it listens for hello packets from Router A. If Router B doesn't receive the hello packet, it'll take over the role of active router by assuming control of the virtual addresses. Host X is totally unaffected by this because it's still using the virtual addresses to send its information.

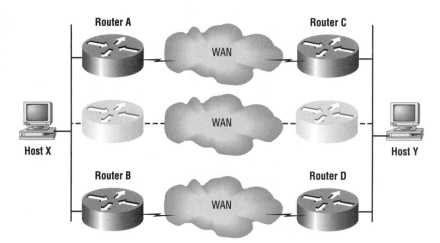

After Router B has taken over for failed Router A, the packets are sent through Router B's WAN link so that they're still able to reach Host Y. The connectivity between hosts depends on the fact that the network was also designed to be fully redundant. If this weren't so, neither of the routers could get to a specified destination. Figure 2.3 demonstrates that Host Y can be reached by either WAN link.

Backup

All of the above scenarios and network designs were based on providing redundancy. Depending on the use and type of applications running on your network, it really could be overkill to design a fully redundant network encompassing all three layers of the Cisco hierarchy. Doing so consumes a lot of resources—in terms of personnel and probably money, too. Often, it's more appropriate to design a backup system in case of network failure instead of committing to a fully redundant network.

And here again, you have a lot of choices when it comes to designing a backup system for a network. No worries, though, because this array of choices is a good thing, providing the flexibility to choose a backup design that best matches the specifics of your network—the applications running on it and the needs of its typical end user.

As with redundancy, there are different types of backup systems—ISDN, leased lines, and analog modems can all be used to provide backup connections for a network. And again, it's imperative to first assess exactly what's required of a particular network before you can design a proper backup system using appropriate technology.

Analog Modems   Analog lines can be used as backup connections into a LAN or WAN from remote sites. If the circuit that connects the network to the outside world goes down and the administrator isn't on-site when that occurs, an analog modem connection can provide connectivity back into the network. Predictably, the limiting factor with analog modems is line speed, but modems that run at 56Kbps can be implemented in conjunction with a 56Kbps leased line. So, if cost and transfer delays aren't major concerns, this could be a great solution to employ as a very reliable backup system.

ISDN   But what about that ubiquitous speed factor—what should you do when speed is an issue? If being quick is a real priority, you should consider ISDN instead of relying on slow analog modem systems. Another important point is that ISDN not only transports data, it supports voice and video. These factors make ISDN a truly attractive option. With it, you get lots of available bandwidth at a relatively low cost.

There are two types of ISDN interfaces: Basic Rate Interface (BRI) and Primary Rate Interface (PRI). Choosing between these interfaces depends on what the line will be used for. BRI is supported on routers that run Cisco IOS 10 or higher; PRI is supported in Cisco IOS 10.2 or higher. Several different devices within Cisco's product line are used for ISDN connections, but it's important to note that Cisco 750 series routers don't run Cisco IOS. Cisco no longer markets 750 series routers—they've collapsed the line of ISDN routers into the Cisco 700 series, including 76*x* and 77*x* routers. And no worries—their 766 router does run Cisco IOS.

BRI uses two B channels and one D channel. Each of the two B channels runs at 64Kbps bi-directionally; the D channel runs at 16Kbps. The B channels are used for transmitting and receiving data. The two B channels are automatically added to a rotary group. The D channel is used for protocol communications and signaling.

In contrast, PRI uses 23 B channels and 1 D channel. All 23 B channels are added to a rotary group as well. The D channel runs at the same line speed as the B channels—64Kbps. Because of the D channel's additional line speed, PRI has the equivalent line speed of a T1 circuit (1.5Mbps). And in Europe, PRI offers 30 B channels and 1 D channel, making it the equivalent of an E1 circuit.

Software   Now that you're familiar with the types of available backup hardware, we can move on to how this hardware can be utilized in designing a backup system. Both analog modems and ISDN routers use leased lines for their connectivity, but the hardware alone isn't enough to provide backup communication between sites. As we saw with redundancy, for a backup system to work properly, the hardware and software aspects of it must work hand in hand. We've discussed the hardware options, but we haven't yet looked into the role that software plays in designing a solid backup connection.

Dial-on-demand routing (DDR) provides the missing software ingredient for creating a fully functional backup system. Versatile DDR can be used over several different types of connections, and is supported in Cisco IOS version 10 and later. It supports the following networking protocols:

- IP

- IPX

- AppleTalk

- DECnet

And DDR's flexibility reaches even further. It can be used over several different types of interfaces—synchronous and asynchronous serial interfaces, as well as ISDN.

If you opt to use DDR as a backup connection, keep a few little details in mind: Since DDR interfaces are usually inactive, no dynamic routing information can be learned from those interfaces. This means that you'll need static routes (and zones if using AppleTalk) configured so that the router will know of the available routes on the other side of the backup link. And here's another issue—recall that static routes have an administrative distance of zero, and will override any dynamically learned route. Why does this matter? Well, if the router were configured with a plain static route, the DDR would become that router's primary link instead of a backup link—yikes! We definitely do not want that to happen. But there is a way to avoid this disturbing event—you must weight the static routes with the following command:

```
ip route 10.1.2.3 255.255.255.0 10.5.6.7 1-255
```

Here, *1-255* is the distance metric specified to weight the static route. BGP (Border Gateway Protocol) routes usually have an administrative distance of 20, internal EIGRP routes have a default distance of 90, and external EIGRP routes have a default distance of 170. With a specified distance greater than 200, the static route won't be used to initiate a DDR connection unless all other routes are absent, or if they're unreachable via the interface from which they were discovered.

OSPF, BGP, or IS-IS (Intermediate System–to–Intermediate System) cannot be used in a DDR environment. These protocols require an acknowledgment from their neighbor for routing updates to be sent, and due to the nature of DDR links, it's very possible that the interface won't be active when a response needs to be sent. This really isn't a big deal when using DDR as a backup connection, because with it, static routes are used to establish routes to desired destinations instead of routing protocols.

With the proper static routes set so that the backup line is activated only when the dynamic routes become unreachable, DDR follows four steps to establish communication with the other site. At this point, it's important to remember that the routers on both sides of the backup line have DDR set up on the interfaces. Before a DDR link can be established, the following four criteria have to be met:

1. The router verifies that there's a route to the intended destination.

2. Via the static route, the router finds the DDR interface that's connected to the desired destination.

3. The router checks to see if the DDR interface is already active and connected to the destination.

4. Finally, the router determines if the packet is either interesting or uninteresting. This decision is based upon the access lists applied to the DDR interface. Interesting packets pass right on through the access list, but the uninteresting ones won't be allowed passage.

If the packet's an interesting one and there's not already a connection, the router will establish one, and the packets will be sent through that interface. If the packet is uninteresting and doesn't pass the access list, no connection will be made, and the packet will be dropped.

Topologies   Three topologies can be designed using DDR. As with all other topology designs, these three are point-to-point, star, and fully meshed. As we discussed in the redundancy section, cost and actual needs should be accurately assessed when designing backup links. Next, we'll present these topology options for you in visual form.

Point-to-point topology can be used when you need to have only a backup link as an exit point from the network. Figure 2.4 shows that if Router A's primary connection to the WAN fails, all that would be needed to provide a backup connection is a DDR interface connected via a leased line that's also connected to the WAN. In Figure 2.4, the solid line symbolizes the primary link, and the dashed line represents the backup dial-up line that DDR will use if the primary link becomes unavailable.

FIGURE 2.4

Point-to-point
topology using DDR
as backup

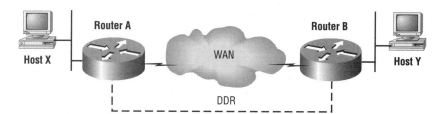

The star topology is often used when remote locations access applications at a central site. Figure 2.5 depicts a scenario where it's necessary to provide backup DDR links to each edge site. This is done so that if the primary link fails, the backup link can still provide enough speed to both access and use the applications available from the hub router, Router A.

WARNING   Time-sensitive applications may not work properly when using DDR because of the time involved in establishing communication with the destination router.

The fully meshed topology permits any site to dial any other site. Depending on which static routes have been configured on it, Router A can dial Router B, Router C, Router D, or Router E. The same goes for the other routers. If a fully meshed topology is used, it's a good idea to limit its size because of the extensive configuration required for each site. Static routes

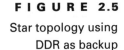

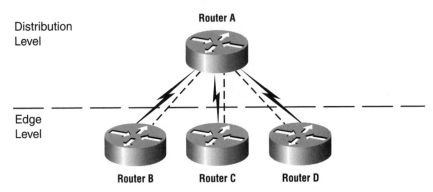

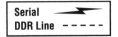

must be mapped to each router from the DDR interface. When the mesh grows, the management of myriad static routes can become complex. Figure 2.6 shows a mesh between five routers—you can see the many links that'll all require static routes to the other routers. Compare that scenario to the one depicted in Figure 2.7, which shows a mesh with only three routers.

So basically, while both redundant and backup designs work well in many different topologies, the deciding factors on whether to use a redundant or backup design depend on the production network requirements. If there's little to no tolerance for downtime, you need a redundant solution. If applications aren't time sensitive and a link is established to provide communication, a backup system could very well be sufficient.

Alternate Path Routing

A redundant network design gives you fault tolerance. Moreover, with it, other methods can be used to help increase network availability. Not only can alternate links be used when primary links fail, alternate links can be used simultaneously to increase availability by expanding the available bandwidth. The concept of alternate path routing is realized when a network device such as a router maintains multiple paths to a given destination.

FIGURE 2.6

Full mesh (five routers) using DDR as backup

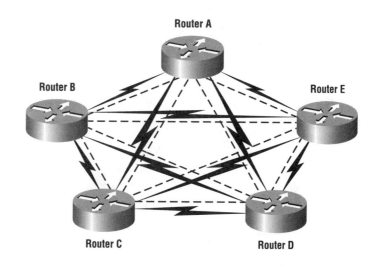

FIGURE 2.7

Full mesh (three routers) using DDR as backup

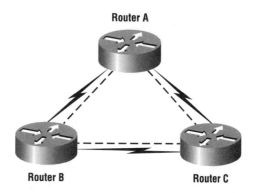

Figure 2.8 displays a complex network layout. Though it's not a very realistic design, it's useful in showing how alternate path routing works. We're using EIGRP as the routing protocol in this example.

FIGURE 2.8

Enhanced IGRP
alternate path routing

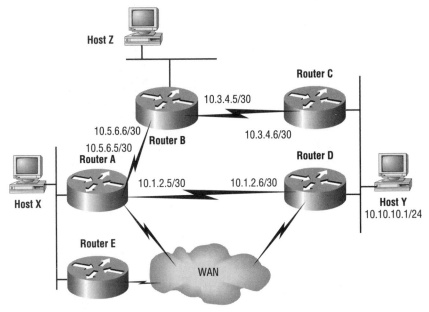

Possible routes
—Topology table

Router A will have Host Y's address in its
topology table via the following interfaces:
• Router B
• WAN
• Router E
• Router D

Let's say Host X's default gateway is set to Router A, and that it wants to talk to Host Y. To initiate communication, it will send a packet to Router A, which will then have to decide which interface it will use to forward the packet. Assuming that all the WAN links are of equal bandwidth and that circumstances are normal, it's a good bet that the packet will be forwarded to Router D. Router D will then forward the packet on to Host Y. We can assume this because we know that EIGRP will provide only one route to the host—the route having the best local metric.

Let's stop here and make sure you're clear on how EIGRP works. Look again at Figure 2.8. You can see that Router A has four connections attached to it, and also that all four of those links have a path to Host Y. In case those four paths aren't readily recognizable to you, we'll list them:

- Router A > Router B > Router C > Host Y

- Router A > Router E > WAN > Router D > Host Y

- Router A > WAN > Router D > Host Y

- Router A > Router D > Host Y

EIGRP actually has all this information stored in the router, and with the following command, you can see how many different ways a route is actually learned.

Show ip eigrp topology *A.B.C.D* <cr>

Typing in that command and substituting A.B.C.D with the IP network for Host Y (not the specific IP address) would give you the following information:

```
IP-EIGRP topology entry for 10.10.10.0/24
   State is Passive, Query origin flag is 1, 1 Successor(s),
FD is 283648
   Routing Descriptor Blocks:
   10.1.2.6 (Serial1), from 10.1.2.6, Send flag is 0x0
      Composite metric is (283648/281600), Route is Internal
      Vector metric:
         Minimum bandwidth is 10000 Kbit
         Total delay is 1080 microseconds
         Reliability is 255/255
         Load is 1/255
         Minimum MTU is 1500
         Hop count is 1
   10.5.6.6 (Serial2), from 10.5.6.6, Send flag is 0x0
      Composite metric is (2246656/2221056), Route is
External
      Vector metric:
         Minimum bandwidth is 1544 Kbit
         Total delay is 23000 microseconds
         Reliability is 255/255
         Load is 1/255
         Minimum MTU is 1500
         Hop count is 2
```

```
External data:
      Originating router is 10.5.6.6
      AS number of route is 104
      External protocol is IGRP, external metric is 8676
      Administrator tag is 0 (0x00000000)
   10.9.10.14 (Serial3), from 10.9.10.14, Send flag is 0x0
      Composite metric is (3424567/3327643), Route is
External
      Vector metric:
         Minimum bandwidth is 1544 Kbit
         Total delay is 21000 microseconds
         Reliability is 255/255
         Load is 3/255
         Minimum MTU is 1500
         Hop count is 3
   10.11.12.18 (Ethernet0), from 10.11.12.18, Send flag is
0x0
Composite metric is (3564379/3499372), Route is Internal
Vector metric:
   Minimum bandwidth is 1544 Kbit
   Total delay is 24000 microseconds
   Reliability is 255/255
   Load is 5/255
   Minimum MTU is 1500
   Hop count is 4
```

By looking over the topology database, you can see the four different sources from which Router A learned about the network that Host Y is on. Normally, and by default, EIGRP will make the choice of one of these routes based on the lowest metric, and then enter it into the route table. This routing decision leaves the other three links unused until the metric on the preferred route becomes higher than the metric for one of them. That usually happens when the load gets heavy enough that the preferred route's metric increases, and since EIGRP always opts for the link with the lowest metric, it will then establish a new preferred route.

Cisco has developed a way to utilize the unused links, and increase bandwidth and network availability, through something it calls *unequal-cost load balancing*. They've done this by configuring EIGRP *feasible successor* relationships with the other routes in the EIGRP topology table. This is also considered alternate path routing. You can configure EIGRP topology routes as feasible successors by using the Variance command. Here's the syntax for it:

variance *multiplier*

From within the variance command, the multiplier can be any value from 1 to 128, with the default being 1, and you have to use it inside the EIGRP protocol configuration.

Figure 2.9 illustrates how the variance command works.

FIGURE 2.9

Feasible successor configuration

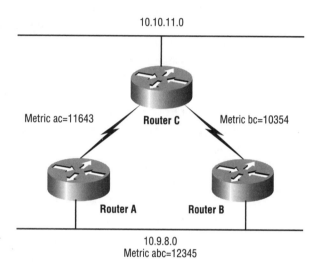

In Figure 2.9, both Routers A and B have individual routes to network 10.10.11.0, and each connection has a metric associated with it. In this example, the metric between Router A and Router C is *ac*, and the metric between Router B and Router C is *bc*. The route from Router A to Router C through Router B also has a metric: *abc*. Let's say that we want to configure the route from Router A to Router C via Router B as a feasible successor. For that to happen, two criteria would have to be met:

- Metric *ac* would have to be greater than metric *bc*. We're OK with this one because *ac*=11345, and *bc*=10345.

- After using the Variance command, the product of the *multiplier* times the metric *ac* must be equal to or greater than the metric *abc*. So if we set the *multiplier* to two, it's equal, and this criteria is met.

Conditions satisfied, route *abc* then becomes an advertised route. A maximum of six routes per destination can be extracted from the EIGRP topology table and tagged as feasible successors. These six routes will then be added into the route table and advertised.

Adaptable Networking

Planning for future change and growth is integral to designing a successful network. As a company evolves, sites are often added, so to accurately address business requirements, the network has to be scalable. Each site added means that new applications and protocols will be introduced, and their network needs to be able to adapt to these changes. Formerly, networking was centered on the need to access mainframe computers—these outmoded systems are now faced with the challenge of fluidly connecting to other company networks and the outside world.

Obviously, these changes introduce many factors into the functionality of a network. Often, the more sites that are added to a network, the more protocols that are present on it—some routable, others not. To function well, the network must not only be able to adapt to these changes, it has to deal with them efficiently.

Joining LANs as a network grows can sometimes cause problems because each existing LAN has its networks and routing already established. And as an enterprise network expands, it becomes necessary to connect remote sites—each of which is likely to have networks that'll have to be routed and advertised to the other remote sites. This can be accomplished through redistribution, because under most routing protocols, it's possible to redistribute other types of protocols. As an example, the following protocols can be redistributed into EIGRP during a session:

```
Gw-RouterA(config-router)#redistribute ?
  bgp        Border Gateway Protocol (BGP)
  connected  Connected
  egp        Exterior Gateway Protocol (EGP)
  eigrp      Enhanced Interior Gateway Routing Protocol
  (EIGRP)
  igrp       Interior Gateway Routing Protocol (IGRP)
  isis       ISO IS-IS
  iso-igrp   IGRP for OSI networks
```

```
mobile    Mobile routes
ospf      Open Shortest Path First (OSPF)
rip       Routing Information Protocol (RIP)
static    Static routes
```

The list is similar for OSPF and other routing protocols. This redistribution allows LANs to share network information across a WAN, and it's possible only when a network is flexible and adaptable. To accomplish that, not only does your design require the right type of hardware, it needs the right IOS. Why? Because earlier versions of the Cisco IOS don't support EIGRP or OSPF.

Complicating things further, protocols like SNA and NetBIOS aren't routable. As if this weren't enough, they're also time sensitive, so if you're thinking the solution is bridging—sorry. This alone just won't always work for you. The full answer comes in the form of queuing mechanisms that give encapsulated protocols first priority when transitioning a network. This priority status means they won't experience the average delay that other packets will.

Though these tools will make a network adaptable, we have to underscore the fact that it's really important to use the right versions of software and hardware with them. The advances made in recent IOS versions allow the advances in hardware to work with more flexibility and adaptability, thereby helping you to maximize your network's efficiency.

Improving Network Performance

Maximizing network availability is a wonderful thing, but actualizing a network's full potential doesn't end there—improving the network's performance is equally important. Just like computers, networks do only what we tell them to do—even when our instructions are incorrect or deficient. Our purpose here is to teach you how to be both efficient and correct when fine-tuning the routers present on your network to optimize its performance.

There are several different ways to approach the optimization goal, but the changes you can make to that end fall into three major categories:

- Making the network efficient

- Minimizing perceived network delay

- Managing protocol responsiveness

The larger a network gets, the more vital it becomes that it's efficient. If the network's routers are improperly tuned and configured, the resource most affected is likely to be the network's precious bandwidth. Broadcasts, talkative network protocols, and routing updates all eat away at it, but fine-tuning the protocols that run on routers will really help to lighten the load.

In this chapter, we'll introduce the various methods used in fine-tuning a network and improving its performance. They'll be covered in greater detail in later chapters.

Making the Network Efficient

First things first: The most effective way of making a network run more efficiently is to optimize the way the available bandwidth is used. You can achieve this by making configuration changes at all three levels of Cisco's three-layer model. The following list details the different ways to optimize bandwidth along with the corresponding functions:

- **Access lists:** Used to permit or deny a specific type of packet, whether it's a routing update, broadcast, or data packet. These can be fairly simple, or very detailed, extensive, complicated, and lengthy. So be aware that extremely long access lists can have quite an impact on CPU utilization and even increase delay.

- **Distribution lists:** This command can be used to limit the number of networks advertised by permitting advertisements only to those specified. Distribution lists are applied from within a routing protocol to manipulate which route updates are sent and accepted on the specified interface. For networks where the edge routers rely only on the default route, advertising a few choice networks to them is all that's necessary. Reducing the advertised routes conserves bandwidth and reduces the load on the edge router.

- **Route summarization:** This command takes all of the specific routes that a router knows about and summarizes them into major network boundaries. Like distribution lists, this also reduces the number of networks that are advertised, and is a very easy and effective way to conserve bandwidth and lower CPU utilization on the router.

- **Incremental updates:** More advanced routing protocols such as OSPF and EIGRP send new updates only when they occur instead of sending the entire route table.

- **Snapshot updates:** Adjacent routers exchange full tables upon establishing communication, and then only at specified intervals.

- **DDR:** With it, connections are initiated only when bandwidth or certain destinations must be accessed. So it's handy when a certain location doesn't need to be continually connected, and it's efficient because the connection is established only when it's needed.

- **Compression:** Software compression can be done with Cisco IOS. It's useful if bandwidth utilization is near saturation, but the downside is that it can cause significant overhead on the routers handling the task of compressing and decompressing data. The amount of overhead is proportional to the amount of compression being done, so the busier the router becomes, the more overhead will be generated. In header compression, the sending router has to read the header, compress it, then route it; the receiving router has to decompress the header, read it, then if compression is enabled, recompress it before routing it. There are two other types of WAN compression: payload compression and link compression.

- **Switching using X.25 or Frame Relay:** Provides the opportunity for global connectivity. Using Frame Relay allows you to connect to a service provider's Frame Relay cloud, which provides circuits to large cities and many other locations.

Minimizing Perceived Network Delay

The network-delay problem can also be solved in different ways, with the easiest method being to simply add more bandwidth. However, doing that can also easily eat up the budget—it's an expensive solution. So if the get-more-bandwidth approach isn't an option for you, it's good to know about the different ways built into the Cisco IOS to manage and maximize existing bandwidth while minimizing network delay. Even if you can afford it, it's a good idea to try these approaches before adding costly bandwidth—you might find that you really don't need more after all!

Cisco IOS includes features such as queuing, fast-switching, optimum-switching, cache flow-switching, and autonomous-switching. These are great tools for effectively managing packets and optimizing bandwidth usage, while simultaneously placing less overhead on the router itself.

Queuing works by defining which type of traffic is given the highest priority, as well as how much bandwidth it's allowed to use. This feature works very well for time-sensitive applications, because packets tagged as high priority are sent immediately. This helps to prevent session time-out errors. Cisco uses first in, first out (FIFO) priority, custom, and weighted fair queuing algorithms. We'll discuss all of these algorithms in greater detail in a later chapter.

In addition to Cisco's queuing algorithms, the Cisco IOS also provides switching paths. Switching paths allow packets to be forwarded to the next hop without looking up all of the header information, thereby saving time and CPU utilization because less has to be done with each incoming packet. Cisco IOS allows process-switching, fast-switching, autonomous-switching, silicon-switching, optimum-switching, distributed-switching, and Netflow-switching, each of which has a distinct feature set and situations in which it can and should be used. We'll talk about these more extensively later in this book.

The perceived network delay can be reduced significantly with these tools, or through a solution combining several of them. As networks grow, so does their need for bandwidth. Lately, there's been a lot of talk about the use and importance of caching, and this too is an excellent way to reduce network delay. Instead of a client having to download an entire Web page from the Internet—utilizing bandwidth and experiencing delay—a cache server can be located within the network that stores many frequently accessed files.

Managing Protocol Responsiveness

Another piece of the performance puzzle is protocol responsiveness. If the network and routing protocols don't respond quickly to requests and changes, the network can't function at its best. Protocol responsiveness can be broken down into two areas: network protocols and routing protocols.

Network protocols such as IPX and AppleTalk function well on the LAN side of the router, but because they're such noisy protocols, it's foolish to allow them to transit WAN links without some type of fine-tuning done on the router. This can be accomplished with filter lists and tunnels, which can be used to link two or more LANs together.

Filter lists stop unwanted broadcasts and protocol announcements from transiting the WAN, and *tunnels* provide encapsulation so that the WAN doesn't have to know about the LAN protocols until the packet gets to its destination. At the other end of the tunnel, the router must provide route information to locally connected LANs so that they can reach the remote

LANs connected on the originating side of the tunnel. Doing this requires redistributing a network protocol into a routing protocol, and when there are many updates, the routing protocol sometimes gets confused, resulting in a lack of responsiveness.

To manage protocol responsiveness, additional configuration steps must be added to maintain the routing protocol's stability and reliability. Just jumping in and redistributing protocols into each other usually causes some type of routing problem. The `default-metric` command allows an administrator to set a metric value to a redistributed protocol. Each redistributed protocol has specific metric requirements—a Cisco command summary manual or Web page should be consulted. The `distance` command is also used to modify the behavior of routing protocols.

So, fine-tuning the protocols running on a router will result in faster route convergence, and when protocols are configured correctly, the network runs smoothly with fewer problems. These factors are integral to creating and running an optimized network.

Summary

In this chapter, we've covered the following key points:

- Redundancy and backup connectivity—both of these elements need to be considered when designing an adaptable, scalable, reliable, and secure network. You must assess the needs of the users and the network itself so that you can make proper decisions.

- Redundancy, backups, alternate path routing, and adaptable networks must all be used in conjunction for a network design to be successful.

- After a network has been designed and implemented, it is important to make the network adaptable so that it can grow with changing needs and technologies. If the network is unable to adjust to new requirements placed upon it, it will soon become obsolete because it cannot support the applications that run across it.

- Constant adjustment is required to maintain an efficient and responsive network. New software features are released that provide the ability to refine network operation even more. It is vital that a network administrator be aware of all of the current software and hardware releases available to them. That knowledge will allow them to make sound decisions concerning what should be done on the routers to constantly improve performance and availability.

- Several different technologies that assist in creating a stable and reliable network—DDR, HSRP, switching, queuing, and others—were all described in detail.

Review Questions

1. What are the three methods used to increase network availability?

   A. Bandwidth, RAM and Cisco IOS

   B. Redundancy, bandwidth, and backup connections

   C. Dynamic routing protocols, bandwidth, and redundancy or backup connectivity

   D. Power, connectivity, and high-end routers

2. Which of the following are the three physical elements of a redundant network design?

   A. Multiple-link topology, meshed-link topology, and power systems

   B. Replacement hardware, multiple links, and power systems

   C. Multiple machines (HSRP), multiple links, and meshed links

   D. Dual links, fully redundant routers, and DDR lines

3. Which topology can be made redundant?

   A. Point-to-point

   B. Hub-and-spoke

   C. Meshed

   D. Both A and B

4. What is required to implement HSRP?

   A. Cisco IOS

   B. Multiple machines and multiple links

   C. Redundant machines running Cisco IOS (rev. 10)

   D. Both A and B

5. You want DDR to be activated only as a backup connection. Which of the following configuration changes will ensure that the DDR link will be used only when the router's primary connection to a given destination fails?

A. A static route

B. A static route with a high administrative distance assigned to it

C. A route in the routing table

D. Simply configuring DDR on the desired interface

6. Why shouldn't BGP, OSPF, and IS-IS protocols be used in a DDR environment?

A. These are time-sensitive protocols

B. These protocols require an acknowledgment from their neighbor before routing updates can be sent

C. DDR does not support these protocols

D. These protocols do not scale well

7. Which of the following are steps that routers take when deciding whether to establish a connection? (Choose all that apply.)

A. Verifying a route to the destination

B. Passing the access list applied to the interface

C. Checking to see if a connection has already been established

D. Defining the interface through which the call should be made

E. All of the above

8. What command is used on a Cisco router to show all the ways that the router learned a given route?

    A. `show ip route`

    B. `show ip eigrp topology`

    C. `show ip route *`

    D. `show eigrp topology`

9. How is a feasible successor configured?

    A. As a global command: `ip feasible-successor 0.0.0.0 255.255.255.0 null 0`

    B. As a command under EIGRP: `variance multiplier value`

    C. As a command under EIGRP: `feasible-successor 0.0.0.0 255.255.255.255`

    D. As a global command: `variance multiplier value`

10. Which of the following is the correct command used to control the redistribution of one routing protocol into IGRP or Enhanced IGRP?

    A. `distance weight address mask`

    B. `redistribute-metric bandwidth delay reliability loading mtu`

    C. `default-metric number`

    D. `default-metric bandwidth delay reliability loading mtu`

11. Which is *not* a method of optimizing bandwidth utilization?

    A. DDR or bandwidth on demand

    B. Dynamic routing protocols

    C. Header or data compression

    D. Access lists

12. Which is a method to improve network responsiveness?

    A. Queuing

    B. Data compression

    C. Access list

    D. DDR or bandwidth on demand

13. Which is a cost-effective alternative to provide additional bandwidth?

    A. Leased-line circuits

    B. ISDN

    C. DDR

    D. Point-to-point circuit

14. In which of the Cisco three-layer hierarchy models can redundancy be implemented?

    A. Core

    B. Edge

    C. Distribution

    D. All of the above

15. What is *not* a benefit of using dynamic routing protocols on routers that have multiple or redundant links?

    A. Load balancing

    B. Quicker network convergence

    C. Feasible-successor calculation

    D. Lower processor utilization

16. Which routing protocol supports load balancing?

    A. IGRP

    B. EIGRP

    C. RIP

    D. BGP

17. In which version of Cisco IOS was DDR implemented?

    A. 11.0

    B. 9.3

    C. 10.0

    D. 10.3

18. When should DDR *not* be implemented?

    A. When applications are time sensitive

    B. When additional bandwidth is not needed

    C. When snapshot routing has been implemented

    D. When access lists have been applied to the interface

19. Which software feature optimizes bandwidth without creating higher CPU utilization?

   A. Access lists

   B. Switching

   C. Compression

   D. None of the above

20. Which is *not* a method of reducing routing updates?

   A. Route summarization

   B. Distribution lists

   C. Tunneling

   D. Unthrottled redistribution

CHAPTER

3

IP Traffic Control

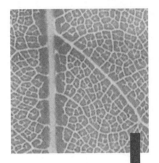

IP access lists are used to control both the amount and types of traffic that transit across a network. They come in a variety of types with many applications, and are used to either permit or deny access to the network, provide security, manage bandwidth, and advertise routes. This chapter will cover the primary types of access lists and their applications.

You can write access lists in many different ways to achieve a particular result, and the numerous ways they can be applied to interfaces and routers provide many additional options. Each different method of application creates a different result.

In this chapter, we'll discuss the difference between standard and extended access lists. Then, we'll cover some alternatives to IP access lists. How to effectively handle directed-broadcast traffic, as well as important security considerations when managing a Cisco router, will also be covered.

The exam objectives covered in this chapter include:

- Configure IP standard access lists

- Configure IP extended access lists

- Verify access list operation

- Limit virtual terminal access

- Configures an alternative to using access lists

- Configure an IP helper address to manage broadcasts

- Introduction to Managing Traffic and Access

IP Access Lists

As mentioned, there are two types of access lists, standard and extended. The standard list is relatively limited in the functions it can provide—it can filter based upon only the source address of the incoming or outgoing packet. The valid numerical assignment for a standard access list is 1 through 99.

On the other hand, extended lists are much more flexible and complex. The different types of traffic they can filter greatly enhance their capabilities. Extended lists can permit or deny based on several different criteria such as the source address, destination address, protocol, and port numbers. The valid numerical identification range is from 100 to 199.

We'll begin our IP access list discussion by examining how standard lists work—their syntax and implementation. After that, we'll show you how extended lists are configured and implemented, giving you many examples of various configurations. You'll also see what actually happens to a packet when it's put through an access list.

Standard Access Lists

A *standard access list* is a sequential list of permit or deny statements based on the source IP address of a packet. When a packet reaches a router, the packet has to follow a different procedure based on whether it's trying to enter or leave an interface. If there's an access list on the interface, the packet must go through every line in it until the packet matches the specified criteria. If the packet goes through the entire list without a match, it is dropped. For the packet to be forwarded, there has to be a permit statement at the end of the list allowing that, or the packet will simply be dropped.

In Cisco IOS, there's an implied deny statement at the end of the access list, so if the purpose of your access list is to deny a few criteria, but forward everything else, you must include a permit statement as the final line of the access list. However, you don't have to end the access list with a deny statement if the list's purpose is to permit only certain criteria and drop the rest—this is automatically understood.

Figure 3.1 shows a flow chart that describes the steps taken when a packet enters or leaves an interface.

Stepping through the flow chart, you can see that the packet arrives at the specific interface through which it must enter or leave. The router's first step is to check whether there's an access list applied to the interface. If so, it will pass through each line of the access list until the packet's source address matches one of the source addresses listed. If the packet fails to match any of the source addresses, it will be denied. However, if the packet's source address *does* find a match in the list, the packet is then subjected to any condition implied on that line of the access list. The two conditional possibilities are to deny the packet or permit it. When a packet is denied, it's dropped; when it's permitted, it's forwarded to the next hop.

Exiting packets are first routed to the exiting interface and then verified by the access list, which determines whether the packet will be dropped or

FIGURE 3.1

Flow-chart process
of an access list

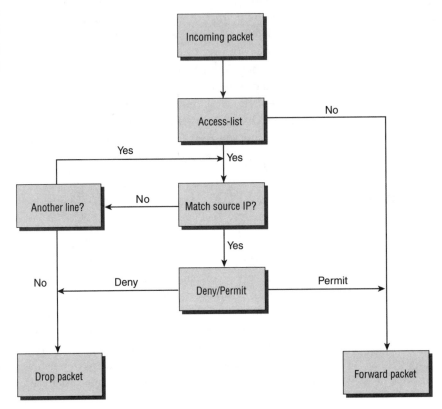

forwarded through the interface. Incoming packets arrive from the forwarding machine or router and are then checked against the access list. If the packet is permitted by the list, the packet will be accepted through the interface and forwarded to the exit interface.

If you're thinking that access lists have the potential of creating a lot of overhead on a router, you're right. They can also cause delays because packets have to be checked against every line in the access list until either they're matched or the list ends. So, when you write an access list, it's really important to plan ahead and write it as efficiently as possible. Place the lines that will receive the most matches at the top of the list, and as lines are added, try to place them according to their projected usage. Be aware of the possibility that the most matched line may not end up where you write it, depending on whether it is a permit or deny statement. Sometimes the IOS will reorder the statements based on the condition. Finally, the shorter the list, the less overhead and delay it will introduce.

Syntax

Now that you know how the standard access list works, we'll show you how they're written. The command is given with the following syntax:

```
access-list access-list-number [deny | permit] source
[source-wildcard]
```

The *access-list-number* is an integer between 1 and 99. After the list number, a deny or permit statement must be added to tell the router what to do if a packet matches this line of the access list. The *source* is the source IP host address or the source IP network address. It's the part of the line used to match the packets being compared against the access list, and can be entered as a four-octet IP address or as the word *any*, which will match any IP address. If more than one host or network needs to be designated, the *source-wildcard* can be added.

The wildcard mask should be written in a four-octet IP address format. The decimal value of each octet converts into a stream of binary zeros and ones. The zeros represent significant bits, meaning that the value must be matched exactly. The ones represent insignificant bits, meaning that the value does not have to be matched exactly. Examples follow in Table 3.1.

T A B L E 3.1: Network Addresses and Wildcard Masks

Network Address	Wildcard Mask (Decimal)	Wildcard Mask (Binary)
172.16 .10.0	0.0.0.255	00000000.00000000.00000000.11111111
172.16 .0.0	0.0.255.15	00000000.00000000.11111111.00001111
172.16 .20.4	0.0.0.3	00000000.00000000.00000000.00000011

These examples show that any address being compared to the IP address and wildcard mask must match the binary value for every place that has a zero assigned. The first example shows that network 172.16.10.0 has a wildcard mask of 0.0.0.255. This means that as long as the first three octets match exactly, the last octet does not matter. The second example is similar in that the Class B network must be matched, but the third octet does not matter. The fourth octet needs to match only every 16th host/network. For the last example, the last two bits of the last octet do not matter.

The syntax for extended lists differs significantly. You can't log matches on a standard list like you can on extended lists. Standard list syntax is much simpler, and so is the matching process that occurs with it. We've included some sample access lists here for you to read through, with an explanation following each list.

```
access-list 1 deny    172.16.40.6
access-list 1 permit 172.16.20.6
```

The access list one is pretty simple and straightforward. The first line identifies the access list as access-list 1. The condition of the first line is to deny any packet that matches the source address specified (in this case, 172.16.40.6). The second line, also identified as part of accesslist one, specifies that the access list will permit any packet that matches the source address of 172.16.20.6. What happens to a packet that doesn't match either of those lines? Remember that in Cisco IOS, the last line (although it may be invisible) of an access list is a *deny any* statement by default. So if you want packets that don't match the specified source addresses to be forwarded, you must add a *permit any* statement at the end of the list, or the packets will be dropped.

The access list two includes a permit any statement:

```
access-list 2 deny    10.0.0.0 0.255.255.255
access-list 2 deny    192.168.0.0 0.0.255.255
access-list 2 permit any
```

In this list, the private networks of 10.0.0.0 and 192.168.0.0 are denied, and everything else is permitted. Access list two has also used the source wildcard mask, indicating that any possible IP address within the Class A address space of 10.0.0.0 will be denied. The same thing was done for 192.168.0.0, indicating that every possible IP address within that Class C supernet range will also be denied. This is because trying to enter a single line for each and every one of the possible Class A and Class C addresses would be an impossibly huge task. Also, notice that access list two ends with *permit any*. If it didn't, nothing would be forwarded.

```
access-list 3 deny    10.1.3.10
access-list 3 deny    10.1.2.10
access-list 3 permit 10.1.4.10
```

Access list three is badly written and inefficient—line one denies host 10.1.3.10; line two denies host 10.1.2.10; line three permits host 10.1.4.10; and the last, invisible line implies a deny any statement. This access list's purpose is to permit one network and drop everything else, and it should be written differently to make it more efficient. The first step would be to remove the first two lines since they're denied by the implied deny at the end of the list anyway. Having them in the list twice just causes needless delay. That change moves the permit statement to the top of the list, allowing the principal condition to be met on the first try, and since the list is very short, it would cause little or no delay—much better!

Executing the command show access-lists displays the following information about the access lists configured on the router:

```
Router_B#show access-lists
Standard IP access list 1
    deny   172.16.40.6
    permit 172.16.20.6
Standard IP access list 2
    deny   10.0.0.0, wildcard bits 0.255.255.255
    deny   192.168.0.0, wildcard bits 0.0.255.255
    permit any
Standard IP access list 3
    deny   10.1.3.10
    deny   10.1.2.10
    permit 10.1.4.10
Router_B#
```

This information gives you a summary of each access list on the router. The access list type is defined (standard), along with the number assigned to it. Each line of the list is displayed individually—if you look at access list two, you can see that the command breaks the line down into its different components. The list also specifies which network is matched using which wildcard mask.

You need to keep a couple of tricks in mind when writing an access list. When you modify an existing access list, your new lines will be placed at the bottom, and that can cause problems. For example, suppose the following is your access list:

```
access-list 4 deny 10.1.2.5
access-list 4 deny 192.168.0.0 0.0.255.255
```

```
access-list 4 permit 10.2.2.3
access-list 4 permit 172.16.0.0 0.0.255.255
access-list 4 deny any
```

In access list four, the deny any statement isn't implicit, and if you add additional lines to this list, they'll be placed after the deny any statement at the bottom. That's important—it won't matter what changes you make because they'll just be dropped by the deny any line preceding them. The easiest way to edit a list is to make a copy of it, paste it into a text editor, and then make the necessary changes. After you've made your changes, delete the original list from the router with the `no ip access-list access-list-number` command. Once the original access list has been removed, simply paste the new one back into the router's configuration. The list may also be modified by deleting the list and simply retyping it.

Before deleting an access list, make sure that it's not applied to any interfaces via the `ip access-group access-list-number [in | out]` command. If an access list is removed while it's applied to an interface, or several interfaces, it could cause the router to crash. So, as a precaution, it's a good idea to remove the application of the access list from the interface to which it is being applied. This is done with the `no ip access-group` command.

After placing your modified access list on the router, go back and reapply the list to the interface(s) it was applied to before you edited it. When an access list is applied to an interface or through a distribute list, but the list doesn't exist on the router, all packets will be freely permitted as though no command applying an access list were present.

Finally, when writing a standard access list for any purpose, plan exactly which source addresses will be blocked and which ones will be permitted. After obtaining a preliminary draft of the networks that will be included in your access list, determine which networks can be aggregated into a single line using wildcard masks so that the list will be shorter, packets will experience less delay, and the router processor won't experience as much load. If you want packets that don't match any line on the list to be forwarded, don't forget to add the permit any statement so that they won't be dropped.

Applying Standard Access Lists

There are two basic ways to apply an access list to an interface—directly or through a routing protocol. To apply an access list directly to an interface, use the following command:

```
ip access-group access-list-number [ in | out ]
```

The *access-list-number* is the number of the list being applied to the interface. If the packet to be forwarded should be checked before its exit onto the line, the out option should be used. If packets coming from outside the router are to be checked against the access list before gaining entry, choose the in option.

Figure 3.2 shows a small network, which we're going to use as the basis for writing an access list to deny Router C access with respect to the originating IP address. In this case, we want to deny access to networks 172.16.10.0 and 172.16.20.0, and permit access to the network that hangs off Router B, 172.16.30.0.

FIGURE 3.2

Configuring and applying access lists

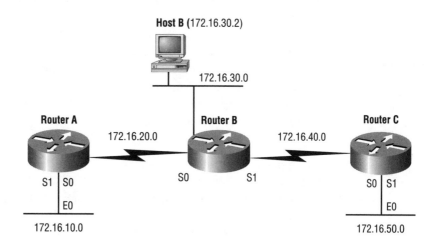

Here is how the access list is configured:

```
Router_C#conf t
Enter configuration commands, one per line.  End with CNTL/Z.
Router_C(config)#access-list 10 deny 172.16.10.0 0.0.0.255
```

```
Router_C(config)#access-list 10 deny 172.16.20.0 0.0.0.255
Router_C(config)#access-list 10 permit 172.16.30.0 0.0.0.255
Router_C(config)#int s0
Router_C(config-if)#ip access-group 10 in
Router_C(config-if)#

interface Serial0
 ip address 172.16.40.6 255.255.255.252
 ip access-group 10 in
!
access-list 10 permit 172.16.30.0 0.0.0.255
access-list 10 deny   172.16.20.0 0.0.0.255
access-list 10 deny   172.16.10.0 0.0.0.255
```

If you look closely at the above configuration, you'll notice that the order in which the statements were added is different from the order in which they're listed in the configuration. That's because the IOS will reorder statements to create a more logical flow. The list ends with the implicit deny, meaning that the list is ordered so that the permit begins it, with all the deny statements placed at the end. If the list ended with a permit any statement, the deny statements would be placed at the top of the list, with the permits at the end instead.

Looking again at Figure 3.2, you can see that the IP address of the serial link that connects Router B and Router C wasn't included in the list. Based on what you already know about access lists, will network 172.16.40.0 be permitted or denied? Instead of just denying access from Router A, we've also denied access to packets originating from Router B. For the access list to deny only packets from Router A, we'd need to modify access list 10. Here's how:

```
Router_C#conf t
Enter configuration commands, one per line.  End with CNTL/Z.
Router_C(config)#int s0
Router_C(config-if)#no ip access-group 10 in
Router_C(config-if)#no access-list 10
Router_C(config)#access-list 10 permit 172.16.30.0 0.0.0.255
Router_C(config)#access-list 10 permit 172.16.40.0 0.0.0.255
```

```
Router_C(config)#int s0
Router_C(config-if)#ip access-group 10 in
Router_C(config-if)#^Z
Router_C#
```

Let's step through each command. The first line (conf t) gains access to the Configuration mode. (The command int s0 is short for *interface serial zero*.) Next, we removed IP access group 10 from the interface. After removing the application of the access list, we deleted access list 10 and then entered the modified version of access list 10. Notice that there are now only two lines to the access list instead of three. The most efficient way of writing this list is to permit the wanted networks and deny everything else. There's no deny any statement at the end of the list because it's implied.

After the list has been modified and applied, it's important to verify that it's working properly. Debugging IP ICMP was turned on to give us an explanation as to why the pings that were executed failed. The results can be seen in the list below. First, a ping was initiated from Router C (172.16.40.6) to Router A (172.16.20.5). It failed because the ICMP echo packet has a source address of 172.16.20.5, which is denied by access list 10 applied to interface serial zero. The ICMP packet actually traveled across Router B and arrived at Router A. Router A then sent back an ICMP echo packet across Router B, to serial zero on Router C. Since the access group is applied inbound on the interface, the packet was dropped before making it through.

```
Router_C#ping 172.16.20.5

Type escape sequence to abort.
Sending 5, 100-byte ICMP Echos to 172.16.20.5, timeout is 2
seconds:

ICMP: dst (172.16.40.6) administratively prohibited
unreachable sent to 172.16.20.5.
ICMP: dst (172.16.40.6) administratively prohibited
unreachable sent to 172.16.20.5.
ICMP: dst (172.16.40.6) administratively prohibited
unreachable sent to 172.16.20.5.
ICMP: dst (172.16.40.6) administratively prohibited
unreachable sent to 172.16.20.5.
ICMP: dst (172.16.40.6) administratively prohibited
unreachable sent to 172.16.20.5.
Success rate is 0 percent (0/5)
Router_C#
```

Another ping was sent from Router A to Router C with similar results (as seen in the list below). In this case, the ICMP packet traveled across Router B and made it to the serial interface on Router C, but was dropped because of the access list applied to the interface.

```
Router_A#ping 172.16.40.6

Type escape sequence to abort.
Sending 5, 100-byte ICMP Echos to 172.16.40.6, timeout is 2
seconds:
U
ICMP: dst (172.16.20.5) administratively prohibited
  unreachable rcv from 172.16.40.6.U
ICMP: dst (172.16.20.5) administratively prohibited
  unreachable rcv from 172.16.40.6.U
ICMP: dst (172.16.20.5) administratively prohibited
  unreachable rcv from 172.16.40.6
Success rate is 0 percent (0/5)
Router_A#
```

When we inspect the debugging messages, they show us exactly what happened. On the first ping, Router C sent an unreachable message to 172.16.20.5 each time the ICMP echo was denied by the access list. On the second ping, a U follows every line, which stands for unreachable. The first debugging messages indicate that the unreachable echo is sent from Router C; the second messages indicate that the unreachable echo is received from Router C as well. The words *administratively prohibited* tell us that packets are being denied on purpose—not because a host or circuit is down.

The following ping is to test the permit condition of the access list. Networks 172.16.30.0 and 172.16.40.0 should be permitted by access list 10. The response is as follows:

```
Router_B#ping 172.16.40.6

Type escape sequence to abort.
Sending 5, 100-byte ICMP Echoes to 172.16.40.6, timeout is
  2 seconds:
!!!!!
Success rate is 100 percent (5/5), round-trip min/avg/max =
  4/7/8 ms
Router_B#
```

From Host B, we see the following results:

```
C:\WINDOWS>ping 172.16.40.6

Pinging 172.16.40.6 with 32 bytes of data:

Reply from 172.16.40.6: bytes=32 time=8ms TTL=254
Reply from 172.16.40.6: bytes=32 time=4ms TTL=254
Reply from 172.16.40.6: bytes=32 time=4ms TTL=254
Reply from 172.16.40.6: bytes=32 time=4ms TTL=254

Ping statistics for 172.16.40.6:
    Packets: Sent = 4, Received = 4, Lost = 0 (0% loss),
Approximate round trip times in milli-seconds:
    Minimum = 4ms, Maximum =  8ms, Average =  5ms
```

From these examples, we can see that the access list is working properly. It's always a good idea to test an access list in a lab environment before actually applying it in a production network.

You can also use access lists to manipulate route advertisements. To demonstrate this, we'll remove the IP access group from serial interface zero on Router C. Here's the route table before any changes are made in the EIGRP session:

```
Router_C#show ip route
Codes: C - connected, S - static, I - IGRP, R - RIP, M -
    mobile, B - BGP, D - EIGRP, EX - EIGRP external, O -
    OSPF, IA - OSPF inter area, N1 - OSPF NSSA external type
    1, N2 - OSPF NSSA external type 2, E1 - OSPF external
    type 1, E2 - OSPF external type 2, E - EGP, i - IS-IS,
    L1 - IS-IS level-1, L2 - IS-IS level-2, * - candidate
    default, U - per-user static route, o - ODR

Gateway of last resort is not set

    172.16.0.0/16 is variably subnetted, 4 subnets, 3 masks
C       172.16.40.4/30 is directly connected, Serial0
D       172.16.30.0/24 [90/2195456] via 172.16.40.5
        , 00:42:51, Serial0
D       172.16.20.4/30 [90/2681856] via 172.16.40.5
        , 02:33:25, Serial0
D       172.16.0.0/16 is a summary, 03:03:56, Null0
Router_C#
```

This information shows that there are three routes learned via EIGRP and one route that's directly connected. Next, we'll filter out the route for the 172.16.30.0 network:

```
Router_C#conf t
Enter configuration commands, one per line.  End with CNTL/Z.
Router_C(config)#access-list 30 deny 172.16.30.0 0.0.0.255
Router_C(config)#access-list 30 permit any
Router_C(config)#router eigrp 100
Router_C(config-router)#distribute-list 30 in serial0
Router_C(config-router)#^Z
Router_C#
```

After applying access list 30 via the distribute-list command, we executed another show ip route on the router. Here is the result:

```
Router_C#show ip route
Codes: C - connected, S - static, I - IGRP, R - RIP, M -
    mobile, B - BGP, D - EIGRP, EX - EIGRP external, O -
    OSPF, IA - OSPF inter area, N1 - OSPF NSSA external type
    1, N2 - OSPF NSSA external type 2, E1 - OSPF external
    type 1, E2 - OSPF external type 2, E - EGP, i - IS-IS,
    L1 - IS-IS level-1, L2 - IS-IS level-2, * - candidate
    default, U - per-user static route, o - ODR

Gateway of last resort is not set

     172.16.0.0/16 is variably subnetted, 3 subnets, 2 masks
C       172.16.40.4/30 is directly connected, Serial0
D       172.16.20.4/30 [90/2681856] via 172.16.40.5,
        00:00:02, Serial0
D       172.16.0.0/16 is a summary, 00:00:02, Null0
Router_C#
```

You can see that the 172.16.30.0 network is no longer in the routing table. This is how the distribute-list command works. However, it would be a lot more efficient if access list 30 were written on Router B and applied to interface serial one as an outbound filter. If we did that, we would avoid the waste of bandwidth resulting from the route being advertised out of the interface and dropped as it gets to Router C. This is really important in large networks—the location of filter application can make a big difference in bandwidth utilization.

Extended Access Lists

Extended access lists offer filtering on port numbers, session-layer protocols, and destination addresses in addition to filtering by source address. Though all these extended filtering features make this kind of access list much more powerful, they can also produce a greater amount of overhead on a router because of their potential complexity.

We'll cover extended lists the same way we covered standard lists—beginning with command syntax, then moving into a demonstration of how they're implemented. The primary difference with extended lists is the syntax of the command.

A packet must follow the same basic process when arriving at an interface with an extended access list applied to it that it does when confronting an interface with an applied standard list. Figure 3.3 illustrates the procedure a packet follows when being compared against an extended list—the only difference is the much greater scope of criteria possible to specify.

FIGURE 3.3

Packet processing through an extended access list

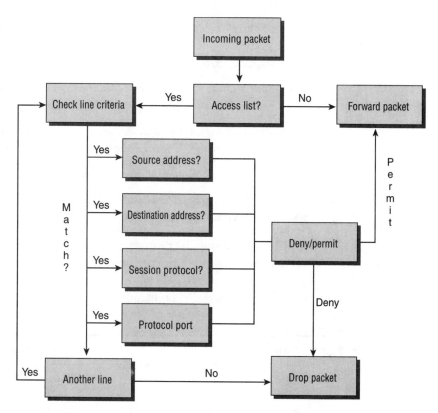

Syntax

Here's where the real differences lie. The syntax for extended lists varies considerably from the syntax of the simpler standard list.

The following syntax is used to configure extended access lists:

```
access-list access-list-number [deny | permit] [protocol |
protocol-keyword] [source-address source wildcard mask |
any] [destination-address destination wildcard mask | any]
[protocol-specific options]
```

The following descriptions are for the syntax of the main extended access list command:

- *access-list-number* is an integer value between 100 and 199.

- *deny|permit* is the condition that's applied to a specific line in the access list.

- *protocol* is the session-layer protocol. EIGRP, GRE, ICMP, IGMP, IGRP, IP, IpinIP, NOS, OSPF, TCP, and UDP are all options here.

- *protocol-keyword* can be ICMP, IGMP, TCP, UDP, and host. These keywords allow other protocol-specific commands. The host command specifies that a single host address will follow.

- *source-address source wildcard mask* is the IP address and wildcard mask. The *any* option specifies any source IP address.

- *destination-address destination wildcard mask* is the IP address and wildcard mask. The *any* options specify any destination IP address.

- The *log* command enables logging for the access list.

As you choose among these different options, additional ones not listed above will become available. These special options are the protocol keywords.

ICMP When using the protocol keyword ICMP, the following options become available after entering the source and destination addresses (see Table 3.2). The names below are used instead of their integer value. We got this list by using the ? command.

T A B L E 3.2	Option	What It Means
ICMP Options	<0-255>	ICMP message type
	administratively-prohibited	Administratively prohibited

TABLE 3.2 *(cont.)*	Option	What It Means
ICMP Options	alternate-address	Alternate address
	conversion-error	Datagram conversion
	dod-host-prohibited	Host prohibited
	dod-net-prohibited	Net prohibited
	echo	Echo (ping)
	echo-reply	Echo reply
	general-parameter-problem	Parameter problem
	host-isolated	Host isolated
	host-precedence-unreachable	Host unreachable for precedence
	host-redirect	Host redirect
	host-tos-redirect	Host redirect for TOS
	host-tos-unreachable	Host unreachable for TOS
	host-unknown	Host unknown
	host-unreachable	Host unreachable
	information-reply	Information replies
	information-request	Information requests
	log	Log matches against this entry
	mask-reply	Mask replies
	mask-request	Mask requests
	mobile-redirect	Mobile host redirect
	net-redirect	Network redirect

T A B L E 3.2 (cont.) ICMP Options	**Option**	**What It Means**
	net-tos-redirect	Net redirect for TOS
	net-tos-unreachable	Network unreachable for TOS
	net-unreachable	Net unreachable
	network-unknown	Network unknown
	no-room-for-option	Parameter required but no room
	option-missing	Parameter required but not present
	packet-too-big	Fragmentation needed and DF set
	parameter-problem	All parameter problems
	port-unreachable	Port unreachable
	precedence	Match packets with given precedence value
	precedence-unreachable	Precedence cutoff
	protocol-unreachable	Protocol unreachable
	reassembly-timeout	Reassembly timeout
	redirect	All redirects
	router-advertisement	Router discovery advertisements
	router-solicitation	Router discovery solicitations
	source-quench	Source quenches
	source-route-failed	Source route failed
	time-exceeded	All time exceededs
	timestamp-reply	Timestamp replies

TABLE 3.2 *(cont.)*	Option	What It Means
ICMP Options	`timestamp-request`	Timestamp requests
	`tos`	Match packets with given TOS value
	`traceroute`	Traceroute
	`ttl-exceeded`	TTL exceeded
	`unreachable`	All unreachables

TCP   When using the protocol keyword TCP, the following options become available after entering the source and destination addresses (see Table 3.3).

TABLE 3.3	Option	What It Means
TCP Options	`eq`	Match only packets on a given port number
	`established`	Match established connections
	`gt`	Match only packets with a greater port number
	`log`	Log matches against this entry
	`lt`	Match only packets with a lower port number
	`neq`	Match only packets not on a given port number
	`precedence`	Match packets with given precedence value
	`range`	Match only packets in the range of port numbers
	`tos`	Match packets with given TOS value
	`<cr>`	Carriage return

The syntax for TCP lines is significantly different from the syntax of normal extended access lists. The command is as follows:

```
access-list access-list-number [permit | deny] tcp [source
source-wildcard | any] [operator source-port | source-port]
[destination destination-wildcard | any] [operator
destination-port | destination-port] [established]
```

Adding the eq option (see Table 3.4) as the operator after the addresses and masks gives us the following options (the number in parentheses is the protocol's port).

T A B L E 3.4 eq Options	Option	What It Means
	<0-65535>	Port number
	bgp	Border Gateway Protocol (179)
	chargen	Character generator (19)
	cmd	Remote commands (rcmd, 514)
	daytime	Daytime (13)
	discard	Discard (9)
	domain	Domain Name Service (53)
	echo	Echo (7)
	exec	Exec (rsh, 512)
	finger	Finger (79)
	ftp	File Transfer Protocol (21)
	ftp-data	FTP data connections (used infrequently, 20)
	gopher	Gopher (70)
	hostname	NIC host-name server (101)
	ident	Ident Protocol (113)

T A B L E 3.4 *(cont.)*	Option	What It Means
eq Options	irc	Internet Relay Chat (194)
	klogin	Kerberos login (543)
	kshell	Kerberos shell (544)
	login	Login (rlogin, 513)
	lpd	Printer service (515)
	nntp	Network News Transport Protocol (119)
	pop2	Post Office Protocol v2 (109)
	pop3	Post Office Protocol v3 (110)
	smtp	Simple Mail Transport Protocol (25)
	sunrpc	Sun Remote Procedure Call (111)
	syslog	System logger (514)
	tacacs	TAC Access Control System (49)
	talk	Talk (517)
	telnet	Telnet (23)
	time	Time (37)
	uucp	Unix-to-Unix Copy Program (540)
	whois	Nicname (43)
	www	World Wide Web (HTTP, 80)

UDP   The syntax for writing a UDP line is the same as with TCP, except there's no established option. When using the protocol keyword UDP and the operator **eq**, the following options (see Table 3.5) become available after entering the source and destination addresses (as with TCP, the protocol port numbers are in parentheses).

TABLE 3.5 UDP Options	Option	What It Means
	<0-65535>	Port number
	biff	Biff (mail notification, comsat, 512)
	bootpc	Bootstrap Protocol (BOOTP) client (68)
	bootps	Bootstrap Protocol (BOOTP) server (67)
	discard	Discard (9)
	dnsix	DNSIX security protocol auditing (195)
	domain	Domain Name Service (DNS, 53)
	echo	Echo (7)
	mobile-ip	Mobile IP registration (434)
	nameserver	IEN116 name service (obsolete, 42)
	netbios-dgm	NetBIOS datagram service (138)
	netbios-ns	NetBIOS name service (137)
	ntp	Network Time Protocol (123)
	rip	Routing Information Protocol (router, inrouted, 520)
	snmp	Simple Network Management Protocol (161)
	snmptrap	SNMP Traps (162)
	sunrpc	Sun Remote Procedure Call (111)
	syslog	System Logger (514)

T A B L E 3.5 *(cont.)*	**Option**	**What It Means**
UDP Options	tacacs	TAC Access Control System (49)
	talk	Talk (517)
	tftp	Trivial File Transfer Protocol (69)
	time	Time (37)
	who	Who service (rwho, 513)
	xdmcp	X Display Manager Control Protocol (177)

Now that you're familiar with the available options gained through extended access list commands, here's an example access list that implements what we've shown you:

```
access-list 101 deny    tcp any any eq chargen
access-list 101 deny    tcp any any eq daytime
access-list 101 deny    tcp any any eq discard
access-list 101 deny    tcp any any eq echo
access-list 101 deny    tcp any any eq finger
access-list 101 deny    tcp any any eq kshell
access-list 101 deny    tcp any any eq klogin
access-list 101 deny    tcp any any eq 37
access-list 101 deny    tcp any any eq uucp
access-list 101 deny    udp any any eq biff
access-list 101 deny    udp any any eq bootpc
access-list 101 deny    udp any any eq bootps
access-list 101 deny    udp any any eq discard
access-list 101 deny    udp any any eq netbios-dgm
access-list 101 deny    udp any any eq netbios-ns
access-list 101 permit  udp host 172.16.10.2 any eq snmp
access-list 101 deny    udp any any eq snmp
access-list 101 permit  udp host 172.16.10.2 any eq snmptrap
access-list 101 deny    udp any any eq snmptrap
access-list 101 deny    udp any any eq who
```

```
access-list 101 permit  udp 172.16.50.0 0.0.0.255 any eq xdmcp
access-list 101 deny    udp any any eq xdmcp
access-list 101 permit tcp any any
access-list 101 permit udp any any
access-list 101 permit icmp any any
access-list 101 permit igmp any any
access-list 101 permit eigrp any any
```

You can spot a lot of protocol-specific lines in this example. The purpose of this list is to provide security against break-ins on servers that are connected to the port where this list is applied. Most of the commands utilized in this list have been defined: eq means equal to, lt means less than, gt means greater than, ge means greater than or equal to, and le means less than or equal to.

Applying Extended Access Lists

Because extended access lists are complex and can create a lot of overhead and delay on routers, it's even more important to strategically place them so that they'll be most efficient and their burden on the network will be minimized.

Extended lists can be applied using the access-group command on any given interface, and each interface can have two access groups applied to them—one inbound and one outbound. There are some important considerations when deciding where to apply an extended access list. For example, if the list's purpose is to provide security as it was above, it should be applied to the interface where the machines are connected. However, if the list is for stopping certain types of traffic from transiting the network, it should be applied as close as possible to the origin of the unwanted traffic, which avoids the problem of wasted bandwidth. You don't want traffic to move across the core just to be denied on the destination router's side.

An extended list can also become long—if it does, examine it to see if it could be streamlined if you applied it closer to the edge devices. Another good strategy—if the same list is applied outbound to the majority of the interfaces on the router—is to apply it inbound on the interface that points upstream instead. All these tricks can really help manage access lists by providing ways to implement them efficiently.

Limiting Virtual Terminal Access

So far, we haven't applied access lists to virtual interfaces—only physical and logical ones. By default, access lists are not effective for packets that originate from the router, leaving a security hole. The five virtual terminals on the router are vulnerable to unrestricted access, but you can apply standard access lists to them as well.

The virtual or *vty* ports are numbered zero through four. The good news is that you can implement security and configure all these ports at the same time. Here's how:

```
Router_A#conf t
Router_A(config)#line vty 0 4
Router_A(config-line)#access-class 50 in
Router_A(config-line)#^Z
Router_A#
```

Notice that the access-class command was used instead of access-group. The access-class command syntax is as follows:

```
access-class access-list-number [in | out]
```

The *access-list-number* in this command is a value from 1 to 99, meaning that it must be a standard access list. Remember that standard access lists match source IP addresses only.

Alternatives to Access Lists

Using an access list can be overkill when all you really want to do is localize traffic to its own network—you may just be creating unnecessary overhead.

There's a better way to isolate traffic. With the Cisco IOS, pointing to a software interface of Null 0 can create static routes. Null 0 doesn't exist on the router as a physical, virtual, or logical interface—it exists only in the IOS software.

The Null 0 interface is like a dump where packets are simply dropped without any CPU processing. Null interfaces are often used for this very reason—they don't require any processor time. Packets are sent to the Null 0 via an entry in the routing table. The route is entered in the routing table by configuring a static route like so:

```
ip route [source] [mask] null 0
```

According to this configuration, any source address listed in the static router will be routed to Null 0 and subsequently dropped. This is an effective way to eliminate unwanted traffic from transiting your WAN, because the static route can be implemented anywhere you want.

In Figure 3.4, you can see that network 10.1.2.0 hangs off Router C. If you wanted to prevent packets from arriving at network 10.1.2.0, a static route would have to be added to Router A and Router B. If the static routes are redistributed into a routing protocol, all neighbors would learn of a route to network 10.1.2.0, making it unnecessary to configure the route individually on each router. Once the packet hits a router destined for network 10.1.2.0, the static route will forward it to the Null 0 dump.

F I G U R E   3.4

Static route to
Null 0

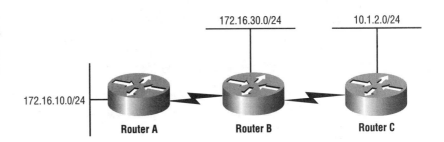

Here's the configuration you'd implement on Router A:

```
Router_A#conf t
Router_A(config)#ip route 10.1.2.0 255.255.255.0 null 0
Router_A(config)#router eigrp 100
Router_A(config-router)#redistribute static
Router_A(config-router)#^Z
Router_A#
```

Directed-Broadcast Handling

By default, routers don't forward broadcast messages to prevent broadcast storms. Though this is generally good, it can create a problem. What if a client needs access to a server on a different network? If that client doesn't have the IP address of the server, it will send out a broadcast requesting it, but since the router won't forward a broadcast, the server won't receive the client's request.

Cisco has a solution—configuring IP helper addresses. Helper addresses convert the broadcast message into a unicast, or directed-broadcast message, destined for the server.

The helper command syntax is as follows:

```
ip helper-address address
```

Eight protocols and ports can be forwarded using this command:

- TFTP (69)
- DNS (53)
- Time (37)
- TACACS (49)
- BOOTP client (68)
- BOOTP server (67)
- NetBIOS name service (137)
- NetBIOS datagram service (138)

When one server exists on a different network, you can use the host address of that server for easy configuration. If multiple servers exist on a different subnet from the client, the broadcast address of the server's subnet may be used. Figure 3.5 illustrates how this is done.

FIGURE 3.5

Configuring helper addresses

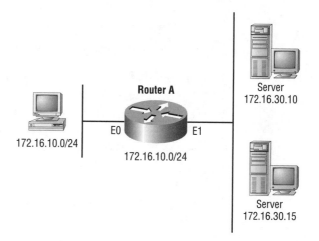

The following configuration text shows how a helper address may be configured for multiple servers on the same subnet.

```
Router_A#conf t
Router_A(config)#int e0
Router_A(config-int)#ip helper-address 172.16.30.255
Router_A(config-int)#^Z
Router_A#
```

When multiple servers exist on different subnets, the interface will need multiple IP helper-address lines. Figure 3.6 shows servers on different networks.

FIGURE 3.6

Multiple servers and multiple subnets

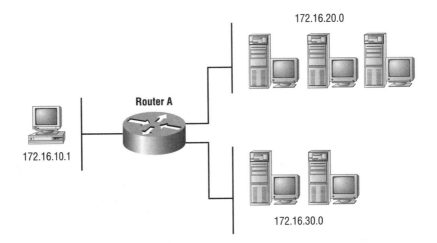

The configuration would look as follows:

```
Router_A#conf t
Router_A(config)#int e0
Router_A(config-int)#ip helper-address 172.16.30.255
Router_A(config-int)#ip helper-address 172.16.20.255
Router_A(config-int)#^Z
Router_A#
```

You can also use the `forward-protocol` command in conjunction with the IP helper address. The `forward-protocol` command allows the IP helper address to refine the type of broadcasts it will convert and forward.

Here's the syntax for the `forward-protocol` command:

```
ip forward-protocol [udp[port] | nd | sdns]
```

This command is used to permit and deny certain UDP port numbers and is also applied to the interface with the IP helper addresses. It works somewhat like an access list.

Security Considerations

Establishing security on a router isn't limited to access lists—you can also lock the door with AAA (authentication, authorization, and accounting), security server protocols, and data encryption, with each one of these methods providing a different type of security.

Access lists provide filtering and security for traffic that transits the router. These other security measures limit who can access and perform administration on the router, and encryption provides security for router passwords and other data.

AAA

AAA (authentication, authorization, and accounting) is configured on the router with global commands. Each division of AAA fulfills a specific function contributing to establishing security. AAA is a scalable and flexible solution that not only provides security, but documents login information.

Authentication handles the task of authenticating the user who is trying to access the router. We won't cover a huge amount of available commands because of the sheer number of them. However, the Cisco Web page, Cisco Connection Online, will equip you with a great list of all the different syntax commands for implementing AAA authentication.

Authorization defines the privileges a user will have once they have gained access to the router through use of a database that maintains their individual profiles. This database is most often housed on a server that the router can access when it receives a login request. AAA authorization works in tandem with RADIUS, TACACS, and TACACS+ servers.

AAA accounting provides logs for auditing and reporting, and is also done via RADIUS and TACACS servers. Again, you can obtain complete configuration guidelines and syntax on the Cisco Web site.

Three security server protocols work with AAA security:

- RADIUS

- TACACS

- Kerberos

They rely on AAA router configurations to supply the protocol with the specified attributes.

Encryption

Data encryption is used to provide secure data transfer between two Cisco routers in an unsecured network environment. Data encryption can create some pretty significant overhead on the router because of the relevant tasks that have to take place at each end of the circuit.

Some other security measures include Cisco encrypted enable passwords and other IP security commands. The command for an encrypted enable password is as follows:

```
enable secret [level level] {password | encryption-type
encrypted-password}
```

You can implement any and all of these flexible and scalable security methods to control who accesses the router and what they can do to the router once it's accessed. Some create more overhead than others (especially network data encryption), but some run in a near transparent manner, creating little or no overhead.

Summary

In this chapter, we've covered the following key topics:

- Differences between regular and extended access lists. Extended lists are much more robust and can be made with greater granularity.

- Restricting virtual terminal access.

- Alternatives to access lists by using the static route to Null 0.

- How to enable clients to contact services on different subnets.

- Security options that may be implemented. This is done by using AAA, TACACS, and RADIUS.

All of this information is used to control IP traffic and provide router security. You can use these tools individually or together to provide greater utilization, security, and control.

Review Questions

1. What range of integers is used to signify a standard access list?

   A. 0–100

   B. 1–100

   C. 1–99

   D. 101–199

2. What range of integers is used to signify an extended access list?

   A. 100–199

   B. 1–99

   C. 100–200

   D. 101–199

3. What is the criterion used to match a packet on a standard access list?

   A. Destination address

   B. Session-layer protocol

   C. Source address

   D. Protocol port number

4. What is the proper syntax for writing a standard access list?

   A. `ip access-list access-list-number {deny | permit} source source-wildcard`

   B. `access-list access-list-number {deny | permit} source source-wildcard`

   C. `access-list access-list-number {deny | permit} source source-mask`

   D. `access-list access-list-number {deny | permit} [protocol] source source-wildcard destination destination-wildcard`

5. What is the proper syntax for an extended access list?

   A. `access-list access-list-number {deny | permit} [protocol | protocol-keyword] [source-address source wildcard mask | any] [destination-address destination wildcard mask | any] [protocol specific options]`

   B. `ip access-list access-list-number {deny | permit} [protocol | protocol-keyword] [source-address source wildcard mask | any] [destination-address destination wildcard mask | any] [protocol specific options]`

   C. `access-list access-list-number {deny | permit} source source-wildcard`

   D. `ip access-list access-list-number source source wildcard destination destination wildcard {permit | deny} [protocol protocol keyword]`

6. Which command is used to apply an access list to a physical interface?

 A. `access-class access-list-number {in | out}`

 B. `access-list access-list-number {in | out}`

 C. `access-group access-list-number {in | out}`

 D. `ip access-group access-list-number {in | out}`

7. Which command is issued to apply a standard access list to a virtual interface?

 A. `access-class access-list-number {in | out}`

 B. `access-list access-list-number {in | out}`

 C. `access-group access-list-number {in | out}`

 D. `Ip access-class access-list-number {in | out}`

8. After looking at the following configuration lines, choose the answer that best explains their effect.

```
Router_X(config)#access-list 20 permit 172.16.0.0
   0.0.255.255
Router_X(config)#access-list 20 permit 10.0.0.0
   0.255.255.255
Router_X(config)#line vty 0 4
Router_X(config-line)#access-class 20 in
Router_X(config-line)#^Z
Router_X#
```

 A. Access list 20 is applied to the virtual interfaces zero through four

 B. Access list 20 permits networks `172.16.0.0` and `10.0.0.0`

 C. Access list 20 is applied to virtual interfaces zero through four, permits all hosts/networks within `172.16.0.0` and `10.0.0.0`, and denies everything else

 D. Access list 20 permits all hosts/networks for `172.16.0.0` and `10.0.0.0`

9. Which of the following commands is used as an alternative to access lists?

A. ip route address mask null 0

B. ip route address wildcard null 0

C. ip route destination mask null 0

D. Ip route destination wildcard null 0

10. If clients need to reach multiple servers on network 172.16.30.0 /24, which command will allow the clients to reach all of the servers?

A. ip helper address 172.16.30.0

B. ip helper address 172.16.30.255

C. ip helper-address 172.16.30.0

D. ip helper-address 172.16.30.255

11. It is alright to simply enter additional access list lines after the scripting of the original access list.

A. True

B. False

12. Routers can reorder access-list statements in which of the following ways?

A. Placing the implicit deny statement at the beginning of the list

B. Manipulating source networks to match the wildcard mask

C. Grouping permit and deny statements

D. Placing all permit statements at the end of the list

E. Placing all deny statements at the end of the list

13. What is the proper syntax to apply an access list to a routing protocol? The command must be issued from within the routing protocol configuration.

A. `ip access-group access-list-number {in | out}`

B. `ip distribute-list access-list-number {in | out}`

C. `distribute-list access-list-number {in | out} interface-type interface-number`

D. `filter-list access-list-number {in | out} interface-type interface-number`

14. Which command(s) may be issued to provide specific information on access list functionality?

A. `show ip access list access-list-number`

B. `show access-list access-list-number`

C. `debug ip icmp`

D. `show ip icmp packets`

15. Which command is used to refine the broadcast domain in conjunction with IP helper addresses?

A. `ip forward-protocol [udp[port] | nd | sdns]`

B. `forward-helper [udp[port] | nd | sdbs]`

C. `ip helper-protocol [udp[port] | nd | sdbs]`

D. None of the above

16. Choose the best explanation of the following access list line:

`access-list 101 permit udp host 172.16.10.2 any eq snmp`

    A. This line permits any node to access host `172.16.10.2` using SNMP

    B. This line permits host `172.16.10.2` to communicate to any destination using SNMP

    C. This line permits host `172.16.10.2` to communicate to any destination using UDP

    D. This line permits any node to communicate with host `172.16.10.2` using UDP

17. Why are null interfaces used in place of an access list?

    A. When RIP is the only protocol running on the router

    B. When security needs to be configured on a loopback interface

    C. To save CPU utilization

    D. To globally deny access to a network

18. Which option is a valid option when applying access lists on an interface?

    A. One list inbound and one list outbound

    B. Two lists inbound or two lists outbound

    C. Only one list may be applied, either inbound or outbound

    D. Two lists inbound and two lists outbound

19. What is accomplished by the following configuration line?

`Access-list 55 permit 172.16.10.0 0.0.0.255`

   A. An extended access list is created that will allow all hosts on network 172.16.10.0 to be forwarded

   B. A standard access list is created that will allow all hosts on network 172.16.10.0 to be forwarded

   C. An extended list is created that will filter traffic destined for network 172.16.10.0

   D. A standard list is created that will permit all traffic destined for network 172.16.10.0

20. What command can be used to encrypt Cisco router password information?

   A. `enable password string encrypt level`

   B. `encrypt level string enable password string`

   C. `enable secret [level level] password | encryption-type encrypted-password]`

   D. `enable secret [encryption-type | level] password`

Laboratory Exercises

Refer to Figure 3.7 to complete the lab exercises below.

FIGURE 3.7

Lab diagram

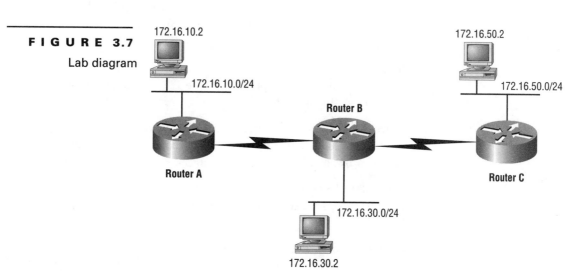

FIGURE 3.7   Lab diagram

1. Write a standard access list or lists to accomplish the following (specify the router and interface where the access list(s) should be applied):

   A. Do not allow network 172.16.10.0 to access network 172.16.50.0, but allow host 172.16.10.2 and all other networks to access network 172.16.50.0.

   B. Network 172.16.30 allows access only from network 172.16.10.0.

   C. Network 172.16.10.0 allows access to all networks except 172.16.50.0.

2. Create extended access lists that will fulfill the following requirements (specify the router and interface where the access list(s) should be applied):

A. Host 172.16.30.2 is not permitted to receive an ICMP ping from the 172.16.10.0 network. All other traffic from all networks is to be allowed.

B. Host 172.16.50.2 is not to deny all Telnet access, but it's supposed to deny ICMP pings from the 172.16.30.0 network. All other protocols and traffic are to be permitted.

3. Protect Router A from vty access from all networks except 172.16.10.0 and 172.16.20.0. Make sure to specify the command used to implement the access list. In addition, which interfaces is the list applied to?

4. Deny all traffic bound for 172.16.10.0 that originates from networks 172.16.30.0, 172.16.40.0, and 172.16.50.0 without using an access list.

5. Configure a helper address that will allow clients on the 172.16.30.0 network to reach servers that are located on the 172.16.10.0 and 172.16.50.0 networks. Specify the commands used, and the router and interfaces where they were applied.

CHAPTER

4

Managing Router Performance

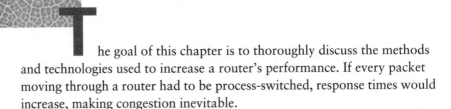

he goal of this chapter is to thoroughly discuss the methods and technologies used to increase a router's performance. If every packet moving through a router had to be process-switched, response times would increase, making congestion inevitable.

The Cisco IOS and hardware provide ways of making a router more efficient through onboard cache pools and flexible software. Utilizing the router's physical architecture to the full potential can enhance its performance. Different types of switching and queuing sustained by the router provide the basis for an optimum performance level, with additional options of this type available with the high-end router product lines such as the Cisco 7200 or 7500 series.

This chapter will cover important distinctions between the switching and queuing options available for Cisco routers, as well as establish how each of these technologies functions within the router. Configuration instructions and examples will also be provided.

In addition to covering the following exam objectives, we'll substantiate the case for switching and discuss the commands associated with configuring path switching on a router. The exam objectives covered in this chapter include:

- Describe the need for queuing in a large network

- Describe weighted fair queuing operation

- Configure priority

- Configure custom queuing

- Verify queuing operation

Switching Paths and Router Architecture

Switching path—the logical path that a packet follows when it's being switched—takes place at Layer 3 of the OSI model. The closer a layer is to the physical layer, the faster the packet can be transported; the faster a packet can leave the router, the less delay and overhead incurred on the router. By using switching, extra lookups in route tables are eliminated, and processing overhead is reduced.

The router's physical design and its interfaces allow for switching processes on the router. This frees up the processor to focus on other tasks instead of looking up the source and destination information for every packet that enters the router.

First, we'll discuss the switching processes available on low-end routers, and then move on to the capabilities of the high-end machines. During the explanation of each switching technology, we'll provide configuration syntax and examples.

Low-End Router Architecture

It's much simpler to state that high-end routers include those found in the 7200 and 7500 router families than it is to define what exactly constitutes a low-end router. So, for the purposes of this book, we'll define low-end routers as all those not belonging to either of the two high-end router families.

Two types of switching occur on low-end routers: process-switching—performed by the processor using routing tables—and fast-switching—through the use of a fast-switching cache.

Process-Switching

As a packet arrives on a router to be forwarded, it's copied to the router's process buffer, and the router performs a lookup on the Layer 3 address. Using the route table, an exit interface is associated with the destination address. The processor forwards the packet with the added new information to the exit interface, while the router initializes the fast-switching cache. Subsequent packets bound for the same destination address follow the same path as the first packet.

Overhead ensues because the processor is occupied with Layer 3 lookups, determining which interface the packet should exit from and calculating the

CRC for the packets. If every packet required all of that to be routed, the processor could get really bogged down. The answer is to use fast-switching whenever and wherever possible.

Fast-Switching

Fast-switching is the low-end architecture's enhancement from process-switching. The first packet of a new session is copied to memory, then compared against the fast-switching cache to find the best interface through which to send it out to its destination. When this is completed, the packet is rewritten and forwarded to the chosen interface.

Instead of the route processor calculating the CRC, the individual interface processors do this, relieving the route processor of a great deal of work.

Fast-switching is also on by default, and if it's been turned off, you can turn it back on by using the following command:

```
ip route-cache
```

So why would it be turned off? Sometimes it's necessary to turn fast-switching off when troubleshooting network problems. Since packets don't move across the route processor after the first packet has been process-switched, you can't see them with packet-level tracing. It's also helpful to turn off fast-switching if the interface card's memory is limited or consumed, or to alleviate congestion when low-speed interfaces become flooded with information from high-speed interfaces.

High-End Router Architecture

The high-end Cisco routers offer a greater variety of switching algorithms, which are also more efficient than both process-switching and fast-switching. Even so, both process- and fast-switching are available on high-end routers.

Due to their advanced hardware design, a high-end router's switching processes can take place closer to the interface, greatly increasing switching speed and efficiency. They offer autonomous-switching, silicon-switching, optimum-switching, distributed-switching, Netflow-switching, and Cisco Express Forwarding.

Autonomous-Switching

Autonomous-switching works by comparing packets against the autonomous-switching cache found on the interface processor, instead of the route or switch processor. Because the CiscoBus controller manages the switching job for autonomous-switching, the route processor isn't interrupted. Thanks to the onboard processor cache, switching speed is increased. Instead of having to send the packet across the backplane of the router to the route processor, the needed cache is right there in the interface board processor.

Autonomous-switching is available only on AGS+ and Cisco 7000 series routers that have highspeed controller interface cards. The command to enable autonomous-switching is as follows:

```
ip route-cache autonomous
```

Silicon-Switching

Silicon-switching is available only on the Cisco 7000 with an SSP (Silicon Switch Processor). Silicon-switched packets are compared to the silicon-switching cache on the SSE (Silicon Switching Engine). The SSP is a dedicated switch processor that offloads the switching process from the route processor, providing a fast-switching solution, but packets must still traverse the backplane of the router to get to the SSP and then back to the exit interface.

Optimum-Switching

Optimum-switching follows the same procedure as the other switching algorithms. When a new packet enters the interface, it is compared to the optimum-switching cache, rewritten, and sent to the chosen exit interface. Other packets associated with the same session will then follow the same path. All processing is carried out on the interface processor including the CRC. Optimum-switching is faster than both fast-switching and Netflow-switching, unless you have implemented several access lists.

You need to enter the command for optimum-switching on each individual interface—however, it's on by default on high-end routers, taking the place of fast-switching. Its command syntax is as follows:

```
ip route-cache optimum
```

Optimum-switching also needs to be turned off to view packets while troubleshooting a network problem.

Distributed-Switching

Distributed-switching happens on the VIP (Versatile Interface Processor) cards, which have a switching processor onboard, so it's very efficient. All required processing is done right on the VIP processor, which maintains a copy of the router's routing cache. With this arrangement, even the first packet doesn't need to be sent to the route processor to initialize the switching path like it does with the other switching algorithms. Router efficiency increases as more VIP cards are added.

Netflow-Switching

Netflow-switching is really more of an administration tool than a performance-enhancement tool. It collects detailed data for use in conjunction with circuit accounting and application utilization information. Due to all the additional data that Netflow collects (and may export), expect an increase in router overhead—possibly as much as a 5% increase in CPU utilization.

Netflow-switching can be configured on most interface types and can be used in a switched environment. ATM, LAN, and VLAN technologies all support Netflow-switching, and the Cisco 7200 and 7500 series routers provide its implementation.

As we touched on, Netflow-switching does much more than just switching—it also gathers statistical data including protocol, port, and user information. All of this is stored in the Netflow-switching cache according to the individual flow that's defined by the packet information (destination address, source address, protocol, source and destination port, and the incoming interface). The data can be sent to a network management station to be stored and processed there.

The Netflow-switching process is very efficient—an incoming packet is processed by the fast- or optimum-switching process, and then all path and packet information is copied to the Netflow cache. The remaining packets that belong to the flow are compared to the Netflow cache and forwarded accordingly.

The first packet that's copied to the Netflow cache contains all security and routing information, and if an access list is applied to an interface, the first packet will be matched against it. If it matches the access list criteria, the cache is flagged so that the remaining packets in the flow can be switched without being compared to the list—very effective when there's a large amount of access list processing required.

Do you remember us saying that distributed-switching on VIP cards is really efficient because it lessens the load to the RSP? Well, Netflow-switching can also be configured on VIP interfaces.

You have to configure the Netflow function on the desired interfaces. The export command is global. Netflow-switching and data exportation are configured with the following commands:

```
ip route-cache flow
ip flow-export ip-address udp-port [version 1] *version 1 is
the default
```

If you're using version 5 software, the export command changes a little to provide a few more options. However, by default, the AS information isn't exported. Here's the version 5 example:

```
ip flow-export ip-address udp-port version 5 [origin-as |
peer-as]
```

Netflow gives you amenities such as the security flag in the cache that allows subsequent packets of an established flow to avoid access list processing. It's comparable to optimum- and distributed-switching, and is much better if access lists (especially long ones) will be placed in the switching path. However, the detailed information Netflow gathers and exports does load down the system, so plan carefully before implementing Netflow-switching on a router.

Cisco Express Forwarding

Cisco Express Forwarding (CEF) is a switching function designed for high-end backbone routers. It functions on Layer 3 of the OSI model, and its biggest asset is the ability to remain stable in a large network. However, it's also more efficient than both the fast and optimum default switching paths.

CEF is wonderfully stable in large environments because it doesn't rely on cached information. Instead of using a CEF cache, it refers to two alternate resources. The Forwarding Information Base (FIB) consists of information duplicated from the IP route table. Every time routing information changes, the changes are propagated to the FIB, so instead of comparing old cache information, a packet looks to the FIB for its forwarding information. CEF stores the Layer 2 MAC addresses of connected routers (or next hop) in the *adjacency table*.

Even though CEF features advanced capabilities, you should consider several restrictions before implementing CEF on a router. According to the document "Cisco Express Forwarding" from the Cisco Web page CCO, system requirements are quite high—the processor should have at least 128MB of RAM, and the line cards should have 32MB each. CEF takes the place of VIP distributed- and fast-switching on VIP interfaces. The following features aren't supported by CEF:

- ATM dixie
- Token Ring
- Multipoint PPP
- Access lists on the GSR
- Policy routing
- NAT
- SMDS

Nonetheless, CEF does many things—even load balancing made possible through FIB. If there are multiple paths to the same destination, the IP route table will know about them all. This information is also copied to the FIB, which CEF consults for its switching decisions.

The command used to enable CEF on a router interface is as follows:

```
ip cef switch
```

A global command can be issued that will enable Distributed CEF (dCEF) on all interfaces, allowing switching between two port adapters. This is basically distributed-switching with CEF.

```
ip cef distributed switch
```

Load balancing can be configured in two different modes. The first mode is load balancing based on the destination and is called per-destination load balancing; the second mode is based on the packet and is called per-packet load balancing. Per-destination load balancing is on by default and must be turned off to enable per-packet load balancing. The commands are shown below.

```
ip load-sharing per-destination
    Enables per-destination load sharing
```

```
ip load-sharing per-packet
    Enables per-packet load sharing
```

Accounting may also be configured for CEF, which furnishes you with detailed statistics about CEF traffic. Two specifications can be made when collecting CEF statistics:

- To collect information on traffic that's forwarded to a specific destination

- To collect statistics for traffic that's forwarded through a specific destination

To enable accounting, use the following commands:

```
ip cef accounting per-prefix
    Data forwarded to a specific address
ip cef accounting non-recursive
    Data forwarded through specific address
```

To view the information collected by CEF accounting, issue the following command:

```
show ip cef
```

CEF was designed for large networks—if reliable and redundant switching paths are necessary, CEF is the way to go. However, keep in mind that its hardware requirements are really high, and it lacks support for many Cisco IOS features. CEF is definitely not the answer for all networks, at least not yet.

Router Performance Planning

When mulling over which router you really need, consider what will be required of it. Is it going to be a campus router or a backbone router—which services does it need to provide? To determine this, make a list of all necessary interfaces and the functions they'll need to perform. It's easy to oversubscribe a chassis with different port adapters, so by fully researching all interesting products, you can establish actual port adapter and chassis capabilities and prevent acquiring a bunch of stuff you don't need.

You'll also save yourself a bunch of dough—with any design implementation, cost is a big player. Thanks to the variety of available products, you might be able to get yourself a scaled-down model that will perform beautifully at a much lower cost than a fully loaded high-end router.

An additional consideration is the potential problems that can result when you try to upgrade and add new capabilities to a router. For instance, individual cards each run at their own speed, which might be faster than the backplane of the existing chassis. This would create a bottleneck at the interface point of the card and the backplane, and you'd have to upgrade the chassis to get around it. So keep in mind that installing a large number of high-speed interface cards on a router may oversubscribe the backplane.

Backplane speed isn't the only issue when choosing the proper equipment—don't forget about CPU and memory requirements. If a router will serve as a firewall that will have several access lists applied—or other processor-intensive attributes—make sure that the processor can *comfortably* handle the load. We can't stress the *comfort* factor enough! If you ask a router to continually maintain a high level of CPU utilization, all processes requiring CPU time will be affected, which will probably cause latency. So it may be necessary to upgrade, for example, from an RSP2 to an RSP4 to lower CPU utilization levels and allow the router to perform more efficiently.

Routers contain buffers that store processed packets, but don't forward them. These are utilized when congestion occurs. Routers set default buffer sizes for different categories, and it's usually a good idea to leave the buffers at their default settings.

Executing a show buffers command on a router will display the following list:

```
Router_A#show buffers
Buffer elements:
    499 in free list (500 max allowed)
    28753345 hits, 0 misses, 0 created

Public buffer pools:
Small buffers, 104 bytes (total 90, permanent 50):
    50 in free list (20 min, 150 max allowed)
    8454394 hits, 0 misses, 0 trims, 0 created
    0 failures (0 no memory)
Middle buffers, 600 bytes (total 25, permanent 25):
    23 in free list (10 min, 150 max allowed)
```

```
    1676303 hits, 51 misses, 153 trims, 153 created
    0 failures (0 no memory)
Big buffers, 1524 bytes (total 50, permanent 50):
    50 in free list (5 min, 150 max allowed)
    1255286 hits, 0 misses, 0 trims, 0 created
    0 failures (0 no memory)
VeryBig buffers, 4520 bytes (total 10, permanent 10):
    10 in free list (0 min, 100 max allowed)
    34842 hits, 0 misses, 0 trims, 0 created
    0 failures (0 no memory)
Large buffers, 5024 bytes (total 0, permanent 0):
    0 in free list (0 min, 10 max allowed)
    0 hits, 0 misses, 0 trims, 0 created
    0 failures (0 no memory)
Huge buffers, 18024 bytes (total 0, permanent 0):
    0 in free list (0 min, 4 max allowed)
    0 hits, 0 misses, 0 trims, 0 created
    0 failures (0 no memory)

Interface buffer pools:
Ethernet0 buffers, 1524 bytes (total 96, permanent 96):
    29 in free list (0 min, 96 max allowed)
    5474 hits, 1998 fallbacks
    32 max cache size, 29 in cache
Ethernet1 buffers, 1524 bytes (total 96, permanent 96):
    24 in free list (0 min, 96 max allowed)
    154 hits, 265 fallbacks
    32 max cache size, 32 in cache


Router_A#
```

We can view six buffer distinctions in this output: small, middle, big, very big, large, and huge, with each division allocated a different amount of buffer space accordingly. The output details the buffer name and its size, with the buffer size following immediately after its name. The (total 90, permanent 50) for the small pool specifies that there are a total of 90 spaces allocated to the small pool, 50 of which are permanently assigned. In the following field, you can see the number of free buffer spaces that are open to accepting a packet. Each pool maintains a minimum and maximum threshold, which it uses to decide if more buffer space needs to be allocated to the pool. This is seen in the `min` and `max` allowed.

The last two lines of information given for each pool describe the activity happening there. This information includes all hits, misses, trims, created, and failures. These are described in the following list:

Hits: Represents how many times the pool was used successfully.

Misses: Represents the number of times a packet tried to find a space within a pool, but found no available spaces. The packet is subsequently dropped.

Trims: Represents the number of spaces removed from the pool because the amount exceeded the number of *allowed* buffer spaces.

Created: Represents the number of spaces created to accommodate requests for space when there wasn't enough at the time the request was made.

Failures: Represents how many times a buffer pool tried to create space, but was unsuccessful. When a failure occurs, the requesting packet is dropped.

The last field is the `no memory` field, which records the number of failures that occurred due to the lack of sufficient system memory required to create additional buffer space.

If you observe a significant increase in the number of misses while monitoring buffers with the `show buffers` command, the pool can be tuned by assigning different values to the `max-free`, `min-free`, and `permanent` parameters. Increasing the values for these parameters will override the system defaults—instead of having to create additional spaces on demand within a pool, the spaces can be statically allocated and assigned. This will help you avoid racking up missed and failed packet statuses.

You can adjust these parameters with the following command:

```
buffers {small | middle | big | verybig | large | huge | type
number} {permanent | max-free | min-free | initial} number
```

The *type* represents interface type, and *number* is the number to be assigned to the specified parameter.

Table 4.1 depicts the sizes of the buffer within a pool. When a packet needs to be stored in a buffer, it will request space from the pool in proportion to its size requirement. Included in the output from the show buffers command is information pertaining to interface buffers. The information is the same as it is for the system buffers, only it pertains to specific interfaces. Interface buffers are monitored and tuned in the same manner as system buffers, but the command does vary a bit—instead of specifying a pool, you specify the interface. The syntax is the same, but the *type number* needs to be entered instead of using pool syntax

T A B L E 4.1 Sizes of the Buffer within a Pool	Pool Name	Buffer Size (in Bytes)
	Small	104
	Middle	600
	Big	1524
	Very Big	4520
	Large	5024
	Huge	18,024

Controlling Traffic: Queuing Methods

Bandwidth has to be available for time-sensitive applications, because if it isn't, packets will be dropped and retransmit requests will be sent back to the originating host. Time-sensitive applications aren't the only type of traffic needing to access bandwidth—it's just flat-out important that bandwidth is there when it's needed.

Since trying to increase bandwidth capacity can be an expensive pursuit, it might be wise to explore alternatives—such as queuing—first. The Cisco IOS allows for several different types of queuing:

- FIFO
- Weighted fair

- Priority

- Custom

Each queuing algorithm provides a solution to different routing problems, so have a clear picture of your desired result before you configure queuing on an interface.

Queuing works especially well on links that experience bursty traffic.

Queuing generally refers to several different criteria to define the priority of incoming or outgoing packets:

- TCP port number

- Packet size

- Protocol type

- MAC address

- LLC SAP

After the packet's priority is determined by the router, it's assigned to a buffered queue. Each queue has a priority globally assigned to it, and is processed according to that priority and the algorithm it's using. Because each algorithm has specific features intended to solve specific traffic problems, and because solidly understanding queuing features will make it easier to make decisions regarding which management technique will really solve a given problem, we'll explain the features in detail.

But first, understand that you should take certain steps before you select a queuing algorithm.

1. Accurately assess the network need—thoroughly analyze the network to determine the types of traffic present, and isolate any special needs to meet.

2. Know which protocols and traffic sessions can be delayed, because once you implement queuing, any traffic assigned a higher priority status will push other traffic offline if necessary.

3. Configure and then test the appropriate queuing algorithm.

FIFO Queuing

This is the most basic form of queuing—FIFO stands for first in, first out. Strangely enough, FIFO does not help much with time-sensitive traffic. Working chronologically, all it does is send the oldest packet in the queue out first.

Weighted Fair Queuing

Weighted fair queuing provides equal amounts of bandwidth to each conversation that traverses the interface using a process that refers to the timestamp found on the last bit of a packet as it enters the queue.

Assigning Priorities

Weighted fair queuing assigns a high priority to all low-volume traffic. Figure 4.1 demonstrates how the timing mechanism for priority assignment occurs. The algorithm determines which frames belong to either a high-volume or low-volume conversation, and forwards out the low-volume packets from the queue first. Through this timing convention, remaining packets can be assigned an exiting priority. In Figure 4.1, packets are labeled A through H. As depicted in the diagram, Packet A will be forwarded out first because it's part of a low-volume conversation, even though the last bit of session B arrived before the last bit of the packets associated with Packet A did. The remaining packets are divided between the two high-traffic conversations, with their timestamps determining the order in which they will exit the queue. (A more detailed picture of how bandwidth is shared among conversations will be shown in Figure 4.2.)

FIGURE 4.1

Priority assignment using weighted fair queuing

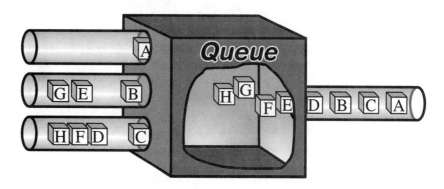

Assigning Conversations

We've discussed how priority is assigned to a packet or conversation, but it's also important to understand the type of information the processor needs to associate a group of packets with an established conversation.

The most common elements used to establish a conversation are as follows:

- Source and destination IP addresses
- MAC addresses
- Port numbers
- Type of service
- The DLCI number assigned to an interface

Figure 4.2 shows two conversations. The router, using some or all of the above factors to determine which conversation a packet belongs to, allocates equal amounts of bandwidth for the conversations. Each of the two conversations receives half of the available bandwidth.

F I G U R E   4.2

Bandwidth allocation with weighted fair queuing

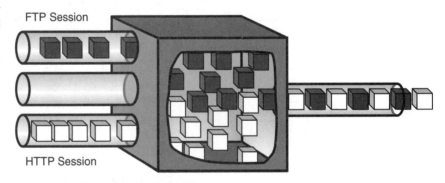

Configuring Weighted Fair Queuing

You're now ready to learn how to configure weighted fair queuing. For all interfaces having a line speed equal to or lower than 2.048Mbps (E1 speed), weighted fair queuing is on by default. Here's an example of how weighted fair queuing is configured on an interface. You can use this command to alter the default settings:

```
Router_C#conf t
Enter configuration commands, one per line. End with CNTL/Z.
```

```
Router_C(config)#int s0
Router_C(config-if)#fair-queue 96
Router_C(config-if)#^Z
Router_C#
```

To understand what was done, let's look at the syntax of the command:

```
fair-queue {congestive-discard-threshold [dynamic-queues
[reservable-queues]]}
```

- The *congestive-discard-threshold* is a value from 1 to 512 that specifies the number of conversations that can exist within the queue. Once this number is exceeded, the following conversations won't be allocated their equal amount of bandwidth. Without a place in the queue, new conversations will be dropped. The default value is 64.

- *Dynamic-queues* are exactly that—queues established dynamically to handle conversations that don't have special requirements. The valid values for this option are 16, 32, 64, 128, 256, 512, 1024, 2048, and 4096, with the default value being 256.

- The *reservable-queues* option defines the number of queues established to handle conversations. The available range is from zero to 1000, with the default being zero. These queues are for interfaces that use RSVP (Resource Reservation Protocol).

Verifying Weighted Fair Queuing

Now that weighted fair queuing is configured on our router's Serial 0 interface, let's look to see what it's doing. To verify the configuration and operation of the queuing system, we can issue the following two commands:

```
show queueing [fair | priority | custom]
show queue [interface-type interface-number]
```

Results from these commands on Router C can be seen below. Since weighted fair queuing is the only type of queuing that's been enabled on this router, it wasn't necessary to issue the optional command of fair, custom, or priority.

```
Router_C#show queueing
Current fair queue configuration:

   Interface  Discard      Dynamic       Reserved
              threshold    queue count   queue count
   Serial0    96           256           0
   Serial1    64           256           0


Current priority queue configuration:
Current custom queue configuration:
Current RED queue configuration:
Router_C#
```

This command shows us that weighted fair queuing is enabled on both serial interfaces, and that the discard threshold for Serial 0 was changed from 64 to 96. There's a maximum of 256 dynamic queues for both interfaces—the default value. The lines following the interface information are empty because their corresponding queuing algorithms haven't been configured yet.

The next command displays more detailed information pertaining to the specified interface:

```
Router_C#show queue serial0
 Input queue: 0/75/0 (size/max/drops); Total output drops: 0
 Queueing strategy: weighted fair
 Output queue: 0/1000/96/0 (size/max total/threshold/drops)
   Conversations 0/1/256 (active/max active/max total)
   Reserved Conversations 0/0 (allocated/max allocated)


Router_C#
```

The input queue information is explained, as is the size of the queue, the maximum size of the queue, and the number of conversations that have been dropped. The algorithm is defined as weighted fair queuing. The output queue (usually the one with the most activity) defines the size, maximum number of output queues, the number of conversations per queue, and the number of conversations dropped. The number of conversations represents the number of conversations in the queue, and active describes the number of active conversations in it. The max active keeps a record of the maximum number of active conversations, and finally a `max total` gives the number of all conversations within the queue. Reserved queues are also displayed by issuing the following command:

```
show queue serial0
```

Priority Queuing

Priority queuing happens on a packet basis instead of on a session basis, and is ideal in network environments that carry time-sensitive applications or protocols. When congestion occurs on low-speed interfaces, priority queuing guarantees that traffic assigned a high priority will be sent first. In turn, if the queue for high-priority traffic is always full, monopolizing bandwidth, packets in the other queues will be delayed or dropped.

Assigning Priorities

The header information that priority queuing uses consists of either the TCP port or the protocol being used to transport the data. When a packet enters the router, it's compared against a list that will assign a priority to it and forward it to the corresponding queue.

Priority queuing has four different priorities it can assign to a packet: high, medium, normal, and low, with a separate dispatching algorithm to manage the traffic in all four. Figure 4.3 shows how these queues are serviced—you can see that the algorithm starts with the high-priority queue processing all of the data there. When that queue is empty, the dispatching algorithm moves down to the medium-priority queue, and so on down the priority chain, performing a cascade check of each queue before moving on. So if the algorithm finds packets in a higher-priority queue, it will process them first before moving on, and this is where problems can develop. Traffic in the lower queues could be totally neglected in favor of the higher ones if they're continually busy with new packets arriving.

Configuring Priority Queuing

Implementing priority queuing on an interface requires three steps:

1. A priority list must be created that the processor will use to determine packet priority.

2. If desired, the size of the queues can be adjusted.

3. The priority list can be applied to the desired interfaces.

FIGURE 4.3

Dispatching algorithm
in priority queuing

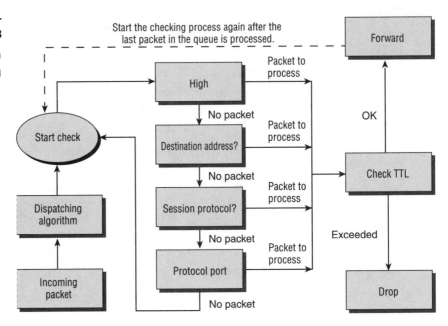

So let's go over how to build a priority list. Start by using the following command:

```
priority-list list-number {[protocol protocol-name] |
[interface interface-type] (high | medium | normal | low) |
default | queue-limit]} queue-keyword
```

The *list-number* identifies the list, and the valid values for it are 1 through 16. The protocol option directs the list to assign priorities based on the protocol, and *protocol-name* defines which protocol to match. With the interface option, the physical interface is listed along with the type of queue that pertains to it. Next, after specifying the protocol or interface, the type of queue needs to be defined—high, medium, normal, or low.

The same priority-list command can be used to configure a default queue for traffic that doesn't match the priority list and that you do not want to be placed in the *normal* queue.

The *queue-limit* is used to create the size limits of the queue. Configuring the size of the queues must be handled carefully, because if a packet is forwarded to the appropriate queue, but the queue is full, the packet will be discarded—even if there is bandwidth available. This means that enabling priority queuing on an interface can be useless (even destructive) if queues aren't accurately configured to respond to actual network needs. It's really important to make the queues large enough to accommodate congestion so that the influx of packets can be accepted and stored until they can be forwarded.

The *queue-keyword* allows packets to be compared by their byte count, existing access list, protocol port number, or name and fragmentation.

The above commands create the priority list, which you can then apply to an interface with the following command:

```
priority-group list
```

The *list* is the priority list number from 1 to 16. Once the list is applied to the interface, it is implicitly applied outbound. All packets will be checked against the priority list before entering their corresponding queue. The ones that don't match will be placed in the default queue.

Here's an example:

```
Router_C#conf t
Enter configuration commands, one per line. End with CNTL/Z.
Router_C(config)#priority-list 1 protocol ip high gt 1500
Router_C(config)#priority-list 1 protocol ip low lt 256
Router_C(config)#priority-list 1 protocol ip normal
Router_C(config)#priority-list 1 interface serial 1 normal
Router_C(config)#priority-list 1 interface ethernet 0 high
Router_C(config)#priority-list 1 default normal
Router_C(config)#priority-list 1 queue-limit 40 80 120 160
Router_C(config)#interface serial 0
Router_C(config-if)#priority-group 1
Router_C(config-if)#^Z
Router_C#
```

The first line of the priority list assigns high priority to all IP traffic with a packet size greater than 1500, and the second line assigns low priority to IP traffic with a packet size lower than 256. The next line assigns all remaining IP traffic to the normal queue. The following line (line four) assigns all incoming traffic on Serial 1 to the normal queue also. All incoming traffic on Ethernet 0 is assigned a high priority, and any remaining traffic will be assigned normal priority. The size of all of the queues is defined by the `queue-limit`, and their numbers follow the order of their high, medium, normal, and low queue sizes.

Below there's an example of what the interface configuration looks like. The priority list has been assigned to the interface with the `priority-group` command. You can see the final form of the applied priority list following the interface configuration.

```
!
interface Serial0
 ip address 172.16.40.6 255.255.255.252
 priority-group 1
!
priority-list 1 protocol ip high gt 1500
priority-list 1 protocol ip low lt 256
priority-list 1 protocol ip normal
priority-list 1 interface Serial1 normal
priority-list 1 interface Ethernet0 high
priority-list 1 queue-limit 40 80 120 180!
```

Verifying Priority Queuing

To make sure the queuing configuration is working and configured properly, you can use the same command used to verify weighted fair queuing with the added option for priority queuing.

The following information summarizes the above priority list:

```
Router_C#show queueing priority
Current priority queue configuration:

List  Queue Args
1   high  protocol ip     gt 1500
1   low   protocol ip     lt 256
1   normal protocol ip
1   normal interface Serial1
1   high  interface Ethernet0
1   high  limit 40
1   medium limit 80
1   normal limit 120
1   low   limit 160
Router_C#
```

Custom Queuing

Custom queuing functions based upon the concept of sharing bandwidth among traffic types. Instead of assigning a priority classification to a specific traffic or packet type, custom queuing forwards traffic in the different queues by referencing FIFO. Custom queuing offers the ability to customize the amount of actual bandwidth used by a specified traffic type.

While remaining within the limits of the physical line's capacity, virtual pipes are configured through the custom queuing option. Varying amounts of the total bandwidth are reserved for various specific traffic types, and if the bandwidth isn't being fully utilized by its assigned traffic type, other types can access it. The configured limits go into effect during high levels of utilization or when congestion on the line causes different traffic types to compete for bandwidth.

Figure 4.4 shows each queue being processed, one after the other. Once this begins, the algorithm checks the first queue, processes the data within it, then moves to the next—if it comes across an empty one, it will simply move on without hesitating. The amount of data that will be forwarded is specified by the *byte-count* for each queue, which directs the algorithm to move to the next queue once it's been attained. Custom queuing permits a maximum of 16 configurable queues.

Figure 4.5 shows how the bandwidth allocation via custom queuing looks relative to the physical connection. Bandwidth allocations are configured by using the frame size of the protocols and configuring the *byte-count* for each different queue.

Configuring Custom Queuing

Configuring custom queuing is similar to configuring priority queuing, but instead of having to complete three tasks, you have to go through five. As with priority queuing, you have to configure a list that will be used to separate types of incoming traffic into their desired queues. After that, you have to configure a default queue for the traffic unassigned to any of the other queues. Once your specific and default queues are defined, the capacity or size of each queue can be adjusted, or you can just stick with the default settings.

When that's complete, you have to specify the transfer rate or *byte-count* for each queue. This is important—the *byte-count* determines the percentage of bandwidth reserved for a specified queue. After these parameters are set, apply them to an interface.

F I G U R E 4.4

Custom queuing
algorithm

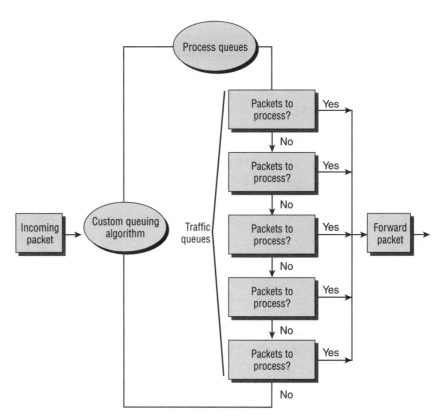

F I G U R E 4.5

Bandwidth allocation
using custom queuing

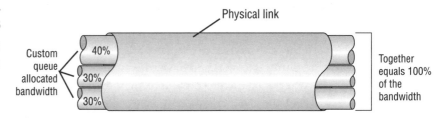

The commands used to configure the queuing list, default queue, queue
size, and transmit rate follow. Here's the command syntax:

```
queue-list list-number {default | interface [interface-type
    interface-number] | lowest-custom | protocol [protocol-name]
```

```
| queue [queue-number byte-count | limit ] | stun } queue-
number queue-keyword keyword-value
```

The syntax may be presented in many different ways to configure the desired command. The *list-number* is a value from 1 to 16 and associates the list with the given number. The following are all available options:

Default: Designates a custom queue for packets that didn't match the `queue-list`

Interface: Assigns priorities for packets incoming on the specified physical interface

Lowest-custom: Specifies the lowest queue number considered a custom queue

Protocol: Indicates that the packets are to be sorted by protocol

Queue: Allows for specific queue parameters to be configured

Stun: Establishes queuing priority for STUN packets

When the interface option is specified, you must supply the *interface-type* and *interface-number* as well. The *interface-type* is the type of physical interface, and the *interface-number* is the physical port of the interface.

The `protocol` option also requires additional information. Obviously, the *protocol-name* must be specified. In Table 4.2, we show a list of the available protocol names. After supplying the *queue-number,* the *keyword-value* may be supplied to refine the protocols and port numbers used for filtering.

T A B L E 4.2 Available Protocol Names	**Protocol Name**	**Description**
	Aarp	AppleTalk ARP
	Appletalk	AppleTalk
	Arp	IP ARP
	Bridge	Bridging
	Cdp	Cisco Discovery Protocol
	Compressedtcp	Compressed TCP

T A B L E 4.2 *(cont.)*	**Protocol Name**	**Description**
Available Protocol Names	Decnet	DECnet
	Decnet_node	DECnet Node
	Decnet_router-l1	DECnet Router L1
	Decnet_router-l2	DECnet Router L2
	Ip	IP
	Llc2	Llc2
	Pad	PAD links
	Snapshot	Snapshot routing support
	Ipx	Novell IPX

Table 4.3 lists the available keyword values.

T A B L E 4.3	**Keyword Value**	**Description**
Available Keyword Values	Fragments	Prioritize IP fragments
	Gt	Greater than specified value
	List	Access list
	Lt	Less than specified value
	Tcp	TCP packets
	Udp	UDP packets

To define the parameter of the custom queues, you use the queue option. After specifying the *queue-number,* you're given two different parameters to configure:

- The limit option allows you to change the size of the queue.

- The byte-count command option specifies the rate at which the queues will be emptied.

Configuring Byte Count   Configure the byte-count queues carefully, because if the setting is too high, the algorithm will take a longer time than necessary to move from one queue to the next. This is not a problem while the processor empties the queue, but if it takes the processor too long to get back to the queue, the queue could fill up and start dropping packets.

So it's important to understand how to configure the bandwidth percentage relationship using the byte-count command. Since frame sizes vary from protocol to protocol, you'll need to know the exact frame sizes of the protocols transiting the custom queued interface to define the byte-count efficiently. You do this using simple math.

Suppose you have a router that uses IP, IPX, and SNA as its protocols. Let's arbitrarily assign frame sizes, realizing that the values aren't the real ones. We'll assign a frame size of 800 bytes to IP, 1000 bytes to IPX, and 1500 bytes to SNA. You calculate a simple ratio by taking the highest frame value and dividing it by the frame size of each protocol:

IP = 1500/800 = 1.875

IPX = 1500/1000 = 1.5

SNA = 1500/1500 = 1.0

These values equal your frame size ratios. To assign correct percentages of bandwidth, multiply each ratio by the percentage of the bandwidth you want to assign to that protocol. For example, let's assign 40 percent to IP, 30 percent to IPX, and 30 percent to SNA.

IP = 1.875 (0.4) = 0.75

IPX = 1.5 (0.3) = 0.45

SNA = 1 (0.3) = 0.35

These values now need to be normalized by dividing the results by the smallest value.

IP = 0.75/0.3 = 2.5

IPX = 0.45/0.3 = 1.5

SNA = 0.3/0.3 = 1

Custom queuing will send only complete frames, so because the ratios are fractions, you must round them up to the nearest integer values that maintain the same ratio. To arrive at the nearest integer value, multiply the original ratios by a common number that will cause the ratios to become integers. In this case, you can multiply everything by two, and get the resulting ratio of 5:3:2. What does this mean? Well, five frames of IP, three frames of IPX, and two frames of SNA will be sent. Because of the protocols' varying frame size, it turns out the bandwidth percentage works out just the way we calculated.

IP = 5 frames × 800 bytes = 4000 bytes

IPX = 3 frames × 1000 bytes = 3000 bytes

SNA = 2 frames × 1500 bytes = 3000 bytes

Total bandwidth is 10,000 bytes. Percentages are verified by dividing the protocol rate by the total. After doing the math, we verify that IP=40 percent, IPX=30 percent, and SNA=30 percent.

Now that the `byte-count` is calculated (4000, 3000, and 3000), you can apply the results in the `queue-list` command. The custom queuing algorithm will forward 4000 bytes worth of IP packets, move on to the IPX queue and forward 3000 bytes, and then go to the SNA queue and forward 3000 bytes.

Check out this example of how to configure and apply custom queuing lists:

```
Router_B#conf t
Enter configuration commands, one per line. End with CNTL/Z.
Router_B(config)#queue-list 1 interface Ethernet0 1
Router_B(config)#queue-list 1 protocol ip 2 tcp 23
Router_B(config)#queue-list 1 protocol ip 3 tcp 80
Router_B(config)#queue-list 1 protocol ip 4 udp snmp
```

```
Router_B(config)#queue-list 1 protocol ip 5
Router_B(config)#queue-list 1 default 6
Router_B(config)#queue-list 1 queue 1 limit 40
Router_B(config)#queue-list 1 queue 5 byte-count 4000
Router_B(config)#queue-list 1 queue 4 byte-count 500
Router_B(config)#queue-list 1 queue 3 byte-count 4000
Router_B(config)#queue-list 1 queue 2 byte-count 1000
Router_B(config)#int serial0
Router_B(config-if)#custom-queue-list 1
Router_B(config-if)#^Z
Router_B#
```

After analyzing the list, you can see that six different queues were configured. The first one was configured to handle incoming traffic from interface Ethernet 0, and the second is reserved for Telnet traffic. Queue number three is for WWW traffic, and the fourth is configured to handle SNMP traffic. The fifth queue will deal with all other IP traffic, and the default queue where all unspecified traffic will go is assigned as queue six. A limit of 40 packets was placed on queue one, and the byte-count was changed from the default value of 1500 for queues two, three, four, and five. Finally, after the list was written, it was applied to interface Serial 0.

Here is what the configuration looks like:

```
!
interface Serial0
 no ip address
 shutdown
 custom-queue-list 1
!
queue-list 1 protocol ip 2 tcp telnet
queue-list 1 protocol ip 3 tcp www
queue-list 1 protocol ip 4 udp snmp
queue-list 1 protocol ip 5
queue-list 1 default 6
queue-list 1 interface Ethernet0 1
queue-list 1 queue 1 limit 40
queue-list 1 queue 2 byte-count 1000
```

```
queue-list 1 queue 3 byte-count 4000
queue-list 1 queue 4 byte-count 500
queue-list 1 queue 5 byte-count 4000
```

As with the other queuing algorithms, you need to be able to verify both the configuration and the status of custom queuing. This is done by issuing the same command as before, except this time, substitute custom for priority:

```
Router_B#show queueing custom
Current custom queue configuration:

List  Queue Args
1    6    default
1    1    interface Ethernet0
1    2    protocol ip     tcp port telnet
1    3    protocol ip     tcp port www
1    4    protocol ip     udp port snmp
1    5    protocol ip
1    1    limit 40
1    2    byte-count 1000
1    3    byte-count 4000
1    4    byte-count 500
1    5    byte-count 4000
Router_B#
```

This output information gives you a breakdown of the custom queue list, detailing queue assignments and any limits or byte counts assigned to the queue.

Summary

The three main types of queuing are as follows:

- Weighted fair

- Priority

- Custom

Each algorithm has a distinct way of processing the queues used by it. Because of these differences, queuing can be adapted to individual network needs. Bandwidth management is a cost-effective way of dealing with network congestion.

The significant differences between each queuing algorithm are as follows:

- Weighted fair queuing: Shares equally with all traffic, but gives low-volume traffic higher priority. Instead of assigning priorities to each packet, this algorithm tracks the session that a packet belongs to. There is no queue list to configure or apply to the interface.

- Priority queuing: A very stringent algorithm that can cause one type of traffic to monopolize available bandwidth, because as long as there are high-priority packets in the queue, they'll be processed first. Other traffic is processed only when there's available bandwidth left over from high-priority traffic. It gives you four queues.

- Custom queuing: An equitable, controllable algorithm allowing an administrator to configure the amount of bandwidth reserved for specified traffic types. All traffic will be processed in turn. Custom queuing allows for the configuration of 16 queues.

Review Questions

1. What is the correct syntax for implementing weighted fair queuing?

    A. `weighted-fair queue`

    B. `fair-queue`

    C. `queue-fair`

    D. None of the above

2. To which type of traffic does weighted fair queuing assign the highest priority?

    A. SNA

    B. IPX

    C. High volume

    D. Low volume

3. When should weighted fair queuing be used?

    A. To provide priority to interactive traffic

    B. To provide priority to file transfers

    C. To allow all traffic to be forwarded

    D. A and C

    E. A and B

4. Where is the most effective place to implement queuing?

    A. High-speed LAN links

    B. T1/E1 links only

    C. Any WAN link whose capacity is 2Mbps and slower

    D. All interfaces

5. When should priority queuing be used?

    A. When traffic has a hierarchical order of importance

    B. When delay doesn't matter

    C. When all traffic must be forwarded

    D. None of the above

6. Which one of the following steps is *not* part of configuring priority queuing?

    A. Configuring a default queue

    B. Configuring a priority list

    C. Configuring the queue transfer rate

    D. Assigning the priority list to an interface

7. How many queues are defined by priority queuing?

    A. 1–16

    B. No limit

    C. 4

    D. 1–10

8. When should custom queuing be used?

    A. When traffic has a hierarchical order of importance

    B. To overcome the possible problem that is introduced with priority queuing.

    C. When trying to provide bandwidth sharing for all traffic

    D. When delay is not important

9. Which step is *not* part of configuring custom queuing?

 A. Defining the custom queuing filter

 B. Assigning a default queue

 C. Configuring the transfer rate per queue

 D. Assigning a priority queue list to the interface

10. What is accomplished by configuring the byte-count for a queue?

 A. Allocating a percentage of the total bandwidth to defined queues

 B. Setting the size of the queue

 C. Setting the amount of data that will be processed before moving on to the next queue

 D. A and C

11. Which statement best describes weighted fair queuing?

 A. Queues based on the source and destination of packets

 B. Shares bandwidth among all traffic types, giving priority to low-volume traffic

 C. Shares bandwidth among high-priority traffic only

 D. Queues using FIFO

12. Which statement best describes priority queuing?

 A. Processes all queues in a round-robin fashion

 B. Queues based on the destination address of the packet

 C. Queues based on the traffic type; processes all queues equally

 D. Queues based on the traffic type; will always process the highest-priority traffic first

13. Which statement best describes custom queuing?

   A. Queues based on traffic type; processes all queues equally

   B. Queues based on traffic type; always processes the high-priority traffic first

   C. Queues based on bandwidth allocation

   D. Processes packets based on the source address

14. What is accomplished by the following configuration?

```
Router_C(config)#priority-list 1 protocol ip low lt 256
Router_C(config)#interface serial 0
Router_C(config-if)#priority-group 1
Router_C(config-if)#^Z
Router_C#
```

   A. IP is held to a packet size less than 256

   B. Priority list one is applied to serial interface zero and permits packet sizes less than 256

   C. IP packets with sizes less than 256 are assigned to the low-priority queue, and the list is applied to serial interface zero

   D. IP packets with sizes less than 256 are assigned a low priority, and the list is applied to serial interface zero

15. Which of the following is *not* used to establish a conversation for weighted fair queuing?

   A. Source address

   B. Destination address

   C. Packet size

   D. Port number

16. Why is queue size important when configuring queuing?

    A. If the queue is full, the packet will be discarded

    B. If the queue is full, the interface will become congested

    C. If the queue is full, the algorithm halts and allows FIFO queuing

    D. None of the above

17. Which of the following commands should be used to assign all traffic from serial interface one to queue one?

    A. Router_B(config-int)#**queue 1**

    B. Router_B(config)#**priority-list 1 interface Serial 1 1**

    C. Router_B(config)#**queue-list 1 interface Serial1 1**

    D. Router_B(config-int)#**queue-list 1 queue-number 1**

18. How many separate priority lists may be written for priority queuing?

    A. 4

    B. 8

    C. 12

    D. 16

19. Which algorithm does custom queuing use within each defined queue to forward packets?

    A. Priority

    B. Weighted fair

    C. FIFO

    D. None of the above

20. When should the default `byte-count` for custom queuing be changed?

- **A.** When available bandwidth needs to be allocated as a percentage of the total bandwidth

- **B.** When the application uses larger packet sizes

- **C.** It should never be changed from the default setting

- **D.** To utilize all available bandwidth

Laboratory Exercises

Use the network diagram in Figure 4.6 to complete the tasks in this lab.

FIGURE 4.6

Network diagram for
Chapter 4 lab

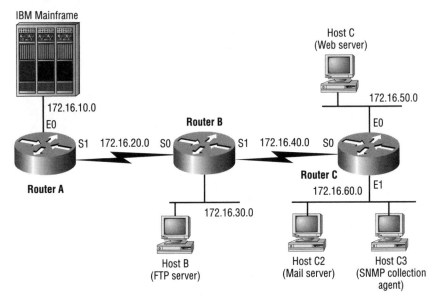

FIGURE 4.6 Network diagram for Chapter 4 lab

1. Configure the queuing algorithm that will give the SNA traffic from the IBM mainframe highest priority across the 172.16.20.0 network. Apply queuing to the appropriate router and interface.

2. Configure the queuing algorithm that will allow all traffic to be processed, yet will give precedence to WWW traffic over file transfer sessions. Apply the queuing to the appropriate router and interface(s).

3. Configure the correct queuing algorithm that will allocate 50 percent of the bandwidth to WWW traffic, 25 percent to SMTP, and 25 percent to SNMP. For this example, use the following frame size information:

- WWW=500 bytes

- SMTP=300 bytes

- SNMP=200 bytes

4. Show the details of all the queuing that was configured in the above tasks.

CHAPTER

5

TCP/IP Routing

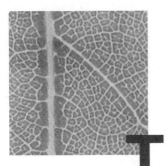

This chapter will provide an overview of TCP/IP routing; in it, you'll learn the basics of how routing is accomplished. Several factors influence TCP/IP routing, including (but not limited to) unique addresses, hierarchical design, and advertisement of unique addresses.

Due to the growth of commercial, corporate, and private networks, the depletion of IP addresses is imminent. So to preserve IP address space, it's imperative to implement new methods that use existing address space more efficiently. We'll discuss these technologies in detail and demonstrate ways to implement them in today's networking environments.

The exam objectives covered in this chapter are as follows:

- List the key information routers needed to route data

- Given an IP address, use VLSMs to extend the use of the IP address

- Given a network plan that includes IP addressing, explain if a route summarization is or is not possible

- Define private addressing and determine when it can be used

- Define network address translation and determine when it can be used

Variable-Length Subnet Masks (VLSMs)

IP addresses are comprised of a network portion and a host portion that can be thought of like a two-part zip code with its five-digit prefix and four-digit suffix. The prefix directs the post office to a general destination—the city and state—and the suffix resolves to a street address or P.O. box. An IP address, with its network and node portions, works much the same way, as shown in Figure 5.1 below.

FIGURE 5.1

The makeup of an
IP address

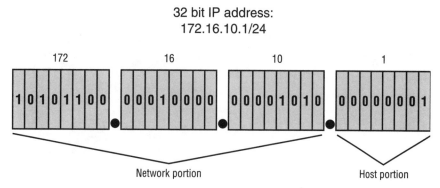

32 bit IP address:
172.16.10.1/24

172 16 10 1

1 0 1 0 1 1 0 0   0 0 0 1 0 0 0 0   0 0 0 0 1 0 1 0   0 0 0 0 0 0 0 1

Network portion   Host portion

The network portion works just like the five-digit prefix of a zip code, and the node or host portion is the unique identifier, similar to the four-digit suffix of a zip code. An IP address consists of 32 bits broken down into four 8-bit segments known as octets. As shown in Figure 5.1, the first three octets define the network portion, and the last octet defines the host. We'll discuss how the network and host portions may be changed by providing certain information a bit later in the chapter.

For a router to route data, it obviously needs to know where to send it. Routers don't maintain information for every unique address in their tables because doing so would make their tables so huge that they would require enormous amounts of memory and processing time. It is much more practical and efficient for them to maintain a table that contains only the network information. If a unique host or address isn't directly connected to a router, it looks in its table to find the appropriate path on which to send the data for them to reach their particular destination. So a router doesn't need to know a specific host's address, its only concern is to accurately identify the network on which it's located.

The specification of the host and network portions within an IP address establishes an inherent hierarchy, consisting of different network lengths being advertised throughout a network or over the Internet. Using a hierarchy when implementing IP addressing provides two main benefits. Since IP addresses can be broken down into smaller subnets to accommodate addressing requirements, address space is conserved. Secondly, route information can be summarized, greatly reducing the size of route tables and the need for the router to know a route to every network.

Figure 5.2 shows what we mean by varying network portion length.

FIGURE 5.2

Hierarchical IP
address structure

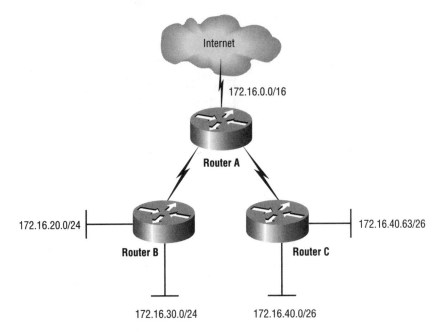

Longer network prefixes reside near the bottom of the network tree. The network length is depicted by a /24 or /26 suffixed to an IP address, which specifies the number of bits (beginning from the left) that define the network portion. In this figure, the address 172.16.20.0/24 is a Class C address. You can tell that because the first 24 bits are used to define the network portion, leaving 254 host addresses available. The first 24 binary bits are equal to the first three octets in the dotted decimal format of an IP address.

As you move up through the network diagram, you can see that the network prefix gets smaller—decreasing from /24 and /26 down to /16. This hierarchy enables routers to determine where to send data when the packet's destination isn't directly connected to the local router. A good example of this can be seen in Figure 5.3, which portrays three different WANs connected to the Internet.

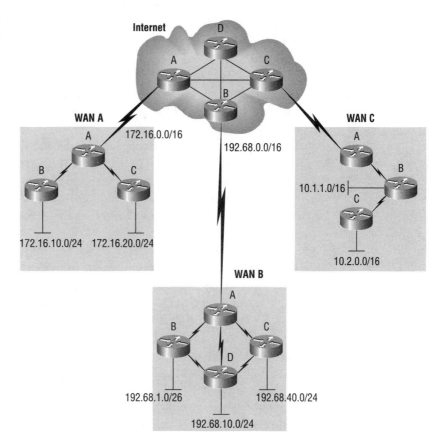

FIGURE 5.3

Hierarchical routing decisions

Each WAN has a specific network that it advertises to the Internet, but it doesn't reveal every host that resides within the network. It advertises information to the Internet only in the most general manner possible.

WAN A advertises the network 172.16.0.0/16 (equivalent to advertising the 172.16.0.0 network as a Class B IP address). Many different host addresses exist within WAN A that fall within the IP address range specified by the /16 subnet. However, to preserve the hierarchy, only a general address is advertised.

So if a host that's on WAN C wants to reach a host on WAN B (192.68.10.2), it will send the packet to the default gateway router. At this point, the router's interested only in the network portion of the IP address in the packet's header, and after determining which network the packet is destined for, the router will forward the packet to the next hop. In this case, the packet will be forwarded to Router A within WAN C, and then to Internet Router C. Then Internet Router C learns about network 192.68.0.0/16 from Internet Router B. So as you can see, no information has been advertised about where 192.68.10.0 is located. Since WAN B advertised general information (that it knows about all 192.68.0.0/16 addresses), it doesn't need to advertise that it has routes to 192.68.10.0/24, 192.68.1.0/26, and 192.68.40.0/24.

All of this can be made clear by working back down the hierarchical tree. Once the packet is forwarded to the border router in WAN B, that device is the one that needs to know the more specific information. At the border router's level, each subnet is advertised. Therefore, a proper routing decision can be made, and the packet will reach its correct destination on network 192.68.10.0.

How is the length of the network prefix determined? To answer that, let's review a little about IP addressing. In the beginning (referencing RFC 760), IP addresses weren't assigned classes. Instead, the network portion of the address was assigned to the first octet. This allowed for only 254 IP networks. To resolve this dilemma, RFC 791 was defined and written. This RFC converted a previously classless IP address structure into specific classes—five to be exact. The three most common ones are Classes A, B, and C, and prefix lengths were defined as 8 bits, 16 bits, and 24 bits, corresponding respectively to Classes A, B, and C. The first 3 bits in the first octet were used to determine the IP address class.

Table 5.1 shows how classes were defined.

T A B L E 5.1 RFC 791 IP Class Assignments	**Address Class**	**Bit Specification**
	A	0
	B	10
	C	110

These bit specifications not only defined the IP class, but also predefined the shortest subnet mask for the address.

The assigned masks are depicted in Table 5.2 below, wherein the prefix for each class varies from 8 bits to 24 bits. You can see a prefix of 8 bits with the first bit set to 0 (2^7), which allows for 128 Class A networks. The Class B prefix of 16 bits, with the first bit set to 1 and the second set to 0 (2^{14}), allows for 16,384 Class B networks. Finally, the Class C prefix of 24 bits, with 3 bits being used for class definition (2^{21}), allows for 2,097,152 Class C networks. So as you can see, the available network numbers, using the classfull scheme, are finite. Although 2,097,152 networks seems like a great number of networks, when you look at it within a global frame of reference, you can see that they can eventually run out.

T A B L E 5.2 Classfull IP Subnet Mask Assignments	**Address Class**	**Subnet Mask**
	A	255.0.0.0
	B	255.255.0.0
	C	255.255.255.0

To deal with (and work around) these inherent limits, new methods of subnetting needed to be developed and implemented—the variable-length subnet mask (VLSM) is one of those methods. Because it provides much greater flexibility when deploying IP addresses, it's much more efficient than just using standard classfull subnets. Instead of being forced to use pre-defined masks, a network designer can be more specific in regards to the number of hosts that can be assigned to a given segment.

We have discussed the importance of an addressing hierarchy and the information routers need to route data, as well as the difference between classic IP subnets and the VLSM approach. Now we'll move on to discuss in detail important design considerations when planning a network.

VLSM Design Considerations

If we look at the 32-bit IP address again—understanding that address is divided into the network and host (node) portions—using VLSM, we can create the division between the two at any point desired. To understand what is meant by dividing the network and host portions, refer to Figure 5.4.

F I G U R E 5.4

VLSM subnet
adjustment

Classfull Class C address and subnet

24 bits   8 bits

/24
1Class C

VLSM subnet assignment

25 bits for network portion   7 bits host portion

/25
1/2 Class C

20 bits for network portion   12 bits

/20
1/16 Class C

30 bits for network portion   2 bits

/30
1/64 Class C

Figure 5.4 depicts a generic 32-bit IP address. The dark line signifies the division between the network and host portions of the address. As discussed previously, in classfull IP subnets, the division could take place only after 8, 16, and 24 bits. It was those divisions that created the subnet masks shown in Table 5.2.

However, by using VLSM, the division can be slid to the left or right to adjust the subnet mask. Why is this important? Because as the division between network and host identifying bits is moved, the number of hosts on the defined network changes respectively. For reference, take the classfull

Class C address: A Class C address contains 254 host nodes—254 because 0 and 255 are reserved for network and broadcast. As depicted in Figure 5.4, when the mask is between the 24th and 25th bit, it is a Class C address with 254 hosts. On the second sample—the first example of a VLSM manipulated IP address—you can see that the division lies between the 25th and 26th bits. This allows 7 bits for host identification and is the equivalent of one-half of a Class C address. The numerical definition would be 0 to 127, and because 0 and 127 are reserved for network and broadcast addresses, one-half of the remaining Class C gives you 126 host addresses.

Two more examples follow in Figure 5.4, with the VLSMs' equivalency to a Class C address shown at the right. With the third example, the network portion is 20 bits long, leaving 12 bits for host addresses. So referencing these numbers, you can see that the range is from 0 to 4095. If you subtract 2, you're left with 4094 possible hosts for this network. The fourth example is a network that reserves only 2 bits for host addresses, permitting two hosts per network.

Because greater flexibility can be achieved through VLSM IP address assignment within a network, it's an efficient method to choose if you need to accommodate a large number of hosts. This increase in availability is made possible simply by moving the division between network and host addresses to the left. So conversely, if you need more networks, all you have to do is move the division to the right.

VLSM goes much further than just increasing subnet mask tractability for the network. Traditionally, only one subnet could be assigned to a network. However, VLSM allows for more than one subnet to be assigned to a network—but there's a catch.

Discontinuous IP addresses should be avoided. To implement VLSM properly, the networks you're working with should be physically connected to the same router. Why is this important? Take a core router for example. These usually have many connections from other routers and switches—even other LAN segments linked into them. To get a picture of the architecture, let's look at Figure 5.5.

In this figure, we have a core router with several connections. Instead of using a separate Class C address for each link, VLSM can be implemented to more efficiently utilize a classfull Class B network.

The Class B network has been broken down into six different networks with each one providing only for the number of hosts necessary. When connecting two routers, only two IP host addresses are needed, and setting the subnet mask to /30 (or 255.255.255.252) defines two host IP addresses for

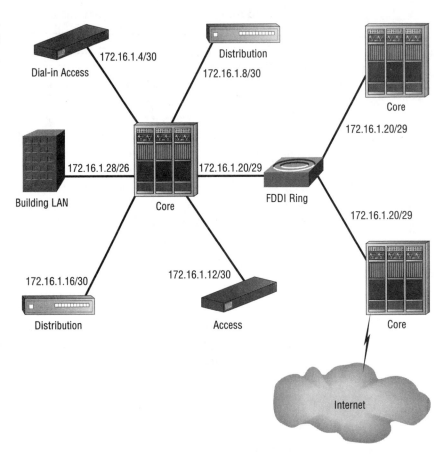

FIGURE 5.5
VLSM implementa-
tion example

the network. The network numbers in Figure 5.5 designate that the links connecting the core router to either a distribution or an access router will use a subnet of /30. This specifies one address for the core router interface and one IP address for the opposite end of the link.

Look at the network diagram again—do you see subnets /26 and /29? Subnet /26 is used to connect to a switch, and using the /26 mask allocates 64 IP addresses to the switch's segment. However, remember that two of those addresses are reserved, so in reality, 62 machines (including the switch and router) can possibly be configured on this segment. The last mask of /29 allows for even fewer hosts. There are only three routers connected to the FDDI ring, and six host addresses can be used within the 172.16.1.20 network.

If more routers were added to the FDDI ring, the subnet mask could be modified to allow for more hosts.

The subnet mask can be modified only if there's room for the increase. In this example, we really couldn't increase the subnet for the FDDI interface using the same network, because the network connected to the switch uses network 172.16.1.28.0, preventing network 172.16.1.20 from growing. We could get around this obstacle by readdressing the FDDI interface. Since the next useable network is 172.16.1.92/28, we would be allowed 14 host addresses by doing that.

The beauty of VLSM is that it has allowed us to take a Class B address and break it down into a Class C equivalent CIDR (Classless Interdomain Routing) block (172.16.1.0), and then create six subnets from that. Why is this useful? Because not only does it conserve IP addresses, it also creates a hierarchy within the core router. This gives the router different networks for each active interface and allows it to just route instead of relying on the ARP table. Can you imagine wasting an entire Class B network on one router? If the Class B were used without subnetting, the network would be flat, with no hierarchy.

We've used three different masks—/26, /29, and /30—and it's recommended that you don't use more than two or three different masks for each network.

So far it looks pretty easy, doesn't it? But don't forget—a great number of networks were designed when VLSM wasn't yet available, and routing protocols like RIP and IGRP don't carry subnet mask information along with the IP address. So networks designed and implemented before routing protocols like EIGRP, OSPF, and RIP2 were available could have IP addresses allocated in a way that just doesn't facilitate grouping them into blocks for VLSM implementation. With cases like these, you would have to renumber IP addresses—a rather deplorable task that many network administrators don't want anything to do with—to implement VLSM.

However, VLSM can greatly enhance potential IP address allocation and simultaneously create a hierarchical architecture within the network. So if renumbering the network is necessary to implement VLSM, it's well worth it in the long run. If you do, you'll be able to utilize IP address space more efficiently, plus (believe it or not) network management will be much easier. For instance, just imagine how much easier it is to write access lists on a router that uses a block of addresses instead of separate networks.

Discontiguous Addressing

We've written a little about what a router needs to know to route a packet. The route information a router possesses depends on the advertisements received from its neighbors or peers, and if a router doesn't receive an advertisement about a specific network, it definitely won't be able to route to it.

So what is *discontiguous addressing*? It's when two subnets of the same classfull network are separated by a different network address. Figure 5.6 shows an example of this.

Campus A has a subnet within the 172.16.0.0 network—172.16.10.0. The WAN link connecting Campus A and Campus B uses a network address of 10.5.4.0, and Campus B uses subnet 172.16.1.0 from the network 172.16.0.0.

At first glance, this may seem just fine, but if you look closely, there's an underlying problem. Remember that some routing protocols, such as RIP and IGRP, don't advertise subnet information in their routing updates. In situations where discontiguous networks exist, RIP or IGRP must issue the default-router command to be able to select a default route. For example, if Router C wanted to send to a host on Campus B, it would look for a route advertisement for network 172.16.1.0/24. If RIP or IGRP are used as the routing protocols, a problem will begin to surface. Let's say both campuses are running RIP as their routing protocols. When Router C attempts to find subnet 172.16.1.0, it won't because the only network advertised will be 172.16.0.0. The problem only worsens, because within the WAN cloud, there are two sources for network 172.16.0.0–one from Campus A and the other from Campus B.

Let's look at some router configurations to understand what's really happening. Refer to Figure 5.7 as a visual aid while we move through the explanation of the router configurations and route tables.

Router B and Router C are both running RIP, and the Ethernet interface on Router B uses a subnet of the 10.0.0.0 network. The purpose of this configuration is to demonstrate that RIP doesn't advertise subnet information.

F I G U R E 5.6

Discontiguous network addresses

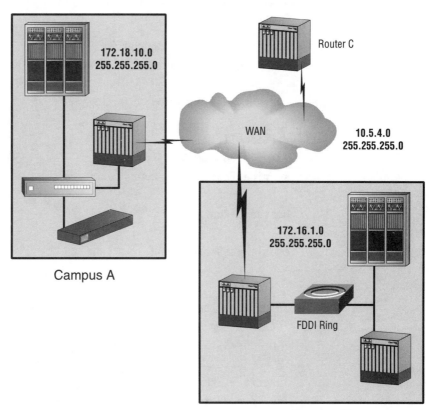

Campus A

Campus B

F I G U R E 5.7

Discontiguous network route advertisement

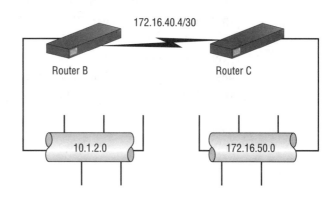

After looking at the configuration, we'll show you the route tables, first from Router B and then from Router C.

```
Router_B#show running-config
Building configuration...

Current configuration:
!
version 11.1
service udp-small-servers
service tcp-small-servers
!
hostname Router_B
!
enable password aloha
!
!
interface Ethernet0
 description Host_B
 ip address 10.1.2.1 255.255.255.0
!
interface Ethernet1
 no ip address
!
interface Serial0
 description Connection to Router A
 ip address 172.16.20.6 255.255.255.252
!
interface Serial1
 description Connection to Router C
 ip address 172.16.40.5 255.255.255.252
!
router rip
 network 10.0.0.0
 network 172.16.0.0
 !
```

```
ip classless
!
line con 0
 password aloha
line aux 0
 password aloha
line vty 0 2
 password aloha
 login
line vty 3 4
 login
!
end
```

```
Router_B#
```

You can see that Ethernet is configured as a /24 subnet of the /8 network 10.0.0.0. (Notice that we've removed the EIGRP session that we used previously.) The network statements within the RIP session default to their classfull form. In a bit, you'll see that the same thing happens with EIGRP and other routing protocols. Now let's look at the configuration for Router C:

```
Router_C#show running-config
Building configuration...

Current configuration:
!
version 11.2
no service password-encryption
no service udp-small-servers
no service tcp-small-servers
!
hostname Router_C
!
enable password aloha
!
!
```

```
interface Ethernet0
 ip address 172.16.50.1 255.255.255.0
 no ip route-cache
 no ip mroute-cache
!
interface Serial0
 ip address 172.16.40.6 255.255.255.252
 clockrate 4000000
 dce-terminal-timing-enable
!
interface Serial1
 no ip address
 no ip route-cache
 no ip mroute-cache
 shutdown
!
router eigrp 100
 network 172.16.0.0
!
router rip
 network 172.16.0.0
!
no ip classless
!
line con 0
line aux 0
line vty 0 4
 password aloha
 login
!
end

Router_C#
```

Router C has two routing protocols configured, but it uses only RIP because that's what its neighbor (Router B) is using to communicate. Now let's jump back to Router B and see what the routing table looks like:

```
Router_B#show ip route
Codes: C - connected, S - static, I - IGRP, R - RIP, M -
mobile, B - BGP
        D - EIGRP, EX - EIGRP external, O - OSPF, IA - OSPF
          inter area
        E1 - OSPF external type 1, E2 - OSPF external type 2,
          E - EGP
        i - IS-IS, L1 - IS-IS level-1, L2 - IS-IS level-2, *
          - candidate default
        U - per-user static route

Gateway of last resort is not set

      10.0.0.0/24 is subnetted, 1 subnets
C        10.1.2.0 is directly connected, Ethernet0
      172.16.0.0/30 is subnetted, 2 subnets
C        172.16.40.4 is directly connected, Serial1
C        172.16.20.4 is directly connected, Serial0
Router_B#
```

Router B is well aware that the /24 subnet is configured on its Ethernet interface. You can tell this by the statement 10.0.0.0/24 is subnetted, 1 subnets, which proves that the router does handle subnet information. However, the problem is that we know RIP won't advertise the subnet information that Router B knows about to Router C. To prove it, let's look at the routing table for Router C:

```
Router_C#sho ip route
Codes: C - connected, S - static, I - IGRP, R - RIP, M -
mobile, B - BGP
        D - EIGRP, EX - EIGRP external, O - OSPF, IA - OSPF
          inter area
        N1 - OSPF NSSA external type 1, N2 - OSPF NSSA
          external type 2
```

```
             E1 - OSPF external type 1, E2 - OSPF external type 2,
               E - EGP
             i - IS-IS, L1 - IS-IS level-1, L2 - IS-IS level-2, *
               - candidate default
             U - per-user static route, o - ODR

      Gateway of last resort is not set

      R     10.0.0.0/8 [120/1] via 172.16.40.5, 00:00:07, Serial0
            172.16.0.0/16 is variably subnetted, 2 subnets, 2 masks
      C        172.16.40.4/30 is directly connected, Serial0
      D        172.16.0.0/16 is a summary, 00:56:16, Null0
      Router_C#
```

Just as we thought, Router C knows the route of 10.0.0.0/8 from Router
B via the RIP routing protocol that's specified by the R in the far-left column.
But what happened to the /24 subnet information? RIP didn't send it. It
shared only the classfull mask for the IP address.

So what do we do? Well, there are several different solutions available to
resolve this issue. Routing protocols that send subnet information, and IP
unnumbered and secondary addressing, can all be used to overcome discontiguous network advertisement. In fact, we'll show you how EIGRP can be
used in the following configurations to solve this little problem.

Let's look at the route tables after we enable EIGRP on Router B. As
before, we'll look at Router B's configuration to see the changes that were
made, and then we'll compare the route tables of both routers.

```
      Router_B#show running-config
      Building configuration...

      Current configuration:
      !
      version 11.1
      service udp-small-servers
      service tcp-small-servers
      !
      hostname Router_B
      !
      enable password aloha
```

```
!
!
interface Ethernet0
 description Host_B
 ip address 10.1.2.1 255.255.255.0
!
interface Ethernet1
 ip address 10.2.1.1 255.255.0.0
!
interface Serial0
 description Connection to Router A
 ip address 172.16.20.6 255.255.255.252
!
interface Serial1
 description Connection to Router C
 ip address 172.16.40.5 255.255.255.252
!
router eigrp 100
 network 10.0.0.0
 network 172.16.0.0
 no auto-summary
!
ip classless
!
line con 0
 password aloha
line aux 0
 password aloha
line vty 0 2
 password aloha
 login
line vty 3 4
 login
!
end

Router_B#
```

You can see that RIP has been removed and that now we're running only EIGRP 100—the same session running on Router C. It's also important to note that for this example, auto-summary was turned off, because if it weren't, we would still see only the summarized route 10.0.0.0/8 from Router B. Let's move on and look at the routing table for Router B:

```
Router_B#show ip route
Codes: C - connected, S - static, I - IGRP, R - RIP, M -
       mobile, B - BGP
       D - EIGRP, EX - EIGRP external, O - OSPF, IA - OSPF
       inter area
       E1 - OSPF external type 1, E2 - OSPF external type 2,
       E - EGP
       i - IS-IS, L1 - IS-IS level-1, L2 - IS-IS level-2, *
       - candidate default
       U - per-user static route

Gateway of last resort is not set

     10.0.0.0/24 is subnetted, 1 subnets
C       10.1.2.0 is directly connected, Ethernet0
     172.16.0.0/30 is subnetted, 2 subnets
C       172.16.40.4 is directly connected, Serial1
C       172.16.20.4 is directly connected, Serial0
Router_B#
```

Not much has changed—actually, nothing has changed from the previous RIP routing table. But what will Router C tell us? We should see the subnet information for the 10.1.2.0/24 subnet. Let's find out:

```
Router_C#show ip route
Codes: C - connected, S - static, I - IGRP, R - RIP, M -
       mobile, B - BGP
       D - EIGRP, EX - EIGRP external, O - OSPF, IA - OSPF
       inter area
       N1 - OSPF NSSA external type 1, N2 - OSPF NSSA
       external type 2
       E1 - OSPF external type 1, E2 - OSPF external type 2,
       E - EGP
       i - IS-IS, L1 - IS-IS level-1, L2 - IS-IS level-2, *
       - candidate default
```

```
       U - per-user static route, o - ODR

Gateway of last resort is not set

     10.0.0.0/24 is subnetted, 1 subnets
D        10.1.2.0 [90/2195456] via 172.16.40.5, 00:02:03,
           Serial0
     172.16.0.0/16 is variably subnetted, 3 subnets, 2 masks
C        172.16.40.4/30 is directly connected, Serial0
D        172.16.20.4/30 [90/2681856] via 172.16.40.5,
           00:02:03, Serial0
D        172.16.0.0/16 is a summary, 00:07:15, Null0
Router_C>
```

You can see that Router C now has the subnet information for the 10.1.2.0/24 subnet in the routing table. This subnet information allows discontiguous networks to be reachable from the outside world.

So basically, the most effective way of dealing with a discontiguous network is to use routing protocols that handle subnet information, such as RIP2, EIGRP, OSPF, and IS-IS. However, if the IOS running on the router doesn't support these protocols, you may also use secondary addresses.

Route Summarization

Route summarization, or aggregation, is a method by which contiguous networks can be grouped together and advertised as one large network. By summarizing several Class C addresses into one supernet, routing tables can be streamlined and tidy with fewer entries. A supernet is created when the division between the network and host address portions is moved to the left. By doing this, the network prefix shrinks and absorbs all the addresses that define individual networks. Figure 5.8 gives us an example of how this is done.

For this example, let's say that we've been assigned three /24 CIDR addresses—the equivalent of three Class C addresses. These three networks can be advertised in two ways. The first would be to advertise each individual network; if we did that, our route table would look something like this:

```
172.16.1.0/24
172.16.2.0/24
172.16.3.0/24
```

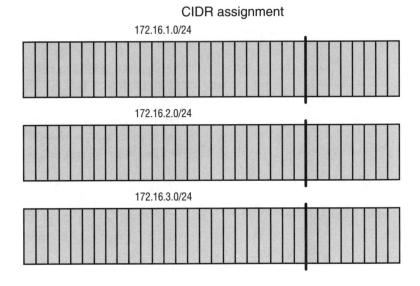

CIDR assignment

172.16.1.0/24

172.16.2.0/24

172.16.3.0/24

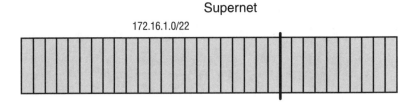

Supernet

172.16.1.0/22

The second way would be to summarize these three networks into one larger network and then advertise it. Doing that would make the route table look like this:

`172.16.1.0/22`

This is one-third the size of the original route table, which saves a lot of memory and processing power. That's why IP route summarization is such a popular thing to do.

OK, great. But how does this work? Let's look at Figure 5.8 again. You can see that the three /24 networks have been summarized into one /22 network—this is possible because the three /24 networks are contiguous. After doing the binary math, your calculation should cause you to arrive at the conclusion that to summarize three /24 networks, you must move the network/host division over two bits to 22. That means your supernet becomes 172.16.1.0/ 22. The /22 subnet includes three networks: 1, 2, and 3.

Table 5.3 details the binary breakdown of how this is done.

T A B L E   5.3:   Creating a Supernet Network Address

CIDR Network	Decimal Mask	Binary Mask
172.16.1.0/24	255.255.255.0	11111111.11111111.11111111.00000000
172.16.2.0/24	255.255.255.0	11111111.11111111.11111111.00000000
172.16.3.0/24	255.255.255.0	11111111.11111111.11111111.00000000
172.16.1.0/22	255.255.252.0	11111111.11111111.11111100.00000000

Each of the /24 networks has the same subnet mask. If you look closely at the last entry in the table, you'll see that it's the supernet entry for all three /24 networks. Plus, you can see that the subnet mask changes for the supernet address. This is best explained by the binary mask shown in the table—the *ones* are the significant bits. The *significant bits* are the bits to which a route processor will refer to determine how many bits represent the network portion of the address and how many represent the host portion. The supernet mask changes from 255 to 252 in the third octet, modifying the division between network and host to the left by two bits. Now you understand how route summarization works. But when would you use it? The following three factors confirm when it's good to use route summarization:

1. IP networks must be contiguous, meaning that the binary enumeration must be the same for the high-order bits.

2. Routing tables must have the capacity to support classless routing.

3. Routing protocols must be able to manage both prefix length and subnet information along with the IP address.

Let's use two examples: The first one is depicted in Figure 5.9 (A) and displays a network that can use route summarization to reduce route table size (and therefore, overhead) on its routers. The second example, shown in Figure 5.9 (B), can't use route summarization. For each of these examples, the routers have been configured for, and are capable of handling, IP classless information.

FIGURE 5.9 (A)

Example one: Route
summarization
possible

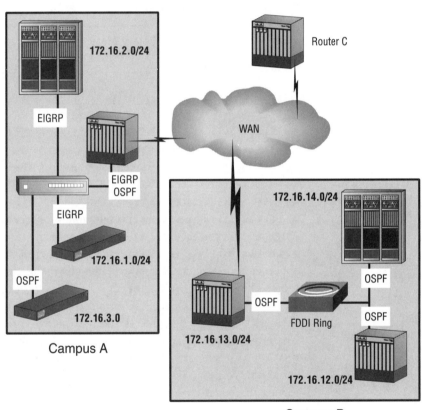

Campus A

Campus B

The network depicted in Figure 5.9 (A) can be summarized because it conforms to rules 1 and 3 listed above. Each of the routers is addressed so that the higher bits are contiguous, and they're all running routing protocols that can advertise subnet and prefix information along with the IP address. So in this example, both campuses can be summarized.

Conversely, in the example depicted in Figure 5.9 (B), you can see that even though the routers support classless routing, summarization isn't possible for either campus. That's because Campus A has contiguous addresses deployed, but none of its routers use routing protocols that will advertise subnet information. Campus B has a different problem. It's running protocols that fulfill rule 3 above, but the addresses it has implemented are discontiguous. These factors combine to make route summarization impossible.

F I G U R E 5.9 (B)

Example two: Route summarization not possible

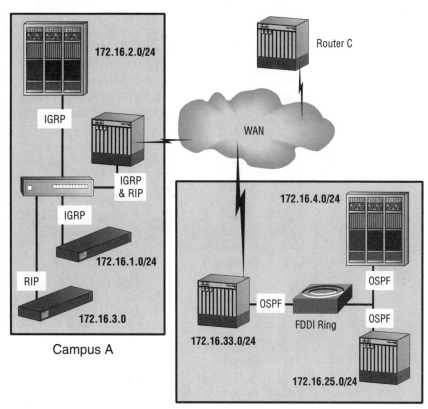

Summarization can be a really useful and efficient tool, but as is true with many good things, you can oversummarize a network. Predictably, the consequences of overdoing it have to do with routing. For instance, if a route is oversummarized, it may conflict with another one that has the same prefix being advertised from a different source. Figure 5.10 shows what we're talking about.

FIGURE 5.10

Oversummarization

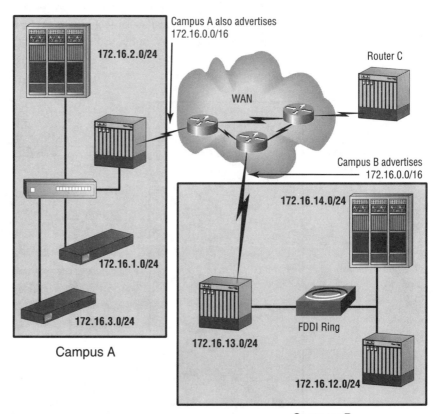

Campus A also advertises
172.16.0.0/16

172.16.2.0/24

Router C

WAN

Campus B advertises
172.16.0.0/16

172.16.14.0/24

172.16.1.0/24

172.16.3.0/24

Campus A

FDDI Ring

172.16.13.0/24

172.16.12.0/24

Campus B

Here we have two campuses of a corporate network, and both oversummarize the IP networks that have been assigned to them. Since both campuses are advertising 172.16.0.0, the routers within the WAN won't be able to decide where to route to reach a specific host. So when Router C needs to send to a destination host on Campus A, it will fail.

When a router is trying to locate a specific host, it will always follow the route of the most specific network. To make this clear, assume that Router C wants to find a host on network 172.16.1.0. When Router C performs its lookup, it will check to see if there's an entry in its table for network 172.16.1.0/24 first. If it doesn't find a route for the specific network, it will then search for the next most specific network entry, and it will discover an entry for a /16 network. Router C will then send the packet to the WAN router. However, since both campuses advertise the /16 network, the WAN router will be totally confused about which one to send it to, and will simply handle the situation by dropping the packet.

To solve this problem, we'd make Campus A summarize its addresses using the supernet 172.16.1.0/22, and make Campus B summarize using 172.16.12.0/22. Why will this work? Because changing the supernet advertisement to these values preserves the hierarchy, equipping Router C with the clarity it needs to be able to find a route to the specified host on Campus A. Basically, since the more specific routes are the ones that have been advertised, the problem is solved. Now, when a packet arrives at the WAN router that borders Router C, it will perform the lookup for the specific address, and learn that it knows about specific network 172.16.1.0/22 via the WAN router connected to Campus A. The packet will be forwarded to the destination host located on Campus A. So by avoiding unnecessary summarization, routing integrity is preserved, and fewer routes populate the route table.

Private Addressing

Another aspect of TCP/IP routing has to do with private networks. Private IP addresses can be used within a network that doesn't need to be reached by outside machines. IANA (Internet Assigned Numbers Authority) allocated three blocks of IP addresses for private network use, shown in Table 5.4.

T A B L E 5.4 IANA Assigned Private Networks	**Network**	**Mask**	**Block**
	10.0.0.0	255.0.0.0	1 Class A network
	172.16.0.0	255.240.0.0	16 Class B networks
	198.168.0.0	255.255.0.0	256 Class C networks

These addresses are for use by corporate networks that don't connect to the global Internet. However, if they're used within a network that also contains a globally unique IP address, the addresses must be filtered by access lists to avoid advertising them to the Internet. Since many companies use private IP address space, it's imperative that these routes aren't announced to the Internet. Although ISPs will not allow private networks to be advertised by their routers, it is a good practice to make sure that your enterprise or campus routers do not advertise private networks to the ISP.

So if a host machine is assigned a private IP address, it won't be able to communicate via TCP/IP to the outside world, because private network advertisements aren't included in Internet routing tables—unless you provide the privately addressed host with a proxy server that has a globally unique address. All the client's requests for information will then have the source IP address of the proxy machine and will be able to communicate through it.

You should implement private addressing schemes with the same plan in mind as with global IP addressing schemes—assign contiguous addresses to defined regions so that you can apply summarization. Use VLSM for subnetting to more efficiently utilize allocated networks. Finally, don't forget to run routing protocols that support classless routing.

Remember to always consider the future of the network when you implement private addresses—someday, some of those machines on what is presently a private network will likely need access to the Internet. Once a network moves from not needing global connectivity to needing globally unique IP addresses, you'll have to readdress.

Using private addresses really helps to conserve your allotment of IP addresses. Since every computer on the network probably doesn't need to access the outside world directly, it's wise to make good use of those private addresses and save the unique ones for machines that require global connectivity.

Network Address Translation (NAT)

NAT is Cisco proprietary software that runs on Cisco IOS, and its basic function is to map private IP addresses to the globally unique IP addresses used to communicate with other Internet hosts. It's available in version 11.2 in the *s* feature set, and you enable it on a border router—one that's located between an enterprise and Internet router.

You can use NAT on an entirely private IP network or on one inhabited by a mix of registered and private addresses. There's a very extensive list of possible NAT-oriented scenarios, but overall, it's used to provide connectivity between globally and privately addressed hosts. For connectivity between the two types of hosts to be established—for it to happen at all—a source address modification of the privately addressed host must occur. NAT provides this translation.

Let's walk through the NAT process. To help visualize what happens with NAT, refer to Figure 5.11.

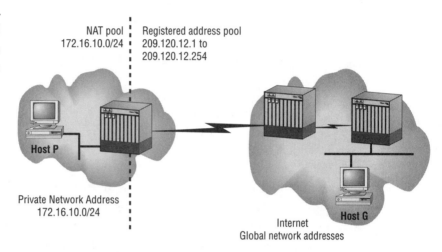

Host P wants to connect with Host G, but since private networks aren't advertised to the Internet, Host G won't be able to respond to Host P— there's no route back to its private address.

So what should a network do? Well, with NAT enabled, a conversion occurs that changes the private address into a globally unique address. With NAT enabled, Host G can respond to Host P's request. How? OK, we'll dissect it for you.

You begin with a pool of registered IP addresses that's specified on the router, and then write an access list to delimit which private addresses will be allowed to be assigned registered addresses from the NAT pool. You must configure the interface connecting the enterprise router to the Internet as the NAT *outside* interface, and the other interfaces may be configured as *inside* interfaces. The inside / outside commands inform the router in which direction the translation is to occur. *Inside* tells the router that NAT should map a registered IP address back to the private IP address, and *outside* indicates the reverse—that NAT should map a private IP address to a registered IP address.

We could discuss several NAT scenarios and configurations, but won't go into those details here because they're outside the scope of this book. However, we will cover the basic configuration of NAT on a border router. First, you have to make some preliminary configuration changes to the router, and then you apply an access list to interface Ethernet 0 that denies all private network traffic. Here are the results of a ping to host 172.16.10.10:

```
C:\WINDOWS>ping 172.16.10.10

Pinging 172.16.10.10 with 32 bytes of data:

Request timed out.
Request timed out.
Request timed out.
Request timed out.

Ping statistics for 172.16.10.10:
    Packets: Sent = 4, Received = 0, Lost = 4 (100% loss),
Approximate round trip times in milli-seconds:
    Minimum = 0ms, Maximum =  0ms, Average =  0ms


C:\WINDOWS>
```

You can see from this output that the ping was unsuccessful. After NAT is implemented on the router, you should have full connectivity between the Internet and your private network, 172.16.10.0/24.

Here's how this is done:

```
Router_B#conf t
Enter configuration commands, one per line.  End with CNTL/Z.
Router_B(config)#ip nat pool CCNP 209.120.12.1
  209.120.12.254 netmask 255.255.255.0
Router_B(config)#access-list 55 permit 172.16.10.0 0.0.0.255
Router_B(config)#access-list 55 deny any
```

```
Router_B(config)#ip nat inside source list 55 pool CCNP
Router_B(config)#interface Ethernet 0
Router_B(config-if)#ip nat inside
Router_B(config-if)#interface Serial 0
Router_B(config-if)#ip nat outside
Router_B(config-if)#^Z
Router_B#
```

Let's check out the final configuration and then verify that connectivity is really happening:

```
Router_B#sho run
Building configuration...

Current configuration:
!
version 11.2
no service password-encryption
service udp-small-servers
service tcp-small-servers
!
hostname Router_B
!
enable password aloha
!
ip nat pool CCNP 209.120.12.1 209.120.12.254 netmask
  255.255.255.0
ip nat inside source list 20 pool CCNP
!
interface Ethernet0
 description Host_B
 ip address 155.99.121.126 255.255.255.0
 ip access-group 10 out
 ip nat outside
!
interface Ethernet1
 ip address 172.16.10.1 255.255.255.0
```

```
 ip nat inside
!
interface Serial0
 description Connection to Router A
 ip address 172.16.20.6 255.255.255.252
!
interface Serial1
 description Connection to Router C
 ip address 172.16.40.5 255.255.255.252
!
router eigrp 100
 network 172.16.0.0
 network 155.99.0.0
 distribute-list 10 out Ethernet0
 no auto-summary
!
ip classless
access-list 10 deny    10.0.0.0 0.255.255.255
access-list 10 deny    172.16.0.0 0.15.255.255
access-list 10 deny    192.168.0.0 0.0.0.255
access-list 10 permit any
access-list 20 permit 172.16.10.0 0.0.0.255
!
!
line con 0
 password aloha
line aux 0
 password aloha
line vty 0 2
 password aloha
 login
line vty 3 4
 login
!
end
```

```
Router_B#
```

```
C:\WINDOWS>ping 172.16.10.10
```

```
Pinging 172.16.10.10 with 32 bytes of data:
```

```
Reply from 172.16.10.10: bytes=32 time=2ms TTL=31
Reply from 172.16.10.10: bytes=32 time=2ms TTL=31
Reply from 172.16.10.10: bytes=32 time=2ms TTL=31
Reply from 172.16.10.10: bytes=32 time=2ms TTL=31
```

```
Ping statistics for 172.16.10.10:
    Packets: Sent = 4, Received = 4, Lost = 0 (0% loss),
Approximate round trip times in milli-seconds:
    Minimum = 2ms, Maximum =  2ms, Average =  2ms
```

```
C:\WINDOWS>
```

Remember that this is a very basic configuration for NAT. In the first line, you can see a pool defined by the name CCNP that's been assigned a block of registered addresses. These addresses range from 209.120.12.1 to 209.120.12.254 with a netmask of 255.255.255.0. After you define the pool of registered addresses, you write an access list set up so that only IP addresses from the 172.16.10.0 network would be permitted to utilize NAT.

Now that the preliminary configuration is done, you must apply it to the necessary interfaces, according to which interface connects the router to the Internet, and which has addresses that match the access list. Here, the Ethernet port is assigned NAT inside, and the serial interface that connects to the Internet is configured as NAT outside. (Only one interface per router may be configured as NAT outside.) When configuring NAT on a bunch of routers, it's really important that your pools have the same range of registered addresses in them.

Here are a few factors to keep in mind to help you decide whether to use NAT:

- The cost of purchasing registered IP addresses

- The number of nodes currently configured with private addresses

- The importance of logging, traceability, and security

- Transport delay

- Application sensitivity

As always, the cost of implementing something needs to be considered. Getting a hold of registered addresses for use with NAT will cost you much, and you'll have to pony up unless the provider allocates those without additional cost. Since procuring registered addresses has a dollar factor whether you're going to use NAT or not, it might be possible to just readdress the current network and bypass NAT altogether. When is this a good idea? It's probably easier to just renumber if there aren't a lot of private nodes on the network. Also, when NAT is used end to end, identity of machines is lost. So if an existing policy mandates strict management information, NAT may not work for you. Because the router must process every packet, there will be delay incurred in packet transport. Some applications simply rely on the end-to-end information that NAT just can't provide. If you have those applications running on your network, implementing NAT could break them.

But all things considered, there are still advantages to using NAT—if your network is huge with a multitude of private addresses, it would be much easier to implement NAT instead of renumbering that monster. Since NAT allows only specific networks to use the registered IP addresses, it gives you some degree of control over who's able to reach Internet hosts and who isn't.

Summary

Routers need the following information to route packets:

- A destination address

- Peers, from which to learn path information

- A route table with potential paths to a given destination

- A selected route from the route table that has the best metric

- Verification that the route is valid

VLSMs extend the use of IP addresses in the following ways:

- Subnets can be configured on nonclassfull boundaries.

- Multiple subnets (two or three) can be configured per network.

The problem of discontiguous networks may be solved by using the following:

- A routing protocol that supports classless routing

- Secondary addresses

- IP unnumbered

Route summarization condenses route information to decrease CPU and memory utilization. The following guidelines indicate when route summarization should be used:

- IP networks must be contiguous, meaning that the binary enumeration must be the same for the high-order bits.

- Routing tables must have the capacity to support classless routing.

- Routing protocols must be able to manage both prefix length and subnet information along with the IP address.

Private networks assigned by IANA are used to conserve IP address space. These addresses cannot be used if a machine must have global connectivity. Private networks are not advertised to or by the Internet.

NAT (network address translation) can be used to convert private network addresses into globally unique addresses to provide global connectivity for the specified hosts.

Review Questions

1. Which of the following is needed for a router to route data?

   A. TCP port number

   B. Destination address

   C. Default gateway

   D. Protocol type

   E. Potential routes

   F. A source for route information

2. Given the network 192.168.10.0, how can this address space be more efficiently used?

   A. By assigning only a mask of /16 (255.255.0.0)

   B. By assigning only a mask of /24 (255.255.255.0)

   C. By assigning only a mask of /8 (255.0.0.0)

   D. By assigning multiple masks to the network

3. What does VLSM (variable-length subnet mask) do? (Choose one.)

   A. Allows multiple subnet masks to be assigned to one IP network

   B. Allows the mask on an IP address to change as needed

   C. Enables classless routing on a router

   D. Allows multiple subnets to be used on a router

4. Identify the host and network addresses from the following VLSM address:

`172.16.10.4/30`

A. 2 and 3 are host addresses; 1 is the network; and 4 is the broadcast address

B. 4 and 5 are host addresses; 3 is the network; and 6 is the broadcast address

C. 4 is the network; 5 and 6 are host addresses; and 7 is the broadcast address

D. 4 through 8 are hosts, with 3 and 9 being the network and broadcast addresses respectively

5. What are the benefits of using a hierarchical IP addressing scheme?

A. A more organized network

B. No routing table needed, just a `default-network` statement

C. Increased availability of IP addresses

D. Reduced size of route tables

6. How can discontiguous networks be advertised? (Choose two.)

A. EIGRP, OSPF, and ISIS

B. RIP, IGRP, EIGRP, and OSPF

C. Secondary addresses

D. Static routes

7. How can RIP or IGRP select a default route when the routers are separated by a discontiguous address?

   A. With the use of helper addresses

   B. By issuing the `ip classless` command on the router

   C. By issuing the `ip default-network` command on the router

   D. By configuring the router to auto-summarize

8. What does RIP or IGRP advertise when only one subnet of a classfull network is connected to a router?

   A. The entire classfull network

   B. The subnet only

   C. Nothing

   D. Both the network and the subnet information

9. What's route summarization?

   A. Using only one subnet so that the network is flattened out

   B. Grouping multiple networks and advertising them as one larger network

   C. Using supernets on all access-level equipment

   D. Advertising only one network for the entire enterprise or campus

10. When can/should route summarization be used? (Choose all that apply.)

 A. Always

 B. When route tables become too large

 C. When a campus or enterprise router owns several contiguous subnets that share equal high-order bit patterns

 D. When routing protocols are capable of handling prefix length and subnet mask information

 E. When the router IOS is capable of IP classless routing (meaning that the network prefix may be any length, including 32 bits long)

11. Given the following configuration lines, is route summarization possible?

```
interface Ethernet 0
  ip address 172.16.12.1 255.255.255.0
interface Ethernet 1
  ip address 172.16.13.1 255.255.255.0
!
router eigrp 100
  network 172.16.0.0
!
```

 A. Yes

 B. No

12. How should the following networks be summarized?

172.16.12.0/24
172.16.13.0/24
172.16.14.0/24

A. 172.16.0.0/16

B. 172.16.14.0/24

C. 172.16.12.0/22

D. 172.16.14.0/22

13. How should the following networks be summarized?

172.16.1.0/24
172.16.2.0/24
172.16.3.0/24

A. They can't be summarized

B. 172.16.1.0/24 *and* 172.16.2.0/23

C. 172.16.1.0/22

D. 172.16.0.0

14. What's the risk of oversummarization?

A. None

B. Slower response times due to route convergence

C. Routing loops

D. Routing failure

15. What's private addressing?

   A. Network blocks set aside by IANA for networks that aren't connected to the global Internet

   B. Networks blocks that IANA doesn't allow for commercial use

   C. Network blocks used by private industry

   D. A block of three Class B addresses allocated by IANA for anyone to use

16. Which network is not part of IANA allocated private address blocks?

   A. 172.31.0.0

   B. 10.0.0.0

   C. 198.162.0.0

   D. 192.168.0.0

17. Where can private addressing be used?

   A. Anywhere

   B. In any network that's not connected to the global Internet or that restricts private addresses from being announced to the global Internet

   C. Only in networks that are not connected to the global Internet

   D. Only in networks that have a connection to the global Internet

18. What is NAT?

A. Network anonymous transport: Used to transfer data from privately addressed hosts to the global Internet

B. Network address translation: Used to renumber a privately addressed network

C. Network address translation: Used to convert a private IP address into a registered IP address so that connectivity with the global Internet may be established

D. Network address translation: Uses one address and then proxies connections from a private network to the global Internet

19. When can NAT be used? (Choose all that apply.)

A. When application sensitivity isn't an issue (delay)

B. When end-to-end traceability isn't needed

C. After the private address blocks have been fully utilized

D. When a network uses only private addresses

E. When a network has both private and registered addresses

20. How many outside interfaces may be configured per router?

A. As many as desired

B. Only one

C. Two

D. Serial interfaces only

Laboratory Exercise

1. Implement NAT using the following information:

- Private network to permit translation for 192.168.0.0

- Registered address block: 198.68.10.1 to 198.68.10.254

- Pool name: LAB5

- The Internet connects via interface Ethernet zero, and serial interfaces one and two have private addresses from the private block 192.168.0.0

CHAPTER

6

TCP/IP Routing Protocols

Routing protocols are responsible for the exchange of IP address information on enterprise, intranet, and Internet scales. The information shared by routers enables two separate end systems to find a path from one to another, thus establishing communication. As we discussed in Chapter 5, IP addressing schemes establish a hierarchy that makes path information both distinct and efficient. Routers receive route information via a given interface and then advertise that information out their other physical interfaces. The routing process occurs on Layer 3 of the OSI model.

In this chapter, we will discuss each of the following routing protocols:

- IGRP (Internal Gateway Routing Protocol)

- EIGRP (Enhanced Internal Gateway Routing Protocol)

- OSPF (Open Shortest Path First)

- BGP (Border Gateway Protocol)

Each of these protocols is distinct in the way it functions, and there are two major types: link-state and distance vector. We'll discuss each type's features and differences at the beginning of this chapter, because understanding how each protocol functions is a very important part of being able to troubleshoot a routing problem. Once you understand how a protocol calculates a route, you can fine-tune the protocol with configuration changes to make it perform at peak efficiency.

Cisco routers implement several different protocols—some are Cisco proprietary, and others are open standard. The proprietary protocols we'll discuss are IGRP and Enhanced IGRP. OSPF is an open standard routing protocol that allows Cisco routers to share routing information with other Cisco and non-Cisco routers.

The test objectives covered in this chapter are as follows:

- Compare distance vector and link-state protocol operation

- Describe Enhanced IGRP features and operation

- Configure Enhanced IGRP

- Verify Enhanced IGRP operation

- Select and configure the different ways to control route update traffic

- Configure route redistribution in a network that does not have redundant paths between dissimilar routing processes

- Configure route redistribution in a network that has redundant paths between dissimilar routing processes

- Resolve path selection problems that result in a redistributed network

- Verify route redistribution

- Explain why OSPF is better than RIP in a large internetwork

- Explain how OSPF discovers, chooses, and maintains routes

- Configure OSPF for proper operation

- Verify OSPF operation

- Describe the issues with interconnecting multiple areas and how OSPF addresses

- Explain the differences between the possible types of areas, routers, and LSAs

- Configure a multiarea OSPF network

- Verify OSPF operation

- Describe when to use BGP to connect to an ISP

- Describe methods to connect to an ISP using static and default routes, and BGP

Scalability Features of Routing Protocols

As networks grow, the extent to which a routing protocol will scale becomes a very critical issue. Network growth imposes a great number of changes to the network environment— the number of hops between end systems, the number of routes in the route table, the different ways a route was learned, and route convergence are all seriously affected by network growth.

So to maintain a stable routing environment, it's absolutely crucial to use a scalable protocol. When the results of network growth manifest, whether your network's routers will be able to meet those challenges is up to the routing protocol the routers are running. For instance, if you use a protocol that's limited by the number of hops it can transverse, how many routes it can store in its table, or even the inability to communicate with other protocols, you have a protocol that will likely stunt the growth of your network.

That last area—a protocol's interoperability—becomes really important when the need to connect multivendor networks arises. Not every network is constructed solely of Cisco equipment, so it's necessary to have a protocol that will allow different vendor types to share routing information.

All the issues we've brought up so far are general scalability considerations—we'll now discuss each protocol type separately with respect to these considerations. Each type has pros and cons (along with scalability issues), and we'll analyze all of these factors in the following sections.

Scalability Limitations of Distance Vector Protocols

In small networks (fewer than 100 routers) where the environment is much more forgiving of routing updates and calculations, distance vector protocols perform pretty well. However, you'll run into several problems when attempting to scale a distance vector protocol to a larger network—convergence times, router overhead (CPU utilization), and bandwidth utilization all become factors that hinder scalability.

A network's convergence time is determined by the ability of the protocol to propagate changes within the network topology. Distance vector protocols don't use formal neighbor relationships between routers. A router using distance vector algorithms becomes aware of a topology change in two ways:

- If a router fails to receive a routing update from a directly connected router

- When a router receives an update from a neighbor notifying it of a topology change somewhere in the network

Routing updates are sent out on a default, or specified, time interval, so when a topology change occurs, it could take up to 90 seconds before a neighboring router realizes what's happened. When the router finally recognizes the change, it recalculates its route table and sends the whole thing out to all its neighbors.

Not only can this cause significant network convergence delay, it also devours bandwidth—just think about 100 routers all sending out their entire routing tables and imagine the impact on your bandwidth. It's not exactly a sweet scenario, and the larger the network, the worse it gets, because a greater percentage of bandwidth is needed for routing updates.

As the size of the routing table increases, so does CPU utilization, because it takes more processing power to calculate the effects of topology changes and then converge using the new information. Also, as more routes populate a route table, it becomes increasingly complex to determine the best path and next hop for a given destination. The following list provides a summary of scalability limitations inherent in distance vector algorithms:

- Network convergence delay

- Increased CPU utilization

- Increased bandwidth utilization

Scalability Limitations of Link-State Protocols

Link-state routing protocols assuage the scalability issues faced by distance vector protocols because the algorithm uses a different procedure for route calculation and advertisement, which enables them to scale along with the growth of the network.

Addressing distance vector's problem with network convergence, link-state protocols maintain a formal neighbor relationship with directly connected routers that allows for faster route convergence. They establish peering by exchanging hello packets during a session, which cements the neighbor relationship between two directly connected routers. This relationship expedites network convergence because neighbors are immediately notified of topology changes. Hello packets are sent at short intervals (typically every 10 seconds), and if an interface fails to receive hello packets from a neighbor within a predetermined hold time, the neighbor is considered down, and the router will then flood the update out all physical interfaces. This is done before the new route table is calculated, so it saves time. Neighbors receive the update, copy it, flood it out their interfaces, and *then* calculate the new routing table—the procedure is followed until the topology change has been propagated throughout the network.

It's noteworthy that the router sends an update concerning only the *new* information—not the entire route table. So the update is a lot smaller, which saves both bandwidth and CPU utilization. Plus, if there aren't any network changes, updates are sent out only at specified, or default, intervals, which differ among specific routing protocols and can range from 30 minutes to 2 hours.

These are key differences that permit link-state protocols to function well in large networks—they don't really have any limitations when it comes to scaling, other than the fact that they're a bit more complex to configure than distance vector routing protocols.

IGRP (Interior Gateway Routing Protocol)

IGRP is a Cisco proprietary routing protocol that uses a distance vector algorithm because it uses a vector (a one-dimensional array) of information to calculate the best path. This vector consists of four elements:

- Bandwidth
- Delay
- Load
- Reliability

MTU (maximum transfer unit) information is included in the final route information, but it's used as part of the vector of metrics. Each element will be described in detail in a little while.

IGRP is intended to replace RIP and create a stable, quickly converging protocol that would scale with increased network growth. As we mentioned, it's preferable to implement a link-state protocol in large networks because of the overhead and delay that results from using a distance vector protocol.

IGRP Features and Operation

IGRP has several features included in the algorithm—these features and a brief description can be found in Table 6.1. These features were added to make IGRP more stable, and a few were created to deal with routing updates and make network convergence happen faster.

T A B L E 6.1	**Feature**	**Description**
IGRP Features	Configurable metrics	Metrics involved in the algorithm responsible for calculating route information may be configured by the user.
	Flash update	Updates are sent out prior to the default time setting. This occurs when the metrics for a route change.
	Poison reverse updates	Implemented to prevent routing loops. These updates place a route in *holddown*. Holddown means that the router won't accept any new route information on a given route for a certain period of time.
	Unequal-cost load balancing	Allows packets to be shared/distributed across multiple paths.

IGRP is a classfull protocol, which means it doesn't include any subnet information about the network with route information. Three types of routes are recognized by IGRP:

Interior Networks directly connected to a router interface.

System Routes advertised by other IGRP neighbors within the same AS (autonomous system). The AS number identifies the IGRP session, because it's possible for a router to have multiple IGRP sessions.

Exterior Routes learned via IGRP from a different AS number, which provide information used by the router to set the *gateway of last resort*. The gateway of last resort is the path a packet will take if a specific route isn't found on the router.

To really understand how IGRP routes, it's important to understand the difference between these route types, which are detailed in Figure 6.1.

When we talked about the scalability of distance vector protocols, we told you that they don't establish a formal neighbor relationship with directly

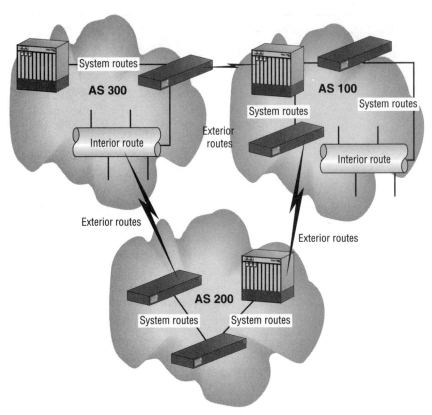

FIGURE 6.1

Route types recognized
by IGRP

connected routers, and that routing updates are sent at designated intervals. IGRP's interval is 90 seconds, which means that every 90 seconds IGRP will broadcast its entire routing table to all directly connected IGRP neighbors.

Figure 6.2 portrays how IGRP routing updates work. It depicts three routers all within the same AS. On the left side of the figure, relative times (in seconds) for each of the routers are listed—notice they're not the actual clock times. The first line shows Routers A and C sending their route tables to Router B. Router B timestamps the routing updates from both routers and will expect to receive updates from them every 90 seconds thereafter. At the next time increment (30 seconds later), Router B broadcasts its routing table to both Routers A and C, which they in turn timestamp. They will also expect to receive an update from Router B every 90 seconds based on that timestamp.

FIGURE 6.2

IGRP route
update process

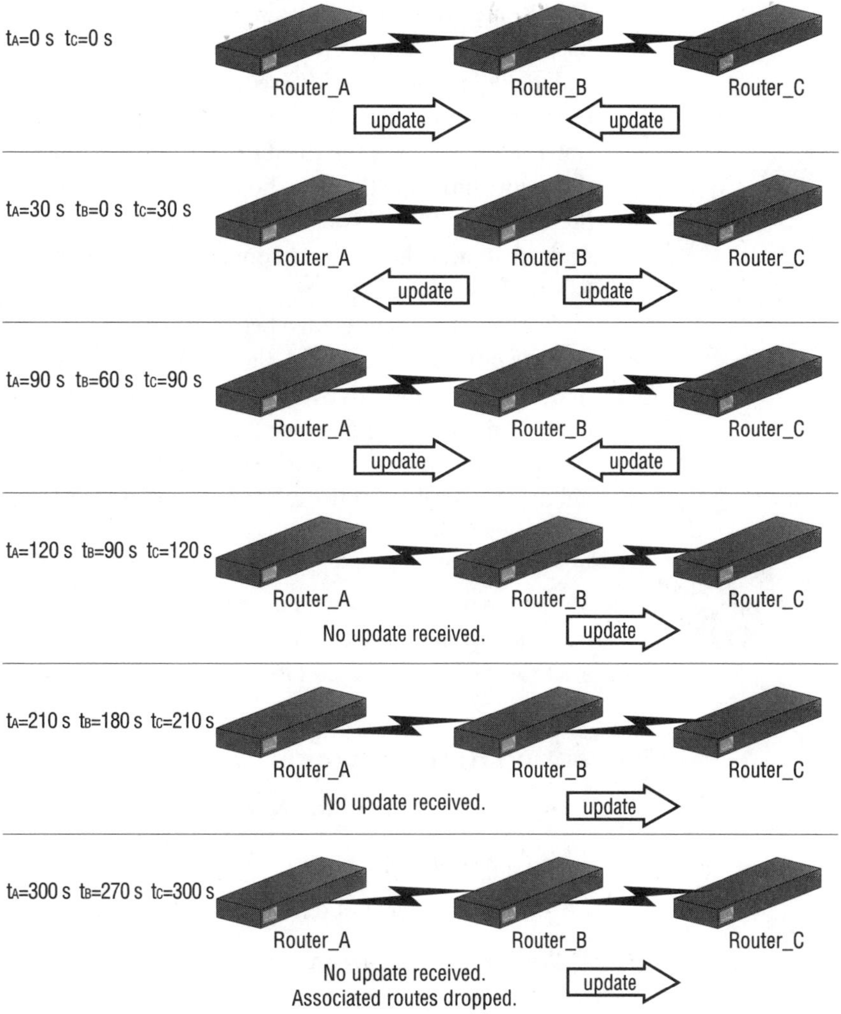

t_A=0 s t_C=0 s

Router_A   Router_B   Router_C
update →   ← update

t_A=30 s t_B=0 s t_C=30 s

Router_A   Router_B   Router_C
← update   update →

t_A=90 s t_B=60 s t_C=90 s

Router_A   Router_B   Router_C
update →   ← update

t_A=120 s t_B=90 s t_C=120 s

Router_A   Router_B   Router_C
No update received.   update →

t_A=210 s t_B=180 s t_C=210 s

Router_A   Router_B   Router_C
No update received.   update →

t_A=300 s t_B=270 s t_C=300 s

Router_A   Router_B   Router_C
No update received.   update →
Associated routes dropped.

Once the timers for Routers A and C reach 90 seconds, they broadcast their route tables to Router B. Router B then resets its receive timer and expects to receive route updates within 90 seconds. Router B's transmit timer continues to count to 90 seconds and broadcasts the route table when that period elapses. Notice that Router C received an update, but Router A didn't. Because of that, Router C resets its receive timer, but Router A's timer continues to count.

Another 90 seconds elapse, so Router B sends out another update. Again, only Router C receives it. Router A's clock is now at 180 seconds because it hasn't yet received an update.

Finally, an additional 90 seconds passes when Router B broadcasts the route table, and again Router C receives the broadcast and resets its receive timer. However, for the third time, Router A doesn't receive the update, so the algorithm flags the next-hop Router B as unreachable and assigns it a higher metric. After Router A recalculates a new table, it will send out flash updates to all other routers connected to Router A notifying them that Router B is unreachable.

The total time that passed between the first update received from Router B and the point that Router A flagged Router B as unreachable was 270 seconds. Three consecutive failures to receive an update from a directly connected router are required for IGRP to consider a neighbor unreachable and assign it a new metric. After seven failures, any routes associated with Router B will be removed from the table and no longer advertised.

More than one route can be associated with a next-hop router, so once it's been determined that a next-hop is down, a router will remove all associated routes from its route table.

Preventing Routing Loops

Two methods are used to prevent routing loops:

- Split horizon

- Poison reverse updates

With split horizon, route information learned from a given interface isn't sent back out the same interface. Using Figure 6.3 as a reference, we'll explain split horizon updates.

Router D advertises network 10.2.1.0/24 to Routers A and B. After Router B receives the update and recalculates its own route table, a broadcast update is sent. However, specific route information learned from Router D isn't advertised back to Router D.

Poison reverse updates use a function within IGRP called *holddown,* which stops the router from being confused about multiple routes to a given network. If a router has a bunch of routers connected to it, it's possible for

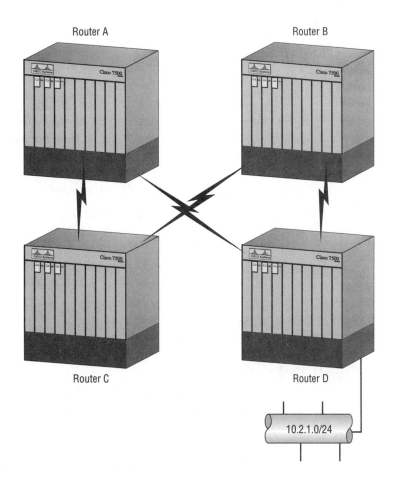

FIGURE 6.3

Poison reverse and holddown

it to receive duplicate route advertisements. Figure 6.3 shows a router that's meshed with three other routers. Router A learns of network 10.2.1.0/24 from Routers C and D. If the Ethernet segment connected to Router D fails, Router D will advertise the change to Routers A and B. So Router A will receive information from Router D that network 10.2.1.0/24 is unreachable—a fact that increases its metrics. Router B must recalculate the route table before it can update Router C. At this point, Router A has a higher metric for the 10.2.1.0/24 network. Due to the change in the metric, the router will place the route in holddown so that updates regarding the network are ignored unless they're received from the router that advertised the increased metric. During holddown, the network is advertised to other routers with the increased metric.

IGRP Metrics

Metrics are the key for route selection—the higher the metric associated with a route, the less desirable it is. The overall metric assigned to a route is created by the Bellman-Ford algorithm using the following equation:

$$CM=(K_1/B_e + [K_2 \times D_c])r$$

- *CM* is the composite metric assigned to the route.
- K_1 and K_2 are equation constants.
- B_e is the bandwidth capacity. This is the capacity without any traffic.
- D_c is the delay associated with the link to the next hop in the path to the network.
- *r* is the reliability of the physical link. If a circuit has several outages, this is calculated into the composite metric.

Configuring IGRP

You can configure many functions within IGRP, and its configuration can range from simple to complex. The most basic configuration is simply implementing the protocol on the router. After the network session begins, networks connected to the router are added into it. If redistribution is taking place, the metrics for redistributed routes may be configured. We'll show you how to do that a bit later.

To enable IGRP on a router, follow this example:

```
Router_B#conf t
Enter configuration commands, one per line.  End with CNTL/Z.
Router_B(config)#router igrp 300
Router_B(config-router)#network 172.16.0.0
Router_B(config-router)#network 10.0.0.0
Router_B(config-router)#^Z
Router_B#
```

The first command is used to enable IGRP and associate it with an autonomous system number—in this case, 300. The AS number is an external number used to allow other routers with the same AS to communicate and exchange routes. Network statements are used to add directly connected networks that are intended to be advertised via IGRP 300—in this example, those would be networks 172.16.0.0 and 10.0.0.0.

The above example shows all you need to get IGRP started on a router, but it's possible to add other configuration lines for several other features under the IGRP session. IGRP uses broadcasts to send route table updates on LAN media. If it is necessary to send updates to only a subset of neighbors, point-to-point updates may be used. Configure passive interfaces to stop sending routing updates on the specified interfaces, and then configure specific neighbors to which updates will be sent. A separate copy of each routing update is sent to each neighbor. Take a look at the next example:

```
Router_B#conf t
Enter configuration commands, one per line.  End with CNTL/Z.
Router_B(config)#router igrp 300
Router_B(config)#passive-interface ethernet 0
Router_B(config-router)#neighbor 172.16.20.5
Router_B(config-router)#^Z
Router_B#show running-configuration
Current configuration:
!
!
!
router igrp 300
 network 172.16.0.0
 network 10.0.0.0
 passive-interface ethernet 0
neighbor 172.16.20.5
!
!
```

Here, a point-to-point relationship is established within IGRP 300 to allow route information to be sent directly to 172.16.20.5 instead of relying on the normal broadcast routine, which sends a broadcast update to all neighbors on Ethernet 0. We've also shown the running configuration for the IGRP session.

Traffic distribution is another IGRP feature. When multiple paths exist, it may not be a very bright idea to send traffic over the path with a higher metric. So, to use only the best route and also have multiple paths around in case of failure on the primary link, use the following command:

```
traffic-share balanced | min
```

The *balanced* option tells the router to load the link inversely, proportional to the metric for the link, and *min* indicates that traffic should be sent across only links with a minimal metric.

We talked about how poison reverse updates put routes into a holddown status, but the holddown feature can also be turned off in Configuration mode for the IGRP session. You do that with the following command:

```
no metric holddown
```

IGRP uses a default network diameter of 100 hops, which means that a route with a hop count greater than 100 isn't advertised to other IGRP neighbors. You can change this value with the `maximum-hops` command:

```
metric maximum-hops hops
```

When a route is received from a neighbor, the source IP address of the router sending the update is verified to ensure that the update is originating from a router that belongs to the same network as the receiving interface. This feature is on by default, but it can be disabled using the *no* form of the following command:

```
validate-update-source
```

Many of these functions are on by default, but can be disabled if necessary, and all can be configured when you implement IGRP. Other metrics can be changed to influence the way the router chooses the best route—we'll talk about this next.

Tuning Metrics

If necessary, you can adjust metrics within the router configuration interface. Metrics are tuned to change the manner in which routes are calculated. After you enable IGRP on a router, metric weights can be changed using the following command:

```
metric weights tos K1 K2 K3 K4 K5
```

Each constant is used to assign a weight to a specific variable. This means that when the metric is calculated, the algorithm will assign a greater importance to the specified metric. By assigning a weight, you are able to specify what is most important. If bandwidth is of greatest concern to a network administrator, a greater weight would be assigned to K1. If delay is unacceptable, the K2 constant should be assigned a greater weight. The *tos* variable is the type of service. Table 6.2 shows the relationship between the constant and the metric it affects.

TABLE 6.2 Metric Association of *K* Values	Constant	Metric
	K1	Bandwidth (B_e)
	K2	Delay (D_c)
	K3	Reliability (r)
	K4	Load (utilization on path)
	K5	MTU

As well as tuning the actual metric weights, you can do other tunings. All routing protocols have an administrative distance associated with the protocol type. If multiple protocols are running on one router, the administrative distance value helps the router decide which path is best. The protocol with the lower administrative distance will be chosen. IGRP has a default administrative distance of 100. The tuning of this value is accomplished with the distance command:

```
distance 1-255
```

Valid values for the administrative distance range from 1 to 255. Again, the lower the value, the better.

When redistributing static routes or other protocol types within IGRP, metrics may be set for these routes as well by using the `default-metric` command:

`default-metric` *bandwidth delay reliability load MTU*

Bandwidth and delay have a range of values from 0 to 4,294,967,295 (in Kb per second) and 0 to 4,294,967,295 (in 10-microsecond units), respectively. Reliability ranges from 0 to 255, with 255 being the most reliable. Load ranges from 0 to 255; however, 255 means that the link is completely loaded. Finally, the value of the MTU has the same range as the bandwidth variable: 0 to 4,294,967,295.

Unequal-Cost Load Balancing: Tuning Variance

When a router receives multiple routes for a specific network, one of the routes must be chosen as the best route from all of the advertisements. The router still knows that it is possible to get to a given network over multiple interfaces, yet all data defaults to the best route.

IGRP provides the ability of unequal-cost load balancing. This was discussed in detail in Chapter 2. In review, the `variance` command is used to assign a weight to each feasible successor. As long as the secondary route conforms to the following three criteria, an unequal-cost load balancing session may be established:

- A limit of four feasible successors may be used.

- The feasible successor's metric must fall within the specified variance of the local metric.

- The local metric must be greater than the metric for the next-hop router.

Remember that a lower metric signifies a better route.

Redistribution Limitations

As an enterprise network grows, there is a possibility that more than one protocol will run on the router. An example is when a company acquires another company and needs to merge the two existing networks. The problem surfaces when the routes of the purchasing company need to be advertised to the newly acquired company. IGRP solves the problem with route redistribution.

When multiple protocols run on a router, you can configure IGRP to redistribute routes from specified protocols. Since different protocols calculate metrics distinctly, adjustments must be made when redistributing protocols. These adjustments cause some limitations in how the redistribution works. The adjustments are made by using the `default-metric` command as seen previously

IGRP may also be redistributed to other routing protocols such as RIP, other IGRP sessions, EIGRP, and OSPF. Metrics are also configured using the `default-metric` command.

Now that we have discussed IGRP, let's move on to Enhanced IGRP (EIGRP).

EIGRP (Enhanced IGRP)

This section is dedicated to Enhanced Interior Gateway Routing Protocol and its features. Details on how to configure, fine-tune, and troubleshoot EIGRP will be given throughout the section.

Enhanced IGRP was created to resolve some of the problems with IGRP. These problems are that the entire route table is sent when changes are made in the network and the lack of formal neighbor relationships with connected routers. EIGRP is a hybrid of both link-state and distance vector routing algorithms, which brings the best of both worlds together.

EIGRP allows for equal-cost load balancing, incremental routing updates, and formal neighbor relationships, overcoming the limitations of IGRP. This enhanced version uses the same distance vector information as IGRP, yet with a different algorithm. EIGRP uses DUAL (diffused update algorithm) for metric calculation.

EIGRP Features and Operation

EIGRP's specific features are detailed in Table 6.3. Each item will be addressed within this section of the chapter. The features offered by EIGRP make it a stable and scalable protocol. Just as IGRP is a Cisco proprietary protocol, so is EIGRP.

T A B L E 6.3	Feature	Description
EIGRP Features	Route tagging	Distinguishes routes learned via different EIGRP sessions.
	Formal neighbor relationships	Uses the Hello protocol to establish peering.
	Incremental routing updates	Only changes are advertised instead of the entire route table.
	Classless routing	EIGRP supports subnet and VLSM information.
	Configurable metrics	Metric information can be set through configuration commands.
	Equal-cost load balancing	Allows traffic to be sent equally across multiple connections.

To aid in the calculation of the best route and load sharing, EIGRP utilizes several databases of information. These databases are as follows:

- The route database where the best routes are stored

- The topology database where all route information resides

- A neighbor table that is used to house information concerning other EIGRP neighbors

Each of these databases exists for IP-EIGRP, IPX-EIGRP, AT-EIGRP, and AppleTalk-EIGRP. Therefore, it is possible for EIGRP to have nine active databases when all three protocols are configured on the router.

Route Tagging

EIGRP functions within defined autonomous systems on a router. It is possible for multiple sessions of EIGRP to run on a single router. Each session is distinguished by the AS number assigned to it. Routers that have Enhanced IGRP sessions running under the same AS number speak to each other and share routing information among the other routers in the same AS. Routes learned via other routers within the AS are considered internal EIGRP routes. It is also possible for one AS session to learn routes from a different EIGRP AS session through redistribution (redistribution will be covered later in this section). When this occurs, the routes are tagged as being learned from an external EIGRP session. Each type of route is assigned its own administrative distance value.

Neighbor Relationships

The manner in which EIGRP establishes and maintains neighbor relationships is derived through its link-state properties. EIGRP uses the Hello protocol (just as OSPF does) to establish and maintain peering relationships with directly connected routers. Hello packets are sent between EIGRP routers to determine the state of the connection between them. Once the neighbor relation is established via the Hello protocol, the routers can exchange route information.

Each router establishes a neighbor table in which it stores important information regarding the neighbors that are directly connected. The information consists of the neighbor's IP address, hold time interval, smooth round trip timer (SRTT), and queue information. These data are used to help determine when the link-state changes.

When two routers initialize communication, their entire route tables are shared. Thereafter, only changes to the route table are propagated. These changes are shared with all directly connected EIGRP-speaking routers. Each of these steps is summarized below.

1. Hello packets are multicast out all of the router's interfaces.

2. Replies to the hello packets include all routes in the neighbor router's topology database including the metrics. Routes that are learned from the originating router are not included in the reply.

3. The originating router acknowledges the update to each neighbor via an Ack packet.

4. The topology database is then updated with the newly received information.

5. Once the topology database has been updated, the originating router will then advertise its entire table to all the new neighbors.

6. Neighbor routers acknowledge the receipt of the route information from the originating router by sending back an Ack packet.

These steps are used in the initialization of EIGRP neighbors and change somewhat when only updates are sent to existing neighbors.

Route Calculation and Updates

Because EIGRP uses distance vector and link-state information when calculating routes using the DUAL algorithm, convergence is much faster than with IGRP. The trick behind the convergence speed is that EIGRP calculates new routes only when a change in the network directly affects the routes contained in its route table. To make that a little clearer, let's look at Figure 6.4. In this figure, we see three routers meshed, and each has an Ethernet segment connected as well.

F I G U R E 6.4

Route updates
vs. calculation

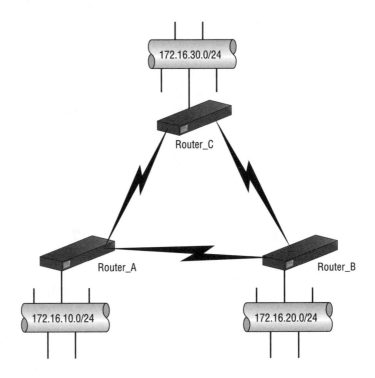

It is important to understand the difference between accepting a routing update and calculating a new route. If a change occurs to a network that is directly connected to a router, all of the relevant information is used to *calculate* a new metric and route entry for it. After the router has calculated the new route, it is advertised to the neighbors.

Using Figure 6.4 as our example, let's assume that Ethernet 0 on Router C is very congested due to high traffic volumes. Router C then uses the distance and link information to calculate a new metric for network 172.16.30.0. With the new metric in place, the change is propagated to Routers A and B. To understand completely, we need to recognize that the other routers don't do any calculation—they just receive the update. Routers A and B don't need to calculate a new route for network 172.16.30.0 because they learn it from Router C.

On the other hand, if the link between Router A and Router C becomes congested, both routers would have to calculate a new route metric. The change is then advertised to Router B by both Routers A and C.

Now that we understand the difference between a route update and a route calculation, we can summarize the steps that a router takes to calculate, learn, and propagate route update information.

Calculation and Selection   The topology database stores all routes and metrics known via adjacent routers. Six routes can be stored for each destination network. From these six routes, the router must select a primary and backup route—the primary route will be added to the route table. While the best route is being chosen for a destination, the route is considered to be in an *active* state. After the route has been chosen, the route status changes to *passive*.

Through the use of existing metric information such as bandwidth and delay from both the local and adjacent routers, a composite metric is calculated. The local router adds its cost to the cost advertised by the adjacent router. *Cost* is another word for metric. By looking at Figure 6.5, we can learn how cost is used to select the successor (best route) and the feasible successor (backup route).

We'll use Router A as our example. Router A has three different routes that tell it how to get to Host Y. We can see that each link has been assigned a cost. Numbers in bold represent *advertised distances,* and numbers in italics represent *feasible distances*. Advertised distances are costs that routers advertise to neighbors.

In this example, Routers C and D and the WAN all have advertised costs that they send to Router A. In turn, Router A has a feasible distance for every

FIGURE 6.5

Best-route selection

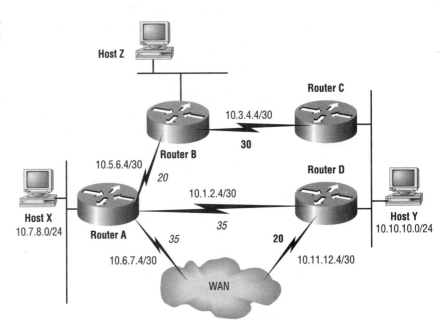

router to which it is connected. The feasible distance is the cost assigned to the link that connects adjacent routers.

The feasible and advertised costs are added together to provide a total cost to reach a specific network. Let's calculate the lowest cost for Host X to get to Host Y. We will use the path from Host X ➢ Router A ➢ Router B ➢ Router C ➢ Host Y for our first path calculation. To calculate the total cost, we add 20 (Router A ➢ Router B) to 30 (Router B ➢ Router C), for a final value of 50.

The next path calculated is from Host X ➢ Router A ➢ Router D ➢ Host Y. In this case, there is no advertised cost, so the final value consists of only the feasible cost—35. The final path is calculated in the same manner to give us the result of 55.

Since the lowest cost was 35, the route to `10.10.10.0/24` learned via Router D will be chosen as the successor or primary route. The other two routes remain in the topology table as feasible successors and are used if the successor to Host Y fails.

Information given in Table 6.4 closely represents what is contained in an actual topology table, though not exactly. The "Status" field shows whether a new route is being calculated or if a primary route has been selected. In our example, the route is in passive state because it has already selected the primary route.

T A B L E 6.4:   Topology Table Information

Status	Route—Adjacent Router's Address (Metrics)	Number of Successors	Feasible Distance
P	10.10.10.0/24 via 10.1.2.6 (3611648/3609600) via 10.5.6.6 (4121600/3609600) via 10.6.7.6 (5031234/3609600)	1 (Router C)	3611648

The route with the best metric (lower is better) is chosen as the primary route. The backup route is chosen by selecting the route with the second lowest metric. Primary routes are moved to the route table after selection. It is possible to have more than one primary route—this will be discussed in the "Load Balancing and Variance" subsection.

EIGRP uses the same vector information as IGRP: bandwidth, delay, reliability, load, and MTU. Bandwidth and delay are the two metrics used by default; the others can be configured manually. When you configure reliability, load and MTU can cause the topology table to be calculated more often.

Updates and Changes   EIGRP also has link-state properties. One of these properties is that it propagates only changes in the route table instead of sending an entire new route table to its neighbors. When changes occur in the network, a regular distance vector protocol will send the entire route table to neighbors. By avoiding sending the entire route table, less bandwidth is consumed. Neighboring routers don't have to re-initialize the entire route table—causing convergence issues—they just have to insert the new route changes. This is one of the big enhancements over IGRP.

Updates can follow two paths. If a route update contains a better metric or a new route, the routers simply exchange the information. If the update contains information that a network is unavailable or the metric is worse than before, an alternate path must be found. The flow chart in Figure 6.6 describes the steps that must be taken to choose a new route.

The router first searches the topology database for feasible successors. If no feasible successors are found, a multicast request is sent to all adjacent routers. Each router will then respond to the query. Depending on how the router answers, different paths will be taken. After the intermediate steps are taken, two final actions can occur. If route information is eventually found, the route is added to the route table, and an update is sent. If the responses from the adjacent routers do not contain any route information, the route is removed from the topology and route tables. After the route table has been updated, the new information is sent to all adjacent routers via a multicast.

EIGRP Metrics

Metrics used by EIGRP are the same as those used by IGRP. As with IGRP, metrics decide how routes are selected. The higher the metric associated with a route, the less desirable the route is. The overall metric assigned to a route is created by the Bellman-Ford algorithm using the following equation:

$$CM=(K_1/B_e + [K_2 \times D_c])r$$

- *CM* is the composite metric assigned to the route.

- K_1 and K_2 are equation constants.

- B_e is the bandwidth capacity. This is the capacity without any traffic.

- D_c is the delay associated with the link to the next hop in the path to the network.

- *r* is the reliability of the physical link. If a circuit has several outages, this is calculated into the composite metric.

Just as with IGRP, you can set these metrics manually from within the Configuration mode. Details on how to change metrics will be explained after we discuss how EIGRP is configured.

Configuring EIGRP

EIGRP supports several different protocols. Each protocol has specific commands that are used to enable EIGRP. EIGRP can be configured for IP, IPX,

Handling route changes

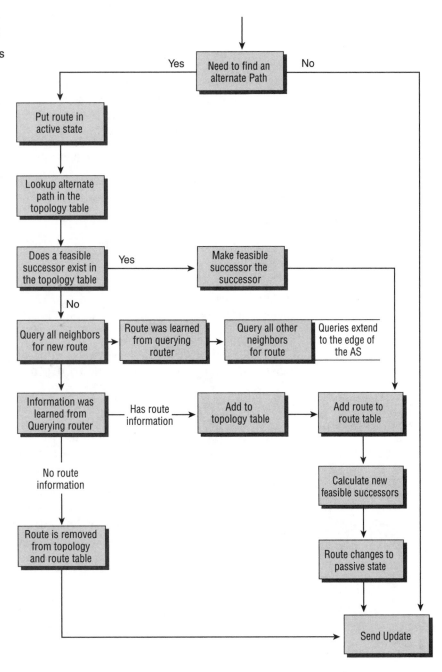

and AppleTalk. In this subsection, we will describe in detail how EIGRP is implemented for each of these protocols.

IP

An autonomous system must be defined for each EIGRP session on a router. To start an EIGRP session on a router, use the command listed just below. After the session has been started, networks that belong to that session need to be added. The networks should be directly connected.

```
router eigrp autonomous-system-number
```

The command to enter the networks must be entered within the EIGRP session configuration. The command and an example follow.

```
network network-number
```

- *network-number* is the IP address of a network connected to the router.

```
Router_B#conf t
Enter configuration commands, one per line.  End with CNTL/Z.
Router_B(config)#router eigrp 200
Router_B(config-router)#network 172.16.0.0
Router_B(config-router)#network 10.0.0.0
Router_B(config-router)#^Z
Router_B#
```

EIGRP assumes that serial connections use T1 speeds. However, it is possible to have slower links, such as 56Kbps or other values, connected to a serial interface. As we have learned previously, bandwidth is one of the two default metrics used to calculate a route's metric. If the bandwidth is slower than T1 speeds, EIGRP will still assign a metric value equivalent to that of a T1. To avoid this confusion, the bandwidth assigned to that interface should be changed. To do this, issue the following command within the Interface Configuration mode:

```
bandwidth bandwidth
```

- *bandwidth* is an integer value between 1 and 10,000,000 defining the kilobits of bandwidth.

You can stop routing updates from exiting the router via specified inter-faces by flagging them as a passive interface from within the EIGRP session. Here is the command:

`passive-interface` *interface-type interface-number*

- *interface-type* defines the type of interface.

- *interface-number* defines the number of the interface.

If all that you want to do is allow only certain networks to be advertised, use the `distribute-list` command. This command was discussed in Chapter 3, but we will review it here as well. The command is issued within the EIGRP session.

`distribute-list` *access-list-number* `[in | out]` *interface-type interface-number*

- *access-list-number* is the number of a predefined access list.

IPX

To use EIGRP as the routing protocol for IPX, you must turn on the IPX pro-tocol. Once IPX is enabled, EIGRP is defined as the routing protocol. The commands, along with descriptions and examples, follow.

`ipx routing`

`ipx router [eigrp` *autonomous-system-number* `| rip | nlsp]`

```
Router_A#conf t
Enter configuration commands, one per line.  End with CNTL/Z.
Router_A(config)#ipx routing
Router_A(config)#ipx router eigrp 400
Router_A(config-ipx-router)#^Z
Router_A#
```

As you can see by the command syntax, it is possible to use RIP, NLSP, and EIGRP as the routing protocols. We're going to use EIGRP at this time. The above example first initializes IPX routing and then defines EIGRP 400 as the routing protocol that IPX will use.

The Novell networks should be added to the IPX-EIGRP session. Networks are added with the same network command that was used in IP EIGRP configuration. Here is an example and the resulting configuration. The IPX networks are seen under the IPX-routing EIGRP 400 session.

```
Router_A#conf t
Enter configuration commands, one per line.  End with CNTL/Z.
Router_A(config)#ipx router eigrp 400
Router_A(config-ipx-router)#network 10
Router_A(config-ipx-router)#network 20
Router_A(config-ipx-router)#^Z
Router_A#show running-config
Building configuration...

Current configuration:
!
version 11.3
no service password-encryption
!
hostname Router_A
!
ipx routing 0010.7bd9.2880
!
router eigrp 100
 network 10.0.0.0
 network 172.16.0.0
!
ip classless
!
ipx router eigrp 400
 network 10
 network 20
!
```

Just as IP interfaces can be configured to allow or disallow routing updates or portions thereof, so can IPX interfaces. SAP updates can be controlled with the incremental update command. This command tells the router that SAP updates are to be sent only when there is a change in the information, and then, only the change is advertised. The command is not issued under the IPX-EIGRP session, but on the interface itself. Another router running IPX-EIGRP should be on the opposite end of the link for this command to work properly. If no IPX peer exists, SAP updates are sent periodically. The command follows.

```
ipx sap-incremental eigrp autonomous-system-number
   [rsup-only]
```

The `rsup-only` option is used when RIP is used as the routing protocol. It indicates to the router that SAP updates are sent via EIGRP only incrementally.

WAN links have this feature turned on by default; LAN interfaces have this feature turned off by default.

AppleTalk

EIGRP also supports AppleTalk. To enable AT-EIGRP on a router, you must first initialize AppleTalk routing on the router. This is done with the following command:

```
appletalk routing eigrp autonomous-system-number
```

Once this command is entered, AppleTalk route redistribution is turned on as well. Other commands relating to AT-EIGRP can be issued directly from the interface. The following options are available:

`eigrp-bandwidth-percent`	Sets EIGRP bandwidth limit
`eigrp-splithorizon`	Enables split horizon processing, generating AT-EIGRP updates
`eigrp-timers`	Sets AT-EIGRP hello and holdtime timers

RTMP routes are automatically redistributed into AT-EIGRP on IOS versions previous to 11.3. When running IOS 11.3, you need to enable RTMP route redistribution into AT-EIGRP. This is done with the following command under the Global Configuration interface: `appletalk route-redistribution`.

Tuning EIGRP Metrics

Metrics for EIGRP are tuned in the same manner as the metrics for IGRP. Metrics are tuned to change the manner in which routes are calculated. The same command is also used:

```
metric weights tos K1 K2 K3 K4 K5
```

Each constant is used to assign a weight to a specific variable. This means that when the metric is calculated, the algorithm will assign a greater importance to the specified metric. By assigning a weight, you are able to specify what is most important. If bandwidth is of greatest concern to a network administrator, a greater weight would be assigned to K1. If delay is unacceptable, the K2 constant should be assigned a greater weight. The *tos* variable is the type of service. Refer back to Table 6.2 for the relationship between the constant and the metric it affects. Also, remember that EIGRP uses bandwidth and delay by default only when calculating routes.

Other tuning may also be done. All routing protocols have an administrative distance associated with the protocol type. If multiple protocols are running on one router, the administrative distance value helps the router decide which path is best. The protocol with the lower administrative distance will be chosen. EIGRP has a default administrative distance of 90 for internal routes and 170 for external routes. Changes are made by using the following command:

```
distance 1-255
```

Valid values for the administrative distance range from 1 to 255. Again, the lower the value, the better. If an administrative distance of 255 is chosen, routes will be considered unreachable and will be ignored.

When redistributing static routes or other protocol types within EIGRP, metrics may be set for these routes as well by using the `default-metric` command:

`default-metric` *bandwidth delay reliability load MTU*

Bandwidth and delay have a range of values from 0 to 4,294,967,295 (in Kb per second) and 0 to 4,294,967,295 (in 10-microsecond units), respectively. Reliability ranges from 0 to 255, with 255 being the most reliable. Load ranges from 0 to 255; however, 255 means that the link is completely loaded. Finally, the value of the MTU has the same range as the bandwidth variable: 0 to 4,294,967,295. Most of this information should be a review, since it's basically the same info associated with IGRP.

Load Balancing and Variance

One of EIGRP's major enhancements is its ability to select more than one primary route or successor. We have discussed how route costs are calculated, and that up to six routes for every destination can be stored in the topology database. EIGRP capitalizes on this information.

By using multiple LAN or WAN connections from one router to another, multiple routes can exist to the next-hop address. When the links are symmetric (they have the same circuit type and the same bandwidth capacity), the same local cost is assigned to each link.

Since both links have the same feasible distance, the metrics for destinations accessible via the links will be equal. As EIGRP chooses the successor for a route, it looks for the route with the lowest cost. When it sees multiple routes with the same metric, it selects them all as successors. EIGRP will then share traffic loads across each of the multiple links. This is called *load balancing*.

Let's look at Figure 6.7 to get a picture of how load balancing works.

F I G U R E   6.7

Equal-cost load balancing with EIGRP

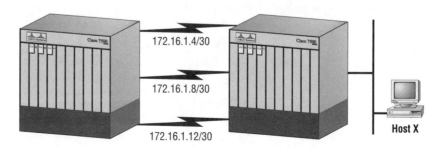

As you can see, Router A has three equal connections to Router B. The topology table will contain a route to Host X. Linked to that route, there are the three routes by which Router A learned of Host X. The topology table would look something like the following listing:

```
IP-EIGRP topology entry for 10.10.10.0/24
    State is Passive, Query origin flag is 1, 1 Successor(s),
      FD is 283648
    Routing Descriptor Blocks:
    172.16.1.6 (Serial1), from 172.16.1.6, Send flag is 0x0
        Composite metric is (283648/281600), Route is Internal
        Vector metric:
          Minimum bandwidth is 1544 Kbit
          Total delay is 1080 microseconds
          Reliability is 255/255
          Load is 1/255
          Minimum MTU is 1500
          Hop count is 1
    172.16.1.10 (Serial2), from 172.16.1.10, Send flag is 0x0
        Composite metric is (283648/281600), Route is Internal
        Vector metric:
          Minimum bandwidth is 1544 Kbit
          Total delay is 1080 microseconds
          Reliability is 255/255
          Load is 1/255
          Minimum MTU is 1500
          Hop count is 1
    172.16.1.14 (Serial3), from 172.16.1.14, Send flag is 0x0
        Composite metric is (283648/281600), Route is Internal
        Vector metric:
          Minimum bandwidth is 1544 Kbit
          Total delay is 1080 microseconds
          Reliability is 255/255
          Load is 1/255
          Minimum MTU is 1500
          Hop count is 1
```

Because the feasible distance is the same for all three links, traffic will be shared across all three links equally.

There will also be situations where there are multiple links to a given destination, but the links have different next-hops. The metric for these links will not likely be the same. Even though each link may have a different cost assigned to it, EIGRP does allow for unequal-cost load balancing.

This is achieved by using the variance command. It is the same command used in IGRP for unequal-cost load balancing:

```
variance multiplier
```

In the variance command, the *multiplier* can be an integer value from 1 to 128. The default setting for the multiplier is 1. This command must be used inside the EIGRP protocol configuration.

To illustrate how the variance command works, let's look at Figure 6.8. In this figure, both Router A and Router B have individual routes to network 10.1.2.0/24. Each connection has a metric associated with it. In this example, the metric between Router A and Router C is *ac*. The metric between Router B and Router C is *bc*. There is also a metric associated with the route from Router A to Router C if it goes through Router B. This metric would be *abc*.

FIGURE 6.8

Unequal-cost load balancing and variance

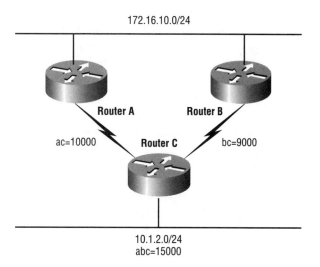

For a network listed in the EIGRP topology table to be tagged as a feasible successor, two criteria must be met. We want to configure the route from Router A to Router C via Router B to be a feasible successor. Let's see if the criteria are met.

1. Metric *ac* must be greater than metric *bc*. In our example, this criterion has been met (*ac*=10,000; *bc*=9000).

2. After the variance command is used, the product of the multiplier and the metric ac must be equal to or greater than the metric *abc*. Assuming that the multiplier was set to 2, this criterion would also be met.

Since both criteria were met, the route *abc* becomes an advertised route. Thus, the unequal path can also be used to load balance even though the metric is higher than that of the primary route.

Route Redistribution

A router may have multiple protocols configured as well as multiple sessions of a protocol. Sessions are defined by the autonomous system number used when implementing the routing protocol (this is true only for IGRP and EIGRP). With all of the different protocols and sessions running on a router, it becomes important that the information learned by each session can be shared with the other protocols and sessions. *Route redistribution* is the feature that allows for the exchange of route information among multiple protocols and multiple sessions.

The router where multiple protocols or sessions meet is called the autonomous system boundary router (ASBR). When routes from one protocol or session are injected or redistributed into another protocol or session, the routes are tagged as external routes. Let's look at a simple example of a route table that has external routes:

```
Router_X#sho ip route eigrp
     172.16.0.0/16 is variably subnetted, 301 subnets,
     10 masks
D EX    172.16.27.230/32
            [170/24827392] via 172.16.131.82, 02:33:32, ATM6/
            0/0.3114
D EX    172.16.237.16/29
            [170/40542208] via 172.16.131.82, 23:40:32, ATM6/
            0/0.3114
```

```
                   [170/40542208] via 172.16.131.74, 23:40:32, ATM6/
                   0/0.3113
D EX    172.16.237.24/29
                   [170/40542208] via 172.16.131.82, 23:40:32, ATM6/
                   0/0.3114
                   [170/40542208] via 172.16.131.74, 23:40:32, ATM6/
                   0/0.3113
D EX    172.16.52.192/26
                   [170/2202112] via 172.16.131.82, 23:40:27, ATM6/
                   0/0.3114
D EX    172.16.41.216/29
                   [170/46232832] via 172.16.131.82, 23:40:28, ATM6/
                   0/0.3114
D EX    172.16.38.200/30
                   [170/2176512] via 172.16.131.82, 23:40:27, ATM6/
                   0/0.3114
D EX    172.16.237.0/29
                   [170/40542208] via 172.16.131.82, 23:40:32, ATM6/
                   0/0.3114
                   [170/40542208] via 172.16.131.74, 23:40:32, ATM6/
                   0/0.3113
D       172.16.236.0/24
                   [90/311808] via 172.16.131.82, 23:40:32, ATM6/0/
                   0.3114
                   [90/311808] via 172.16.131.74, 23:40:32, ATM6/0/
                   0.3113
D       172.16.235.0/24
                   [90/311808] via 172.16.131.82, 23:40:32, ATM6/0/
                   0.3114
--More-
```

As you can see, there are internal routes and external routes in this route
table. The external routes are flagged with EX, while the internal routes have
no flag. The D stands for an EIGRP learned route.

While redistribution allows multiple protocols to share routing information, it can cause routing loops, slow convergence, and inconsistent route
information. This is caused by the different algorithms and methods used by
each protocol. It is not a good practice to redistribute bidirectionally. If, for
example, you have both IGRP 100 and EIGRP 200 routing sessions running

on your router, bidirectional redistribution would occur if you entered redistribution commands under each protocol session. Here is an example:

```
Router_A#conf t
Enter configuration commands, one per line.  End with CNTL/Z.
Router_A(config)#router igrp 100
Router_A(config-router)#redistribute eigrp 200
Router_A(config-router)#router eigrp 200
Router_A(config-router)#redistribute igrp 100
Router_A(config-router)#^Z
Router_A#
```

It is not recommended that protocols be redistributed bidirectionally.

When a route from RIP, IGRP, or OSPF is injected into EIGRP, the route loses its identity, and its metrics are converted from the original format to EIGRP's format. This can cause confusion within the router.

You can reset metrics to help alleviate this problem. This is done by using the default-metric command as follows:

default-metric *bandwidth delay reliability load MTU*

This command takes the metrics for the protocol being injected into EIGRP and converts them directly to values that EIGRP can use. The *bandwidth* is the capacity of the link; *delay* is the time in microseconds; *reliability* and *load* are values from 1 to 255; and *MTU* is the maximum transmission unit in bytes.

Finally, you can also change the distance values that are assigned to EIGRP (90 internal; 170 external). The distance value tells the router which protocol to believe. The lower the distance value, the more believable the protocol. The distance values for EIGRP are changed with the following command from within the EIGRP session:

distance eigrp *internal-distance external-distance*

- *internal-distance* and *external-distance* have a range of values from 1 to 255.

Remember that a value of 255 tells the router to ignore the route. So unless you want the routes from the protocol to be ignored, never use the value 255.

Troubleshooting EIGRP

Cisco provides several commands to aid in troubleshooting EIGRP functionality. Table 6.5 contains all of the commands that are used in conjunction with verifying EIGRP operation.

T A B L E 6.5 EIGRP Troubleshooting Commands	**Command**	**Description/Function**
	`show ip route eigrp`	Shows EIGRP entries in the route table
	`show ip eigrp neighbors`	Shows all EIGRP neighbors
	`show ip eigrp topology`	Shows entries in the EIGRP topology table
	`show ip eigrp traffic`	Shows the packet count for EIGRP packets sent and received
	`show ip protocols`	Shows information about the active protocol sessions
	`show ip eigrp events`	Shows a log of EIGRP events—for example, routes being added or removed from the route table

You can use these commands to gain a clearer understanding of the information discussed in this section as well as to diagnose a network problem.

Troubleshooting skills are obtained after you work through many network problems. Each situation may call for a different method. The following descriptions are intended solely to illustrate a general method—by no means should troubleshooting be restricted to the information provided below.

When troubleshooting an EIGRP problem, it is always a good idea to get a picture of the network. The most relevant picture is provided by the `show ip eigrp neighbors` command. This command shows all adjacent routers that share route information within a given autonomous system. If neighbors are missing, check the configuration and link status on both routers to verify that the protocol has been configured correctly.

If all neighbors are present, verify the routes learned. By executing the `show ip route eigrp` command, you gain a quick picture of the routes in the route table. If the route does not appear in the route table, verify the source of the route. If the source is functioning properly, check the topology table.

The topology table is displayed by using the `show ip eigrp topology` command. If the route is in the topology table, it is safe to assume that there is a problem between the topology database and the route table. There must be a reason why the topology database is not injecting the route into the route table.

Other commands such as `show ip eigrp traffic` can be used to see if updates are being sent. If the counters for EIGRP input and output packets don't increase, no EIGRP information is being sent between peers.

The `show ip eigrp events` command is an undocumented command. This command displays a log of every EIGRP event—when routes are injected and removed from the route table, and when EIGRP adjacencies reset or fail. This information can be used to see if there are routing instabilities in the network.

Again, these commands are meant to be used at the discretion of the system administrator when troubleshooting a problem in the network. The information provided by these commands can be used for many more issues than have been discussed in this section.

OSPF (Open Shortest Path First)

You can implement several types of OSPF areas—each of these types will be discussed in detail. Configuration examples and information specific to OSPF, such as metrics, redistribution, and filtering, will be provided.

OSPF differs from IGRP and Enhanced IGRP in that it is a pure link-state routing technology. Also, it is an open standard routing protocol, which means that it was not developed solely by Cisco. OSPF was designed and developed by the IETF to provide a scalable, quickly converging, and efficient routing protocol that could be used by all routing equipment. Complete details for OSPF are found in RFC2178.

OSPF is an enhancement over RIP that provides a scalable routing solution. It supports several features that RIP does not—for example, VLSM and route summarization are supported.

The hop count was eliminated with OSPF, thus giving it limitless reachability. RIP was limited to 16 hops. Due to the algorithm used to calculate and advertise routes, network convergence is fast with OSPF. OSPF is like EIGRP in that it sends route updates only when changes occur in the network. A formal neighbor relationship is established with all adjacent OSPF routers.

Areas are used within OSPF to define a group of routers and networks belonging to the same OSPF session. Links connect routers, and the information about each link is defined by its link state. On each broadcast or multi-access network segment, two routers must be assigned the responsibilities of designated router (DR) and backup designated router (BDR).

Like EIGRP, OSPF maintains three databases: adjacency, topology, and route. The adjacency database is similar to the neighbor database used by EIGRP. It contains all information about OSPF neighbors and the links connecting them. The topology database maintains *all* route information. The best routes from the topology database are placed in the route database, or route table.

Now that we have a general understanding of how OSPF is set up, let's move on and discuss its features and operation in detail.

Features and Operation

OSPF operation can be divided into several categories. We will start with how OSPF initializes and creates a peering relationship with adjacent routers. After an OSPF area is defined, we will discuss how the designated and backup designated routers are chosen and what their responsibilities are. Once the area is established and functioning, routing information must be learned and shared.

Initializing OSPF

The Hello protocol is used to establish peering sessions between routers. Hello packets are multicast out every interface. The information that is multicast includes the router ID, timing intervals, existing neighbors, area identification, router priority, designated and backup router information, authentication password, and stub area information. All this information is used when establishing new peers. Descriptions of each element can be found in Table 6.6.

T A B L E 6.6 OSPF Multicast Information	Information	Description
	Router ID	The highest active IP address on the router.
	Time intervals	Contains intervals between hello packets and the dead time interval.
	Existing neighbors	Addresses for any existing OSPF neighbors.
	Area identification	OSPF area number and link information must be the same for a peering session to be established.
	Router priority	This value is used when choosing the DR and BDR.
	DR and BDR	If they have already been chosen, their information is contained in the hello packet.
	Authentication password	All peers must have the same authentication password if authentication is enabled.
	Stub area flag	This is a special area—two routers must share the same stub information. This is not necessary to initiate a regular peering session with another OSPF router.

Figure 6.9 displays a flow chart that depicts each step of the initialization process. The process starts by sending out hello packets. Every listening router will then add the originating router to the adjacency database. The responding routers will reply with all of their hello information so that the originating router can add them to its adjacency table.

Once adjacencies have been established, the DR and BDR need to be chosen before route information and link-state information can be exchanged. After the DR and BDR are chosen, route information is exchanged, and the OSPF peers continue to multicast hello packets every 10 seconds to determine if neighbors are still reachable.

Before we go any further with peer initialization, we need to discuss several terms specific to OSPF. These terms are important for understanding OSPF and how it functions.

The easiest way to understand OSPF is to build from what we already know about EIGRP. We learned that EIGRP uses autonomous system numbers to specify routing processes and the routing process to which individual routers belong. OSPF uses areas in place of an autonomous system. An OSPF area consists of a group of routers or interfaces on a router that are assigned to a common area.

OSPF also allows and uses different area types. When deploying OSPF, there must be a backbone area. Standard and stub connect to the backbone area. Below, there is a list of each router type, followed by a short description of the area type.

Backbone This area accepts all LSAs and is used to connect multiple areas.

Stub This area will not accept any external routing update, but will accept summary LSAs.

Totally stub These areas are closed off from accepting external or summary advertisements.

Standard This is the normal area that accepts internal and external LSAs and summary information.

From the previous area descriptions, you probably noticed the frequent use of the term LSA. Let's move on now to explain the different types of link-state advertisements (LSAs). LSAs are the heart of OSPF's information exchange. Different types of LSAs represent different types of route information. All of the LSA types are summarized in Table 6.7.

Different LSA types represent the type of route that is being advertised and assist in restricting the number and type of routes that are accepted by a given area. As shown in Table 6.7, an LSA of type 5 is sent only by the autonomous system border router. Now we need to define the different router types that belong to OSPF areas.

Multiple router types can exist within an OSPF area. Table 6.8 lists all of the OSPF router types and the role that each plays within the area.

FIGURE 6.9
OSPF peer initialization

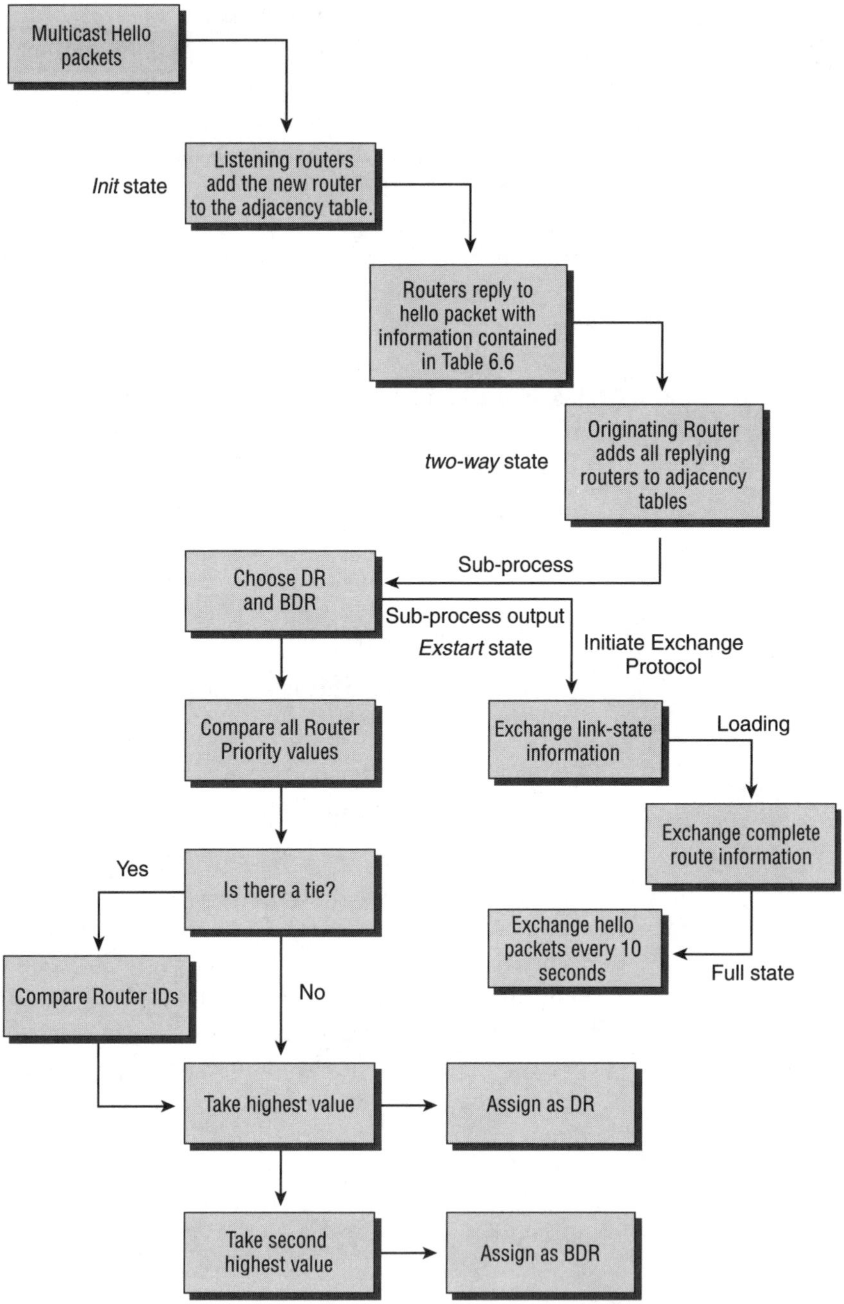

T A B L E 6.7 OSPF LSA Types	**LSA Type**	**Description**
	1. Router link entry	This LSA is broadcast only within its defined area. The LSA contains all of the default link-state information.
	2. Network entry	This LSA is multicast to all area routers by the DR. This update contains network-specific information.
	3./4. Summary entry	Type 3 LSAs contain route information for internal networks and are sent to backbone routers. Type 4 LSAs contain information about ASBRs. Summary information is multicast by the ABR, and the information reaches all backbone routers.
	5. Autonomous system entry	As the name indicates, these advertisements originate from the ASBR. These packets contain information about external networks.

T A B L E 6.8 OSPF Router Types	**Router Type**	**Description**
	Internal	All interfaces are defined on the same area. All internal routers have an identical link-state database.
	Backbone	Have at least one interface assigned to area 0.
	Area border router (ABR)	Interfaces are connected to multiple OSPF areas. Information specific to each area is stored on this type of router.
	Autonomous system border router (ASBR)	This type of router has an interface connected to an external network or a different AS.

In addition to the listed responsibilities, a router can also be assigned additional responsibilities. These additions are assumed when a router is assigned the role of DR or BDR.

Designated and Backup Designated Routers

The DR and BDR are focal points within each multi-access network segment. These special routers act as a central point for information. Routers on any given segment will exchange link-state information with the DR and BDR instead of with each other. After a router has updated the DR and BDR with its information, the DR or BDR multicasts this information to all other routers on this segment. The DR and BDR are also in charge of making sure that all routers have the same version of link-state information. The BDR listens to all updates, but sends OSPF information on a segment only when the DR fails.

Once a DR and BDR have been established, new routers will establish adjacencies only with the DR and BDR.

Initializing and Maintaining Route Information

Routes are discovered via the Exchange protocol (as indicated in Figure 6.9). The Exchange protocol commences only after the DR and BDR have been chosen. The Exstart state depicted in Figure 6.9 creates peering relationships with the DR, BDR, and each individual router within the area.

The following steps are taken when route information is exchanged (also known as database synchronization):

1. Master-slave relationships are established between routers—the router with the highest router ID is the master.

2. Master and slaves exchange database description packets (DBDs or DDPs). These packets contain link-state advertisement (LSA) information. LSA information consists of the IP address of the advertising router, cost, and sequence number or data concerning how recent the link-state information is.

3. After the slave router receives the DBD or DDP, it sends back an LSAck (link-state acknowledgement) packet. It also compares new information to the existing information. If the information provided by the DBD is newer than the existing information, an LSR (link-state request) is sent back to the master router. The link-state request tells

the master router to send complete information. The sending of LSRs occurs in the *loading* state.

4. The master responds with an LSU (link-state update).

5. The slave replies with another LSAck packet.

6. All routers within the area receive the link-state information via the DR.

7. A router will continue to send LSRs until it receives all the information that it needs. Once it has all of the information it needs, it will change to the *full* state.

8. Once a router is in full state, it can route traffic. At this point in the exchange, all routers should have the same link-state database.

Let's look at an example in Figure 6.10. This is a protocol trace from a network. We're just going to look at the final exchange between the master sending out the LSU and then other routers replying with LSAck packets. Note that the destination address of all the LSUs and LSAck packets are multicast addresses.

FIGURE 6.10

OSPF LSU and LSAck exchange

Packet	Source	Destination	Flag	Size	Time-Stamp	Protocol
541	00:10:7b:53:a7:b2	01:80:c2:00:00:00	*	64	13:04:42.139000	802.1
542	IP-131.31.194.141	IP-224.0.0.5		94	13:04:42.586000	OSPF LSU
543	IP-131.31.194.129	IP-224.0.0.6		94	13:04:42.594000	OSPF LSU
544	IP-131.31.194.141	IP-224.0.0.5		94	13:04:42.596000	OSPF LSU
545	IP-131.31.194.142	IP-224.0.0.5		94	13:04:42.773000	OSPF Hlo
546	IP-131.31.194.129	IP-224.0.0.5		94	13:04:42.839000	OSPF Hlo
547	AT-1105.179	AT-0.255	*	64	13:04:42.901000	RTMP Data
548	00:10:7b:a4:4a:a1	00:10:7b:a4:4a:a1		64	13:04:43.413000	Loopback
549	00:10:7b:53:a7:b0	01:80:c2:00:00:00	*	64	13:04:44.138000	802.1
550	00:10:7b:53:a7:b1	01:80:c2:00:00:00	*	64	13:04:44.138000	802.1
551	00:10:7b:53:a7:b2	01:80:c2:00:00:00	*	64	13:04:44.138000	802.1
552	00:10:7b:a4:4a:a1	Ethernet Brdcast	*	178	13:04:44.169000	NW SAP
553	IP-131.31.194.129	IP Broadcast		110	13:04:44.598000	UDP RIP
554	IP-131.31.194.140	IP-224.0.0.6		102	13:04:45.087000	OSPF LSA
555	IP-131.31.194.129	IP-224.0.0.6		82	13:04:45.087000	OSPF LSA
556	IP-131.31.194.142	IP-224.0.0.5		102	13:04:45.088000	OSPF LSA

Now that we have seen the trace, let's look at the actual packets. First, we'll see the LSU packet, then the LSAcks after the LSUs have been sent.

```
IP Header - Internet Protocol Datagram
    Version:            4
    Header Length:      5
    Precedence:         6
```

```
        Type of Service:        %000
        Unused:                 %00
        Total Length:           76
        Identifier:             14145
        Fragmentation Flags:    %000
        Fragment Offset:        0
        Time To Live:           1
        IP Type:                0x59  OSPF
        Header Checksum:        0x5ba6
        Source IP Address:      131.31.194.141
        Dest. IP Address:       224.0.0.5
        No Internet Datagram Options
OSPF - Open Shortest Path First Routing Protocol
        Version:                2
        Type:                   4  Link State Update
        Packet Length:          56
        Router IP Address:      153.53.193.1
        Area ID:                1
        Checksum:               0x6aa5
        Authentication Type:    0  No Authentication
        Authentication Data:
        ........         00 00 00 00 00 00 00 00
        # Of Advertisements:    1
Link State Advertisement Header
        Age:                    3600  seconds
        Options:                %00100010
            No AS External Link State Advertisements
        Type:                   3  Summary Link (IP Network)
        ID:                     0x90fb6400
        Advertising Router:     153.53.193.1
        Sequence Number:        2147483708
        Checksum:               0x3946
        Link State Length:      28
Summary Links Advertisement (IP Network)
        Network Mask:           0xffffff00
        Type Of Service:        0
```

```
   Metric:                    0xffffff
Frame Check Sequence:  0x20536f66
```

From this packet decode, we can see that the IP type is OSPF. From there, skip down to the OSPF header information—it indicates that the packet is a link-state update (LSU). Also in the packet decode, we can find the IP address of the advertising router and the LSA header. The LSA includes summary information.

Now let's look at just one of the acknowledgements to the LSU:

```
IP Header - Internet Protocol Datagram
   Version:               4
   Header Length:         5
   Precedence:            6
   Type of Service:       %000
   Unused:                %00
   Total Length:          84
   Identifier:            1285
   Fragmentation Flags:   %000
   Fragment Offset:       0
   Time To Live:          1
   IP Type:               0x59  OSPF
   Header Checksum:       0x8dda
   Source IP Address:     131.31.194.140
   Dest. IP Address:      224.0.0.6
   No Internet Datagram Options
OSPF - Open Shortest Path First Routing Protocol
   Version:                  2
   Type:                     5  Link State Acknowledgment
   Packet Length:            64
   Router IP Address:        142.42.193.1
   Area ID:                  1
   Checksum:                 0x6699
   Authentication Type:      0  No Authentication
   Authentication Data:
   ........              00 00 00 00 00 00 00 00
Link State Advertisement Header
```

```
        Age:                        3600  seconds
        Options:                    %00100010
            No AS External Link State Advertisements
        Type:                       3  Summary Link (IP Network)
        ID:                         0x90fb6400
        Advertising Router:         153.53.193.1
        Sequence Number:            2147483708
        Checksum:                   0x3946
        Link State Length:          28
    Link State Advertisement Header
        Age:                        3600  seconds
        Options:                    %00100010
            No AS External Link State Advertisements
        Type:                       3  Summary Link (IP Network)
        ID:                         0x90fb6400
        Advertising Router:         131.31.193.1
        Sequence Number:            2147483650
        Checksum:                   0x25c0
        Link State Length:          28
    Frame Check Sequence:   0x00000000
```

This decode shows us that the packet is a link-state acknowledgement. The IP address is the IP address of the responding router. Other LSAs were also picked up on the trace, because each router responds to the LSU.

Now that we have discussed how route information is exchanged between OSPF routers, let's discuss how each router selects its routes and maintains the route table.

Link-state protocols choose their routes differently than distance vector protocols do. Bandwidth is one of the most important metrics for route selection within OSPF. The Dijkstra algorithm is used to choose the lowest cost link for route selection.

Costs of the local router are added to the cost required to reach the destination. The route with the lowest cost is selected as the primary route. Just as with EIGRP, OSPF can hold six equal-cost routes for each destination. Changes in link-state status change the cost of the link.

Every time a link state changes, LSUs are sent to the DR and BDR. The DR relays the information to all other routers within the segment, causing the route table to be recalculated. We have already seen the trace and decode for this process when we discussed the route initialization process. If there are many link-state changes within a short period, network convergence may never be reached. OSPF prevents this problem by using holddown times. The default holddown time for route calculation is 10 seconds.

Let's summarize how route information is calculated and shared between other routers:

1. A link-state change occurs.

2. An LSU packet with the new LSA attached is sent to all DRs. The multicast address 224.0.0.6 is used by a router to send to all DRs and BDRs.

3. The DR then notifies all other adjacent routers by multicasting an LSU on address 224.0.0.5.

4. Each adjacent router responds with an LSAck.

5. Other networks receive updates via LSUs sent by the other network's DR.

6. The receiving router updates the link-state database.

7. The SPF algorithm is used to calculate the new route table and control when the router begins to use the new table.

OSPF Metrics

The metrics associated with OSPF are different from those associated with IGRP and EIGRP. OSPF uses bandwidth as the main metric in selecting a route. The cost is calculated using the bandwidth for the link. The equation is 10^8 divided by the bandwidth. You may change bandwidth on the individual interface.

The cost is manipulated by changing the value to a number within the range of 1 to 65,535. Since the cost is assigned to each link, the value must be changed on each interface. The command to do this follows:

```
ip ospf cost
```

NOTE Cisco bases link cost on bandwidth. Other vendors may use other metrics to calculate the link's cost. When connecting links between routers from different vendors, you may have to adjust the cost to match the other router. Both routers must assign the same cost to the link for OSPF to work.

You can configure the OSPF distance with the following command:

```
distance ospf [external | Intra-area | Inter-area] distance
```

This command allows the distance metric to be defined for external OSPF, and intra-area and inter-area routes. Intra-area and inter-area routes will be discussed during the "Configuring OSPF" subsection. Distance values range from 1 to 255, and the lower the distance, the better.

Other values important to OSPF's operation are not actually metrics, but can be configured as well. Values such as the router ID and router priority are important in router initialization and DR and BDR selection. You can change these values with some minor configuration changes.

To change the router priority, use the following command on the desired interface:

```
ip ospf priority number
```

The *number* can range from 0 to 255; the higher value indicates a higher priority when choosing the DR and BDR for the area.

A loopback interface must be added to the router to change the router ID. The IP address of the loopback can be a private address or a fake address. If the IP address is to be announced, a private IP address should be used. To implement a loopback interface on the router, use the following command:

```
interface loopback number
 ip address A.B.C.D
```

You can inject the address used on the loopback interface into OSPF by using the `network area` command.

Configuring OSPF

Initial configuration for OSPF is simple and straightforward—although, for connectivity to be established between routers from different vendors, other configuration commands may have to be issued.

Configuration can be broken down into two groups. The first group is for routers within an area; the second is for routers that connect different areas.

Internal Routers

When you're initializing OSPF on a router, the session is defined by a process identification. Unlike EIGRP's autonomous system number, the process identification number does not have to be uniform across all the routers within the OSPF area. Instead of using the process ID to identify the OSPF area, the networks that are added to the session are assigned to an OSPF area. This means that all networks assigned to a given area make up that area.

To initiate OSPF on a router, the first step is to assign the routing protocol with the process ID. After that is done, networks are added and assigned to the desired OSPF area. The commands follow:

```
router ospf process-id
network address wildcard-mask area area-id
```

The *process-id* is an integer from 1 to 65,535; the *area-id* is an integer from 0 to 4,294,967,295. Let's look at a configuration example:

```
Router_A#conf t
Enter configuration commands, one per line.  End with CNTL/Z.
Router_A(config)#router ospf 1
Router_A(config-router)#network 172.16.20.0 0.0.0.255 area 20
Router_A(config-router)#network 10.1.2.0 0.0.0.255 area 20
Router_A(config-router)#^Z
Router_A#

Router_A#show running-config
Building configuration...
Current configuration:
!
version 11.3
```

```
no service password-encryption
!
hostname Router_A
!
enable password aloha
!
interface Ethernet0/0
 ip address 172.16.10.1 255.255.255.0
!
interface Serial0/0
 ip address 172.16.20.5 255.255.255.252
 no ip mroute-cache
 no fair-queue
!
interface Ethernet0/1
 ip address 10.1.2.1 255.255.255.0
!
router ospf 1
 network 10.1.2.0 0.0.0.255 area 20
 network 172.16.20.0 0.0.0.255 area 20
!
ip classless
!
line con 0
line aux 0
line vty 0 4
 password aloha
 login
!
end
Router_A#
```

The example shows that the OSPF process was defined as *one*. Two networks were added to OSPF area 20. As you can see, the configuration is quite simple. Again, this configuration is the simplest form of OSPF implementation.

Now let's move on to multiple-area configurations.

Multiple Areas

Configuration for multiple-area routers is the same as it is for internal routers. The different types of routers are defined by the area assignment of the connected networks. For example, if a router has two networks, with one assigned to area 10 and the other assigned to area 30, by default the router becomes an area border router (ABR). A similar example may be given with a backbone router—if an interface or network is assigned to area zero, it becomes a backbone router.

Route Summarization

Route summarization in OSPF is used for the same reasons that other routing protocols use it. When a route table becomes large, it taxes the router in multiple ways: CPU utilization, and bandwidth and memory consumption.

OSPF supports two types of route summarization: inter-area and external. As with many inter-area functions, the ABR is in charge of summarizing area routes. External summarization is exactly that—only external routes are summarized by the autonomous system border router (ASBR).

The summarization commands must be issued on the respective routers. Inter-area summarization must be configured on the ABR with the following command within the OSPF routing session:

```
area area-id range address mask
```

The *area-id* is the OSPF area number. The *address* and *mask* define the range of IP addresses that will be summarized for the specified area. To configure external summarization, the following command must be entered within the OSPF routing session on the ASBR:

```
summary-address address mask
```

Notice that the area ID was not used in the command. This is because only external routes will be summarized. The address and mask define the range of external IP addresses that will be summarized.

Stub Areas

When the size of route tables and link-state databases grows too large and can't be remedied with route summarization alone, the area may be configured as a stub or totally stub area.

The difference between a stub area and a normal area is that intra- and inter-area routes are the only routes allowed inside the stub area. To communicate with networks that are not present in the route table, the stub area relies on a default route of 0.0.0.0. This means that when a router does not have a route to the destination address, it will forward the packet to the ABR from which it learned the default network 0.0.0.0. The ABR will then do the route lookup and forward the packet accordingly.

A stub area contains all routes from its area and other areas that are connected via the backbone and ABRs. It does not contain any external routes.

To further shrink a route table for an area, you can make the route table totally stubby. A totally stub area contains an even smaller route table because the only routes it knows are the routes from within its own area. To contact networks outside the area, the default route 0.0.0.0 is used as well. The ABR is responsible for forwarding packets to the correct destination.

Configuring Stub Areas

Now that we know what stub and totally stub areas are, let's learn how to configure them. To configure a stub area, the following command should be implemented on an internal router that is not an ASBR and not connected to the backbone. It is also important to issue this command on every router within the stub or totally stub area.

```
area area-id stub
```

The command is self-explanatory—the *area-id* simply defines the stub area.

To make an area totally stubby, the same command is used with one modification. It must be issued on the ABR for the area.

```
area area-id stub no-summary
```

You cannot configure routers as stub routers if they belong to the backbone. An area cannot be defined as a stub area if an ASBR is part of the area.

Redistribution

OSPF supports redistribution for many protocols. A listing directly from a router gives the protocols supported:

```
Router_A(config-router)#redistribute ?
  bgp        Border Gateway Protocol (BGP)
  connected  Connected
  egp        Exterior Gateway Protocol (EGP)
  eigrp      Enhanced Interior Gateway Routing Protocol
             (EIGRP)
  igrp       Interior Gateway Routing Protocol (IGRP)
  isis       ISO IS-IS
  iso-igrp   IGRP for OSI networks
  mobile     Mobile routes
  odr        On Demand stub Routes
  ospf       Open Shortest Path First (OSPF)
  rip        Routing Information Protocol (RIP)
  static     Static routes
```

Just as with EIGRP, new metrics must be assigned to route information that is injected into the OSPF session. The command is much simpler than the command used when assigning metrics for EIGRP or IGRP—it is almost the same, but only one metric is assigned. The value of the metric is the cost for the route.

```
default-metric cost
```

OSPF Filtering Considerations

Normal methods of route filtering done by distribution lists are effective when filtering route information. The most effective method of filtering OSPF is by implementing the filters on the ASBR as outbound filters. Inbound filters are effective in filtering routes, but since they are inbound filters, LSA packets are still propagated.

Cisco recommends that you filter within other protocols and that you don't filter OSPF if possible. This is done by implementing outbound filters on other protocols, which keeps unwanted networks from even entering the OSPF area.

BGP (Border Gateway Protocol)

This subsection is dedicated to BGP and connecting to Internet service providers (ISPs). We will discuss the different types of BGP. Details and examples of BGP configuration will follow. BGP route selection, management, and monitoring will be addressed as well.

The Internet consists of a number of commercial networks that connect to each other via tier-one providers such as Sprint, WorldCom/MCI, UUNet, Qwest, and others. Each enterprise network or ISP must be identified by an autonomous system number. This number allows a hierarchy to be maintained when sharing route information.

We are now familiar with several IGPs (Interior Gateway Protocols), such as IGRP, EIGRP, and OSPF. For enterprise networks to communicate with other autonomous systems or ISPs, the IGP information has to be injected into BGP. The Border Gateway Protocol is used by all network entities that comprise the Internet.

BGP is an open standard protocol that was developed and defined in several RFCs: 1163, 1267, 1654, and 1655. Complete technical details can be found in these articles. One of the requirements of BGP was that it needed to be a loop-free protocol.

The two types of BGP are iBGP and eBGP. There are several differences between the two. Primarily, iBGP (internal BGP) is used to share BGP information with routers within the same AS, while eBGP (external BGP) is used to share route information between two different autonomous systems. More details will be given as we discuss each type separately.

BGP may not always be the right solution for connecting to an Internet service provider. Let's move on and discuss when it *is* the right time to use BGP before we discuss how it works.

ISP Connectivity Considerations

The following scenarios are examples of when BGP should be used:

- You are connecting two or more ISPs—NAPs (network access points) and exchange points.

- You are multi-homing—an enterprise network connects to multiple ISPs.

Static or default routes may be used in situations where the complexity of BGP is not needed—for example, when an enterprise network is connected to multiple ISPs, but the second connection is used only as a backup. Another example would be a campus network that is not worried about receiving exterior routes—any route that was not in its routing table will be sent to the ISP.

iBGP (Internal Border Gateway Protocol)

Internal BGP is used by routers that belong to the same autonomous system. iBGP may use loopback interfaces to provide greater reachability. This is possible because the IGP can provide multiple routes to any given destination address if the network has redundant or multiple links to each router. If one interface on a router goes down, the TCP connection to the loopback address can be maintained by using redundant interfaces.

It is important to understand that before any BGP route information can be exchanged between two routers, a TCP connection has to be established. The TCP connection is made by a three-way handshake using a SYN, ACK, SYN sequence. Once a TCP connection has been established, route info can be exchanged.

An important feature of iBGP is that route information from one peer is not advertised to another iBGP peer. This avoids inconsistent route information and routing loops. To share route information between all iBGP routers, establish a logical mesh (Figure 6.11 shows us a picture of what is meant by this). Route information is exchanged only between routers. Router B can learn BGP networks only from Router A. When Router C sends its BGP information, only its information is sent. Routes learned from Router A are not included.

Configuration details and examples will be given in the "Configuring BGP" section.

eBGP (External Border Gateway Protocol)

External BGP is used to exchange route information between two different autonomous systems. When only one link connects two autonomous systems, the IP address of the connected interface is used to establish the BGP session. It is also possible to use other IP addresses, but the address must be reachable without using an IGP. This is accomplished by using static routes

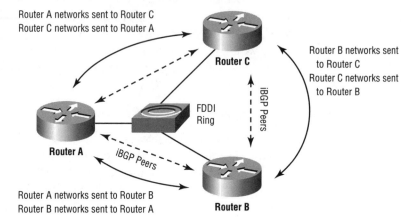

FIGURE 6.11

iBGP information
exchange

or additional BGP commands when configuring eBGP. If multiple links are used to connect to the other AS, using loopback addresses is the best option.

The purpose of eBGP is to inject routes owned by the enterprise network into another AS. Two prerequisites need to be met for internal routes to be propagated via BGP:

- The route to be advertised must be present in the router's IGP route table.

- BGP must learn the route.

You can fulfill the first condition by using one of three methods: inject the routes into a router's route table via an IGP, a static route, or directly connected networks. BGP has a synchronization option that requires BGP and the IGP routes to synchronize before BGP will advertise IGP learned networks. The no version of the command indicates that BGP and the IGP do not have to synchronize before BGP will advertise the routes.

You can also accomplish the second prerequisite in one of three ways: BGP learns of networks that it needs to advertise through other BGP advertisements, network statements, and redistribution of an IGP into BGP. The last option is not recommended because of the instability incurred—redistribution can cause routing loops and route flapping.

Configuring BGP

BGP configuration can be very complicated. Several different options may be configured to optimize BGP routing. When only one link is used to peer with another AS or ISP, the configuration can be straightforward. As more links are used, or multiple ISPs or autonomous systems are connected to a router, the configuration becomes increasingly complex.

BGP is initiated on the router by using the following command:

```
router bgp autononous-system
```

This command defines the AS to which the router belongs. The next step is to establish peers. The only difference between establishing an external peer and an internal one is the autonomous system number used in the neighbor command.

```
neighbor address remote-as autonomous-system-number
```

In this command, *address* is the IP address of the neighboring router. It can be the loopback or the directly connected IP address. The *autonomous-system-number* is the peer's AS number. If the *autonomous-system-number* is the same as the *autonomous-system* defined in the router bgp command, the neighbor is an iBGP peer. If the numbers are different, the neighbor is an eBGP peer.

After you have configured neighbors, you must add network statements for the router to propagate enterprise networks to another AS. Network statements must be added since redistribution on an IGP into BGP is not recommended. Networks are added with the following command:

```
network network-number
```

The *network-number* represents the network that is to be advertised via BGP. The IP network specified in the BGP network statement does not have to be directly connected to the router. Network statements within the BGP protocol session allow BGP to advertise routes learned via the IGP that are contained in the route table.

When a logical BGP mesh exists, each iBGP session should have network statements only for routes that it learns directly from the IGP. In other words, network statements should not be duplicated among iBGP routers.

It was mentioned before that the loopback IP address can be used for both iBGP and eBGP peers. Additional commands must be used when creating a peering session with a loopback interface.

For iBGP sessions, the only additional command is the `update-source` command. The syntax follows:

```
neighbor [address | peer-group-name] update-source
interface-type interface-number
```

In this command, the IP address of the loopback should be used. Since the loopback interface is being used as the source of the BGP session, the *interface-type* should be entered as the loopback. The *interface-number* is the number of the loopback interface that is being used for BGP peering.

Several other options can be configured within BGP, but are beyond the scope of this book. Some of these options will be discussed in the "Large-Scale BGP Networking" section.

BGP Route Selection

BGP uses several metrics and criteria when selecting a route. Each metric can be configured manually. Other criteria that influence BGP route selection may also be configured.

To quickly understand how BGP selects a route, review Figure 6.12. This figure summarizes the steps that the BGP process takes to choose the best route. Ten different criteria are used in path selection, several of which are configurable.

Now let's discuss some of these criteria separately. We will also learn how to configure them.

Weight

The weight metric allows a system administrator to manually assign a value to all paths learned from other BGP peers. The larger the weight value, the more desirable the path.

This metric is particularly helpful when a router is connected to multiple autonomous systems. The weight assigned stays local to the router on which it is configured. When paths are learned from multiple sources, the weight metric can be used to force BGP to select a specified interface over the others.

This metric is configured using the following command from within the BGP routing session:

```
neighbor [ip-address | peer-group-name] weight weight
```

FIGURE 6.12

BGP path-selection
diagram

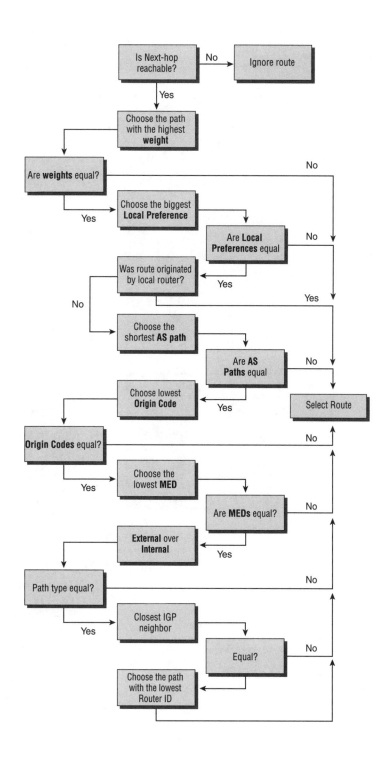

The *ip-address* is the IP address of the neighbor. The peer group may be used when assigning weight to all routes learned via the BGP peer group. The *weight* value has a range from 0 to 65,535. The default value is 32,768.

Local Preference

Local preference is used to assign metric values that are used among iBGP peers. We learned that the weight metric remains local to a router. The local preference is useful when multiple iBGP peers have their own eBGP peers. Figure 6.13 gives us a picture of how local preference works.

FIGURE 6.13

Local preference
operation

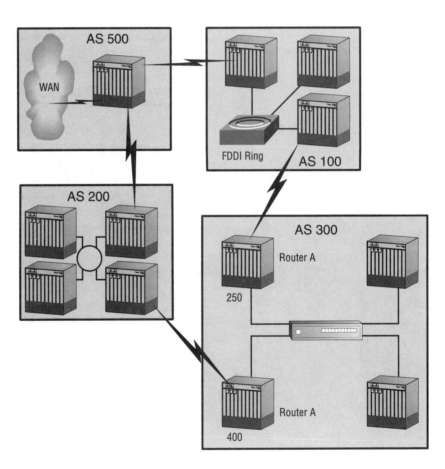

When a path is learned via two different border routers, both paths are advertised to other iBGP peers. Either path is valid and can be used. However, if one path is to be used only as a backup route, you can set local preference values on both routers.

The diagram in Figure 6.13 shows that Router A and Router B both have paths to AS 500. If we want Router B to be the primary route, we can assign local preference values to both Routers A and B. The local preference value is propagated throughout AS 300. We assign local preferences of 400 to Router B and 250 to Router A. When any router inside of AS 300 wants to reach AS 500, it will use Router B's path.

Local preference is configured by using the following command. The command must be issued within the BGP session configuration.

```
bgp default local-preference value
```

Acceptable values for the local preference range from 0 to 4,294,967,295. Higher values are preferred over lower values.

MED (Multi-Exit Discriminator)

While the previous metrics inform local AS routers which path to select when leaving the AS, MEDs inform the neighboring AS which link to use to receive traffic.

MEDs are used when two autonomous systems are connected via multiple links or multiple routers. MED values are not propagated to other autonomous systems.

Configuring MEDs is more complicated than configuring weight or local preference values. Because of the complexity of the configuration, more CPU resources are needed. MEDs are set using route maps. Route maps are a form of access lists. Here is an example of a BGP configuration using MEDs:

```
Router_A#conf t
Enter configuration commands, one per line.  End with CNTL/Z.
Router_A(config)#router bgp 300
Router_A(config-rou)#neighbor 172.16.24.15 route-map
    EXAMPLE out
Router_A(config-rou)#exit
Router_A(config)#route-map EXAMPLE permit 10
Router_A(config-rou)#match ip address 1
Router_A(config-rou)#set metric 25
Router_A(config-rou)#exit
```

```
Router_A(config)#route-map EXAMPLE permit 20
Router_A(config-rou)#exit
Router_A(config)#access-list 1 permit 172.16.0.0 0.0.255.255
Router_A(config)#^Z
Router_A#


router bgp 300
 network 172.16.0.0
 neighbor 172.16.24.15 remote-as 500
 neighbor 172.16.24.15 route-map EXAMPLE out
!
ip classless
access-list 1 permit 172.16.0.0 0.0.255.255
route-map EXAMPLE permit 10
 match ip address 1
 set metric 25
!
route-map EXAMPLE permit 20
!
```

This configuration sets an MED of 25 for all networks belonging to
172.16.0.0. AS 500 is the AS that will use this value. The lower MED value
is preferred. The second permit statement of the route-map EXAMPLE permits all other networks to be advertised, but does not assign an MED value.

Managing BGP

You manage BGP by changing the previous metrics. Other items can also be
manipulated to manage BGP routing. As we saw in Figure 6.12, AS path
length is also considered when selecting a route. With the use of route maps,
the AS path may be lengthened by adding false AS numbers. This is called *AS
path pre-pending*. It is another way to influence route selection.

In addition to manipulating route selection, BGP has features that allow
network advertisements to be aggregated before they are advertised to neighboring autonomous systems.

Router confusion and high CPU utilization can occur when routes flap. A
route flap is defined as a change in the state of the route. Once a route is
established and then removed from the BGP table, one flap has occurred. To

prevent routing problems, issue the bgp dampening command. The dampening command maintains a threshold for route flaps—when the threshold is exceeded, the route is put into holddown. A timing mechanism then monitors the route status—if the route stops flapping for a given period of time, the route is allowed back into the BGP table and can be advertised.

It is often important to define what type of AS you are administering. When multiple autonomous systems interconnect, one or all of the ASs can become a transit AS. Depending on your network policy, this can be a good or bad thing.

It is considered bad if other ISPs use your circuits, equipment, and bandwidth to connect to a neighboring AS instead of using their own resources. Figure 6.14 depicts three autonomous systems. Each AS is connected to the other. AS 200 does not want to permit traffic originating from AS 300 to reach AS 100 using AS 200's resources.

This task is accomplished by using AS path filters. By using regular expressions, AS path information can be compared, and then either permitted or denied. Here is a sample configuration detailing how AS filters can be implemented:

```
router bgp 200
 no synchronization
 bgp dampening
 neighbor 172.16.65.10 remote-as 100
 neighbor 172.16.65.10 filter-list 10 in
 neighbor 172.16.65.10 filter-list 1 out
 neighbor 172.16.65.11 remote-as 300
 neighbor 172.16.65.11 filter-list 11 in
 neighbor 172.16.65.11 filter-list 1 out
!
!
ip as-path access-list 1 permit ^200$
ip as-path access-list 10 permit ^100$
ip as-path access-list 11 permit ^300$
!
!
```

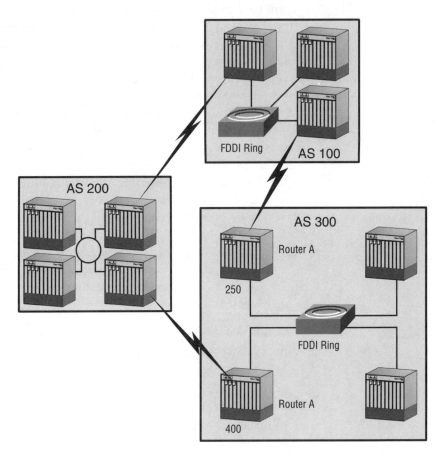

FIGURE 6.14

Nontransit AS

The filters are applied using the `neighbor` command. The AS path filters block routes that contain AS path information that does not match the regular expression. For access list 1, we see that only routes that originate from AS 200 will be allowed to be sent to the respective neighbors. For access lists 10 and 11, routes that do not originate within AS 100 and AS 300, respectively, will not be accepted.

Large-Scale BGP Networking

Several methods exist to help manage large BGP networks:

- Using private AS numbers
- Creating peer groups

- Creating confederations

- Creating route reflectors

Each of these methods can become quite complex. We will give a brief overview of what each does.

When a router reaches 100 BGP sessions, it is recommended that you configure route reflectors. By using route reflectors, a router needs to peer only with the reflector instead of with each individual router. A route reflector maintains the route table for all internal peers connected to it. A router can learn the same number of routes from a route reflector as it could by participating in a full mesh.

Confederations are used to control the size of iBGP meshes. The idea behind confederations is to break up the AS. Several sub-AS numbers can be configured inside of the real AS. Sub-ASs must use private AS numbers. The routers within each sub-AS are fully meshed, then one of the routers peers with one of the routers from another sub-AS—the overhead on each router is reduced, while a complete BGP table for the entire AS is preserved.

Monitoring BGP

When BGP implementation becomes widespread, it is important to be able to monitor peering sessions and route information. Several commands enable the user to get detailed BGP information.

Table 6.9 summarizes all of the commands that can be used to monitor BGP.

T A B L E 6.9 BGP Monitoring Command Summary	**Command**	**Description**
	show ip bgp neighbors	Shows all configured BGP neighbors. It provides detailed statistics and information about each neighbor.
	show ip bgp inconsistent-as	Displays routes learned via BGP speakers that have a different AS from the AS of the originating router.
	show ip bgp regexp	Allows the user to enter a regular expression to search for specific BGP information.

T A B L E 6.9 *(cont.)*	**Command**	**Description**
BGP Monitoring Command Summary	`show ip bgp community`	Used to display routes belonging to the specified community.
	`show ip bgp cidr-only`	Displays classless routes.
	`show ip bgp filter-list`	Displays AS path lists.
	`show ip bgp paths`	Displays all path information for the local router.
	`show ip bgp peer-group`	Provides information on the members of the specified peer group.

The detailed use of some of these commands will be explained in the next section, "Troubleshooting BGP."

 At the time we wrote this chapter, some of these show commands can cause the router to reload. Cisco is aware of the problem and has bug tickets on them. The problem occurs in later 11.1 and 11.3 IOS versions.

Troubleshooting BGP

The most important part of troubleshooting is verifying the status of the peering router. When you issue the show ip bgp neighbors command, basic troubleshooting information is displayed. Let's look at an example:

```
Router_A#sho ip bgp neighbors 172.16.65.10
BGP neighbor is 172.16.65.10, remote AS 500, external link
 Index 1, Offset 0, Mask 0x2
  BGP version 4, remote router ID 10.1.2.1
  BGP state = Established, table version = 508, up for 3d20h
  Last read 00:00:45, hold time is 180, keepalive interval
    is 60 seconds
  Minimum time between advertisement runs is 30 seconds
```

Received 5579 messages, 0 notifications, 0 in queue
Sent 5703 messages, 0 notifications, 0 in queue
Inbound path policy configured
Outbound path policy configured
Incoming update AS path filter list is 10
Outgoing update AS path filter list is 1
Connections established 1; dropped 0
Last reset never
No. of prefix received 10
Connection state is ESTAB, I/O status: 1, unread input
  bytes: 0
Local host: 172.16.65.1, Local port: 179
Foreign host: 172.16.65.10, Foreign port: 29768

Enqueued packets for retransmit: 0, input: 0 mis-ordered: 0
  (0 bytes)

Event Timers (current time is 0x14322791):

Timer	Starts	Wakeups	Next
Retrans	5677	1	0x0
TimeWait	0	0	0x0
AckHold	5578	4246	0x0
SendWnd	0	0	0x0
KeepAlive	0	0	0x0
GiveUp	0	0	0x0
PmtuAger	0	0	0x0
DeadWait	0	0	0x0

iss: 1337567913 snduna: 1337679159 sndnxt: 1337679159
  sndwnd: 15066
irs: 4270375806 rcvnxt: 4270482004 rcvwnd: 15548
  delrcvwnd: 836

SRTT: 309 ms, RTTO: 708 ms, RTV: 45 ms, KRTT: 0 ms
minRTT: 4 ms, maxRTT: 453 ms, ACK hold: 300 ms
Flags: passive open, nagle, gen tcbs

```
Datagrams (max data segment is 1460 bytes):
Rcvd: 11252 (out of order: 0), with data: 5579, total data
    bytes: 106216
Sent: 9996 (retransmit: 1), with data: 5675, total data
    bytes: 111245
Router_A#
```

As you can see, a great deal of information is provided by the `neighbor` command. When a peering relationship has trouble getting established, use this command to see if the TCP connection has failed. This will give you a starting point for troubleshooting.

When the problem seems to be route information–oriented, you can use the following command:

```
show ip bgp regexp regular-expression
```

Use this command to see which routes are being learned from the neighboring AS. If the neighboring AS is not receiving given routes from your AS, you can use the following command to see what you are advertising to the AS:

```
show ip bgp neighbor address advertised-routes
```

A quick `summary` command can be used to verify connectivity via BGP:

```
show ip bgp summary
```

These are just a few of the commands that you can use when troubleshooting BGP. Many other commands and procedures can be used to accomplish this task, but they are beyond the scope of this book.

Summary

This has been a very extensive chapter—a lot of information has been covered. Let's review the major points discussed in this chapter:

- We compared the differences and limitations of both distance vector and link-state routing protocols. The conclusion was made that link-state protocols (or a hybrid of link-state and distance vector) provide for greater scalability and stability.

- Enhanced IGRP is a hybrid of link-state and distance vector protocols. It provides greater stability than IGRP and also allows for equal-cost load balancing, controlled routing updates, and formal neighbor adjacencies.

- Routing updates can also be controlled by applying access lists with the `distribute-list` command from within a routing protocol session. Updates can also be stopped from exiting an interface by using the `passive-interface` command.

- We learned the importance of assigning correct metric information when configuring redistribution among dissimilar protocols.

- There was a great deal of information discussed about OSPF. We learned that OSPF uses areas, and that within each area, different router types exist. LSAs and LSUs are used to communicate route information and changes. The different types of LSA packets were also discussed.

- In addition to all of the information provided about IGPs, we also learned about BGP and ISP connectivity issues. BGP should be used only when a network meets a few specific criteria as outlined in this chapter. BGP metrics and how to change them were discussed at length.

Review Questions

1. What are two benefits of using a link-state routing protocol?

   A. It uses the Hello protocol to establish adjacencies

   B. It uses several components to calculate the metric of a route

   C. Updates are sent only when changes occur in the network

   D. It is a better protocol than distance vector is

2. Which protocol does not use a topology table?

   A. EIGRP

   B. IGRP

   C. RIP1

   D. OSPF

3. Which route type must be redistributed by a routing protocol if other routers are to learn about it?

   A. RIP

   B. Default routes

   C. Connected routes

   D. Static routes

4. Which command should be used to ensure proper metric conversion when redistributing routes from different protocols?

   A. `distance distance-value`

   B. `default-metric`

   C. `distribute-list`

   D. `default-information`

5. Why are passive interfaces used within routing protocols such as EIGRP and OSPF?

    A. To stop unwanted route information from entering the specified interface

    B. To allow route information to be filtered by an access list

    C. To allow routes to be sent out the specified interface, but deny route information to enter the interface

    D. To allow routes to enter the interface, but deny any route information to exit the specified interface

6. How is a feasible successor chosen when the successor fails?

    A. The route with the next lowest metric is chosen

    B. If a router doesn't have a feasible successor, queries are multicast to neighboring routers in search of a feasible successor

    C. The route is removed from the route table

    D. The route is flagged as an active state

7. Which of the following is a prerequisite for incremental SAP updates to work with EIGRP IPX instead of periodic updates?

    A. IPX must be running on the router

    B. The `ipx sap-incremental eigrp` command must be issued

    C. The neighbor connected to the configured interface must also have EIGRP IPX enabled

    D. Different AS numbers must be used

8. How is EIGRP implemented on a router?

    A. `ip router eigrp autonomous-system-number`

    B. `router ip eigrp autonomous-system-number`

    C. `router eigrp process-id`

    D. `router eigrp autonomous-system-number`

9. Which of the following are *not* features of EIGRP?

    A. Incremental updates

    B. Only one route per destination

    C. Support for IP, IPX, and AT

    D. Hybrid distance vector and link-state protocol

    E. Not a scalable protocol

    F. Hello protocol used to establish adjacencies

10. Which commands can be used for troubleshooting EIGRP problems?

    A. `show ip eigrp route`

    B. `show ip route eigrp`

    C. `show ip eigrp topology`

    D. `show ip eigrp neighbors`

    E. `show ip eigrp events`

11. What configuration option changes a stub area to a totally stub area?

    A. `area area-id stub no-summary`

    B. `area area-id total stub`

    C. `area process-id stub`

    D. `area process-id stub no-summary`

12. Which OSPF initialization states allow routers to actually exchange route information?

    A. The loading state

    B. The two-way state

    C. The full state

    D. The exchange state

13. Which state indicates that link-state databases have been synchronized among OSPF area routers?

    A. The loading state

    B. The two-way state

    C. The Exstart state

    D. The exchange state

14. What two characteristics distinguish a stub area from a totally stub area?

    A. A totally stub area accepts summary routes

    B. A totally stub area is Cisco proprietary

    C. A totally stub area contains only intra-area routes

    D. A totally stub area contains only inter-area routes

15. What command is used to assign a cost to summary routes advertised to a stub area?

    A. `area area-id default-cost cost`, issued on the ABR

    B. `area area-id default-cost cost`, issued on the ASBR

    C. `area process-id default-cost`, issued on the ABR

    D. `area area-id default-cost cost`, issued on any stub router

16. What three enhancements were made to OSPF to make it better than RIP1?

    A. No hop-count limit

    B. Use of distance vector algorithm

    C. Use of classfull routing

    D. Incremental routing updates

    E. Route tables are calculated after the change has been propagated

17. Which commands are used to verify correct operation of OSPF?

    A. `show ip ospf area-id`

    B. `show ospf database`

    C. `show ip ospf border-routers`

    D. `show ip ospf process-id`

    E. `show ip ospf links`

    F. `show ip ospf database [network | summary | asbr-summary | external | database-summary]`

    G. `show ip ospf virtual-links`

18. What is a summary LSA?

    A. A type 3 or 4 LSA that describes links between the ABR and local area routers

    B. A type 2 LSA that is propagated by the DR about all local routes

    C. A type 3 or 4 LSA that is multicast by the ASBR containing a summary of all external routes

    D. A type 5 LSA that contains a summary of all external routes

19. What are the commands needed to implement OSPF on a router? (Choose two.)

A. router ip ospf *area-id*

B. router ospf *area-id*

C. router ospf *process-id*

D. network *address mask area-id*

E. network *address wildcard-mask area-id*

F. network *address wildcard-mask* area *area-id*

20. What is the difference between an ABR and an ASBR?

A. An ABR is the border router between two or more defined areas, and an ASBR is a border router between an OSPF area and external autonomous system

B. An ASBR is the border router between two or more defined areas, and an ABR is a border router between an OSPF area and external autonomous system

C. An ABR is the area backbone router that connects the backbone routers, and an ASBR borders different autonomous systems

D. An ASBR is the autonomous system backbone router that connects the backbone to other autonomous systems, and the ABR is the area border router

21. Which of the following is an example of how to configure eBGP?

A. router ip bgp 10
network 10.1.1.1 100

B. router bgp 10
network 10.1.1.1 remote-as 10

C. router bgp 100
neighbor 10.1.1.1 remote-as 100

D. router bgp 100
neighbor 10.1.1.1 remote-as 200

22. Which of the following is an example of how to configure iBGP?

    A. `router ip bgp 10`
       `network 10.1.1.1 100`

    B. `router bgp 10`
       `network 10.1.1.1 remote-as 10`

    C. `router bgp 100`
       `neighbor 10.1.1.1 remote-as 100`

    D. `router bgp 100`
       `neighbor 10.1.1.1 remote-as 200`

23. Which command shows the BGP routes?

    A. `show ip bgp route`

    B. `show ip bgp`

    C. `show ip route bgp`

    D. `show ip bgp paths`

24. How is a BGP session established between two routers?

    A. Telnet

    B. Hello packets

    C. UDP (SYN, ACK, SYN)

    D. TCP (SYN, ACK, SYN)

25. When should BGP be used?

    A. When multi-homing

    B. When connecting multiple ISPs

    C. When connecting routers within the same AS

    D. When configuring backup links

Laboratory Exercises

Refer to Figure 6.15 to complete lab exercises 1–3.

FIGURE 6.15

Lab diagram

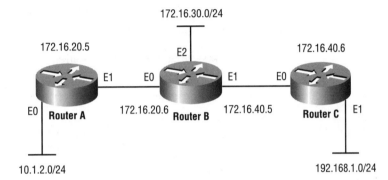

1. IGRP—You are building the network shown in Figure 6.15. All IP addresses have been configured on the router.

   A. Implement IGRP on all three routers. Assign AS 100 to Router A, and AS 200 to Routers B and C. Make sure to include the correct networks.

   B. Redistribute AS 100 into AS 200.

   C. Verify that routes are being redistributed.

2. EIGRP—Using the same information provided in Figure 6.15, complete the following tasks. All IGRP sessions have been removed.

   A. Implement EIGRP on all routers. Use AS 100 for all routers.

   B. Display the topology table for Router B.

   C. Configure Router A so that no routing updates are sent to Router B.

   D. Implement EIGRP IPX on Routers B and C, and configure interface E1 on Router B to send incremental SAP updates.

3. OSPF—Continue to use the same diagram (shown in Figure 6.15). Complete the following tasks.

A. Configure OSPF on all routers.

- Assign interface E0 on Router A to area 1.

- Assign all `172.16.0.0` networks to area 0.

- Assign interface E1 on Router C to area 2.

B. Make area 1 a stub area.

C. Make area 2 a totally stub area.

Use Figure 6.16 to complete lab exercise 4.

F I G U R E 6.16

BGP diagram

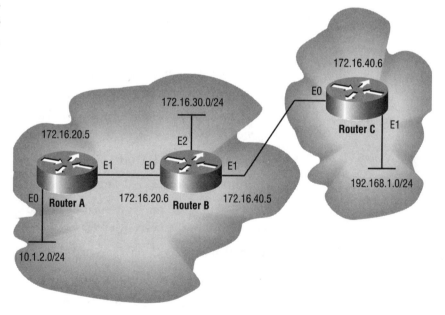

4. BGP—Complete the following tasks. Assume that the IGP is already configured.

    A. Configure iBGP between Routers A and B, then configure eBGP between Routers B and C.

    B. On Router B, set the weight for all incoming routes from Router C to 500.

    C. Show a summary of all BGP connections from Router B.

CHAPTER

7

IPX Traffic Control

What—a chapter on IPX? Doesn't the whole world—even Novell—use TCP/IP? Well actually, no. There's still a multitude of installed IPX networks. At the time of this writing, Novell claims on their Web site to have over 81 million users and 4 million installed NetWare servers, and a huge installed base like that leaves little room for doubt—IPX configuration skills will be valuable for years to come.

Cisco has reduced the focus on other protocols such as DECnet and Banyan in ACRC over the last few years, and their continued coverage of IPX as a significant network protocol is due to the legion of installed IPX nodes.

This chapter will cover the following exam objectives:

- Describe IPX/SPX traffic management issues

- Filter IPX traffic using IPX access lists

- Manage IPX/SPX traffic over WAN

- Verify IPX/SPX filter operation

Introduction to IPX Traffic

As a prerequisite to understanding IPX traffic management, we'll pause to review some fundamentals of how IPX operates. You must fully comprehend *why* IPX packets are generated before you can really understand *how* to control them.

From a router's perspective, all IPX traffic falls into one of two categories:

- Client-server communications

- Server-server communications

Routing updates could rightly be considered a subset of server-server communications, and in larger internetworks, they're best managed with advanced IPX routing protocols. (We'll talk about these protocols in detail in Chapter 8.)

Client-Server Communication

Novell NetWare adheres to a strict client-server model—a NetWare node is either a client or a server, and that is that. You won't find *peer* machines that both provide and consume network resources here. Clients can be workstations running operating systems such as DOS, MacOS, Windows NT, or Windows 95/98. Servers generally run Novell NetWare versions 3.*x*–5.

With the release of NetWare 5, Novell NetWare servers and clients can now fully communicate using TCP/IP instead of IPX, but NetWare 5 still supports IPX as a client-server communication protocol.

NetWare clients depend upon servers to locate all network resources, and they basically view the internetwork as one big LAN regardless of its actual size. Every NetWare server builds a SAP table, which includes all the network resources it knows of (we'll explain how it does this in a bit). When clients need to access any resource, they transmit an IPX broadcast called a GNS (get nearest server), assuming that it will be both heard and answered by a server. The servers that receive the GNS check their SAP tables to find a NetWare server that matches the client's request, and then respond to the client with another GNS, which includes the address of the server the client may contact for the resource it requested. If none of the servers hearing the client's GNS request have a server in their SAP tables that hosts the requested resource, they simply don't respond, leaving the requesting client without access.

Why do we care? Well, for two reasons: First, we want clients to succeed and actually find the resources they need—remember that client machines do all kinds of useful things, such as printing our paychecks. This means we must make sure that the GNS IPX broadcasts the clients send out do in fact reach the devices capable of responding to them. Second, we very much want to control IPX broadcast propagation—especially in WAN environments.

OK, so how do we achieve these two goals? Well, one solution stems from the fact that Cisco routers build SAP tables and can respond to client GNS requests just as if they were NetWare servers. (This doesn't mean they *offer* the services that NetWare servers do, just that their responses are identical when it comes to locating services.) So a GNS response to a client can come from a local NetWare server, a remote NetWare server, or a Cisco router. If any local NetWare servers are present, they'll usually respond to the client. However, if none are present, a local Cisco router that's connected to the client's segment can respond to its GNS request instead. This saves clients the time they would've spent waiting for remote NetWare servers to respond. A second advantage to this arrangement is that precious WAN bandwidth isn't occupied with GNS conversations between clients on a segment with access to remote NetWare servers only, as shown in Figure 7.1.

FIGURE 7.1

Remote IPX clients on a serverless network

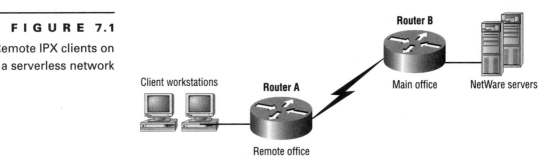

This figure depicts client workstations at a remote office site that require access to server resources at the main office. In this situation, Router A would answer client GNS requests from its SAP table rather than forwarding the request across the WAN to the servers at the main office. The clients never realize that there isn't a NetWare server present on their LAN. For this process to run smoothly, the administrator needs to ensure only that the SAP table on Router A is correctly populated.

This communication method insulates the client from the task of locating and tracking available network resources and places that burden on the server instead. The client simply broadcasts a GNS, then waits for a response. From the client's perspective, all network resources respond as though they were local, regardless of their actual physical location in the internetwork.

Now let's use EtherPeek to observe a conversation between client and server. The workstation's MAC address is 00:60:08:9e:2e:44, and the first thing we see is the client GNS request:

```
Flags:     0x80 802.3
 Status:     0x00
```

```
Packet Length:64
Timestamp:  22:56:14.565643 10/07/1998
```
802.3 Header
Destination: ff:ff:ff:ff:ff:ff Ethernet Brdcast
Source: 00:60:08:9e:2e:44
LLC Length: 38
802.2 Logical Link Control (LLC) Header
 Dest. SAP: 0xe0 NetWare
 Source SAP: 0xe0 NetWare *Individual LLC Sublayer Management Function*
 Command: 0x03 *Unnumbered Information*
IPX - NetWare Protocol
 Checksum: 0xffff
 Length: 34
 Transport Control:
  Reserved: %0000
  Hop Count: %0000
 Packet Type: 0 *Novell*
 Destination Network: 0x00000000
 Destination Node: ff:ff:ff:ff:ff:ff Ethernet Brdcast
 Destination Socket: 0x0452 *Service Advertising Protocol*
 Source Network: 0xf3df9b36
 Source Node: 00:60:08:9e:2e:44
 Source Socket: 0x4000 *IPX Ephemeral*
SAP - Service Advertising Protocol
 Operation: 3 *NetWare Nearest Service Query*
 Service Type: 4 *File Server*
Extra bytes (Padding):
 ....   00 04 00 04 00 04 00 04 00
Frame Check Sequence: 0x00000000

Did you notice that this was a broadcast to the local segment, not a directed
request to any server? The client just assumed its broadcast would be heard
and answered. OK—here's the response from the server, ECORP:

```
 Flags:     0x80 *802.3*
  Status:     0x00
  Packet Length:118
  Timestamp:  22:56:14.565643 10/07/1998
 802.3 Header
  **Destination:** 00:60:08:9e:2e:44
```

Source: 00:60:08:9d:2a:8e

LLC Length: 99

<u>802.2 Logical Link Control (LLC) Header</u>

Dest. SAP: 0xe0 NetWare

Source SAP: 0xe0 NetWare *Group LLC Sublayer Management Function*

Command: 0x03 *Unnumbered Information*

<u>IPX - NetWare Protocol</u>

Checksum: 0xffff

Length: 96

<u>Transport Control:</u>

 Reserved: %0000

 Hop Count: %0000

Packet Type: 4 *PEP*

Destination Network: 0xf3df9b36

Destination Node: 00:60:08:9e:2e:44

Destination Socket: 0x4000 *IPX Ephemeral*

Source Network: 0xf3df9b36

Source Node: 00:60:08:9d:2a:8e

Source Socket: 0x0452 *Service Advertising Protocol*

<u>SAP - Service Advertising Protocol</u>

 Operation: 4 *NetWare Nearest Service Response*

Service Advertising Set #1

 Service Type: 4 *File Server*

 Service Name: ECORP.....................................

 Network Number: 0x34b62f24

 Node Number: 00:00:00:00:00:01

 Socket Number: 0x0451

 Hops to Server: 1

Extra bytes (Padding):

  .   00

Frame Check Sequence: 0x00000000

So did you notice that this time the packet wasn't a broadcast, that it was directed from the server answering the request right to the client? The client received the IPX address (network and node) information to find the service type—in this case, a file server—for which it was looking.

Server-Server Communication

The communication between two NetWare servers is a bit more complicated than that of client-server communications. Servers exchange service information using a protocol called SAP (Service Advertising Protocol). As the name suggests, SAP communicates information about services offered by individual servers.

As mentioned earlier, servers are responsible for maintaining SAP tables that chronicle all available network resources whether those resources are local to the server's segment or not.

NetWare servers use SAP to advertise the services they offer by sending out an SAP broadcast on all interfaces every 60 seconds, which includes their available services plus any others that the server has learned of from other servers. All servers receiving the SAP broadcast incorporate the information into their own SAP tables, and propagate it through their own SAP updates. It's like a room full of people who each have a secret, but can't keep it—leave them there long enough, and eventually everyone will know all the secrets. Because SAP information is shared between all servers, all servers ultimately become aware of all available services, thereby equipping them to respond to client GNS requests. As new services are introduced, they're added into SAP tables on local servers, and then rebroadcasted until every server knows that they exist and where to find them.

Great—but where do Cisco routers fit in? As far as SAPs are concerned, the router acts just like another NetWare server. By default, an SAP broadcast won't cross a Cisco router, which catalogs all the SAPs it has received on any of its IPX-enabled interfaces into its own SAP table. The router then broadcasts the whole table from each of those interfaces at 60 second intervals (unless you change the settings), just as NetWare servers do. This is an important point—especially when it comes to WAN links. The router isolates SAP broadcasts to individual segments, and passes along only the summarized information to each segment.

So let's take a look at an SAP broadcast with our EtherPeek analyzer:

```
Flags:     0x00
 Status:    0x00
 Packet Length:306
 Timestamp:  16:55:39.868873 10/09/1998
```

<u>Ethernet Header</u>
 Destination: ff:ff:ff:ff:ff:ff Ethernet Brdcast
 Source: 00:80:5f:ad:e4:83
 Protocol Type:81-37 NetWare
<u>IPX - NetWare Protocol</u>
 Checksum: 0xffff
 Length: 288
 <u>Transport Control:</u>
  Reserved: %0000
  Hop Count: %0000
 Packet Type: 4 *PEP*
 Destination Network: 0xcc715b00
 Destination Node: ff:ff:ff:ff:ff:ff Ethernet Brdcast
 Destination Socket: 0x0452 *Service Advertising Protocol*
 Source Network: 0xcc715b00
 Source Node: 00:80:5f:ad:e4:83
 Source Socket: 0x0452 *Service Advertising Protocol*
<u>SAP - Service Advertising Protocol</u>
 Operation: 2 *NetWare General Service Response*
 Service Advertising Set *#1*
  Service Type: 263 *NetWare 386*
  Service Name: BORDER2...................................
  Network Number: 0x00000001
  Node Number: 00:00:00:00:00:01
  Socket Number: 0x8104
  Hops to Server: 1
 Service Advertising Set *#2*
  Service Type: 4 *File Server*
  Service Name: BORDER2...................................
  Network Number: 0x00000001
  Node Number: 00:00:00:00:00:01
  Socket Number: 0x0451
  Hops to Server: 1
 Service Advertising Set *#3*
  Service Type: 632
  Service Name: BORDER_____@@@H@@@@@@D.PJ..

```
Network Number:  0x00000001
Node Number:    00:00:00:00:00:01
Socket Number:  0x4006
Hops to Server:  1
Service Advertising Set #4
Service Type:    993
Service Name:    BORDER2....................................
Network Number:  0x00000001
Node Number:    00:00:00:00:00:01
Socket Number:  0x9056
Hops to Server:  1
Frame Check Sequence: 0x00000000
```

We can see that this SAP is from a NetWare server named Border 2. Also, notice that it's advertising four distinct services that it offers. Those services, and their address and socket information, would be included in the SAP table of all IPX-enabled devices attached to this network—including routers—and rebroadcast throughout the internetwork.

We'll take a closer look at managing all this GNS and SAP traffic in the following sections.

WARNING   Complete management of IPX traffic requires that you pay attention to routing table maintenance in addition to the details of the client requests and services location. (Flip to Chapter 8 for information on controlling IPX routing protocols.)

IPX Filtering

A quick review of IPX addressing will help you once we begin building access lists to control IPX traffic.

IPX addresses use 80 bits, or 10 bytes, of data. They are hierarchical, and divided into a network and node portion. The first 4 bytes represent the network address, and the last 6 represent the node address. The network portion of the address is assigned by administrators and must be unique on the entire

IPX internetwork. Node addresses are *automatically* assigned to every node. In most cases, the MAC address of the machine is used as the node portion of the address. IPX addresses are most often written in hex, as in the following example:

```
00007C80.0000.8609.33E9
```

The first 8 hex digits (00007C80) represent the network portion of the address; the remaining 12 hex digits (0000.8609.33E9) represent the node portion and are the MAC address of the workstation. When referring to the IPX network, it's a common IPX custom to drop leading zeros. With this done, the above network address would simply be referred to as IPX network 7C80. The node portion is commonly divided into three sections of 4 hex digits divided by periods, as shown above.

Just as IP uses port addresses to identify separate services running on a host, IPX uses a *socket* address to identify services provided by a server. Services of the same type are always advertised using the same socket address. Remember these facts when building your access lists.

Access lists for IPX fall into three categories:

- Standard access lists

- Extended access lists

- SAP filters

Standard IPX Access Lists

Standard IPX access lists give us the ability to permit or deny packets based on source and/or destination IPX addresses. They're powerful tools that you can use to protect the network from unwelcome access. Remember that IPX clients view the internetwork as a big, friendly LAN, even though the CNE who runs your accounting department's servers doesn't. With proper use of both standard and extended access lists, you can enforce almost any IPX access policy.

Each line of an IPX standard access list includes the following fields:

```
access-list number permit/deny source destination
```

Let's say that we have IPX configured in our network as outlined in Figure 7.2.

FIGURE 7.2

Our IPX internetwork

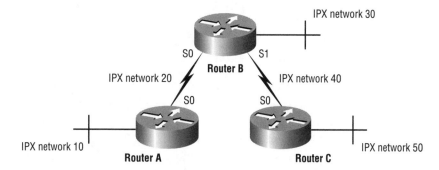

Now suppose that we want to set up an IPX access list allowing IPX network 30 to access IPX network 10, but prohibiting IPX network 50 from accessing that same network.

Here are the two steps for doing that:

1. While in Global Configuration mode, enter the access list.

2. While in Interface Configuration mode, apply the access list to either inbound or outbound traffic.

Here's how we'll set up who gets to access what using the two steps mentioned above:

```
RouterA#config t
Enter configuration commands, one per line. End with CNTL/Z.
RouterA(config)#access-list 810 permit 30 10
RouterA(config)#access-list 810 deny 50 10
RouterA(config)#int e0
RouterA(config-if)#ipx access-group 810 out
RouterA(config-if)#^Z
RouterA#
```

Let's break down the two lines of access list 810 to make the syntax clearer:

Access List	Number	Permit/Deny	Source	Destination
access-list	810	permit	30	10
access-list	810	deny	50	10

The number 810 falls within the range of 800–899 that's reserved for IPX standard access lists. The permit/deny is the same as it is with IP packets. Here, we've specified the source and destination based upon the IPX network addresses from our diagram. (We could have used –1 to specify all IPX networks, or defined a complete, 80-bit IPX address to specify a particular host.)

Do you remember that implicit *deny* at the end of every access list? In this case, any networks other than 30 will be denied access to network 10. Functionally, we could have omitted the entire second line—the implicit *deny* would have denied packets from IPX network 50 (along with every other IPX network).

OK—so if we want to allow access for all IPX networks except 50, we could proceed by again using the two steps we mentioned earlier:

```
RouterA#config t
Enter configuration commands, one per line. End with CNTL/Z.
RouterA(config)#access-list 811 deny 50 10
RouterA(config)#access-list 811 permit -1 -1
RouterA(config)#int e0
RouterA(config-if)#ipx access-group 811 out
RouterA(config-if)#^Z
RouterA#
```

Once again, let's isolate these two lines to get a clear picture of what's going on:

Access List	Number	Permit/Deny	Source	Destination
access-list	811	deny	50	10
access-list	811	permit	-1	-1

The –1 network address is important here because it refers to any IPX network address in IPX access list convention. Although there's an implicit *deny* at the end of this list, it will be overridden by the second line, which dictates to allow any IPX packet through. Functionally, this list denies all packets from IPX network 50 that are destined for IPX network 10, but allows everything else to pass.

If this syntax gets confusing (and it certainly can), just remember that online help is always available to guide you to the next parameter.

Here's an example of how one line from the above example could be entered using the online help:

```
RouterA(config)#access-list ?
  <1-99>    IP standard access list
  <100-199>  IP extended access list
  <1000-1099> IPX SAP access list
  <1100-1199> Extended 48-bit MAC address access list
  <1200-1299> IPX summary address access list
  <200-299>  Protocol type-code access list
  <300-399>  DECnet access list
  <600-699>  Appletalk access list
  <700-799>  48-bit MAC address access list
  <800-899>  IPX standard access list
  <900-999>  IPX extended access list


RouterA(config)#access-list 810 ?
  deny  Specify packets to reject
  permit Specify packets to permit


RouterA(config)#access-list 810 permit ?
  -1      Any IPX net
  <0-FFFFFFFF> Source net
  N.H.H.H    Source net.host address
  <cr>


RouterA(config)#access-list 810 permit 30 ?
  -1      Any IPX net
  <0-FFFFFFFF> Destination net
  N.H.H.H    Destination net.host address
  <cr>


RouterA(config)#access-list 810 permit 30 10 ?
  <cr>


RouterA(config)#access-list 810 permit 30 10
```

Remember that when access lists are being entered into the router, they must be methodically entered line by line, in the proper order. There's no way to enter the second line, then the first, then the fifth—you must enter the first line, then the second, and so on. And be warned—if you make a mistake on a line, you have to use the no access-list command to remove everything you've entered, and start all over.

Here is an example of this dismal event—in it, the author mistakenly entered the second line first, and had to remove his work and begin again:

```
RouterA#config t
Enter configuration commands, one per line. End with CNTL/Z.
RouterA(config)#access-list 811 permit -1 -1
RouterA(config)#no access-list 811
RouterA(config)#access-list 811 deny 50 10
RouterA(config)#access-list 811 permit -1 -1
RouterA(config)#int e0
RouterA(config-if)#ipx access-group 811 out
RouterA(config-if)#^Z
RouterA#
```

Most of the time, it's a whole lot easier to Telnet into the router and then use an external text editor to compose the access list instead of typing it directly into the router. Once the list is correct in the text editor, you can just cut and paste it into your router configuration screen. Even if you don't make typos, this can still be handy—we all appreciate a good shortcut.

Extended IPX Access Lists

Extended IPX access lists function the same way that standard IPX access lists do—the difference is one of degrees. With standard IPX access lists, your filtering capacity is limited to the source or destination address, but with extended IPX access lists, you can filter based upon any of the following criteria:

- Source network/node
- Destination network/node
- IPX protocol (SAP, SPX, etc.)
- IPX socket

Extended access lists live in the 900–999 range. They're configured just like standard access lists are, only with the addition of protocol and socket information. Let's take a look at a template for building lines in an IPX extended access list:

```
access-list number permit/deny protocol source socket
destination socket log
```

When progressing from standard to extended access lists, you simply gain the ability to filter based on protocol and socket (port for IP). There are several options when specifying the protocol:

- −1 for any protocol
- 1 for RIP
- 4 for IPX
- 5 for SPX

The source and destination addresses are specified as they are with standard IPX access lists, and the socket information includes the following:

- 0 for all sockets
- 452 for SAP

Let's take access list 811 from our above example and implement it as an extended access list:

```
RouterA#config t
Enter configuration commands, one per line. End with CNTL/Z.
RouterA(config)#access-list 910 deny -1 50 0 10 0
RouterA(config)#access-list 910 permit -1 -1 0 -1 0
RouterA(config)#int e0
RouterA(config-if)#ipx access-group 910 out
RouterA(config-if)#^Z
RouterA#
```

Once again, online help is available if you need it to wade through the syntax. Here's a look at the online help while entering one of the above lines:

```
RouterA#config t
Enter configuration commands, one per line. End with CNTL/Z.
```

```
RouterA(config)#access-list ?
 <1-99>     IP standard access list
 <100-199>  IP extended access list
 <1000-1099> IPX SAP access list
 <1100-1199> Extended 48-bit MAC address access list
 <1200-1299> IPX summary address access list
 <200-299>  Protocol type-code access list
 <300-399>  DECnet access list
 <600-699>  Appletalk access list
 <700-799>  48-bit MAC address access list
 <800-899>  IPX standard access list
 <900-999>  IPX extended access list

RouterA(config)#access-list 910 ?
 deny   Specify packets to reject
 permit Specify packets to permit

RouterA(config)#access-list 910 deny ?
 -1     Any IPX protocol type
 <0-255> Protocol type number (DECIMAL)
 <cr>

RouterA(config)#access-list 910 deny -1 ?
 -1      Any IPX net
 <0-FFFFFFFF> Source net
 N.H.H.H     Source net.host address
 <cr>

RouterA(config)#access-list 910 deny -1 50 ?
 <0-FFFFFFFF> Source Socket (0 for all sockets) HEXIDECIMAL
 <cr>

RouterA(config)#access-list 910 deny -1 50 0 ?
 -1      Any IPX net
 <0-FFFFFFFF> Destination net
 N.H.H.H     Destination net.host address
 <cr>
```

```
RouterA(config)#access-list 910 deny -1 50 0 10 ?
 <0-FFFFFFFF> Destination Socket (0 for all sockets)
HEXIDECIMAL
 <cr>


RouterA(config)#access-list 910 deny -1 50 0 10 0 ?
 <cr>


RouterA(config)#access-list 910 deny -1 50 0 10 0
```

There are variations in syntax, depending on which IOS version you are running. Online help is useful in navigating these variations.

IPX SAP Filters

IPX SAP filters are central to controlling IPX SAP traffic, and they're implemented using the same tools we've been discussing so far in this chapter. Why is controlling this traffic important? If you control the SAPs, you control the access to IPX devices. We'll use access lists in the 1000–1099 range to specify IPX SAP filters. Here's the template for each line of an IPX SAP filter:

```
access-list number permit/deny source service type
```

So on our Admin network, we have three NetWare servers, but we want only the one with the internal IPX network address 11.0000.0000.0001 to be seen by the outside world. To accomplish that, we'd configure and apply an access list as follows:

```
RouterA#config t
Enter configuration commands, one per line. End with CNTL/Z.
RouterA(config)#access-list 1010 permit 11.0000.0000.0001 0
RouterA(config)#int e0
RouterA(config-if)#ipx input-sap-filter 1010
RouterA(config-if)#^Z
RouterA#
```

You can apply SAP filters to interfaces as either input or output filters using the keywords `ipx input-sap-filter` and `ipx output-sap-filter`. Input SAP filters prevent services advertised to an interface from being added to the router's SAP table, while output SAP filters prevent a router from advertising services in its SAP table out an interface. In this case, we want to prevent the router from learning of (and thus advertising) all file servers except the one with internal network 11, so we use the `ipx input-sap-filter` command.

Here's how that one command line in the above access list maps to the template:

Access List	Number	Permit /Deny	Source	Service Type
access-list	1010	permit	11.0000.0000.0001	0

The 1010 falls into the range 1000–1099 reserved for IPX SAP filters. The source network is the network/node address of the server. The resulting access list allows updates about 11.0000.0000.0001 to enter the Ethernet interface and be included in SAP updates across the network. As with other access lists, an implicit *deny* blocks all other SAP updates arriving at the router on the Ethernet interface. Finally, we entered a zero for service type, which indicates that all services should be allowed:

```
RouterA#config t
Enter configuration commands, one per line. End with CNTL/Z.
RouterA(config)#access-list 1010 permit 11.0000.0000.0001 ?
  <0-FFFF> Service type-code (0 matches all services)
  N.H.H.H  Source net.host mask
  <cr>
```

There are several common service types, including the following:

- 3 for print queue

- 4 for file server

- 7 for print server

Here's the above line entered using the online help:

```
RouterA(config)#access-list ?
  <1-99>     IP standard access list
  <100-199>  IP extended access list
  <1000-1099> IPX SAP access list
  <1100-1199> Extended 48-bit MAC address access list
  <1200-1299> IPX summary address access list
```

```
<200-299>  Protocol type-code access list
<300-399>  DECnet access list
<600-699>  Appletalk access list
<700-799>  48-bit MAC address access list
<800-899>  IPX standard access list
<900-999>  IPX extended access list
RouterA(config)#access-list 1010 ?
 deny  Specify packets to reject
 permit Specify packets to forward
RouterA(config)#access-list 1010 permit ?
 -1       Any IPX net
 <0-FFFFFFFF> Source net
 N.H.H.H     Source net.host address
RouterA(config)#access-list 1010 permit 11.0000.0000.0001 ?
 <0-FFFFFFFF> Service type-code (0 matches all services)
 N.H.H.H     Source net.host mask
 <cr>
RouterA(config)#access-list 1010 permit 11.0000.0000.0001 0 ?
 WORD A SAP server name
 <cr>
RouterA(config)#access-list 1010 permit 11.0000.0000.0001 0
RouterA(config)#
```

Verifying IPX Access List Operation

Once you have your access lists in place, there are several ways to verify their actual operation. We'll cover four commands that you can use to verify that your access lists are actually working:

- show ipx servers
- show ipx int
- show ipx traffic
- show access-list

Of course, if you forget the exact syntax, online help is always available:

```
RouterA#show ipx ?
 accounting  The active IPX accounting database
 cache     IPX fast-switching cache
 compression IPX compression information
 eigrp     IPX EIGRP show commands
 interface  IPX interface status and configuration
 nhrp      NHRP information
 nlsp      Show NLSP information
 route     IPX routing table
 servers    SAP servers
 spx-spoof  SPX Spoofing table
 traffic    IPX protocol statistics
RouterA#show ipx
```

The show ipx servers command displays the contents of the router's SAP table. This can be extremely helpful when troubleshooting SAP filters to test their operation. For example, if you specify ipx input-sap-filter on an interface, it will prevent the router from learning SAPs of the specified type being heard on that interface. The output should look as follows:

```
RouterA#show ipx servers
Codes: S - Static, P - Periodic, E - EIGRP, N - NLSP, H -
  Holddown, + = detail
9 Total IPX Servers

Table ordering is based on routing and server info

    Type Name         Net   Address Port   Route Hops Itf
 P  4 BORDER1       350ED6D2.0000.0000.0001:0451   2/01  1
    Et0
 P  4 BORDER2          1.0000.0000.0001:0451   2/01  1 Et0
 P  107 BORDER1      350ED6D2.0000.0000.0001:8104   2/01  1
    Et0
 P  107 BORDER2         1.0000.0000.0001:8104   2/01  1 Et0
 P  26B BORDER_____ 350ED6D2.0000.0000.0001:0005
    2/01  1 Et0
 P  278 BORDER_____   1.0000.0000.0001:4006   2/01
    1 Et0
```

```
P   278 BORDER_____  350ED6D2.0000.0000.0001:4006
    2/01  1 Et0
P   3E1 BORDER1        350ED6D2.0000.0000.0001:9056   2/01  1
    Et0
P   3E1 BORDER2            1.0000.0000.0001:9056   2/01  1 Et0
RouterA#
```

You can use the show ipx interface command to see which interfaces have IPX enabled, as well as which (if any) of the access lists we have discussed have been applied. The output reads as follows:

```
RouterA#show ipx interface
Ethernet0 is up, line protocol is up
  IPX address is CC715B00.0000.0c47.6f4f, ARPA [up] line-up,
    RIPPQ: 0, SAPPQ: 0
  Delay of this IPX network, in ticks is 1 throughput 0 link
    delay 0
  IPXWAN processing not enabled on this interface.
  IPX SAP update interval is 1 minute(s)
  IPX type 20 propagation packet forwarding is disabled
  Incoming access list is not set
  Outgoing access list is not set
  IPX helper access list is not set
  SAP GNS processing enabled, delay 0 ms, output filter list
    is not set
  SAP Input filter list is not set
  SAP Output filter list is not set
  SAP Router filter list is not set
  Input filter list is not set
  Output filter list is not set
  Router filter list is not set
  Netbios Input host access list is not set
  Netbios Input bytes access list is not set
  Netbios Output host access list is not set
  Netbios Output bytes access list is not set
  Updates each 60 seconds, aging multiples RIP: 3 SAP: 3
  SAP interpacket delay is 55 ms, maximum size is 480 bytes
  RIP interpacket delay is 55 ms, maximum size is 432 bytes
  IPX accounting is disabled
```

```
IPX fast switching is configured (enabled)
RIP packets received 1850, RIP packets sent 1
SAP packets received 1850, SAP packets sent 1
```

The show ipx traffic command will display information about the total number of IPX packets both sent and received. Information on routing and SAP is included here. The output reads as follows:

```
RouterA#show ipx traffic
System Traffic for 0.0000.0000.0001 System-Name: RouterA
Rcvd:  13388 total, 1579 format errors, 0 checksum errors, 0
  bad hop count,
    926 packets pitched, 12462 local destination, 0
      multicast
Bcast: 13386 received, 2 sent
Sent:  2 generated, 0 forwarded
    0 encapsulation failed, 0 no route
SAP:  0 SAP requests, 0 SAP replies, 9 servers
    1850 SAP advertisements received, 0 sent
    0 SAP flash updates sent, 0 SAP format errors
RIP:  2 RIP requests, 0 RIP replies, 3 routes
    1848 RIP advertisements received, 0 sent
    0 RIP flash updates sent, 0 RIP format errors
Echo:  Rcvd 0 requests, 0 replies
    Sent 0 requests, 0 replies
    0 unknown: 0 no socket, 0 filtered, 0 no helper
    0 SAPs throttled, freed NDB len 0
Watchdog:
    0 packets received, 0 replies spoofed
Queue lengths:
    IPX input: 0, SAP 0, RIP 0, GNS 0
    SAP throttling length: 0/(no limit), 0 nets pending lost
      route reply
    Delayed process creation: 0
EIGRP: Total received 0, sent 0
    Updates received 0, sent 0
    Queries received 0, sent 0
    Replies received 0, sent 0
    SAPs received 0, sent 0
NLSP:  Level-1 Hellos received 0, sent 0
```

```
        PTP Hello received 0, sent 0
        Level-1 LSPs received 0, sent 0
        LSP Retransmissions: 0
        LSP checksum errors received: 0
        LSP HT=0 checksum errors received: 0
        Level-1 CSNPs received 0, sent 0
        Level-1 PSNPs received 0, sent 0
        Level-1 DR Elections: 0
        Level-1 SPF Calculations: 0
        Level-1 Partial Route Calculations: 0
RouterA#
```

Finally, you can use the show access-list command to display the access lists currently configured on your routers. With this command, all access lists on the route will be displayed. The output reads as follows:

```
RouterA#show access-list
Novell access list 910
   deny -1 50 0 10 0
Novell SAP access list 1010
   permit 11.0000.0000.0001 0
RouterA#
```

WAN Considerations for IPX

The main drawback associated with running IPX in the WAN is the frequency of routing and service advertisement updates. We'll cover how to control routing updates in the next chapter, but we'll look at the SAP issues now.

As we mentioned, routers exchange SAP tables with each other just like NetWare servers do, and their exchanges occur at the default update interval of every 60 seconds. If you are dealing with a slow WAN link, that default is likely to be more frequent than necessary. Also, if your router's SAP tables are sufficiently large, these events will surely eat up more serial link time than you find acceptable. One approach to this problem is to reduce the SAP update interval over a WAN connection. Consider the network shown in Figure 7.3.

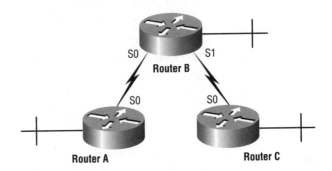

FIGURE 7.3

Internetwork 2

We can reduce the update interval on the serial links between Router A and Router B, and between Router B and Router C, so that it will occur every 10 minutes instead of each minute.

When modifying the default SAP update interval, you must make sure to configure the same update interval on the serial interfaces of both routers. If they don't agree, services may expire from one table before updates are received; thus, they won't be continuously advertised.

Let's take a look at how to accomplish this on Router A:

```
RouterA#config t
Enter configuration commands, one per line. End with CNTL/Z.
RouterA(config)#interface serial0
RouterA(config-if)#ipx sap-interval 10
RouterA(config-if)#^Z
RouterA#
```

Then repeat the same procedure on Router B Serial 0. From now on, SAP updates will occur only every 10 minutes across our serial link. This reduction in bandwidth does not come for free, however. Since Router A and Router B exchange SAP information only every 10 minutes now, as new services become available (or old services disappear), these updates may take significantly longer to propagate across the internetwork.

Summary

We've detailed the operation of three types of IPX access lists:

- We started with standard IPX access lists and their basic functionality level of making packet forward/deny decisions based on source and destination IPX addresses.

- We then introduced extended IPX access lists and their additional ability to evaluate protocol and socket information.

- Finally, we discussed IPX SAP filters and how they can affect both what routers enter into their own SAP tables and what SAP information they will forward to other devices.

We also covered four valuable commands for evaluating the performance of configured access lists:

- `show ipx servers`
- `show ipx int`
- `show ipx traffic`
- `show access-list`

Lastly, we introduced the `ipx sap-interval` command for reducing the frequency of SAP broadcasts across WAN links.

Review Questions

1. Which of the following is a valid IPX standard access list entry?

A. `access-list 888 permit 50 -1`

B. `access-group 888 permit 50 -1`

C. `access list 888 permit 50 -1`

D. `access-list permit 50 any`

E. `access list permit 50 any`

2. Which of the following is valid syntax to apply access list 810 to interface E0 incoming (assuming you are already in Interface Configuration mode)?

A. `access group 810 in`

B. `access group 801 incoming`

C. `access-group 810 in`

D. `access-group 810 incoming`

E. `ipx input-sap-filter 810`

3. Which of the following are valid IPX addresses?

A. `00007132.0000.8609.33E9`

B. `-1`

C. `0000.8609.33E9`

D. `7132.0000.8609.33E9`

4. Suppose that you want only to advertise services on IPX network 3B out the serial interface of your router. Which of the following would you use?

A. access-list 1010 permit 3b 0
access-list 1010 deny –1 0
interface s0
ipx input-sap-filter 1010

B. access-list 1010 permit 3b 0
access-list 1010 deny –1 0
interface s0
ipx output-sap-filter 1010

C. access-list 1010 permit -1 0
access-list 1010 deny –1 0
interface s0
ipx output-sap-filter 1010

D. access-list 1010 permit 3b -1
access-list 1010 deny –1 0
interface s0
ipx output-sap-filter 1010

5. Suppose that you want to learn only of services on IPX network 3B on the Serial 0 interface of your router. Which of the following would you use?

A. `access-list 1011 permit 3b 0`
`access-list 1011 deny -1 0`
`interface s0`
`ipx output-sap-filter 1011`

B. `access-list 1011 permit 3b 0`
`access-list 1011 deny -1 any`
`interface s0`
`ipx output-sap-filter 1011`

C. `access-list 1011 deny 3b 0`
`access-list 1011 deny -1 0`
`interface s0`
`ipx input-sap-filter 1011`

D. `access-list 1011 permit 3b 0`
`access-list 1011 deny -1 0`
`interface s0`
`ipx input-sap-filter 1011`

6. Suppose that you want to block access to IPX network 30 by all packets from network 50, but allow access to packets from network 10. Suppose that you also do not want to block any traffic to other IPX networks. Which of the following lists would work?

A. `access-list 850 deny 50 30`
`access-list 850 permit 10 30`
`access-list 850 permit −1 −1`

B. `access-list 850 deny 30 50`
`access-list 850 permit 30 50`
`access-list 850 permit −1 −1`

C. `access-list 850 deny 50 −1`
`access-list 850 permit −1 −1`

D. `access-list 850 deny 50 30`
`access-list 850 permit −1 −1`

E. `access-list 850 permit −1 −1`
`access-list 850 deny 50 30`

7. Which of the following is the correct way to readjust the SAP update interval on Serial 0 to 30 minutes (assuming you are already in Interface Configuration mode)?

A. `ipx sap-update-interval 30`

B. `ipx sap-update-interval 1800`

C. `ipx sap-interval 30`

D. `ipx sap-interval 1800`

E. `ipx sap update interval 30`

F. `ipx sap update interval 1800`

8. Which of the following commands would you use to see which interfaces have SAP filter 1012 enabled?

A. show running-config

B. show access-list

C. show ip interface

D. show ipx interface

E. show ipx servers

9. Which commands can you use to verify that your router is receiving SAP updates?

A. show running-config

B. show ipx sap

C. show ipx traffic

D. show ipx interface

E. show ipx servers

10. Suppose that you need to switch your outbound IPX access list from 830 to 831. Assuming you are already in Interface Configuration mode, which of the following will work?

A. ipx access-group 831 in

B. ipx access-group 831 out

C. no ipx access-group 830 in
ipx access-group 831 in

D. no ipx access-group 830 out
ipx access-group 831 out

11. Suppose that you want to prevent all IPX traffic from network 7D from leaving your Ethernet interface. Which of the following would you use?

A. IPX extended access list

B. IPX standard access list

C. IPX SAP filter

D. IPX RIP filter

12. Suppose that you want to prevent your print services on network 7D from being advertised beyond your Ethernet interface. Which of the following would you use?

A. IPX extended access list

B. IPX standard access list

C. IPX SAP filter

D. IPX RIP filter

13. Suppose that you want to prevent your router from including in its SAP table anything not in network 8A. Which of the following would you use?

A. IPX extended access list

B. IPX standard access list

C. IPX SAP filter

D. IPX RIP filter

14. When IPX clients attempt to locate services, which protocol do they use to find them?

   A. SAP

   B. RIP

   C. NLSP

   D. GNS

   E. ARP

15. When IPX servers are exchanging information on their respective services, which protocol do they use?

   A. SAP

   B. RIP

   C. NLSP

   D. GNS

   E. ARP

16. When IPX servers are responding to client requests, which protocol do they use?

   A. SAP

   B. RIP

   C. NLSP

   D. GNS

   E. ARP

17. What is the default broadcast interval for SAP traffic?

   A. 10 seconds

   B. 20 seconds

   C. 60 seconds

   D. 120 seconds

   E. 10 minutes

18. Suppose that you have modified the default SAP interval on your router and are experiencing inconsistencies when using the show ipx servers command on your router from time to time. Which of the following is the most likely cause?

   A. Incorrectly configured standard access list

   B. Incorrectly configured SAP list

   C. Incorrectly configured routing protocol

   D. Incorrectly configured SAP interval

19. Suppose that you need to implement an access list and log packets that meet certain lines within your list. Which of the following could you use?

   A. IPX extended access list

   B. IPX standard access list

   C. IPX SAP filter

   D. IPX RIP filter

20. Suppose that you need to filter based on socket number. Which of the following could you use?

   A. IPX extended access list

   B. IPX standard access list

   C. IPX SAP filter

   D. IPX RIP filter

Laboratory Exercises

1. Before configuring access lists, you need to enable IPX routing. So, configure your router to route IPX, and prepare to configure interfaces in the next lab.

2. Add IPX network numbers to your router's interfaces.

3. Configure an IPX SAP access list and apply it to your Ethernet interface.

4. Configure a standard IPX access list to protect your internal IPX network from unwanted external access. Assume that your Ethernet interface is configured to be on IPX network 8C.

CHAPTER

8

IPX Routing

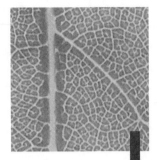

In this chapter, we will continue discussing the management of IPX traffic. In Chapter 7, we covered IPX access lists; here, we will talk about alternatives to running SAP and RIP across your internetwork. Some pretty hot options are available, and we will cover the best of them.

First, we will review the problems that arise with RIP and SAP as networks grow. Then, we will cover NLSP, which is roughly Novell's equivalent of OSPF for the IPX world. Next, we will take a look at IPX Enhanced IGRP, Cisco's slick answer to IPX routing. Finally, we will examine IPX tunneling. While not a routing protocol, it is a way to transport IPX traffic across your WAN (well, kind of—we'll get there).

The following CCNP test objectives are covered in this chapter:

- Describe IPX/SPX traffic management issues

- Manage IPX/SPX traffic over WAN

IPX SAP and RIP

Before we talk about how to fix the problem, let's take a second to define the problem. In Chapter 7, we spent a fair amount of time reviewing just how RIP and SAP work. The point is, *they do work*, so why go any further? Well, just as we saw with RIP in IP networks, the answer concerns growth. If your network consists of 3 routers, T1 lines, and 5 servers, you can probably run RIP and SAP forever and be perfectly happy. However, when that network grows to 300 routers, 500 servers, and occasional 56Kbps lines, RIP and SAP will run out of juice. They will *try* to work if you let them, and they might just kill your internetwork in the process. So what will break in this large internetwork? Here are just a few problems that RIP and SAP will encounter.

Bandwidth

SAP and RIP broadcast everything that they know every 60 seconds. On a small network, this is no problem. The updates are pretty reasonably sized. However, what if you really do have 500 servers? Imagine that SAP updates advertising all those servers are crossing your 56Kbps circuit every 60 seconds. Your network could be spending so much time keeping itself up to date that it would have no time to pass any other traffic (such as user data).

Convergence

Once again, the problem here for RIP and SAP is size. Consider Figure 8.1.

FIGURE 8.1

10-hop IPX network

As you can see, we have 10 segments separating East Router and West Router. Now, suppose that West Server goes down. West Router will wait until West Server has missed three RIP and SAP broadcasts before it removes West Server's internal IPX network address from its routing table and West Server's services from its SAP table. The next time that West Router sends out RIP and SAP updates, the news that West Server is gone will begin to cross the 10 hops. At each hop, the news has to wait for the next scheduled broadcast.

Convergence asks the question, How long will it be after West Server goes down before East Router removes West Server's internal IPX network address and services from its tables? The answer here is *way too long*. RIP and SAP routers can't initiate a connection and say, "Hey, I just heard..." They have to wait for the broadcast at their scheduled interval. As mentioned earlier, if you have only three routers, your convergence is probably acceptable.

However, if you expand your network to the limit of 15 hops, then install 1000 or so services (all of which can go up and down), your network may spend more time converging than being converged.

Scalability

This is really the bottom line for the problems with RIP and SAP—they just don't scale. As we mentioned, as your network grows, RIP and SAP will eat your bandwidth and leave your network more confused than converged. You can overcome these problems with patience and stacks of cash (to purchase bandwidth). However, once a certain point is exceeded, your network will die. This point is hop count for RIP.

To prevent routing loops from routing packets forever, RIP will define networks more that 15 hops away as *unreachable*. What if your network really is more that 15 segments wide? At this point, RIP is broken. It was probably sweating once you exceeded 6 or so hops and was barely functioning when you hit 12, but after 15, it just stopped. You will no longer be able to have IPX connectivity from one end of your network to the other. At this point, you have to look to a different solution.

NLSP

NLSP (Novell Link State Protocol) is Novell's answer to the problems mentioned above.

Overview

NLSP is based on ISO's IS-IS routing protocol. It is a link-state routing protocol, not a distance vector protocol like RIP. Most of the problems with RIP listed above are common to all distance vector routing protocols. NLSP is not subject to these problems.

The current version of NLSP, version 1.1, supports a multitude of advanced routing features, such as:

- Multiple areas

- Route aggregation

- Hierarchical addressing
- Network summarization

NLSP is similar to IS-IS in that it defines areas. It offers solutions to many of the problems that we discussed with RIP and SAP, and can actually work as a replacement for all RIP and SAP communication between servers (or routers).

Let's look at each of the three problems mentioned above with RIP and SAP to learn how NLSP solves the problems.

Bandwidth

With NLSP, updates no longer have to be sent at frequently scheduled intervals. NLSP will consume some bandwidth when everything is first turned on, but once the network converges, it sends updates only when there is a change to report. If there are no changes to report, NLSP will need to communicate only once every two hours by default. That is a huge improvement over every 60 seconds.

Convergence

We traced the problem with RIP and convergence to the fixed 60-second interval. If a RIP router has just made its scheduled broadcast, then learns something important (such as a new route), it has to wait 59 more seconds before it can share that information. NLSP is not so constrained. If an NLSP router hears of a change, it will immediately share that information with the rest of the network, thus significantly reducing total time to convergence. Also, because NLSP is a link-state routing protocol, every router communicates with every other router in the network (we will discuss how this happens shortly). There is no second- or third-hand information, and thus problems such as routing loops are nonexistent with NLSP. With NLSP, the routing tables converge quicker and thus are more reliable than with RIP.

Scalability

Like OSPF, NLSP uses a cost metric that goes to 128. No hops or ticks are used as metrics as with RIP, and thus there is no limitation equivalent to the 15-hop rule with RIP. Your networks can grow much larger than they ever could with RIP and still maintain complete IPX communication end to end.

Features and Operation

Every NLSP router (remember that NLSP-enabled NetWare servers are NLSP routers) builds and maintains three databases:

- Adjacency
- Link state
- Forwarding

These three databases are listed in the order in which they are built. The adjacency database can be unique on every router. Each router will, on each of its NLSP-enabled interfaces, meet every other NLSP router on that network segment. On an Ethernet interface, for example, there could be several other NLSP-enabled devices (other routers, servers, etc.). On a point-to-point WAN interface, there will be only one other device. All of this information goes into the adjacency database, and once it is built, each router will know all of its NLSP neighbors on all connected networks.

The information in the adjacency database is used to create the link state database. Once the routers know all of their adjacencies, they share that information with every other router in what is called the area (we will cover this process and define an area next). At that point, every router knows not only its own adjacencies, but every other router's as well. From this, each router builds a link state database that represents every router in the area and every path between them. Since every router builds this database with the same information (all unique adjacency databases from all routers), the link state database will be identical on every router in the area.

Once the link state database is built and all routers agree upon it, each router builds from the link state database a forwarding database. This is really just a routing table. It lists all networks and the best path for each individual router to take to get to these networks. Because each router can occupy a unique position in the area, each router will have a unique forwarding database.

Now that we have been through the basics, let's step back for a second and marvel at just how cool this process really is. Every router goes out and meets its neighbors, then at a block party, they all share this information with every other router in the neighborhood. They all go home, and now that they know who lives next to whom, they draw a map. Since they all have the same information, they all draw the same map. Another party is held, and once they agree on the map, each one goes home and decides the best path to take from its location to each of its neighbors. What a great way to keep order!

Let's look at this whole process in a bit more detail. We are going to examine how NLSP devices communicate at three different levels, starting from the smallest (a single network) and going to the largest (an internetwork).

Within the Network

NLSP-enabled devices broadcast hello packets on network segments to find other NLSP devices in the same broadcast domain. By sending the hellos at regular intervals, the devices are able to build their adjacency database. This is a list of all NLSP devices on a given segment. Here is a look at one of these hello packets:

```
Flags:          0x80  802.3
  Status:         0x00
  Packet Length:92
  Timestamp:      00:55:25.715452 10/21/1998
802.3 Header
  Destination:    ff:ff:ff:ff:ff:ff Ethernet Brdcast
  Source:         00:00:0c:3e:82:2a
  Length:         74
IPX - NetWare Protocol
  Checksum:               0xffff
  Length:                 73
  Transport Control:
    Reserved:             %0000
    Hop Count:            %0000
  Packet Type:            0  Novell
  Destination Network:    0x00000000
  Destination Node:       ff:ff:ff:ff:ff:ff Ethernet Brdcast
  Destination Socket:     0x9001  IPX Static
  Source Network:         0x00000010
  Source Node:            00:00:0c:3e:82:2a
  Source Socket:          0x9001  IPX Static
  IPX Data Area:
```

```
...........>.*.     83 1b 02 00 0f 01 00 00 11 00 00 0c 3e
                    82 2a 00
..+@...>.*.À....    01 00 2b 40 00 00 0c 3e 82 2a 01 c0 08
                    00 00 00
.....À...           00 00 00 00 00 c5 04 00 00
Extra bytes (Padding):
 .Ü.                05 dc 06
Frame Check Sequence:   0x00000000
```

Notice in the 802.3 header that this really is an Ethernet broadcast.

Once all NLSP machines on a network segment have introduced themselves, they are ready to select a king. They call their king DR (designated router). There is one DR per LAN segment. The main responsibility of the DR is to represent all other routers on the network segment in internetwork communications. This means that whenever NLSP information about that network segment needs to be communicated to the rest of the area, instead of having every router on the network segment communicate, only the DR will communicate. This saves redundant information from being passed by every router on the network and is a big improvement over RIP, where every router on a network broadcasts the same (redundant) information. The routers agree via hello packets whom the DR will be.

Within the Area

We have been freely using the term area without really defining it. NLSP, like OSPF and IS-IS, groups networks into collections called *areas*. It is within an area that all routers exchange adjacency databases and build a common link state database. An NLSP area does not have to be any specific topology—it is a logical grouping of IPX networks.

We have already introduced the DR. Within an area, each DR creates from its adjacency database an LSP (link state packet), which it then floods to all other routers in the area. Note that a flood is not a broadcast. The hello packet we discussed above was a broadcast—it will not cross a router. A flood will cross routers until it reaches every router in the area. Each LSP contains both route and service information. From this flood of LSPs, each router will receive a complete, identical collection of LSPs. Each router will then build its link state database from the same set of information, and thus all routers will end up with an identical logical map of the entire area.

Beyond the Area

As with OSPF, it is possible to make NLSP networks larger by combining multiple areas. Routing domains are composed of multiple areas. These routing domains can then be combined to form an internetwork. From this hierarchy, three types of routers can be defined:

- Level-1 routers communicate within an area.

- Level-2 routers communicate between areas.

- Level-3 routers communicate between routing domains.

Within each of its areas, a level-2 router will act as a level-1 router. Each level-1 router will contain the entire link state database for its area.

Configuring NLSP

Are you ready to see NLSP work? Before we configure NLSP, we must complete a few prerequisites:

- We must have IPX routing enabled.

- Our router must have an internal IPX network number.

- Interfaces must have IPX network numbers and encapsulation types.

Suppose that our network is set up as in Figure 8.2.

FIGURE 8.2

Our internetwork

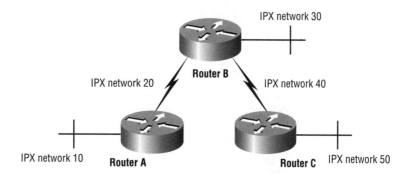

IPX network 30

Router B

IPX network 20   IPX network 40

IPX network 10   **Router A**   **Router C** IPX network 50

Let's take a look at these three steps to configure NLSP on Router C in our internetwork:

```
RouterC#conf t
Enter configuration commands, one per line.  End with CNTL/Z.
RouterC(config)#ipx routing
RouterC(config)#ipx internal-network c
RouterC(config)#int s0
RouterC(config-if)#ipx network 40
RouterC(config-if)#int e0
RouterC(config-if)#ipx network 50
RouterC(config-if)#exit
RouterC(config)#
```

After enabling ipx routing, we used the ipx internal-network command to make the internal network 0000000C for this router. We then configured both active interfaces with IPX addresses using the default encapsulation (HDLC on Serial 0, novell-ether on Ethernet 0). We are now ready to configure NLSP:

```
RouterC#conf t
Enter configuration commands, one per line.  End with CNTL/Z.
RouterC(config)#ipx router nlsp
RouterC(config-ipx-router)#area-address 0 0
RouterC(config-ipx-router)#int s0
RouterC(config-if)#ipx nlsp enable
```

We completed several steps here. We first used the ipx router nlsp command to enable NLSP on the router. In our example here, we did not use any additional parameters with this command. However, we could have entered a tag number at the end of the command to specify the NLSP process to the IOS. This parameter is not required if you are running only one NLSP process:

```
RouterC#config t
Enter configuration commands, one per line.  End with CNTL/Z.
RouterC(config)#ipx router nlsp ?
  WORD  ISO routing area tag
  <cr>

RouterC(config)#
```

One command is required when configuring NLSP—the `area-address` command. This command is used to define which IPX addresses are part of the area. The syntax is as follows:

```
area-address address mask
```

Here, we used zero for the address and zero for the mask. This indicates that all addresses are to be included in this area; i.e., we have only one NLSP area for the entire visible IPX internetwork. If we had specified an address of 1000 and a mask of FF00, that would have indicated networks 1000 through 10ff. Finally, we used the `ipx nlsp enable` command on the serial interface to enable NLSP communication on that interface.

That's it! We can use a few commands to verify NLSP operation:

- show ipx route
- show ipx servers
- show ipx nlsp neighbors

Let's start and verify that the IPX routing table is getting NLSP information:

```
RouterC#sho ipx route
Codes: C - Connected primary network,    c - Connected
          secondary network
       S - Static, F - Floating static, L - Local
          (internal), W - IPXWAN
       R - RIP, E - EIGRP, N - NLSP, X - External, A -
          Aggregate
       s - seconds, u - uses


7 Total IPX routes. Up to 1 parallel paths and 16
   hops allowed.


No default route known.


L         C is the internal network
C         40 (HDLC),        Se0
C         50 (NOVELL-ETHER), Et0
N         A [72][13/02] via        B.0000.0000.0001,
          1990s, Se0
```

```
N          B [27][02/01] via        B.0000.0000.0001,
           1991s, Se0
N          10 [72][12/02] via       B.0000.0000.0001,
           1991s, Se0
N          30 [27][01/01] via       B.0000.0000.0001,
           1991s, Se0
RouterC#
```

Notice from the N in the first column that routes are being learned via NLSP. Now, here is a list of services:

```
RouterC#sho ipx servers
Codes: S - Static, P - Periodic, E - EIGRP, N - NLSP, H -
Holddown, + = detail
3 Total IPX Servers


Table ordering is based on routing and server info


        Type Name                      Net     Address     Port
             Route Hops Itf
N       4 server1                      10.0000.0000.0001:0000
        12/02   3   Se0
N       4 server2                      10.0000.0000.0002:0000
        12/02   3   Se0
N       4 server3                      10.0000.0000.0003:0000
        12/02   3   Se0
RouterC#
```

Here, we are showing three servers, all on network 10. Once again, all three services were learned via NLSP. Finally, here are the NLSP neighbors:

```
RouterC#sho ipx nlsp neighbors
NLSP Level-1 Neighbors: Tag Identifier = notag


System Id   Interface State  Holdtime  Priority   Circuit Id
RouterB       Se0      Up     55          0          04
RouterC#
```

Router C has one NLSP neighbor: Router B. If we wish, we can get more detailed information:

```
RouterC#sho ipx nlsp neighbors detail
NLSP Level-1 Neighbors: Tag Identifier = notag

System Id   Interface  State  Holdtime  Priority  Circuit Id
RouterB     Se0        Up     43        0         04
  IPX Address: B.0000.0000.0001
  IPX Areas:   00000000/00000000
  Uptime: 01:13:09
RouterC#
```

We can use a few additional commands. You may wish to turn RIP and SAP off on interfaces—here is how you can do it:

```
RouterC#conf t
Enter configuration commands, one per line.  End with CNTL/Z.
RouterC(config)#int s0
RouterC(config-if)#ipx nlsp rip off
RouterC(config-if)#ipx nlsp sap off
RouterC(config-if)#^Z
RouterC#
```

Using the off command will prevent RIP and SAP updates from ever crossing this interface. Instead, only NLSP updates will be used. There are actually three versions of these commands:

- ipx nlsp rip off—never send out RIP updates

- ipx nlsp rip on—always send out RIP updates

- ipx nlsp rip auto—send RIP updates only if you hear someone else using them

We can use these three commands to limit SAP traffic as well—just replace the keyword RIP with the keyword SAP above.

EIGRP

We have already introduced EIGRP and discussed its functionality in the chapters on IP routing. Here, we will take a quick look at how it improves IPX routing over RIP and SAP, then jump right into some configurations.

Overview

Just like NLSP, EIGRP fixes many of the problems with RIP and SAP. The three problems with RIP and SAP that we discussed were bandwidth utilization, convergence time, and scalability. Here is how EIGRP takes on these problems.

Bandwidth

You will recall that SAP can clog your WAN by broadcasting everything it knows every 60 seconds. EIGRP gives you greater control over SAP update intervals. By default, on WAN interfaces running IPX EIGRP, SAP updates are incremental rather than periodic, which means that information crosses the WAN only when a change occurs, rather than every 60 seconds. On LAN interfaces, SAP will operate normally by default (unless you modify it).

Devices on your LAN may depend upon periodic SAP updates, so use caution when suppressing periodic SAP updates on LAN interfaces.

Convergence

Just like OSPF, EIGRP does not have to wait until a scheduled interval to share route or service updates. It can go ahead and propagate information when it receives it. Thus, convergence times are significantly lower than with RIP and SAP.

Scalability

Do you remember that maximum number of hops under RIP? Well, with EIGRP, you can go to 224 instead of 15. Have you ever seen a network more than 224 hops wide? (I didn't think so.) Additionally, EIGRP uses bandwidth and delay as metrics for route selection, which means that EIGRP has the information to make intelligent decisions on route selection. You may recall that RIP used ticks and hops, a less effective solution.

Configuring EIGRP

IPX EIGRP is a breeze to configure. However, we need to get a few prerequisites out of the way:

- We must have IPX routing enabled.

- Interfaces must have IPX network numbers and encapsulation types.

Notice that no internal IPX network is required as with NLSP. Once these prerequisites are taken care of, there are only a few steps left. Here is the configuration for our internetwork (assume the above have already been completed):

```
RouterA#config t
RouterA(config)#ipx router eigrp 1
RouterA(config-ipx-router)#network 10
RouterA(config-ipx-router)#network 20
RouterA(config-ipx-router)#ipx router rip
RouterA(config-ipx-router)#no network 20
RouterA(config-ipx-router)#^Z
RouterA#

RouterB#config t
RouterB(config)#ipx router eigrp 1
RouterB(config-ipx-router)#network 20
RouterB(config-ipx-router)#network 30
RouterB(config-ipx-router)#network 40
RouterB(config-ipx-router)#ipx router rip
RouterB(config-ipx-router)#no network 20
RouterB(config-ipx-router)#no network 40
RouterB(config-ipx-router)#^Z
RouterB#

RouterC#config t
RouterC(config-if)#ipx router eigrp 1
```

```
RouterC(config-ipx-router)#network 40
RouterC(config-ipx-router)#network 50
RouterC(config-ipx-router)#ipx router rip
RouterC(config-ipx-router)#no network 40
RouterC(config-ipx-router)#^Z
RouterC#
```

Notice that when we specify the AS (autonomous system) for EIGRP, we are consistent across all three routers. While configuring EIGRP, we also have to tell it which IPX networks are part of the EIGRP AS. Finally, we enter ipx router rip and remove the networks where we don't want RIP used. In the above example, we disable RIP on the serial WAN IPX networks (SAP is set to incremental by default on these interfaces).

As always, we need to verify that this is actually working. Let's start with a look at the IPX routing table on Router C:

```
RouterC#sho ipx route
Codes: C - Connected primary network,    c - Connected
           secondary network
         S - Static, F - Floating static, L - Local
           (internal), W - IPXWAN
         R - RIP, E - EIGRP, N - NLSP, X - External, A -
           Aggregate
         s - seconds, u - uses


5 Total IPX routes. Up to 1 parallel paths and 16 hops
   allowed.


No default route known.


C        40 (HDLC),         Se0
C        50 (NOVELL-ETHER),  Et0
E        10 [46763776/0] via          40.0000.0c5d.6ec8, age
         00:26:04,
                         4u, Se0
E        20 [46738176/0] via          40.0000.0c5d.6ec8, age
         00:26:05,
                         1u, Se0
E        30 [2195456/0] via           40.0000.0c5d.6ec8, age
         00:26:05,
```

```
                           1u, Se0
RouterC#
```

Sure enough, networks 10, 20, and 30 were learned via EIGRP. Next, let's verify that Router C learned about the servers on IPX network 10:

```
RouterC#sho ipx servers
Codes: S - Static, P - Periodic, E - EIGRP, N - NLSP, H -
  Holddown, + = detail
3 Total IPX Servers


Table ordering is based on routing and server info


     Type Name                        Net      Address    Port
        Route Hops Itf
E      4 server1                      10.0000.0000.0001:0000
    46763776/00   1  Se0

E      4 server2                      10.0000.0000.0002:0000
    46763776/00   1  Se0

E      4 server3                      10.0000.0000.0003:0000
    46763776/00   1  Se0
RouterC#
```

As expected, the services were learned of via EIGRP as well.

IPX Tunneling

Tunneling is a unique solution to transporting IPX across your internetwork. It assumes that you already have IP routing enabled, and makes use of work that has already been done by IP to transport IPX traffic.

Overview

Question: Can you carry IPX with OSPF? Answer: Yes! (RFC purists read on....) OSPF is a routing protocol for IP, not IPX. So how can we use it to carry IPX? The solution is to let IP carry the IPX traffic. Consider the internetwork in Figure 8.3.

FIGURE 8.3

IPX tunnel network

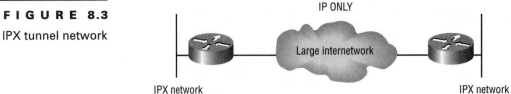

FIGURE 8.3

IPX tunnel network

Suppose that the two IPX networks need to communicate. You could use the techniques that we have discussed thus far to enable IPX routing across the entire IP internetwork, which might involve configuration on many routers. Or, you could configure a tunnel. A *tunnel* is basically a virtual circuit between the two routers that acts like a directly connected IPX interface. It may actually be something very different, but for purposes of IPX connectivity, that is irrelevant.

Configuring IPX Tunneling

Consider the internetwork in Figure 8.4.

FIGURE 8.4

Our IP internetwork

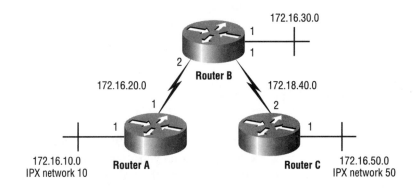

We have the Ethernet network on Router A configured as IPX network 10, and the Ethernet network on Router C configured as IPX network 50. There is no IPX connectivity between Router A and Router C, but there is IP connectivity. Several configuration steps are required to configure the tunnel between these two routers:

1. Create a tunnel interface.

2. Assign the tunnel interface an IPX address.

3. Set the tunnel source address.

4. Set the tunnel destination address.

Configuration Tasks

Let's take a look at how tunneling works, beginning with Router A:

```
RouterA#conf t
Enter configuration commands, one per line.  End with CNTL/Z.
RouterA(config)#interface tunnel0
RouterA(config-if)#ipx network 20
RouterA(config-if)#tunnel source 172.16.20.1
RouterA(config-if)#tunnel destination 172.16.40.2
RouterA(config-if)#^Z
RouterA#
```

We first specify the interface tunnel 0, then proceed to give it an IPX network address just as if it were an actual interface. We then specify the tunnel's source and destination addresses. In our example, we configure them as the appropriate serial interface addresses on Routers A and C, although any router interface (including a loopback interface) will work. Next, we configure Router C:

```
RouterC#conf t
Enter configuration commands, one per line.  End with CNTL/Z.
RouterC(config)#interface tunnel0
RouterC(config-if)#ipx network 20
RouterC(config-if)#tunnel source 172.16.40.2
RouterC(config-if)#tunnel destination 172.16.20.1
RouterC(config-if)#^Z
RouterC#
```

Same as before—notice that the tunnel interface gets the same IPX network address as the tunnel interface on Router A. Don't be fooled just because there is not a single physical medium between these two routers—for IPX purposes, this is a point-to-point connection, and thus both interfaces get the same IPX network address. We did switch the source and destination addresses—from Router C's perspective, they are the opposite of Router A's.

Verification Tasks

We can use several standard IPX verification commands to verify the function of the tunnel interface just created:

- sho ipx route
- sho ipx servers
- sho ipx interface

Here is a look at Router A:

```
RouterA#
RouterA#sho ipx route
Codes: C - Connected primary network,    c - Connected
   secondary network
        S - Static, F - Floating static, L - Local
            (internal), W - IPXWAN
        R - RIP, E - EIGRP, N - NLSP, X - External, A -
            Aggregate
        s - seconds, u - uses


3 Total IPX routes. Up to 1 parallel paths and 16 hops
   allowed.

No default route known.

C        10 (NOVELL-ETHER),   Et0
C        20 (TUNNEL),         Tu0
R        50 [151/01] via       20.0000.0c4a.520f,   46s,
         Tu0


RouterA#sho ipx servers
```

Codes: S - Static, P - Periodic, E - EIGRP, N - NLSP, H - Holddown, + = detail
2 Total IPX Servers

Table ordering is based on routing and server info

	Type Name Route Hops Itf	Net	Address	Port
S	4 server1 conn 1 Et0		10.0000.0000.0001:0000	
P	4 server2 151/01 2 Tu0		50.0000.0000.0001:0000	

RouterA#**sho ipx interface tunnel0**
Tunnel0 is up, line protocol is up
  IPX address is 20.0000.0c3e.822a [up]
  Delay of this IPX network, in ticks is 150 throughput 0
   link delay 0
  IPXWAN processing not enabled on this interface.
  IPX SAP update interval is 1 minute(s)
  IPX type 20 propagation packet forwarding is disabled
  Incoming access list is not set
  Outgoing access list is not set
  IPX helper access list is not set
  SAP GNS processing enabled, delay 0 ms, output filter list
   is not set
  SAP Input filter list is not set
  SAP Output filter list is not set
  SAP Router filter list is not set
  Input filter list is not set
  Output filter list is not set
  Router filter list is not set
  Netbios Input host access list is not set
  Netbios Input bytes access list is not set
  Netbios Output host access list is not set
  Netbios Output bytes access list is not set

```
Updates each 60 seconds, aging multiples RIP: 3 SAP: 3
SAP interpacket delay is 55 ms, maximum size is 480 bytes
RIP interpacket delay is 55 ms, maximum size is 432 bytes
Watchdog processing is disabled, SPX spoofing is disabled,
  idle time 60
IPX accounting is disabled
IPX fast switching is configured (enabled)
RIP packets received 38, RIP packets sent 42
SAP packets received 38, SAP packets sent 42
RouterA#
```

Notice that in the sho ipx route command, the router knows of only three networks: 10, 20, and 50. In the sho ipx servers command, the router knows of servers on 10 and 50. Here is the same information on Router C:

```
RouterC#sho ipx route
Codes: C - Connected primary network,    c - Connected
  secondary network
        S - Static, F - Floating static, L - Local
            (internal), W - IPXWAN
        R - RIP, E - EIGRP, N - NLSP, X - External, A -
            Aggregate
        s - seconds, u - uses


3 Total IPX routes. Up to 1 parallel paths and 16 hops
allowed.


No default route known.


C       20 (TUNNEL),        Tu0
C       50 (NOVELL-ETHER),  Et0
R       10 [151/01] via     20.0000.0c3e.822a,    8s,
        Tu0



RouterC#sho ipx servers
Codes: S - Static, P - Periodic, E - EIGRP, N - NLSP, H -
  Holddown, + = detail
```

2 Total IPX Servers

Table ordering is based on routing and server info

	Type Name Route Hops Itf	Net	Address	Port
S	4 server2 conn 1 Et0		50.0000.0000.0001:0000	
P	4 server1 151/01 2 Tu0		10.0000.0000.0001:0000	

RouterC#**sho ipx interface tunnel0**
Tunnel0 is up, line protocol is up
  IPX address is 20.0000.0c4a.520f [up]
  Delay of this IPX network, in ticks is 150 throughput 0
    link delay 0
  IPXWAN processing not enabled on this interface.
  IPX SAP update interval is 1 minute(s)
  IPX type 20 propagation packet forwarding is disabled
  Incoming access list is not set
  Outgoing access list is not set
  IPX helper access list is not set
  SAP GNS processing enabled, delay 0 ms, output filter list
    is not set
  SAP Input filter list is not set
  SAP Output filter list is not set
  SAP Router filter list is not set
  Input filter list is not set
  Output filter list is not set
  Router filter list is not set
  Netbios Input host access list is not set
  Netbios Input bytes access list is not set
  Netbios Output host access list is not set
  Netbios Output bytes access list is not set
  Updates each 60 seconds, aging multiples RIP: 3 SAP: 3
  SAP interpacket delay is 55 ms, maximum size is 480 bytes

```
    RIP interpacket delay is 55 ms, maximum size is 432 bytes
    Watchdog processing is disabled, SPX spoofing is disabled,
      idle time 60
    IPX accounting is disabled
    IPX fast switching is configured (enabled)
    RIP packets received 41, RIP packets sent 42
    SAP packets received 41, SAP packets sent 42
RouterC#
```

Just as with Router A, Router C knows of the three networks and two servers. We know that they are connected via Router B and actually are passing IPX traffic through Router B's serial interfaces. Let's see what Router B knows:

```
RouterB#sho ipx route
%IPX not running
RouterB#sho ipx servers
%IPX not running
```

Router B has no clue that IPX traffic is crossing its interfaces, because that IPX traffic is buried inside of IP packets.

Summary

In this chapter, we covered several alternatives to the default RIP/SAP strategy for IPX routing:

- We first reviewed the problems with RIP and SAP, including bandwidth troubles, slow conversion, and scalability.

- Then, we covered NLSP, Novell's link-state routing protocol for IPX. We saw how it fixed the problems associated with RIP and SAP. We discussed how it works in areas, and how routers communicate with other routers within an area.

- Next, we covered IPX EIGRP, Cisco's solution to the RIP and SAP problem.

- Finally, we got to IPX tunneling, a neat trick for getting IPX traffic across a large IP network.

Review Questions

1. What is the default update interval for IPX RIP?

    A. 10 seconds

    B. 20 seconds

    C. 30 seconds

    D. 60 seconds

2. Which of the following are problems with RIP and SAP?

    A. Convergence time

    B. Multivendor interoperability

    C. AppleTalk incompatibility

    D. Bandwidth utilization

    E. CPU utilization

    F. Scalability

3. What is the maximum number of hops allowed by IPX RIP?

    A. 5

    B. 10

    C. 15

    D. 20

    E. 25

4. NLSP is based on which of the following ISO routing protocols?

    A. IS-IS

    B. OSPF

    C. EIGRP

    D. RTMP

    E. CDP

5. At what regular interval does NLSP send out service and route updates?

   A. Every 30 seconds

   B. Every 60 seconds

   C. Every 300 seconds

   D. Every two hours

   E. Never

6. Which of the following best describes why convergence is slower with RIP than with other IPX routing protocols?

   A. RIP requires more CPU cycles to process

   B. RIP is limited to periodic updates

   C. RIP has to use split-horizon to suppress routing loops

   D. RIP has to coordinate directly with SAP

7. Which of the following databases are identical on all NLSP routers within an area?

   A. Adjacency

   B. Link state

   C. Routing

   D. Forwarding

   E. DR

8. You want to add NLSP to your router. Which of the following must be completed before you can add NLSP?

   A. IPX RIP must be disabled

   B. IPX routing must be enabled

   C. IPX internal network must be configured on the router

   D. At least one NetWare server must be running

   E. Interfaces must be configured for IPX

9. Which of the following commands is required for every NLSP configuration?

   A. `area-address x y`

   B. `show ipx interfaces`

   C. `ipx external-network x`

   D. `ipx nlsp run`

10. You want to have IPX networks 100–1FF in your NLSP area. Which of the following `area-address` statements would you use?

   A. `area-address 100 0ff`

   B. `area-address 100 f00`

   C. `area-address 100-1ff`

   D. `area-address 100 1ff`

11. Once you have configured NLSP, how would you configure an interface to send out RIP and SAP updates only if there are other devices present that use these protocols? (Assume you are already in Interface Configuration mode.)

A. `ipx nlsp rip on`
`ipx nlsp sap on`

B. `ipx nlsp rip off`
`ipx nlsp sap off`

C. `ipx nlsp rip discover`
`ipx nlsp sap discover`

D. `ipx nlsp rip auto`
`ipx nlsp sap auto`

12. True or False. IPX EIGRP automatically suppresses SAP updates on LAN interfaces.

13. True or False. IPX EIGRP automatically suppresses SAP updates on WAN interfaces.

14. What is the maximum number of hops IPX EIGRP will support?

A. 15

B. 150

C. 224

D. Unlimited

15. What metrics does IPX EIGRP use when making routing decisions?

A. Ticks

B. Bandwidth

C. Reliability

D. Hops

E. Delay

16. You want to add IPX EIGRP to your router. Which of the following must be completed before you can add IPX EIGRP?

   A. IPX RIP must be disabled

   B. IPX routing must be enabled

   C. IPX internal network must be configured on the router

   D. At least one NetWare server must be running

   E. Interfaces must be configured for IPX

17. Which of the following commands will add network 50 to your IPX router EIGRP?

   A. `area-address 50 ff`

   B. `area-address 50 00`

   C. `area-address 50 11`

   D. `network 50`

18. IPX EIGRP is supported by which of the following internetwork devices?

   A. Novell servers

   B. NT servers

   C. Cisco routers

   D. Bay routers

19. Which of the following are required to configure an IPX tunnel?

   A. Creating a tunnel interface

   B. Configuring an internal IPX address on the router

   C. Setting the tunnel destination address

   D. Assigning the tunnel interface an IPX address

   E. Assigning the tunnel interface an IP address

   F. Setting the tunnel source address

20. When configuring the tunnel interface on two routers, the _____ address on one router should be the same as the _____ address on the router at the other end of the tunnel.

A. source; destination

B. internal IPX; internal IPX

C. destination; source

D. IP; IP

Laboratory Exercises

1. Configure your router with basic SAP and RIP, and configure interfaces for IPX.

2. Continue from lab exercise 1 and enable NLSP routing on your router.

3. Continue from lab exercise 1 and enable EIGRP routing on your router.

CHAPTER

9

AppleTalk

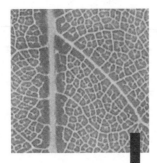

In this chapter, we'll introduce several techniques for controlling AppleTalk traffic on your internetwork. A significant portion of this book deals with optimizing performance (especially on the WAN), and if you tune IP and IPX, but not AppleTalk, life will be less than sweet. You could even end up less than employed!

So, with that in mind, we'll take some time to go over AppleTalk operation and addressing. We'll also introduce several methods of controlling access to AppleTalk devices, including zone, RTMP, and NBP filtering, and cover how to turn RTMP (AppleTalk's default routing protocol) off and use AppleTalk EIGRP to carry routing information instead.

The following CCNP test objectives are covered in this chapter:

- Identify potential sources of congestion in an AppleTalk network
- Configure zone filters
- Configure RTMP filters
- Configure NBP filters

AppleTalk Review

For quite some time, many network administrators have believed that AppleTalk is an unworthy internetwork protocol that's best confined to the LAN. Even though Apple has made some significant improvements, this belief continues among network staff today. These perceptions are not without basis—AppleTalk is often considered a "chatty" protocol. Such is the price paid for the incredible functionality and ease of use AppleTalk offers users and network staff. Don't expect that a protocol that essentially releases the administrator from doing DHCP, DNS, and VLAN will do all that for free.

Anyway, given the profound loyalty of many Macintosh users, opinion among IS staff can be pretty irrelevant. Few end users are as devoted to their platform as Mac users are (hey, the humble author of this chapter is sitting in front of his faithful PowerMac). Let's face it, when the new CEO stacks their PC in the hall outside their office saying, "I use a Mac," or your newest client wants you to integrate their graphics department across the company's internetwork, you'll need the information presented in this chapter.

AppleTalk Communication

Just as IP and IPX had their own rules, AppleTalk has its own way of doing things. Addressing, location of services, and communication are a bit different than with other protocols. There are also several concepts that just don't have parallels elsewhere, such as AppleTalk zones.

AppleTalk Zones

What are AppleTalk zones, and how do they relate to the internetwork? Technically, a *zone* is a logical network, independent of the physical network segment. A *logical network* is a network that you define based on your *users* instead of your *wiring*. Why would you want to do that? Figure 9.1 shows an example of how it's useful.

FIGURE 9.1

AppleTalk zone example

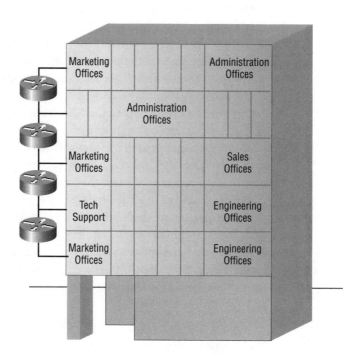

Let's say that on each floor of your building, you have a single network (you have to cross a router to communicate floor to floor as shown in Figure 9.1), and that each floor has a unique network address (no worries, we'll discuss addressing next). The physical network on each floor is the *broadcast domain*, and all users on a given floor share that one broadcast domain. AppleTalk uses broadcasts to locate services, which implies that your users on each floor can locate services on that floor using broadcasts—right? However, we're going to complicate things a bit—let's suppose that because of space considerations, Marketing has offices on the first, third, and fifth floors. It gets worse—also assume that Engineering has offices on the first and second floors. So, to summarize: Your *physical networks* are segmented by floor, but your *departments* segment your users—you have a problem because your physical network doesn't match your departmental needs.

AppleTalk is a wonderfully dynamic protocol for users locating network services, but as we said, it depends on broadcasts. End nodes within a department like Marketing need to be able to send and receive broadcast traffic to every other end node in Marketing *regardless of the physical topology of the network*. What's a network administrator to do? Use AppleTalk zones, that's what.

The idea behind zones is to group your users and network resources into a logical zone that's independent of physical network constraints, thus allowing all users within those zones to exchange broadcast traffic. Referring to the above example, you'd want to create a zone called Marketing, then ensure that all broadcasts to the Marketing zone reached the first-, third-, and fifth-floor network segments. For your logical Engineering zone, broadcasts would need to reach the first and second floors. With zones set up like that, your users in Marketing could exchange broadcast traffic and locate network services even though they span three separate segments—and AppleTalk takes care of this for you.

When you define the Marketing zone and tell the router interfaces on the first, third, and fifth floors that they're part of the Marketing zone, the routers build tables of zones and associated network addresses. In Marketing's case, there would be three networks. The routers then take care of forwarding broadcast requests to the other network segments within the zone and forwarding the replies back to the source workstation's network segment.

Location of Services

Mac users launch an application called Chooser to locate resources on the internetwork. Once users launch the Chooser application, they select an AppleTalk zone and type of resource (file server, printer, etc.). Chooser then builds a dynamic list of workstation names that offers the requested service in the selected zone. The user selects one of the names, then proceeds with their work. Let's get a more detailed idea of how this works:

1. The user launches the Chooser application.

2. The Chooser queries the router for available zones and presents the list of available zones to the user.

3. The user selects a zone and the type of resource requested.

4. The user's Mac issues an NBP request identifying the requested type of resource and zone.

5. The routers ensure that the NBP broadcast is forwarded to all specified network segments for that zone.

6. All nodes in the requested zone receive the NBP broadcast, and the nodes that provide the requested service reply to the requesting workstation.

7. Routers forward the responses to the requesting workstation's segment.

8. The Chooser builds a list of available services.

9. The user selects a service and proceeds with their work.

With this arrangement, it's pretty obvious that the proper forwarding of broadcasts is crucial to locating resources on the internetwork. From the users' perspective, they can just use the dynamic Chooser to find out which resources are available on the internetwork. If you get a new laser printer, you simply plug it in and tell it which zone it's in, and Chooser will automatically let users looking for that type of printer know that it's available.

So let's take a look at how this works in an actual network. We are going to configure our internetwork as outlined in Figure 9.2.

FIGURE 9.2

Our internetwork
with AppleTalk

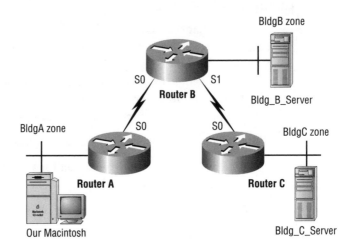

We have the workstation located in the BldgA zone, and we want to attach to the server Bldg_B_Server in the BldgB zone. Here is what EtherPeek sees in the BldgA zone, starting with step 2 from above:

```
Flags:          0x80  802.3
Status:         0x00
Packet Length:64
Timestamp:      14:44:52.508000 06/18/1998
```
802.3 Header
Destination: 00:00:0c:5d:6e:c8
Source: 08:00:07:7f:62:cf
LLC Length: 29
802.2 Logical Link Control (LLC) Header
Dest. SAP: 0xaa   SNAP
Source SAP: 0xaa   SNAP *Group LLC Sublayer Management Function*
Command: 0x03   *Unnumbered Information*
Protocol: 08-00-07-80-9b   ETalkPh2
Long DDP Header - Datagram Delivery Protocol
Unused: %00
Hop Count: %0000
Datagram Length: 21

DDP Checksum: 0x0000

Dest. Network: 107

Source Network: 101

Dest Node: 1

Source Node: 217

Dest. Socket: 6 *Zone Information*

Source Socket: 245

DDP Type: 3 *ATP*

ATP Header – AppleTalk Transaction Protocol

Function Code: 1 *TReq*

Control Information: %000 *ALO*

TRel Timeout Indicator: %000 *30 seconds*

Bitmap: %00000001 *Need Packet(s) 0*

Transaction ID: 2374

ZIP – Zone Information Protocol

Function: 8 *GetZoneList*

Unused: 0

Start Index: 1

Extra bytes (Padding):

.... 00 00 00 00 00 00 00 00 00 00 00 00 00
00 00 00

.   00

Frame Check Sequence: 0x00000000

We can see in the ZIP header at the end of this packet that it's a type 8 (GetZoneList). So the workstation is requesting the zone list from the router. Notice that this is not a broadcast—it's a directed request between the workstation and router. This is important—the workstation learned of the router because it heard the router's RTMP broadcasts. Workstations do not build routing tables, but in AppleTalk they do listen to routing protocols to learn the address of the router. This essentially is what you are doing in IP when you assign a default gateway to a host. With AppleTalk, the workstation learns its gateway dynamically. Now let's take a look at the router's response:

Flags: 0x80 *802.3*

 Status: 0x00

 Packet Length:69

```
       Timestamp:      14:44:52.513000 06/18/1998
```
802.3 Header
  Destination: 08:00:07:7f:62:cf
  Source: 00:00:0c:5d:6e:c8
  LLC Length: 51
802.2 Logical Link Control (LLC) Header
  Dest. SAP: 0xaa SNAP
  Source SAP: 0xaa SNAP
  Command: 0x03 *Unnumbered Information*
  Protocol: 08-00-07-80-9b ETalkPh2
Long DDP Header - Datagram Delivery Protocol
  Unused: %00
  Hop Count: %0000
  Datagram Length: 43
  DDP Checksum: 0xe151
  Dest. Network: 101
  Source Network: 107
  Dest Node: 217
  Source Node: 1
  Dest. Socket: 245
  Source Socket: 6 *Zone Information*
  DDP Type: 3 *ATP*
ATP Header - AppleTalk Transaction Protocol
  Function Code: 2 *TResp*
  Control Information: %010 *ALO EOM*
  TRel Timeout Indicator: %000 *30 seconds*
  Sequence Number: 0 *Here is Packet 0*
  Transaction ID: 2374
ZIP - Zone Information Protocol
  Last Flag: 1
  Unused: 0
  Number of Zones: 4
  Zone: BldgA
  Zone: BldgB
  Zone: BldgC
  Zone: WAN

Frame Check Sequence: 0x00000000

Again, in the ZIP header, we can see that the router has listed the four zones on our internetwork for the requesting workstation. This information will be presented to the user by the Chooser application.

After the user selects a type of service and a zone, we can capture the packet as described in step 4:

```
Flags:          0x80  802.3
  Status:         0x00
  Packet Length:64
  Timestamp:      14:44:55.319000 06/18/1998
802.3 Header
  Destination:    00:00:0c:5d:6e:c8
  Source:         08:00:07:7f:62:cf
  LLC Length:     46
802.2 Logical Link Control (LLC) Header
  Dest. SAP:      0xaa  SNAP
  Source SAP:     0xaa  SNAP  Group LLC Sublayer Management Function
  Command:        0x03  Unnumbered Information
  Protocol:       08-00-07-80-9b  ETalkPh2
Long DDP Header - Datagram Delivery Protocol
  Unused:           %00
  Hop Count:        %0000
  Datagram Length:  38
  DDP Checksum:     0x0000
  Dest. Network:    107
  Source Network:   101
  Dest Node:        1
  Source Node:      217
  Dest. Socket:     2  Name Information
  Source Socket:    253
  DDP Type:         2  NBP
NBP - Name Binding Protocol
  Function:       1  BrRq - Broadcast Request
  Tuple Count:    1
  NBP ID:         6
```

<u>NBP Tuple # 1</u>

Node Address: 101.217

Socket Number: 253

Enumerator: 0

Object: =

Type: AFPServer

Zone: BldgB

Frame Check Sequence: 0x00000000

In this packet, we can tell from the NBP header that the request was for an AFP Server (AppleShare File Protocol Server) in zone BldgB. Since the current segment isn't part of that zone, the router forwards the request to the appropriate segment. The broadcast is made on all physical segments that are part of zone BldgB. Finally, we can see the response from the server on the remote segment coming back to the requesting workstation as described in step 7 above:

Flags: 0x80 802.3

Status: 0x00

Packet Length: 72

Timestamp: 14:44:58.547000 06/18/1998

<u>802.3 Header</u>

Destination: 08:00:07:7f:62:cf

Source: 00:00:0c:5d:6e:c8

LLC Length: 54

<u>802.2 Logical Link Control (LLC) Header</u>

Dest. SAP: 0xaa SNAP

Source SAP: 0xaa SNAP Group LLC Sublayer Management <u>Function</u>

Command: 0x03 Unnumbered Information

Protocol: 08-00-07-80-9b ETalkPh2

<u>Long DDP Header - Datagram Delivery Protocol</u>

Unused: %00

Hop Count: %0010

Datagram Length: 46

DDP Checksum: 0x0000

Dest. Network: 101

```
Source Network:   204
Dest Node:        217
Source Node:      1
Dest. Socket:     253
Source Socket:    2   Name Information
DDP Type:         2   NBP
NBP - Name Binding Protocol
  Function:       3   LkUp-Reply
  Tuple Count:    1
  NBP ID:         6
NBP Tuple # 1
  Node Address:   204.1
  Socket Number:  251
  Enumerator:     1
  Object:         BLDG_B_SERVER
  Type:           AFPServer
  Zone:           *
Frame Check Sequence:  0x00000000
```

Here we can see in the NBP response the network address of the responding device (204.1), the device's type (an AFP Server), and its name (BLDG_B_SERVER). The requesting workstation now knows everything it needs to know to communicate across the internetwork with the server.

As mentioned earlier, AppleTalk is considered a "chatty" protocol. We also mentioned how powerful and dynamic it is. The above example illustrates both of these characteristics. Later in this chapter, we will take a look at how we can control and scale AppleTalk.

AppleTalk Addressing

AppleTalk uses a 24-bit address written in dotted decimal format—*network.node*. The network portion is always 16 bits long; the node portion is always 8 bits long. So as with IPX, there's no subnetting and no classes. There are two versions of AppleTalk—Phase 1 and Phase 2. In Phase 1, there were some rather nasty limitations in addressing (see Table 9.1).

Wow—we're limited to 127 host addresses per segment because the node address is defined in only 8 bits. Since you can have only one network address per segment, the number of nodes per segment is also really limited. If that

T A B L E 9.1	Item	Amount
AppleTalk Phase 1 Addressing	Network addresses per segment	1
	Host addresses per network	127
	Server addresses per network	127
	Zones per network	1

isn't enough, there's also an imposed limitation of one zone per network, obliterating an administrator's ability to create multiple logical networks within the same segment. There must be a better way! Thankfully, Apple thought so too. Let's take a look at some changes made for AppleTalk Phase 2 (see Table 9.2).

T A B L E 9.2	Item	Amount
AppleTalk Phase 2 Addressing	Network addresses per segment	Unlimited
	Host addresses per network	Unlimited
	Server addresses per network	Unlimited
	Zones per network	255

Now we're talking—with Phase 2, there can be an unlimited number of network addresses per segment. Plus, there are ample node addresses available, despite the fact that network addresses are still only 8 bits long.

There really isn't an unlimited number of networks available per segment—you're still limited by the 16-bit network portion of the address, giving you approximately 65,000 potential networks. However, it's highly unlikely that you'd ever need anywhere near 65,000 network addresses for a single network.

Also, we can now have multiple zones per network, allowing us to create multiple logical networks (zones) within a single network segment.

As is the case with IP, there are a few reserved network and node addresses. Network address 0 (zero) is reserved for use by nodes that haven't yet learned their segment's address, so it can't be assigned. Node addresses 254 and 255 are also reserved and can't be assigned to nodes.

The technique used by AppleTalk Phase 2 to assign multiple network addresses to a single segment is called *extended addressing*. Instead of having a single network address on a segment, you can assign a range—an extension—of addresses to a segment. Here's an example: A nonextended address for a segment could be network 100, and an extended address for the same segment could be network 100-110—a range of 11 network addresses. However, what if you need even more node addresses? Well, how about network 100-1000 (901 network addresses)? Need fewer node addresses? Try network 100-100 (1 network address). All you have to do is specify a range of network addresses that you want included on the segment in the extended address. Pretty easy, huh?

AppleTalk nodes dynamically obtain node addresses upon startup. When a new machine starts up, it sends out a ZIP to find the network address, or the address range if extended addressing is being used. The machine then selects a random node address and issues an AARP (AppleTalk Address Resolution Protocol) to see if anyone is using that particular network node address. If there's no response, the machine will continue using that address. Node addressing is completely dynamic and requires no administration.

When an AppleTalk node starts up, it sets up a provisional address. If the node is being started for the very first time, it chooses, at random, a network number between 65,280 and 65,534. This range is referred to as the startup range. The node number is also chosen at random. If the node has been started before, it will use its previous address as a *hint*. In either case, the node will use AARP to check whether the selected provisional address is in use. If the address is in use, it will select another node number and check again. If the node is using a hint and subsequently exhausts all available node numbers without finding an unused address, it will choose a new network address from the startup range and a new node number, and then repeat the check for an unused address.

Once the node has selected an unused provisional address, it can send a ZIP `GetNetInfo` request to a router to determine the actual segment's cable range. If the network number for the provisional address falls between the segment's cable range, the address is kept. Otherwise, a new network number is chosen from this cable range, and the resulting node address will be checked using AARP. If the address is in use, the node will select another node number. If it runs out of node numbers, it will choose another network number from within the segment's cable range and repeat the node address check process. Once the node has found an unused network number and node number combination, this will become its final node address. The address will be saved and used as a future hint.

Enabling AppleTalk on Cisco Routers

Basic AppleTalk configuration comes in two steps. First, we'll enable Apple-Talk routing in Global Configuration mode. Then, we'll configure each individual interface with the appropriate network and zone information.

Enabling AppleTalk Routing

Let's get started configuring our test network. We'll set up the networks and zones as illustrated in Figure 9.2 earlier in the chapter.

We will be using extended network addresses on all segments. The Ethernet networks will be assigned a range of 11 network addresses, and the serial networks will be assigned 1. Also, every segment, including the serial networks, is assigned to a zone. Assigning all serial interfaces to a single WAN zone is a fairly common practice.

Without this first step—enabling AppleTalk routing from Global Configuration mode—we couldn't move on to configure individual interfaces:

```
RouterA#config t
Enter configuration commands, one per line.  End with CNTL/Z.
RouterA(config)#appletalk routing
RouterA(config)#^Z
RouterA#
```

Configuring AppleTalk on Interfaces

Our next step is to configure AppleTalk on each individual interface. We'll configure both network and zone information:

```
RouterA#config t
Enter configuration commands, one per line.  End with CNTL/Z.
RouterA(config)#int e0
```

```
RouterA(config-if)#appletalk cable-range 100-110
RouterA(config-if)#appletalk zone BldgA
RouterA(config-if)#int s0
RouterA(config-if)#appletalk cable-range 200-200
RouterA(config-if)#appletalk zone WAN
RouterA(config-if)#^Z
RouterA#
```

The command to assign extended network addresses is as follows:

```
appletalk cable-range range
```

If we wanted to assign nonextended network addresses, we could use the `appletalk address` *address* command. As detailed above, it's still possible to assign a single network address when using extended addressing. Here, we've used the `cable-range` command for consistency.

That's it! The router is now configured. However, before we go into monitoring AppleTalk, here are the configurations for Router B and Router C.

Router B

```
RouterB#config t
Enter configuration commands, one per line.  End with CNTL/Z.
RouterB(config)#appletalk routing
RouterB(config)#int e0
RouterB(config-if)#appletalk cable-range 300-310
RouterB(config-if)#appletalk zone BldgB
RouterB(config-if)#int s0
RouterB(config-if)#appletalk cable-range 200-200
RouterB(config-if)#appletalk zone WAN
RouterB(config-if)#int s1
RouterB(config-if)#appletalk cable-range 400-400
RouterB(config-if)#appletalk zone WAN
RouterB(config-if)#^Z
RouterB#
```

Router C

```
RouterC#config t
Enter configuration commands, one per line.  End with CNTL/Z.
```

```
RouterC(config)#appletalk routing
RouterC(config)#int e0
RouterC(config-if)#appletalk cable-range 500-510
RouterC(config-if)#appletalk zone BldgC
RouterC(config-if)#int s0
RouterC(config-if)#appletalk cable-range 400-400
RouterC(config-if)#appletalk zone WAN
RouterC(config-if)#^Z
RouterC#
```

Notice that when we configured the two serial interfaces on a common segment, they received identical cable-range and zone information. Whenever you have multiple interfaces on a common segment, their network and zone configuration must be identical for AppleTalk to function properly.

At this point, you may be wondering when we're going to configure a routing protocol. The answer is that we already have. When we entered the command

```
RouterA(config)#appletalk routing
```

in Global Configuration mode, we automatically enabled RTMP on all interfaces that we subsequently configured for AppleTalk. RTMP is the default routing protocol—we will change it later in the chapter. RTMP is similar to RIP. One major difference is that RTMP broadcasts its entire routing table every 10 seconds, rather than every 60 seconds as for RIP.

Now that the network is set up and running, here is an EtherPeek look at an RTMP update from Router A's Ethernet interface:

```
Flags:          0x80  802.3
 Status:         0x00
 Packet Length:73
 Timestamp:      20:56:30.689000 06/18/1998
802.3 Header
 Destination:   09:00:07:ff:ff:ff
 Source:        00:00:0c:5d:6e:c8
 LLC Length:    55
802.2 Logical Link Control (LLC) Header
 Dest. SAP:     0xaa  SNAP
 Source SAP:    0xaa  SNAP  Null LSAP
```

Command: 0x03 *Unnumbered Information*
Protocol: 08-00-07-80-9b *ETalkPh2*

Long DDP Header - Datagram Delivery Protocol

Unused: %00
Hop Count: %0000
Datagram Length: 47
DDP Checksum: 0xd978
Dest. Network: 0
Source Network: 106
Dest Node: 255
Source Node: 74
Dest. Socket: 1 *RTMP*
Source Socket: 1 *RTMP*
DDP Type: 1 *RTMP Response or Data*

RTMP - Routing Table Maintenance Protocol

Router's Net: 106
ID Length: 8
Router's Node ID: 74

RTMP Tuple # 1

Range Start: 100
Range Flag: %100 *Extended*
Distance: 0
Range End: 110
Version: 0x82

RTMP Tuple # 2

Range Start: 300
Range Flag: %100 *Extended*
Distance: 1
Range End: 210
Version: 0x82

RTMP Tuple # 3

Range Start: 500
Range Flag: %100 *Extended*
Distance: 2
Range End: 310
Version: 0x82

RTMP Tuple # 4

Range Start:	200
Range Flag:	%100 *Extended*
Distance:	0
Range End:	1000
Version:	0x82

RTMP Tuple # 5

Range Start:	400
Range Flag:	%100 *Extended*
Distance:	1
Range End:	1001
Version:	0x82
Frame Check Sequence:	0x00000000

It really does look like RIP. Notice that just as we expected, each of our network cable ranges is listed in the RTMP update. Take a look at Figure 9.3.

F I G U R E 9.3

AppleTalk RTMP
updates

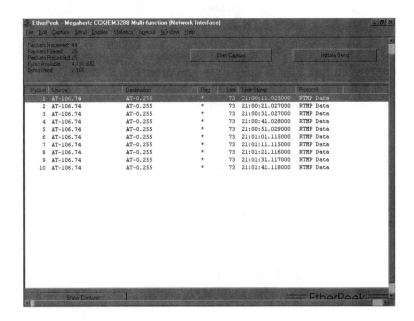

Notice that the timestamps on each of the RTMP updates received from Router A are at equal 10-second intervals—again, just as we expected.

Before we go on, let's take a look at our current router configurations.

Router A

```
RouterA#wr t
Building configuration...

Current configuration:
!
version 11.3
no service password-encryption
!
hostname RouterA
!
enable secret 5 $1$YMNO$Pz1r4tEg1E91wcKrNUIOHO
enable password password
!
appletalk routing
!
interface Ethernet0
 ip address 172.16.10.1 255.255.255.0
 appletalk cable-range 100-110 101.83
 appletalk zone BldgA
 no mop enabled
!
interface Serial0
 ip address 172.16.20.1 255.255.255.0
 no ip mroute-cache
 appletalk cable-range 200-200 200.5
 appletalk zone WAN
!
interface Serial1
 no ip address
 shutdown
!
```

```
router rip
 redistribute connected
 network 172.16.0.0
!
ip classless
!
line con 0
line aux 0
line vty 0 4
 password password2
 login
!
end

RouterA#
```

Router B

```
RouterB#wr t
Building configuration...

Current configuration:
!
version 11.3
no service password-encryption
!
hostname RouterB
!
enable secret 5 $1$hbRx$RuNTv6S.oJYs6L/OEEcey/
enable password password
!
appletalk routing
!
interface Ethernet0
 ip address 172.16.30.1 255.255.255.0
 appletalk cable-range 300-310 304.210
 appletalk zone BldgB
```

```
 no mop enabled
!
interface Serial0
 ip address 172.16.20.2 255.255.255.0
 no ip mroute-cache
 bandwidth 56
 appletalk cable-range 200-200 200.77
 appletalk zone WAN
 clockrate 56000
!
interface Serial1
 ip address 172.16.40.1 255.255.255.0
 bandwidth 56
 appletalk cable-range 400-400 400.79
 appletalk zone WAN
 clockrate 56000
!
router rip
 redistribute connected
 network 172.16.0.0
!
ip classless
!
line con 0
line aux 0
line vty 0 4
 password password2
 login
!
end

RouterB#
```

Router C
```
RouterC#wr t
Building configuration...
```

```
Current configuration:
!
version 11.3
no service password-encryption
!
hostname RouterC
!
enable secret 5 $1$D6/k$SDGQc4haThdggG1I7LOWM1
enable password password
!
appletalk routing
!
interface Ethernet0
 ip address 172.16.50.1 255.255.255.0
 appletalk cable-range 500-510 506.192
 appletalk zone BldgC
!
interface Serial0
 ip address 172.16.40.2 255.255.255.0
 no ip mroute-cache
 appletalk cable-range 400-400 400.216
 appletalk zone WAN
!
interface Serial1
 no ip address
 shutdown
!
router rip
 redistribute connected
 network 172.16.0.0
!
ip classless
!
line con 0
line aux 0
```

```
line vty 0 4
 password password2
 login
!
end


RouterC#
```

Monitoring AppleTalk Traffic

Several useful commands are used to monitor AppleTalk once the interfaces have been configured. As always, remember to use the context-sensitive help when exploring IOS commands.

To verify zone information, we'll use the show appletalk zone command on Router A:

```
RouterA#show appletalk zone
Name                               Network(s)
BldgA                              100-110
BldgB                              300-310
BldgC                              500-510
WAN                                200-200 400-400
Total of 4 zones
RouterA#
```

Notice that all zones are listed by the router along with corresponding network cable-range information.

Next, let's check out the AppleTalk routing table on Router A by using the show appletalk route command:

```
RouterA#show appletalk route
Codes: R - RTMP derived, E - EIGRP derived, C - connected, A
  - AURP
      S - static  P - proxy
5 routes in internet

The first zone listed for each entry is its default
  (primary) zone.
```

```
C Net 100-110 directly connected, Ethernet0, zone BldgA
R Net 300-310 [1/G] via 200.77, 0 sec, Serial0, zone BldgB
R Net 500-510 [2/G] via 200.77, 0 sec, Serial0, zone BldgC
C Net 200-200 directly connected, Serial0, zone WAN
R Net 400-400 [1/G] via 200.77, 0 sec, Serial0, zone WAN
RouterA#
```

Here we have `Net 100-110` and `200-200` directly connected, with the remaining networks accessible via Serial 0. The `R` in the first column indicates that the routes were learned via RTMP.

 RTMP uses hop count as a metric and reports the number of hops to remote networks. For the route to `Net 500-510`, the `[2/G]` indicates that network `500-510` is 2 hops away, as seen in the above output. The maximum number of hops allowed by RTMP is 30.

There are several ways to view AppleTalk interface information. The first is to use the `show appletalk interface brief` command, as follows:

```
RouterA#show appletalk interface brief
Interface   Address     Config       Status/Line Protocol    Atalk Protocol
Ethernet0   101.83      Extended     up                      up
Serial0     200.5       Extended     up                      up
Serial1     unassigned  not config'd administratively down   n/a
RouterA#
```

This command summarizes each interface's AppleTalk configuration on a single line, and it's helpful to get a quick look at all of the router's interfaces. Now, let's use the `show appletalk interface` command to get some more detailed information:

```
RouterA#show appletalk interface
Ethernet0 is up, line protocol is up
  AppleTalk cable range is 100-110
  AppleTalk address is 101.83, Valid
  AppleTalk zone is "BldgA"
  AppleTalk address gleaning is disabled
  AppleTalk route cache is enabled
```

```
Serial0 is up, line protocol is up
  AppleTalk cable range is 200-200
  AppleTalk address is 200.5, Valid
  AppleTalk zone is "WAN"
  AppleTalk port configuration verified by 200.77
  AppleTalk address gleaning is not supported by hardware
  AppleTalk route cache is enabled
Serial1 is administratively down, line protocol is down
  AppleTalk protocol processing disabled
RouterA#
```

We now have more detailed information about each interface, including cable-range and zone information. Let's take a look at the overall AppleTalk configuration using the show appletalk globals command, which summarizes the overall AppleTalk activities of the router:

```
RouterA#show appletalk globals
AppleTalk global information:
  Internet is incompatible with older, AT Phase1, routers.
  There are 5 routes in the internet.
  There are 4 zones defined.
  Logging of significant AppleTalk events is disabled.
  ZIP resends queries every 10 seconds.
  RTMP updates are sent every 10 seconds.
  RTMP entries are considered BAD after 20 seconds.
  RTMP entries are discarded after 60 seconds.
  AARP probe retransmit count: 10, interval: 200 msec.
  AARP request retransmit count: 5, interval: 1000 msec.
  DDP datagrams will be checksummed.
  RTMP datagrams will be strictly checked.
  RTMP routes may not be propagated without zones.
  Routes will not be distributed between routing protocols.
  Routing between local devices on an interface will not be
performed.
  IPTalk uses the udp base port of 768 (Default).
  AppleTalk EIGRP is not enabled.
  Alternate node address format will not be displayed.
  Access control of any networks of a zone hides the zone.
RouterA#
```

AppleTalk Filters

Now that we have had a review of AppleTalk operation, we can discuss how to control it. We had to review *why* AppleTalk nodes communicate the way they do before we could control them. There are two real reasons to control AppleTalk traffic:

- To control access to resources
- To reduce traffic levels

In this section, we will discuss how to control access to (i.e., protect) resources in AppleTalk internetworks. Later, we will look at some traffic reduction strategies, specifically on WAN links.

Access Lists

By now, you should be an expert on access lists, but just in case we need to remind you, they're the tools that we're going to use to control access to AppleTalk resources. AppleTalk access lists all fall in the 600–699 range, and there are no extended or standard versions like there are with IP and IPX—there are just plain old AppleTalk access lists. The same rules that we've been following all along still apply, and the patterns of use are pretty much the same too—create the access list, then apply it to an interface. As you'll see, you can get pretty creative with the application of AppleTalk access lists to interfaces, and as always, online help can walk you through the many options. Here is an example of the range of options available via the online help:

```
RouterC#conf t
Enter configuration commands, one per line.  End with CNTL/Z.
RouterC(config)#access-list 600 permit ?
  <1-65279>         Appletalk network number
  additional-zones  Default filter action for unspecified
     zones
  cable-range       Filter on cable range
  includes          Filter on cable range inclusively
  nbp               Specify nbp filter
  network           Filter an appletalk network
  other-access      Default filter action
  other-nbps        Default filter action for nbp
```

```
        within          Filter on cable range exclusively
        zone            Filter on appletalk zone
RouterC(config)#
```

When working with AppleTalk access lists, much of the magic occurs when the list is applied to an interface. There are many ways to apply a list, and functionality varies greatly depending on which method you use. Let's look at some specific applications and examples.

Zone Filtering

There are two methods of zone filtering, each with its own unique functionality. One method (GZL filtering) is used to control zone information passing between workstations and routers; the other (ZIP reply filtering) controls zone information passing between routers.

GetZoneList Filter

Remember that when a Macintosh user fires up Chooser to locate a remote device, the Mac sends a directed request to a router on its segment with a GZL (GetZoneList) request. The router is supposed to respond with a list of all available zones on the internetwork. If you can control the router's response (which zones the router tells the workstation about), you can control the workstation's access to zones. Here are a few points to keep in mind:

- You cannot control which router a workstation will query on a given segment. Therefore, if you have multiple routers on any segment, you must configure them all to respond identically—i.e., they must have the same GZL filters.

- A very clever user could get around this if they knew the actual AppleTalk address of a device (highly unlikely, but not impossible). This method controls only the GZL response.

- Since this filter affects only the communication between clients and routers, there is no reason to use it on a serial interface, where there cannot be any AppleTalk clients.

Suppose that in our internetwork, we want to prevent users from seeing our WAN zone, where we have been placing all of our serial interfaces. We could proceed as follows:

```
RouterC#config t
Enter configuration commands, one per line.  End with CNTL/Z.
RouterC(config)#access-list 610 deny zone WAN
```

```
RouterC(config)#access-list 610 permit additional-zones
RouterC(config)#int e0
RouterC(config-if)#appletalk getzonelist-filter 610
RouterC(config-if)#^Z
RouterC#
```

Notice that the access list is composed to deny zone WAN and permit any other zone. The trick to make this access list a GZL filter comes when we apply it to an interface. We use the `appletalk getzonelist-filter 610` command on the Ethernet interface. This tells the router that whenever it responds to a GZL request on the Ethernet interface, it must use access list 610 when composing the reply. The end result is that workstations on the Ethernet segment with cable range 500-510 will no longer see zone WAN in their Chooser windows (the first line of access list 610 takes care of this). However, they will be able to see every other zone that the router knows about (the second line of access list 610 does this).

ZIP Reply Filter

`GetZoneList` filters worked between clients and routers; ZIP reply filters work between routers. After all, if we can prevent routers from learning about zones, we don't have to worry about clients serviced by those routers learning about them either.

Make sure that any cable ranges you advertise have at least one zone name advertised with them. Do not use ZIP reply filters on advertised cable ranges that have only one zone name associated with them.

Suppose that we have a small group called Payroll in Building C. We could create a zone for them—it would be associated with cable range 500-510—along with zone BldgC. Suppose that we don't want any other sites to learn about the Payroll zone. We could proceed as follows:

```
RouterC#config t
Enter configuration commands, one per line.  End with CNTL/Z.
RouterC(config)#interface ethernet0
RouterC(config-if)#appletalk zone Payroll
RouterC(config-if)#exit
```

```
RouterC(config)#access-list 611 deny zone Payroll
RouterC(config)#access-list 611 permit additional-zones
RouterC(config)#int s0
RouterC(config-if)#appletalk zip-reply-filter 611
RouterC(config-if)#^Z
RouterC#
```

The first step was to add the Payroll zone to the Ethernet interface. As said, it's perfectly legal to assign two zone names to the same cable segment with Phase 2 addressing. The access list is similar to the one we used in GZL filters. Once again, the trick is in *how* the access list is applied. This time we used the `appletalk zip-reply-filter 611` command on the serial interface. The end result is that Router C will advertise out cable range 500-510, but it won't tell anyone else about the Payroll zone—only the original BldgC zone.

RTMP Filtering

Zone filtering allows us to control zone information; RTMP filtering gives us control over cable-range information. With RTMP filters, we can control the actual AppleTalk cable ranges that we advertise to the outside world.

Suppose that in our network we don't want Router B forwarding information about range 100-110 to Router C. We could use the following technique to achieve our goal:

```
RouterB#config t
Enter configuration commands, one per line.  End with CNTL/Z.
RouterB(config)#access-list 612 deny cable-range 100-110
RouterB(config)#access-list 612 permit other-access
RouterB(config)#access-list 612 permit additional-zones
RouterB(config)#int s1
RouterB(config-if)#appletalk distribute-list 612 out
RouterB(config-if)#^Z
RouterB#
```

This access list is similar to others that we have done. The application to an interface bears some explanation. First, note that when the `distribute-list` command is used, access list 612 will not filter *packets* from cable range 100-110, but will filter *routing updates* about network 100-110. Also, notice here that when applying the access list to the interface, we used a direction. out will filter what a router advertises; in will filter what a router will listen to in routing updates that it hears.

NBP Filtering

We have covered how to control both zone and network address propagation. These tools will cover many situations. However, what if you need more granular control, such as limiting access to a particular file server or printer within a zone? To take this next step and filter access to specific devices within zones, we will introduce NBP filtering. Before we can begin, we need to take another look at how NBP works. In our example earlier in this chapter, we had a workstation requesting file services from the BldgB zone. We captured the following packet:

```
Flags:            0x80   802.3
  Status:         0x00
  Packet Length:64
  Timestamp:      14:44:55.319000 06/18/1998
802.3 Header
  Destination:    00:00:0c:5d:6e:c8
  Source:         08:00:07:7f:62:cf
  LLC Length:     46
802.2 Logical Link Control (LLC) Header
  Dest. SAP:      0xaa   SNAP
  Source SAP:     0xaa   SNAP   Group LLC Sublayer Management Function
  Command:        0x03   Unnumbered Information
  Protocol:       08-00-07-80-9b   ETalkPh2
Long DDP Header - Datagram Delivery Protocol
  Unused:         %00
  Hop Count:      %0000
  Datagram Length: 38
  DDP Checksum:   0x0000
  Dest. Network:  107
  Source Network: 101
  Dest Node:      1
  Source Node:    217
```

```
Dest. Socket:      2  Name Information
Source Socket:     253
DDP Type:          2  NBP
NBP - Name Binding Protocol
  Function:        1  BrRq - Broadcast Request
  Tuple Count:     1
  NBP ID:          6
NBP Tuple # 1
  Node Address:  101.217
  Socket Number:253
  Enumerator:      0
  Object:          =
  Type:            AFPServer
  Zone:            BldgB
Frame Check Sequence:   0x00000000
```

Let's focus on the NBP information here. Notice that this is a broadcast request, and that in the section titled NBP Tuple #1, we are requesting an object, type, and zone. AppleTalk nodes are classified by these three properties:

Object: Refers to the name of the node (= is a wildcard for any object)

Type: Refers to the service the node offers—e.g., AFP Server, LaserWriter, etc. (= is a wildcard for any type)

Zone: Refers to the zone name (* signifies the user's current zone)

Notice in the above packet that we are looking for any objects of type AFP Server in the BldgB zone. Now that we know these three pieces used by NBP to refer to a node (called an *entity name*), we can create some filters to limit responses by any of these fields.

Suppose in our sample internetwork that we don't want AppleTalk users in Buildings A or B to access any resources in Building C other than file services. We could create the following NBP filter to accomplish this:

```
RouterB#config t
Enter configuration commands, one per line.  End with CNTL/Z.
RouterB(config)#access-list 615 permit nbp 1 type AFPServer
RouterB(config)#access-list 615 permit nbp 1 object =
RouterB(config)#access-list 615 permit nbp 1 zone BldgC
```

```
RouterB(config)#access-list 615 permit other-access
RouterB(config)#int s1
RouterB(config-if)#appletalk access-group 615
RouterB(config-if)#^Z
RouterB#
```

The 1 after the nbp command is called a *sequence number*. It ties the type, object, and zone statements together. The permit other-access line is critical—it allows the rest of the DDP traffic to pass. AppleTalk access lists applied to interfaces using the access-group command are applied incoming; therefore, we applied this filter on Router B's S1 interface.

NBP filters are powerful tools, but don't be afraid to play with them. They offer a level of control beyond the capabilities of zone and RTMP filters.

AppleTalk EIGRP

As you know, the EIGRP routing protocol is capable of routing IP, IPX, and AppleTalk, and the real advantage to running AppleTalk EIGRP is seen on WAN links. We've discussed how clients need to hear RTMP updates to find their routers. This means that whenever you have a LAN (unless that LAN contains only routers—perhaps an FDDI interface), you must not disable all RTMP broadcasts, and Macintosh workstations don't understand EIGRP. Generally, bandwidth is more of a concern on a WAN than on a LAN anyway, and this is one area where AppleTalk EIGRP really shines.

Consider our internetwork: We have three buildings, each separated by WAN links. We have five segments—three Ethernet and two serial—and we have to leave RTMP running on the three Ethernet interfaces because there are clients there that need to hear those broadcasts. However, we *can* remove RTMP and install AppleTalk EIGRP in its place on the two remaining serial links. Remember that RTMP is similar to RIP in that it broadcasts everything it knows every 10 seconds. Conversely, AppleTalk EIGRP communicates only when network changes occur, and that saves valuable WAN bandwidth. Below, the configurations for all three routers are listed:

Router A
```
RouterA#config t
```

```
Enter configuration commands, one per line.  End with CNTL/Z.
RouterA(config)#appletalk routing eigrp 200
RouterA(config)#int s0
RouterA(config-if)#appletalk protocol eigrp
RouterA(config-if)#no appletalk protocol rtmp
RouterA(config-if)#^Z
RouterA#
```

Router B

```
RouterB#config t
Enter configuration commands, one per line.  End with CNTL/Z.
RouterB(config)#appletalk routing eigrp 200
RouterB(config)#int s0
RouterB(config-if)#appletalk protocol eigrp
RouterB(config-if)#no appletalk protocol rtmp
RouterB(config-if)#int s1
RouterB(config-if)#appletalk protocol eigrp
RouterB(config-if)#no appletalk protocol rtmp
RouterB(config-if)#^Z
RouterB#
```

Router C

```
RouterC#config t
Enter configuration commands, one per line.  End with CNTL/Z.
RouterC(config)#appletalk routing eigrp 200
RouterC(config)#int s0
RouterC(config-if)#appletalk protocol eigrp
RouterC(config-if)#no appletalk protocol rtmp
RouterC(config-if)#^Z
RouterC#
```

From this point forward, only AppleTalk EIGRP will cross the WAN
links between buildings. Notice that we had to turn off RTMP on each link.
If we had not, both routing protocols would have crossed the serial link,
negating any benefit. Redistribution between RTMP and AppleTalk EIGRP
is automatically enabled when AppleTalk EIGRP is started.

Summary

We began by reviewing AppleTalk operation and looking at a few examples of how AppleTalk nodes communicate. We then discussed four types of filters to control access to AppleTalk devices across our test internetwork. They were as follows:

- GetZoneList filters
- ZIP reply filters
- RTMP filters
- NBP filters

We then looked at how to replace RTMP with AppleTalk EIGRP on our WAN links, reducing the amount of bandwidth used by routing updates.

Review Questions

1. What AppleTalk protocol handles routing?

   A. RTMP

   B. DDP

   C. ZIP

   D. AURP

   E. NCP

2. When configuring AppleTalk, how many zones can you have per cable range?

   A. None

   B. At least one

   C. Many

3. How do AppleTalk clients learn of routers on their segments?

   A. They issue broadcasts

   B. They listen to RTMP updates

   C. Routers always have node address 1

   D. They listen to NBP broadcasts

4. What type of request does an AppleTalk client issue when attempting to get a current list of zones?

   A. GZL broadcast request

   B. GZL directed request

   C. NBP broadcast request

   D. NBP directed request

   E. DDP broadcast request

   F. DDP directed request

5. When you enter the command `appletalk routing` in Global Configuration mode, what process have you started?

A. Router RIP

B. Router EIGRP

C. Router NBP

D. Router RTMP

6. What is the appropriate range for AppleTalk access list numbers?

A. 200–299

B. 400–499

C. 600–699

D. 800–899

7. You have just configured a GZL filter and need to apply it to an interface. Which of the following choices are appropriate?

A. Int e0
`appletalk getzonelist-filter 610`

B. Int s0
`appletalk getzonelist-filter 610`

C. int e0
`appletalk getzonelist filter 610`

D. int s0
`appletalk getzonelist filter 610`

E. int e0
`appletalk get zone list filter 610`

F. int s0
`appletalk get zone list filter 610`

8. Which of the following GZL filters will report all zones other than Marketing to GZL requests?

A. `access-list 690 permit Marketing`
`access-list 690 permit other`

B. `access-list 690 deny Marketing`
`access-list 690 permit additional-zones`

C. `access-list 690 deny zone Marketing`
`access-list 690 permit additional-zones`

D. `access-list 690 deny Marketing`
`access-list 690 permit any-zones`

9. You have just configured a ZIP reply filter and need to apply it to an interface. Which of the following choices are appropriate?

A. `appletalk zip reply filter 611`

B. `appletalk zip-reply filter 611`

C. `appletalk zip-reply-filter 611`

D. `appletalk zip filter 611`

E. `appletalk zip-filter 611`

F. `appletalk access-group 611`

10. When applying ZIP reply filters, to which interfaces should you apply them?

A. LAN

B. Serial

C. Both

11. Suppose that you are configuring your router, and you want it to advertise only zone Engineering out the serial interface. Which of the following lists could you use?

A. `access-list 678 deny Engineering`
   `access-list 678 permit additional-zones`

B. `access-list 678 permit Engineering`

C. `access-list 678 permit Engineering`
   `access-list 678 permit additional-zones`

D. `access-list 678 deny zone not Engineering`

12. How many zone names must you advertise out for each cable segment that you advertise out?

A. None

B. One

C. Two

D. Many

13. You have just configured an RTMP filter and need to apply it to an interface. Your filter will prevent your router from learning of cable ranges in other parts of your internetwork. Which of the following choices is appropriate? (Assume that you are already in Interface Configuration mode.)

A. `appletalk cable-range-filter 610 in`

B. `appletalk cable-range-filter 610 out`

C. `appletalk distribute-list 610 in`

D. `appletalk distribute-list 610 out`

E. `appletalk rtmp-filter 610 in`

F. `appletalk rtmp-filter 610 out`

14. What are the three portions of an entity name?

   A. Name

   B. Type

   C. Tuple

   D. Zone

   E. Object

   F. Cable range

15. Which of the following access list lines would deny all file servers as part of an NBP filter?

   A. `access-list 631 deny nbp object AFPServer`

   B. `access-list 631 deny nbp object =`

   C. `access-list 631 deny nbp zone *`

   D. `access-list 631 deny nbp type =`

   E. `access-list 631 deny nbp type AFPServer`

16. Which of the following filters allows you to control access to individual machines or types of resources?

   A. GZL filters

   B. RTMP filters

   C. NBP filters

   D. ZIP filters

17. Which of the following filters allows you to control advertisement of cable ranges?

   A. GZL filters

   B. RTMP filters

   C. NBP filters

   D. ZIP filters

18. Which of the following filters allows you to control which zones routers learn?

   A. GZL filters

   B. RTMP filters

   C. NBP filters

   D. ZIP filters

19. Suppose that you do the following configuration:

```
router#config t
Enter configuration commands, one per line.  End with
  CNTL/Z.
router(config)#appletalk routing
router(config)#appletalk routing eigrp 250
router(config)#int e0
router(config-if)#appletalk cable-range 1000-1001
router(config-if)#appletalk zone Marketing
router(config-if)#appletalk protocol eigrp
router(config-if)#^Z
router#
```

Which AppleTalk routing protocols are currently running on e0?

   A. RTMP

   B. RIP

   C. AppleTalk EIGRP

   D. NBP

20. What do you have to do to ensure that redistribution happens between RTMP and EIGRP?

- **A.** Use the `appletalk route-redistribution` command

- **B.** Redistribute EIGRP in router RTMP, and redistribute RTMP in router EIGRP

- **C.** Enable AppleTalk EIGRP

- **D.** Nothing

Laboratory Exercises

1. Turn on AppleTalk routing and configure the interfaces on your router to pass AppleTalk traffic.

2. From lab exercise 1, suppose that you do not want your users on Ethernet 0 to see a zone called Engineering learned on the serial interface. You will need to configure a filter to prevent your router from including the Engineering zone in GZL replies.

3. From lab exercise 1, suppose that you do not want your router advertising the Marketing zone out its Serial 0 interface. You will need to create a filter to prevent this zone from being included in your ZIP updates.

4. From lab exercise 1, suppose that the router you connect to out your Serial 0 interface is already configured for AppleTalk EIGRP using AS 250. You need to configure your router to use AppleTalk EIGRP instead of RTMP across the serial interface.

CHAPTER

10

Bridging

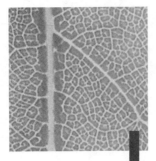

In this chapter, we will introduce and explore bridging. Bridging is fundamentally different from routing in that it operates on a completely different level. We will discuss transparent bridging, then go on to configure integrated routing and bridging (IRB). Finally, we will spend some time on source-route bridging (SRB) and some of its variations.

The CCNP test objectives covered in this chapter are as follows:

- Define routable and nonroutable protocols and give an example of each
- Define various bridging types and describe when to use each type
- Configure transparent bridging
- Configure integrated Routing and Bridging (IRB)
- Describe the basic functions of source-route bridging (SRB)
- Configure SRB
- Configure source-route transparent bridging (SRT)
- Configure source-route translational bridging (SR/TLB)
- Verify SRB operation

Introduction to Bridging

Bridging is a method of connecting individual network segments so that they look like a single LAN. Bridging takes place at layer 2 of the OSI model, as opposed to routing, which takes place at layer 3. See Figure 10.1.

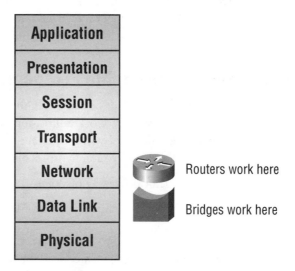

FIGURE 10.1

OSI-model bridge routing

Traffic must be bridged rather than routed for many reasons. For starters, some network protocols cannot be routed and must be bridged. We will take a look at several of those shortly. With Ethernet networks, bridging is a common method of controlling collisions and reducing contention for the media. If you haven't heard of Ethernet switches over the last few years, you must not have been paying attention, because they are everywhere! Well, that flashy Ethernet switch is really nothing more than a multiport bridge (on steroids, of course). Its operation is similar to that of the transparent bridges we will discuss later.

Since bridges operate at layer 2 rather than layer 3 of the OSI model, they don't see all of the protocol-dependent things with which routers have to deal. For example, IP and IPX packets are really indistinguishable to a bridge. IP and IPX are layer 3 specifications, and the bridge really doesn't care about their differences. The bridge simply focuses on the layer 2 frames, and avoids the hassle of looking any further. This simplifies the configuration of bridges, and is one reason why this book can cover bridging in 1 chapter, while routing takes 12 chapters.

Bridging creates a single, extended, data-link network. This is often referred to as a *flat* network. With Cisco IOS, all routable protocols can be bridged. However, don't think that this is an easy shortcut to avoid routing. Bridging creates its own special concerns. For example, bridges will forward broadcasts, while routers will block them, which means that while 1500 workstations will work nicely in a routed network, they may melt the wire with broadcasts alone in a bridged one.

Let's take a quick look at some situations where you have to bridge.

Routable and Non-Routable Protocols

Some protocols cannot be routed. In their specifications, they simply do not provide for layer 3 network addressing. That means they must share a common data-link network (layer 2) to communicate, which calls for bridging. These non-routable protocols are as follows:

- LAT (Local Area Transport)

- MOP (Maintenance Operation Protocol)

- NetBIOS

NetBIOS can be encapsulated in IP or IPX, which makes it routable. However, with the popularity of Microsoft Windows NT (which uses NetBIOS), some networks must be bridged.

With NT, you can configure IP or IPX as the default protocol. However, if you have machines on multiple segments using NetBEUI as the sole communications protocol, you will have to bridge between those segments so that those machines can communicate.

Transparent Bridging

A transparent bridge can connect two or more network segments into a single data-link LAN. It is called a transparent bridge because the devices on the network are unaware that the bridge is even there. The bridge simply listens to frames and passes them along. It does not address, modify, or receive frames. It really is transparent to the devices on the network.

Transparent bridging is generally used with Ethernet. To be transparent to network devices, the bridge performs certain functions:

1. Learning MAC addresses

2. Forwarding packets

3. Filtering packets

These functions allow the bridge to act transparently. Additionally, with multiple bridges, there is the possibility of an endless loop, so the bridge is required to perform a fourth function:

4. Avoiding loops

We will discuss each of these steps in more detail.

Learning MAC Addresses

When you hook a transparent bridge to an Ethernet segment, it will actually receive all frames transmitted on that segment (remember the *MA—Multiple Access* in CSMA/CD). Now, suppose you have the bridge in Figure 10.2.

FIGURE 10.2

Transparent bridge

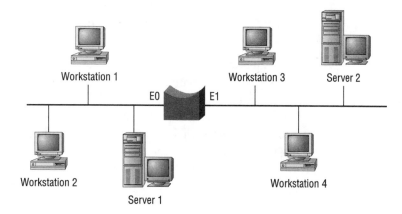

When Workstation 1 is communicating with Server 1, the bridge over-hears all of this traffic on its E0 interface. It quietly notes the source MAC address of each frame received on E0, and enters those into a table as origi-nating from E0. It does the same for all traffic received by its E1 interface. Pretty soon, the bridge will have a fairly comprehensive database of all attached devices (their MAC addresses) out each of its interfaces. The bridge updates the database each time it receives a frame to keep the database cur-rent. If the bridge does not see a frame from a device for some predetermined period of time (typically five minutes), the entry for that device is removed from the database.

In this sense, a transparent bridge can accurately be called a *learning* bridge. By simply listening to traffic, it can quickly learn the location of all network devices on those segments to which it is attached. By continuously updating the database and discarding stale entries, the map of the network remains accurate.

Forwarding Packets

Suppose that in the previous figure (10.2), we have just turned on the bridge, so it has an empty database. It will immediately begin populating its database with MAC addresses from frames that it receives. Now, suppose that the first frame the bridge receives is the one shown in Figure 10.3.

F I G U R E   10.3

WS1➤S1 frame

The bridge now knows that Workstation 1 is out its E0 interface, and makes an appropriate entry into its database. However, it still does not know where Server 1 is. The bridge will *flood* the frame—it will forward the frame out all interfaces except the one on which the frame was received. This is to ensure that no matter where Server 1 is (and the bridge still does not know where Server 1 is), Server 1 will still receive the frame addressed to it. Now, we know from the above diagram that this is not necessary, but the bridge does not know that (yet). However, consider what happens next. Server 1 receives the frame from Workstation 1, and generates a reply as pictured in Figure 10.4.

F I G U R E   10.4

S1➤WS1 frame

The bridge receives this frame on its E0 interface, makes an entry for Server 1 in its database, and now knows that both of these devices are located on the same segment. At this point, the transparent bridge can begin the next step: filtering.

Some frames must always be flooded by the bridge—whenever they are received, they must be forwarded to all interfaces (other than the one on which they were received). They include the following types:

- Frames destined for unknown MAC addresses

- Broadcast frames

- Multicast frames

We will discuss some of the ramifications of this requirement in the "Avoiding Loops" section.

Filtering Packets

Let's continue with our above example. Now that the bridge knows the MAC address of Workstation 1 and Server 1, and knows that they are on the same segment (i.e., out the same bridge interface), it no longer needs to flood packets exchanged between those two machines out its other interfaces.

Suppose that now Workstation 1 sends out a packet to Server 2. If the bridge does not recognize the MAC address of Server 2, it will flood the packet. However (assuming Server 2 is running), it will immediately learn Server 2's location when it responds to Workstation 1's request. From that point forward, the bridge will filter (drop) packets between Workstation 1 and Server 1, because they are on the same segment and do not require the bridge's help to communicate. The bridge will forward frames between Workstation 1 and Server 2, because without the bridge's help, these two devices would not be able to communicate. Finally, if Workstation 2 addresses a frame to an unknown device, the bridge will flood the frame (and hopefully learn the new device's location when it responds).

The bridge has the following three options whenever it receives a frame:

- Filter

- Forward

- Flood

The MAC address database is kept in cache on the bridge to speed up the decision-making process.

Avoiding Loops

Loops can be good or bad. When they work correctly, redundant paths provide fault tolerance for certain failures. However, when loops do not work correctly, they can cause complete network failure. Consider the network shown in Figure 10.5.

FIGURE 10.5

Redundant bridges

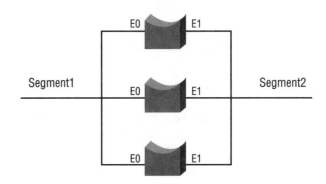

Three bridges connect Segment 1 and Segment 2. All three bridges hear all frames on each segment; all three bridges also build MAC address databases. However, what if all three bridges forward frames? Suppose a frame on Segment 1 is destined for a device on Segment 2, and all three bridges forward the frame. How will the destination device react when it receives three identical frames? It will probably be a bit confused.

There is, however, a worse case. Suppose that a *broadcast* is issued on Segment 1. All three bridges would pick it up and flood it to Segment 2. But now, each bridge hears two broadcasts on Segment 2 (one from each of the other two bridges). They are actually copies of the same broadcast, but since these are transparent bridges, there is no way to know that. So, each bridge floods the two broadcasts it received on Segment 2 back to Segment 1. Now we have 6 frames on Segment 1, which becomes 12 frames on Segment 2, which becomes 24 frames on Segment 1, ... This is called a *broadcast storm*, and it is a real problem with topological loops and bridges. As the above example shows, a single broadcast frame can cause a broadcast storm that will consume all available bandwidth in seconds.

This problem results from the transparent nature of the bridges. Routers tear apart and rebuild packets, and therefore can address issues such as TTL, number of hops, etc. They also handle broadcasts much differently from bridges. However, transparent bridges by definition do not modify packets. They just filter, forward, or flood. Of course, there is a solution.

The Spanning Tree Protocol solves this problem. It allows multiple paths to exist for fault tolerance, yet creates a loop-free topology to reduce the risk of broadcast storms. It does this by turning off (blocking) unnecessary interfaces until they are needed. For example, in our above example, we may end up with the situation illustrated in Figure 10.6.

FIGURE 10.6

Spanning Tree implemented

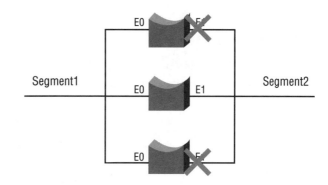

Spanning Tree will turn off (block) the interfaces, which would cause loops, and then re-enable the interfaces when necessary for fault tolerance (in case another active path fails, for example).

Cisco supports two Spanning Tree Protocols for transparent bridging. They are not compatible—they will not communicate with each other. They are as follows:

- DEC
- IEEE 802.1D

The IEEE protocol was actually derived from work done by DEC. Nevertheless, they are not compatible.

Spanning Tree Protocol and bridging are covered in much more depth in *CCNP: CLSC Cisco LAN Switch Configuration Study Guide*, also by Sybex.

Spanning Tree works in the following manner:

- All bridges in the Spanning Tree environment agree on a *root* bridge (we will show you how to control which bridge is the root in the "Configuration Tasks" section).

- Each bridge discovers all possible paths to the root, then selects the lowest-cost path.

- Each bridge blocks all other interfaces to prevent loops.

Configuration Tasks

Configuration of transparent bridging is relatively simple. Suppose we have the scenario shown in Figure 10.7.

FIGURE 10.7

NT network

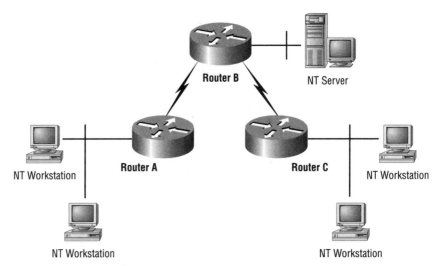

We have Windows NT workstations and servers on different segments. If we are running NetBEUI, we will need to bridge so that these devices can communicate with each other. Here are the configuration steps:

Router A

```
RouterA#config t
Enter configuration commands, one per line.  End with CNTL/Z.
```

```
RouterA(config)#bridge 1 protocol ieee
RouterA(config)#int s0
RouterA(config-if)#bridge-group 1
RouterA(config-if)#int e0
RouterA(config-if)#bridge-group 1
RouterA(config-if)#^Z
RouterA#
```

Router B

```
RouterB#config t
Enter configuration commands, one per line.  End with CNTL/Z.
RouterB(config)#bridge 1 protocol ieee
RouterB(config)#bridge 1 priority 0
RouterB(config)#int s0
RouterB(config-if)#bridge-group 1
RouterB(config-if)#int s1
RouterB(config-if)#bridge-group 1
RouterB(config-if)#int e0
RouterB(config-if)#bridge-group 1
RouterB(config-if)#^Z
RouterB#
```

Router C

```
RouterC#config t
Enter configuration commands, one per line.  End with CNTL/Z.
RouterC(config)#bridge 1 protocol ieee
RouterC(config)#int s0
RouterC(config-if)#bridge-group 1
RouterC(config-if)#int e0
RouterC(config-if)#bridge-group 1
RouterC(config-if)#^Z
RouterC#
```

We started on each router using the bridge 1 protocol ieee command.
The 1 indicates the bridge-group number that we used on each individual
interface. This command is not required. You could omit this command to
disable Spanning Tree Protocol. Notice that on Router B, we also used the
bridge 1 priority 0 command in Global Configuration mode. This sets

the priority by setting the Spanning Tree root to zero on Router B, meaning that it will most likely become the root. You need to do this on only one router per bridge group. This command is also not required unless you wish to influence the root election process. Make sure to select a router near the center of your bridge-group network.

Finally, on each interface, after entering Interface Configuration mode, we used the `bridge-group 1` command to make that interface a member of the bridge group. Any interfaces with this command applied will be part of the same bridged network. At this point, all five segments in our sample network (three Ethernet, two serial) are part of the same flat network. Our NT workstations running NetBEUI will now be able to communicate with the NT server without any problems.

There are significant drawbacks and even dangers to bridging multiple LANs together. Once again, the Sybex *CLSC* book is a source of further information on bridging large environments.

Verification

You can use a few commands to verify operation of your bridge. We will look at two.

```
RouterC#show bridge

Total of 300 station blocks, 298 free
Codes: P - permanent, S - self

Bridge Group 1:

    Address       Action   Interface   Age   RX count   TX count
    0000.0c5d.6ec8  forward  Ethernet0   1     1          0
    0000.0c3e.822a  forward  Ethernet0   4     1          0

RouterC#
```

The show bridge command displays the contents of the database of learned MAC addresses. The Total of 300 station blocks, 298 free refers to the database entries. When the number of free blocks falls below 25, another block of 300 will be issued. The two entries are listed under bridge group 1. Their MAC address, action (discard or forward), interface where they are located, and age are displayed.

```
RouterC#sho span

Bridge Group 1 is executing the IEEE compatible Spanning
  Tree protocol
  Bridge Identifier has priority 32768, address
    0000.0c3e.822a
  Configured hello time 2, max age 20, forward delay 15
  Current root has priority 0, address 0000.0c5d.6ec8
  Root port is 3 (Serial0), cost of root path is 17857
  Topology change flag not set, detected flag not set
  Times:  hold 1, topology change 30, notification 30
          hello 2, max age 20, forward delay 15, aging 300
  Timers: hello 0, topology change 0, notification 0

Port 2 (Ethernet0) of bridge group 1 is forwarding
   Port path cost 100, Port priority 128
   Designated root has priority 0, address 0000.0c5d.6ec8
   Designated bridge has priority 32768, address
     0000.0c3e.822a
   Designated port is 2, path cost 17857
   Timers: message age 0, forward delay 0, hold 1

Port 3 (Serial0) of bridge group 1 is forwarding
   Port path cost 17857, Port priority 128
   Designated root has priority 0, address 0000.0c5d.6ec8
   Designated bridge has priority 0, address 0000.0c5d.6ec8
   Designated port is 3, path cost 0
   Timers: message age 1, forward delay 0, hold 0


RouterC#
```

The show span command displays Spanning Tree information such as the direction to the root and the Spanning Tree Protocol being used. Perhaps most useful is the interface information, showing both ports in Forwarding mode. Other possible statuses for ports include:

- Down
- Listening
- Learning
- Blocking

Before we go on, let's look at an example where Spanning Tree has to turn off an interface (see Figure 10.8).

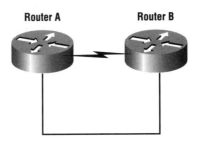

FIGURE 10.8

Spanning Tree shutdown example

If we bridge all ports, we would expect that one would have to be shut down to avoid a loop, right? Let's see if we can find it.

Router A

RouterA#**sho span**

```
Bridge Group 1 is executing the IEEE compatible Spanning
  Tree protocol
  Bridge Identifier has priority 32768, address
    0000.0c3e.822a
  Configured hello time 2, max age 20, forward delay 15
  Current root has priority 0, address 0000.0c5d.6ec8
  Root port is 2 (Ethernet0), cost of root path is 100
  Topology change flag set, detected flag not set
  Times:  hold 1, topology change 30, notification 30
          hello 2, max age 20, forward delay 15, aging 300
  Timers: hello 0, topology change 13, notification 0
```

```
Port 2 (Ethernet0) of bridge group 1 is forwarding
   Port path cost 100, Port priority 128
   Designated root has priority 0, address 0000.0c5d.6ec8
   Designated bridge has priority 0, address 0000.0c5d.6ec8
   Designated port is 2, path cost 0
   Timers: message age 1, forward delay 0, hold 0

Port 3 (Serial0) of bridge group 1 is blocking
   Port path cost 17857, Port priority 128
   Designated root has priority 0, address 0000.0c5d.6ec8
   Designated bridge has priority 0, address 0000.0c5d.6ec8
   Designated port is 3, path cost 0
   Timers: message age 1, forward delay 0, hold 0


RouterA#
```

Router B

```
RouterB#sho span

Bridge Group 1 is executing the IEEE compatible Spanning
   Tree protocol
   Bridge Identifier has priority 0, address 0000.0c5d.6ec8
   Configured hello time 2, max age 20, forward delay 15
   We are the root of the spanning tree
   Topology change flag not set, detected flag not set
   Times:  hold 1, topology change 30, notification 30
           hello 2, max age 20, forward delay 15, aging 300
   Timers: hello 1, topology change 0, notification 0

Port 2 (Ethernet0) of bridge group 1 is forwarding
   Port path cost 100, Port priority 128
   Designated root has priority 0, address 0000.0c5d.6ec8
   Designated bridge has priority 0, address 0000.0c5d.6ec8
   Designated port is 2, path cost 0
   Timers: message age 0, forward delay 0, hold 0
```

```
Port 3 (Serial0) of bridge group 1 is forwarding
  Port path cost 17857, Port priority 128
  Designated root has priority 0, address 0000.0c5d.6ec8
  Designated bridge has priority 0, address 0000.0c5d.6ec8
  Designated port is 3, path cost 0
  Timers: message age 0, forward delay 0, hold 0


RouterB#
```

As expected, one of the ports (Serial 0 on Router A) is blocking.

Integrated Routing and Bridging

Integrated routing and bridging (IRB) is an IOS 11.2 feature that allows you to route *and* bridge the same protocol within a single router. Normally, you cannot have packets cross a single router between routed and bridged interfaces. However, with IRB, you can.

This is accomplished by creating a bridge-group virtual interface (BVI), which represents the bridge group in the routed environment. The interface number of the BVI must correspond to the bridge-group number you wish to include in IRB. The BVI can then be configured, and will act, just like any other routed interface.

This type of configuration can be useful when you have to connect bridged and routed networks, or perhaps when you need to preserve network addresses (such as IP) yet still route those protocols to a larger internetwork.

Consider Figure 10.9. Suppose that we need to bridge from Router A to Router C, but we want to route to the Ethernet interface on Router B. We could then configure IRB on Router B. Here is the configuration:

```
RouterB#conf t
Enter configuration commands, one per line.  End with CNTL/Z.
RouterB(config)#bridge irb
RouterB(config)#interface bvi1
RouterB(config-if)#ip address 171.16.20.2 255.255.255.0
```

```
RouterB(config-if)#exit
RouterB(config)#bridge 1 route ip
RouterB(config)#no bridge 1 bridge ip
RouterB(config)#^Z
RouterB#
```

FIGURE 10.9

IRB example

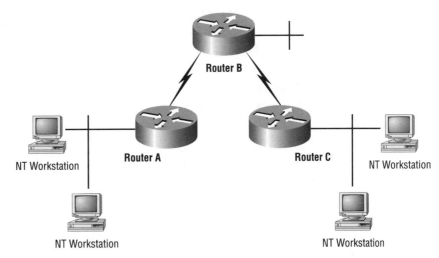

Router B

Router A   **Router C**

NT Workstation   NT Workstation

NT Workstation   NT Workstation

There are several steps to the configuration:

1. Use the `bridge irb` command to enable IRB.

2. Use the `interface bvi1` command to create the BVI with the appropriate bridge-group number.

3. Configure the BVI (we gave it an IP address).

4. Back in Global Configuration mode, enter the `bridge 1 route ip` command. This allows the BVI to accept IP packets from bridge group 1 and route them.

5. Enter the `no bridge 1 bridge ip` command to tell the BVI *not* to bridge IP packets (we already told it to route them). By default, it will bridge them unless we route them.

Here is our final configuration:

RouterB#**show running**

```
<clip>

interface Ethernet0
 ip address 172.16.30.1 255.255.255.0
!
interface Serial0
 no ip address
 bandwidth 56
 clockrate 56000
 bridge-group 1
!
interface Serial1
 no ip address
 bandwidth 56
 clockrate 56000
 bridge-group 1
!
interface BVI1
 ip address 171.16.20.2 255.255.255.0
!
router rip
 network 172.16.0.0
!
no ip classless
bridge irb
bridge 1 protocol ieee
 bridge 1 route ip
 no bridge 1 bridge ip
bridge 1 priority 0
```

We can verify the function of the BVI using the show interface command, and verify the status of bridged and routed protocols in individual interfaces using the show interface int irb command. Output from these commands follows.

```
RouterB#sho int bvi1
BVI1 is up, line protocol is up
  Hardware is BVI, address is 0000.0ced.e620 (bia
    0000.0000.0000)
  Internet address is 171.16.20.2/24
  MTU 1500 bytes, BW 10000 Kbit, DLY 5000 usec, rely 255/
    255, load 1/255
  Encapsulation ARPA, loopback not set, keepalive set (10 sec)
  ARP type: ARPA, ARP Timeout 04:00:00
  Last input never, output never, output hang never
  Last clearing of "show interface" counters never
  Queueing strategy: fifo
  Output queue 0/0, 0 drops; input queue 0/75, 0 drops
  5 minute input rate 0 bits/sec, 0 packets/sec
  5 minute output rate 0 bits/sec, 0 packets/sec
    0 packets input, 0 bytes, 0 no buffer
    Received 0 broadcasts, 0 runts, 0 giants, 0 throttles
    0 input errors, 0 CRC, 0 frame, 0 overrun, 0 ignored, 0
      abort
    0 packets output, 0 bytes, 0 underruns
    0 output errors, 0 collisions, 0 interface resets
    0 output buffer failures, 0 output buffers swapped out
RouterB#sho int s0 irb

Serial0

  Routed protocols on Serial0:
   ip

  Bridged protocols on Serial0:
    appletalk  decnet     ip        ipx

  Software MAC address filter on Serial0
    Hash Len    Address      Matches Act      Type
```

```
      0x00:   0 ffff.ffff.ffff       0 RCV Physical broadcast
      0x2A:   0 0900.2b01.0001       0 RCV DEC spanning tree
      0x2C:   0 0000.0ced.e620       0 RCV Bridge-group Virtual
         Interface
      0xC2:   0 0180.c200.0000       0 RCV IEEE spanning tree
      0xC4:   0 0000.0c5d.6ec8       0 RCV Interface MAC
         address
   RouterB#
```

Source-Route Bridging

IBM created source-route bridging (SRB) in the mid-1980s to connect corporate Token Rings to their IBM mainframes. With SRB, the source knows the entire route to a destination before any data are transmitted. It is called source-route bridging because the source device gets to choose the entire route to the destination device. SRB is part of the IEEE 802.5 Token Ring specification.

SRB was not designed for large internetworks. The specifications for IBM Token Ring define a maximum of 8 rings and 7 bridges. 802.5 defines up to 14 rings and 13 bridges.

Types of Explorer Packets

A source device determines the best path to a destination device by sending explorer packets. There are three types of explorer packets:

Local explorer packets Used to find local destination devices.

Spanning explorer packets Used to find the best route to the final destination.

All-routes explorer packets Used to find all routes to a destination host by checking all rings.

All-routes explorer packets are also known as all-rings explorer packets, and spanning explorer packets are also known as single-route and limited-route explorer packets.

Here is how the three types of explorer packets work together to find a route to a destination device:

- A NetBIOS or SNA device generates a local explorer packet to determine if the destination device is connected to the local ring.

- If the destination device is not located on the local ring, the transmitting device sends either a spanning or an all-routes explorer packet. (A NetBIOS device sends a spanning explorer packet, while the SNA device sends an all-routes explorer packet.)

- The destination device responds to the explorer packets, which then return to the originating device. By examining the RIF (route information field), the source can determine the route to take to the destination.

From that point forward, the source will determine the path, hence the name source-route bridging.

Configuring Cisco SRB

Consider the router shown in Figure 10.10.

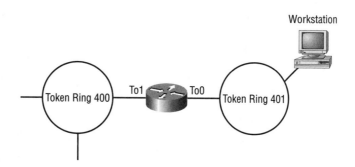

In this situation, we can use a manual Spanning Tree configuration. Here is the configuration example:

```
RouterB#conf t
Enter configuration commands, one per line.  End with CNTL/Z.
RouterB(config)#interface to0
RouterB(config-if)#source-bridge 401 5 400
```

```
RouterB(config-if)#source-bridge spanning
RouterB(config-if)#interface to1
RouterB(config-if)#source-bridge 400 5 401
RouterB(config-if)#source-bridge spanning
RouterB(config-if)#^Z
RouterB#
```

We use the `source-bridge 401 5 400` command on interface To0 to indicate that the local ring is 401, the target ring is 400, and the bridge number is 5. We do the inverse on interface To1. The `source-bridge spanning` command indicates that we are using a manual Spanning Tree configuration. To enable automatic Spanning Tree configuration, we would proceed as follows:

```
RouterB#conf t
Enter configuration commands, one per line.  End with CNTL/Z.
RouterB(config)#bridge 10 protocol ibm
RouterB(config)#interface to0
RouterB(config-if)#source-bridge 401 5 400
RouterB(config-if)#source-bridge spanning 10
RouterB(config-if)#interface to1
RouterB(config-if)#source-bridge 400 5 401
RouterB(config-if)#source-bridge spanning 10
RouterB(config-if)#^Z
RouterB#
```

Source-Route Transparent Bridging

Source-route transparent bridging (SRT) was introduced by IBM in 1990. In SRT, both SRB and transparent bridging occur within the same device. You can use SRT on Token Ring networks where some devices are doing SRB, but some are not. SRT does not translate between two bridging domains—the SRB and transparent bridging systems do not communicate via the SRT. If the traffic arrives with SRB routing information, SRB is used. If not, transparent bridging is used. Token Ring to Ethernet communication is not provided by SRT.

Configuration is simply a marriage of transparent bridging and SRB. Using our earlier example, to implement SRT instead of SRB, we simply do as follows:

```
RouterB#conf t
Enter configuration commands, one per line.  End with CNTL/Z.
```

```
RouterB(config)#bridge 1 protocol ieee
RouterB(config)#interface to0
RouterB(config-if)#source-bridge 401 5 400
RouterB(config-if)#source-bridge spanning
RouterB(config-if)#bridge-group 1
RouterB(config-if)#interface to1
RouterB(config-if)#source-bridge 400 5 401
RouterB(config-if)#source-bridge spanning
RouterB(config-if)#bridge-group 1
RouterB(config-if)#^Z
RouterB#
```

Notice that as mentioned, this is simply the combination of transparent bridging and SRB commands.

Source-Route Translational Bridging

Source-route translational bridging (SR/TLB) is used when bridging domains must be crossed. With SRT, it was possible to do both SRB and transparent bridging. With SR/TLB, SRB and transparent bridging domains can now communicate. With SRT, communication from Ethernet to Token Ring was not supported. With SR/TLB, that issue can be addressed. SRB generally runs on a Token Ring network, while transparent bridging is generally associated with Ethernet. We should point out that SR/TLB is a Cisco IOS feature, and is not an industry standard.

WARNING The spanning tree packets used to prevent loops in transparent bridging environments will *not* cross SRB environments. It is crucial that no redundant paths are configured between the two domains, because spanning tree will not be able to detect and thus disable them.

When bridging between Ethernet and Token Ring, a number of issues must be addressed:

- MTU size
- Lack of support for RIF in Ethernet frames
- Different systems for MAC addresses

There are significant technical challenges when bridging between dissimilar media. Cisco has documented problems with bridging Novell IPX, DECnet Phase IV, AppleTalk, VINES, XNS, and IP from Token Ring to other media, and recommends that these protocols be routed rather than bridged whenever possible.

To configure SR/TLB, you must first configure multiport SRB and transparent bridging as described earlier in this chapter. Then, you use the `source-bridge ring-group` command to configure a virtual ring, to which all SRB interfaces bridge. Finally, you use the `source-bridge transparent` command to enable bridging between the two environments. Syntax for this command is as follows:

```
Source-bridge transparent [ring-group] [psuedo-ring]
    [bridge-number] [tb-group] [oui]
```

- `ring-group` is the virtual ring created by the `source-bridge ring-group` command.

- `pseudo-ring` is the ring number by which the transparent bridging domain will be known to the SRB domain.

- `bridge-number` is the SRB number of the router.

- `tb-group` is the number of the translational bridge group.

- `oui` is the organizational unit identifier. This optional parameter can be set to 90-compatible, Cisco, or standard.

Continuing with our above example, we would have the following configuration:

```
RouterB#conf t
Enter configuration commands, one per line.  End with CNTL/Z.
RouterB(config)#bridge 1 protocol ieee
RouterB(config)#source-bridge ring-group 450
RouterB(config)#source-bridge transparent 450 451 5 1
RouterB(config)#interface to0
RouterB(config-if)#source-bridge 401 5 450
RouterB(config-if)#source-bridge spanning
RouterB(config-if)#interface e0
RouterB(config-if)#bridge-group 1
```

```
RouterB(config-if)#^Z
RouterB#
```

At this point, the SRB environment out interface To0 will see the entire bridge group 1 as ring 451.

Verification

You can use several commands to verify operation of SRB. As always, `show interface` commands are useful to display interface operations. There are also several other helpful `show` commands:

- `show rif`
- `show source-bridge`

Below, the output of the `show rif` command is shown:

```
RouterB#show rif
Codes: * interface, - static, + remote
Hardware Addr   How   Idle (min)   Routing Information Field

RouterB#
```

As you can see, this command will display four pieces of information about each RIF entry:

- `Hardware Addr` is the hardware address.
- `How` indicates how the information was learned, via either a specific interface or RG (ring group).
- `Idle` is the amount of time since this node was last heard from.
- `Routing Information Field` is the contents of the RIF.

Summary

In this chapter:

- We began with an overview of bridging and its associated problems and solutions.

- We developed the idea of a transparent bridge, and reviewed how it learned of devices, made decisions about what to do with different types of frames, and avoided topological loops using Spanning Tree.

- We reviewed the configuration of both transparent bridging and integrated routing and bridging (IRB).

- Finally, we introduced source-route bridging (SRB) and spent a few pages describing its functionality, and then viewed configurations of SRB, source-route transparent bridging (SRT), and source-route translational bridging (SR/TLB).

Review Questions

1. Bridges work at which layer of the OSI model?

   A. 1

   B. 2

   C. 3

   D. 4

2. Routers work at which layer of the OSI model?

   A. 1

   B. 2

   C. 3

   D. 4

3. Which of the following are routable protocols?

   A. IPX

   B. NetBIOS

   C. MOP

   D. AppleTalk

   E. LAT

   F. TCP/IP

4. Transparent bridges operate differently on which of the following layer 3 protocols?

   A. IPX

   B. DDP (AppleTalk)

   C. IP

   D. None of the above

5. Which of the following are functions of a transparent bridge?

   A. Avoiding loops

   B. Filtering packets

   C. Forwarding packets

   D. Learning MAC addresses

   E. All of the above

6. Which of the following are legal Spanning Tree types on Cisco routers?

   A. CCITT

   B. IEEE

   C. ARPA

   D. DEC

   E. IPX

7. When configuring bridging, which command must be entered before interfaces can be configured?

   A. `bridge 1 protocol ieee`

   B. `bridge-group 1 protocol ieee`

   C. `bridge 1 protocol dec`

   D. `bridge-group 1 protocol dec`

8. Suppose that you have already enabled bridging, and you want this router to be the root of the spanning tree. Which command would you use?

   A. `bridge 1 priority 0`

   B. `bridge 1 priority 32768`

   C. `bridge 1 priority high`

   D. `bridge 1 priority top`

9. Which of the following commands will configure an interface to be part of bridge group 1? (Assume you are already in Interface Configuration mode.)

A. `bridge group 1`

B. `bridge group 1 protocol ieee`

C. `bridge-group 1`

D. `bridge-group 1 protocol ieee`

E. `bridge group 1 priority 32768`

10. Suppose you have a loop in your network topology. Which of the following describes what the Spanning Tree Protocol will do?

A. Locate a point of redundancy, then load balance

B. Locate a point of redundancy, then disable the interface until it is needed

C. Locate a point of redundancy, then permanently disable the interface

D. Locate a point of redundancy, then block all packets with expired TTLs

11. Suppose you have a loop in your network topology. Which of the following commands is the best way to verify what Spanning Tree did in question 10?

A. `show spanning-tree`

B. `show interface`

C. `show irb`

D. `show bridge`

12. Which of the following can be possible statuses of a bridge interface?

    A. Down

    B. Disabled

    C. Listening

    D. Flooding

    E. Spanning

    F. Learning

    G. Blocking

    H. Forwarding

13. In which of the following situations would you use IRB?

    A. When layer 3 network addresses are scarce

    B. When serial interfaces are necessary

    C. When more than one protocol must be bridged

    D. When routed and bridged networks of the same layer 3 protocol are merged

14. Which of the following commands is required to enable IRB?

    A. `bridge irb`

    B. `bridge irb protocol ip`

    C. `bridge-group 1 irb`

    D. `bridge irb 1`

15. Which of the following describes how routed and bridged interfaces communicate when using IRB?

    A. Via bridge group 1

    B. Via routing protocols

    C. Via BVIs

    D. Via Ethernet switches

16. In which of the following ways does SRB locate routes to destinations?

   A. Discoverer

   B. Explorer

   C. Voyager

   D. Flood

17. Which IEEE standard defines Token Ring?

   A. 802.1

   B. 802.1D

   C. 802.3

   D. 802.5

18. Which of the following commands will set up bridge 15 between local ring 50 and target ring 51?

   A. `source-bridge 50 15 51`

   B. `source-bridge 51 15 50`

   C. `source-bridge 50 51 15`

   D. `source-bridge 15 50 51`

19. Which commands are used only for SRT—not in other bridging configurations?

   A. `bridge srt`

   B. `bridge map srb transparent`

   C. `bridge-group srt`

   D. None of the above

20. Which of the following can be addressed only with SR/TLB?

   A. IP to SNA communication

   B. IPX to SNA communication

   C. Transparent bridging

   D. Ethernet to Token Ring bridging

Laboratory Exercises

1. Enable transparent bridging.

2. Enable IRB. (This lab continues from lab exercise 1.)

CHAPTER

11

WAN Scalability

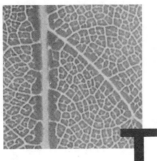

This chapter's focus is the strategies for scaling WANs with Cisco routers. The packet switching protocols covered in this chapter include Frame Relay, X.25, SMDS, and ATM.

We will cover the basic WAN connection considerations and talk about the different Cisco connection services. We'll then cover the details of configuring and monitoring the Cisco packet switched networks.

The CCNP test objectives covered in this chapter are as follows:

- Compare the differences between WAN connection types: dedicated, asynchronous dial-in, dial-on-demand, and packet switched services

- List at least four common issues to be considered when evaluating WAN services

WAN Scalability

LANs are defined as a network that is restricted to a floor or building. LAN users often rely on asynchronous connections to access the remote services available outside the confines of their local LAN.

However, as organizations evolve and expand, they're often faced with the need to make their networks efficiently support WAN services to the Internet and remote divisions at LAN-type speeds. Achieving that is simply beyond the capabilities of asynchronous connections.

Because it just isn't always feasible for an organization to create its very own private, dedicated WAN connection, alternative approaches to forging connections across public networks have been sought and expansively developed.

Connection Considerations

When a company grows, it's imperative that its internetwork grows with it. The network's administrator must not only understand the various user-group differences regarding their specialized needs for the mélange of LAN and WAN resources, they must find a way to meet—or better yet—exceed these requirements, while planning for growth as well. Below, we've listed important factors to consider when defining and researching business requirements for the purposes of internetwork design or refinement.

Availability Because networks are so heavily relied upon—they're ideally up and running 24 hours a day, 365 days a year—failures and downtime must be minimized. It's also vital that when a failure does occur, it's easy to isolate so that the time needed to troubleshoot the problem is reduced.

Bandwidth Accurately determining the actual and eventual bandwidth requirements with information gathered from both users and management is crucial. It can be advantageous to contract with a service provider to establish connectivity between remote sites. Bandwidth considerations are also an important element for the next consideration—cost.

Cost In a perfect world, we could just install nothing but Cisco Catalyst 5000 series switches that provide switched 100Mbps to each desktop with gigabit speeds between data closets and remote offices. However, since the world's not perfect, and often budget constraints simply won't allow for doing that, Cisco offers an abundance of switches and routers tailored to many wallet sizes. This is one very big reason why it's so important to accurately assess actual needs. A budget must be carefully delimited when designing an internetwork.

Ease of management The ramifications such as the degree of difficulty associated with creating any network connections must be understood and regarded carefully. Factors associated with configuration management include analyses of both the initial configuration and the ongoing configuration tasks related to running and maintaining the entire internetwork. Traffic management issues—the ability to adjust to different traffic rates, especially in bursty networks—also apply here.

Type of application traffic This can be typically comprised of small to very large packets, and the internetwork design must reflect and regard the typical traffic type to meet business requirements.

Routing protocols The characteristics of these protocols can cause some ugly problems and steal a lot of precious bandwidth in networks where they're either not understood or not configured properly.

Cisco Connection Services

Cisco supports many different types of services, providing ample flexibility and many options for meeting internetworking business requirements. These services include:

- Dedicated leased lines
- Dial-in modems
- Dial-up connections using Cisco routers (DDR)
- Packet switched services

Dedicated

Point-to-point serial links are dedicated links that provide full-time connectivity. Cisco router serial ports are used to gain access at a rate of up to 45Mbps. They connect into a channel service unit/data service unit (CSU/DSU), which then plugs into the demarc provided by the telephone company.

Figure 11.1 shows how point-to-point connections can be made between remote offices and the corporate office.

FIGURE 11.1

Point-to-point connections between branches and the corporate office

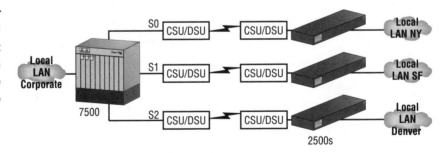

If the established business requirements dictate that constant connection and steady data flow must prevail, a dedicated point-to-point connection can be an optimal solution—but even so, this approach does have a disadvantage associated with it. Point-to-point connections require paying tariffs for them even when the connection is in an idle state with no data being transmitted.

Asynchronous Dial-In

Any user with an asynchronous modem can make connections to an internetwork using the public switched telephone network (PSTN), and there are many common situations requiring this type of access. Users who are traveling can dial in to gather e-mails or update a database, while others may want to dial in from home to finish projects, send and retrieve e-mails, and even print documents to be available for them when they arrive at work the next day.

Cisco answers this need by providing a variety of asynchronous dial-in products such as the AS5200 access server. This device provides up to 48 asynchronous modems for both dial-in and dial-out services, and it runs the Cisco IOS, so it can also perform routing, authentication, and security-related tasks. If demands don't dictate the need for that many ports, there are Cisco products that offer a lower port density.

Dial-on-Demand Routing

DDR (dial-on-demand routing) allows wide area links to be used selectively. With it, the administrator can define "interesting" traffic on the router, and initiate WAN links based upon that traffic. Access lists define interesting traffic, so there's a great deal of flexibility given to the administrator. For instance, an expensive ISDN connection to the Internet could be initiated to retrieve e-mail, but not for a WWW request. DDR is an effective tool in situations where WAN access is charged in some time interval, and it's best to use it in situations where WAN access is infrequent.

Dial-on-demand routing provides the missing software ingredient for creating a fully functional backup system. Versatile DDR can be used over several different types of connections, and is supported in Cisco IOS version 9 and later. It supports the following networking protocols: IP, IPX, AppleTalk, and others. DDR's flexibility reaches even further. It can be used over several different types of interfaces—synchronous and asynchronous serial interfaces, as well as ISDN.

Packet Switched Services

Packet switched services are usually run over a publicly maintained network, such as the public switched telephone network, but if necessary, a large organization can build a private packet switched network (PSN).

PSN data delivery can take place within frames, packets, or cells, and occurs transparently to end users.

Frame Relay, X.25, SMDS, and ATM are some of the topologies that employ packet switching technology—they'll be discussed next.

Packet Switched Networks

As we said, PSNs can be either private or public networks. Switching devices forward packets using an internal addressing scheme, which can be entirely different from what's used on the LAN. This is because a switch that's located at the WAN provider's office will typically check the address field of the packets only, and then carry out the forwarding based upon the static routes configured by an administrator.

An administrator must understand how switching protocols operate to customize the internetwork according to the specific characteristics of the switched network. For example, Frame Relay will perform a CRC only at the Data Link layer of the frame, so if the application you need to run on the WAN doesn't support upper-layer error checking, Frame Relay may not be the best solution for you. Because X.25 supports more extensive error checking, that would be a better choice.

The most popular switching protocols are as follows:

- Frame Relay
- X.25
- SMDS/ATM

Frame Relay

Recently, the high-performance WAN encapsulation method known as Frame Relay has become one of the most popular technologies in use. It operates at the Physical and Data Link layers of the OSI reference model, and was originally designed for use across Integrated Services Digital Network (ISDN) interfaces. But today, Frame Relay is used over a variety of other network interfaces.

Cisco Frame Relay supports the following protocols:

- IP
- DECnet

- AppleTalk

- Xerox Network Service (XNS)

- Novell IPX

- Connectionless Network Service (CLNS)

- International Organization for Standards (ISO)

- Banyan Vines

- Transparent bridging

Frame Relay provides a communications interface between DTE (data terminal equipment) and DCE (data circuit-terminating equipment—such as packet switches) devices. DTE consists of terminals, PCs, routers, and bridges—customer-owned end node and internetworking devices. DCE consists of carrier-owned internetworking devices.

Popular opinion maintains that Frame Relay is more efficient and faster than X.25 because it assumes error checking will be done through higher-layer protocols and application services.

Frame Relay provides connection-oriented, Data Link layer communication via virtual circuits just as X.25 does. These virtual circuits are logical connections created between two DTEs across a packet switched network, which is identified by a DLCI. (We'll get to DLCIs in a bit.) Also, like X.25, Frame Relay uses both PVCs and SVCs, although most Frame Relay networks use PVCs.

Frame Relay with Cisco Routers

When configuring Frame Relay on Cisco routers, you need to specify it as an encapsulation on serial interfaces. There are only two encapsulation types: Cisco and IETF (Internet engineering task force). The following router output shows the two different encapsulation methods when choosing Frame Relay on your Cisco router:

```
RouterA(config)#int s0
RouterA(config-if)#encapsulation frame-relay ?
  ietf  Use RFC1490 encapsulation
  <cr>
```

The default encapsulation is Cisco unless you manually type in IETF, and Cisco is the type used when connecting two Cisco devices. You'd opt for the IETF-type encapsulation if you needed to connect a Cisco device to a non-Cisco device with Frame Relay. So before choosing an encapsulation type, check with your ISP and find out which one they use. (If they don't know, hook up with a different ISP!)

Data Link Connection Identifiers

Frame Relay virtual circuits are identified by data link connection identifiers (DLCIs). A Frame Relay service provider, such as the telephone company, typically assigns DLCI values, which are used by Frame Relay to distinguish between different virtual circuits on the network. Since many virtual circuits can be terminated on one multipoint Frame Relay interface, many DLCIs are often affiliated with it.

For the IP devices at each end of a virtual circuit to communicate, their IP addresses need to be mapped to DLCIs. This mapping can function as a multipoint device—one that can identify to the Frame Relay network the appropriate destination virtual circuit for each packet that is sent over the single physical interface.

Frame Relay uses DLCIs the same way that X.25 uses X.121 addresses, and every DLCI number can be given either global or local meaning everywhere within the Frame Relay network. However, the customary implementation is to give each DLCI local meaning. What does this do? It makes two DTE devices connected via a virtual circuit use different DLCI values when referring to the same connection.

Configuring a DLCI number to be applied to an interface is shown below:

```
RouterA(config-if)#frame-relay interface-dlci ?
  <16-1007> Define a DLCI as part of the current
  subinterface
RouterA(config-if)#frame-relay interface-dlci 16
```

Prioritizing DLCI Traffic   To control which path traffic will take through a Frame Relay cloud, you can configure virtual circuits that match parameters within a priority queue list. These queues can then be matched to a specific DLCI, providing a traffic management tool to minimize congestion problems with slower links. This can be really helpful if your network commonly sustains traffic from sources with high-speed access that's queued at destination sites with lower-speed access, and can be achieved by applying priority levels to the DLCI.

The steps to configure DLCI priority levels are as follows:

1. Define a global priority list.

2. Enable Frame Relay on the serial interface.

3. Define either inverse ARP or static mappings.

4. Configure the LMI.

DLCI priority levels provide a way to define multiple DLCIs and associate each with different types of traffic. However, don't confuse DLCI priorities with router priority queues.

You can enable queuing and then use the same DLCIs for queuing by placing the higher-priority DLCIs into the high-priority queues.

To assign protocol traffic to match the specified parameters of a priority queue, you use the priority-list protocol command:

```
Router(config)#priority-list ?
  <1-16>  Priority list number

Router(config)#priority-list 1 ?
  default     Set priority queue for unspecified datagrams
  interface   Establish priorities for packets from a named
                interface
  protocol    Priority queueing by protocol
  queue-limit Set queue limits for priority queues

Router(config)#priority-list 1 protocol ?
  aarp             AppleTalk ARP
  appletalk        AppleTalk
  arp              IP ARP
  bridge           Bridging
  bstun            Block Serial Tunnel
  cdp              Cisco Discovery Protocol
  compressedtcp    Compressed TCP
  decnet           DECnet
  decnet_node      DECnet Node
  decnet_router-l1 DECnet Router L1
```

```
        decnet_router-12   DECnet Router L2
        decnet_router-12   DECnet Router L2
        ip                 IP
        ipx                Novell IPX
        llc2               llc2
        pad                PAD links
        rsrb               Remote Source-Route Bridging
        snapshot           Snapshot routing support
        stun               Serial Tunnel

Router(config)#priority-list 1 protocol ip ?
  high
  medium
  normal
  low


Router(config)#priority-list 1 protocol ip high ?
  fragments  Prioritize fragmented IP packets
  gt         Prioritize packets greater than a specified
               size
  list       To specify an access list
  lt         Prioritize packets less than a specified size
  tcp        Prioritize TCP packets 'to' or 'from' the
               specified port
  udp        Prioritize UDP packets 'to' or 'from' the
               specified port
  <cr>
Router(config)#priority-list 1 protocol ip high gt ?
  <0-65535>  Packet size (include MAC encapsulation bytes)
```

The list below provides an explanation of the router output listed above.

- The priority list number represents the number of the priority list—a value between 1 and 16.

- The protocol name represents the name of the protocol being specified.

- The priority level represents the name of the queue—high, medium, normal, or low.

- The equality (gt) represents the conditional value.
- The byte count represents the number of bytes within the packet, including the frame header.

To establish the DLCIs for use by each of the four individual priority queues that apply the specified priority list to an interface, you use the frame relay priority-dlci-group command:

```
Router(config-if)#frame priority-dlci-group ?
  <1-16>  Assign priority group

Router(config-if)#frame priority-dlci-group 1 ?
  <16-1007>  DLCI for high priority

Router(config-if)#frame priority-dlci-group 1 16 ?
  <16-1007>  DLCI for medium priority
  <cr>

Router(config-if)#frame priority-dlci-group 1 16 17 ?
  <16-1007>  DLCI for normal priority
  <cr>

Router(config-if)#frame priority-dlci-group 1 16 17 18 ?
  <16-1007>  DLCI for low priority
  <cr>
```

The list below explains the meaning of the router output above.

- The priority group number represents the number of the priority that's applied to the interface, between 1 and 16.
- The high DLCI represents the DLCI number that's assigned to the high queue.
- The medium DLCI represents the DLCI number that's assigned to the medium queue.
- The normal DLCI represents the DLCI number that's assigned to the normal queue.
- The low DLCI represents the DLCI number that's assigned to the low queue.

If a DLCI value isn't configured for a queue, the last assigned DLCI value used will be propagated to complete the syntax by default.

Setting Access Lists with Priorities   If you want to define an access list to use a high-priority queue, use the `list` parameter as shown in the following example:

```
Router(config)#priority-list 1 protocol ip high ?
  fragments  Prioritize fragmented IP packets
  gt         Prioritize packets greater than a specified
             size
  list       To specify an access list
  lt         Prioritize packets less than a specified size
  tcp        Prioritize TCP packets 'to' or 'from' the
             specified port
  udp        Prioritize UDP packets 'to' or 'from' the
             specified port
  <cr>

Router(config)#priority-list 1 protocol ip high list ?
  <1-199>  IP access list

Router(config)#priority-list 1 protocol ip high list 10 ?
  <cr>
```

You can choose any access list between 1 and 199, which covers IP standard and IP extended access lists.

Local Management Interface (LMI)

The LMI (Local Management Interface) was developed in 1990 by Cisco Systems, StrataCom, Northern Telecom, and Digital Equipment Corporation, and became known as the Gang-of-Four LMI or Cisco LMI. This gang took the basic Frame Relay protocol from the CCIT and added extensions onto the protocol features that allow internetworking devices to communicate easily with a Frame Relay network.

LMI messages provide information about the current DLCI values, whether their significance is global or local, and they report the status of virtual circuits.

Beginning with IOS version 11.2, the LMI type is autosensed. This enables the interface to determine the LMI type supported by the switch.

To configure the LMI type, you need to do as follows:

- Set the LMI type.

- Set the LMI keepalive interval.

- Set the LMI polling and timer intervals (not required).

If you're not going to use the autosense feature, you'll need to check with your Frame Relay provider to find out which type to use instead. The default type is Cisco, but you may need to change to ANSI or Q.933A. The three different LMI types are depicted in the router output below.

```
RouterA(config-if)#frame-relay lmi-type ?
  cisco
  ansi
  q933a
```

As seen in the output, all three standard LMI signaling formats are supported:

Cisco LMI defined by the gang of four (default)

ANSI Annex D defined by ANSI standard T1.617

ITU-T (q933a) Annex A defined by Q.933

To establish the interval at which your router will send keepalive messages, use the `frame-relay keepalive` command. The default period is every 10 seconds, but be aware that this value must be set to less than that of the corresponding interval on the switch.

```
Router(config-if)#keepalive ?
  <0-32767>  Keepalive period (default 10 seconds)
  <cr>
```

The 10-second default interval can also be seen by using the `sh int` command:

```
Router#sh int s0
Serial0 is administratively down, line protocol is down
  Hardware is HD64570
  MTU 1500 bytes, BW 1544 Kbit, DLY 20000 usec, rely
    255/255, load 1/255
  Encapsulation FRAME-RELAY, loopback not set, keepalive set
    (10 sec)
```

```
LMI enq sent  0, LMI stat recvd 0, LMI upd recvd 0, DTE
  LMI down
LMI enq recvd 0, LMI stat sent  0, LMI upd sent  0
LMI DLCI 1023  LMI type is CISCO  frame relay DTE
```

 The above output was edited for brevity.

You can set the LMI polling and timer intervals by using the `frame-relay lmi-n39x` command. This specifies the interval between full status requests made to the Frame Relay switch from your router.

```
Router(config-if)#frame-relay lmi?
lmi-n391dte  lmi-n392dce  lmi-n392dte  lmi-n393dce  lmi-n393dte
lmi-t392dce  lmi-type
```

The list below describes the different LMI polling and timer commands.

- The `lmi-n391dte` sets a full status polling interval on a DTE interface or NNI (Network-to-Network Interface).

- The `lmi-n392dce` sets the DCE and NNI error threshold.

- The `lmi-n392dte` sets the DTE and NNI error threshold.

- The `lmi-n393dce` sets the DCE and NNI monitored events count.

- The `lmi-n393dte` sets the DTE and NNI monitored events count.

- The `lmi-t392dce` sets the polling verification timer on a DCE interface or NNI.

Subinterfaces

You can have multiple virtual circuits on a single serial interface and yet treat each as a separate interface. These are known as *subinterfaces*. Think of a subinterface as a hardware interface defined by the IOS software.

An advantage gained through using subinterfaces is the ability to assign different network layer characteristics to each subinterface and virtual circuit, such as IP routing on one virtual circuit and IPX on another. Figure 11.2 shows how a single physical interface simulates multiple logical interfaces.

FIGURE 11.2

Subinterfaces
representing several
logical interfaces

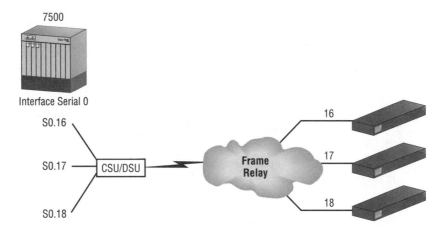

You define subinterfaces with the int s0.*subinterface number* command as shown below.

```
RouterA(config)#int s0.?
  <0-4294967295>  Serial interface number
RouterA(config)#int s0.16 ?
  multipoint      Treat as a multipoint link
  point-to-point  Treat as a point-to-point link
```

You can define a limitless number of subinterfaces on a given physical interface (keeping router memory in mind). In the above example, we chose to use subinterface 16 because that represents the DLCI number assigned to that interface. However, you can choose any number between 0 and 4,292,967,295.

There are two types of subinterfaces:

Point-to-point Used when a single virtual circuit connects one router to another

Multipoint Used when the router is the center of a star of virtual circuits

An example of a production router running multiple subinterfaces is shown below, and corresponds to Figure 11.3. Notice that the subinterface number matches the DLCI number. Also notice that there is no LMI type defined, which means they're running in autosense mode.

F I G U R E 11.3

Subinterface example

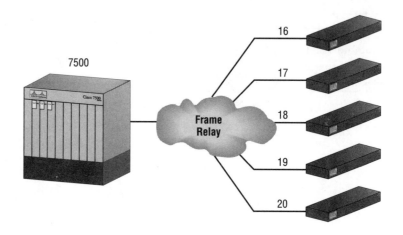

```
interface Serial0.16 point-to-point
ip address 192.168.2.22 255.255.255.252
 ipx network 101
 frame-relay interface-dlci 16
!
interface Serial0.17 point-to-point
ip address 192.168.2.101 255.255.255.252
 ipx network 102
 frame-relay interface-dlci 17
!
interface Serial0.18 point-to-point
ip address 192.168.2.113 255.255.255.252
 ipx network 103
 frame-relay interface-dlci 18
!
interface Serial0.19 point-to-point
ip address 192.168.2.109 255.255.255.252
 ipx network 104
 frame-relay interface-dlci 19
!
interface Serial0.20 point-to-point
ip address 192.168.2.105 255.255.255.252
 ipx network 105
 frame-relay interface-dlci 20
```

Partial Meshed Networks

You can use subinterfaces to mitigate partial meshed Frame Relay networks and split horizon protocols. For example, say you were running the IP protocol on a LAN network. If on the same physical network, Router A can talk to Router B, and Router B can talk to Router C—you can usually assume that Router A can talk to Router C. Though this is true with a LAN, it's not true with a Frame Relay network, unless Router A has a virtual circuit to Router C.

In Figure 11.4, Network 1 is configured with five locations. To be able to make this network function, you would have to create a meshed network as shown in Network 2. However, even though Network 2's example works, it's an expensive solution—configuring subinterfaces as shown in the Network 3 solution is much more cost effective.

FIGURE 11.4

Partial meshed network examples

Network 1

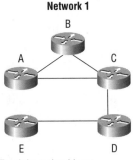

Partial mesh without full connectivity and without subinterfaces.

Network 2

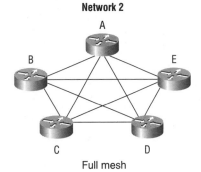

Full mesh

Network 3

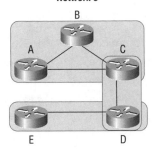

Partial mesh with full connectivity using subinterfaces

In Network 3, configuring subinterfaces actually works to subdivide the Frame Relay network into smaller subnetworks—each with its own network number. So locations A, B, and C connect to a fully meshed network, while locations C and D, and D and E, are connected via point-to-point connections. Locations C and D connect to two subinterfaces and forward packets.

Mapping Frame Relay

As we mentioned earlier in the chapter, for IP devices on opposite ends of a virtual circuit to communicate, their addresses must be properly mapped to the DLCIs. There are two ways to ensure that the address-to-DLCI mapping takes place:

- Via the `frame-relay map` command
- Via the inverse ARP function

Inverse ARP (IARP) uses a dynamic address mapping process to request the next hop protocol address for a specific connection, given its known DLCI number. The responses to the IARP are entered in an address-to-DLCI mapping table, which is then used to supply the next hop protocol address of the DLCI for outgoing traffic.

IARP is enabled by default, but can be disabled on a by-protocol basis. This allows you to run dynamic mapping with some protocols and static mappings with others.

Static mappings link a specific next hop protocol address to a specific DLCI number. Since you don't need IARP functioning on an interface that's using static mapping, the IARP function is automatically disabled for a specified protocol on a specific DLCI.

Here's an example using the `frame-relay map` command:

```
RouterA(config)#int s0.16
RouterA(config-if)#encap frame-relay ietf
RouterA(config-if)#no inverse-arp
RouterA(config-if)#ip address 172.16.30.1 255.255.255.0
RouterA(config-if)#frame-relay map ip 172.16.30.17 30 cisco
   broadcast
```

```
RouterA(config-if)#frame-relay map ip 172.16.30.18 50
  broadcast
RouterA(config-if)#frame-relay map ip 172.16.30.19 40
```

Here's what we did: First, we chose our subinterface, then added the encapsulation command using IETF. We then turned off IARP, and mapped three virtual circuits to their corresponding DLCI numbers. Notice the cisco encapsulation on the first virtual circuit. The other two use the encapsulation method specified in the interface command (IETF). The frame-relay map command is the only way to mix both Cisco and IETF encapsulation types.

The broadcast at the end of the map command directs the router to forward the broadcasts for this interface to the specified virtual circuit (50). This means Router A will forward broadcasts when multicasting isn't enabled. It also means that you're allowed to send broadcasts of routing protocols such as OSPF down a Frame Relay link without having to specify the OSPF neighbor command.

The no inverse-arp command wasn't really necessary because it is automatically disabled for the protocol specified in the static map (IP). However, by typing **no inverse-arp**, you turn it off for all protocols. If you want to turn off inverse ARP for a specific protocol only, use the protocol argument instead.

When using the inverse-arp function, you don't have to use the map command. This approach makes the configuration look as follows instead:

```
RouterA(config)#int s0.16
RouterA(config-if)#encap frame-relay ietf
RouterA(config-if)#ip address 172.16.30.1 255.255.255.0
```

Yes, you're right—that *is* a whole lot easier! However, it's not as stable as using the map command. Why? Sometimes, when using the inverse-arp function, configuration errors can occur because virtual circuits can be insidiously and dynamically mapped to unknown devices.

Monitoring Frame Relay

The Cisco IOS provides many different Exec tasks with which to monitor Frame Relay connections. Table 11.1 shows the commands and tasks you can perform on your Frame Relay networks.

T A B L E 11.1 Monitoring Frame Relay	**Exec Command**	**Function**
	`Clear frame-relay-inarp`	Clears dynamically created Frame Relay maps created by inverse ARP
	`Sh int type [number]`	Displays the information about Frame Relay DLCIs and the LMI
	`Sh frame-relay lmi [type number]`	Displays LMI statistics
	`Sh frame-relay map`	Displays the current Frame Relay map entries
	`Sh frame-relay pvc [type number [dlci]]`	Displays the PVC statistics
	`Sh frame-relay traffic`	Displays the Frame Relay traffic statistics
	`Sh frame-relay route`	Displays the configured static routes
	`Sh frame-relay svc maplist`	Displays all the SVCs under a specified map list

Broadcasting on Frame Relay

Frame Relay is a nonbroadcast network. This means it definitely will not propagate normal routing and routed protocol broadcasts across the Frame cloud without special configurations in place. However, there is a way to make this happen anyway. Frame Relay can replicate broadcast traffic and retransmit broadcast packets to multiple DLCIs with Frame Relay encapsulation.

Frame Relay has its very own queue that includes its own buffers and configurable service rate, which is independent of the other, normal interface queues.

To create a queue so that Frame Relay has a place to hold broadcast traffic, use the `frame-relay broadcast-queue` command. The example below specifies a broadcast queue holding 180 packets (the default is 64), a maximum byte transmission rate of 128,000 bytes per second (default is 256,000), and a maximum packet transmission rate of 160 packets per second (default is 36).

```
Router(config-if)#fram broadcast-queue ?
  <1-65535>  Queue size for broadcasts

Router(config-if)#fram broadcast-queue 180 ?
  <1000-1000000>  Byte rate per sec. for broadcasts
    transmission

Router(config-if)#fram broadcast-queue 180 128000 ?
  <1-999>  Max. packets/S broadcasts transmission

Router(config-if)#fram broadcast-queue 180 128000 160
```

Novell Broadcasts   If you're running Novell IPX over Frame Relay, you must configure SAP traffic to advertise NetWare services. The only problem is that both SAP and RIP transmitting from a Novell device by default every 60 seconds can cause some very real bandwidth problems. The answer lies in controlling all the SAP traffic—you can do that with:

- SAP filters created with special access lists

- SAP timers used to change the SAP and RIP timers

- Broadcast queues that impose a limit on the amount of bandwidth made available to a broadcast

OSPF

And then there's OSPF—no stranger to the cherished routing protocol pastime of broadcasting to say hello to a neighbor. Even though this isn't necessarily a bad thing, if it's not configured correctly, it can cause some serious problems on your Frame Relay network.

To configure OSPF to broadcast to neighboring routers through the Frame Relay cloud, you can either use the neighbor commands or just tell the whole Frame network that things have changed and now it supports routing and routed protocol broadcasts. Of course, telling your router that it's on a broadcast network is easier, but doing that comes with a price that's paid out of your throughput.

When running OSPF in its native environment (a nonbroadcast network), you can use the `neighbor` command to encapsulate the broadcasts in a Frame Relay packet.

You can assign a priority number to set the priority of the neighbor (the default is zero). If a neighbor doesn't respond, the poll interval sets the interval at which polls are sent until the neighbor comes online—the default is 120 seconds.

To set your routers to redefine the Frame Relay network as a broadcast network, use the `ip ospf` network command:

```
Router(config-if)#ip ospf ?
  authentication-key   Authentication password (key)
  cost                 Interface cost
  dead-interval        Interval after which a neighbor is
                         declared dead
  demand-circuit       OSPF demand circuit
  hello-interval       Time between HELLO packets
  message-digest-key   Message digest authentication
                         password (key)
  network              Network type
  priority             Router priority
  retransmit-interval  Time between retransmitting lost link
                         state
                       advertisements
  transmit-delay       Link state transmit delay
Router(config-if)#ip ospf network ?
  broadcast            Specify OSPF Type of Network
  non-broadcast        Specify OSPF Type of Network
  point-to-multipoint  Specify OSPF Type of Network
```

If you use the `broadcast` argument, it will establish the network as a broadcast network. The `non-broadcast` option will set the network back to the default, and the `point-to-multipoint` option configures a router interface to work in a multipoint network environment.

Frame Relay Switching

If you use the PVC switching feature, you can build an entire Frame Relay network using Cisco routers.

There are two parts to Frame Relay switching:

- Frame Relay DTE (router)
- Frame Relay DCE (switch)

Cisco allows for two types of frame switching:

- Local Frame Relay switching configures your router to forward Frame Relay frames based on the DLCI number in the frame's header.
- Remote Frame Relay switching enables the router to encapsulate frames in an IP packet, which is then tunneled across an IP backbone.

Figure 11.5 shows the two different types of Frame Relay switching configurable on a Cisco router.

FIGURE 11.5

Frame Relay switching

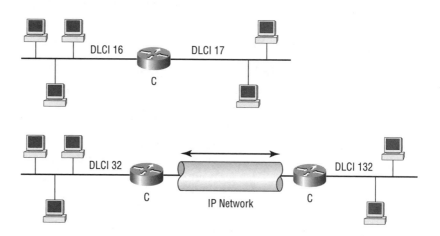

To configure a Cisco router for Frame Relay switching, you must follow the three steps below:

1. Enable Frame Relay switching.

2. Configure the DTE device, DCE switch, or Network-to-Network Interface (NNI) support.

3. Specify the static routes.

The following router configuration demonstrates how to configure Frame Relay switching.

```
Router(config)#frame-relay switching
Router(config)#int s0
Router(config-if)#frame-relay intf-type ?
  dce  Configure a FR DCE
  dte  Configure a FR DTE
  nni  Configure a FR NNI
Router(config-if)#frame-relay intf-type dce
Router(config-if)#frame-relay route ?
  <16-1007>  input dlci to be switched
Router(config-if)#frame-relay route 16 ?
  interface  outgoing interface for pvc switching
Router(config-if)#frame-relay route 16 int s1 ?
  <16-1007>  output dlci to use when switching
Router(config-if)#frame-relay route 16 int s1 39
```

X.25 Networks

X.25 was born in a different world from that of today's digital networks. Originally designed in the 1970s when circuits were both analog and noisy, X.25 is way over-built for today's needs.

It uses addressing defined by X.121, where addresses are between 1 and 14 decimal digits long. The first four bits are the DNIC (Data Network Identifier Code), and the remaining ones are free to be assigned by the administrator.

X.25 defines point-to-point communications between DTEs and DCEs. As mentioned earlier, DTE stands for data terminating equipment, and is usually a router of some sort; DCE stands for data circuit-terminating equipment, and is usually a modem or CSU/DSU. The DCE connects to the X.25 service provider's network with the ultimate goal of establishing a virtual circuit between two DTE devices. X.25 supports both switched and permanent virtual circuits.

Regardless of the type of system connected to the network, versatile X.25 works well. It's heavily used in the packet switched networks (PSNs) of telephone companies that charge their customers based on how much they use the network. So it makes sense that the development of the X.25 standard was begun by common carriers. In the 1970s, there was a need for WAN protocols that could provide connectivity across public data networks (PDNs), and X.25 is now administered as an international standard by the ITU-T.

X.25 network devices can typically be placed in one of three categories:

Data terminating equipment (DTE) End systems that communicate over an X.25 network, such as host systems, terminals, and PCs that belong to the individual subscriber, and are present at the same site.

Data circuit-terminating equipment (DCE) Specific communications equipment, such as modems and packet switches, that interface between a packet switching exchange (PSE) and DTE devices. They're typically found in carrier facilities.

Packet switching exchange (PSE) These switches constitute the majority of a carrier's network and handle the transfer of data between DTE devices via the X.25 packet switched network.

X.25 Sessions

X.25 sessions are established using the following process:

1. One DTE device contacts another requesting a communication session.

2. The receiving DTE device either accepts or refuses the connection.

3. If the request is accepted, the two systems begin full-duplex information transfer.

4. Either DTE device can terminate the connection.

After the session has been terminated, any further communication requires establishing a new session.

Virtual Circuits

Virtual circuits are logical, not physical, connections that are formed so that reliable communication between network devices can take place. A virtual circuit represents a logical, bi-directional path from one DTE device to another over an X.25 network. The connection can physically pass through *x* amount of transitional nodes like PSEs and DCE devices. Plus, a whole bunch of virtual circuits can be multiplexed onto one physical circuit, then demultiplexed at the remote end—the data are then sent to the proper destinations.

X.25 uses two types of virtual circuits.

SVC SVC stands for switched virtual circuit. An *SVC* is a temporary connection used for intermittent data transfers, and requires two DTE devices to establish, maintain, and then terminate a session every time they need to talk.

PVC PVCs (permanent virtual circuits) are established and used for recurrent, steady data transfer. Since they don't need sessions to be established and terminated, a DTE can transmit data whenever necessary—the session is already set up and active, and remains that way.

X.25 Protocol Suite

The X.25 protocol suite maps to the lower three layers—Physical through Network layers—of the OSI reference model. The following protocols are typically used in X.25 implementations:

- Packet Layer Protocol (PLP)

- Link Access Procedure, Balanced (LAPB)

- X.21bis and other Physical layer serial interfaces (such as EIA/TIA-232, EIA/TIA-449, EIA-530, G.703, and so forth)

Packet Layer Protocol The packet layer protocol (PLP) is X.25's Network layer protocol. It manages packet exchanges between DTE devices across virtual circuits, but PLP can also run over Logical Link Control 2 (LLC2) implementations on LANs, and Integrated Services Digital Network (ISDN) interfaces running Link Access Procedure on the D channel (LAPD).

Here are PLP's five modes of operation:

Call Setup mode Used to establish SVCs between DTE devices. To initially set up a virtual circuit, PLP uses X.121's addressing scheme. Different virtual circuits can be in different modes at the same time because Call Setup mode is deployed as individual virtual circuits require it. This mode is used only with SVCs, not with PVCs.

Data Transfer mode Used for data transfer between two DTE devices via a virtual circuit. Tasks such as segmentation, reassembly, bit padding, and error and flow control occur in this mode. Just like Call Setup mode, Data Transfer mode is also deployed on a per–virtual circuit basis, but unlike Call Setup, it's used with both SVCs and PVCs.

Idle mode Used when a virtual circuit is established, but no transfer of data occurs. It's deployed on a per–virtual circuit basis, and only with SVCs.

Call Clearing mode Used to terminate communication sessions between DTE devices as well as SVCs. It's also deployed on a per–virtual circuit basis, and only with SVCs.

Restarting mode Used to synchronize the transmission between a DCE device that's locally connected and a DTE device—tasks such as communication and packet framing between DTE and DCE devices happen here. Since it affects all the established virtual circuits of the DTE device, it isn't deployed on a per–virtual circuit basis.

LAPB LAPB's job is to make sure that frames are error free and properly sequenced, and it's a bit-oriented protocol. Below, we've listed the three different frame types of LAPB.

Information frames (I-frames) Transport upper-layer information and a bit (no pun intended) of control information. I-frames schlep both send and receive sequence numbers, and relate to jobs such as sequencing, flow control, error detection, and recovery.

Supervisory frames (S-frames) Bearing control information, S-frames handle both requesting and suspending transmissions, plus they report on status and acknowledge that I-frames have been received. S-frames only receive sequence numbers.

Unnumbered frames (U-frames) Also bearing control information, they handle things such as link setup and disconnection, and error reporting. U-frames don't schlep any sequence numbers at all.

X.21bis Used in X.25 at the physical layer, the X.21bis protocol specifies the electrical and mechanical processes for the use of the physical media. It oversees both activation and deactivation of whatever physical media connects the DTE and DCE devices. At a speed of up to 19.2Kbps, X21bis supports point-to-point connections and synchronous, full-duplex transmission over four-wire media.

X.25 on Cisco Routers

Cisco routers support X.25 encapsulation via the encap x25 command, which you can apply while in Interface Configuration mode. There are many tuneable features with X.25, as shown below.

```
RouterA#config t
Enter configuration commands, one per line.  End with CNTL/Z.
RouterA(config)#int s0
RouterA(config-if)#encap x25
RouterA(config-if)#x25 ?
  accept-reverse        Accept all reverse charged calls
  address               Set interface X.121 address
  alias                 Define an alias address pattern
  default               Set protocol for calls with
                          unknown Call User Data
  facility              Set explicit facilities for
                          originated calls
  hic                   Set highest incoming channel
  hoc                   Set highest outgoing channel
  hold-queue            Set limit on packets queued per
                          circuit
  hold-vc-timer         Set time to prevent calls to a
                          failed destination
  htc                   Set highest two-way channel
  idle                  Set inactivity time before
                          clearing SVC
  ip-precedence         Open one virtual circuit for
                          each IP TOS
  ips                   Set default maximum input
                          packet size
  lic                   Set lowest incoming channel
  linkrestart           Restart when LAPB resets
  loc                   Set lowest outgoing channel
  ltc                   Set lowest two-way channel
  map                   Map protocol addresses to
                          X.121 address
  modulo                Set operating standard
  nvc                   Set maximum VCs simultaneously
                          open to one host per protocol
```

ops	Set default maximum output packet size
pad-access	Accept only PAD connections from statically mapped X25 hosts
pvc	Configure a Permanent Virtual Circuit
suppress-called-address	Omit destination address in outgoing calls
suppress-calling-address	Omit source address in outgoing calls
t20	Set DTE Restart Request retransmission timer
t21	Set DTE Call Request retransmission timer
t22	Set DTE Reset Request retransmission timer
t23	Set DTE Clear Request retransmission timer
threshold	Set packet count acknowledgement threshold
use-source-address	Use local source address for forwarded calls
win	Set default input window (maximum unacknowledged packets)
wout	Set default output window (maximum unacknowledged packets)

```
RouterA(config-if)#
```

X.121 addresses aren't burned into ROM like LAN addresses, so you need to tell your Cisco router about the local X.121 address on an X.25 serial interface. However, if your router does not start or terminate X.25 calls, this is optional. You set the X.121 address with the x25 address command, as shown below.

```
RouterA(config)#int s0
RouterA(config-if)#x25 address ?
  X.121 Addr  X.121 address
RouterA(config-if)#x25 address 12345678
```

The default packet size of 128 bytes doesn't work with every vendor's implementation of X.25. But have no worries, you can configure your Cisco routers with the correct input packet size (IPS) and output packet size (OPS) with the commands x25 ips and x25 ops, as shown below.

```
RouterA(config-if)#x25 ips ?
  <16-4096>  Bytes (power of two)
RouterA(config-if)#x25 ips 256
RouterA(config-if)#x25 ops 256
```

Also, you might need to adjust your window size for packets that are used by flow control mechanisms. The default window size is two, but you can change this with x25 win (window input size) and x25 wout (window output size), as shown below.

```
RouterA(config-if)#x25 win ?
  <1-127>  Packets
RouterA(config-if)#x25 win 7
RouterA(config-if)#x25 wout 7
```

Cisco also supports the modulo, which sets the interface's data packet sequencing. Eight is the default. Use the x25 modulo command to set the number:

```
Router(config-if)#x25 modulo ?
  128  Packet numbering modulus
Packet numbering modulus
```

You can use the x25 map command to establish a static map between a Network layer protocol and the X.121 address used within the X.25 network. It will permit you to put in nine different addresses when configuring a single x25 map command:

```
Router(config-if)#x25 map ip ?
  A.B.C.D  Protocol specific address

Router(config-if)#x25 map ip 172.16.10.5 ?
  X.121 Addr     Destination host address
  appletalk      AppleTalk
  compressedtcp  Compressed TCP
  decnet         DECnet
  ip             IP
  ipx            Novell IPX
```

```
         qllc          qllc protocol

Router(config-if)#x25 map ip 172.16.10.5 ipx ?
  N.H.H.H  Protocol specific address

Router(config-if)#x25 map ip 172.16.10.5 ipx
  100.1234.1234.1234 ?
  X.121 Addr      Destination host address
  appletalk       AppleTalk
  compressedtcp   Compressed TCP
  decnet          DECnet
  ip              IP
  ipx             Novell IPX

Router(config-if)#x25 map ip 172.16.10.5 ipx
  100.1234.1234.1234 12345678 ?
  accept-reverse  Accepting incoming reverse-charged calls
  broadcast       Send broadcasts to this host
  compress        Specify Packet By Packet Compression
  cug             Specify a Closed User Group number
  idle            Specify VC idle timer
  method          Specify encapsulation method
  no-incoming     Do not use map for incoming Calls
  no-outgoing     Do not use map for outgoing Calls
  nudata          Specify user formatted network user ID
  nuid            Specify Cisco formatted network user ID
  nvc             Set number of virtual circuits for this
                    map
  packetsize      Request maximum packet sizes for
                    originated calls
  passive         Compress outgoing TCP packets only if
                    incoming TCP packets
                  are compressed
  reverse         Use reverse charging on originated calls
  rpoa            Specify RPOA
  throughput      Request bandwidth in X.25 network
  transit-delay   Specify transit delay (msec)
  windowsize      Request window sizes for originated calls
```

```
<cr>

Router(config-if)#$172.16.10.5 ipx 100.1234.1234.1234
12345678 nvc 8
```

The x25 nvc command is used to set the maximum number (up to eight) of SVCs that a host or router can open.

The x25 facilities command forces optional fields on a per-call basis for calls initiated by the router interface:

```
Router(config-if)#x25 facility ?
  cug             Specify a Closed User Group number
  packetsize      Specify maximum packet sizes
  reverse         Use reverse charging on originated calls
  rpoa            Specify transit RPOA list in Call Requests
  throughput      Request bandwidth in X.25 network
  transit-delay   Specify maximum acceptable transit delay
  windowsize      Specify window sizes
```

OSPF

As with Frame Relay, you need to specifically configure X.25 for it to propagate OSPF broadcasts. Also as with Frame Relay, you can either configure X.25 to send encapsulated broadcasts to specified locations or configure the entire network as a broadcast network.

To configure X.25 to encapsulate the broadcasts and send them to a specific destination, use the x25 map command:

```
Router(config-if)#x25 map ?
  appletalk      AppleTalk
  bridge         Bridging
  cdp            Cisco Discovery Protocol
  compressedtcp  Compressed TCP
  decnet         DECnet
  ip             IP
  ipx            Novell IPX
  pad            PAD links
  qllc           qllc protocol
  qllc           qllc protocol
Router(config-if)#x25 map ip 172.16.10.1 ?
  X.121 Addr     Destination host address
```

```
    appletalk      AppleTalk
    compressedtcp  Compressed TCP
    decnet         DECnet
    ip             IP
    ipx            Novell IPX
    qllc           qllc protocol
Router(config-if)#x25 map ip 172.16.10.1 12345678 ?
    accept-reverse  Accepting incoming reverse-charged calls
    broadcast       Send broadcasts to this host
    compress        Specify Packet By Packet Compression
    cug             Specify a Closed User Group number
    idle            Specify VC idle timer
    method          Specify encapsulation method
    no-incoming     Do not use map for incoming Calls
    no-outgoing     Do not use map for outgoing Calls
    nudata          Specify user formatted network user ID
    nuid            Specify Cisco formatted network user ID
    nvc             Set number of virtual circuits for this
                      map
    packetsize      Request maximum packet sizes for
                      originated calls
    passive         Compress outgoing TCP packets only if
                      incoming TCP packets
                    are compressed
    reverse         Use reverse charging on originated calls
    rpoa            Specify RPOA
    throughput      Request bandwidth in X.25 network
    transit-delay   Specify transit delay (msec)
    windowsize      Request window sizes for originated calls
    <cr>
Router(config-if)#x25 map ip 172.16.10.1 12345678 broadcast
```

To make OSPF regard the network as a broadcast network, use the `ip ospf network` broadcast command. Doing this will save you a lot of work because you won't have to define all the neighbors. However, it will cost you in terms of throughput.

Here's the `ip ospf network` broadcast command in action:

```
Router(config-if)#ip ospf network ?
  broadcast             Specify OSPF Type of Network
  non-broadcast         Specify OSPF Type of Network
  point-to-multipoint   Specify OSPF Type of Network
```

The same split horizon–oriented problems that were mentioned in the Frame Relay section can also be the bane of the X.25 network. But have no worries—you can also use the subinterface strategy to solve this problem if you're using a partial mesh network.

Switching

You can locally route X.25 virtual circuits between serial ports on Cisco routers. You can create an X.25 switching environment by using static routing statements to map X.121 addresses to serial interfaces, and by using X.25-over-TCP (XOT) commands. This will enable X.25 interfaces to make SVC connections.

However, first you have to enable X.25 routing on the routers that you want to connect before adding your routes. Here is how to enable `x25 routing` and an `x25 route`:

```
Router(config)#x25 routing
Router(config)#x25 route ?
  #<number>  Optional positional parameter
  WORD       X.121 address pattern to match
```

Using the `x25 routing` command transforms the router into an X.25 router. The position value (if used) tells the router where to put this entry in the table. By default, it will be placed on the bottom, and read sequentially from top to bottom:

```
Router(config)#x25 route 20 ?
  alias              Treat the X.121 address as local
  cud                Called User Data pattern to match
  interface          Route to a local interface
  ip                 Route to a remote Cisco router
  substitute-dest    Specify destination rewrite pattern
  substitute-source  Specify source rewrite pattern

Router(config)#x25 route 20 cud ?
  WORD  CUD pattern to match
```

```
Router(config)#x25 route 20 cud ^pad$ int s0
Router(config)#x25 route 20 int s1
Router(config)#x25 route .* ip 172.16.10.10
```

Thus configured, the routing table will now forward all calls for X.121 address 20 out Interface s0. However, if the call doesn't match the call user data (CUD) string pad, it will be forwarded out Interface s1. The x25 route .* command tells the router to forward all calls that don't match the X.121 address 20 to IP address 172.16.10.10.

SMDS Networks

Switched Multimegabit Data Service (SMDS) is a digital WAN service provided by Regional Bell Operating Companies (RBOCs) and MCI. SMDS is a connectionless cell-relay WAN topology that runs on top of a full-meshed fiber technology.

You need some special equipment to run SMDS:

- CSC-MCI or CSC-SCI serial interface controller cards, and an HSSI interface—or you can use the serial port on any Cisco router

- EIA/TIA-449 or V.25 applique on chassis-based systems, or EIA/TIA-449 transition cable on any Cisco router

- A special SMDS DSU (which costs a whole lot more than a normal DSU)

- Packet switched IOS software

SDSU

An SMDS Data Service Unit (SDSU) is used to encapsulate packets as they enter the cell network. Like ATM, SMDS uses fixed-size packets, which are 53 octets in size.

SMDS Addressing

The service provider assigns SMDS addresses. Two different types of addresses can be used within your Cisco configuration:

E Multicast addresses used to broadcast a packet to multiple end points

C Unicast address for identifying individual network devices

These addresses are 64 bits (15 digits) long, with the first 4 bits representing the address type (E or C), and the other 60 representing the device address. Addresses in this format are known as E.164 addresses, and are depicted in Figure 11.6.

F I G U R E   11.6

SMDS address format

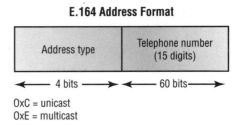

E.164 Address Format

Here's an example of an E.164 15-digit SMDS address:

C25266672424FFFF

The 60-bit device portion of the address is represented in binary-coded decimal (BCD) format. Each section of 4 bits represents a single telephone number digit and can be a value of up to 15 digits. Sometimes you may be assigned only 11 digits, in which case the last 4 will be occupied with ones as in the above example.

It's also possible to enter the address in Ethernet-style notation, as in the following example:

C252.6666.2323.FFFF

And a multicast address would look as follows:

E291.1000.9999.FFFF

Configuring SMDS

Your first step is to obtain your SMDS addresses from your service provider. Next, enable SMDS on your router interface(s).

You set the encapsulation method just as you do for Frame Relay, X.25, etc. Use the `encap smds` command, then add the SMDS address that will apply to the interface using the `smds address` command:

```
Router#config t
Enter configuration commands, one per line.  End with CNTL/Z.
```

```
Router(config)#int s0
Router(config)#ip address 172.16.10.2 255.255.255.0
Router(config-if)#encap smds
Router(config-if)#smds ?
  address      Set an interface SMDS address
  dxi-mode     SMDS DXI3.2 mode
  enable-arp   Enable ARP processing
  glean-mode   SMDS GLEAN mode
  multicast    Set an SMDS multicast (or broadcast) address
  nec-mode     SMDS NEC mode
  static-map   Map high level protocol address to SMDS address
Router(config-if)#smds address C252.6666.2323.FFFF
```

SMDS routing tables are typically dynamic, but you can configure static tables by using the smds static-map command. This is important because you need to define static mappings if your routing protocols don't support dynamic routing.

Here's the smds static-map command in action:

```
Router(config-if)#smds static-map ?
  A.B.C.D     Protocol specific address
  appletalk   AppleTalk
  decnet      DECnet
  ip          IP
  ipx         Novell IPX
  pad         PAD links
Router(config-if)#smds static-map ip 172.16.10.1
C252.5678.3434.FFFF
```

Notice all the different protocols available for use. You also can add a broadcast argument at the end of the line to indicate whether broadcast traffic will be carried.

To map an SMDS group address to a multicast address used by higher-layer protocols (such as IP), use the smds multicast command:

```
Router(config-if)#smds multicast ?
  aarp          AppleTalk ARP
  appletalk     AppleTalk
  arp           IP ARP
  bridge        Bridging
```

```
cdp                  Cisco Discovery Protocol
decnet               DECnet
decnet_node          DECnet Node
decnet_prime_router  DECnet Prime Router
decnet_router-l1     DECnet Router L1
decnet_router-l2     DECnet Router L2
ip                   IP
ipx                  Novell IPX
Router(config-if)#smds multicast ip E291.1000.1234.1243
172.16.10.4 ?
A.B.C.D  IP address mask
Router(config-if)#$ast ip E291.1000.1234.1243 172.16.10.4
255.255.255.0
```

An additional approach is to enable dynamic Address Resolution Protocol (ARP) or use static ARP entries. To create a static entry, use the `arp` command. To enable dynamic ARP, use the `smds enable-arp` command:

```
Router(config-if)#smds enable-arp
```

You can enable dynamic address mapping when using IPX by using the `smds glean-mode ipx` command:

```
Router(config-if)#smds glean-mode ?
  ipx  Novell IPX
Router(config-if)#smds glean-mode ipx ?
  <1-65535>  TIMEOUT value (minutes)
  broadcast  Make SMDS address in dynamic maps a broadcast
    address
  <cr>
Router(config-if)#smds glean-mode ipx 10 broadcast
```

ATM Networks

Asynchronous Transmission Mode (ATM) is another cell-switching multiplexing technology that uses circuit-switching for constant transmission delay with guaranteed capacity, combined with packet-switching for flexibility and efficiency.

ATM is connection oriented, and employs virtual path identifiers (VPIs) and a virtual channel identifier (VCI) to create a single virtual circuit. This virtual circuit is a private connection between two devices on the network, meaning that each ATM device must make a separate connection between every device with which it needs to communicate.

Cisco supports the following hardware for ATM transmission (depending on router type):

- ATM interface processor (AIP)

- ATM port adapter (PA)

- ATM network processor module (NPM)

If you have a router that doesn't support any of the interfaces listed above, you can use a serial interface configured for multiprotocol encapsulation over the Asynchronous Transfer Mode Data Exchange Interface (ATM-DXI) instead.

The RFC supports two different methods for transporting multiprotocol connectionless network interconnect traffic over an ATM network:

- A single PVC

- Different VCs for each protocol used (e.g., IP, IPX, etc.)

Like SMDS, ATM uses a pricey and special DSU called an ADSU. This provides the ATM interface to the network, and converts outgoing packets into cells and incoming packets into packets. It is also responsible for deducing the DXI frame address (DFA) from the VPI and VCI running on each PVC.

Configuring ATM

To configure ATM, you must first assign the protocols you're going to run on it. If you're using a serial interface, assign ATM-DXI encapsulation by using the encap atm-dxi command:

```
Router(config)#int s0
Router(config-if)#ip address 172.16.10.1 255.255.255.0
Router(config-if)#ipx network 172abc
Router(config-if)#apple address 10.172
Router(config-if)#encap atm-dxi
```

If you're running multiple protocols, you'll need to set up a PVC for each one. You can do this via the dxi pvc command:

```
Router(config-if)#dxi pvc ?
  <0-15>  VPI
Router(config-if)#dxi pvc 1 ?
  <0-63>  VCI
Router(config-if)#dxi pvc 1 1 ?
  mux    MUX Encapsulation
  nlpid  NLPID Encapsulation
  snap   LLC/SNAP Encapsulation
  <cr>
Router(config-if)#dxi pvc 1 1 snap
Router(config-if)#dxi pvc 2 2 snap
Router(config-if)#dxi pvc 3 3 snap
```

The MUX option is used to specify that only one protocol will be carried on the PVC (remember—only one protocol is configured per PVC). The Subnetwork Access Protocol allows the LLC to read the protocols within each PVC.

Network Layer Protocol Identification (NLPID) was used before LLC. SNAP is the default encapsulation starting in IOS 10.3. The default encapsulation was NLPID prior to 10.3.

To map ATM protocol addresses to VCIs and VPIs, use the dxi map command:

```
Router(config-if)#dxi map ?
  appletalk  AppleTalk
  bridge     Bridging
  decnet     DECnet
  ip         IP
  ipx        Novell IPX
  qllc       qllc protocol
  snapshot   Snapshot routing support
Router(config-if)#dxi map ip 172.16.10.5 ?
  <0-15>  VPI
```

```
Router(config-if)#dxi map ip 172.16.10.5 1 ?
  <0-63>  VCI
Router(config-if)#dxi map ip 172.16.10.5 1 1 ?
  broadcast  Broadcasts should be forwarded to this address
  <cr>
Router(config-if)#dxi map ip 172.16.10.5 1 1 broadcast
Router(config-if)#dxi map ipx 10.2345.2345.2345 2 2 broadcast
Router(config-if)#dxi map appletalk 10.172 3 3 broadcast
```

You must use the map command for each protocol.

Monitoring ATM on the ATM-DXI Interface

You can display the status of your serial interface, the PVC, and maps with the commands shown in Table 11.2.

T A B L E 11.2	Command	Function
ATM Monitoring Commands	sh int atm [slot/port]	Displays the serial ATM interface status
	sh dxi pvc	Displays the ATM-DXI PVC information
	sh dxi map	Displays the ATM-DXI map information

Summary

In this chapter, the following points were covered:

- The common issues to be considered when evaluating a WAN service.

  Availability How the internetwork must stay working 24 hours a day.

  Bandwidth Accurately determining the actual and eventual bandwidth requirements with information gathered from both users and management.

  Cost Cisco offers an abundance of switches and routers tailored to many wallet sizes.

Ease of management The ramifications, such as the degree of difficulty associated with creating any network connections, must be understood and regarded carefully.

Type of application traffic This can be typically comprised of small to very large packets.

Routing protocols The characteristics of these protocols must be understood and then configured properly.

- The differences between WAN connection types: dedicated, asynchronous dial-in, dial-on-demand, and packet switched services. Dedicated point-to-point serial links are dedicated links that provide full-time connectivity. Cisco answers the asynchronous need by providing a variety of asynchronous dial-in products, such as the AS5200 access server. DDR (dial-on-demand routing) allows wide area links to be used selectively. We also found out how PSN data delivery can take place within frames, packets, or cells, and how that occurs transparently to end users.

- Cisco's main packet switching network types: Frame Relay, X.25, SMDS, and ATM.

Review Questions

1. What encapsulation method would you use to configure ATM on a serial port?

    A. ATM-Serial

    B. HDLC

    C. ATM-DXI

    D. ATM

2. When would it be necessary to prioritize DLCI traffic?

    A. When bandwidth is at a premium

    B. When you have traffic from sites with high-speed access being queued at destination sites with lower-speed access

    C. When running X.25 at remote locations

    D. When you need to prioritize queues

3. Which command would you use to assign protocol traffic that would match the specified parameters to a priority queue?

    A. queue

    B. protocol queue

    C. priority-queue

    D. priority-list

4. For which of the following is X.21bis used?

   A. Frame Relay 56Kbps lines

   B. Frame types used in X.25

   C. X.25 Physical layer specifications

   D. PLP Call Setup mode

5. How many Frame Relay encapsulation methods are used with Cisco routers?

   A. Two

   B. Three

   C. Four

   D. Five

6. How many LMI types are supported?

   A. Two

   B. Three

   C. Four

   D. Five

7. Which of the following is true about LMI?

   A. LMIs map DLCI numbers to virtual circuits

   B. LMIs map X.121 addresses to virtual circuits

   C. LMIs report the status of virtual circuits

   D. LMI messages provide information about the current DLCI values

8. What are X.121 addresses used for?

A. Mapping DLCI addresses to logical interfaces

B. Mapping X.25 addresses to logical hardware addresses

C. Receiving LMI messages

D. Providing information about the current DLCI values

9. Which of the following commands will define access list 10 to use a high-priority queue?

A. `frame priority-dlci-group 10`

B. `access-list 10 permit eq high`

C. `priority-list 10 protocol ip high list 5`

D. `priority-list 5 protocol ip high list 10`

10. What is a disadvantage to having point-to-point connections?

A. A point-to-point connection requires that tariffs be paid even when the connection is in an idle state and no data are being transmitted

B. A point-to-point connection requires users to dial the connection manually when data need to be transmitted

C. A point-to-point connection requires interesting traffic to be defined on the router with access lists when data need to be transmitted

D. A point-to-point connection requires a lease through an ISP using a point-to-point routing protocol

11. What command do you use to set the LMI polling and timer intervals?

   A. `frame-relay n39x-lmi`

   B. `frame-relay lmi-xn39`

   C. `frame-relay lmi-n39x`

   D. `frame-relay lmi-x39n`

12. How do you configure OSPF to broadcast to other routers through the Frame Relay cloud?

   A. By creating subinterfaces

   B. IARP

   C. By mapping X.121 addresses

   D. With the `neighbor` command

13. What command would you use to create a queue so that Frame Relay has a place to hold broadcast traffic?

   A. `frame-relay queue 16 eq broadcast`

   B. `frame-relay broadcast-queue`

   C. `frame-relay broadcast 16 eq queue 16`

   D. `frame-relay queue 1 low 16 broadcast 16`

14. What command should you use to set your routers to redefine the Frame Relay network as an OSPF broadcast network?

   A. `ip ospf network`

   B. `ip ospf broadcast`

   C. `network ospf broadcast all`

   D. `network ospf broadcast` *network number*

15. What are the two parts of Frame Relay switching?

    A. Frame Relay DTE (switch)

    B. Frame Relay DTE (router)

    C. Frame Relay DCE (router)

    D. Frame Relay DCE (switch)

16. What are the two types of frame switching?

    A. Local

    B. Remote

    C. Standby

    D. Cut-through

17. What is the solution for using partial meshed Frame Relay networks with split-horizon protocols?

    A. DLCI addressing

    B. X.121 addresses

    C. Secondary Ethernet interfaces

    D. Subinterfaces

18. What are the three types of LMI methods used by Cisco routers?

    A. Cisco

    B. ANSI

    C. IETF

    D. q933a

19. What is IARP used for?

   A. Mapping X.121 addresses to X.25 addresses

   B. Mapping DLCIs to network protocol addresses

   C. SMDS addressing

   D. Mapping ATM addresses to virtual addresses

20. Which two of the following are true regarding SMDS addressing?

   A. E: multicast addresses

   B. E: unicast addresses

   C. C: unicast addresses

   D. C: multicast addresses

CHAPTER

12

Cisco Serial Line Support

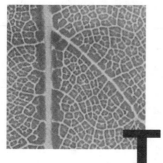

This chapter will cover Cisco's serial line options. Cisco routers support multiple encapsulation methods and different compression algorithms in addition to channelized T1/E1 interfaces.

The encapsulation methods we'll look at include SDLC, HDLC, ISDN, PPP, and LAPB. The compression methods that Cisco supports are header, payload (data), and link (both header and data). LAPB has its own compression methods called Predictor and Stacker, which are each used in different environments. We'll present all of these together with how each can be used within various environments.

The chapter will conclude with a perusal of channelized T1/E1 and instruction on how to configure channel groups, clock sources, framing, and linecode with Cisco routers.

The CCNP test objectives covered in the chapter are as follows:

- Determine when to use PPP, HDLC, LAPB, and IETF encapsulation types

- Describe the components that make up ISDN connectivity

- Configure ISDN BRI

- Configure MultiLink PPP operation

- Verify MultiLink PPP operation

- Identify channelized T1 and E1 configuration

- Identify ISDN PRI configuration commands

Serial Line Options

We'll begin by describing the different encapsulation methods supported by Cisco and demonstrating how to configure serial encapsulation methods. To make solid networking business decisions, it's imperative that you thoroughly understand WAN connectivity.

The serial encapsulation methods supported by Cisco include:

- SDLC
- HDLC
- ISDN
- PPP
- LAPB

All of these protocols are configured with the subcommand `encapsulation`, which is used to set the serial encapsulation method for a particular interface. This command sets the framing type for data transmission. The framing type is generally protocol specific.

SDLC

IBM originally developed SDLC (Synchronous Data Link Control) for use by their SNA protocol. SDLC was the predecessor to HDLC and is a bit-synchronous Data Link layer protocol.

SDLC was developed by IBM during the mid-1970s for use in Systems Network Architecture (SNA) environments. Subsequent to the implementation of SDLC by IBM, SDLC formed the foundation for numerous similar protocols, including HDLC and LAPB.

Bit-synchronous protocols owe their success to their expanded efficiency, flexibility, and in some cases greater speed, with SDLC in the lead as the chief SNA link layer protocol for WAN links. Versatile SDLC supports many link types and topologies, such as:

- Point-to-point and multipoint links
- Bounded and unbounded media
- Half-duplex and full-duplex transmission facilities
- Circuit and packet switched networks

SDLC also supports two network node types:

Primary stations Control the operation of other stations; poll secondaries in a predetermined order; and set up, tear down, and manage links.

Secondary stations Controlled by a primary station. If a secondary is polled, it can transmit outgoing data. An SDLC secondary can send information only to the primary, and even then only after the primary grants permission.

HDLC

The High-Level Data Link Control (HDLC) protocol is a popular ISO-standard, bit-oriented, link layer protocol that specifies an encapsulation method for data on synchronous serial data links.

HDLC's development began when the International Standardization Organization (ISO) modified SDLC and came up with HDLC. Thereafter, the International Telecommunication Union Telecommunication Standardization Sector (ITU-T) tweaked HDLC a bit more and released Link Access Procedure (LAP), and then Link Access Procedure, Balanced (LAPB). After that, the Institute of Electrical and Electronic Engineers (IEEE) went to work on HDLC, and the result was the IEEE 802.2 specification.

HDLC is the default encapsulation used by Cisco routers over synchronous serial links. Cisco's HDLC is proprietary—it won't communicate with any other vendor's HDLC implementation. But don't give Cisco grief for it—everyone's HDLC implementation is proprietary. When we brought up our routers in Chapter 5, we were using HDLC encapsulation on all of our serial links.

The sh int command displays the encapsulation method in the following output:

```
RouterA#show int s0
Serial0 is up, line protocol is up
  Hardware is HD64570
  Internet address is 172.16.20.1/24
  MTU 1500 bytes, BW 1544 Kbit, DLY 20000 usec, rely
    255/255, load 1/255
  Encapsulation HDLC, loopback not set, keepalive set (10 sec)
  Last input 00:00:05, output 00:00:01, output hang never
  Last clearing of "show interface" counters never
  Input queue: 0/75/0 (size/max/drops); Total output drops: 0
  Queueing strategy: weighted fair
  Output queue: 0/1000/64/0 (size/max total/threshold/drops)
    Conversations  0/2/256 (active/max active/max total)
    Reserved Conversations 0/0 (allocated/max allocated)
  5 minute input rate 0 bits/sec, 2 packets/sec
  5 minute output rate 0 bits/sec, 1 packets/sec
    1363 packets input, 59515 bytes, 0 no buffer
    Received 1242 broadcasts, 0 runts, 0 giants, 0 throttles
    0 input errors, 0 CRC, 0 frame, 0 overrun, 0 ignored,
      0 abort
```

```
          1403 packets output, 59222 bytes, 0 underruns
          0 output errors, 0 collisions, 24 interface resets
          0 output buffer failures, 0 output buffers swapped out
          25 carrier transitions
          DCD=up  DSR=up  DTR=up  RTS=up  CTS=up
     RouterA#
```

Did you notice that fifth line? It reported our encapsulation as (surprise) HDLC.

Transfer Modes

HDLC supports the following transfer modes:

Normal Response mode (NRM) The transfer mode implemented with SDLC. Under NRM, a secondary can't communicate with a primary until the primary asks it to.

Asynchronous Response mode (ARM) This mode allows secondaries to communicate with a primary without permission from it.

Asynchronous Balanced mode (ABM) This mode introduced the combined node—one that can act as either a primary or a secondary station. All ABM communication takes place between a number of combined nodes, and combined stations can originate transmissions without permission.

LAPB Integrated into the X.25 protocol stack, LAPB shares the same frame format, frame types, and field functions as both SDLC and HDLC. It's confined to the ABM transfer mode, and with it, you can establish circuits with either data terminal equipment (DTE) or data circuit-terminating equipment (DCE). Devices that initiate communication are deemed primaries, and those that respond are deemed secondaries.

ISDN

ISDN (Integrated Services Digital Network) is a digital service designed to run over existing telephone networks—the ability to deliver a true digital service across your existing local loop is very cool indeed. ISDN can support both data and voice—a telecommuter's dream. ISDN applications require bandwidth because typical ISDN applications and implementations include high-speed image applications (such as Group IV facsimile), high-speed file transfer, video conferencing, and multiple links into homes of telecommuters.

ISDN is actually a set of communication protocols proposed by telephone companies, which allows them to carry data and voice, etc. It gives us a group of digital services that simultaneously convey data, text, voice, music, graphics, and video to end users, and it was designed to achieve this over the telephone systems already in place. ISDN is referenced by a suite of ITU-T standards encompassing the OSI model's Physical, Data Link, and Network layers.

ISDN Terminals

Devices connecting to the ISDN network are known as terminals, and there are two types:

TE1 Terminal equipment type 1 refers to those terminals that understand ISDN standards.

TE2 Terminal equipment type 2 refers to those that predate ISDN standards. To use a TE2, you have to use a terminal adapter (TA).

ISDN Reference Points

ISDN has four reference points that define logical interfaces:

R reference point Defines the reference point between non-ISDN equipment and a TA.

S reference point Defines the reference point between user terminals and an NT2.

T reference point Defines the reference point between NT1 and NT2 devices.

U reference point Defines the reference point between NT1 devices and line-termination equipment in a carrier network. (This is only in North America where the NT1 function isn't provided by the carrier network.)

ISDN Protocols

ISDN protocols are defined by the ITU, and there are several series of protocols dealing with diverse issues:

- Protocols beginning with the letter *E* deal with using ISDN on the existing telephone network.

- Protocols beginning with the letter *I* deal with concepts, terminology, and services.

- Protocols beginning with the letter *Q* cover switching and signaling.

ISDN Switch Types

We can credit AT&T and NorTel for the majority of the ISDN switches in place today, but additional companies also make them. In Table 12.1 under "Keyword," you'll find the right keyword to use along with the `isdn switch-type` command to configure a router for the variety of switches to which it's going to connect. If you don't know which switch your provider is using at their central office, simply call them to find out.

T A B L E 12.1: ISDN Switch Types	**Switch Type**	**Keyword**
	AT&T basic rate switch	`basic-5ess`
	NorTel DMS-100 basic rate switch	`basic-dms100`
	National ISDN-1 switch	`basic-ni1`
	AT&T 4ESS (ISDN PRI only)	`primary-4ess`
	AT&T 5ESS (ISDN PRI only)	`primary-5ess`
	NorTel DMS-100 (ISDN PRI only)	`primary-dms100`

Basic Rate Interface

ISDN Basic Rate Interface (BRI) service provides two B channels and one D channel. The BRI B-channel service operates at 64Kbps and carries data, while the BRI D-channel service operates at 16Kbps and usually carries control and signaling information. The D-channel signaling protocol spans the OSI reference model's Physical, Data Link, and Network layers. BRI also provides framing control for a total bit rate of up to 144Kbps.

When configuring ISDN BRI, you'll need to obtain SPIDs (Service Profile Identifiers), and you should have one SPID for each B channel—two for BRI. You can think of SPIDs as the telephone number of each B channel. The ISDN device gives the SPID to the ISDN switch, which then allows the device to access the network for BRI or PRI service. Without an SPID, many ISDN switches don't allow an ISDN device to place a call on the network. Not all configurations require unique SPIDs, however. Some are autosensed. Ask your service provider to be sure.

Primary Rate Interface

The ISDN Primary Rate Interface (PRI) service delivers 23 B channels and 1 64Kbps D channel in North America and Japan, for a total bit rate of up to 1.544Mbps.

In Europe, Australia, and other parts of the world, ISDN provides 30 B channels and 1 64Kbps D channel, for a total bit rate of up to 2.048Mbps.

PPP

PPP (Point-to-Point Protocol) is a data-link protocol that can be used over either asynchronous (dial-up) or synchronous (ISDN) media and that uses LCP (Link Control Protocol) to build and maintain data-link connections. LCP is packed with a number of features, including:

- Authentication using either PAP (Password Authentication Protocol) or CHAP (Challenge Handshake Authentication Protocol)

- Compression of data for transmission across media

These features weren't available in PPP's predecessor, SLIP (Serial Line IP), so this is progress.

Another new feature is the support for multiple protocols. SLIP supported only IP, but through NCP (Network Control Protocol), PPP supports IP, IPX, AppleTalk, DECnet, OSI/CLNS, and transparent bridging. NCP is actually a family of protocols—one for each layer-3 protocol supported by PPP. PPP specifies an authentication mechanism, while CHAP and PAP are typically used. It is extensible so other companies (like Microsoft) can implement their own security.

To configure PPP on a serial link, you use the encapsulation ppp command. The ppp authentication subcommand allows you to specify the type of PPP authentication and the type of authentication protocol. The following example uses an ISDN dialer interface with PPP encapsulation and authentication:

```
Router#config t
Enter configuration commands, one per line.  End with CNTL/Z.
Router(config)#int s0
Router(config-if)#int dialer 1
Router(config-if)#encap ppp
Router(config-if)#ppp auth ?
   chap  Challenge Handshake Authentication Protocol (CHAP)
```

```
       pap    Password Authentication Protocol (PAP)

Router(config-if)#ppp auth chap ?
  callin  Authenticate remote on incoming call only
  pap     Password Authentication Protocol (PAP)
  <cr>

Router(config-if)#ppp auth chap pap ?
  callin  Authenticate remote on incoming call only
  <cr>

Router(config-if)#ppp auth chap pap callin
```

Multilink PPP

By using ISDN with PPP encapsulation, Cisco routers can support multiple connections over the same physical interface. This allows Cisco routers to use dial-up connections to establish more than one connection at a time to an access server. Why would you want a router to be able to do that? Because if it can, you're granted twice the bandwidth of a single dial-up line. The capacity to increase bandwidth between point-to-point dial-up connections by grouping interfaces, then splitting and recalculating packets to run over that group of interfaces, is called *multilink*.

Before you can run multilink, you must define the interesting packets using the dialer-list global command. This command directs the router to search for specific network protocols for making and keeping a link active. You can apply a dialer list to an interface using the subcommand dialer-group.

In the following example, we enabled ISDN dialer one to support PPP multilink:

```
Router#config t
Enter configuration commands, one per line.  End with CNTL/Z.
Router(config)#int dialer 1
Router(config-if)#ppp multilink
Router(config-if)#dialer-group 1
Router(config-if)#dialer-list 1 protocol ip list 102
Router(config)#access-list 110 permit tcp any any eq www
Router(config)#access-list 110 permit tcp any any eq 53
Router(config)#^Z
```

You can also specify dynamic IP addressing of ISDN PPP hosts and PPP multilink hosts by using the subcommand peer default ip address. Doing this will assign a unique IP address to each individual ISDN interface from a pool of them. You can provide a DNS name server and WINS server to ISDN dial-up users as well using the global commands async-bootp dns-server and async-bootp nbns-server.

You can supply multiple IP addresses for both DNS and WINS, as the example below shows:

```
Router#config t
Enter configuration commands, one per line.  End with CNTL/Z.
Router(config)#int dialer 1
Router(config-if)#peer default ip address pool isdn-group1
Router(config-if)#ip local pool isdn-group1 172.16.20.1
   172.16.20.254
Router(config-if)#async-bootp dns-server 172.16.10.253
   172.16.10.254
Router(config-if)#async-bootp nbns-server 172.16.10.251
   172.16.10.252
Router(config-if)#^Z
```

LAPB

LAPB encapsulation is great when you need to configure a simple, reliable serial connection. LAPB can be implemented if you have a private serial line, or with X.25 encapsulation.

LAPB's job is to make sure that frames are error free and properly sequenced. It's a bit-oriented protocol, and below we've listed the three different LAPB frame types:

Information frames (I-frames) Transport upper-layer information and a bit (no pun intended) of control information. I-frames schlep both send and receive sequence numbers, and relate to jobs such as sequencing, flow control, error detection, and recovery.

Supervisory frames (S-frames) Bearing control information, S-frames handle both requesting and suspending transmissions, plus they report on status and acknowledge that I-frames have been received. S-frames only receive sequence numbers.

Unnumbered frames (U-frames) Also bearing control information, they handle things such as link setup and disconnection, and error reporting. U-frames don't schlep any sequence numbers.

Opting for LAPB instead of HDLC encapsulation is a good solution if you're experiencing noisy serial links and you're not running time-sensitive applications, because unlike HDLC, which expects the upper layers to be responsible for missing data, LAPB will retransmit missing frames. However, if your serial link is solid, HDLC encapsulation is the better choice because of its lower overhead.

Compression

By default, Cisco routers transmit data across serial links in an uncompressed format, but by using Cisco serial compression techniques, you can make more efficient use of your available bandwidth. It's true that any compression method will cause overhead on the router's CPU, but the benefits of compression on slower links can outweigh that disadvantage.

Three types of compression are used in a Cisco internetworking environment:

Header compression Cisco uses the Van Jacobson algorithm to compress the headers of IP packets before sending them out onto WAN links. This method leaves the data intact, compressing only the header information, and can be used for applications (e.g., Telnet) and HDLC or X.25 encapsulation. However, it doesn't allow for protocol independence.

Payload compression This approach compresses the data, but leaves the header intact. Because the packet's header isn't changed, it can be switched through a network. So this method is the one generally used for switching services such as X.25, SMDS, Frame Relay, and ATM.

Link compression This method is a combination of both header and payload compression, and for you to be able to use it, the data must be encapsulated in either PPP or LAPB. Link compression allows for protocol independence.

TCP header compression is achieved using the `ip tcp header-compression` command:

```
Router(config)#int s0
Router(config-if)#ip tcp ?
  compression-connections  Maximum number of compressed
    connections
  header-compression       Enable TCP header compression
```

```
Router(config-if)#ip tcp header-compression ?
  passive  Compress only for destinations which send
    compressed headers
  <cr>
```

The passive argument is optional and used to add restrictions to outbound TCP traffic. If you don't include the passive argument, all TCP traffic will be compressed. If you do use it, outgoing TCP traffic will be compressed only if the data received on the same interface are compressed.

LAPB Compression

Serial interfaces using LAPB or multi-LAPB can employ software compression to reduce the size of an LAPB frame. Multi-LAPB is used when running multiple protocols over X.25.

Software compression can significantly affect router CPU performance, and the Cisco rule of thumb is that the routers' CPU load must not exceed 65% when running software compression. If it does, you'd be better off just disabling any compression method.

Use the sho process cpu EXEC command to see the CPU load.

LAPB can use two different types of compression methods:

Predictor This approach should be used to solve bottleneck problems caused by a heavy load on the router. The Predictor algorithm learns data patterns and "predicts" the next character. This is sometimes referred to as *lossless* because no data are lost during the compression and decompression process.

Stacker Opt for this method when bottlenecks are related to bandwidth issues.

Don't use compression if you're running a T1 or greater. The added processing time will slow down a faster link's performance. However, Cisco has hardware compression processors (Compression Service Adapter) that can offload the compression tasks from the route processor. This allows compression without affecting main processor performance.

In the example below, we turned on LAPB encapsulation with Predictor compression, and set the maximum transmission unit (MTU) and the LAPB N1 parameters:

```
Router#config t
Enter configuration commands, one per line.  End with CNTL/Z.
Router(config)#int s0
Router(config-if)#encap lapb
Router(config-if)#compress ?
predictor  predictor compression type
stac       stac compression algorithm
Router(config-if)#compress predictor
Router(config-if)#mtu 1510
Router(config-if)#lapb n1 1296
```

The LAPB N1 represents the number of bits in an LAPB frame, which holds an X.25 packet. It is set to eight times the MTU size, plus any overhead when using LAPB over leased lines. For instance, the N1 is specified at 1280 (1510×8) plus 16 bits for protocol overhead. The LAPB N1 parameter can cause major problems if it's not configured correctly and most often should be left at its default value. Even so, it can be really valuable if you need to set the MTU size.

Channelized T1/E1

Large businesses have typically used point-to-point connections with DSU/CSUs to connect two sites together. In turn, these connected to low- and high-speed serial interfaces on routers—usually Cisco routers. The router backplane and the amount of interfaces the router could handle determined how well it supported a WAN connection.

The Cisco 7000 series of routers supports the Fast Serial Interface Processor (FSIP), which provides either four or eight serial ports, permitting the same amount of point-to-point connections to remote offices.

The Cisco series of routers also supports the MultiChannel Interface Processor (MIP), which furnishes support for two full T1/E1 ports in the 7000 series and one port in the 4000 series.

T1s run at 1.544Mbps, which uses 24 channels in contrast to E1s, which use 30 channels and run at 2.048Mbps. E1 is mainly used in Europe, and both T1 and E1 are considered wide area digital transmission schemes.

Each port in the MIP can support 24 DS0 channels of 64Kbps each when using a T1, and 30 DS0 channels when using an E1. The MIP refers to each line as a subchannel, which allows each channel to be configured individually. Subchannels have all the characteristics and options of regular serial interfaces.

Figure 12.1 shows how an imaginary, but typical, serial WAN could be configured, compared to how it could be configured using a MIP card.

FIGURE 12.1

Using a MultiChannel Interface Processor

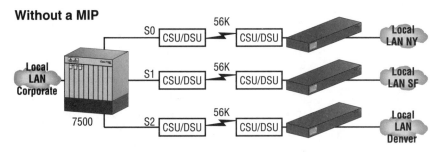

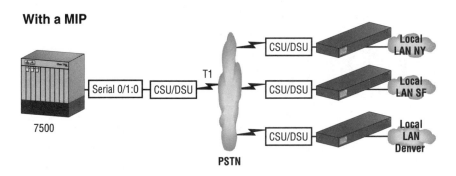

Configuring T1

The serial links connect into either a private data network or a service provider's network. Both the line encoding and the framing must match the service provider's equipment. To configure a T1 on a serial link, you must supply the following information:

Channel type Either T1 or E1.

Frame type When using a T1, this can be either Super Frame or Extended Super Frame (ESF). Super Frame can also be referred to as D4 framing, which consists of 12 frames each with 193 bits. The last bit is used for error checking. Extended Super Frame is an enhanced version of Super Frame that uses 24 frames each with 192 bits. ESF is typically used in the U.S.

Linecode This will be either alternate mark inversion (AMI) or binary 8-zero substitution (B8ZS). B8ZS is typically used in the U.S.; however, most legacy phone systems still use AMI.

Which time slots the T1 uses By using the channel-group command on your subchannel, you can define the subchannels associated with each time slot.

In the following example, we chose to configure Slot 1, Port 0 of the MIP card in our 7000 router, and we opted for ESF framing, with B8ZS line coding. The pri-group 0 timeslots 1 indicates that circuit zero has only one time slot. Since no speed was specified, it's running the default of 56Kbps. Channel group one has six time slots running at 64Kbps. We could choose up to 24 DS0s, but purchased only 6 from our provider. Here's a look at the output:

```
Router#config t
Enter configuration commands, one per line.  End with CNTL/Z.
Router(config)#controller T1 1/0
Router(config-if)#framing esf
Router(config-if)#linecode b8zs
Router(config-if)#channel-group 0 timeslots 1
Router(config-if)#channel-group 1 timeslots 6 3,4,8-11 speed 64
Router(config-if)#^Z
```

An IP address and the serial encapsulation method (HDLC is the default) then need to be assigned to each interface, as shown in the following example:

```
Router#config t
Enter configuration commands, one per line.  End with CNTL/Z.
Router(config)#int s 0/1:0
Router(config-if)#encap ppp
Router(config-if)#ip address 172.16.30.5 255.255.255.252
Router(config)#int s 0/1:1
Router(config-if)#encap hdlc
Router(config-if)#ip address 172.16.30.5 255.255.255.252
Router(config-if)#^Z
```

When connecting two MIP cards together, you must specify the clock source. This is done with the `clock source` command.

Configuring E1

The E1 configuration is similar to the T1 configuration, but has different parameters.

Framing The E1 framing types available are crc4, no-crc4, and australia. The default is crc4, and it specifies CRC error checking, with no-crc4 specifying that CRC checking is (surprise) disabled. The australia framing method is used when configuring an E1 in (another surprise) Australia.

Linecode This is either AMI or HDB3 when configuring an E1, with AMI as the default.

In the following example, we specified Slot 0, Port 1 on our MIP card, and by using the crc4 framing type, we're actually specifying the ESF frame type. The provider has defined HDB3 as the linecode (AMI is the default) to match the carrier's equipment. Primary group zero with a time slot of one specifies that there is only 1 time slot with circuit zero. However, primary group one is using 12 time slots, with up to 30 available if purchased.

```
Router#config t
Enter configuration commands, one per line.  End with CNTL/Z.
Router(config)#controller T1 1/0
```

```
Router(config-if)#framing esf
Router(config-if)#linecode b8zs
Router(config-if)#channel-group 0 timeslots 1
Router(config-if)#channel-group 1 timeslots 12 12-23 speed 64
Router(config-if)#^Z
```

You then need to specify the IP address and encapsulation methods used just as we did in the T1 example.

Summary

In this chapter, we discussed the different encapsulation types to help you determine when to use each one:

- PPP

- HDLC

- ISDN

- LAPB

For example, you could use LAPB instead of HDLC in circumstances where the leased line is noisy and error checking must be done.

The different ISDN connectivity components discussed were as follows:

- Terminals: Devices connecting to the ISDN network.

- Reference points: Logical interfaces.

- ISDN protocols: Defined by the ITU.

- ISDN Basic Rate Interface (BRI): Provides two B channels and one D channel. B channels operate at 64Kbps and carry data; BRI D-channel service operates at 16Kbps and usually carries control and signaling information.

By using ISDN with PPP encapsulation, Cisco routers can support multiple connections over the same physical interface, making it possible for them to use dial-up connections and establish more than one connection at a time to an access server.

Review Questions

1. What different types of compression does Cisco support with LAPB? (Choose all that apply.)

    A. Interesting

    B. Predictor

    C. X.121

    D. Stacker

2. What does the I protocol specify in ISDN?

    A. ISDN on the existing telephone network

    B. Bandwidth on demand

    C. Concepts, terminology, and services

    D. Switching and signaling

3. Which is true regarding HDLC?

    A. HDLC has a reachability limit of 15

    B. HDLC uses TCP sequencing and acknowledgements

    C. HDLC is a byte-oriented protocol

    D. HDLC is a bit-oriented protocol

4. Which command enables Predictor data compression with LAPB? X.25 Predictor compress

    A. LAPB compress Predictor passive

    B. Compress Predictor

    C. Predictor compress

5. What does BRI provide?

    A. 2 B channels and 1 D channel

    B. 23 B channels and 1 64Kbps D channel

    C. 2 D channels and 1 B channel

    D. 23 D channels and 1 64Kbps B channel

6. What does PRI provide?

    A. 2 B channels and 1 D channel

    B. 23 B channels and 1 64Kbps D channel

    C. 2 D channels and 1 B channel

    D. 23 D channels and 1 64Kbps B channel

7. Which of the following is true regarding Super Frames?

    A. Used only with PPP encapsulation methods

    B. Used only with LAPB encapsulation methods

    C. Consist of 12 frames each with 193 bits

    D. Consist of 24 frames each with 192 bits

8. Which of the following is true regarding Extended Super Frames?

    A. Used only with PPP encapsulation methods

    B. Used only with LAPB encapsulation methods

    C. Consist of 12 frames each with 193 bits

    D. Consist of 24 frames each with 192 bits

9. Which of the following is true?

   A. T1s run at 2.048Mbps and use 30 channels, in contrast to E1s, which use 24 channels and run at 1.544Mbps

   B. T1s run at 1.544Mbps and use 30 channels, in contrast to E1s, which use 24 channels and run at 2.048Mbps

   C. T1s run at 1.544Mbps and use 24 channels, in contrast to E1s, which use 30 channels and run at 2.048Mbps

   D. T1s run at 2.048Mbps and use 24 channels, in contrast to E1s, which use 30 channels and run at 1.544Mbps

10. Which of the following is true regarding multilink?

   A. It is the ability to dial a link when the router finds interesting packets

   B. Multilink is used as a secondary link when the main link drops

   C. It creates logical interfaces on a serial interface by using DDR

   D. It is the ability to increase bandwidth between point-to-point dial-up connections by grouping interfaces.

11. What does the Q protocol specify in ISDN?

   A. ISDN on the existing telephone network

   B. Bandwidth on demand

   C. Concepts, terminology, and services

   D. Switching and signaling

12. Which is true about link compression?

   A. It compresses the data, but leaves the header intact

   B. It compresses only the header information and leaves the data intact

   C. It is the combination of both header and payload compression

   D. It can be used only with LAPB encapsulation

13. If a Cisco router dials up more than one connection and splits the traffic over both interfaces, what type of protocol or device are you using?

    A. Payload compression

    B. Multi-dial-up

    C. Switched access

    D. Multilink

14. Which is true about payload compression?

    A. It compresses the data, but leaves the header intact

    B. It compresses only the header information and leaves the data intact

    C. It is the combination of both header and payload compression

    D. It can be used only with LAPB encapsulation

15. What does the E protocol in ISDN specify?

    A. ISDN on the existing telephone network

    B. Bandwidth on demand

    C. Concepts, terminology, and services

    D. Switching and signaling

16. The `isdn switch-type` command provides what function?

    A. Aggregates traffic over multiple ISDN channels simultaneously

    B. Encapsulates ISDN over PPP encapsulations

    C. Specifies the type of ISDN switch with which the router communicates

    D. Configures the framing, either IETF or AMI

17. Which is true regarding header compression?

    A. It compresses the data, but leaves the header intact

    B. It compresses only the header information and leaves the data intact

    C. It is the combination of both header and payload compression

    D. It can be used only with LAPB encapsulation

18. What is the default serial encapsulation on Cisco routers?

    A. IETF

    B. LAPB

    C. HDLC

    D. ISDN

19. What command will encapsulate PPP on a serial link?

    A. `ppp encapsulation`

    B. `encap ppp`

    C. `encapsulation lppp`

    D. `line encapsulation ppp`

20. What can be thought of as basically the telephone number of each B channel?

    A. DDR

    B. E protocols

    C. SPIDs

    D. Priority lists

13

Bandwidth on Demand

Although you can possibly have too much money—maybe even too much fun—you can never have too much bandwidth. So in this chapter, we will discuss ways to provide and maximize bandwidth when it's needed, and how not to waste this precious resource when it's not needed.

Some pretty powerful IOS tools are available that supply significant flexibility when implementing WAN services. We'll discuss dial-on-demand routing (DDR), both legacy DDR and the new dialer profiles. After that, we'll present some advanced DDR features such as PPP authentication, dial backup, multilink, DDR for IPX, and snapshot routing.

The CCNP test objectives covered in this chapter are as follows:

- Configure Legacy dial-on-demand routing (DDR)

- Configure dialer profiles

- Verify DDR operation

- Configure dial backup

- Verify dial backup operation

- Configure snapshot routing

- Configure IPX spoofing

Dial-on-Demand Routing (DDR)

Sometimes it just isn't worth the cost to install expensive, dedicated WAN circuits—why pay for 7×24 connectivity when all you really need is about four to five hours per week? This type of scenario is where DDR really shines. Basically, any situation where only occasional connectivity is needed screams for DDR. For example, consider the network shown in Figure 13.1.

FIGURE 13.1

Sample DDR internetwork

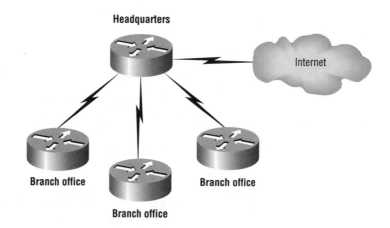

Suppose that the remote sites need to communicate with headquarters only once per day to report total sales orders, and maybe once every couple of hours to check for or send new e-mail. Traditionally, there are two options:

- Install a dedicated WAN

- Configure some sort of manual dial-up

DDR fits neatly between these two options, capturing the best of both solutions. With DDR implemented, the branch office routers will initiate connections with the headquarters router only when necessary (as with a typical dial-up solution). However, with DDR in place, the routers will initiate, maintain, and close this connection without requiring user intervention—*not* a typical dial-up solution. From the user's perspective, network operation is no different than it is with dedicated WAN links. Whenever users need to access the WAN, they just do—they don't have to do anything to set it up. However, when the time comes to pay the bill for these WAN services, the bill is for the actual time spent rather than for dedicated circuits. So you get fully functional WAN services at dial-up prices—what a deal! What more could you want?

While DDR is a truly awesome solution for many situations, it's not for every WAN situation. Here are some situations where DDR really excels:

- Low bandwidth requirements

- Infrequent usage

- Periodic rather than continuous traffic patterns

- ISDN or PSTN (dial-up, circuit switched WAN services)

In these situations, DDR can provide most of the functionality of a traditional WAN, and frequently does so at significant savings over traditional WAN costs.

Whenever DDR is configured, the administrator can define which types of traffic will trigger calls. Consider our example in Figure 13.1. Now suppose we don't want to connect for WWW requests, but we do want to connect to upload sales orders and for e-mail traffic. You can do this by defining what Cisco calls *interesting traffic*. As the administrator, you can control whether calls are made for every request or only when certain types of requests are made. As you'll see, the tool used for this definition is an access list (these should be old friends by now). Plus, as the administrator, you can also specify exactly how long to remain connected after last seeing interesting traffic. By configuring a *dialer idle timeout*, you can mandate the connection to be closed after being connected for *x* period of time without seeing any sales orders or e-mail traffic.

Before doing any actual configurations, we'll introduce the steps by which DDR operates, because a few of the steps are common to all DDR implementations:

1. Upon receiving traffic, the router will check its routing table to see if it knows of a route to the specified destination network. If it finds one, the router then checks to see if the outbound interface uses DDR. If it does, the router finally checks to see if the traffic is defined as interesting, because only interesting packets can initiate DDR connections.

2. After determining that there is indeed a route to the destination network, the next hop router is located, and the router determines dialing instructions for the interface.

3. The router will then check to see if the interface is currently connected. If not, the router will initiate the call (assuming the traffic has been deemed interesting). If the interface is currently connected, the traffic will be sent. If the traffic was defined as interesting, the dialer idle timeout will be reset.

4. The connection is maintained, and all traffic is routed until the idle timeout expires. Once the timeout expires, the call is terminated.

Once the link is up, the router will transmit both interesting and uninteresting traffic. However, unless interesting traffic is continuous (more frequent than the dialer idle timeout setting), the link will close. So uninteresting traffic can take advantage only of a call that's been established and maintained by interesting traffic—uninteresting traffic can't keep a call established by itself.

Designing DDR Networks

When designing your DDR network topology, you'll have to decide whether the remote sites are going to answer calls, place calls, or both place and receive calls. Cisco has three basic DDR topologies that you can follow when designing your DDR internetwork:

- Point-to-point
- Hub-and-spoke
- Fully meshed

Point-to-Point

This isn't much different from having a dedicated leased line between two sites, except it's a dial-up connection. You configure each site with a dialer interface, then map the other site's address to a telephone number. You can configure more than one DDR interface for bandwidth-on-demand capability.

Hub-and-Spoke

In this topology, one main location can dial several remote locations simultaneously. However, the remote locations communicate directly only with the main location—not with any other remote locations. This topology is pictured in Figure 13.2.

Rotary groups (covered later in this chapter) are used to map the main location to remote locations, and using them allows a router to choose any interface that's not being used at the time. If you're not using rotary groups, you must configure each interface as a separate, dedicated interface.

Since hub-and-spoke topologies are mapped to only a central location, they're easier to configure than a meshed topology. Hub-and-spoke was designed for communication servers with higher port density, or routers with PRIs or multiple BRIs.

F I G U R E 13.2

Hub-and-spoke
DDR topology

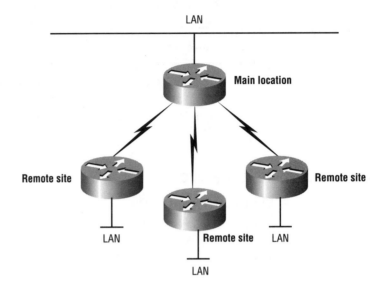

F I G U R E 13.2

Hub-and-spoke
DDR topology

If you need remote sites to communicate with each other within a hub-and-spoke physical topology, you must disable split horizons at the hub router interfaces. Why? Because split horizon mandates that an interface that receives information about a route isn't allowed to advertise that information out the same interface. That means remote sites won't be able to communicate with each other when routers are running in this mode. Remember that this is a feature, not a bug. If you need the remote sites to communicate, you just have to disable split horizons on the hub routers. An alternative is to disable routing protocols and use static routes and default routes instead. While this may not be appropriate for larger or dynamic environments, if it is an option for you, it might just save a few headaches.

Fully Meshed

This topology has a connection from each location to every other location and should be used when you need remote locations to call any other site directly instead of going through a central location as with hub-and-spoke topology. Figure 13.3 pictures a fully meshed topology.

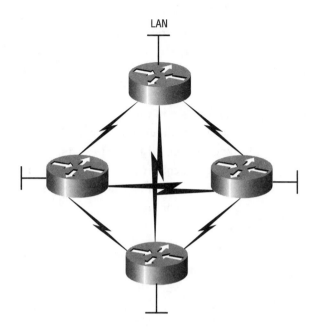

This topology obviously has a more complex configuration than hub-and-spoke physical topology, because each site must have a mapping configured for every other site. As with hub-and-spoke, without a rotary group configured, there must be an interface for each link.

So now that we've introduced the basics, let's take a look at some configuration specifics and special features.

Legacy DDR

Legacy DDR is the router's ability to make a call and establish a connection when appropriate. As an administrator, you control what is or is not an appropriate criterion for placing a call by defining interesting traffic. There are three steps involved in configuring legacy DDR:

1. Specify interesting traffic (what kind of traffic is required to bring up the link).

2. Define the static routes (teach the router how to get to a destination).

3. Configure dialer information (the number to call, how to place the call).

Interesting Traffic

Interesting traffic is specified using the dialer-list command. A dialer list is created much like an access list is, and the syntax is similar as well.

Suppose we want IP traffic—but not IPX or AppleTalk traffic—to be able to initiate a call. We could proceed as follows:

```
RouterC#configure term
Enter configuration commands, one per line.  End with CNTL/Z.
RouterC(config)#dialer-list 5 protocol ip permit
RouterC(config)#dialer-list 5 protocol ipx deny
RouterC(config)#dialer-list 5 protocol appletalk deny
RouterC(config)#^Z
RouterC#
```

After entering Configuration mode, we use the dialer-list command, followed by a dialer-group number, the protocol keyword, then a permit or deny. By default, all traffic is defined as interesting and will initiate a connection. As with access lists, there's an implicit deny at the end of each dialer list. The dialer-list 5 above and dialer-list 6 below are equivalent.

```
RouterC#configure term
Enter configuration commands, one per line.  End with CNTL/Z.
RouterC(config)#dialer-list 6 protocol ip permit
RouterC(config)#^Z
RouterC#
```

Also as with access lists, the context-sensitive help can be extremely useful when you're wading through the syntax:

```
RouterC#configure term
Enter configuration commands, one per line.  End with CNTL/Z.
RouterC(config)#dialer-list ?
  <1-10>  Dialer group number

RouterC(config)#dialer-list 6 ?
  protocol  Permit or Deny based on protocols
```

```
RouterC(config)#dialer-list 6 protocol ?
  appletalk         AppleTalk
  bridge            Bridging
  clns              OSI Connectionless Network Service
  clns_es           CLNS End System
  clns_is           CLNS Intermediate System
  decnet            DECnet
  decnet_node       DECnet node
  decnet_router-L1  DECnet router L1
  decnet_router-L2  DECnet router L2
  ip                IP
  ipx               Novell IPX
  llc2              LLC2
  netbios           NETBIOS
  vines             Banyan Vines
  xns               XNS

RouterC(config)#dialer-list 6 protocol ip ?
  deny    Deny specified protocol
  list    Add access list to dialer list
  permit  Permit specified protocol

RouterC(config)#dialer-list 6 protocol ip permit ?
  <cr>

RouterC(config)#dialer-list 6 protocol ip permit
RouterC(config)#^Z
RouterC#
```

You can see that you have the ability to decide which protocols will be defined as interesting, but what if (as in our earlier example) you want to define some traffic within a protocol stack as interesting, and other traffic within the same protocol stack as uninteresting? The answer lies in using access lists. Regard the following lines from our help example above:

```
RouterC(config)#dialer-list 6 protocol ip ?
  deny    Deny specified protocol
```

```
list    Add access list to dialer list
permit  Permit specified protocol
```

RouterC(config)#**dialer-list 6 protocol ip ?**

We can, of course, permit or deny based on protocol, or we can use the `list` keyword and specify an access list to define interesting traffic. If you need more granular control than just specifying an entire protocol stack to define interesting traffic, you can use this option, then build extremely detailed access lists to define the type of interesting traffic you need. Let's look at an example:

```
RouterC#configure term
Enter configuration commands, one per line.  End with CNTL/Z.
RouterC(config)#access-list 101 permit tcp any any eq smtp
RouterC(config)#access-list 101 permit tcp any any eq pop3
RouterC(config)#access-list 101 deny ip any any
RouterC(config)#dialer-list 7 protocol ip list 101
RouterC(config)#^Z
RouterC#
```

In access-list 101, we specified that both checking and sending of e-mail should be allowed, but all other IP traffic is denied. So in `dialer-list 7`, we then stated that `access-list 101` is to be used as a criteria for testing whether traffic is interesting.

access-list 101 will not actually permit or deny any packets unless it's applied to an interface with an access-group command. It will be used only to decide if the packets are interesting. Even though IP packets other than e-mail are not interesting, they would still be routed (assuming that the link is up).

We could have entered IPX or AppleTalk access lists and used those as well as our IP access list in `dialer-list 7`. Also, only one access list per protocol is allowed in a dialer list, just as with interface configuration.

Static Routing

Obviously, routing updates between routers can't be sent over a link that doesn't exist or is inactive (we will examine this issue later in the section on snapshot routing). In most networks, routers build routing tables using dynamic routing algorithms such as RIP, IGRP, or EIGRP. However, since routing updates are not sent over DDR inactive links, the administrator of the network (you) will usually configure static routes in each router so that hosts can still find network services when the DDR link is inactive. After all, having routing updates initiate calls at regular intervals may very well negate any gains afforded by DDR over a leased line. In these situations, static routing is generally preferable to any form of dynamic routing. Consider the following listing:

```
RouterC#configure term
Enter configuration commands, one per line.  End with CNTL/Z.
RouterC(config)#ip route 172.16.50.0 255.255.255.0 bri0
RouterC(config)#^Z
RouterC#
```

Here we've defined that any traffic destined for the 172.16.50.0 network is to be sent via BRI0.

As you saw, if you want to create a static route, you use the ip route command. You might not have known that you could then distribute these static routes to the other routers in your internetwork with the redistribute command. This is shown in the following example:

```
Router(config)#router igrp 109
Router(config-router)#network 131.108.0.0
Router(config-router)#redistribute ?
  bgp        Border Gateway Protocol (BGP)
  connected  Connected
  egp        Exterior Gateway Protocol (EGP)
  eigrp      Enhanced Interior Gateway Routing Protocol
             (EIGRP)
  igrp       Interior Gateway Routing Protocol (IGRP)
  isis       ISO IS-IS
  iso-igrp   IGRP for OSI networks
  mobile     Mobile routes
```

```
    odr        On Demand stub Routes
    ospf       Open Shortest Path First (OSPF)
    rip        Routing Information Protocol (RIP)
    static     Static routes
Router(config-router)#redistribute static ?
    metric     Metric for redistributed routes
    route-map  Route map reference
    <cr>
Router(config-router)#redistribute static metric ?
    <1-4294967295>  Bandwidth metric in Kbits per second
```

You don't need to set the metric for the static route, but you can use this to weight the link higher than a directly connected T1 link, which can be really helpful in dial backup situations.

If you don't have dynamic or static routes in place to all networks, your routers won't be able to find them. However, creating a default route on your routers will cause them to forward unknown packets to the default networks. You can effect this with the ip default-network command. Also, you can use the passive command to stop broadcasts from routing protocols from triggering a DDR link. This command tells the router not to transmit routing information on the specified interface. The use of both the ip default-network and the passive commands is demonstrated below.

```
Router#config t
Enter configuration commands, one per line.  End with CNTL/Z.
Router(config)#ip default-network ?
    A.B.C.D  IP address of default network

Router(config)#ip default-network 172.16.50.0
Router(config)#router rip
Router(config-router)#network 172.16.50.0
Router(config-router)#passive s0
```

Configuring the Dialer

Once you've selected the interface to be configured, you must complete the following steps:

- Configure a network address for the interface

- Configure an encapsulation type
- Configure the dialer group (interesting traffic)
- Configure the dialer map (destination)

Also, you might want to complete the following optional step:

- Configure the dialer idle timeout

Here is an example of these configurations on our BRI0 interface:

```
RouterC#configure term
Enter configuration commands, one per line.  End with CNTL/Z.
RouterC(config)#int bri0
RouterC(config-if)#ip address 172.16.20.1 255.255.255.0
RouterC(config-if)#encapsulation ppp
RouterC(config-if)#dialer-group 5
RouterC(config-if)#dialer map ip 172.16.20.2 name RouterC
  5556677
RouterC(config-if)#dialer idle-timeout 300
RouterC(config-if)#^Z
RouterC#
```

Since DDR isn't an encapsulation method, you need to run it with an encapsulation method that Cisco supports. One of the following data link encapsulations will do:

- Cisco recommends Point-to-Point Protocol (PPP) because it can be used with asynchronous, synchronous, and ISDN interfaces; has multiprotocol support; and provides authentication security via CHAP and PAP.

- High-Level Data Link Control (HDLC) supports multiple protocols, but can be run on only synchronous and ISDN interfaces. It also doesn't provide for any authentication.

- Serial Line Interface Protocol (SLIP) is an older protocol that can run on only asynchronous interfaces. It can't use multiple protocols (IP only), and has no provision for authentication.

- X.25 can be run on ISDN and synchronous interfaces.

The `dialer-group` interface command assigns the DDR interface to a dialer access group. You use the group number (a value between 1 and 10) to specify which group the DDR interface belongs to, and this number must match the value of the dialer list. This command is also used to connect the DDR interface to access-list statements, which identify interesting packets. The `dialer map` interface command is used to define the phone numbers (one or multiple) for a DDR interface connecting to the DCE device. The `dialer map` and `dialer-group` commands work together to initiate dialing by associating interesting packets. You can also choose specific protocols (IP, IPX, or AppleTalk) with the `protocol` keyword. The `dialer idle-timeout` interface command specifies how long a link stays active after the last interesting packet was passed—the default is 120 seconds.

Verifying Calls

Once you've completed these three steps for configuring legacy DDR (specifying interesting traffic, setting up static routing, and configuring the dialer), you're ready to verify and test your configuration. The following commands are useful when testing legacy DDR configuration:

- `ping`—establishes a connection with a remote network (assuming you defined it as interesting)

- `show dialer`—gives the current status of a link

- `show isdn status`—gives the status of ISDN connection

- `show ip route`—displays and verifies routes

- `debug q921`—call setup and teardown

- `debug dialer`—call setup and teardown

Dialer Profiles

There's one major problem with the legacy DDR configuration we just reviewed. When we configured the interface, we were actually configuring the physical interface with parameters such as network address, encapsulation, etc. However, what if we wanted to use that same interface to dial a different number and use different parameters when establishing that connection? With legacy DDR, the interface configuration is statically assigned. Dialer profiles alleviate this problem.

Dialer profiles allow us to create multiple virtual interfaces (called dialer interfaces) that have different configurations for different circumstances. All physical interfaces are placed in a *dialer pool*, and can be used by any dialer interface that has access to that pool. This abstraction separates the physical interface from the configuration, so it allows multiple configurations to be used on the same physical interface. Dialer profiles are a relatively new feature—they were introduced in IOS version 11.2.

The steps for creating a dialer profile are similar to the steps used in legacy DDR:

1. Specify interesting traffic—what kind of traffic is required to bring up the link.

2. Define the static routes—direct the router on how to get to a destination.

3. Configure the dialer interface—configuration goes here, not on the physical interface.

4. Configure the physical interface—make it a member of a dialer pool.

We used the following example for the legacy DDR configuration:

```
RouterC#configure term
Enter configuration commands, one per line.  End with CNTL/Z.
RouterC(config)#int bri0
RouterC(config-if)#ip address 172.16.20.1 255.255.255.0
RouterC(config-if)#encapsulation ppp
RouterC(config-if)#dialer-group 5
RouterC(config-if)#dialer map ip 172.16.20.2 name RouterC
   5556677
RouterC(config-if)#dialer idle-timeout 300
RouterC(config-if)#^Z
RouterC#
```

Now let's take a look at the same configuration using a dialer profile:

```
RouterC#configure term
Enter configuration commands, one per line.  End with CNTL/Z.
RouterC(config)#interface dialer1
RouterC(config-if)#ip address 172.16.20.1 255.255.255.0
RouterC(config-if)#encapsulation ppp
```

```
RouterC(config-if)#dialer remote-name RouterC
RouterC(config-if)#dialer string 5556677
RouterC(config-if)#dialer-group 5
RouterC(config-if)#dialer pool 10
RouterC(config-if)#dialer idle-timeout 300
RouterC(config-if)#exit
RouterC(config)#int bri0
RouterC(config-if)#no ip address
RouterC(config-if)#dialer pool-member 10
RouterC(config-if)#^Z
RouterC#
```

Notice that the entire configuration is now on the dialer1 interface, and our actual physical interface (BRI0) is just a member of dialer pool 10. At this point, we could configure additional dialer interfaces with distinct parameters, and also to use dialer pool 10 (and thus use BRI0).

PPP Authentication

Security and authentication shouldn't be an afterthought when you're designing your DDR network—they must be considered when you're designing the DDR topology. Authentication is responsible for identifying who is calling in so that the called router can correctly forward packets to the correct interface. Most of the time this is required when using dialer rotary groups where multiple sites will be calling into a single router.

The Point-to-Point Protocol (PPP) has two different security and authentication methods that can be used with DDR:

- Challenge Handshake Authentication Protocol (CHAP)
- Password Authentication Protocol (PAP)

CHAP

CHAP is used with PPP encapsulation methods to grant authentication and security. The username and password are encrypted before being sent over the link. When a remote device tries to connect to a local router, the local router receives a challenge response. The local router will verify the connection by looking up the remote device's name in the configuration and making sure the passwords match on both the remote and local router.

The names and passwords are configured using the `username` command. The example below shows a router configuration allowing a username of todd to call into the router:

```
Router(config)#hostname Sales
Router(config)#username todd password goodguy
Router(config)#int bri1
Router(config-int)#encapsulation ppp
Router(config-int)#ppp authentication chap
```

PAP

PAP is also used with PPP for authentication purposes, but it's not as secure as CHAP because PAP sends the complete password and username in clear text across the link.

The `username` command is used to verify a user in the router configuration and grants the user access. The following example shows a username entry and an ISDN interface configured for PAP:

```
Router(config)#username todd password goodguy
Router(config)#int bri1
Router(config-int)#encapsulation ppp
Router(config-int)#ppp authentication pap
```

Rotary Groups

You can create a group of physical serial interfaces that act as one by using a rotary group. This was used in the hub-and-spoke topology mentioned earlier, and it's helpful when you need a single location to dial multiple locations simultaneously as in Figure 13.4.

If you have a device with multiple DDR interfaces, you can configure the router to share the interfaces instead of dedicating an interface to each location. The router checks for a free interface in the rotary group when a connection is needed. Incoming calls will also use the first available interface found.

The following listing is an example of using rotary groups with DDR:

```
Router(config)#Interface dialer 9
Router(config)#int bri0
Router(config-int)#dialer rotary-group 9
Router(config-int)#encapsulation ppp
```

```
Router(config-int)#int bri1
Router(config-int)#dialer rotary-group 9
Router(config-int)#encapsulation ppp.
```

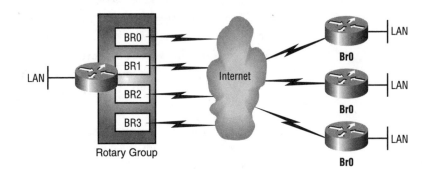

FIGURE 13.4

Using rotary groups
with DDR

Advanced DDR

There are many advanced DDR features—we'll introduce only a few of them briefly here. Many are covered in greater detail in *CCNP: Configuring, Monitoring, and Troubleshooting Dialup Services (CMTD),* coming soon from Sybex. In this chapter, we'll acquaint you with four advanced topics:

- Dial backup
- Multilink PPP
- DDR for IPX
- Snapshot routing

Dial Backup

Dial backup allows you to use a DDR connection to back up a regular primary connection, meaning that if a primary connection fails, the DDR connection will come to life and continue to pass traffic. Failure can be defined in two ways: loss of connectivity or saturation of bandwidth. The first one's obvious—when your T1 goes down, that's failure. However, the second one isn't quite so apparent. When your T1 reaches 90% utilization and a user needs to download a mega-file from the Internet, the link is as good as down as far as your user is concerned. In this case, dial backup can sense that the bandwidth utilization is high and use DDR to provide an additional path for traffic to follow, thus responding to peak demand. Let's take a look at each of these situations.

Primary-Link Failure

In this scenario, a DDR link is configured to back up a failed primary link. Consider the following configuration:

```
RouterC#configure term
Enter configuration commands, one per line.  End with CNTL/Z.
RouterC(config)#int bri0
RouterC(config-if)#backup interface serial0
RouterC(config-if)#backup delay 5 60
RouterC(config-if)#^Z
RouterC#
```

We configured interface BRI0 to back up interface serial 0. The backup delay command tells the BRI0 interface to wait 5 seconds after the failure of serial 0 before starting up, and if the ISDN connection is established, to wait 60 seconds after serial 0 recovers before tearing it down. So now when your frame's away, your users can still play—using ISDN, of course.

Primary-Link Bandwidth Saturation

In this scenario, a DDR link will back up a saturated primary link. Here's the configuration:

```
RouterC#configure term
Enter configuration commands, one per line.  End with CNTL/Z.
RouterC(config)#int bri0
RouterC(config-if)#backup interface serial0
RouterC(config-if)#backup load 80 30
RouterC(config-if)#^Z
RouterC#
```

In this scenario, BRI0 will come alive and help interface serial 0 when it becomes too busy. When we entered the backup load command, we specified that the ISDN call would not be placed until 80% of serial 0's available bandwidth was in use, and that it would remain available until serial 0's bandwidth use was less than 30%.

Multilink PPP

Multilink PPP is basically the ability to aggregate several separate physical interfaces into a single virtual pipe. Through the use of multilink PPP, multiple ISDN channels can be combined to form a single, faster channel—at least virtually. Consider Figure 13.5.

F I G U R E 13.5

Multilink PPP

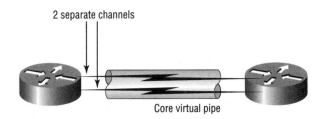

2 separate channels

Core virtual pipe

Even though the routers are connected via two separate channels, the two channels will act as a single connection when using multilink.

Configuration is relatively straightforward. Consider the following legacy DDR configuration:

```
RouterC#configure term
Enter configuration commands, one per line.  End with CNTL/Z.
RouterC(config)#int bri1
RouterC(config-if)#ppp multilink
RouterC(config-if)#dialer load-threshold 100 either
RouterC(config-if)#^Z
RouterC#
```

Here we assume that BRI1 was already configured for legacy DDR. We added the ppp multilink, which will enable multilink on both B channels. Next, we used the dialer load-threshold command to specify that once utilization exceeds 40%, either inbound or outbound, the additional link should be used.

Configuration is similar on dialer profile configurations, although with dialer profiles, the modifications aren't made to the physical interface, they're applied to the dialer interface. Be aware that all physical interfaces included in the dialer pool are potential candidates to be added into the multilink bundle.

DDR for IPX

NetWare servers are good sheepdogs—they keep track of their clients. Consider Figure 13.6.

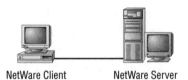

NetWare Client   NetWare Server

Under normal circumstances, the NetWare server will send an IPX watchdog packet to the workstation if it hasn't heard from the workstation in a while. This assures the server that the workstation is still alive and working—it's just not currently using the server's resources. Now, suppose that the workstation is running an application such as RCONSOLE that requires that the server and workstation establish an SPX connection. In an effort to maintain its connection, SPX will send periodic keepalive packets between the two machines. No problem? Well, consider the same client and server in Figure 13.7.

NetWare Client   DDR Connection   NetWare Server

The server and workstation have a DDR connection between them. (Remember that IPX doesn't care about your internetwork—it wants to work like it's on a huge LAN.) You have a problem—either you can have the DDR link up all the time, or you can risk having your SPX and watchdog timers time out. However, there is a solution for this one—it involves fooling the IPX servers.

The trick is to have the router answer the watchdog request or SPX keep-alive as if it were the actual workstation or server. In the above figure, if the router on the Ethernet segment local to the server can respond to the watchdog request destined for the workstation across the DDR link, the DDR link never has to be started. Likewise, if the router on the same Ethernet segment as the workstation can respond to any SPX keepalives destined for the server, we can again protect our DDR link from unnecessary usage.

The configuration of these responses is called *spoofing*, and is as follows:

```
RouterC#configure term
Enter configuration commands, one per line.  End with CNTL/Z.
RouterC(config)#int bri0
RouterC(config-if)#no ipx route-cache
RouterC(config-if)#ipx spx-spoof
RouterC(config-if)#ipx watchdog-spoof
RouterC(config-if)#ipx spx-idle-time 240
RouterC(config-if)#^Z
RouterC#
```

The BRI0 interface will spoof both the SPX keepalive and watchdog packets rather than initiate a call. The `no ipx route-cache` command is required before entering the `spoof` commands. Remember that you can't just define the keepalive and watchdog as uninteresting to protect your DDR link, because if you do that, you'll cause timeouts on servers and work-stations. You have to set up the spoofs shown here to protect your DDR link and keep your NetWare servers and clients happy too.

Snapshot Routing

Snapshot routing is another method of controlling traffic across DDR links. We spent some time earlier discussing how to use static and default routes instead of running dynamic routing protocols. The primary reason for avoiding dynamic routing is that routers running dynamic routing protocols have this nasty habit of trying to communicate at regular intervals. Even link-state routing protocols exchange hellos. If DDR links come up for every routing update, most benefits of DDR over dedicated links would be lost. If DDR links don't come up, routers will assume that remote networks have gone away and will eventually expire routes from their routing tables.

Snapshot routing fixes this problem by allowing some dynamic routing protocols to be run across DDR links (thus saving administrators the burden of configuring and maintaining static routes). It fixes the problems listed above with dynamic routing. With snapshot routing, DDR links are not required to be up all of the time. Also, routers configured with snapshot routing will not expire routes learned via the DDR links (as they normally would when the links go down). Snapshot routing works only with distance vector routing protocols (IP RIP, IPX RIP, RTMP, and IGRP). Link-state protocols, including EIGRP, are not candidates for snapshot routing.

Snapshot routing works best in hub-and-spoke topologies. With meshed DDR networks, static routing is still a better option. Also, snapshot routing is not for every hub-and-spoke network. A small network that is not likely to have many changes would probably still be easier to manage using static routing. Snapshot routing is most useful in large, dynamic hub-and-spoke DDR networks.

Operation is relatively straightforward. There are three main steps:

1. Client (spoke) routers are configured with a routing update interval. This determines how often the client will contact the server (hub) router to exchange routing information. The server router will wait for the client router to contact it to exchange routing information.

2. When the interval is reached, the client router connects with the server router and exchanges routing information.

3. After exchanging routing information, the client router takes a snapshot of the newly updated routing table and "freezes" it. No updates to the routing table take place until the next scheduled update (even if the DDR link comes up for interesting traffic).

While waiting for the next scheduled update, the server routers will broadcast route updates to the rest of the network at normal intervals as if they really were connected to the client routers. They will not expire routes.

Configuration is also relatively simple—only two commands are required on both client and server routers. Both commands are entered in Interface Configuration mode (physical or dialer interface):

- Enable snapshot routing using the `snapshot client` or `snapshot server` command.

- Define a dialer map using the `dialer map` command.

In the example below, Router A is a client router, and Router B is the server router. Both routers are already configured for DDR—we will add the snapshot routing commands:

```
RouterA#config t
RouterA(config)#int BRIO
RouterA(config-if)#snapshot client 5 480 dialer
RouterA(config-if)#dialer map snapshot 1 name RouterB
   5556677
RouterA(config-if)#^Z
RouterA#

RouterB#config t
RouterB(config)#int dialer1
RouterB(config-if)#snapshot server 5 dialer
RouterB(config-if)#dialer map snapshot 1 name RouterA
   5556688
RouterB(config-if)#^Z
RouterB#
```

On Router A, when we entered the `snapshot client` command, the 5 specifies the time in minutes that the routers will spend communicating once they connect to exchange routing information. Notice that on Router B, we use the same parameter. On Router A, we specify 480 as the number of minutes between connections (six hours). As mentioned, the client router controls the connection interval, so while both routers must know and agree on the amount of time that they will connect for, only the client needs to know the interval at which they will connect—the server does not receive this information. The `dialer` keyword is optional and is used to allow the client to dial the server if the DDR link is not already up.

Summary

In this chapter, the following topics were covered:

- We introduced legacy DDR, where we defined interesting traffic and then configured an interface to use that definition to determine when to dial and when to hang up.

- We examined dialer profiles, the newest method of abstracting details away from the physical interface and freeing it up to participate in a dialer pool.

- We then studied PPP authentication, rotary groups, dial backup, and multilink.

- We introduced you to watchdog and SPX spoofing, and demonstrated their configuration.

- Finally, we discussed snapshot routing. This is an effective method of running dynamic routing protocols in a DDR network.

Review Questions

1. Which of the following are valid reasons to implement DDR?

   A. Low bandwidth requirements

   B. ISDN connections

   C. Continuous rather than periodic traffic patterns

   D. Interoperability

   E. Periodic rather than continuous traffic patterns

   F. Infrequent usage

2. Which of the following best describes the comparison of DDR against traditional dial-up services and traditional leased-line services?

   A. It's more expensive than leased-line and easier to use than traditional dial-up

   B. It's less expensive than leased-line and easier to use than traditional dial-up

   C. It's easier to use than leased-line and more expensive than traditional dial-up

   D. It's easier to use than leased-line and less expensive than traditional dial-up

3. You need to set up spoofing for IPX with DDR. Write in the four commands that you should use.

Router#**configure term**

Enter configuration commands, one per line. End with CNTL/Z.

Router(config)#int bri0

Router(config-if)#_____

Router(config-if)#_____

Router(config-if)#_____

Router(config-if)#_____

4. Which of the following best describes the function of the dialer timeout?

   A. After the specified number of seconds, the connection will be closed

   B. After the specified number of seconds has passed without having any traffic cross the interface, the connection will be closed

   C. After the specified number of seconds has passed without having any interesting traffic cross the interface, the connection will be closed

   D. After the specified number of interesting packets have crossed the interface, the connection will be closed

5. True or False. The router will check to see if the interface is currently connected before checking to see whether the traffic is interesting.

6. True or False. The router will check to see if the interface uses DDR before checking to see if the traffic is interesting.

7. When configuring legacy DDR, which of the following are valid steps?

   A. Configuring interesting traffic

   B. Configuring the dialer interface

   C. Configuring static routes

   D. Configuring the dialer

   E. Configuring the watchdog

8. When configuring legacy DDR, which of the following must the dialer group match?

   A. The access list

   B. The dialer list

   C. The dialer interface number

   D. The timeout value

9. Suppose that you want to use access list 155 to specify interesting traffic. Which of the following is valid dialer-list syntax to accomplish this?

   A. `dialer-list 5 protocol ipx list 155`

   B. `dialer-list 5 ip protocol list 155`

   C. `dialer-list 5 ipx protocol list 155`

   D. `dialer-list 5 protocol ip list 155`

   E. `dialer-list 5 protocol ipx list 155`

10. Suppose you want to state that AppleTalk is interesting traffic, but IP is not. Which of the following is valid dialer-list syntax to accomplish this?

A. `dialer-list 6 protocol appletalk permit`

B. `dialer-list 6 protocol appletalk permit`
   `dialer-list 6 protocol ip deny`

C. `dialer-list 6 protocol appletalk permit`
   `dialer-list 5 protocol ip deny`

D. `dialer-list 6 protocol appletalk allow`
   `dialer-list 6 protocol ip deny`

E. `dialer-list 5 protocol appletalk permit`
   `dialer-list 6 protocol ip deny`

11. When configuring legacy DDR, which of the following must you specify?

A. A network address for the interface

B. An encapsulation type

C. The dialer idle timeout

D. The dialer map

E. The dialer group

12. Which of the following best describes the function of a dialer profile?

A. Dialer information is configured at the physical interface

B. Dialer information is configured on a logical interface

C. A secondary link will be brought up if a primary link fails

D. A group of physical interfaces will be available to a dialer interface

E. A method for bundling multiple physical links into one logical link will be available

13. Which of the following best describes the function of multilink PPP?

   A. Dialer information is configured at the physical interface

   B. Dialer information is configured on a logical interface

   C. A secondary link will be brought up if a primary link fails

   D. A group of physical interfaces will be available to a dialer interface

   E. A method for bundling multiple physical links into one logical link will be available

14. Which of the following best describes the function of a dialer pool?

   A. Dialer information is configured at the physical interface

   B. Dialer information is configured on a logical interface

   C. A secondary link will be brought up if a primary link fails

   D. A group of physical interfaces will be available to a dialer interface

   E. A method for bundling multiple physical links into one logical link will be available

15. Which of the following best describes the function of legacy DDR?

   A. Dialer information is configured at the physical interface

   B. Dialer information is configured on a logical interface

   C. A secondary link will be brought up if a primary link fails

   D. A group of physical interfaces will be available to a dialer interface

   E. A method for bundling multiple physical links into one logical link will be available

16. Which of the following best describes the function of dial backup?

   A. Dialer information is configured at the physical interface

   B. Dialer information is configured on a logical interface

   C. A secondary link will be brought up if a primary link fails

   D. A group of physical interfaces will be available to a dialer interface

   E. A method for bundling multiple physical links into one logical link will be available

17. Suppose that you want to configure dial backup to connect if your serial 0 link goes down. Suppose as well that you want the DDR link to be established only if the serial 0 link is down longer than 30 seconds, and that the DDR link should disconnect after the serial 0 link has been reestablished for 60 seconds. Which of the following configurations is valid? (Assume you're already in Interface Configuration mode.)

   A. `backup interface serial 0`
       `backup delay 30 60`

   B. `backup interface serial 0`
       `Backup-delay 60 30`

   C. `backup interface 60 30`
       `backup delay serial 0`

   D. `backup interface serial 0`
       `Backup-delay 30 30`

18. Suppose that you want to configure dial backup to connect if your serial 0 link exceeds 70% utilization and disconnect if its utilization drops below 20%. Which of the following configurations is valid? (Assume you are already in Interface Configuration mode.)

A. `backup interface serial 0`
`Backup-load 70 20`

B. `backup interface 70 20`
`backup load serial 0`

C. `backup interface serial 0`
`Backup-load 20 70`

D. `backup interface serial 0`
`backup load 70 20`

19. Which of the following commands will enable multilink when utilization exceeds 50% inbound?

A. `dialer load-threshold 127 in`

B. `dialer load-threshold 127 inbound`

C. `dialer load threshold 127 in`

D. `dialer load threshold 127 inbound`

20. Which command must you enter first if you want to enable watchdog spoofing and SPX keepalive spoofing?

A. `no ipx-route`

B. `no ipx route cache`

C. `no ipx route-cache`

D. `no ipx-route-cache`

Laboratory Exercises

1. Suppose that you want to define FTP and Telnet as interesting traffic, but no other IP traffic as interesting.

2. Continue from lab exercise 1 and enable legacy DDR.

3. Continue from lab exercise 2 and create a dialer profile.

APPENDIX

A

Answers to Review Questions

Chapter 1

1. Which of the following can you use to alleviate congestion in an internetwork (if used correctly)?

   A. Repeaters

   B. Routers

   C. DLC

   D. Switches

   E. Bridges

   Answer: B, D, E

2. Choose the three layers Cisco uses for building its hierarchical internetwork model.

   A. Fundamental

   B. Distribution

   C. IGRP

   D. Core

   E. Backbone

   F. Access

   Answer: B, D, F

3. Identify the characteristics of a scalable internetwork.

   A. Reliability

   B. Responsiveness

   C. Efficiency

   D. Adaptability

   E. Accessibility

   F. All of the above

   Answer: F

4. What is the primary function of the Core layer?

   A. To distribute client-server router information

   B. To provide an optimized and reliable transport structure

   C. To provide access to various parts of the internetwork, as well as to services

   D. To provide access to corporate resources for a workgroup or users on a local segment

Answer: B

5. What is the primary function of the Distribution layer?

   A. To distribute client-server router information

   B. To provide an optimized and reliable transport structure

   C. To provide access to various parts of the internetwork, as well as to services

   D. To provide access to corporate resources for a workgroup or users on a local segment

Answer: C

6. What is the purpose of the Access-layer functions?

   A. To distribute client-server router information

   B. To provide an optimized and reliable transport structure

   C. To provide access to various parts of the internetwork, as well as to services

   D. To provide access to corporate resources for a workgroup or users on a local segment

Answer: D

7. How do LAN switches improve performance on a LAN?

A. By filtering via logical address

B. By regenerating the digital signal

C. By employing packet-switching that permits high-speed data exchanges

D. By employing frame-switching that permits high-speed data exchanges

Answer: D

8. What is a benefit of bridge segmentation?

A. Regeneration and propagation

B. Segmenting or breaking up your network into smaller, more manageable pieces

C. LAN queuing

D. Bridges begin forwarding the frame before reception is complete

Answer: B

9. How does cut-through switching provide better performance than other switching methods?

A. LAN queuing

B. Microsegmentation

C. Receiving the entire frame onto onboard buffers, running a CRC, and then forwarding the frames out the destination port

D. Forwarding the frame before reception is complete

Answer: D

10. LAN segmentation with switches is also called what?

A. Filtering

B. Microsegmenting

C. Bridging

D. Routing

Answer: B

11. Which router layers govern access to Core-layer resources?

A. Distribution

B. Core

C. Backbone

D. Access

Answer: A

12. Which layer has services that enhance communication between routes in different logical groups?

A. Backbone

B. Core

C. Distribution

D. Access

Answer: B

13. How do bridges filter a network?

A. By logical address

B. By IP address

C. By hardware address

D. By digital signaling

Answer: C

14. How do routers filter a network? (Choose all that apply.)

   A. By logical address

   B. By IP address

   C. By digital signaling

   D. By hardware address

   E. By IPX address

   Answer: A, B, E

15. How do switches segment a network?

   A. By logical address

   B. By IP address

   C. By hardware address

   D. By IPX address

   Answer: C

16. What is a drawback of filtering a network with bridges?

   A. It segments the network

   B. It creates internetworks

   C. It passes datagram broadcasts

   D. It filters frames

   Answer: C

17. How can you reduce route table entries?

   A. Route summarization

   B. Incremental updates

   C. Filtering

   D. VLANs

   Answer: A

18. Which Cisco IOS features are available to help reduce bandwidth usage? (Choose all that apply.)

  A. Access lists

  B. Snapshot routing

  C. Compression of WANs

  D. TTL

  E. DDR

  F. Incremental updates

  Answer: A, B, C, E, F

19. Which Cisco IOS features serve to provide stability and availability? (Choose all that apply.)

  A. Reachability

  B. Convergence

  C. Alternative path routing

  D. Snapshot routing

  E. Tunneling

  F. Dial backup

  G. Load balancing

  Answer: C, D, E, F

20. The Cisco IOS provides mitigation for the latency needs of each protocol running on your internetwork with which features? (Choose all that apply.)

  A. Snapshot routing

  B. Weighted fair queuing

  C. Priority queuing

  D. Custom queuing

  Answer: B, C, D

Chapter 2

1. What are the three methods used to increase network availability?

   A. Bandwidth, RAM and Cisco IOS

   B. Redundancy, bandwidth, and backup connections

   C. Dynamic routing protocols, bandwidth, and redundancy or backup connectivity

   D. Power, connectivity, and high-end routers

   Answer: C

2. Which of the following are the three physical elements of a redundant network design?

   A. Multiple-link topology, meshed-link topology, and power systems

   B. Replacement hardware, multiple links, and power systems

   C. Multiple machines (HSRP), multiple links, and meshed links

   D. Dual links, fully redundant routers, and DDR lines

   Answer: A

3. Which topology can be made redundant?

   A. Point-to-point

   B. Hub-and-spoke

   C. Meshed

   D. Both A and B

   Answer: D

4. What is required to implement HSRP?

   A. Cisco IOS

   B. Multiple machines and multiple links

   C. Redundant machines running Cisco IOS (rev. 10)

   D. Both A and B

   Answer: C

5. You want DDR to be activated only as a backup connection. Which of the following configuration changes will ensure that the DDR link will be used only when the router's primary connection to a given destination fails?

    A. A static route

    B. A static route with a high administrative distance assigned to it

    C. A route in the routing table

    D. Simply configuring DDR on the desired interface

Answer: B

6. Why shouldn't BGP, OSPF, and IS-IS protocols be used in a DDR environment?

    A. These are time-sensitive protocols

    B. These protocols require an acknowledgment from their neighbor before routing updates can be sent

    C. DDR does not support these protocols

    D. These protocols do not scale well

Answer: B

7. Which of the following are steps that routers take when deciding whether to establish a connection? (Choose all that apply.)

    A. Verifying a route to the destination

    B. Passing the access list applied to the interface

    C. Checking to see if a connection has already been established

    D. Defining the interface through which the call should be made

    E. All of the above

Answer: E

8. What command is used on a Cisco router to show all the ways that the router learned a given route?

A. show ip route

B. show ip eigrp topology

C. show ip route *

D. show eigrp topology

Answer: B

9. How is a feasible successor configured?

A. As a global command: ip feasible-successor 0.0.0.0 255.255.255.0 null 0

B. As a command under EIGRP: variance multiplier value

C. As a command under EIGRP: feasible-successor 0.0.0.0 255.255.255.255

D. As a global command: variance multiplier value

Answer: B

10. Which of the following is the correct command used to control the redistribution of one routing protocol into IGRP or Enhanced IGRP?

A. distance weight address mask

B. redistribute-metric bandwidth delay reliability loading mtu

C. default-metric number

D. default-metric bandwidth delay reliability loading mtu

Answer: D

11. Which is *not* a method of optimizing bandwidth utilization?

    A. DDR or bandwidth on demand

    B. Dynamic routing protocols

    C. Header or data compression

    D. Access lists

Answer: B

12. Which is a method to improve network responsiveness?

    A. Queuing

    B. Data compression

    C. Access list

    D. DDR or bandwidth on demand

Answer: A

13. Which is a cost-effective alternative to provide additional bandwidth?

    A. Leased-line circuits

    B. ISDN

    C. DDR

    D. Point-to-point circuit

Answer: C—You may think the answer could also be B. However, the correct answer is DDR. This holds because DDR is used only when needed. ISDN can be implemented on leased lines as well as DDR.

14. In which of the Cisco three-layer hierarchy models can redundancy be implemented?

A. Core

B. Edge

C. Distribution

D. All of the above

Answer: D

15. What is *not* a benefit of using dynamic routing protocols on routers that have multiple or redundant links?

A. Load balancing

B. Quicker network convergence

C. Feasible-successor calculation

D. Lower processor utilization

Answer: D

16. Which routing protocol supports load balancing?

A. IGRP

B. EIGRP

C. RIP

D. BGP

Answer: B

17. In which version of Cisco IOS was DDR implemented?

A. 11.0

B. 9.3

C. 10.0

D. 10.3

Answer: C

18. When should DDR *not* be implemented?

    A. When applications are time sensitive

    B. When additional bandwidth is not needed

    C. When snapshot routing has been implemented

    D. When access lists have been applied to the interface

Answer: A

19. Which software feature optimizes bandwidth without creating higher CPU utilization?

    A. Access lists

    B. Switching

    C. Compression

    D. None of the above

Answer: B

20. Which is *not* a method of reducing routing updates?

    A. Route summarization

    B. Distribution lists

    C. Tunneling

    D. Unthrottled redistribution

Answer: D

Chapter 3

1. What range of integers is used to signify a standard access list?

   A. 0–100

   B. 1–100

   C. 1–99

   D. 101–199

   Answer: C

2. What range of integers is used to signify an extended access list?

   A. 100–199

   B. 1–99

   C. 100–200

   D. 101–199

   Answer: A

3. What is the criterion used to match a packet on a standard access list?

   A. Destination address

   B. Session-layer protocol

   C. Source address

   D. Protocol port number

   Answer: C

4. What is the proper syntax for writing a standard access list?

   A. `ip access-list access-list-number {deny | permit} source source-wildcard`

   B. `access-list access-list-number {deny | permit} source source-wildcard`

   C. `access-list access-list-number {deny | permit} source source-mask`

   D. `access-list access-list-number {deny | permit} [protocol] source source-wildcard destination destination-wildcard`

   Answer: B

5. What is the proper syntax for an extended access list?

A. `access-list access-list-number {deny | permit} [protocol | protocol-keyword] [source-address source wildcard mask | any] [destination-address destination wildcard mask | any] [protocol specific options]`

B. `ip access-list access-list-number {deny | permit} [protocol | protocol-keyword] [source-address source wildcard mask | any] [destination-address destination wildcard mask | any] [protocol specific options]`

C. `access-list access-list-number {deny | permit} source source-wildcard`

D. `ip access-list access-list-number source source wildcard destination destination wildcard {permit | deny} [protocol protocol keyword]`

Answer: A

6. Which command is used to apply an access list to a physical interface?

A. `access-class access-list-number {in | out}`

B. `access-list access-list-number {in | out}`

C. `access-group access-list-number {in | out}`

D. `ip access-group access-list-number {in | out}`

Answer: D

7. Which command is issued to apply a standard access list to a virtual interface?

A. `access-class access-list-number {in | out}`

B. `access-list access-list-number {in | out}`

C. `access-group access-list-number {in | out}`

D. `Ip access-class access-list-number {in | out}`

Answer: A

8. After looking at the following configuration lines, choose the answer that best explains their effect.

```
Router_X(config)#access-list 20 permit 172.16.0.0
  0.0.255.255
Router_X(config)#access-list 20 permit 10.0.0.0
  0.255.255.255
Router_X(config)#line vty 0 4
Router_X(config-line)#access-class 20 in
Router_X(config-line)#^Z
Router_X#
```

A. Access list 20 is applied to the virtual interfaces zero through four

B. Access list 20 permits networks 172.16.0.0 and 10.0.0.0

C. Access list 20 is applied to virtual interfaces zero through four, permits all hosts/networks within 172.16.0.0 and 10.0.0.0, and denies everything else

D. Access list 20 permits all hosts/networks for 172.16.0.0 and 10.0.0.0

Answer: C

9. Which of the following commands is used as an alternative to access lists?

A. ip route address mask null 0

B. ip route address wildcard null 0

C. ip route destination mask null 0

D. Ip route destination wildcard null 0

Answer: A

10. If clients need to reach multiple servers on network 172.16.30.0 /24, which command will allow the clients to reach all of the servers?

A. ip helper address 172.16.30.0

B. ip helper address 172.16.30.255

C. ip helper-address 172.16.30.0

D. ip helper-address 172.16.30.255

Answer: D

11. It is alright to simply enter additional access list lines after the scripting of the original access list.

    A. True

    B. False

    Answer: B. Any lines that are simply added to an existing access list will be put at the end of the list. These commands may or may not be utilized.

12. Routers can reorder access-list statements in which of the following ways?

    A. Placing the implicit deny statement at the beginning of the list

    B. Manipulating source networks to match the wildcard mask

    C. Grouping permit and deny statements

    D. Placing all permit statements at the end of the list

    E. Placing all deny statements at the end of the list

    Answer: B and C

13. What is the proper syntax to apply an access list to a routing protocol? The command must be issued from within the routing protocol configuration.

    A. `ip access-group access-list-number {in | out}`

    B. `ip distribute-list access-list-number {in | out}`

    C. `distribute-list access-list-number {in | out} interface-type interface-number`

    D. `filter-list access-list-number {in | out} interface-type interface-number`

    Answer: C

14. Which command(s) may be issued to provide specific information on access list functionality?

A. `show ip access list access-list-number`

B. `show access-list access-list-number`

C. `debug ip icmp`

D. `show ip icmp packets`

Answer: B and C

15. Which command is used to refine the broadcast domain in conjunction with IP helper addresses?

A. `ip forward-protocol [udp[port] | nd | sdns]`

B. `forward-helper [udp[port] | nd | sdbs]`

C. `ip helper-protocol [udp[port] | nd | sdbs]`

D. None of the above

Answer: A

16. Choose the best explanation of the following access list line:

`access-list 101 permit udp host 172.16.10.2 any eq snmp`

A. This line permits any node to access host 172.16.10.2 using SNMP

B. This line permits host 172.16.10.2 to communicate to any destination using SNMP

C. This line permits host 172.16.10.2 to communicate to any destination using UDP

D. This line permits any node to communicate with host 172.16.10.2 using UDP

Answer: B

17. Why are null interfaces used in place of an access list?

  A. When RIP is the only protocol running on the router

  B. When security needs to be configured on a loopback interface

  C. To save CPU utilization

  D. To globally deny access to a network

  Answer: C

18. Which option is a valid option when applying access lists on an interface?

  A. One list inbound and one list outbound

  B. Two lists inbound or two lists outbound

  C. Only one list may be applied, either inbound or outbound

  D. Two lists inbound and two lists outbound

  Answer: A

19. What is accomplished by the following configuration line?

  `Access-list 55 permit 172.16.10.0 0.0.0.255`

  A. An extended access list is created that will allow all hosts on network `172.16.10.0` to be forwarded

  B. A standard access list is created that will allow all hosts on network `172.16.10.0` to be forwarded

  C. An extended list is created that will filter traffic destined for network `172.16.10.0`

  D. A standard list is created that will permit all traffic destined for network `172.16.10.0`

  Answer: B

20. What command can be used to encrypt Cisco router password information?

   A. `enable password string encrypt level`

   B. `encrypt level string enable password string`

   C. `enable secret [level level] password | encryption-type encrypted-password]`

   D. `enable secret [encryption-type | level] password`

   Answer: D

Chapter 4

1. What is the correct syntax for implementing weighted fair queuing?

   A. `weighted-fair queue`

   B. `fair-queue`

   C. `queue-fair`

   D. None of the above

   Answer: B

2. To which type of traffic does weighted fair queuing assign the highest priority?

   A. SNA

   B. IPX

   C. High volume

   D. Low volume

   Answer: D

3. When should weighted fair queuing be used?

   A. To provide priority to interactive traffic

   B. To provide priority to file transfers

   C. To allow all traffic to be forwarded

   D. A and C

   E. A and B

Answer: A

4. Where is the most effective place to implement queuing?

   A. High-speed LAN links

   B. T1/E1 links only

   C. Any WAN link whose capacity is 2Mbps and slower

   D. All interfaces

Answer: C

5. When should priority queuing be used?

   A. When traffic has a hierarchical order of importance

   B. When delay doesn't matter

   C. When all traffic must be forwarded

   D. None of the above

Answer: A

6. Which one of the following steps is *not* part of configuring priority queuing?

   A. Configuring a default queue

   B. Configuring a priority list

   C. Configuring the queue transfer rate

   D. Assigning the priority list to an interface

Answer: C

7. How many queues are defined by priority queuing?

   A. 1–16

   B. No limit

   C. 4

   D. 1–10

   Answer: C

8. When should custom queuing be used?

   A. When traffic has a hierarchical order of importance

   B. To overcome the possible problem that is introduced with priority queuing.

   C. When trying to provide bandwidth sharing for all traffic

   D. When delay is not important

   Answer: B

9. Which step is *not* part of configuring custom queuing?

   A. Defining the custom queuing filter

   B. Assigning a default queue

   C. Configuring the transfer rate per queue

   D. Assigning a priority queue list to the interface

   Answer: D

10. What is accomplished by configuring the `byte-count` for a queue?

   A. Allocating a percentage of the total bandwidth to defined queues

   B. Setting the size of the queue

   C. Setting the amount of data that will be processed before moving on to the next queue

   D. A and C

   Answer: D

11. Which statement best describes weighted fair queuing?

    A. Queues based on the source and destination of packets

    B. Shares bandwidth among all traffic types, giving priority to low-volume traffic

    C. Shares bandwidth among high-priority traffic only

    D. Queues using FIFO

Answer: B

12. Which statement best describes priority queuing?

    A. Processes all queues in a round-robin fashion

    B. Queues based on the destination address of the packet

    C. Queues based on the traffic type; processes all queues equally

    D. Queues based on the traffic type; will always process the highest-priority traffic first

Answer: D

13. Which statement best describes custom queuing?

    A. Queues based on traffic type; processes all queues equally

    B. Queues based on traffic type; always processes the high-priority traffic first

    C. Queues based on bandwidth allocation

    D. Processes packets based on the source address

Answer: A

14. What is accomplished by the following configuration?

```
Router_C(config)#priority-list 1 protocol ip low lt 256
Router_C(config)#interface serial 0
Router_C(config-if)#priority-group 1
Router_C(config-if)#^Z
Router_C#
```

A. IP is held to a packet size less than 256

B. Priority list one is applied to serial interface zero and permits packet sizes less than 256

C. IP packets with sizes less than 256 are assigned to the low-priority queue, and the list is applied to serial interface zero

D. IP packets with sizes less than 256 are assigned a low priority, and the list is applied to serial interface zero

Answer: C

15. Which of the following is *not* used to establish a conversation for weighted fair queuing?

A. Source address

B. Destination address

C. Packet size

D. Port number

Answer: C

16. Why is queue size important when configuring queuing?

A. If the queue is full, the packet will be discarded

B. If the queue is full, the interface will become congested

C. If the queue is full, the algorithm halts and allows FIFO queuing

D. None of the above

Answer: A

17. Which of the following commands should be used to assign all traffic from serial interface one to queue one?

    A. `Router_B(config-int)#queue 1`

    B. `Router_B(config)#priority-list 1 interface Serial 1 1`

    C. `Router_B(config)#queue-list 1 interface Serial1 1`

    D. `Router_B(config-int)#queue-list 1 queue-number 1`

Answer: C

18. How many separate priority lists may be written for priority queuing?

    A. 4

    B. 8

    C. 12

    D. 16

Answer: D

19. Which algorithm does custom queuing use within each defined queue to forward packets?

    A. Priority

    B. Weighted fair

    C. FIFO

    D. None of the above

Answer: C

20. When should the default `byte-count` for custom queuing be changed?

    A. When available bandwidth needs to be allocated as a percentage of the total bandwidth

    B. When the application uses larger packet sizes

    C. It should never be changed from the default setting

    D. To utilize all available bandwidth

Answer: A

Chapter 5

1. Which of the following is needed for a router to route data?

   A. TCP port number

   B. Destination address

   C. Default gateway

   D. Protocol type

   E. Potential routes

   F. A source for route information

   Answer: B, E, F

2. Given the network 192.168.10.0, how can this address space be more efficiently used?

   A. By assigning only a mask of /16 (255.255.0.0)

   B. By assigning only a mask of /24 (255.255.255.0)

   C. By assigning only a mask of /8 (255.0.0.0)

   D. By assigning multiple masks to the network

   Answer: D

3. What does VLSM (variable-length subnet mask) do? (Choose one.)

   A. Allows multiple subnet masks to be assigned to one IP network

   B. Allows the mask on an IP address to change as needed

   C. Enables classless routing on a router

   D. Allows multiple subnets to be used on a router

   Answer: A

4. Identify the host and network addresses from the following VLSM address:

172.16.10.4/30

A. 2 and 3 are host addresses; 1 is the network; and 4 is the broadcast address

B. 4 and 5 are host addresses; 3 is the network; and 6 is the broadcast address

C. 4 is the network; 5 and 6 are host addresses; and 7 is the broadcast address

D. 4 through 8 are hosts, with 3 and 9 being the network and broadcast addresses respectively

Answer: C

5. What are the benefits of using a hierarchical IP addressing scheme?

A. A more organized network

B. No routing table needed, just a `default-network` statement

C. Increased availability of IP addresses

D. Reduced size of route tables

Answer: C, D

6. How can discontiguous networks be advertised? (Choose two.)

A. EIGRP, OSPF, and ISIS

B. RIP, IGRP, EIGRP, and OSPF

C. Secondary addresses

D. Static routes

Answer: A, C

7. How can RIP or IGRP select a default route when the routers are separated by a discontiguous address?

   A. With the use of helper addresses

   B. By issuing the `ip classless` command on the router

   C. By issuing the `ip default-network` command on the router

   D. By configuring the router to auto-summarize

   Answer: C

8. What does RIP or IGRP advertise when only one subnet of a classfull network is connected to a router?

   A. The entire classfull network

   B. The subnet only

   C. Nothing

   D. Both the network and the subnet information

   Answer: A

9. What's route summarization?

   A. Using only one subnet so that the network is flattened out

   B. Grouping multiple networks and advertising them as one larger network

   C. Using supernets on all access-level equipment

   D. Advertising only one network for the entire enterprise or campus

   Answer: B

10. When can/should route summarization be used? (Choose all that apply.)

   A. Always

   B. When route tables become too large

   C. When a campus or enterprise router owns several contiguous subnets that share equal high-order bit patterns

   D. When routing protocols are capable of handling prefix length and subnet mask information

   E. When the router IOS is capable of IP classless routing (meaning that the network prefix may be any length, including 32 bits long)

Answer: C, D, E

11. Given the following configuration lines, is route summarization possible?

```
interface Ethernet 0
  ip address 172.16.12.1 255.255.255.0
interface Ethernet 1
  ip address 172.16.13.1 255.255.255.0
!
router eigrp 100
  network 172.16.0.0
!
```

   A. Yes

   B. No

Answer: A

12. How should the following networks be summarized?

```
172.16.12.0/24
172.16.13.0/24
172.16.14.0/24
```

A. 172.16.0.0/16

B. 172.16.14.0/24

C. 172.16.12.0/22

D. 172.16.14.0/22

Answer: C

13. How should the following networks be summarized?

```
172.16.1.0/24
172.16.2.0/24
172.16.3.0/24
```

A. They can't be summarized

B. 172.16.1.0/24 *and* 172.16.2.0/23

C. 172.16.1.0/22

D. 172.16.0.0

Answer: B. Networks must share the same high-order bits. Look at the binary values to understand more clearly.

14. What's the risk of oversummarization?

A. None

B. Slower response times due to route convergence

C. Routing loops

D. Routing failure

Answer: D. Another campus or enterprise may be over advertising as well, therefore outside packets won't be able to find a route back to your network.

15. What's private addressing?

    A. Network blocks set aside by IANA for networks that aren't connected to the global Internet

    B. Networks blocks that IANA doesn't allow for commercial use

    C. Network blocks used by private industry

    D. A block of three Class B addresses allocated by IANA for anyone to use

Answer: A

16. Which network is not part of IANA allocated private address blocks?

    A. 172.31.0.0

    B. 10.0.0.0

    C. 198.162.0.0

    D. 192.168.0.0

Answer: C

17. Where can private addressing be used?

    A. Anywhere

    B. In any network that's not connected to the global Internet or that restricts private addresses from being announced to the global Internet

    C. Only in networks that are not connected to the global Internet

    D. Only in networks that have a connection to the global Internet

Answer: B

18. What is NAT?

A. Network anonymous transport: Used to transfer data from privately addressed hosts to the global Internet

B. Network address translation: Used to renumber a privately addressed network

C. Network address translation: Used to convert a private IP address into a registered IP address so that connectivity with the global Internet may be established

D. Network address translation: Uses one address and then proxies connections from a private network to the global Internet

Answer: C

19. When can NAT be used? (Choose all that apply.)

A. When application sensitivity isn't an issue (delay)

B. When end-to-end traceability isn't needed

C. After the private address blocks have been fully utilized

D. When a network uses only private addresses

E. When a network has both private and registered addresses

Answer: A, B, D, and E

20. How many outside interfaces may be configured per router?

A. As many as desired

B. Only one

C. Two

D. Serial interfaces only

Answer: B

Chapter 6

1. What are two benefits of using a link-state routing protocol?

   A. It uses the Hello protocol to establish adjacencies

   B. It uses several components to calculate the metric of a route

   C. Updates are sent only when changes occur in the network

   D. It is a better protocol than distance vector is

   Answer: A, C

2. Which protocol does not use a topology table?

   A. EIGRP

   B. IGRP

   C. RIP1

   D. OSPF

   Answer: C

3. Which route type must be redistributed by a routing protocol if other routers are to learn about it?

   A. RIP

   B. Default routes

   C. Connected routes

   D. Static routes

   Answer: D

4. Which command should be used to ensure proper metric conversion when redistributing routes from different protocols?

   A. `distance distance-value`

   B. `default-metric`

   C. `distribute-list`

   D. `default-information`

   Answer: B

5. Why are passive interfaces used within routing protocols such as EIGRP and OSPF?

A. To stop unwanted route information from entering the specified interface

B. To allow route information to be filtered by an access list

C. To allow routes to be sent out the specified interface, but deny route information to enter the interface

D. To allow routes to enter the interface, but deny any route information to exit the specified interface

Answer: D

6. How is a feasible successor chosen when the successor fails?

A. The route with the next lowest metric is chosen

B. If a router doesn't have a feasible successor, queries are multicast to neighboring routers in search of a feasible successor

C. The route is removed from the route table

D. The route is flagged as an active state

Answer: A. B is not the correct answer because that is how a new successor is chosen.

7. Which of the following is a prerequisite for incremental SAP updates to work with EIGRP IPX instead of periodic updates?

A. IPX must be running on the router

B. The `ipx sap-incremental eigrp` command must be issued

C. The neighbor connected to the configured interface must also have EIGRP IPX enabled

D. Different AS numbers must be used

Answer: C

8. How is EIGRP implemented on a router?

   A. `ip router eigrp autonomous-system-number`

   B. `router ip eigrp autonomous-system-number`

   C. `router eigrp process-id`

   D. `router eigrp autonomous-system-number`

   Answer: D

9. Which of the following are *not* features of EIGRP?

   A. Incremental updates

   B. Only one route per destination

   C. Support for IP, IPX, and AT

   D. Hybrid distance vector and link-state protocol

   E. Not a scalable protocol

   F. Hello protocol used to establish adjacencies

   Answer: B, E

10. Which commands can be used for troubleshooting EIGRP problems?

   A. `show ip eigrp route`

   B. `show ip route eigrp`

   C. `show ip eigrp topology`

   D. `show ip eigrp neighbors`

   E. `show ip eigrp events`

   Answer: B, C, D, E

11. What configuration option changes a stub area to a totally stub area?

   A. `area area-id stub no-summary`

   B. `area area-id total stub`

   C. `area process-id stub`

   D. `area process-id stub no-summary`

   Answer: A

12. Which OSPF initialization states allow routers to actually exchange route information?

A. The loading state

B. The two-way state

C. The full state

D. The exchange state

Answers: A, C

13. Which state indicates that link-state databases have been synchronized among OSPF area routers?

A. The loading state

B. The two-way state

C. The Exstart state

D. The exchange state

Answer: D

14. What two characteristics distinguish a stub area from a totally stub area?

A. A totally stub area accepts summary routes

B. A totally stub area is Cisco proprietary

C. A totally stub area contains only intra-area routes

D. A totally stub area contains only inter-area routes

Answer: B, C

15. What command is used to assign a cost to summary routes advertised to a stub area?

A. area *area-id* default-cost cost, issued on the ABR

B. area *area-id* default-cost cost, issued on the ASBR

C. area *process-id* default-cost, issued on the ABR

D. area *area-id* default-cost cost, issued on any stub router

Answer: A

16. What three enhancements were made to OSPF to make it better than RIP1?

    A. No hop-count limit

    B. Use of distance vector algorithm

    C. Use of classfull routing

    D. Incremental routing updates

    E. Route tables are calculated after the change has been propagated

    Answer: A, D, E

17. Which commands are used to verify correct operation of OSPF?

    A. `show ip ospf area-id`

    B. `show ospf database`

    C. `show ip ospf border-routers`

    D. `show ip ospf process-id`

    E. `show ip ospf links`

    F. `show ip ospf database [network | summary | asbr-summary | external | database-summary]`

    G. `show ip ospf virtual-links`

    Answer: C, D, F, G

18. What is a summary LSA?

    A. A type 3 or 4 LSA that describes links between the ABR and local area routers

    B. A type 2 LSA that is propagated by the DR about all local routes

    C. A type 3 or 4 LSA that is multicast by the ASBR containing a summary of all external routes

    D. A type 5 LSA that contains a summary of all external routes

    Answer: A

19. What are the commands needed to implement OSPF on a router? (Choose two.)

A. router ip ospf *area-id*

B. router ospf *area-id*

C. router ospf *process-id*

D. network *address mask area-id*

E. network *address wildcard-mask area-id*

F. network *address wildcard-mask area area-id*

Answer: C, F

20. What is the difference between an ABR and an ASBR?

A. An ABR is the border router between two or more defined areas, and an ASBR is a border router between an OSPF area and external autonomous system

B. An ASBR is the border router between two or more defined areas, and an ABR is a border router between an OSPF area and external autonomous system

C. An ABR is the area backbone router that connects the backbone routers, and an ASBR borders different autonomous systems

D. An ASBR is the autonomous system backbone router that connects the backbone to other autonomous systems, and the ABR is the area border router

Answer: A

21. Which of the following is an example of how to configure eBGP?

A. router ip bgp 10
network 10.1.1.1 100

B. router bgp 10
network 10.1.1.1 remote-as 10

C. router bgp 100
neighbor 10.1.1.1 remote-as 100

D. router bgp 100
neighbor 10.1.1.1 remote-as 200

Answer: D

22. Which of the following is an example of how to configure iBGP?

   A. `router ip bgp 10`
      `network 10.1.1.1 100`

   B. `router bgp 10`
      `network 10.1.1.1 remote-as 10`

   C. `router bgp 100`
      `neighbor 10.1.1.1 remote-as 100`

   D. `router bgp 100`
      `neighbor 10.1.1.1 remote-as 200`

Answer: C

23. Which command shows the BGP routes?

   A. `show ip bgp route`

   B. `show ip bgp`

   C. `show ip route bgp`

   D. `show ip bgp paths`

Answer: B

24. How is a BGP session established between two routers?

   A. Telnet

   B. Hello packets

   C. UDP (SYN, ACK, SYN)

   D. TCP (SYN, ACK, SYN)

Answer: D

25. When should BGP be used?

    A. When multi-homing

    B. When connecting multiple ISPs

    C. When connecting routers within the same AS

    D. When configuring backup links

    Answer: A, B

Chapter 7

1. Which of the following is a valid IPX standard access list entry?

    A. `access-list 888 permit 50 -1`

    B. `access-group 888 permit 50 -1`

    C. `access list 888 permit 50 -1`

    D. `access-list permit 50 any`

    E. `access list permit 50 any`

    Answer: A

2. Which of the following is valid syntax to apply access list 810 to interface E0 incoming (assuming you are already in Interface Configuration mode)?

    A. `access group 810 in`

    B. `access group 801 incoming`

    C. `access-group 810 in`

    D. `access-group 810 incoming`

    E. `ipx input-sap-filter 810`

    Answer: C

3. Which of the following are valid IPX addresses?

   A. 00007132.0000.8609.33E9

   B. -1

   C. 0000.8609.33E9

   D. 7132.0000.8609.33E9

   Answer: A, D

4. Suppose that you want only to advertise services on IPX network 3B out the serial interface of your router. Which of the following would you use?

   A.
```
access-list 1010 permit 3b 0
access-list 1010 deny -1 0
interface s0
ipx input-sap-filter 1010
```

   B.
```
access-list 1010 permit 3b 0
access-list 1010 deny -1 0
interface s0
ipx output-sap-filter 1010
```

   C.
```
access-list 1010 permit -1 0
access-list 1010 deny -1 0
interface s0
ipx output-sap-filter 1010
```

   D.
```
access-list 1010 permit 3b -1
access-list 1010 deny -1 0
interface s0
ipx output-sap-filter 1010
```

   Answer: B

5. Suppose that you want to learn only of services on IPX network 3B on the Serial 0 interface of your router. Which of the following would you use?

A. `access-list 1011 permit 3b 0`
`access-list 1011 deny -1 0`
`interface s0`
`ipx output-sap-filter 1011`

B. `access-list 1011 permit 3b 0`
`access-list 1011 deny -1 any`
`interface s0`
`ipx output-sap-filter 1011`

C. `access-list 1011 deny 3b 0`
`access-list 1011 deny -1 0`
`interface s0`
`ipx input-sap-filter 1011`

D. `access-list 1011 permit 3b 0`
`access-list 1011 deny -1 0`
`interface s0`
`ipx input-sap-filter 1011`

Answer: D

6. Suppose that you want to block access to IPX network 30 by all packets from network 50, but allow access to packets from network 10. Suppose that you also do not want to block any traffic to other IPX networks. Which of the following lists would work?

   A. `access-list 850 deny 50 30`
      `access-list 850 permit 10 30`
      `access-list 850 permit -1 -1`

   B. `access-list 850 deny 30 50`
      `access-list 850 permit 30 50`
      `access-list 850 permit -1 -1`

   C. `access-list 850 deny 50 -1`
      `access-list 850 permit -1 -1`

   D. `access-list 850 deny 50 30`
      `access-list 850 permit -1 -1`

   E. `access-list 850 permit -1 -1`
      `access-list 850 deny 50 30`

   Answer: A, D

7. Which of the following is the correct way to readjust the SAP update interval on Serial 0 to 30 minutes (assuming you are already in Interface Configuration mode)?

   A. `ipx sap-update-interval 30`

   B. `ipx sap-update-interval 1800`

   C. `ipx sap-interval 30`

   D. `ipx sap-interval 1800`

   E. `ipx sap update interval 30`

   F. `ipx sap update interval 1800`

   Answer: C

8. Which of the following commands would you use to see which interfaces have SAP filter 1012 enabled?

A. `show running-config`

B. `show access-list`

C. `show ip interface`

D. `show ipx interface`

E. `show ipx servers`

Answer: A, D

9. Which commands can you use to verify that your router is receiving SAP updates?

A. `show running-config`

B. `show ipx sap`

C. `show ipx traffic`

D. `show ipx interface`

E. `show ipx servers`

Answer: C, E

10. Suppose that you need to switch your outbound IPX access list from 830 to 831. Assuming you are already in Interface Configuration mode, which of the following will work?

A. `ipx access-group 831 in`

B. `ipx access-group 831 out`

C. `no ipx access-group 830 in`
   `ipx access-group 831 in`

D. `no ipx access-group 830 out`
   `ipx access-group 831 out`

Answer: B, D. While both will work, the first line in D is not really necessary. The router will automatically remove the first access list from the interface when the new one is added. Remember—only one list per protocol, per interface, per direction.

11. Suppose that you want to prevent all IPX traffic from network 7D from leaving your Ethernet interface. Which of the following would you use?

A. IPX extended access list

B. IPX standard access list

C. IPX SAP filter

D. IPX RIP filter

Answer: B

12. Suppose that you want to prevent your print services on network 7D from being advertised beyond your Ethernet interface. Which of the following would you use?

A. IPX extended access list

B. IPX standard access list

C. IPX SAP filter

D. IPX RIP filter

Answer: C

13. Suppose that you want to prevent your router from including in its SAP table anything not in network 8A. Which of the following would you use?

A. IPX extended access list

B. IPX standard access list

C. IPX SAP filter

D. IPX RIP filter

Answer: C

14. When IPX clients attempt to locate services, which protocol do they use to find them?

A. SAP

B. RIP

C. NLSP

D. GNS

E. ARP

Answer: A, D. GNS is actually a type of SAP, so both answers could be considered correct.

15. When IPX servers are exchanging information on their respective services, which protocol do they use?

A. SAP

B. RIP

C. NLSP

D. GNS

E. ARP

Answer: A

16. When IPX servers are responding to client requests, which protocol do they use?

A. SAP

B. RIP

C. NLSP

D. GNS

E. ARP

Answer: A, D

17. What is the default broadcast interval for SAP traffic?

   A. 10 seconds

   B. 20 seconds

   C. 60 seconds

   D. 120 seconds

   E. 10 minutes

   Answer: C

18. Suppose that you have modified the default SAP interval on your router and are experiencing inconsistencies when using the show ipx servers command on your router from time to time. Which of the following is the most likely cause?

   A. Incorrectly configured standard access list

   B. Incorrectly configured SAP list

   C. Incorrectly configured routing protocol

   D. Incorrectly configured SAP interval

   Answer: D. While B could cause you to not see services you expected to see in your router's SAP table, they would most likely be consistent. Only D would cause SAP entries to appear and disappear.

19. Suppose that you need to implement an access list and log packets that meet certain lines within your list. Which of the following could you use?

   A. IPX extended access list

   B. IPX standard access list

   C. IPX SAP filter

   D. IPX RIP filter

   Answer: A

20. Suppose that you need to filter based on socket number. Which of the following could you use?

A. IPX extended access list

B. IPX standard access list

C. IPX SAP filter

D. IPX RIP filter

Answer: A

Chapter 8

1. What is the default update interval for IPX RIP?

A. 10 seconds

B. 20 seconds

C. 30 seconds

D. 60 seconds

Answer: D

2. Which of the following are problems with RIP and SAP?

A. Convergence time

B. Multivendor interoperability

C. AppleTalk incompatibility

D. Bandwidth utilization

E. CPU utilization

F. Scalability

Answer: A, D, F

3. What is the maximum number of hops allowed by IPX RIP?

   A. 5

   B. 10

   C. 15

   D. 20

   E. 25

   Answer: C

4. NLSP is based on which of the following ISO routing protocols?

   A. IS-IS

   B. OSPF

   C. EIGRP

   D. RTMP

   E. CDP

   Answer: A

5. At what regular interval does NLSP send out service and route updates?

   A. Every 30 seconds

   B. Every 60 seconds

   C. Every 300 seconds

   D. Every two hours

   E. Never

   Answer: D

6. Which of the following best describes why convergence is slower with RIP than with other IPX routing protocols?

A. RIP requires more CPU cycles to process

B. RIP is limited to periodic updates

C. RIP has to use split-horizon to suppress routing loops

D. RIP has to coordinate directly with SAP

Answer: B

7. Which of the following databases are identical on all NLSP routers within an area?

A. Adjacency

B. Link state

C. Routing

D. Forwarding

E. DR

Answer: B

8. You want to add NLSP to your router. Which of the following must be completed before you can add NLSP?

A. IPX RIP must be disabled

B. IPX routing must be enabled

C. IPX internal network must be configured on the router

D. At least one NetWare server must be running

E. Interfaces must be configured for IPX

Answer: B, C, E

9. Which of the following commands is required for every NLSP configuration?

A. `area-address x y`

B. `show ipx interfaces`

C. `ipx external-network x`

D. `ipx nlsp run`

Answer: A

10. You want to have IPX networks 100–1FF in your NLSP area. Which of the following `area-address` statements would you use?

A. `area-address 100 0ff`

B. `area-address 100 f00`

C. `area-address 100-1ff`

D. `area-address 100 1ff`

Answer: B

11. Once you have configured NLSP, how would you configure an interface to send out RIP and SAP updates only if there are other devices present that use these protocols? (Assume you are already in Interface Configuration mode.)

A. `ipx nlsp rip on`
   `ipx nlsp sap on`

B. `ipx nlsp rip off`
   `ipx nlsp sap off`

C. `ipx nlsp rip discover`
   `ipx nlsp sap discover`

D. `ipx nlsp rip auto`
   `ipx nlsp sap auto`

Answer: D

12. True or False. IPX EIGRP automatically suppresses SAP updates on LAN interfaces.

Answer: False

13. True or False. IPX EIGRP automatically suppresses SAP updates on WAN interfaces.

Answer: True

14. What is the maximum number of hops IPX EIGRP will support?

   A. 15

   B. 150

   C. 224

   D. Unlimited

   Answer: C

15. What metrics does IPX EIGRP use when making routing decisions?

   A. Ticks

   B. Bandwidth

   C. Reliability

   D. Hops

   E. Delay

   Answer: B, D, E

16. You want to add IPX EIGRP to your router. Which of the following must be completed before you can add IPX EIGRP?

   A. IPX RIP must be disabled

   B. IPX routing must be enabled

   C. IPX internal network must be configured on the router

   D. At least one NetWare server must be running

   E. Interfaces must be configured for IPX

   Answer: B, E

17. Which of the following commands will add network 50 to your IPX router EIGRP?

A. `area-address 50 ff`

B. `area-address 50 00`

C. `area-address 50 11`

D. `network 50`

Answer: D

18. IPX EIGRP is supported by which of the following internetwork devices?

A. Novell servers

B. NT servers

C. Cisco routers

D. Bay routers

Answer: C

19. Which of the following are required to configure an IPX tunnel?

A. Creating a tunnel interface

B. Configuring an internal IPX address on the router

C. Setting the tunnel destination address

D. Assigning the tunnel interface an IPX address

E. Assigning the tunnel interface an IP address

F. Setting the tunnel source address

Answer: A, C, D, F

20. When configuring the tunnel interface on two routers, the _____ address on one router should be the same as the _____ address on the router at the other end of the tunnel.

    A. source; destination

    B. internal IPX; internal IPX

    C. destination; source

    D. IP; IP

Answer: A, C

Chapter 9

1. What AppleTalk protocol handles routing?

    A. RTMP

    B. DDP

    C. ZIP

    D. AURP

    E. NCP

Answer: A

2. When configuring AppleTalk, how many zones can you have per cable range?

    A. None

    B. At least one

    C. Many

Answer: B, C. You are required to have at least one zone per cable range and can have more than one.

3. How do AppleTalk clients learn of routers on their segments?

   A. They issue broadcasts

   B. They listen to RTMP updates

   C. Routers always have node address 1

   D. They listen to NBP broadcasts

Answer: B

4. What type of request does an AppleTalk client issue when attempting to get a current list of zones?

   A. GZL broadcast request

   B. GZL directed request

   C. NBP broadcast request

   D. NBP directed request

   E. DDP broadcast request

   F. DDP directed request

Answer: B. GZL (`GetZoneList`) requests are directed requests from clients to routers.

5. When you enter the command `appletalk routing` in Global Configuration mode, what process have you started?

   A. Router RIP

   B. Router EIGRP

   C. Router NBP

   D. Router RTMP

Answer: D

6. What is the appropriate range for AppleTalk access list numbers?

   A. 200–299

   B. 400–499

   C. 600–699

   D. 800–899

   Answer: C

7. You have just configured a GZL filter and need to apply it to an interface. Which of the following choices are appropriate?

   A. Int e0
      ```
      appletalk getzonelist-filter 610
      ```

   B. Int s0
      ```
      appletalk getzonelist-filter 610
      ```

   C. int e0
      ```
      appletalk getzonelist filter 610
      ```

   D. int s0
      ```
      appletalk getzonelist filter 610
      ```

   E. int e0
      ```
      appletalk get zone list filter 610
      ```

   F. int s0
      ```
      appletalk get zone list filter 610
      ```

   Answer: A. Remember that it makes sense to apply this type of filter only to a LAN interface.

8. Which of the following GZL filters will report all zones other than
Marketing to GZL requests?

A. `access-list 690 permit Marketing`
`access-list 690 permit other`

B. `access-list 690 deny Marketing`
`access-list 690 permit additional-zones`

C. `access-list 690 deny zone Marketing`
`access-list 690 permit additional-zones`

D. `access-list 690 deny Marketing`
`access-list 690 permit any-zones`

Answer: C

9. You have just configured a ZIP reply filter and need to apply it to an
interface. Which of the following choices are appropriate?

A. `appletalk zip reply filter 611`

B. `appletalk zip-reply filter 611`

C. `appletalk zip-reply-filter 611`

D. `appletalk zip filter 611`

E. `appletalk zip-filter 611`

F. `appletalk access-group 611`

Answer: C

10. When applying ZIP reply filters, to which interfaces should you
apply them?

A. LAN

B. Serial

C. Both

Answer: C. ZIP reply filters can be used on any interface where
another router may be present on the same segment, either LAN or serial.

11. Suppose that you are configuring your router, and you want it to advertise only zone Engineering out the serial interface. Which of the following lists could you use?

A. `access-list 678 deny Engineering`
`access-list 678 permit additional-zones`

B. `access-list 678 permit Engineering`

C. `access-list 678 permit Engineering`
`access-list 678 permit additional-zones`

D. `access-list 678 deny zone not Engineering`

Answer: B

12. How many zone names must you advertise out for each cable segment that you advertise out?

A. None

B. One

C. Two

D. Many

Answer: B. If you advertise cable ranges without advertising at least one zone name, you risk flooding your network with ZIP packets. You can advertise two or more, but you must advertise at least one.

13. You have just configured an RTMP filter and need to apply it to an interface. Your filter will prevent your router from learning of cable ranges in other parts of your internetwork. Which of the following choices is appropriate? (Assume that you are already in Interface Configuration mode.)

A. `appletalk cable-range-filter 610 in`

B. `appletalk cable-range-filter 610 out`

C. `appletalk distribute-list 610 in`

D. `appletalk distribute-list 610 out`

E. `appletalk rtmp-filter 610 in`

F. `appletalk rtmp-filter 610 out`

Answer: C. You must apply the list inbound to prevent your router from learning other cable ranges. You would apply the list outbound to prevent your router from advertising cable ranges it already knows.

14. What are the three portions of an entity name?

A. Name

B. Type

C. Tuple

D. Zone

E. Object

F. Cable range

Answer: B, D, E

15. Which of the following access list lines would deny all file servers as part of an NBP filter?

A. `access-list 631 deny nbp object AFPServer`

B. `access-list 631 deny nbp object =`

C. `access-list 631 deny nbp zone *`

D. `access-list 631 deny nbp type =`

E. `access-list 631 deny nbp type AFPServer`

Answer: E

16. Which of the following filters allows you to control access to individual machines or types of resources?

A. GZL filters

B. RTMP filters

C. NBP filters

D. ZIP filters

Answer: C

17. Which of the following filters allows you to control advertisement of cable ranges?

A. GZL filters

B. RTMP filters

C. NBP filters

D. ZIP filters

Answer: B

18. Which of the following filters allows you to control which zones routers learn?

A. GZL filters

B. RTMP filters

C. NBP filters

D. ZIP filters

Answer: D

19. Suppose that you do the following configuration:

```
router#config t
Enter configuration commands, one per line.  End with
  CNTL/Z.
router(config)#appletalk routing
router(config)#appletalk routing eigrp 250
router(config)#int e0
router(config-if)#appletalk cable-range 1000-1001
router(config-if)#appletalk zone Marketing
router(config-if)#appletalk protocol eigrp
router(config-if)#^Z
router#
```

Which AppleTalk routing protocols are currently running on e0?

A. RTMP

B. RIP

C. AppleTalk EIGRP

D. NBP

Answer: A, C. Remember that if you don't remove RTMP, it will run on any AppleTalk-enabled interface.

20. What do you have to do to ensure that redistribution happens between RTMP and EIGRP?

   A. Use the `appletalk route-redistribution` command

   B. Redistribute EIGRP in router RTMP, and redistribute RTMP in router EIGRP

   C. Enable AppleTalk EIGRP

   D. Nothing

   Answer: C

Chapter 10

1. Bridges work at which layer of the OSI model?

   A. 1

   B. 2

   C. 3

   D. 4

   Answer: B

2. Routers work at which layer of the OSI model?

   A. 1

   B. 2

   C. 3

   D. 4

   Answer: C

3. Which of the following are routable protocols?

   A. IPX

   B. NetBIOS

   C. MOP

   D. AppleTalk

   E. LAT

   F. TCP/IP

   Answer: A, D, F

4. Transparent bridges operate differently on which of the following layer 3 protocols?

   A. IPX

   B. DDP (AppleTalk)

   C. IP

   D. None of the above

   Answer: D. Transparent bridges do not see layer 3 information.

5. Which of the following are functions of a transparent bridge?

   A. Avoiding loops

   B. Filtering packets

   C. Forwarding packets

   D. Learning MAC addresses

   E. All of the above

   Answer: E

6. Which of the following are legal Spanning Tree types on Cisco routers?

A. CCITT

B. IEEE

C. ARPA

D. DEC

E. IPX

Answer: B, D

7. When configuring bridging, which command must be entered before interfaces can be configured?

A. `bridge 1 protocol ieee`

B. `bridge-group 1 protocol ieee`

C. `bridge 1 protocol dec`

D. `bridge-group 1 protocol dec`

Answer: A, C

8. Suppose that you have already enabled bridging, and you want this router to be the root of the spanning tree. Which command would you use?

A. `bridge 1 priority 0`

B. `bridge 1 priority 32768`

C. `bridge 1 priority high`

D. `bridge 1 priority top`

Answer: A

9. Which of the following commands will configure an interface to be part of bridge group 1? (Assume you are already in Interface Configuration mode.)

A. `bridge group 1`

B. `bridge group 1 protocol ieee`

C. `bridge-group 1`

D. `bridge-group 1 protocol ieee`

E. `bridge group 1 priority 32768`

Answer: C

10. Suppose you have a loop in your network topology. Which of the following describes what the Spanning Tree Protocol will do?

A. Locate a point of redundancy, then load balance

B. Locate a point of redundancy, then disable the interface until it is needed

C. Locate a point of redundancy, then permanently disable the interface

D. Locate a point of redundancy, then block all packets with expired TTLs

Answer: B

11. Suppose you have a loop in your network topology. Which of the following commands is the best way to verify what Spanning Tree did in question 10?

A. `show spanning-tree`

B. `show interface`

C. `show irb`

D. `show bridge`

Answer: A

12. Which of the following can be possible statuses of a bridge interface?

    A. Down

    B. Disabled

    C. Listening

    D. Flooding

    E. Spanning

    F. Learning

    G. Blocking

    H. Forwarding

    Answer: A, C, F, G, H

13. In which of the following situations would you use IRB?

    A. When layer 3 network addresses are scarce

    B. When serial interfaces are necessary

    C. When more than one protocol must be bridged

    D. When routed and bridged networks of the same layer 3 protocol are merged

    Answer: A, D

14. Which of the following commands is required to enable IRB?

    A. `bridge irb`

    B. `bridge irb protocol ip`

    C. `bridge-group 1 irb`

    D. `bridge irb 1`

    Answer: A

15. Which of the following describes how routed and bridged interfaces communicate when using IRB?

   A. Via bridge group 1

   B. Via routing protocols

   C. Via BVIs

   D. Via Ethernet switches

   Answer: C

16. In which of the following ways does SRB locate routes to destinations?

   A. Discoverer

   B. Explorer

   C. Voyager

   D. Flood

   Answer: B

17. Which IEEE standard defines Token Ring?

   A. 802.1

   B. 802.1D

   C. 802.3

   D. 802.5

   Answer: D

18. Which of the following commands will set up bridge 15 between local ring 50 and target ring 51?

   A. source-bridge 50 15 51

   B. source-bridge 51 15 50

   C. source-bridge 50 51 15

   D. source-bridge 15 50 51

   Answer: A

19. Which commands are used only for SRT—not in other bridging configurations?

A. `bridge srt`

B. `bridge map srb transparent`

C. `bridge-group srt`

D. None of the above

Answer: D. SRT does not introduce any new commands.

20. Which of the following can be addressed only with SR/TLB?

A. IP to SNA communication

B. IPX to SNA communication

C. Transparent bridging

D. Ethernet to Token Ring bridging

Answer: D

Chapter 11

1. What encapsulation method would you use to configure ATM on a serial port?

A. ATM-Serial

B. HDLC

C. ATM-DXI

D. ATM

Answer: C

2. When would it be necessary to prioritize DLCI traffic?

A. When bandwidth is at a premium

B. When you have traffic from sites with high-speed access being queued at destination sites with lower-speed access

C. When running X.25 at remote locations

D. When you need to prioritize queues

Answer: B

3. Which command would you use to assign protocol traffic that would match the specified parameters to a priority queue?

A. queue

B. protocol queue

C. priority-queue

D. priority-list

Answer: D

4. For which of the following is X.21bis used?

A. Frame Relay 56Kbps lines

B. Frame types used in X.25

C. X.25 Physical layer specifications

D. PLP Call Setup mode

Answer: C

5. How many Frame Relay encapsulation methods are used with Cisco routers?

   A. Two

   B. Three

   C. Four

   D. Five

   Answer: A

6. How many LMI types are supported?

   A. Two

   B. Three

   C. Four

   D. Five

   Answer: B

7. Which of the following is true about LMI?

   A. LMIs map DLCI numbers to virtual circuits

   B. LMIs map X.121 addresses to virtual circuits

   C. LMIs report the status of virtual circuits

   D. LMI messages provide information about the current DLCI values

   Answer: C, D

8. What are X.121 addresses used for?

   A. Mapping DLCI addresses to logical interfaces

   B. Mapping X.25 addresses to logical hardware addresses

   C. Receiving LMI messages

   D. Providing information about the current DLCI values

   Answer: B

9. Which of the following commands will define access list 10 to use a high-priority queue?

   A. `frame priority-dlci-group 10`

   B. `access-list 10 permit eq high`

   C. `priority-list 10 protocol ip high list 5`

   D. `priority-list 5 protocol ip high list 10`

   Answer: D

10. What is a disadvantage to having point-to-point connections?

   A. A point-to-point connection requires that tariffs be paid even when the connection is in an idle state and no data are being transmitted

   B. A point-to-point connection requires users to dial the connection manually when data need to be transmitted

   C. A point-to-point connection requires interesting traffic to be defined on the router with access lists when data need to be transmitted

   D. A point-to-point connection requires a lease through an ISP using a point-to-point routing protocol

   Answer: A

11. What command do you use to set the LMI polling and timer intervals?

   A. `frame-relay n39x-lmi`

   B. `frame-relay lmi-xn39`

   C. `frame-relay lmi-n39x`

   D. `frame-relay lmi-x39n`

   Answer: C

12. How do you configure OSPF to broadcast to other routers through the Frame Relay cloud?

   A. By creating subinterfaces

   B. IARP

   C. By mapping X.121 addresses

   D. With the `neighbor` command

   Answer: D

13. What command would you use to create a queue so that Frame Relay has a place to hold broadcast traffic?

   A. `frame-relay queue 16 eq broadcast`

   B. `frame-relay broadcast-queue`

   C. `frame-relay broadcast 16 eq queue 16`

   D. `frame-relay queue 1 low 16 broadcast 16`

   Answer: B

14. What command should you use to set your routers to redefine the Frame Relay network as an OSPF broadcast network?

   A. `ip ospf network`

   B. `ip ospf broadcast`

   C. `network ospf broadcast all`

   D. `network ospf broadcast` *network number*

   Answer: A

15. What are the two parts of Frame Relay switching?

   A. Frame Relay DTE (switch)

   B. Frame Relay DTE (router)

   C. Frame Relay DCE (router)

   D. Frame Relay DCE (switch)

   Answer: B, D

16. What are the two types of frame switching?

   A. Local

   B. Remote

   C. Standby

   D. Cut-through

   Answer: A, B

17. What is the solution for using partial meshed Frame Relay networks with split-horizon protocols?

   A. DLCI addressing

   B. X.121 addresses

   C. Secondary Ethernet interfaces

   D. Subinterfaces

   Answer: D

18. What are the three types of LMI methods used by Cisco routers?

   A. Cisco

   B. ANSI

   C. IETF

   D. q933a

   Answer: A, B, D

19. What is IARP used for?

   A. Mapping X.121 addresses to X.25 addresses

   B. Mapping DLCIs to network protocol addresses

   C. SMDS addressing

   D. Mapping ATM addresses to virtual addresses

   Answer: B

20. Which two of the following are true regarding SMDS addressing?

   A. E: multicast addresses

   B. E: unicast addresses

   C. C: unicast addresses

   D. C: multicast addresses

   Answer: A, C

Chapter 12

1. What different types of compression does Cisco support with LAPB? (Choose all that apply.)

   A. Interesting

   B. Predictor

   C. X.121

   D. Stacker

   Answer: B, D

2. What does the I protocol specify in ISDN?

   A. ISDN on the existing telephone network

   B. Bandwidth on demand

   C. Concepts, terminology, and services

   D. Switching and signaling

   Answer: C

3. Which is true regarding HDLC?

   A. HDLC has a reachability limit of 15

   B. HDLC uses TCP sequencing and acknowledgements

   C. HDLC is a byte-oriented protocol

   D. HDLC is a bit-oriented protocol

   Answer: D

4. Which command enables Predictor data compression with LAPB?

    A. X.25 Predictor compress

    B. LAPB compress Predictor passive

    C. Compress Predictor

    D. Predictor compress

Answer: C

5. What does BRI provide?

    A. 2 B channels and 1 D channel

    B. 23 B channels and 1 64Kbps D channel

    C. 2 D channels and 1 B channel

    D. 23 D channels and 1 64Kbps B channel

Answer: A

6. What does PRI provide?

    A. 2 B channels and 1 D channel

    B. 23 B channels and 1 64Kbps D channel

    C. 2 D channels and 1 B channel

    D. 23 D channels and 1 64Kbps B channel

Answer: B

7. Which of the following is true regarding Super Frames?

    A. Used only with PPP encapsulation methods

    B. Used only with LAPB encapsulation methods

    C. Consist of 12 frames each with 193 bits

    D. Consist of 24 frames each with 192 bits

Answer: C

8. Which of the following is true regarding Extended Super Frames?

  A. Used only with PPP encapsulation methods

  B. Used only with LAPB encapsulation methods

  C. Consist of 12 frames each with 193 bits

  D. Consist of 24 frames each with 192 bits

  Answer: D

9. Which of the following is true?

  A. T1s run at 2.048Mbps and use 30 channels, in contrast to E1s, which use 24 channels and run at 1.544Mbps

  B. T1s run at 1.544Mbps and use 30 channels, in contrast to E1s, which use 24 channels and run at 2.048Mbps

  C. T1s run at 1.544Mbps and use 24 channels, in contrast to E1s, which use 30 channels and run at 2.048Mbps

  D. T1s run at 2.048Mbps and use 24 channels, in contrast to E1s, which use 30 channels and run at 1.544Mbps

  Answer: C

10. Which of the following is true regarding multilink?

  A. It is the ability to dial a link when the router finds interesting packets

  B. Multilink is used as a secondary link when the main link drops

  C. It creates logical interfaces on a serial interface by using DDR

  D. It is the ability to increase bandwidth between point-to-point dial-up connections by grouping interfaces.

  Answer: D

11. What does the Q protocol specify in ISDN?

    A. ISDN on the existing telephone network

    B. Bandwidth on demand

    C. Concepts, terminology, and services

    D. Switching and signaling

Answer: D

12. Which is true about link compression?

    A. It compresses the data, but leaves the header intact

    B. It compresses only the header information and leaves the data intact

    C. It is the combination of both header and payload compression

    D. It can be used only with LAPB encapsulation

Answer: C

13. If a Cisco router dials up more than one connection and splits the traffic over both interfaces, what type of protocol or device are you using?

    A. Payload compression

    B. Multi-dial-up

    C. Switched access

    D. Multilink

Answer: D

14. Which is true about payload compression?

    A. It compresses the data, but leaves the header intact

    B. It compresses only the header information and leaves the data intact

    C. It is the combination of both header and payload compression

    D. It can be used only with LAPB encapsulation

Answer: A

15. What does the E protocol in ISDN specify?

   A. ISDN on the existing telephone network

   B. Bandwidth on demand

   C. Concepts, terminology, and services

   D. Switching and signaling

   Answer: A

16. The `isdn switch-type` command provides what function?

   A. Aggregates traffic over multiple ISDN channels simultaneously

   B. Encapsulates ISDN over PPP encapsulations

   C. Specifies the type of ISDN switch with which the router communicates

   D. Configures the framing, either IETF or AMI

   Answer: C

17. Which is true regarding header compression?

   A. It compresses the data, but leaves the header intact

   B. It compresses only the header information and leaves the data intact

   C. It is the combination of both header and payload compression

   D. It can be used only with LAPB encapsulation

   Answer: B

18. What is the default serial encapsulation on Cisco routers?

   A. IETF

   B. LAPB

   C. HDLC

   D. ISDN

   Answer: C

19. What command will encapsulate PPP on a serial link?

   A. `ppp encapsulation`

   B. `encap ppp`

   C. `encapsulation lppp`

   D. `line encapsulation ppp`

Answer: B

20. What can be thought of as basically the telephone number of each B channel?

   A. DDR

   B. E protocols

   C. SPIDs

   D. Priority lists

Answer: C

Chapter 13

1. Which of the following are valid reasons to implement DDR?

   A. Low bandwidth requirements

   B. ISDN connections

   C. Continuous rather than periodic traffic patterns

   D. Interoperability

   E. Periodic rather than continuous traffic patterns

   F. Infrequent usage

Answer: A, E, F

2. Which of the following best describes the comparison of DDR against traditional dial-up services and traditional leased-line services?

A. It's more expensive than leased-line and easier to use than traditional dial-up

B. It's less expensive than leased-line and easier to use than traditional dial-up

C. It's easier to use than leased-line and more expensive than traditional dial-up

D. It's easier to use than leased-line and less expensive than traditional dial-up

Answer: B

3. You need to set up spoofing for IPX with DDR. Write in the four commands that you should use.

```
Router#configure term
Enter configuration commands, one per line.  End with
CNTL/Z.
Router(config)#int bri0
Router(config-if)#_____
Router(config-if)#_____
Router(config-if)#_____
Router(config-if)#_____
```

Answer: no ipx route-cache; **ipx spx-spoof**; **ipx watchdog-spoof**; **ipx spx-idle-time number**

4. Which of the following best describes the function of the dialer timeout?

    A. After the specified number of seconds, the connection will be closed

    B. After the specified number of seconds has passed without having any traffic cross the interface, the connection will be closed

    C. After the specified number of seconds has passed without having any interesting traffic cross the interface, the connection will be closed

    D. After the specified number of interesting packets have crossed the interface, the connection will be closed

Answer: C

5. True or False. The router will check to see if the interface is currently connected before checking to see whether the traffic is interesting.

Answer: False

6. True or False. The router will check to see if the interface uses DDR before checking to see if the traffic is interesting.

Answer: True

7. When configuring legacy DDR, which of the following are valid steps?

    A. Configuring interesting traffic

    B. Configuring the dialer interface

    C. Configuring static routes

    D. Configuring the dialer

    E. Configuring the watchdog

Answer: A, C, D

8. When configuring legacy DDR, which of the following must the dialer group match?

  A. The access list

  B. The dialer list

  C. The dialer interface number

  D. The timeout value

Answer: B

9. Suppose that you want to use access list 155 to specify interesting traffic. Which of the following is valid dialer-list syntax to accomplish this?

  A. `dialer-list 5 protocol ipx list 155`

  B. `dialer-list 5 ip protocol list 155`

  C. `dialer-list 5 ipx protocol list 155`

  D. `dialer-list 5 protocol ip list 155`

  E. `dialer-list 5 protocol ipx list 155`

Answer: D

10. Suppose you want to state that AppleTalk is interesting traffic, but IP is not. Which of the following is valid dialer-list syntax to accomplish this?

  A. `dialer-list 6 protocol appletalk permit`

  B. `dialer-list 6 protocol appletalk permit`
  `dialer-list 6 protocol ip deny`

  C. `dialer-list 6 protocol appletalk permit`
  `dialer-list 5 protocol ip deny`

  D. `dialer-list 6 protocol appletalk allow`
  `dialer-list 6 protocol ip deny`

  E. `dialer-list 5 protocol appletalk permit`
  `dialer-list 6 protocol ip deny`

Answer: A, B

11. When configuring legacy DDR, which of the following must you specify?

A. A network address for the interface

B. An encapsulation type

C. The dialer idle timeout

D. The dialer map

E. The dialer group

Answer: A, B, D, E

12. Which of the following best describes the function of a dialer profile?

A. Dialer information is configured at the physical interface

B. Dialer information is configured on a logical interface

C. A secondary link will be brought up if a primary link fails

D. A group of physical interfaces will be available to a dialer interface

E. A method for bundling multiple physical links into one logical link will be available

Answer: B

13. Which of the following best describes the function of multilink PPP?

A. Dialer information is configured at the physical interface

B. Dialer information is configured on a logical interface

C. A secondary link will be brought up if a primary link fails

D. A group of physical interfaces will be available to a dialer interface

E. A method for bundling multiple physical links into one logical link will be available

Answer: E

14. Which of the following best describes the function of a dialer pool?

   A. Dialer information is configured at the physical interface

   B. Dialer information is configured on a logical interface

   C. A secondary link will be brought up if a primary link fails

   D. A group of physical interfaces will be available to a dialer interface

   E. A method for bundling multiple physical links into one logical link will be available

Answer: D

15. Which of the following best describes the function of legacy DDR?

   A. Dialer information is configured at the physical interface

   B. Dialer information is configured on a logical interface

   C. A secondary link will be brought up if a primary link fails

   D. A group of physical interfaces will be available to a dialer interface

   E. A method for bundling multiple physical links into one logical link will be available

Answer: A

16. Which of the following best describes the function of dial backup?

   A. Dialer information is configured at the physical interface

   B. Dialer information is configured on a logical interface

   C. A secondary link will be brought up if a primary link fails

   D. A group of physical interfaces will be available to a dialer interface

   E. A method for bundling multiple physical links into one logical link will be available

Answer: C

17. Suppose that you want to configure dial backup to connect if your serial 0 link goes down. Suppose as well that you want the DDR link to be established only if the serial 0 link is down longer than 30 seconds, and that the DDR link should disconnect after the serial 0 link has been reestablished for 60 seconds. Which of the following configurations is valid? (Assume you're already in Interface Configuration mode.)

A. backup interface serial 0
backup delay 30 60

B. backup interface serial 0
Backup-delay 60 30

C. backup interface 60 30
backup delay serial 0

D. backup interface serial 0
Backup-delay 30 30

Answer: A

18. Suppose that you want to configure dial backup to connect if your serial 0 link exceeds 70% utilization and disconnect if its utilization drops below 20%. Which of the following configurations is valid? (Assume you are already in Interface Configuration mode.)

A. backup interface serial 0
Backup-load 70 20

B. backup interface 70 20
backup load serial 0

C. backup interface serial 0
Backup-load 20 70

D. backup interface serial 0
backup load 70 20

Answer: D

19. Which of the following commands will enable multilink when utilization exceeds 50% inbound?

A. `dialer load-threshold 127 in`

B. `dialer load-threshold 127 inbound`

C. `dialer load threshold 127 in`

D. `dialer load threshold 127 inbound`

Answer: B

20. Which command must you enter first if you want to enable watchdog spoofing and SPX keepalive spoofing?

A. `no ipx-route`

B. `no ipx route cache`

C. `no ipx route-cache`

D. `no ipx-route-cache`

Answer: C

APPENDIX

B

Answers to Laboratory Exercises

Chapter 3

1(A).

```
Router_C#conf t
Enter configuration commands, one per line.  End with CNTL/Z.
Router_C(config)#access-list 1 permit host 172.16.10.2
Router_C(config)#access-list 1 deny 172.16.10.0 0.0.0.255
Router_C(config)#access-list 1 permit any
Router_C(config)#interface e0
Router_C(config-if)#ip access-group 1 out
Router_C(config-if)#^Z
Router_C#
```

1(B).

```
Router_B#conf t
Enter configuration commands, one per line.  End with CNTL/Z.
Router_B(config)#access-list 2 permit 172.16.10.0 0.0.0.255
Router_B(config)#interface e0
Router_B(config-if)#ip access-group 2 out
Router_B(config-if)#^Z
Router_B#
```

1(C).

```
Router_A#conf t
Enter configuration commands, one per line.  End with CNTL/Z.
Router_A(config)#access-list 3 deny 172.16.50.0 0.0.0.255
Router_A(config)#access-list 3 permit any
Router_A(config)#interface e0
Router_A(config-if)#ip access-group 3 out
Router_A(config-if)#**
Router_A#
```

2(A).

```
Router_B#conf t
Enter configuration commands, one per line.  End with CNTL/Z.
```

```
Router_B(config)#access-list 100 deny icmp 172.16.10.0
    0.0.0.255 host 172.16.30.2 echo
Router_B(config)#access-list 100 permit ip any any
Router_B(config)#interface e0
Router_B(config-if)#ip access-group 100 out
Router_B(config-if)#^Z
Router_B#
```

2(B).

```
Router_C#conf t
Enter configuration commands, one per line.  End with CNTL/Z.
Router_C(config)#access-list 101 deny tcp any host
    172.16.50.2 eq telnet
Router_C(config)#access-list 101 deny icmp 172.16.30.0
    0.0.0.255 host 172.15.50.2 echo
Router_C(config)#access-list 101 permit ip any any
Router_C(config)#interface e0
Router_C(config-if)#ip access-group 101 out
Router_C(config-if)#^Z
Router_C#
```

or

```
Router_C#conf t
Enter configuration commands, one per line.  End with CNTL/Z.
Router_C(config)#access-list 101 deny tcp any host
    172.16.50.2 eq 23
Router_C(config)#access-list 101 deny icmp 172.16.30.0
    0.0.0.255 host 172.15.50.2 echo
Router_C(config)#access-list 101 permit ip any any
Router_C(config)#interface e0
Router_C(config-if)#ip access-group 101 out
Router_C(config-if)#^Z
Router_C#
```

The only difference between the two is that the keyword telnet was used in the first list and the port number (23) was used in the second list. Either answer is correct.

3.

```
Router_A#conf t
Enter configuration commands, one per line.  End with CNTL/Z.
Router_A(config)#access-list 20 permit 172.16.10.0 0.0.0.255
Router_A(config)#access-list 20 permit 172.16.20.0 0.0.0.255
Router_A(config)#line vty 0 4
Router_A(config-line)#access-class 20 in
Router_A(config-line)#^Z
Router_A#
```

4.

```
Router_B#conf t
Enter configuration commands, one per line.  End with CNTL/Z.
Router_B(config)#ip route 172.16.10.0 255.255.255.0 null 0
Router_B(config)#^Z
Router_B#
```

5.

```
Router_B#conf t
Enter configuration commands, one per line.  End with CNTL/Z.
Router_B(config)#interface e0
Router_B(config-if)#ip helper-address 172.16.10.255
Router_B(config-if)#ip helper-address 172.16.50.255
Router_B(config-if)#^Z
Router_B#
```

Chapter 4

1.

```
Router_A#conf t
Enter configuration commands, one per line. End with CNTL/Z.
Router_A(config)#priority-list 1 interface Ethernet0 high
Router_A(config)#interface Serial1
Router_A(config-if)#priority
Router_A(config-if)#priority-group 1
Router_A(config-if)#^Z
Router_A#
```

2.

```
Router_B#conf t
Enter configuration commands, one per line. End with CNTL/Z.
Router_B(config)#interface serial 0
Router_B(config-if)#fair-queue
Router_B(config-if)#interface serial 1
Router_B(config-if)#fair-queue
Router_B(config-if)#^Z
Router_B#
```

3.

```
Router_C#conf t
Enter configuration commands, one per line. End with CNTL/Z.
Router_C(config)#queue-list 1 protocol ip 1 tcp www
Router_C(config)#queue-list 1 protocol ip 2 tcp smtp
Router_C(config)#queue-list 1 protocol ip 3 udp snmp
Router_C(config)#queue-list 1 queue 1 byte-count 2400
Router_C(config)#queue-list 1 queue 2 byte-count 1200
Router_C(config)#queue-list 1 queue 3 byte-count 1200
Router_C(config)#int serial0
Router_C(config-if)#custom-queue-list 1
Router_C(config-if)#^Z
Router_C#
```

For the byte-count information, the ratio is 5(4.8):4:6. These values were found by multiplying the original ratio 1.2:1:1.5 by four to create integers. The ratio values were multiplied by the frame size, thus giving 2400, 1200, and 1200.

4.

```
Router_A#show queueing priority
Router_B#show queueing fair
Router_B#show queue serial1
Router_B#show queue serial0
Router_C#show queueing custom
```

Chapter 5

1.

```
Router_B#conf t
Enter configuration commands, one per line.  End with
CNTL/Z.
Router_B(config)#ip nat pool LAB5 198.68.10.1
  198.68.10.254 netmask 255.255.255.0
Router_B(config)#access-list 20 permit 192.168.0.0
  0.0.255.255
Router_B(config)#ip nat inside source list 20 pool LAB5
Router_B(config)#int e0
Router_B(config-if)#ip nat outside
Router_B(config-if)#int s1
Router_B(config-if)#ip nat inside
Router_B(config-if)#int s0
Router_B(config-if)#ip nat inside
Router_B(config-if)#^Z
Router_B#
```

Chapter 6

1 (A, B).

```
Router_A#conf t
Enter configuration commands, one per line.  End with CNTL/Z.
Router_A(config)#router igrp 100
Router_A(config-router)#network 10.0.0.0
Router_A(config-router)#network 172.16.0.0
Router_A(config-router)#^Z
Router_A#

Router_B#conf t
Enter configuration commands, one per line.  End with CNTL/Z.
Router_B(config)#router igrp 100
Router_B(config-router)#network 172.16.0.0
Router_B(config-router)#router igrp 200
```

```
Router_B(config-router)#network 172.16.0.0
Router_B(config-router)#redistribute igrp 100 <Answer, part B>
Router_B(config-router)#^Z
Router_B#


Router_C#conf t
Enter configuration commands, one per line.  End with CNTL/Z.
Router_C(config)#router igrp 200
Router_C(config-router)#network 172.16.0.0
Router_C(config-router)#network 192.168.0.0
Router_C(config-router)#^Z
Router_C#
```

1 (C).

```
Router_C#show ip route
   Codes: C - connected, S - static, I - IGRP, R - RIP, M -
   mobile, B - BGP, D - EIGRP, EX - EIGRP external, O - OSPF,
   IA - OSPF inter area, N1 - OSPF NSSA external type 1, N2 -
   OSPF NSSA external type 2, E1 - OSPF external type 1, E2 -
   OSPF external type 2, E - EGP, i - IS-IS, L1 - IS-IS
   level-1, L2 - IS-IS level-2, * - candidate default,  U -
   per-user static route, o - ODR


   Gateway of last resort is not set


172.16.0.0/30 is subnetted, 2 subnets
C    172.16.40.4 is directly connected, Ethernet0/0
I    172.16.20.4 [100/1200] via 172.16.40.5, 00:00:28,
       Ethernet0/0
I    10.0.0.0/8 [100/1300] via 172.16.40.5, 00:00:28,
       Ethernet0/0
C    192.168.1.0/24 is directly connected, Ethernet0/1
       Router_C#
```

2 (A).

```
Router_B#conf t
Enter configuration commands, one per line.  End with CNTL/Z.
Router_B(config)#router eigrp 100
```

```
Router_B(config-router)#network 172.16.0.0
Router_B(config-router)#^Z
Router_B#


Router_A#conf t
Enter configuration commands, one per line.  End with CNTL/Z.
Router_A(config)#router eigrp 100
Router_A(config-router)#network 10.0.0.0
Router_A(config-router)#network 172.16.0.0
Router_A(config-router)#^Z
Router_A#


Router_C#conf t
Enter configuration commands, one per line.  End with CNTL/Z.
Router_C(config)#router eigrp 100
Router_C(config-router)#network 172.16.0.0
Router_C(config-router)#network 192.168.1.0
Router_C(config-router)#^Z
Router_C#
```

2 (B).

```
Router_B#show ip eigrp topology
Codes: P - Passive, A - Active, U - Update, Q - Query, R -
  Reply, r - Reply status


P 10.0.0.0/8, 1 successors, FD is 307200
        via 172.16.20.5 (307200/281600), Ethernet0/0
P 192.168.1.0/24, 1 successors, FD is 307200
        via 172.16.40.6 (307200/281600), Ethernet0/1
P 172.16.40.4/30, 1 successors, FD is 281600
        via Connected, Ethernet0/1
P 172.16.20.4/30, 1 successors, FD is 281600
        via Connected, Ethernet0/0
Router_B#
```

2 (C).

```
Router_A#conf t
Enter configuration commands, one per line.  End with CNTL/Z.
```

```
Router_A(config)#router eigrp 100
Router_A(config-router)#passive-interface Ethernet 0/1
Router_A(config-router)#^Z
Router_A#
```

2 (D).

```
Router_B#conf t
Enter configuration commands, one per line.  End with CNTL/Z.
Router_B(config)#ipx routing
Router_B(config)#ipx router eigrp 10
Router_B(config-ipx-router)#network all
Router_B(config-ipx-router)#^Z
Router_B#
```

```
Router_C#conf t
Enter configuration commands, one per line.  End with CNTL/Z.
Router_C(config)#ipx routing
Router_C(config)#ipx router eigrp 10
Router_C(config-ipx-router)#network all
Router_C(config-ipx-router)#^Z
Router_C#
```

```
Router_B#conf t
Enter configuration commands, one per line.  End with CNTL/Z.
Router_B(config)#interface Ethernet 0/1
Router_B(config-if)#ipx sap-incremental eigrp 10
Router_B(config-if)#^Z
Router_B#
```

3 (A).

```
Router_A#conf t
Enter configuration commands, one per line.  End with CNTL/Z.
Router_A(config)#router ospf 1
Router_A(config-router)#network 10.1.2.0 255.255.255.0 area 1
Router_A(config-router)#network 172.16.20.4 255.255.255.252
  area 0
Router_A(config-router)#^Z
```

```
Router_A#

Router_B#conf t
Enter configuration commands, one per line.  End with CNTL/Z.
Router_B(config)#router ospf 2
Router_B(config-router)#network 172.16.20.4 255.255.255.252
  area 0
Router_B(config-router)#network 172.16.40.4 255.255.255.252
  area 0
Router_B(config-router)#^Z
Router_B#

Router_C#conf t
Enter configuration commands, one per line.  End with CNTL/Z.
Router_C(config)#router ospf 3
Router_C(config-router)#network 172.16.40.4 255.255.255.252
  area 0
Router_C(config-router)#network 192.168.1.0 255.255.255.0
  area 2
Router_C(config-router)#^Z
Router_C#
```

3 (B).

```
Router_A#conf t
Enter configuration commands, one per line.  End with CNTL/Z.
Router_A(config)#router ospf 1
Router_A(config-router)#area 1 stub
Router_A(config-router)#^Z
Router_A#
```

3 (C).

```
Router_C#conf t
Enter configuration commands, one per line.  End with CNTL/Z.
Router_C(config)#router ospf 3
Router_C(config-router)#area 2 stub no-summary
Router_C(config-router)#^Z
Router_C#
```

4 (A).

```
Router_B(config)#int loopback 0
Router_B(config-if)#ip address 172.16.60.1 255.255.255.0
Router_B(config-if)#router bgp 500
Router_B(config-router)#neighbor 172.16.70.1 remote-as 500
Router_B(config-router)#neighbor 172.16.70.1 update-source
   loopback0
Router_B(config-router)#neighbor 172.16.70.1 next-hop-self
Router_B(config-router)#neighbor 172.16.40.6 remote-as 200
Router_B(config-router)#network 172.16.0.0
Router_B(config-router)#^Z
Router_B#


Router_A#conf t
Enter configuration commands, one per line.  End with CNTL/Z.
Router_A(config)#interface loopback 0
Router_A(config-if)#ip address 172.16.70.1 255.255.255.0
Router_A(config-if)#router bgp 500
Router_A(config-router)#neighbor 172.16.60.1 remote-as 500
Router_A(config-router)#neighbor 172.16.60.1 update-source
   loopback 0
Router_A(config-router)#neighbor 172.16.60.1 next-hop-self
Router_A(config-router)#network 10.1.2.0
Router_A(config-router)#network 172.16.0.0
Router_A(config-router)#^Z
Router_A#


Router_C#conf t
Enter configuration commands, one per line.  End with CNTL/Z.
Router_C(config)#router bgp 200
Router_C(config-router)#neighbor 172.16.40.5 remote-as 500
Router_C(config-router)#network 172.16.0.0
Router_C(config-router)#network 192.168.1.0
Router_C(config-router)#^Z
Router_C#
```

4 (B).

Router_B#**conf t**
Enter configuration commands, one per line. End with CNTL/Z.
Router_B(config)#**router bgp 500**
Router_B(config-router)#**neighbor 172.16.40.6 weight 500**
Router_B(config-router)#**^Z**
Router_B#

4 (C).

Router_B#**sho ip bgp summary**
BGP table version is 2, main routing table version 2
1 network entries (1/3 paths) using 208 bytes of memory
1 BGP path attribute entries using 116 bytes of memory
0 BGP route-map cache entries using 0 bytes of memory
0 BGP filter-list cache entries using 0 bytes of memory

Neighbor	V	AS	MsgRcvd	MsgSent	TblVer	InQ	OutQ	Up/Down	State/PfxRcd
172.16.20.5	4	500	10	11	2	0	0	00:00:06	1
172.16.40.6	4	200	8	8	2	0	0	00:00:01	0

Chapter 7

1.

A. Press Return to get started and enter your password.

B. Type **enable** at the router prompt and enter your password.

C. Enter Global Configuration mode by typing **configure terminal**.

D. Type **ipx routing**, then hit Return.

E. Press **CTRL+Z** to exit Global Configuration mode.

F. Type **show config** and verify that IPX routing is enabled.

G. What was used as your node address? Where did this come from?

H. Type **exit** to log out of the router.

2.

    A. Log in to your router and enter Privilege mode.

    B. Type **config t**, then specify your router interface.

    C. Type **ipx network** *network number*.

    D. Press **CTRL+Z**.

    E. Type **sh prot**. Is IPX enabled on your interface?

    F. Type **exit**.

3.

    A. Configure your Ethernet interface for IPX and assign it an IPX network number (see lab questions 1 and 2).

    B. Configure an IPX SAP access list that prevents any SAP messages other than those from IPX address 8C.0000.0000.0001 from leaving the Ethernet network.

    C. Apply the IPX SAP access list to the Ethernet interface, using the appropriate keyword `input-sap-filter`.

    D. Verify that the access list is applied by using the `show running-config` and `show ipx interface` commands.

    E. Verify that the access list is entered correctly using the `show access-list` command.

4.

    A. Configure your Ethernet interface for IPX and assign it an IPX network number (see lab questions 1 and 2).

    B. Configure an IPX standard access list that prevents any access to network 8C from networks other than 7D and 6A.

    C. Apply the IPX standard access list to the correct interface, using the correct direction.

    D. Verify that the access list is applied by using the `show running-config` and `show ipx interface` commands.

    E. Verify that the access list is entered correctly by using the `show access-list` command.

Chapter 8

1.

    A. Enter Configuration mode by typing **conf t** at the enable prompt.

    B. Enable IPX routing by typing **ipx routing** while in Configuration mode.

    C. Enable IPX on an interface by typing **int e0**, followed by **ipx network 10**.

    D. Type **CTRL-Z** to leave Configuration mode.

    E. Verify that IPX is enabled using the `show ipx route` and `show ipx interface` commands.

2.

    A. While in Global Configuration mode, give your router an internal IPX address using the `ipx internal-network` command.

    B. Add in NLSP support using the `ipx router nlsp` command.

    C. Use the `area-address` command to indicate that all IPX networks are included in this area.

    D. Enter Interface Configuration mode, and enable NLSP support using the `ipx nlsp enable` command.

    E. Verify that NLSP is enabled using the `show ipx route`, `show ipx servers`, and `show ipx nlsp neighbors` commands.

3.

    A. Add in EIGRP support using the `ipx router eigrp as` command.

    B. Use the `network` command to add in the network address you want EIGRP to use.

    C. Verify that EIGRP is enabled using the `show ipx route` and `show ipx servers` commands.

Chapter 9

1.

    A. After booting your router, type **enable** at the prompt and enter the enable password.

    B. Type **config term**, and hit Enter.

    C. Type **appletalk routing**, and hit Enter. This will enable router RTMP.

    D. Type **interface e0**, and hit Enter.

    E. Type **appletalk cable range 100-110**, and hit Enter.

    F. Type **appletalk zone Marketing**, and hit Enter.

    G. Type **ctrl-Z**, and hit Enter.

Your router is now enabled for AppleTalk, and your Ethernet 0 interface is configured.

    H. Type **show appletalk interface brief** to verify your configuration.

    I. Type **show running-config** to verify your configuration.

    J. Type **config term**, and hit Enter.

    K. Type **interface s0**, and hit Enter.

    L. Type **appletalk cable-range 200-200**, and hit Enter.

    M. Type **appletalk zone WAN**, and hit Enter.

Your Serial 0 interface is now enabled for AppleTalk. Repeat steps H and I to verify.

2.

    A. Type **config term**, and hit Enter.

    B. Enter the appropriate access list.

    C. Apply the access list to interface Ethernet 0 using the appropriate command.

    D. Verify your configuration by typing **show running-config** and hitting Enter.

3.

 A. Type **config term**, and hit Enter.

 B. Type **interface ethernet0**, and hit Enter.

 C. Type **appletalk zone Sales**, and hit Enter.

 D. Type **exit**, and hit Enter.

 E. Enter the appropriate access list.

 F. Apply the access list to the interface Serial 0 using the appropriate command.

 G. Verify your configuration by typing **show running-config** and hitting Enter.

What would have happened if we had not done steps A through D?

4.

 A. Type in **config term**, and hit Enter.

 B. Enter the command to enable AppleTalk EIGRP.

 C. Type in **interface serial0**, and hit Enter.

 D. Type in the command to enable AppleTalk EIGRP on this interface.

 E. Type in the command to disable RTMP on this interface.

 F. Type in **ctrl-Z**, and hit Enter.

What would have happened if you omitted step E?

Chapter 10

1.

 A. Enter Configuration mode by typing **conf t** at the enable prompt.

 B. Enter the command to enable bridging. Use `bridge group 1` and IEEE Spanning Tree.

 C. Enter the command to set the Spanning Tree priority for the bridge to zero (forcing it to be the root).

 D. Configure interfaces to be part of this bridge group.

 E. Verify Spanning Tree and bridge operation.

2.

    A. In Global Configuration mode, enter the command to enable IRB.

    B. Configure the BVI.

    C. Configure the protocols to be routed and the protocols to be bridged.

    D. Enable the BVI for routing.

    E. Verify IRB operation.

Chapter 13

1.

    A. Enter Configuration mode by typing **conf t** at the enable prompt.

    B. Create an access list that allows FTP and Telnet, then denies all other IP traffic.

    C. Create a dialer list that uses the access list you created.

    D. On a dialer interface, assign a dialer group to use the dialer list you created.

2.

    A. Begin by creating a static route entry.

    B. Next, configure an interface with the appropriate configuration. Hint: We are doing legacy DDR here.

    C. What commands could you use to bring up your link? To verify it? To troubleshoot it?

3.

    A. Begin by removing the configuration from your dialer interface from lab exercise 2.

    B. Configure a dialer interface, and make your physical interface part of the appropriate dialer pool.

    C. How would you create additional dialers to use the same interface with a different configuration?

    D. How could you increase the size of the dialer pool?

APPENDIX

C

Glossary

10Base2   10Mbps baseband Ethernet specification using 50-ohm thin coaxial cable. 10Base2, which is part of the IEEE 802.3 specification, has a distance limit of 185 meters per segment. See also Cheapernet, Ethernet, IEEE 802.3, and Thinnet.

10Base5   10Mbps baseband Ethernet specification using standard (thick) 50-ohm baseband coaxial cable. 10Base5, which is part of the IEEE 802.3 baseband physical layer specification, has a distance limit of 500 meters per segment. See also Ethernet and IEEE 802.3.

10BaseF   10Mbps baseband Ethernet specification that refers to the 10BaseFB, 10BaseFL, and 10BaseFP standards for Ethernet over fiber-optic cabling. See also 10BaseFB, 10BaseFL, 10BaseFP, and Ethernet.

10BaseFB   10Mbps baseband Ethernet specification using fiber-optic cabling. 10BaseFB is part of the IEEE 10BaseF specification. It is not used to connect user stations, but instead provides a synchronous signaling backbone that allows additional segments and repeaters to be connected to the network. 10BaseFB segments can be up to 2000 meters long. See also 10BaseF and Ethernet.

10BaseFL   10Mbps baseband Ethernet specification using fiber-optic cabling. 10BaseFL is part of the IEEE 10BaseF specification and, while able to interoperate with FOIRL, is designed to replace the FOIRL specification. 10BaseFL segments can be up to 1000 meters long if used with FOIRL, and up to 2000 meters if 10BaseFL is used exclusively. See also 10BaseF, Ethernet, and FOIRL.

10BaseFP   10Mbps fiber-passive baseband Ethernet specification using fiber-optic cabling. 10BaseFP is part of the IEEE 10BaseF specification. It organizes a number of computers into a star topology without the use of repeaters. 10BaseFP segments can be up to 500 meters long. See also 10BaseF and Ethernet.

10BaseT   10Mbps baseband Ethernet specification using two pairs of twisted-pair cabling (Category 3, 4, or 5): one pair for transmitting data and the other for receiving data. 10BaseT, which is part of the IEEE 802.3 specification, has a distance limit of approximately 100 meters per segment. See also Ethernet and IEEE 802.3.

10Broad36   10Mbps broadband Ethernet specification using broadband coaxial cable. 10Broad36, which is part of the IEEE 802.3 specification, has a distance limit of 3600 meters per segment. See also Ethernet and IEEE 802.3.

100BaseFX   100Mbps baseband Fast Ethernet specification using two strands of multimode fiber-optic cable per link. To guarantee proper signal timing, a 100BaseFX link cannot exceed 400 meters in length. Based on the IEEE 802.3 standard. See also 100BaseX, Fast Ethernet, and IEEE 802.3.

100BaseT   100Mbps baseband Fast Ethernet specification using UTP wiring. Like the 10BaseT technology on which it is based, 100BaseT sends link pulses over the network segment when no traffic is present. However, these link pulses contain more information than those used in 10BaseT. Based on the IEEE 802.3 standard. See also 10BaseT, Fast Ethernet, and IEEE 802.3.

100BaseT4   100Mbps baseband Fast Ethernet specification using four pairs of Category 3, 4, or 5 UTP wiring. To guarantee proper signal timing, a 100BaseT4 segment cannot exceed 100 meters in length. Based on the IEEE 802.3 standard. See also Fast Ethernet and IEEE 802.3.

100BaseTX   100Mbps baseband Fast Ethernet specification using two pairs of either UTP or STP wiring. The first pair of wires is used to receive data; the second is used to transmit. To guarantee proper signal timing, a 100BaseTX segment cannot exceed 100 meters in length. Based on the IEEE 802.3 standard. See also 100BaseX, Fast Ethernet, and IEEE 802.3.

100BaseX   100Mbps baseband Fast Ethernet specification that refers to the 100BaseFX and 100BaseTX standards for Fast Ethernet over fiber-optic cabling. Based on the IEEE 802.3 standard. See also 100BaseFX, 100BaseTX, Fast Ethernet, and IEEE 802.3.

100VG-AnyLAN   100Mbps Fast Ethernet and Token Ring media technology using four pairs of Category 3, 4, or 5 UTP cabling. This high-speed transport technology, developed by Hewlett-Packard, can be made to operate on existing 10BaseT Ethernet networks. Based on the IEEE 802.12 standard. See also IEEE 802.12.

4B/5B local fiber   4-byte/5-byte local fiber. Fiber channel physical media used for FDDI and ATM. Supports speeds of up to 100Mbps over multimode fiber. See also TAXI 4B/5B.

8B/10B local fiber   8-byte/10-byte local fiber. Fiber channel physical media that supports speeds up to 149.76Mbps over multimode fiber.

A&B bit signaling   Procedure used in T1 transmission facilities in which each of the 24 T1 subchannels devotes one bit of every sixth frame to the carrying of supervisory signaling information. Also called 24th channel signaling.

AAL   ATM Adaptation layer. Service-dependent sublayer of the Data Link layer. The AAL accepts data from different applications and presents it to the ATM layer in the form of 48-byte ATM payload segments. AALs consist of two sublayers, CS and SAR. AALs differ on the basis of the source-destination timing used, whether they use CBR or VBR, and whether they are used for connection-oriented or connectionless mode data transfer. At present, the four types of AAL recommended by the ITU-T are AAL1, AAL2, AAL3/4, and AAL5. See AAL1, AAL2, AAL3/4, AAL5, CS, and SAR. See also ATM and ATM layer.

AAL1   ATM Adaptation layer 1. One of four AALs recommended by the ITU-T. AAL1 is used for connection-oriented, delay-sensitive services requiring constant bit rates, such as uncompressed video and other isochronous traffic. See also AAL.

AAL2   ATM Adaptation layer 2. One of four AALs recommended by the ITU-T. AAL2 is used for connection-oriented services that support a variable bit rate, such as some isochronous video and voice traffic. See also AAL.

AAL3/4   ATM Adaptation layer 3/4. One of four AALs (merged from two initially distinct adaptation layers) recommended by the ITU-T. AAL3/4 supports both connectionless and connection-oriented links, but is primarily used for the transmission of SMDS packets over ATM networks. See also AAL.

AAL5   ATM Adaptation layer 5. One of four AALs recommended by the ITU-T. AAL5 supports connection-oriented, VBR services, and is used predominantly for the transfer of classical IP over ATM and LANE traffic. AAL5 uses SEAL and is the least complex of the current AAL recommendations. It offers low bandwidth overhead and simpler processing requirements in exchange for reduced bandwidth capacity and error-recovery capability. See also AAL and SEAL.

AARP   AppleTalk Address Resolution Protocol. Protocol in the AppleTalk protocol stack that maps a data-link address to a network address.

AARP probe packets   Packets transmitted by AARP that determine if a randomly selected node ID is being used by another node in a nonextended AppleTalk network. If the node ID is not being used, the sending node uses that node ID. If the node ID is being used, the sending node chooses a different ID and sends more AARP probe packets. See also AARP.

ABM   Asynchronous Balanced Mode. An HDLC (and derivative protocol) communication mode supporting peer-oriented, point-to-point communications between two stations, where either station can initiate transmission.

ABR   1. available bit rate. QOS class defined by the ATM Forum for ATM networks. ABR is used for connections that do not require timing relationships between source and destination. ABR provides no guarantees in terms of cell loss or delay, providing only best-effort service. Traffic sources adjust their transmission rate in response to information they receive describing the status of the network and its capability to successfully deliver data. Compare with CBR, UBR, and VBR. 2. area border router. Router located on the border of one or more OSPF areas that connects those areas to the backbone network. ABRs are considered members of both the OSPF backbone and the attached areas. They therefore maintain routing tables describing both the backbone topology and the topology of the other areas.

Abstract Syntax Notation One   See ASN.1.

access list   List kept by routers to control access to or from the router for a number of services (for example, to prevent packets with a certain IP address from leaving a particular interface on the router).

access method   1. Generally, the way in which network devices access the network medium. 2. Software within an SNA processor that controls the flow of information through a network.

access server   Communications processor that connects asynchronous devices to a LAN or WAN through network and terminal emulation software. Performs both synchronous and asynchronous routing of supported protocols. Sometimes called a network access server. Compare with communication server.

accounting management   One of five categories of network management defined by ISO for management of OSI networks. Accounting management subsystems are responsible for collecting network data relating to resource usage. See also configuration management, fault management, performance management, and security management.

ACD   automatic call distribution. Device or service that automatically reroutes calls to customers in geographically distributed locations served by the same CO. See also CO.

ACF   Advanced Communications Function. A group of SNA products that provides distributed processing and resource sharing. See also ACF/NCP.

ACF/NCP   Advanced Communications Function/Network Control Program. The primary SNA NCP. ACF/NCP resides in the communications controller and interfaces with the SNA access method in the host processor to control network communications. See also ACF and NCP.

acknowledgment   Notification sent from one network device to another to acknowledge that some event (for example, receipt of a message) has occurred. Sometimes abbreviated ACK. Compare to NAK.

ACR   allowed cell rate. Parameter defined by the ATM Forum for ATM traffic management. ACR varies between the MCR and the PCR, and is dynamically controlled using congestion control mechanisms. See also MCR and PCR.

ACSE   association control service element. An OSI convention used to establish, maintain, or terminate a connection between two applications.

active hub   Multiported device that amplifies LAN transmission signals.

active monitor   Device responsible for managing a Token Ring. A network node is selected to be the active monitor if it has the highest MAC address on the ring. The active monitor is responsible for such management tasks as ensuring that tokens are not lost, or that frames do not circulate indefinitely. See also ring monitor and standby monitor.

ADCCP   Advanced Data Communications Control Protocol. An ANSI standard bit-oriented data link control protocol.

address   Data structure or logical convention used to identify a unique entity, such as a particular process or network device.

Addressed Call mode   Mode that permits control signals and commands to establish and terminate calls in V.25bis. See also V.25bis.

address mapping   Technique that allows different protocols to interoperate by translating addresses from one format to another. For example, when routing IP over X.25, the IP addresses must be mapped to the X.25 addresses so that the IP packets can be transmitted by the X.25 network. See also address resolution.

address mask   Bit combination used to describe which portion of an address refers to the network or subnet and which part refers to the host. Sometimes referred to simply as mask. See also subnet mask.

address resolution   Generally, a method for resolving differences between computer addressing schemes. Address resolution usually specifies a method for mapping Network layer (Layer 3) addresses to Data Link layer (Layer 2) addresses. See also address mapping.

Address Resolution Protocol   See ARP.

adjacency   Relationship formed between selected neighboring routers and end nodes for the purpose of exchanging routing information. Adjacency is based upon the use of a common media segment.

adjacent nodes   1. In SNA, nodes that are connected to a given node with no intervening nodes. 2. In DECnet and OSI, nodes that share a common network segment (in Ethernet, FDDI, or Token Ring networks).

ADM   Add Drop Multiplexer. In OSS, a multiplexer that allows a signal to be added into or dropped out of a SONET span. See also SONET.

administrative distance   A rating of the trustworthiness of a routing information source. Administrative distance is often expressed as a numerical value between 0 and 255. The higher the value, the lower the trustworthiness rating.

administrative weight   A value set by the network administrator to indicate the desirability of a network link. One of four link metrics exchanged by PTSPs to determine the available resources of an ATM network. See PTSP.

ADPCM   adaptive differential pulse code modulation. Process by which analog voice samples are encoded into high-quality digital signals.

ADSL   asymmetric digital subscriber line. One of four DSL technologies. ADSL is designed to deliver more bandwidth downstream (from the central office to the customer site) than upstream. Downstream rates range from 1.5Mbps to 9Mbps, while upstream bandwidth ranges from 16Kbps to 640Kbps. ADSL transmissions work at distances up to 18,000 feet over a single copper twisted pair. Compare with HDSL, SDSL, and VDSL.

ADSU   ATM DSU. Terminal adapter used to access an ATM network via an HSSI-compatible device. See also DSU.

advertising   Router process in which routing or service updates are sent at specified intervals so that other routers on the network can maintain lists of usable routes.

AEP   AppleTalk Echo Protocol. Used to test connectivity between two AppleTalk nodes. One node sends a packet to another node and receives a duplicate, or echo, of that packet.

AFI   authority and format identifier. The portion of an NSAP format ATM address that identifies the type and format of the IDI portion of an ATM address. See also IDI and NSAP.

AFP   AppleTalk Filing Protocol. A presentation-layer protocol that allows users to share data files and application programs that reside on a file server. AFP supports AppleShare and Mac OS File Sharing.

agent   1. Generally, software that processes queries and returns replies on behalf of an application. 2. In NMSs, process that resides in all managed devices and reports the values of specified variables to management stations.

AIN   Advanced Intelligent Network. In SS7, an expanded set of network services made available to the user and under user control that requires improvement in network switch architecture, signaling capabilities, and peripherals. See also SS7.

AIP   ATM Interface Processor. ATM network interface for Cisco 7000 series routers designed to minimize performance bottlenecks at the UNI. The AIP supports AAL3/4 and AAL5. See also AAL3/4 and AAL5.

AIS   alarm indication signal. In a T1 transmission, an all-ones signal transmitted in lieu of the normal signal to maintain transmission continuity and to indicate to the receiving terminal that there is a transmission fault that is located either at, or upstream from, the transmitting terminal. See also T1.

alarm   SNMP message notifying an operator or administrator of a network problem. See also event and trap.

a-law   The ITU-T companding standard used in the conversion between analog and digital signals in PCM systems. A-law is used primarily in European telephone networks and is similar to the North American mu-law standard. See also companding and mu-law.

algorithm   Well-defined rule or process for arriving at a solution to a problem. In networking, algorithms are commonly used to determine the best route for traffic from a particular source to a particular destination.

alignment error   In IEEE 802.3 networks, an error that occurs when the total number of bits of a received frame is not divisible by eight. Alignment errors are usually caused by frame damage due to collisions.

all-rings explorer packet   See all-routes explorer packet.

all-routes explorer packet   Explorer packet that traverses an entire SRB network, following all possible paths to a specific destination. Sometimes called all-rings explorer packet. See also explorer packet, local explorer packet, and spanning explorer packet.

ALO transaction   An ATP transaction in which the request is repeated until a response is received by the requester or until a maximum retry count is reached. This recovery mechanism ensures that the transaction request is executed at least once. See also ATP.

AM   amplitude modulation. Modulation technique whereby information is conveyed through the amplitude of the carrier signal.Compare with FM and PAM. See also modulation.

AMA   Automatic Messaging Accounting. In OSS, the automatic collection, recording, and processing of information relating to calls for billing purposes.

AMADNS   AMA Data Networking System. In OSS, the next generation Bellcore system for the collection and transport of AMA data from central office switches to a billing system. See also AMA.

AMATPS   AMA Teleprocessing System. In OSS, the Bellcore legacy system for collecting and transporting AMA data from central office switches to a billing system. The AMATPS consists of an AMA Transmitter and a collector. See also AMA.

AMI   alternate mark inversion. Line-code type used on T1 and E1 circuits. In AMI, zeros are represented by 01 during each bit cell, and ones are represented by 11 or 00, alternately, during each bit cell. AMI requires that the sending device maintain ones density. Ones density is not maintained independent of the data stream. Sometimes called binary coded alternate mark inversion. Compare with B8ZS. See also ones density.

amplitude   Maximum value of an analog or a digital waveform.

analog transmission   Signal transmission over wires or through the air in which information is conveyed through variation of some combination of signal amplitude, frequency, and phase.

ANSI   American National Standards Institute. Voluntary organization comprised of corporate, government, and other members that coordinates standards-related activities, approves U.S. national standards, and develops positions for the United States in international standards organizations. ANSI helps develop international and U.S. standards relating to, among other things, communications and networking. ANSI is a member of the IEC and the ISO. See also IEC and ISO.

anycast   In ATM, an address that can be shared by multiple end systems. An anycast address can be used to route a request to a node that provides a particular service.

API   application programming interface. Specification of function-call conventions that defines an interface to a service.

Apollo Domain   Proprietary network protocol suite developed by Apollo Computer for communication on proprietary Apollo networks.

APPC   Advanced Program-to-Program Communication. IBM SNA system software that allows high-speed communication between programs on different computers in a distributed computing environment. APPC establishes and tears down connections between communicating programs, and consists of two interfaces, a programming interface and a data-exchange interface. The former replies to requests from programs requiring communication; the latter establishes sessions between programs. APPC runs on LU 6.2 devices. See also LU 6.2.

AppleTalk   Series of communications protocols designed by Apple Computer. Two phases currently exist. Phase 1, the earlier version, supports a single physical network that can have only one network number and be in one zone. Phase 2, the more recent version, supports multiple logical networks on a single physical network and allows networks to be in more than one zone. See also zone.

Application layer   Layer 7 of the OSI reference model. This layer provides services to application processes (such as electronic mail, file transfer, and terminal emulation) that are outside of the OSI model. The Application layer identifies and establishes the availability of intended communication partners (and the resources required to connect with them), synchronizes cooperating applications, and establishes agreement on procedures for error recovery and control of data integrity. Corresponds roughly with the Transaction Services layer in the SNA model. See also Data Link layer, Network layer, Physical layer, Presentation layer, Session layer, and Transport layer.

APPN   Advanced Peer-to-Peer Networking. Enhancement to the original IBM SNA architecture. APPN handles session establishment between peer nodes, dynamic transparent route calculation, and traffic prioritization for APPC traffic. Compare with APPN+. See also APPC.

APPN+   Next-generation APPN that replaces the label-swapping routing algorithm with source routing. Also called high-performance routing. See also APPN.

APaRT   automated packet recognition/translation. Technology that allows a server to be attached to CDDI or FDDI without requiring the reconfiguration of applications or network protocols. APaRT recognizes specific Data Link layer encapsulation packet types and, when these packet types are transferred from one medium to another, translates them into the native format of the destination device.

ARA   AppleTalk Remote Access. Protocol that provides Macintosh users direct access to information and resources at a remote AppleTalk site.

ARCnet   Attached Resource Computer Network. A 2.5Mbps token-bus LAN developed in the late 1970s and early 1980s by Datapoint Corporation.

area   Logical set of network segments (either CLNS-, DECnet-, or OSPF-based) and their attached devices. Areas are usually connected to other areas via routers, making up a single autonomous system. See also autonomous system.

ARM   Asynchronous Response mode. HDLC communication mode involving one primary station and at least one secondary station, where either the primary or one of the secondary stations can initiate transmissions. See also primary station and secondary station.

ARP   Address Resolution Protocol. Internet protocol used to map an IP address to a MAC address. Defined in RFC 826. Compare with RARP. See also proxy ARP.

ARPA   Advanced Research Projects Agency. Research and development organization that is part of DoD. ARPA is responsible for numerous technological advances in communications and networking. ARPA evolved into DARPA, and then back into ARPA again (in 1994). See also DARPA.

ARPANET   Advanced Research Projects Agency Network. Landmark packet-switching network established in 1969. ARPANET was developed in the 1970s by BBN and funded by ARPA (and later DARPA). It eventually evolved into the Internet. The term ARPANET was officially retired in 1990. See also ARPA, BBN, DARPA, and Internet.

ARQ   automatic repeat request. Communication technique in which the receiving device detects errors and requests retransmissions.

ASBR   autonomous system boundary router. ABR located between an OSPF autonomous system and a non-OSPF network. ASBRs run both OSPF and another routing protocol, such as RIP. ASBRs must reside in a non-stub OSPF area. See also ABR, non-stub area, and OSPF.

ASCII   American Standard Code for Information Interchange. 8-bit code for character representation (7 bits plus parity).

ASN.1   Abstract Syntax Notation One. OSI language for describing data types independent of particular computer structures and representation techniques. Described by ISO International Standard 8824. See also BER (basic encoding rules).

ASP   AppleTalk Session Protocol. Protocol that uses ATP to provide session establishment, maintenance, and teardown, as well as request sequencing. See also ATP.

associative memory   Memory that is accessed based on its contents, not on its memory address. Sometimes called content addressable memory (CAM).

AST   automatic spanning tree. Function that supports the automatic resolution of spanning trees in SRB networks, providing a single path for spanning explorer frames to traverse from a given node in the network to another. AST is based on the IEEE 802.1 standard. See IEEE 802.1 and SRB.

ASTA   Advanced Software Technology and Algorithms. Component of the HPCC program intended to develop software and algorithms for implementation on high-performance computer and communications systems. See also HPCC.

asynchronous transmission   Term describing digital signals that are transmitted without precise clocking. Such signals generally have different frequencies and phase relationships. Asynchronous transmissions usually encapsulate individual characters in control bits (called start and stop bits) that designate the beginning and end of each character. Compare with isochronous transmission, plesiochronous transmission, and synchronous transmission.

ATCP   AppleTalk Control Protocol. The protocol that establishes and configures AppleTalk over PPP, as defined in RFC 1378. See also PPP.

ATDM   asynchronous time-division multiplexing. Method of sending information that resembles normal TDM, except that time slots are allocated as needed rather than preassigned to specific transmitters. Compare with FDM, statistical multiplexing, and TDM.

ATG   address translation gateway. Cisco DECnet routing software function that allows a router to route multiple, independent DECnet networks and to establish a user-specified address translation for selected nodes between networks.

ATM   Asynchronous Transfer mode. International standard for cell relay in which multiple service types (such as voice, video, or data) are conveyed in fixed-length (53-byte) cells. Fixed-length cells allow cell processing to occur in hardware, thereby reducing transit delays. ATM is designed to take advantage of high-speed transmission media such as E3, SONET, and T3.

ATM ARP server   A device that provides address-resolution services to LISs when running classical IP over ATM.

ATM endpoint   The point in an ATM network where an ATM connection is initiated or terminated. ATM endpoints includes ATM-attached workstations, ATM-attached servers, ATM-to-LAN switches, and ATM routers.

ATM Forum   International organization jointly founded in 1991 by Cisco Systems, NET/ADAPTIVE, Northern Telecom, and Sprint that develops and promotes standards-based implementation agreements for ATM technology. The ATM Forum expands on official standards developed by ANSI and ITU-T, and develops implementation agreements in advance of official standards.

ATM layer   Service-independent sublayer of the Data Link layer in an ATM network. The ATM layer receives the 48-byte payload segments from the AAL and attaches a 5-byte header to each, producing standard 53-byte ATM cells. These cells are passed to the Physical layer for transmission across the physical medium. See also AAL.

ATMM   ATM management. Process that runs on an ATM switch that controls VCI translation and rate enforcement. See also ATM and VCI.

ATM user-user connection   Connection created by the ATM layer to provide communication between two or more ATM service users, such as ATMM processes. Such communication can be unidirectional, using one VCC, or bidirectional, using two VCCs. See also ATM layer, ATMM, and VCC.

ATP   AppleTalk Transaction Protocol. Transport-level protocol that provides a loss-free transaction service between sockets. This service allows exchanges between two socket clients in which one client requests the other to perform a particular task and to report the results; ATP binds the request and response together to ensure the reliable exchange of request-response pairs.

attenuation   Loss of communication signal energy.

AU   Access unit. Device that provides ISDN access to PSNs. See also PSN.

AUI   attachment unit interface. IEEE 802.3 interface between an MAU and a NIC (network interface card). The term AUI can also refer to the rear panel port to which an AUI cable might attach. Also called transceiver cable. See also IEEE 802.3, MAU, and NIC.

AURP   AppleTalk Update-Based Routing Protocol. Method of encapsulating AppleTalk traffic in the header of a foreign protocol, allowing the connection of two or more discontiguous AppleTalk internetworks through a foreign network (such as TCP/IP) to form an AppleTalk WAN. This connection is called an AURP tunnel. In addition to its encapsulation function, AURP maintains routing tables for the entire AppleTalk WAN by exchanging routing information between exterior routers. See also AURP tunnel and exterior router.

AURP tunnel   Connection created in an AURP WAN that functions as a single, virtual data link between AppleTalk internetworks physically separated by a foreign network (a TCP/IP network, for example). See also AURP.

authority zone   Associated with DNS, an authority zone is a section of the domain-name tree for which one name server is the authority. See also DNS.

automatic call reconnect   Feature permitting automatic call rerouting away from a failed trunk line.

autonomous confederation   Group of autonomous systems that rely on their own network reachability and routing information more than they rely on that received from other autonomous systems or confederations.

autonomous switching   Feature on Cisco routers that provides faster packet processing by allowing the ciscoBus to switch packets independently without interrupting the system processor.

autonomous system   Collection of networks under a common administration sharing a common routing strategy. Autonomous systems are subdivided by areas. An autonomous system must be assigned a unique 16-bit number by the IANA. Sometimes abbreviated AS. See also area and IANA.

autoreconfiguration   Process performed by nodes within the failure domain of a Token Ring network. Nodes automatically perform diagnostics in an attempt to reconfigure the network around the failed areas. See also failure domain.

average rate   The average rate, in kilobits per second (kbps), at which a given virtual circuit will transmit

B8ZS   binary 8-zero substitution. Line-code type, used on T1 and E1 circuits, in which a special code is substituted whenever 8 consecutive zeros are sent over the link. This code is then interpreted at the remote end of the connection. This technique guarantees ones density independent of the data stream. Sometimes called bipolar 8-zero substitution. Compare with AMI. See also ones density.

backbone   The part of a network that acts as the primary path for traffic that is most often sourced from, and destined for, other networks.

back end   Node or software program that provides services to a front end. See also client, front end, and server.

backoff   The (usually random) retransmission delay enforced by contentious MAC protocols after a network node with data to transmit determines that the physical medium is already in use.

backplane   Physical connection between an interface processor or card and the data buses and power distribution buses inside a chassis.

back pressure   Propagation of network congestion information upstream through an internetwork.

backward learning   Algorithmic process used for routing traffic that surmises information by assuming symmetrical network conditions. For example, if node A receives a packet from node B through intermediate node C, the backward-learning routing algorithm will assume that A can optimally reach B through C.

balanced configuration   In HDLC, a point-to-point network configuration with two combined stations.

balun   balanced, unbalanced. Device used for matching impedance between a balanced and an unbalanced line, usually twisted-pair and coaxial cable.

bandwidth   The difference between the highest and lowest frequencies available for network signals. The term is also used to describe the rated throughput capacity of a given network medium or protocol.

bandwidth reservation   Process of assigning bandwidth to users and applications served by a network. Involves assigning priority to different flows of traffic based on how critical and delay-sensitive they are. This makes the best use of available bandwidth, and if the network becomes congested, lower-priority traffic can be dropped. Sometimes called bandwidth allocation. See also call priority.

BARRNet   Bay Area Regional Research Network. Regional network serving the San Francisco Bay Area. The BARRNet backbone is composed of four University of California campuses (Berkeley, Davis, Santa Cruz, and San Francisco), Stanford University, Lawrence Livermore National Laboratory, and NASA Ames Research Center. BARRNet is now part of BBN Planet. See also BBN Planet.

baseband   Characteristic of a network technology where only one carrier frequency is used. Ethernet is an example of a baseband network. Also called narrowband. Contrast with broadband.

bash   Bourne-again shell. Interactive UNIX shell based on the traditional Bourne shell, but with increased functionality. See also root account.

baud   Unit of signaling speed equal to the number of discrete signal elements transmitted per second. Baud is synonymous with bits per second (bps), if each signal element represents exactly 1 bit.

BBN   Bolt, Beranek, and Newman, Inc. High-technology company located in Massachusetts that developed and maintained the ARPANET (and later, the Internet) core gateway system. See also BBN Planet.

BBN Planet   Subsidiary company of BBN that operates a nationwide Internet access network composed in part by the former regional networks BARRNET, NEARNET, and SURAnet. See also BARRNet, BBN, NEARNET, and SURAnet.

Bc   Committed Burst. Negotiated tariff metric in Frame Relay internetworks. The maximum amount of data (in bits) that a Frame Relay internetwork is committed to accept and transmit at the CIR. See also Be and CIR.

B channel   bearer channel. In ISDN, a full-duplex, 64kbps channel used to send user data. Compare to D channel, E channel, and H channel.

BDCS   Broadband Digital Cross-Connect System. A SONET DCS capable of cross connecting DS-3, STS-1 and STS-3c signals. See also DCS.

Be   Excess Burst. Negotiated tariff metric in Frame Relay internetworks. The number of bits that a Frame Relay internetwork will attempt to transmit after Bc is accommodated. Be data is, in general, delivered with a lower probability than Bc data because Be data can be marked as DE by the network. See also Bc and DE.

beacon   Frame from a Token Ring or FDDI device indicating a serious problem with the ring, such as a broken cable. A beacon frame contains the address of the station assumed to be down. See also failure domain.

BECN   backward explicit congestion notification. Bit set by a Frame Relay network in frames traveling in the opposite direction of frames encountering a congested path. DTE receiving frames with the BECN bit set can request that higher-level protocols take flow control action as appropriate. Compare with FECN.

Bellcore   Bell Communications Research. Organization that performs research and development on behalf of the RBOCs.

BER   1. bit error rate. The ratio of received bits that contain errors. 2. basic encoding rules. Rules for encoding data units described in the ISO ASN.1 standard. See also ASN.1.

BERT   bit error rate tester. Device that determines the BER on a given communications channel. See also BER (bit error rate).

best-effort delivery   Describes a network system that does not use a sophisticated acknowledgment system to guarantee reliable delivery of information.

BGP   Border Gateway Protocol. Interdomain routing protocol that replaces EGP. BGP exchanges reachability information with other BGP systems. It is defined by RFC 1163. See also BGP4 and EGP.

BGP4   BGP Version 4. Version 4 of the predominant interdomain routing protocol used on the Internet. BGP4 supports CIDR and uses route aggregation mechanisms to reduce the size of routing tables. See also BGP and CIDR.

BICI   Broadband Inter-Carrier Interface. An ITU-T standard that defines the protocols and procedures needed for establishing, maintaining, and terminating broadband switched virtual connections between public networks.

BIGA   Bus Interface Gate Array. Technology that allows the Catalyst 5000 to receive and transmit frames from its packet-switching memory to its MAC local buffer memory without the intervention of the host processor.

big-endian   Method of storing or transmitting data in which the most significant bit or byte is presented first. Compare with little-endian.

binary   A numbering system characterized by ones and zeros (1 = on, 0 = off).

BinHex   Binary Hexadecimal. A method for converting binary files into ASCII for transmission by applications, such as E-mail, that can only handle ASCII.

BIP bit interleaved parity. In ATM, a method used to monitor errors on a link. A check bit or word is sent in the link overhead for the previous block or frame. Bit errrors in the payload can then be detected and reported as maintenance information.

biphase coding Bipolar coding scheme originally developed for use in Ethernet. Clocking information is embedded into and recovered from the synchronous data stream without the need for separate clocking leads. The biphase signal contains no direct current energy.

BIND Berkeley Internet Name Domain. Implementation of DNS developed and distributed by the University of California at Berkeley. Many Internet hosts run BIND, and it is the ancestor of many commercial BIND implementations.

bipolar Electrical characteristic denoting a circuit with both negative and positive polarity. Contrast with unipolar.

BISDN Broadband ISDN. ITU-T communication standards designed to handle high-bandwidth applications such as video. BISDN currently uses ATM technology over SONET-based transmission circuits to provide data rates from 155 to 622 Mbps and beyond. Contrast with N-ISDN. See also BRI, ISDN, and PRI.

bit Binary digit used in the binary numbering system. Can be 0 or 1.

BITNET "Because It's Time" Networking Services. Low-cost, low-speed academic network consisting primarily of IBM mainframes and 9600bps leased lines. BITNET is now part of CREN. See also CREN.

BITNET III Dial-up service providing connectivity for members of CREN. See also CREN.

bit-oriented protocol Class of Data Link layer communication protocols that can transmit frames regardless of frame content. Compared with byte-oriented protocols, bit-oriented protocols provide full-duplex operation and are more efficient and reliable. Compare with byte-oriented protocol.

bit rate Speed at which bits are transmitted, usually expressed in bits per second (bps).

bits per second Abbreviated bps.

black hole Routing term for an area of the internetwork where packets enter, but do not emerge, due to adverse conditions or poor system configuration within a portion of the network.

blocking In a switching system, a condition in which no paths are available to complete a circuit. The term is also used to describe a situation in which one activity cannot begin until another has been completed.

block multiplexer channel IBM-style channel that implements the FIPS-60 channel, a U.S. channel standard. This channel is also referred to as OEMI channel and 370 block mux channel.

blower Internal cooling fan used in larger router and switch chassis.

BLSR Bidirectional Line Switch Ring. A SONET ring architecture that provides working and protection fibers between nodes. If the working fiber between nodes is cut, traffic is automatically routed onto the protection fiber. See also SONET.

BNC connector Standard connector used to connect IEEE 802.3 10Base2 coaxial cable to an MAU.

BNN   boundary network node. In SNA terminology, a subarea node that provides boundary function support for adjacent peripheral nodes. This support includes sequencing, pacing, and address translation. Also called boundary node.

BOC   Bell operating company. Twenty-two local phone companies formed by the breakup of AT&T. See RBOC.

BOOTP   Bootstrap Protocol. Protocol used by a network node to determine the IP address of its Ethernet interfaces, in order to affect network booting.

boot PROM   boot programmable read-only memory. Chip mounted on a printed circuit board used to provide executable boot instructions to a computer device.

border gateway   Router that communicates with routers in other autonomous systems.

boundary function   Capability of SNA subarea nodes to provide protocol support for attached peripheral nodes. Typically found in IBM 3745 devices.

BPDU   bridge protocol data unit. Spanning-Tree Protocol hello packet that is sent out at configurable intervals to exchange information among bridges in the network. See also PDU.

BRHR   Basic Research and Human Resources. Component of the HPCC program designed to support research, training, and education in computer science, computer engineering, and computational science. See also HPCC.

BRI   Basic Rate Interface. ISDN interface composed of two B channels and one D channel for circuit-switched communication of voice, video, and data. Compare with PRI. See also BISDN, ISDN, and N-ISDN.

bridge   Device that connects and passes packets between two network segments that use the same communications protocol. Bridges operate at the Data Link layer (Layer 2) of the OSI reference model. In general, a bridge will filter, forward, or flood an incoming frame based on the MAC address of that frame. See also relay.

bridge forwarding   Process that uses entries in a filtering database to determine whether frames with a given MAC destination address can be forwarded to a given port or ports. Described in the IEEE 802.1 standard. See also IEEE 802.1.

bridge group   Bridging feature that assigns network interfaces to a particular spanning-tree group. Bridge groups can be compatible with the IEEE 802.1 or the DEC specification.

bridge number   Number that identifies each bridge in an SRB LAN. Parallel bridges must have different bridge numbers.

bridge static filtering   Process in which a bridge maintains a filtering database consisting of static entries. Each static entry equates a MAC destination address with a port that can receive frames with this MAC destination address and a set of ports on which the frames can be transmitted. Defined in the IEEE 802.1 standard. See also IEEE 802.1.

broadband   Transmission system that multiplexes multiple independent signals onto one cable. In telecommunications terminology, any channel having a bandwidth greater than a voice-grade channel (4 kHz). In LAN terminology, a coaxial cable on which analog signaling is used. Also called wideband. Contrast with baseband.

broadcast Data packet that will be sent to all nodes on a network. Broadcasts are identified by a broadcast address. Compare with multicast and unicast. See also broadcast address.

broadcast address Special address reserved for sending a message to all stations. Generally, a broadcast address is a MAC destination address of all ones. Compare with multicast address and unicast address. See also broadcast.

broadcast domain The set of all devices that will receive broadcast frames originating from any device within the set. Broadcast domains are typically bounded by routers because routers do not forward broadcast frames.

broadcast search Propagation of a search request to all network nodes if the location of a resource is unknown to the requester. See also directed search.

broadcast storm Undesirable network event in which many broadcasts are sent simultaneously across all network segments. A broadcast storm uses substantial network bandwidth and, typically, causes network time-outs.

browser GUI-based hypertext client application, such as Internet Explorer, Mosaic, and Netscape Navigator, used to access hypertext documents and other services located on innumerable remote servers throughout the WWW and Internet. See also hypertext, Internet, Mosaic, and WWW.

BSC binary synchronous communication. Character-oriented Data Link layer protocol for half-duplex applications. Often referred to simply as bisync.

BSD Berkeley Standard Distribution. Term used to describe any of a variety of UNIX-type operating systems based on the UC Berkeley BSD operating system.

BT burst tolerance. Parameter defined by the ATM Forum for ATM traffic management. For VBR connections, BT determines the size of the maximum burst of contiguous cells that can be transmitted. See also VBR.

buffer Storage area used for handling data in transit. Buffers are used in internetworking to compensate for differences in processing speed between network devices. Bursts of data can be stored in buffers until they can be handled by slower processing devices. Sometimes referred to as a packet buffer.

US broadcast and unknown server. Multicast server used in ELANs that is used to flood traffic addressed to an unknown destination, and to forward multicast and broadcast traffic to the appropriate clients. See also ELAN.

bus 1. Common physical signal path composed of wires or other media across which signals can be sent from one part of a computer to another. Sometimes called highway. 2. See bus topology.

bus and tag channel IBM channel, developed in the 1960s, incorporating copper multiwire technology. Replaced by the ESCON channel. See also ESCON channel and parallel channel.

bus topology Linear LAN architecture in which transmissions from network stations propagate the length of the medium and are received by all other stations. Compare with ring topology, star topology, and tree topology.

BX.25 An AT&T implementation of X.25. See also X.25.

Bypass mode   Operating mode on FDDI and Token Ring networks in which an interface has been removed from the ring.

bypass relay   Allows a particular Token Ring interface to be shut down and thus effectively removed from the ring.

byte   Term used to refer to a series of consecutive binary digits that are operated upon as a unit (for example, an 8-bit byte).

byte-oriented protocol   Class of data-link communications protocols that use a specific character from the user character set to delimit frames. These protocols have largely been replaced by bit-oriented protocols. Compare with bit-oriented protocol.

byte reversal   Process of storing numeric data with the least-significant byte first. Used for integers and addresses on devices with Intel microprocessors.

cable   Transmission medium of copper wire or optical fiber wrapped in a protective cover.

cable range   Range of network numbers that is valid for use by nodes on an extended AppleTalk network. The cable range value can be a single network number or a contiguous sequence of several network numbers. Node addresses are assigned based on the cable range value.

call admission control   Traffic management mechanism used in ATM networks that determines whether the network can offer a path with sufficient bandwidth for a requested VCC.

call priority   Priority assigned to each origination port in circuit-switched systems. This priority defines the order in which calls are reconnected. Call priority also defines which calls can or cannot be placed during a bandwidth reservation. See also bandwidth reservation.

call setup time   The time required to establish a switched call between DTE devices.

CAM   content-addressable memory. See associative memory.

CAP   Competitive Access Provider. An independent company providing local telecommunications services mainly to business customers in competition with an area's BOC or IOC. Teleport and MFS are the two major CAPs operating in major metropolitan areas in the US. See also BOC and IOC.

carrier   Electromagnetic wave or alternating current of a single frequency, suitable for modulation by another, data-bearing signal. See also modulation.

Category 1 cabling   One of five grades of UTP cabling described in the EIA/TIA-586 standard. Category 1 cabling is used for telephone communications and is not suitable for transmitting data. Compare with Category 2 cabling, Category 3 cabling, Category 4 cabling, and Category 5 cabling. See also EIA/TIA-586 and UTP.

Category 2 cabling   One of five grades of UTP cabling described in the EIA/TIA-586 standard. Category 2 cabling is capable of transmitting data at speeds up to 4 Mbps. Compare with Category 1 cabling, Category 3 cabling, Category 4 cabling, and Category 5 cabling. See also EIA/TIA-586 and UTP.

Category 3 cabling   One of five grades of UTP cabling described in the EIA/TIA-586 standard. Category 3 cabling is used in 10BaseT networks and can transmit data at speeds up to 10 Mbps. Compare with Category 1 cabling, Category 2 cabling, Category 4 cabling, and Category 5 cabling. See also EIA/TIA-586 and UTP.

Category 4 cabling   One of five grades of UTP cabling described in the EIA/TIA-586 standard. Category 4 cabling is used in Token Ring networks and can transmit data at speeds up to 16 Mbps. Compare with Category 1 cabling, Category 2 cabling, Category 3 cabling, and Category 5 cabling. See also EIA/TIA-586 and UTP.

Category 5 cabling   One of five grades of UTP cabling described in the EIA/TIA-586 standard. Category 5 cabling can transmit data at speeds up to 100Mbps. Compare with Category 1 cabling, Category 2 cabling, Category 3 cabling, and Category 4 cabling. See also EIA/TIA-586 and UTP.

catenet   Network in which hosts are connected to diverse networks, which themselves are connected with routers. The Internet is a prominent example of a catenet.

CATV   cable television. Communication system where multiple channels of programming material are transmitted to homes using broadband coaxial cable. Formerly called Community Antenna Television.

CBDS   Connectionless Broadband Data Service. European high-speed, packet-switched, datagram-based WAN networking technology. Similar to SMDS. See also SMDS.

CBR   constant bit rate. QOS class defined by the ATM Forum for ATM networks. CBR is used for connections that depend on precise clocking to ensure undistorted delivery. Compare with ABR, UBR, and VBR.

CCITT   Consultative Committee for International Telegraph and Telephone. International organization responsible for the development of communications standards. Now called the ITU-T. See ITU-T.

CCS   common channel signaling. Signaling system used in telephone networks that separates signaling information from user data. A specified channel is exclusively designated to carry signaling information for all other channels in the system. See also SS7.

CD   Carrier Detect. Signal that indicates whether an interface is active. Also, a signal generated by a modem indicating that a call has been connected.

CDDI   Copper Distributed Data Interface. Implementation of FDDI protocols over STP and UTP cabling. CDDI transmits over relatively short distances (about 100 meters), providing data rates of 100Mbps using a dual-ring architecture to provide redundancy. Based on the ANSI Twisted-Pair Physical Medium Dependent (TPPMD) standard. Compare with FDDI.

CDP   Cisco Discovery Protocol. Media- and protocol-independent device-discovery protocol that runs on all Cisco-manufactured equipment including routers, access servers, bridges, and switches. Using CDP, a device can advertise its existence to other devices and receive information about other devices on the same LAN or on the remote side of a WAN. Runs on all media that support SNAP, including LANs, Frame Relay, and ATM media.

CDPD Cellular Digital Packet Data. Open standard for two-way wireless data communication over high-frequency cellular telephone channels. Allows data transmissions between a remote cellular link and a NAP. Operates at 19.2Kbps.

CDV cell delay variation. A component of cell transfer delay, which is induced by buffering and cell scheduling. CDV is a QOS delay parameter associated with CBR and VBR service. See also CBR and VBR.

CDVT cell delay variation tolerance. In ATM, a QOS parameter for managing traffic that is specified when a connection is setup. In CBR transmissions, CDVT determines the level of jitter that is tolerable for the data samples taken by the PCR. See also CBR and PCR.

cell The basic data unit for ATM switching and multiplexing. Cells contain identifiers that specify the data stream to which they belong. Each cell consists of a 5-byte header and 48 bytes of payload. See also cell relay.

cell payload scrambling Technique used an ATM switch to maintain framing on some medium-speed edge and trunk interfaces.

cell relay Network technology based on the use of small, fixed-size packets, or cells. Because cells are fixed-length, they can be processed and switched in hardware at high speeds. Cell relay is the basis for many high-speed network protocols including ATM, IEEE 802.6, and SMDS. See also cell.

cellular radio Technology that uses radio transmissions to access telephone company networks. Service is provided in a particular area by a low-power transmitter.

Centrex An LEC service that provides local switching applications similar to those provided by an on-site PBX. With Centrex, there is no on-site switching; all customer connections go back to the CO. See also CO and LEC (local exchange carrier).

CEPT Conférence Européenne des Postes et des Télécommunications. Association of the 26 European PTTs that recommends communication specifications to the ITU-T.

CER cell error ratio. In ATM, the ratio of transmitted cells that have errors to the total cells sent in a transmission for a specific period of time.

CERFnet California Education and Research Federation Network. TCP/IP network, based in Southern California, that connects hundreds of higher-education centers internationally while also providing Internet access to subscribers. CERFnet was founded in 1988 by the San Diego Supercomputer Center and General Atomics and is funded by the NSF.

CGI Common Gateway Interface. A set of rules that describe how a Web server communicates with another application running on the same computer and how the application (called a "GI program") communicates with the Web server. Any application can be a CGI program if it handles input and output according to the CGI standard.

chaining SNA concept in which RUs are grouped together for the purpose of error recovery.

channel 1. A communication path. Multiple channels can be multiplexed over a single cable in certain environments. 2. In IBM, the specific path between large computers (such as mainframes) and attached peripheral devices.

channel-attached Pertaining to attachment of devices directly by data channels (input/output channels) to a computer.

channelized E1 Access link operating at 2.048Mbps that is subdivided into 30 B-channels and 1 D-channel. Supports DDR, Frame Relay, and X.25. Compare with channelized T1.

channelized T1 Access link operating at 1.544Mbps that is subdivided into 24 channels (23 B-channels and 1 D-channel) of 64Kbps each. The individual channels or groups of channels connect to different destinations. Supports DDR, Frame Relay, and X.25. Also referred to as fractional T1. Compare with channelized E1.

CHAP Challenge Handshake Authentication Protocol. Security feature supported on lines using PPP encapsulation that prevents unauthorized access. CHAP does not itself prevent unauthorized access, it merely identifies the remote end. The router or access server then determines whether that user is allowed access. Compare to PAP.

chat script String of text that defines the login "conversation" that occurs between two systems. Consists of expect-send pairs that define the string that the local system expects to receive from the remote system and what the local system should send as a reply.

Cheapernet Industry term used to refer to the IEEE 802.3 10Base2 standard or the cable specified in that standard. Compare with Thinnet. See also 10Base2, Ethernet, and IEEE 802.3.

checksum Method for checking the integrity of transmitted data. A checksum is an integer value computed from a sequence of octets taken through a series of arithmetic operations. The value is recomputed at the receiving end and compared for verification.

choke packet Packet sent to a transmitter to tell it that congestion exists and that it should reduce its sending rate.

CICNet Regional network that connects academic, research, nonprofit, and commercial organizations in the Midwestern United States. Founded in 1988, CICNet was a part of the NSFNET and was funded by the NSF until the NSFNET dissolved in 1995. See also NSFNET.

CICS Customer Information Control System. IBM application subsystem allowing transactions entered at remote terminals to be processed concurrently by user applications.

CID Craft Interface Device. A terminal or PC-based interface that enables the performance of local maintenance operations.

CIDR classless interdomain routing. Technique supported by BGP4 and based on route aggregation. CIDR allows routers to group routes together in order to cut down on the quantity of routing information carried by the core routers. With CIDR, several IP networks appear to networks outside the group as a single, larger entity. With CIDR, IP addresses and their subnet masks are written as 4 octets, separated by periods, followed by a forward slash and a two-digit number that represents the subnet mask. See also BGP4.

child peer group A peer group for which another peer group is the parent peer group. See also logical group node, peer group, and parent peer group.

CIP   Channel Interface Processor. Channel attachment interface for Cisco 7000 series routers. The CIP is used to connect a host mainframe to a control unit, eliminating the need for an FEP for channel attachment.

CIR   committed information rate. The rate at which a Frame Relay network agrees to transfer information under normal conditions, averaged over a minimum increment of time. CIR, measured in bits per second, is one of the key negotiated tariff metrics. See also Bc.

circuit   Communications path between two or more points.

circuit group   Grouping of associated serial lines that link two bridges. If one of the serial links in a circuit group is in the spanning tree for a network, any of the serial links in the circuit group can be used for load balancing. This load-balancing strategy avoids data ordering problems by assigning each destination address to a particular serial link.

circuit steering   A mechanism used by some ATM switches to eavesdrop on a virtual connection and copy its cells to another port where an ATM analyzer is attached. Also known as port snooping.

circuit switching   Switching system in which a dedicated physical circuit path must exist between sender and receiver for the duration of the "call." Used heavily in the telephone company network. Circuit switching can be contrasted with contention and token passing as a channel-access method, and with message switching and packet switching as a switching technique.

Cisco FRAD   Cisco Frame Relay access device. Cisco product that supports Cisco IOS Frame Relay SNA services and can be upgraded to be a full-function multiprotocol router. The Cisco FRAD connects SDLC devices to Frame Relay without requiring an existing LAN. However, the Cisco FRAD does support attached LANs and can perform conversion from SDLC to Ethernet and Token Ring. See also FRAD.

CiscoFusion   Cisco internetworking architecture that "fuses" together the scalability, stability, and security advantages of the latest routing technologies with the performance benefits of ATM and LAN switching, and the management benefits of VLANs. See also Cisco IOS software.

Cisco IOS software   Cisco Internetwork Operating System software. Cisco system software that provides common functionality, scalability, and security for all products under the CiscoFusion architecture. The Cisco IOS software allows centralized, integrated, and automated installation and management of internetworks, while ensuring support for a wide variety of protocols, media, services, and platforms. See also CiscoFusion.

CiscoView   GUI-based device-management software application that provides dynamic status, statistics, and comprehensive configuration information for Cisco internetworking devices. In addition to displaying a physical view of Cisco device chassis, CiscoView also provides device monitoring functions and basic trouble-shooting capabilities, and can be integrated with several leading SNMP-based network management platforms

classical IP over ATM   Specification for running IP over ATM in a manner that takes full advantage of the features of ATM. Defined in RFC 1577. Sometimes called CIA.

CLAW   Common Link Access for Workstations. Data Link layer protocol used by channel-attached RISC System/6000 series systems and by IBM 3172 devices running TCP/IP off-load. CLAW improves efficiency of channel use and allows the CIP to provide the functionality of a 3172 in TCP/IP environments and support direct channel attachment. The output from TCP/IP mainframe processing is a series of IP datagrams that the router can switch without modifications.

clear channel   A channel that uses out-of-band signaling (as opposed to in-band signaling) so that the channel's entire bit rate is available.

CLI   command line interface. An interface that allows the user to interact with the operating system by entering commands and optional arguments. The UNIX operating system and DOS provide CLIs. Compare with GUI.

client   Node or software program (front-end device) that requests services from a server. See also back end, front end, and server.

client/server computing   Term used to describe distributed computing (processing) network systems in which transaction responsibilities are divided into two parts: client (front end) and server (back end). Both terms (client and server) can be applied to software programs or actual computing devices. Also called distributed computing (processing). Compare with peer-to-peer computing. See also RPC.

CLNP   Connectionless Network Protocol. OSI network layer protocol that does not require a circuit to be established before data is transmitted. See also CLNS.

CLNS   Connectionless Network Service. OSI network layer service that does not require a circuit to be established before data is transmitted. CLNS routes messages to their destinations independently of any other messages. See also CLNP.

CLP   cell loss priority. Field in the ATM cell header that determines the probability of a cell being dropped if the network becomes congested. Cells with CLP=0 are insured traffic, which is unlikely to be dropped. Cells with CLP=1 are best-effort traffic, which might be dropped in congested conditions in order to free up resources to handle insured traffic.

CLR   cell loss ratio. In ATM, the ratio of discarded cells to cells that are successfully transmitted. CLR can be set as a QOS parameter when a connection is set up.

CLS   Cisco Link Services. A front-end for a variety of data-link control services

CLSI   Cisco Link Services Interface. The messages that are exchanged between CLS and data-link users such as APPN, SNA service point, and DLSw+.

cluster controller   1. Generally, an intelligent device that provides the connections for a cluster of terminals to a data link. 2. In SNA, a programmable device that controls the input/output operations of attached devices. Typically, an IBM 3174 or 3274 device.

CMI   coded mark inversion. ITU-T line coding technique specified for STS-3c transmissions. Also used in DS-1 systems. See also DS-1 and STS-3c.

CMIP   Common Management Information Protocol. OSI network management protocol created and standardized by ISO for the monitoring and control of heterogeneous networks. See also CMIS.

CMIS   Common Management Information Services. OSI network management service interface created and standardized by ISO for the monitoring and control of heterogeneous networks. See also CMIP.

CMNS   Connection-Mode Network Service. Extends local X.25 switching to a variety of media (Ethernet, FDDI, Token Ring). See also CONP.

CMT   connection management. FDDI process that handles the transition of the ring through its various states (off, active connect, and so on), as defined by the ANSI X3T9.5 specification.

CO   central office. Local telephone company office to which all local loops in a given area connect and in which circuit switching of subscriber lines occurs.

CO-IPX   Connection Oriented IPX. A native ATM protocol based on IPX under development by Novell.

coaxial cable   Cable consisting of a hollow outer cylindrical conductor that surrounds a single inner wire conductor. Two types of coaxial cable are currently used in LANs: 50-ohm cable, which is used for digital signaling, and 75-ohm cable, which is used for analog signaling and high-speed digital signaling.

CODEC   coder-decoder. Device that typically uses pulse code modulation to transform analog signals into a digital bit stream, and digital signals back into analog.

coding   Electrical techniques used to convey binary signals.

collapsed backbone   Nondistributed backbone in which all network segments are interconnected by way of an internetworking device. A collapsed backbone might be a virtual network segment existing in a device such as a hub, a router, or a switch.

collision   In Ethernet, the result of two nodes transmitting simultaneously. The frames from each device impact and are damaged when they meet on the physical media. See also collision domain.

collision domain   In Ethernet, the network area within which frames that have collided are propagated. Repeaters and hubs propagate collisions; LAN switches, bridges and routers do not. See also collision.

common carrier   Licensed, private utility company that supplies communication services to the public at regulated prices.

communication   Transmission of information.

communication controller   In SNA, a subarea node (such as an IBM 3745 device) that contains an NCP.

communication server   Communications processor that connects asynchronous devices to a LAN or WAN through network and terminal emulation software. Performs only asynchronous routing of IP and IPX. Compare with access server.

communications line   The physical link (such as wire or a telephone circuit) that connects one or more devices to one or more other devices.

community   In SNMP, a logical group of managed devices and NMSs in the same administrative domain.

Community Antenna Television   Now known as CATV. See CATV.

community string   Text string that acts as a password and is used to authenticate messages sent between a management station and a router containing an SNMP agent. The community string is sent in every packet between the manager and the agent. Also called a community name.

companding   Contraction derived from the opposite processes of compression and expansion. Part of the PCM process whereby analog signal values are logically rounded to discrete scale-step values on a nonlinear scale. The decimal step number is then coded in its binary equivalent prior to transmission. The process is reversed at the receiving terminal using the same nonlinear scale. Compare with compression and expansion. See also a-law and mu-law.

compression   The running of a data set through an algorithm that reduces the space required to store or the bandwidth required to transmit the data set. Compare with companding and expansion.

configuration direct VCC   In ATM, a bi-directional point-to-point VCC set up by a LEC to an LES. One of three control connections defined by Phase 1 LANE. Compare with control distribute VCC and control direct VCC.

configuration management   One of five categories of network management defined by ISO for management of OSI networks. Configuration management subsystems are responsible for detecting and determining the state of a network. See also accounting management, fault management, performance management, and security management.

configuration register   In Cisco routers, a 16-bit, user-configurable value that determines how the router functions during initialization. The configuration register can be stored in hardware or software. In hardware, the bit position is set using a jumper. In software, the bit position is set by specifying a hexadecimal value using configuration commands.

congestion   Traffic in excess of network capacity.

congestion avoidance   The mechanism by which an ATM network controls traffic entering the network to minimize delays. In order to use resources most efficiently, lower-priority traffic is discarded at the edge of the network if conditions indicate that it cannot be delivered.

congestion collapse   A condition in which the re-transmission of frames in an ATM network results in little or no traffic successfully arriving at the destination. Congestion collapse frequently occurs in ATM networks composed of switches that do not have adequate and effective buffering mechanisms complimented by intelligent packet discard or ABR congestion feedback mechanisms.

connectionless   Term used to describe data transfer without the existence of a virtual circuit. Compare with connection-oriented. See also virtual circuit.

connection-oriented   Term used to describe data transfer that requires the establishment of a virtual circuit. See also connectionless and virtual circuit.

CONP   Connection-Oriented Network Protocol. OSI protocol providing connection-oriented operation to upper-layer protocols. See also CMNS.

console   DTE through which commands are entered into a host.

contention   Access method in which network devices compete for permission to access the physical medium. Compare with circuit switching and token passing.

control direct VCC   In ATM, a bidirectional VCC set up by a LEC to a LES. One of three control connections defined by Phase 1 LANE. Compare with configuration direct VCC and control distribute VCC.

control distribute VCC   In ATM, a unidirectional VCC set up from a LES to a LEC. One of three control connections defined by Phase 1LANE. Typically, the VCC is a point-to-multipoint connection. Compare with configuration direct VCC and control direct VCC.

convergence   The speed and ability of a group of internetworking devices running a specific routing protocol to agree on the topology of an internetwork after a change in that topology.

conversation   In SNA, an LU 6.2 session between two transaction programs.

cookie   A piece of information sent by a Web server to a Web browser that the browser is expected to save and send back to the Web server whenever the browser makes additional requests of the Web server.

core gateway   The primary routers in the Internet.

core router   In a packet-switched star topology, a router that is part of the backbone and that serves as the single pipe through which all traffic from peripheral networks must pass on its way to other peripheral networks.

COS   1. class of service. Indication of how an upper-layer protocol requires that a lower-layer protocol treat its messages. In SNA subarea routing, COS definitions are used by subarea nodes to determine the optimal route to establish a given session. A COS definition comprises a virtual route number and a transmission priority field. Also called TOS (type of service). 2. Corporation for Open Systems. Organization that promulgates the use of OSI protocols through conformance testing, certification, and related activities.

COSINE   Cooperation for Open Systems Interconnection Networking in Europe. European project financed by the European Community (EC) to build a communication network between scientific and industrial entities in Europe. The project ended in 1994.

cost   Arbitrary value, typically based on hop count, media bandwidth, or other measures, that is assigned by a network administrator and used to compare various paths through an internetwork environment. Cost values are used by routing protocols to determine the most favorable path to a particular destination: the lower the cost, the better the path. Sometimes called path cost. See also routing metric.

count to infinity   Problem that can occur in routing algorithms that are slow to converge, in which routers continuously increment the hop count to particular networks. Typically, some arbitrary hop-count limit is imposed to prevent this problem.

CP   control point. In SNA networks, element that identifies the APPN networking components of a PU 2.1 node, manages device resources, and can provide services to other devices. In APPN, CPs are able to communicate with logically adjacent CPs by way of CP-to-CP sessions. See also EN and NN.

CPCS   common part convergence sublayer. One of the two sublayers of any AAL. The CPCS is service-independent and is further divided into the CS and the SAR sublayers. The CPCS is responsible for preparing data for transport across the ATM network, including the creation of the 48-byte payload cells that are passed to the ATM layer. See also AAL, ATM layer, CS, SAR, and SSCS.

CPE customer premises equipment. Terminating equipment, such as terminals, telephones, and modems, supplied by the telephone company, installed at customer sites, and connected to the telephone company network.

CPI-C Common Programming Interface for Communications. Platform-independent API developed by IBM and used to provide portability in APPC applications. See also APPC.

cps cells per second.

crankback A mechanism used by ATM networks when a connection setup request is blocked because a node along a selected path cannot accept the request. In this case, the path is rolled back to an intermediate node, which attempts to discover another path to the final destination using GCAC. See also GCAC.

CRC cyclic redundancy check. Error-checking technique in which the frame recipient calculates a remainder by dividing frame contents by a prime binary divisor and compares the calculated remainder to a value stored in the frame by the sending node.

CREN Corporation for Research and Educational Networking. The result of a merger of BITNET and CSNET. CREN is devoted to providing Internet connectivity to its members, which include the alumni, students, faculty, and other affiliates of participating educational and research institutions, via BITNET III. See also BITNET, BITNET III, and CSNET.

CRM cell rate margin. One of three link attributes exchanged using PTSPs to determine the available resources of an ATM network. CRM is a measure of the difference between the effective bandwidth allocation per traffic class as the allocation for sustainable cell rate.

CRV call reference value. A number carried in all Q.931 (I.451) messages that provides an identifier for each ISDN call.

cross talk Interfering energy transferred from one circuit to another.

CS convergence sublayer. One of the two sublayers of the AAL CPCS, responsible for padding and error checking. PDUs passed from the SSCS are appended with an 8-byte trailer (for error checking and other control information) and padded, if necessary, so that the length of the resulting PDU is divisible by 48. These PDUs are then passed to the SAR sublayer of the CPCS for further processing. See also AAL, CPCS, SAR, and SSCS.

CSA Canadian Standards Association. Agency within Canada that certifies products that conform to Canadian national safety standards.

CSLIP Compressed Serial Link Internet Protocol. Extension of SLIP that, when appropriate, allows just header information to be sent across a SLIP connection, reducing overhead and increasing packet throughput on SLIP lines. See also SLIP.

CSMA/CD carrier sense multiple access collision detect. Media-access mechanism wherein devices ready to transmit data first check the channel for a carrier. If no carrier is sensed for a specific period of time, a device can transmit. If two devices transmit at once, a collision occurs and is detected by all colliding devices. This collision subsequently delays retransmissions from those devices for some random length of time. CSMA/CD access is used by Ethernet and IEEE 802.3.

CSNET   Computer Science Network. Large internetwork consisting primarily of universities, research institutions, and commercial concerns. CSNET merged with BITNET to form CREN. See also BITNET and CREN.

CSNP   complete sequence number PDU. PDU sent by the designated router in an OSPF network to maintain database synchronization.

CSU   channel service unit. Digital interface device that connects end-user equipment to the local digital telephone loop. Often referred to together with DSU, as CSU/DSU. See also DSU.

CTD   cell transfer delay. In ATM, the elapsed time between a cell exit event at the source UNI and the corresponding cell entry event at the destination UNI for a particular connection. The CTD between the two points is the sum of the total inter-ATM node transmission delay and the total ATM node processing delay.

CTS   1. Clear To Send. Circuit in the EIA/TIA-232 specification that is activated when DCE is ready to accept data from DTE. 2. common transport semantic. Cornerstone of the IBM strategy to reduce the number of protocols on networks. CTS provides a single API for developers of network software and enables applications to run over APPN, OSI, or TCP/IP.

cut-through packet switching   Packet switching approach that streams data through a switch so that the leading edge of a packet exits the switch at the output port before the packet finishes entering the input port. A device using cut-through packet switching reads, processes, and forwards packets as soon as the destination address is looked up, and the outgoing port determined. Also known as on-the-fly packet switching. Compare with store and forward packet switching.

CxBus   Cisco Extended Bus. Data bus for interface processors on Cisco 7000 series routers. See also SP.

DAC   dual-attached concentrator. FDDI or CDDI concentrator capable of attaching to both rings of an FDDI or CDDI network. It can also be dual-homed from the master ports of other FDDI or CDDI concentrators.

DACS   Digital Access and Cross-connect System. AT&T's term for a digital crossconnect system.

DARPA   Defense Advanced Research Projects Agency. U.S. government agency that funded research for and experimentation with the Internet. Evolved from ARPA, and then, in 1994, back to ARPA. See also ARPA.

DARPA Internet   Obsolete term referring to the Internet. See Internet.

DAS   1. dual attachment station. Device attached to both the primary and the secondary FDDI rings. Dual attachment provides redundancy for the FDDI ring: if the primary ring fails, the station can wrap the primary ring to the secondary ring, isolating the failure and retaining ring integrity. Also known as a Class A station. Compare with SAS. 2. dynamically assigned socket. A socket that is dynamically assigned by DDP upon request by a client. In an AppleTalk network, the sockets numbered 128 to 254 are allocated as DASs.

database object   A piece of information that is stored in a database.

data direct VCC   In ATM, a bi-directional point-to-point VCC set up between two LECs. One of three data connections defined by Phase 1 LANE. Data direct VCCs do not offer any type of QOS guarantee, so they are typically used for UBR and ABR connections. Compare with control distribute VCC and control direct VCC.

Data Flow Control layer Layer 5 of the SNA architectural model. This layer determines and manages interactions between session partners, particularly data flow. Corresponds to the Session layer of the OSI model. See also Data Link Control layer, Path Control layer, Physical Control layer, Presentation Services layer, Transaction Services layer, and Transmission Control layer.

datagram Logical grouping of information sent as a network layer unit over a transmission medium without prior establishment of a virtual circuit. IP datagrams are the primary information units in the Internet. The terms cell, frame, message, packet, and segment are also used to describe logical information groupings at various layers of the OSI reference model and in various technology circles.

Datakit An AT&T proprietary packet switching system widely deployed by the RBOCs.

Data Link Control layer Layer 2 in the SNA architectural model. Responsible for the transmission of data over a particular physical link. Corresponds roughly to the Data Link layer of the OSI model. See also Data Flow Control layer, Path Control layer, Physical Control layer, Presentation Services layer, Transaction Services layer, and Transmission Control layer.

Data Link layer Layer 2 of the OSI reference model. This layer provides reliable transit of data across a physical link. The Data Link layer is concerned with physical addressing, network topology, line discipline, error notification, ordered delivery of frames, and flow control. The IEEE has divided this layer into two sublayers: the MAC sublayer and the LLC sublayer. Sometimes simply called Link layer. Roughly corresponds to the Data Link Control layer of the SNA model. See also Application layer, LLC, MAC, Network layer, Physical layer, Presentation layer, Session layer, and Transport layer.

data sink Network equipment that accepts data transmissions.

data stream All data transmitted through a communications line in a single read or write operation.

DB connector data bus connector. Type of connector used to connect serial and parallel cables to a data bus. DB connector names are of the format DB-x, where x represents the number of wires within the connector. Each line is connected to a pin on the connector, but in many cases, not all pins are assigned a function. DB connectors are defined by various EIA/TIA standards.

DCA Defense Communications Agency. U.S. government organization responsible for DDN networks such as MILNET. Now called DISA. See DISA.

DCC Data Country Code. One of two ATM address formats developed by the ATM Forum for use by private networks. Adapted from the subnetwork model of addressing in which the ATM layer is responsible for mapping network layer addresses to ATM addresses. Compare with ICD.

DCE data communications equipment (EIA expansion) or data circuit-terminating equipment (ITU-T expansion). The devices and connections of a communications network that comprise the network end of the user-to-network interface. The DCE provides a physical connection to the network, forwards traffic, and provides a clocking signal used to synchronize data transmission between DCE and DTE devices. Modems and interface cards are examples of DCE. Compare with DTE.

DCS Digital Cross-connect System. A network element providing automatic cross connection of a digital signal or its constituent parts.

D channel   1. data channel. Full-duplex, 16Kbps (BRI) or 64Kbps (PRI) ISDN channel. Compare to B channel, E channel, and H channel. 2. In SNA, a device that connects a processor and main storage with peripherals.

DDM   Distributed Data Management. Software in an IBM SNA environment that provides peer-to-peer communication and file sharing. One of three SNA transaction services. See also DIA and SNADS.

DDN   Defense Data Network. U.S. military network composed of an unclassified network (MILNET) and various secret and top-secret networks. DDN is operated and maintained by DISA. See also DISA and MILNET.

DDP   Datagram Delivery Protocol. AppleTalk Network layer protocol that is responsible for the socket-to-socket delivery of datagrams over an AppleTalk internetwork.

DDR   dial-on-demand routing. Technique whereby a router can automatically initiate and close a circuit-switched session as transmitting stations demand. The router spoofs keepalives so that end stations treat the session as active. DDR permits routing over ISDN or telephone lines using an external ISDN terminal adapter or modem.

DE   discard eligible. See tagged traffic.

deadlock   1. Unresolved contention for the use of a resource. 2. In APPN, when two elements of a process each wait for action by or a response from the other before they resume the process.

decibels   Abbreviated dB.

DECnet   Group of communications products (including a protocol suite) developed and supported by Digital Equipment Corporation. DECnet/OSI (also called DECnet Phase V) is the most recent iteration and supports both OSI protocols and proprietary Digital protocols. Phase IV Prime supports inherent MAC addresses that allow DECnet nodes to coexist with systems running other protocols that have MAC address restrictions. See also DNA.

DECnet routing   Proprietary routing scheme introduced by Digital Equipment Corporation in DECnet Phase III. In DECnet Phase V, DECnet completed its transition to OSI routing protocols (ES-IS and IS-IS).

decryption   The reverse application of an encryption algorithm to encrypted data, thereby restoring that data to its original, unencrypted state. See also encryption.

dedicated LAN   Network segment allocated to a single device. Used in LAN switched network topologies.

dedicated line   Communications line that is indefinitely reserved for transmissions, rather than switched as transmission is required. See also leased line.

de facto standard   Standard that exists by nature of its widespread use. Compare with de jure standard. See also standard.

default route   Routing table entry that is used to direct frames for which a next hop is not explicitly listed in the routing table.

de jure standard   Standard that exists because of its approval by an official standards body. Compare with de facto standard. See also standard.

delay   The time between the initiation of a transaction by a sender and the first response received by the sender. Also, the time required to move a packet from source to destination over a given path.

demand priority   Media access method used in 100VG-AnyLAN that uses a hub that can handle multiple transmission requests and can process traffic according to priority, making it useful for servicing time-sensitive traffic such as multimedia and video. Demand priority eliminates the overhead of packet collisions, collision recovery, and broadcast traffic typical in Ethernet networks. See also 100VG-AnyLAN.

demarc   Demarcation point between carrier equipment and CPE.

demodulation   Process of returning a modulated signal to its original form. Modems perform demodulation by taking an analog signal and returning it to its original (digital) form. See also modulation.

demultiplexing   The separating of multiple input streams that have been multiplexed into a common physical signal back into multiple output streams. See also multiplexing.

DES   Data Encryption Standard. Standard cryptographic algorithm developed by the U.S. NBS.

designated bridge   The bridge that incurs the lowest path cost when forwarding a frame from a segment to the route bridge.

designated router   OSPF router that generates LSAs for a multiaccess network and has other special responsibilities in running OSPF. Each multiaccess OSPF network that has at least two attached routers has a designated router that is elected by the OSPF Hello protocol. The designated router enables a reduction in the number of adjacencies required on a multiaccess network, which in turn reduces the amount of routing protocol traffic and the size of the topological database.

destination address   Address of a network device that is receiving data. See also source address.

deterministic load distribution   Technique for distributing traffic between two bridges across a circuit group. Guarantees packet ordering between source-destination pairs and always forwards traffic for a source-destination pair on the same segment in a circuit group for a given circuit-group configuration.

DHCP   Dynamic Host Configuration Protocol. Provides a mechanism for allocating IP addresses dynamically so that addresses can be reused when hosts no longer needs them.

DIA   Document Interchange Architecture. Defines the protocols and data formats needed for the transparent interchange of documents in an SNA network. One of three SNA transaction services. See also DDM and SNADS.

dial backup   Feature that provides protection against WAN downtime by allowing the network administrator to configure a backup serial line through a circuit-switched connection.

dial-up line   Communications circuit that is established by a switched-circuit connection using the telephone company network.

differential encoding   Digital encoding technique whereby a binary value is denoted by a signal change rather than a particular signal level.

differential Manchester encoding   Digital coding scheme where a mid-bit-time transition is used for clocking, and a transition at the beginning of each bit time denotes a zero. The coding scheme used by IEEE 802.5 and Token Ring networks.

DIN   Deutsche Industrie Norm. German national standards organization.

DIN connector   Deutsche Industrie Norm connector. Multipin connector used in some Macintosh and IBM PC-compatible computers, and on some network processor panels.

directed search   Search request sent to a specific node known to contain a resource. A directed search is used to determine the continued existence of the resource and to obtain routing information specific to the node. See also broadcast search.

directed tree   A logical construct used to define data streams or flows. The origin of a data stream is the root. Data streams are unidirectional branches directed away from the root and toward targets, and targets are the leaves of the directed tree.

directory services   Services that help network devices locate service providers.

DISA   Defense Information Systems Agency. U.S. military organization responsible for implementing and operating military information systems, including the DDN. See also DDN.

discovery architecture   APPN software that enables a machine configured as an APPN EN to automatically find primary and backup NNs when the machine is brought onto an APPN network.

Discovery mode   Method by which an AppleTalk interface acquires information about an attached network from an operational node and then uses this information to configure itself. Also called dynamic configuration.

distance vector routing algorithm   Class of routing algorithms that iterate on the number of hops in a route to find a shortest-path spanning tree. Distance vector routing algorithms call for each router to send its entire routing table in each update, but only to its neighbors. Distance vector routing algorithms can be prone to routing loops, but are computationally simpler than link state routing algorithms. Also called Bellman-Ford routing algorithm. See also link-state routing algorithm and SPF.

distortion delay   Problem with a communication signal resulting from nonuniform transmission speeds of the components of a signal through a transmission medium. Also called group delay.

DLCI   data-link connection identifier. Value that specifies a PVC or SVC in a Frame Relay network. In the basic Frame Relay specification, DLCIs are locally significant (connected devices might use different values to specify the same connection). In the LMI extended specification, DLCIs are globally significant (DLCIs specify individual end devices). See also LMI.

DLSw   data-link switching. Interoperability standard, described in RFC 1434, that provides a method for forwarding SNA and NetBIOS traffic over TCP/IP networks using Data Link layer switching and encapsulation. DLSw uses SSP (Switch-to-Switch Protocol) instead of SRB, eliminating the major limitations of SRB, including hop-count limits, broadcast and unnecessary traffic, timeouts, lack of flow control, and lack of prioritization schemes. See also DLSw+, SRB, and SSP.

DLSw+   Data Link Switching Plus. Cisco implementation of the DLSw standard for SNA and NetBIOS traffic forwarding. DLSw+ goes beyond the standard to include the advanced features of the current Cisco RSRB implementation, and provides additional functionality to increase the overall scalability of data-link switching. See also DLSw.

DLU   Dependent LU. An LU that depends on the SSCP to provide services for establishing sessions with other LUs. See also LU and SSCP.

DLUR   Dependent LU Requester. The client half of the Dependent LU Requestor/Server enhancement to APPN. The DLUR component resides in APPN ENs and NNs that support adjacent DLUs by securing services from the DLUS. See also APPN, DLU, and DLUS.

DLUR node   In APPN networks, an EN or NN that implements the DLUR component. See also DLUR.

DLUS   Dependent LU Server. The server half of the Dependent LU Requestor/Server enhancement to APPN. The DLUS component provides SSCP services to DLUR nodes over an APPN network. See also APPN, DLU, and DLUR.

DLUS node   In APPN networks, a NN that implements the DLUS component. See also DLUS.

DMA   direct memory access. The transfer of data from a peripheral device, such as a hard disk drive, into memory without that data passing through the microprocessor. DMA transfers data into memory at high speeds with no processor overhead.

DMAC   destination MAC. The MAC address specified in the Destination Address field of a packet. Compare with SMAC. See also MAC address.

DMP   Data Movement Processor. Processor on the Catalyst 5000 that, along with the multiport packet buffer memory interface, performs the frame-switching function for the switch. The DMP also handles translational bridging between the Ethernet and FDDI interfaces, IP segmentation, and intelligent bridging with protocol-based filtering.

DNA   Digital Network Architecture. Network architecture developed by Digital Equipment Corporation. The products that embody DNA (including communications protocols) are collectively referred to as DECnet. See also DECnet.

DNIC   Data Network Identification Code. Part of an X.121 address. DNICs are divided into two parts: the first specifying the country in which the addressed PSN is located and the second specifying the PSN itself. See also X.121.

DNS   Domain Name System. System used in the Internet for translating names of network nodes into addresses. See also authority zone.

DNSIX   Department of Defense Intelligence Information System Network Security for Information Exchange. Collection of security requirements for networking defined by the U.S. Defense Intelligence Agency.

DoD   Department of Defense. U.S. government organization that is responsible for national defense. The DoD has frequently funded communication protocol development.

domain   1. In the Internet, a portion of the naming hierarchy tree that refers to general groupings of networks based on organization-type or geography. 2. In SNA, an SSCP and the resources it controls. 3. In IS-IS, a logical set of networks.

Domain   Networking system developed by Apollo Computer (now part of Hewlett-Packard) for use in its engineering workstations.

dot address   Refers to the common notation for IP addresses in the form n.n.n.n where each number n represents, in decimal, 1 byte of the 4-byte IP address. Also called dotted notation or four-part dotted notation.

DQDB   Distributed Queue Dual Bus. Data Link layer communication protocol, specified in the IEEE 802.6 standard, designed for use in MANs. DQDB, which permits multiple systems to interconnect using two unidirectional logical buses, is an open standard that is designed for compatibility with carrier transmission standards, and is aligned with emerging standards for BISDN. SIP (SMDS Interface Protocol) is based on DQDB. See also MAN.

DRAM   dynamic random-access memory. RAM that stores information in capacitors that must be periodically refreshed. Delays can occur because DRAMs are inaccessible to the processor when refreshing their contents. However, DRAMs are less complex and have greater capacity than SRAMs. See also SRAM.

drop   Point on a multipoint channel where a connection to a networked device is made.

drop cable   Generally, a cable that connects a network device (such as a computer) to a physical medium. A type of AUI. See also AUI.

DS-0   digital signal level 0. Framing specification used in transmitting digital signals over a single channel at 64Kbps on a T1facility. Compare with DS-1 and DS-3.

DS-1   digital signal level 1. Framing specification used in transmitting digital signals at 1.544Mbps on a T1 facility (in the United States) or at 2.108Mbps on an E1 facility (in Europe). Compare with DS-0 and DS-3. See also E1 and T1.

DS-1/DTI   DS-1 domestic trunk interface. Interface circuit used for DS-1 applications with 24 trunks.

DS-3   digital signal level 3. Framing specification used for transmitting digital signals at 44.736Mbps on a T3 facility. Compare with DS-0 and DS-1. See also E3 and T3.

DSAP   destination service access point. The SAP of the network node designated in the Destination field of a packet. Compare to SSAP. See also SAP (service access point).

DSL   digital subscriber line. A public network technology that delivers high bandwidth over conventional copper wiring at limited distances. There are four types of DSLs: ADSL, HDSL, SDSL, and VDSL. All are provisioned via modem pairs, with one modem located at a central office and the other at the customer site. Because most DSL technologies don't use the whole bandwidth of the twisted pair, there is room left for a voice channel. See also ADSL, HDSL, SDSL, and VDSL.

DSP   domain specific part. The part of an NSAP-format ATM address that contains an area identifier, a station identifier, and a selector byte. See also NSAP.

DSPU   downstream physical unit. In SNA, a PU that is located downstream from the host. See also DSPU concentration in the Cisco Systems section.

DSPU concentration   Cisco IOS software feature that enables a router to function as a PU concentrator for SNA PU 2 nodes. PU concentration at the router simplifies the task of PU definition at the upstream host while providing additional flexibility and mobility for downstream PU devices.

DSR   data set ready. EIA/TIA-232 interface circuit that is activated when DCE is powered up and ready for use.

DSU   data service unit. Device used in digital transmission that adapts the physical interface on a DTE device to a transmission facility such as T1 or E1. The DSU is also responsible for such functions as signal timing. Often referred to together with CSU, as CSU/DSU. See also CSU.

DSX-1   Cross-connection point for DS-1 signals.

DTE   data terminal equipment. Device at the user end of a user-network interface that serves as a data source, destination, or both. DTE connects to a data network through a DCE device (for example, a modem) and typically uses clocking signals generated by the DCE. DTE includes such devices as computers, protocol translators, and multiplexers. Compare with DCE.

DTL   designated transit list. A list of nodes and optional link IDs that completely specify a path across a single PNNI peer group.

DTMF   dual tone multifrequency. Use of two simultaneous voice-band tones for dialing (such as touch tone).

DTR   data terminal ready. EIA/TIA-232 circuit that is activated to let the DCE know when the DTE is ready to send and receive data.

DUAL   Diffusing Update Algorithm. Convergence algorithm used in Enhanced IGRP that provides loop-free operation at every instant throughout a route computation. Allows routers involved in a topology change to synchronize at the same time, while not involving routers that are unaffected by the change. See also Enhanced IGRP.

dual counter-rotating rings   Network topology in which two signal paths, whose directions are opposite one another, exist in a token-passing network. FDDI and CDDI are based on this concept.

dual-homed station   Device attached to multiple FDDI rings to provide redundancy.

dual homing   Network topology in which a device is connected to the network by way of two independent access points (points of attachment). One access point is the primary connection, and the other is a standby connection that is activated in the event of a failure of the primary connection.

DVMRP   Distance Vector Multicast Routing Protocol. Internetwork gateway protocol, largely based on RIP, that implements a typical dense mode IP multicast scheme. DVMRP uses IGMP to exchange routing datagrams with its neighbors. See also IGMP.

DXI   Data Exchange Interface. ATM Forum specification, described in RFC 1483, that defines how a network device such as a bridge, router, or hub can effectively act as an FEP to an ATM network by interfacing with a special DSU that performs packet segmentation and reassembly.

dynamic address resolution   Use of an address resolution protocol to determine and store address information on demand.

Dynamic IISP   Dynamic Interim-Interswitch Signaling Protocol. A basic call routing protocol that automatically reroutes ATM connections in the event of link failures. Dynamic IISP is an interim solution until PNNI Phase 1 is completed. Contrast with IISP.

dynamic routing   Routing that adjusts automatically to network topology or traffic changes. Also called adaptive routing.

E1   Wide-area digital transmission scheme used predominantly in Europe that carries data at a rate of 2.048Mbps. E1 lines can be leased for private use from common carriers. Compare with T1. See also DS-1.

E.164   1. ITU-T recommendation for international telecommunication numbering, especially in ISDN, BISDN, and SMDS. An evolution of standard telephone numbers. 2. The name of the field in an ATM address that contains numbers in E.164 format.

E2A   Legacy protocols for providing OAM&P functions between a network element and an operations support system. See also OAM&P.

E3   Wide-area digital transmission scheme used predominantly in Europe that carries data at a rate of 34.368Mbps. E3 lines can be leased for private use from common carriers. Compare with T3. See also DS-3.

early token release   Technique used in Token Ring networks that allows a station to release a new token onto the ring immediately after transmitting, instead of waiting for the first frame to return. This feature can increase the total bandwidth on the ring. See also Token Ring.

EARN   European Academic Research Network. European network connecting universities and research institutes. EARN merged with RARE to form TERENA. See also RARE and TERENA.

EBCDIC   extended binary coded decimal interchange code. Any of a number of coded character sets developed by IBM consisting of 8-bit coded characters. This character code is used by older IBM systems and telex machines. Compare with ASCII.

E channel   echo channel. 64Kbps ISDN circuit-switching control channel. The E channel was defined in the 1984 ITU-T ISDN specification, but was dropped in the 1988 specification. Compare with B channel, D channel, and H channel.

echoplex   Mode in which keyboard characters are echoed on a terminal screen upon return of a signal from the other end of the line indicating that the characters were received correctly.

ECMA   European Computer Manufacturers Association. Group of European computer vendors who have done substantial OSI standardization work.

edge device   1. A physical device that is capable of forwarding packets between legacy interfaces (such as Ethernet and Token Ring) and ATM interfaces based on Data Link and Network layer information. An edge device does not participate in the running of any Network layer routing protocol, but it obtains forwarding descriptions using the route distribution protocol. 2. Any device that isn't an ATM switch that can connect to an ATM switch.

EDI   electronic data interchange. The electronic communication of operational data such as orders and invoices betweenorganizations.

EDIFACT   Electronic Data Interchange for Administration, Commerce, and Transport. Data exchange standard administered by the United Nations to be a multi-industry EDI standard.

EEPROM   electrically erasable programmable read-only memory. EPROM that can be erased using electrical signals applied to specific pins. See also EPROM.

EFCI   Explicit Forward Congestion Indication. In ATM, one of the congestion feedback modes allowed by ABR service. A network element in an impending congestion state or in a congested state may set the EFCI. The destination end-system can implement a protocol that adaptively lowers the cell rate of the connection based on the value of the EFCI. See also ABR.

EGP Exterior Gateway Protocol. Internet protocol for exchanging routing information between autonomous systems. Documented in RFC 904. Not to be confused with the general term exterior gateway protocol. EGP is an obsolete protocol that has been replaced by BGP. See also BGP.

EIA Electronic Industries Association. Group that specifies electrical transmission standards. The EIA and TIA have developed numerous well-known communications standards, including EIA/TIA-232 and EIA/TIA-449. See also TIA.

EIA-530 Refers to two electrical implementations of EIA/TIA-449: RS-422 (for balanced transmission) and RS-423 (for unbalanced transmission). See also RS-422, RS-423, and EIA/TIA-449.

EIA/TIA-232 Common Physical layer interface standard, developed by EIA and TIA, that supports unbalanced circuits at signal speeds of up to 64Kbps. Closely resembles the V.24 specification. Formerly known as RS-232.

EIA/TIA-449 Popular Physical layer interface developed by EIA and TIA. Essentially, a faster (up to 2Mbps) version of EIA/TIA-232 capable of longer cable runs. Formerly called RS-449. See also EIA-530.

EIA/TIA-586 Standard that describes the characteristics and applications for various grades of UTP cabling. See also Category 1cabling, Category 2 cabling, Category 3 cabling, Category 4 cabling, Category 5 cabling, and UTC.

EIP Ethernet Interface Processor. Interface processor card on the Cisco 7000 series routers. The EIP provides high-speed (10Mbps) AUI ports that support Ethernet Version 1 and Ethernet Version 2 or IEEE 802.3 interfaces, and a high-speed data path to other interface processors.

EISA Extended Industry-Standard Architecture. 32-bit bus interface used in PCs, PC-based servers, and some UNIX workstations and servers. See also ISA.

ELAN emulated LAN. ATM network in which an Ethernet or Token Ring LAN is emulated using a client-server model. ELANs are composed of an LEC, an LES, a BUS, and an LECS. Multiple ELANs can exist simultaneously on a single ATM network. ELANs are defined by the LANE specification. See also BUS, LANE, LEC, LECS, and LES.

ELAP EtherTalk Link Access Protocol. The link-access protocol used in an EtherTalk network. ELAP is built on top of the standard Ethernet Data Link layer.

electronic mail Widely used network application in which text messages are transmitted electronically between end users over various types of networks using various network protocols. Often called e-mail.

EMA 1. Enterprise Management Architecture. Digital Equipment Corporation network management architecture, based on the OSI network management model. 2. Electronic Messaging Association. Forum devoted to standards and policy work, education, and development of electronic messaging systems such as electronic mail, voice mail, and facsimile.

EMI electromagnetic interference. Interference by electromagnetic signals that can cause reduced data integrity and increased error rates on transmission channels.

EMIF ESCON Multiple Image Facility. Mainframe I/O software function that allows one ESCON channel to be shared among multiple logical partitions on the same mainframe. See also ESCON.

EMP   electromagnetic pulse. Caused by lightning and other high-energy phenomena. Capable of coupling enough energy into unshielded conductors to destroy electronic devices. See also Tempest.

Emulation mode   Function of an NCP that enables it to perform activities equivalent to those performed by a transmission control unit.

EN   end node. APPN end system that implements the PU 2.1, provides end-user services, and supports sessions between local and remote CPs. ENs are not capable of routing traffic and rely on an adjacent NN for APPN services. Compare with NN. See also CP.

encapsulation   The wrapping of data in a particular protocol header. For example, Ethernet data is wrapped in a specific Ethernet header before network transit. Also, when bridging dissimilar networks, the entire frame from one network is simply placed in the header used by the Data Link layer protocol of the other network. See also tunneling.

encapsulation bridging   Carries Ethernet frames from one router to another across disparate media, such as serial and FDDI lines. Contrast with translational bridging.

encoder   Device that modifies information into the required transmission format.

encryption   The application of a specific algorithm to data so as to alter the appearance of the data making it incomprehensible to those who are not authorized to see the information. See also decryption.

end point   Device at which a virtual circuit or virtual path begins or ends.

Enhanced Monitoring Services   Set of analysis tools on the Catalyst 5000 switch, consisting of an integrated RMON agent and the SPAN. These tools provide traffic monitoring, and network segment analysis and management. See also RMON and span.

Enhanced IGRP   Enhanced Interior Gateway Routing Protocol. Advanced version of IGRP developed by Cisco. Provides superior convergence properties and operating efficiency, and combines the advantages of link state protocols with those of distance vector protocols. Compare with IGRP. See also IGP, OSPF, and RIP.

enterprise network   Large and diverse network connecting most major points in a company or other organization. Differs from a WAN in that it is privately owned and maintained.

entity   Generally, an individual, manageable network device. Sometimes called an alias.

entity identifier   The unique address of an NVE's socket in a node on an AppleTalk network. The specific format of an entity identifier is network-
dependent. See also NVE.

entity name   A name that an NVE may assign to itself. Although not all NVEs have names, NVEs can possess several names (or aliases). An entity name is made up of three character strings: object, entity type, and zone. For example: Bldg 2 LaserJet 5:LaserWriter@Bldg 2 Zone. See also NVE.

entity type   The part of an entity name that describes the entity's class; for example, LaserWriter or AFPServer. See also entity name.

EOM   end of message. An indicator in the AAL that identifies the last ATM cell containing information from a data packet that has been segmented.

EOT   end of transmission. Generally, a character that signifies the end of a logical group of characters or bits.

EPD   early packet discard. A mechanism used by some ATM switches to allow a complete AAL5 frame to be discarded when a threshold condition is met, such as one indicating that congestion is imminent. Useful for avoiding unwanted congestion that jeopardize the switch's ability to properly support existing connections with a guaranteed service. Compare with TPD.

EPROM   erasable programmable read-only memory. Nonvolatile memory chips that are programmed after they are manufactured, and, if necessary, can be erased by some means and reprogrammed. Compare with EEPROM and PROM.

equalization   Technique used to compensate for communications channel distortions.

ER   explicit rate. In ATM, an RMcell used to limit the ACR for a transmission to a specific value. It is initially set by the source to a requested rate, such as the PCR. Later, it may be reduced by any network element in the path to a value that the element can sustain. See also ACR, PCR, and RM.

error control   Technique for detecting and correcting errors in data transmissions.

error-correcting code   Code having sufficient intelligence and incorporating sufficient signaling information to enable the detection and correction of many errors at the receiver.

error-detecting code   Code that can detect transmission errors through analysis of received data based on the adherence of the data to appropriate structural guidelines.

ES   1. end system. Generally, an end-user device on a network. 2. end system. Nonrouting host or node in an OSI network.

ESI   end system identifier. An identifier that distinguishes multiple nodes at the same level when the lower level peer group is partitioned. (Usually an IEEE 802 address.)

ESCON   Enterprise System Connection. IBM channel architecture that specifies a pair of fiber-optic cables, with either LEDs or lasers as transmitters and a signaling rate of 200 Mbps.

ESCON channel   IBM channel for attaching mainframes to peripherals such as storage devices, backup units, and network interfaces. This channel incorporates fiber channel technology. The ESCON channel replaces the bus and tag channel. Compare with parallel channel. See also bus and tag channel.

ESD   electrostatic discharge. Discharge of stored static electricity that can damage electronic equipment and impair electrical circuitry, resulting in complete or intermittent failures.

ESF   Extended Superframe. Framing type used on T1 circuits that consists of 24 frames of 192 bits each, with the 193rd bit providing timing and other functions. ESF is an enhanced version of SF. See also SF.

ES-IS   End System–to–Intermediate System. OSI protocol that defines how end systems (hosts) announce themselves to intermediate systems (routers). See also IS-IS.

ESnet   Energy Sciences Network. Data communications network managed and funded by the U.S. Department of Energy Office of Energy Research (DOE/OER). Interconnects the DOE to educational institutions and other research facilities.

ESS   Electronic Switching System. AT&T's term for an electronic central office switch. A 5ESS is AT&T's digital central office for end office applications and a 4ESS is its digital central office for toll center application.

Ethernet   Baseband LAN specification invented by Xerox Corporation and developed jointly by Xerox, Intel, and Digital Equipment Corporation. Ethernet networks use CSMA/CD and run over a variety of cable types at 10 Mbps. Ethernet is similar to the IEEE 802.3 series of standards. See also 10Base2, 10Base5, 10BaseF, 10BaseT, 10Broad36, FastEthernet, and IEEE 802.3.

EtherTalk   Apple Computer's data-link product that allows an AppleTalk network to be connected by Ethernet.

ETSI   European Telecommunication Standards Institute. Organization created by the European PTTs and the European Community (EC) to propose telecommunications standards for Europe.

EUnet   European Internet. European commercial Internet service provider. EUnet is designed to provide electronic mail, news, and other Internet services to European markets.

event   Network message indicating operational irregularities in physical elements of a network or a response to the occurrence of a significant task, typically the completion of a request for information. See also alarm and trap.

excess rate   In ATM, traffic in excess of the insured rate for a given connection. Specifically, the excess rate equals the maximum rate minus the insured rate. Excess traffic is delivered only if network resources are available and can be discarded during periods of congestion. Compare with insured rate and maximum rate.

EXEC   The interactive command processor of the Cisco IOS software.

expansion   The process of running a compressed data set through an algorithm that restores the data set to its original size. Compare with companding and compression.

expedited delivery   Option set by a specific Protocol layer telling other Protocol layers (or the same Protocol layer in another network device) to handle specific data more rapidly.

explicit route   In SNA, a route from a source subarea to a destination subarea, as specified by a list of subarea nodes and transmission groups that connect the two.

explorer frame   Frame sent out by a networked device in a SRB environment to determine the optimal route to another networked device.

explorer packet   Generated by an end station trying to find its way through a SRB network. Gathers a hop-by-hop description of a path through the network by being marked (updated) by each bridge that it traverses, thereby creating a complete topological map. See also all-routes explorer packet, local explorer packet, and spanning explorer packet.

exterior gateway protocol Any internetwork protocol used to exchange routing information between autonoous systems. Not to be confused with Exterior Gateway Protocol (EGP), which is a particular instance of an exterior gateway protocol.

exterior router Router connected to an AURP tunnel, responsible for the encapsulation and deencapsulation of AppleTalk packets in a foreign protocol header (for example, IP). See also AURP and AURP tunnel.

failure domain Area in which a failure has occurred in a Token Ring, defined by the information contained in a beacon. When a station detects a serious problem with the network (such as a cable break), it sends a beacon frame that includes the station reporting the failure, its NAUN, and everything in between. Beaconing in turn initiates a process called autoreconfiguration. See also autoreconfiguration, beacon, and NAUN.

fallback A mechanism used by ATM networks when rigorous path selection does not generate an acceptable path. The fallback mechanism attempts to determine a path by selectively relaxing certain attributes, such as delay, in order to find a path that meets some minimal set of desired attributes.

fan-out unit Device that allows multiple devices on a network to communicate using a single network attachment.

fantail Panel of I/O connectors that attaches to an equipment rack, providing easy access for data connections to a networking.

Fast Ethernet Any of a number of 100Mbps Ethernet specifications. Fast Ethernet offers a speed increase ten times that of the 10BaseT Ethernet specification, while preserving such qualities as frame format, MAC mechanisms, and MTU. Such similarities allow the use of existing 10BaseT applications and network management tools on Fast Ethernet networks. Based on an extension to the IEEE 802.3 specification. Compare with Ethernet. See also 100BaseFX, 100BaseT, 100BaseT4, 100BaseTX, 100BaseX, and IEEE 802.3.

fast switching Cisco feature whereby a route cache is used to expedite packet switching through a router. Contrast with process switching.

fault management One of five categories of network management defined by ISO for management of OSI networks. Fault management attempts to ensure that network faults are detected and controlled. See also accounting management, configuration management, performance management, and security management.

FCC Federal Communications Commission. U.S. government agency that supervises, licenses, and controls electronic and electromagnetic transmission standards.

FCS frame check sequence. Refers to the extra characters added to a frame for error control purposes. Used in HDLC, Frame Relay, and other Data Link layer protocols.

FDDI Fiber Distributed Data Interface. LAN standard, defined by ANSI X3T9.5, specifying a 100Mbps token-passing network using fiber-optic cable, with transmission distances of up to 2 km. FDDI uses a dual-ring architecture to provide redundancy. Compare with CDDI and FDDI II.

FDDI II ANSI standard that enhances FDDI. FDDI II provides isochronous transmission for connectionless data circuits and connection-oriented voice and video circuits. Compare with FDDI.

FDDITalk   Apple Computer's data-link product that allows an AppleTalk network to be connected by FDDI cable.

FDM   frequency-division multiplexing. Technique whereby information from multiple channels can be allocated bandwidth on a single wire based on frequency. Compare with ATDM, statistical multiplexing, and TDM.

FECN   forward explicit congestion notification. Bit set by a Frame Relay network to inform DTE receiving the frame that congestion was experienced in the path from source to destination. DTE receiving frames with the FECN bit set can request that higher-level protocols take flow-control action as appropriate. Compare with BECN.

FEP   front-end processor. Device or board that provides network interface capabilities for a networked device. In SNA, typically an IBM 3745 device.

FEIP   Fast Ethernet Interface Processor. Interface processor on the Cisco 7000 series routers. The FEIP supports up to two 100Mbps 100BaseT ports.

fiber-optic cable   Physical medium capable of conducting modulated light transmission. Compared with other transmission media, fiber-optic cable is more expensive, but is not susceptible to electromagnetic interference, and is capable of higher data rates. Sometimes called optical fiber.

FID0   format indicator 0. One of several formats that an SNA TH can use. An FID0 TH is used for communication between an SNA node and a non-SNA node. See also TH.

FID1   format indicator 1. One of several formats that an SNA TH can use. An FID1 TH encapsulates messages between two subarea nodes that do not support virtual and explicit routes. See also TH.

FID2   format indicator 2. One of several formats that an SNA TH can use. An FID2 TH is used for transferring messages between a subarea node and a PU 2, using local addresses. See also TH.

FID3   format indicator 3. One of several formats that an SNA TH can use. An FID3 TH is used for transferring messages between a subarea node and a PU 1, using local addresses. See also TH.

FID4   format indicator 4. One of several formats that an SNA TH can use. An FID4 TH encapsulates messages between two subarea nodes that are capable of supporting virtual and explicit routes. See also TH.

field-replaceable unit   Hardware component that can be removed and replaced on-site. Typical field-replaceable units include cards, power supplies, and chassis components.

file transfer   Category of popular network applications that allow files to be moved from one network device to another.

filter   Generally, a process or device that screens network traffic for certain characteristics, such as source address, destination address, or protocol, and determines whether to forward or discard that traffic based on the established criteria.

finger   An software tool for determining whether a person has an account at a particular Internet site. Many sites do not allow incoming finger requests, but some do.

firewall   Router or access server, or several routers or access servers, designated as a buffer between any connected public networks and a private network. A firewall router uses access lists and other methods to ensure the security of the private network.

firmware   Software instructions set permanently or semipermanently in ROM.

FIP   FDDI Interface Processor. Interface processor on the Cisco 7000 series routers. The FIP supports SASs, DASs, dual homing, and optical bypass, and contains a 16-mips processor for high-speed (100Mbps) interface rates. The FIP complies with ANSI and ISO FDDI standards.

flapping   Routing problem where an advertised route between two nodes alternates (flaps) back and forth between two paths due to a network problem that causes intermittent interface failures.

Flash memory   Nonvolatile storage that can be electrically erased and reprogrammed developed by Intel and licensed to other semiconductor companies. Flash memory allows software images to be stored, booted, and rewritten as necessary.

flash update   Routing update sent asynchronously in response to a change in the network topology. Compare with routing update.

flat addressing   A scheme of addressing that does not use a logical hierarchy to determine location. For example, MAC addresses are flat; bridging protocols must flood packets throughout the network in order to deliver the packet to the appropriate location. Compare with hierarchical addressing.

flooding   Traffic passing technique used by switches and bridges in which traffic received on an interface is sent out all of the interfaces of that device except the interface on which the information was originally received.

flow   Stream of data traveling between two endpoints across a network (for example, from one LAN station to another). Multiple flows can be transmitted on a single circuit.

flow control   Technique for ensuring that a transmitting entity, such as a modem, does not overwhelm a receiving entity with data. When the buffers on the receiving device are full, a message is sent to the sending device to suspend the transmission until the data in the buffers has been processed. In IBM networks, this technique is called pacing.

flowspec   The traffic parameters of a flow.

FLT   Full Line Terminal. A multiplexer that terminates a SONET span. See also SONET.

FM   frequency modulation. Modulation technique in which signals of different frequencies represent different data values. Compare with AM and PAM. See also modulation.

FNC   Federal Networking Council. Group responsible for assessing and coordinating U.S. federal agency networking policies and needs.

FOIRL   fiber-optic interrepeater link. Fiber-optic signaling methodology based on the IEEE 802.3 fiber-optic specification. FOIRL is a precursor of the 10BaseFL specification, which is designed to replace it. See also 10BaseFL.

forward channel   Communications path carrying information from the call initiator to the called party.

forward delay interval   Amount of time an interface spends listening for topology change information after that interface has been activated for bridging and before forwarding actually begins.

forwarding   Process of sending a frame toward its ultimate destination by way of an internetworking device.

FOTS   Fiber Optics Transmission Systems. Vendor-proprietary fiber optic transmission equipment.

Fourier transform   Technique used to evaluate the importance of various frequency cycles in a time series pattern.

FRAD   Frame Relay access device. Any network device that provides a connection between a LAN and a Frame Relay WAN. See also Cisco FRAD and FRAS in the Cisco Systems section.

fragment   Piece of a larger packet that has been broken down to smaller units.

fragmentation   Process of breaking a packet into smaller units when transmitting over a network medium that cannot support the original size of the packet. See also reassembly.

frame   Logical grouping of information sent as a Data Link layer unit over a transmission medium. Often refers to the header and trailer, used for synchronization and error control, that surround the user data contained in the unit. The terms cell, datagram, message, packet, and segment are also used to describe logical information groupings at various layers of the OSI reference model and in various technology circles.

frame forwarding   The mechanism by which frame-based traffic, such as HDLC and SDLC, traverses an ATM network.

Frame Relay   Industry-standard, switched Data Link layer protocol that handles multiple virtual circuits using HDLC encapsulation between connected devices. Frame Relay is more efficient than X.25, the protocol for which it is generally considered a replacement. See also X.25.

Frame Relay bridging   Bridging technique, described in RFC 1490, that uses the same spanning-tree algorithm as other bridging functions, but allows packets to be encapsulated for transmission across a Frame Relay network.

FRAS   Frame Relay Access Support. Cisco IOS software feature that allows SDLC, Token Ring, Ethernet, and Frame Relay-attached IBM devices to connect to other IBM devices across a Frame Relay network. See also FRAD.

free-trade zone   Part of an AppleTalk internetwork that is accessible by two other parts of the internetwork that are unable to directly access one another.

frequency   Number of cycles, measured in hertz, of an alternating current signal per unit time.

front end   Node or software program that requests services of a back end. See also back end, client, and server.

FSIP   Fast Serial Interface Processor. The default serial interface processor for Cisco 7000 series routers. The FSIP provides four or eight high-speed serial ports

FST   Fast Sequenced Transport. Connectionless, sequenced transport protocol that runs on top of the IP protocol. SRB traffic is encapsulated inside of IP datagrams and is passed over an FST connection between two network devices (such as routers). Speeds up data delivery, reduces overhead, and improves the response time of SRB traffic.

FTAM File Transfer, Access, and Management. In OSI, an Application layer protocol developed for network file exchange and management between diverse types of computers.

FTP File Transfer Protocol. Application protocol, part of the TCP/IP protocol stack, used for transferring files between network nodes. FTP is defined in RFC 959.

full duplex Capability for simultaneous data transmission between a sending station and a receiving station. Compare with half duplex and simplex.

full mesh Term describing a network in which devices are organized in a mesh topology, with each network node having either a physical circuit or a virtual circuit connecting it to every other network node. A full mesh provides a great deal of redundancy, but because it can be prohibitively expensive to implement, it is usually reserved for network backbones. See also mesh and partial mesh.

Fuzzball Digital Equipment Corporation LSI-11 computer system running IP gateway software. The NSFnet used these systems as backbone packet switches.

G.703/G.704 ITU-T electrical and mechanical specifications for connections between telephone company equipment and DTE using BNC connectors and operating at E1 data rates.

G.804 ITU-T framing standard that defines the mapping of ATM cells into the physical medium.

gateway In the IP community, an older term referring to a routing device. Today, the term router is used to describe nodes that perform this function, and gateway refers to a special-purpose device that performs an Application layer conversion of information from one protocol stack to another. Compare with router.

gateway host In SNA, a host node that contains a gateway SSCP.

gateway NCP NCP that connects two or more SNA networks and performs address translation to allow cross-network session traffic.

GB gigabyte. Approximately 1,000,000,000 bytes.

GBps gigabytes per second.

Gb gigabit. 1,000,000,000 bits.

Gbps gigabits per second.

GCAC generic call admission control. In ATM, a PNNI algorithm designed for CBR and VBR connections. Any node can use GCAC to calculate the expected CAC behavior of another node given than node's advertised link metrics and the QOS of a connection setup request. See also CAC.

GCRA generic cell rate algorithm. An algorithm that defines conformance with respect to the traffic contract of the connection. For each cell arrival, the GCRA determines whether the cell conforms to the traffic contract.

GDP Gateway Discovery Protocol. Cisco protocol that allows hosts to dynamically detect the arrival of new routers as well as determine when a router goes down. Based on UDP. See also UDP in the main glossary.

GGP   Gateway-to-Gateway Protocol. MILNET protocol specifying how core routers (gateways) should exchange reachability and routing information. GGP uses a distributed shortest-path algorithm.

GHz   gigahertz.

gigabit   Abbreviated Gb.

gigabits per second   Abbreviated Gbps.

gigabyte   Abbreviated GB.

gigabytes per second   Abbreviated GBps.

gigahertz   Abbreviated GHz.

gleaning   The process by which a router automatically derives AARP table entries from incoming packets. Gleaning speeds up the process of populating the AARP table. See also AARP.

GNS   Get Nearest Server. Request packet sent by a client on an IPX network to locate the nearest active server of a particular type. An IPX network client issues a GNS request to solicit either a direct response from a connected server or a response from a router that tells it where on the internetwork the service can be located. GNS is part of the IPX SAP. See also IPX and SAP (Service Advertisement Protocol).

GOSIP   Government OSI Profile. U.S. government procurement specification for OSI protocols. Through GOSIP, the government has mandated that all federal agencies standardize on OSI and implement OSI-based systems as they become commercially available.

grade of service   Measure of telephone service quality based on the probability that a call will encounter a busy signal during the busiest hours of the day.

graphical user interface   See GUI.

GRE   generic routing encapsulation. Tunneling protocol developed by Cisco that can encapsulate a wide variety of protocol packet types inside IP tunnels, creating a virtual point-to-point link to Cisco routers at remote points over an IP internetwork. By connecting multiprotocol subnetworks in a single-protocol backbone environment, IP tunneling using GRE allows network expansion across a single-protocol backbone environment

ground station   Collection of communications equipment designed to receive signals from (and usually transmit signals to) satellites. Also called a downlink station.

guard band   Unused frequency band between two communications channels that provides separation of the channels to prevent mutual interference.

GUI   graphical user interface. User environment that uses pictorial as well as textual representations of the input and output of applications and the hierarchical or other data structure in which information is stored. Conventions such as buttons, icons, and windows are typical, and many actions are performed using a pointing device (such as a mouse). Microsoft Windows and the Apple Macintosh are prominent examples of platforms utilizing a GUI.

half duplex   Capability for data transmission in only one direction at a time between a sending station and a receiving station. BSC is an example of a half-duplex protocol. See also BSC. Compare with full duplex and simplex.

handshake   Sequence of messages exchanged between two or more network devices to ensure transmission synchronization.

HBD3   Line code type used on E1 circuits.

H channel   high-speed channel. Full-duplex ISDN primary rate channel operating at 384Kbps. Compare with B channel, D channel, and E channel.

HDLC   High-Level Data Link Control. Bit-oriented synchronous Data Link layer protocol developed by ISO. Derived from SDLC, HDLC specifies a data encapsulation method on synchronous serial links using frame characters and checksums. See also SDLC.

HDSL   High-data-rate digital subscriber line. One of four DSL technologies. HDSL delivers 1.544Mbps of bandwidth each way over two copper twisted pairs. Because HDSL provides T1 speed, telephone companies have been using HDSL to provision local access to T1 services whenever possible. The operating range of HDSL is limited to 12,000 feet, so signal repeaters are installed to extend the service. HDSL requires two twisted pairs, so it is deployed primarily for PBX network connections, digital loop carrier systems, interexchange POPs, Internet servers, and private data networks. Compare with ADSL, SDSL, and VDSL.

headend   The end point of a broadband network. All stations transmit toward the headend; the headend then transmits toward the destination stations.

header   Control information placed before data when encapsulating that data for network transmission. Compare with trailer. See also PCI.

HEC   header error control. An algorithm for checking and correcting an error in an ATM cell. Using the fifth octet in the ATM cell header, ATM equipment may check for an error and correct the contents of the header. The check character is calculated using a CRC algorithm allowing a single bit error in the header to be corrected or multiple errors to be detected.

HELLO   Interior routing protocol used principally by NSFnet nodes. HELLO allows particular packet switches to discover minimal delay routes. Not to be confused with the Hello protocol.

hello packet   Multicast packet that is used by routers for neighbor discovery and recovery. Hello packets also indicate that a client is still operating and network-ready.

Hello protocol   Protocol used by OSPF systems for establishing and maintaining neighbor relationships. Not to be confused with HELLO.

helper address   Address configured on an interface to which broadcasts received on that interface will be sent.

HEPnet   High-Energy Physics Network. Research network that originated in the United States, but that has spread to most places involved in high-energy physics. Well-known sites include Argonne National Laboratory, Brookhaven National Laboratory, Lawrence Berkeley Laboratory, and the Stanford Linear Accelerator Center (SLAC).

hertz   Measure of frequency, abbreviated Hz. Synonymous with cycles per second.

heterogeneous network   Network consisting of dissimilar devices that run dissimilar protocols and in many cases support dissimilar functions or applications.

hierarchical addressing   A scheme of addressing that uses a logical hierarchy to determine location. For example, IP addresses consist of network numbers, subnet numbers, and host numbers, which IP routing algorithms use to route the packet to the appropriate location. Compare with flat addressing.

HIP   HSSI Interface Processor. Interface processor on the Cisco 7000 series routers. The HIP provides one HSSI port that supports connections to ATM, SMDS, Frame Relay, or private lines at speeds up to T3 or E3.

HIPPI   High-Performance Parallel Interface. High-performance interface standard defined by ANSI. HIPPI is typically used to connect supercomputers to peripherals and other devices.

holddown   State into which a route is placed so that routers will neither advertise the route nor accept advertisements about the route for a specific length of time (the holddown period). Holddown is used to flush bad information about a route from all routers in the network. A route is typically placed in holddown when a link in that route fails.

homologation   Conformity of a product or specification to international standards, such as ITU-T, CSA, TUV, UL, or VCCI. Enables portability across company and international boundaries.

hop   Term describing the passage of a data packet between two network nodes (for example, between two routers). See also hop count.

hop count   Routing metric used to measure the distance between a source and a destination. RIP uses hop count as its sole metric. See also hop and RIP.

host   Computer system on a network. Similar to the term node except that host usually implies a computer system, whereas node generally applies to any networked system, including access servers and routers. See also node.

host node   SNA subarea node that contains an SSCP. See also SSCP.

host number   Part of an IP address that designates which node on the subnetwork is being addressed. Also called a host address.

HPCC   High Performance Computing and Communications. U.S. government funded program advocating advances in computing, communications, and related fields. The HPCC is designed to ensure U.S. leadership in these fields through education, research and development, industry collaboration, and implementation of high-performance technology. The five components of the HPCC are ASTA, BRHR, HPCS, IITA, and NREN.

HPCS   High Performance Computing Systems. Component of the HPCC program designed to ensure U.S. technological leadership in high-performance computing through research and development of computing systems and related software. See also HPCC.

HPR   High Performance Routing. Second-generation routing algorithm for APPN. HPR provides a connectionless layer with nondisruptive routing of sessions around link failures, and a connection-oriented layer with end-to-end flow control, error control, and sequencing. Compare to ISR. See also APPN.

HSCI   High-Speed Communications Interface. Single-port interface, developed by Cisco, providing full-duplex synchronous serial communications capability at speeds up to 52Mbps.

HSRP   Hot Standby Router Protocol. Provides high network availability and transparent network topology changes. HSRP creates a Hot Standby router group with a lead router that services all packets sent to the Hot Standby address. The lead router is monitored by other routers in the group, and if it fails, one of these standby routers inherits the lead position and the Hot Standby group address

HSSI   High-Speed Serial Interface. Network standard for high-speed (up to 52Mbps) serial connections over WAN links.

HTTP   Hypertext Transfer Protocol. The protocol used by Web browsers and Web servers to transfer files, such as text and graphic files.

HTML   Hypertext Markup Language. Simple hypertext document formatting language that uses tags to indicate how a given part of a document should be interpreted by a viewing application, such as a Web browser. See also hypertext and web browser.

hub   1. Generally, a term used to describe a device that serves as the center of a star-topology network. 2. Hardware or software device that contains multiple independent but connected modules of network and internetwork equipment. Hubs can be active (where they repeat signals sent through them) or passive (where they do not repeat, but merely split, signals sent through them). 3. In Ethernet and IEEE 802.3, an Ethernet multiport repeater, sometimes referred to as a concentrator.

hybrid network   Internetwork made up of more than one type of network technology, including LANs and WANs.

hypertext   Electronically-stored text that allows direct access to other texts by way of encoded links. Hypertext documents can be created using HTML, and often integrate images, sound, and other media that are commonly viewed using a browser. See also HTML and browser.

IAB   Internet Architecture Board. Board of internetwork researchers who discuss issues pertinent to Internet architecture. Responsible for appointing a variety of Internet-related groups such as the IANA, IESG, and IRSG. The IAB is appointed by the trustees of the ISOC. See also IANA, IESG, IRSG, and ISOC.

IANA   Internet Assigned Numbers Authority. Organization operated under the auspices of the ISOC as a part of the IAB. IANA delegates authority for IP address-space allocation and domain-name assignment to the InterNIC and other organizations. IANA also maintains a database of assigned protocol identifiers used in the TCP/IP stack, including autonomous system numbers. See also IAB, ISOC, and InterNIC.

ICD   International Code Designator. One of two ATM address formats developed by the ATM Forum for use by private networks. Adapted from the subnetwork model of addressing in which the ATM layer is responsible for mapping Network layer addresses to ATM addresses. Compare with DCC.

ICMP   Internet Control Message Protocol. Network layer Internet protocol that reports errors and provides other information relevant to IP packet processing. Documented in RFC 792.

IDI   initial domain identifier. The portion of an NSAP or NSAP-format ATM address that specifies the address allocation and administration authority. See also NSAP.

IDN   International Data Number. See X.121.

IDP   initial domain part. The part of a CLNS address that contains an authority and format identifier and a domain identifier.

IDPR   Interdomain Policy Routing. Interdomain routing protocol that dynamically exchanges policies between autonomous systems. IDPR encapsulates interautonomous system traffic and routes it according to the policies of each autonomous system along the path. IDPR is currently an IETF proposal. See also policy-based routing.

IDRP   IS-IS Interdomain Routing Protocol. OSI protocol that specifies how routers communicate with routers in different domains.

IEC   International Electrotechnical Commission. Industry group that writes and distributes standards for electrical products and components.

IEEE   Institute of Electrical and Electronics Engineers. Professional organization whose activities include the development of communications and network standards. IEEE LAN standards are the predominant LAN standards today.

IEEE 802.1   IEEE specification that describes an algorithm that prevents bridging loops by creating a spanning tree. The algorithm was invented by Digital Equipment Corporation. The Digital algorithm and the IEEE 802.1 algorithm are not exactly the same, nor are they compatible. See also spanning tree, spanning-tree algorithm, and Spanning-Tree Protocol.

IEEE 802.12   IEEE LAN standard that specifies the Physical layer and the MAC sublayer of the Data Link layer. IEEE 802.12 uses the demand priority media-access scheme at 100Mbps over a variety of physical media. See also 100VG-AnyLAN.

IEEE 802.2   IEEE LAN protocol that specifies an implementation of the LLC sublayer of the Data Link layer. IEEE 802.2 handles errors, framing, flow control, and the Network layer (Layer 3) service interface. Used in IEEE 802.3 and IEEE 802.5 LANs. See also IEEE 802.3 and IEEE 802.5.

IEEE 802.3   IEEE LAN protocol that specifies an implementation of the Physical layer and the MAC sublayer of the Data Link layer. IEEE 802.3 uses CSMA/CD access at a variety of speeds over a variety of physical media. Extensions to the IEEE 802.3 standard specify implementations for Fast Ethernet. Physical variations of the original IEEE 802.3 specification include 10Base2, 10Base5, 10BaseF, 10BaseT, and 10Broad36. Physical variations for Fast Ethernet include 100BaseT, 100BaseT4, and 100BaseX.

IEEE 802.4   IEEE LAN protocol that specifies an implementation of the Physical layer and the MAC sublayer of the Data Link layer. IEEE 802.4 uses token-passing access over a bus topology and is based on the token bus LAN architecture. See also token bus.

IEEE 802.5   IEEE LAN protocol that specifies an implementation of the Physical layer and MAC sublayer of the Data Link layer. IEEE 802.5 uses token passing access at 4 or 16Mbps over STP cabling and is similar to IBM Token Ring. See also Token Ring.

IEEE 802.6   IEEE MAN specification based on DQDB technology. IEEE 802.6 supports data rates of 1.5 to 155Mbps. See also DQDB.

IESG   Internet Engineering Steering Group. Organization, appointed by the IAB, that manages the operation of the IETF. See also IAB and IETF.

IETF   Internet Engineering Task Force. Task force consisting of over 80 working groups responsible for developing Internet standards. The IETF operates under the auspices of ISOC. See also ISOC.

IFIP   International Federation for Information Processing. Research organization that performs OSI prestandardization work. Among other accomplishments, IFIP formalized the original MHS model. See also MHS.

I-frame   Information frame. One of three SDLC frame formats. See also S-frame and U-frame.

IGMP   Internet Group Management Protocol. Used by IP hosts to report their multicast group memberships to an adjacent multicast router. See also multicast router.

IGP   Interior Gateway Protocol. Internet protocol used to exchange routing information within an autonomous system. Examples of common Internet IGPs include IGRP, OSPF, and RIP. See also IGRP in the Cisco Systems section, OSPF, and RIP.

IIH   IS-IS Hello. Message sent by all IS-IS systems to maintain adjacencies. See also IS-IS.

IISP   Interim-Interswitch Signaling Protocol. Formerly known as PNNI Phase 0, IISP is an ATM signaling protocol for inter-switch communication using manually configured prefix tables. When a signaling request is received by a switch, the switch checks the destination ATM address against the prefix table and notes the port with the longest prefix match. It then forwards the signaling request across that port using UNI procedures. IISP is an interim solution until PNNI Phase 1 is completed. Contrast with Dynamic IISP.

IITA   Information Infrastructure Technology and Applications. Component of the HPCC program intended to ensure U.S. leadership in the development of advanced information technologies. See also HPCC.

ILMI   Interim Local Management Interface. Specification developed by the ATM Forum for incorporating network-management capabilities into the ATM UNI.

IMP   interface message processor. Old name for ARPANET packet switches. See also packet switch.

INA   Information Networking Architecture. A Bellcore object-oriented architecture for the management of ATM and SONET equipment and services in an operating company environment.

INASoft   The Bellcore implementation of INA. See also INA.

in-band signaling   Transmission within a frequency range normally used for information transmission. Compare with out-of-band signaling.

information element   Used in signaling messages.

infrared   Electromagnetic waves whose frequency range is above that of microwaves, but below that of the visible spectrum. LAN systems based on this technology represent an emerging technology.

INE   Intelligent Network Element. A network element that can be provisioned from a remote OSS.

INOC   Internet Network Operations Center. BBN group that in the early days of the Internet monitored and controlled the Internet core gateways (routers). INOC no longer exists in this form.

insured burst   In an ATM network, the largest burst of data above the insured rate that will be temporarily allowed on a PVC and not tagged by the traffic policing function for dropping in the case of network congestion. The insured burst is specified in bytes or cells. Compare with maximum burst. See also insured rate.

insured rate   The long-term data throughput, in bits or cells per second, that an ATM network commits to support under normal network conditions. The insured rate is 100 percent allocated; the entire amount is deducted from the total trunk bandwidth along the path of the circuit. Compare with excess rate and maximum rate. See also insured burst.

insured traffic   Traffic within the insured rate specified for an ATM PVC. This traffic should not be dropped by the network under normal network conditions. See also CLP and insured rate.

Integrated IS-IS   Routing protocol based on the OSI routing protocol IS-IS, but with support for IP and other protocols. Integrated IS-IS implementations send only one set of routing updates, making it more efficient than two separate implementations. Formerly referred to as Dual IS-IS. Compare with IS-IS.

Integrated Services Internet   An IETF proposal for enhancing IP to allow it to support integrated or multimedia services, including traffic management mechanisms that closely match the traffic management mechanisms of ATM. An example is RSVP.

interarea routing   Term used to describe routing between two or more logical areas. Compare with intraarea routing.

interface   1. Connection between two systems or devices. 2. In routing terminology, a network connection. 3. In telephony, a shared boundary defined by common physical interconnection characteristics, signal characteristics, and meanings of interchanged signals. 4. The boundary between adjacent layers of the OSI model.

interface processor   Any of a number of processor modules used in the Cisco 7000 series routers. See AIP, CIP, EIP, FEIP, FIP, FSIP, HIP, MIP, SIP (Serial Interface Processor), and TRIP.

interference   Unwanted communication channel noise.

International Standards Organization   Erroneous expansion of the acronym ISO. See ISO.

Internet   Term used to refer to the largest global internetwork, connecting tens of thousands of networks worldwide and having a "culture" that focuses on research and standardization based on real-life use. Many leading-edge network technologies come from the Internet community. The Internet evolved in part from ARPANET. At one time, called the DARPA Internet. Not to be confused with the general term internet. See also ARPANET.

internet   Short for internetwork. Not to be confused with the Internet. See internetwork.

Internet protocol   Any protocol that is part of the TCP/IP protocol stack. See TCP/IP.

internetwork   Collection of networks interconnected by routers and other devices that functions (generally) as a single network. Sometimes called an internet, which is not to be confused with the Internet.

internetworking   General term used to refer to the industry that has arisen around the problem of connecting networks together. The term can refer to products, procedures, and technologies.

InterNIC   Organization that serves the Internet community by supplying user assistance, documentation, training, registration service for Internet domain names, and other services. Formerly called Network Information Center (NIC).

interoperability   Ability of computing equipment manufactured by different vendors to communicate with one another successfully over a network.

intra-area routing   Term used to describe routing within a logical area. Compare with interarea routing.

Inverse ARP   Inverse Address Resolution Protocol. Method of building dynamic routes in a network. Allows an access server to discover the network address of a device associated with a virtual circuit.

I/O   input/output.

IOC   Independent Operating Company. An independently owned company providing local telephone services to residential and business customers in a geographic area not served by an RBOC.

IP   Internet Protocol. Network layer protocol in the TCP/IP stack offering a connectionless internetwork service. IP provides features for addressing, type-of-service specification, fragmentation and reassembly, and security. Documented in RFC 791.

IP address   32-bit address assigned to hosts using TCP/IP. An IP address belongs to one of five classes (A, B, C, D, or E) and is written as 4 octets separated by periods (dotted decimal format). Each address consists of a network number, an optional subnetwork number, and a host number. The network and subnetwork numbers together are used for routing, while the host number is used to address an individual host within the network or subnetwork. A subnet mask is used to extract network and subnetwork information from the IP address. Classless interdomain routing (CIDR) provides a new way of representing IP addresses and subnet masks. Also called an Internet address. See also CIDR, IP, and subnet mask.

IPCP   IP Control Protocol. The protocol that establishes and configures IP over PPP. See also IP and PPP.

IP multicast   Routing technique that allows IP traffic to be propagated from one source to a number of destinations or from many sources to many destinations. Rather than sending one packet to each destination, one packet is sent to a multicast group identified by a single IP destination group address.

IPv6   IP Version 6. A replacement for the current version of IP (Version 4). IPv6 includes support for flow ID in the packet header, which can be used to identify flows. Formerly known as IPng (next generation).

IPSO   IP Security Option. U.S. government specification that defines an optional field in the IP packet header that defines hierarchical packet security levels on a per interface basis.

IPX   Internetwork Packet Exchange. NetWare network layer (Layer 3) protocol used for transferring data from servers to workstations. IPX is similar to IP and XNS.

IPXCP   IPX Control Protocol. The protocol that establishes and configures IPX over PPP. See also IPX and PPP.

IPXWAN Protocol that negotiates end-to-end options for new links. When a link comes up, the first IPX packets sent across are IPXWAN packets negotiating the options for the link. When the IPXWAN options have been successfully determined, normal IPX transmission begins. Defined by RFC 1362.

IRDP ICMP Router Discovery Protocol. Enables a host to determine the address of a router that it can use as a default gateway. Similar to ESIS, but used with IP. See also ES-IS.

IRN intermediate routing node. In SNA, a subarea node with intermediate routing capability.

IRSG Internet Research Steering Group. Group that is part of the IAB and oversees the activities of the IRTF. See also IAB and IRTF.

IRTF Internet Research Task Force. Community of network experts that consider Internet-related research topics. The IRTF is governed by the IRSG and is considered a subsidiary of the IAB. See also IAB and IRSG.

IS intermediate system. Routing node in an OSI network.

ISA Industry-Standard Architecture. 16-bit bus used for Intel-based personal computers. See also EISA.

isarithmic flow control Flow control technique that permits travel through the network. Possession of these permits grants the right to transmit. Isarithmic flow control is not commonly implemented.

ISDN Integrated Services Digital Network. Communication protocol, offered by telephone companies, that permits telephone networks to carry data, voice, and other source traffic. See also BISDN, BRI, N-ISDN, and PRI.

IS-IS Intermediate System-to-Intermediate System. OSI link-state hierarchical routing protocol based on DECnet Phase V routing whereby ISs (routers) exchange routing information based on a single metric to determine network topology. Compare with Integrated IS-IS. See also ES-IS and OSPF.

ISO International Organization for Standardization. International organization that is responsible for a wide range of standards, including those relevant to networking. ISO developed the OSI reference model, a popular networking reference model.

ISL Inter-Switch Link. A Cisco-proprietary protocol that maintains VLAN information as traffic flows between switches and routers

ISO 3309 HDLC procedures developed by ISO. ISO 3309:1979 specifies the HDLC frame structure for use in synchronous environments. ISO 3309:1984 specifies proposed modifications to allow the use of HDLC in asynchronous environments as well.

ISO 9000 Set of international quality-management standards defined by ISO. The standards, which are not specific to any country, industry, or product, allow companies to demonstrate that they have specific processes in place to maintain an efficient quality system.

ISOC Internet Society. International nonprofit organization, founded in 1992, that coordinates the evolution and use of the Internet. In addition, ISOC delegates authority to other groups related to the Internet, such as the IAB. ISOC is headquartered in Reston, Virginia, U.S.A. See also IAB.

isochronous transmission   Asynchronous transmission over a synchronous data link. Isochronous signals require a constant bit rate for reliable transport. Compare with asynchronous transmission, plesiochronous transmission, and synchronous transmission.

ISODE   ISO development environment. Large set of libraries and utilities used to develop upper-layer OSI protocols and applications.

ISP   Internet Service Provider. A company that provides Internet access to other companies and individuals.

ISR   Intermediate Session Routing. Initial routing algorithm used in APPN. ISR provides node-to-node connection-oriented routing. Network outages cause sessions to fail because ISR cannot provide nondisruptive rerouting around a failure. ISR has been replaced by HPR. Compare with HPR. See also APPN.

ISSI   Inter-Switching System Interface. Standard interface between SMDS switches.

ITU-T   International Telecommunication Union Telecommunication Standardization Sector. International body that develops worldwide standards for telecommunications technologies. The ITU-T carries out the functions of the former CCITT. See also CCITT.

IXC   inter-exchange carrier. A common carrier providing long distance connectivity between LATAs. The three major IXCs are AT&T, MCI, and Sprint, but several hundred IXCs offer long distance service in the US market.

jabber   1. Error condition in which a network device continually transmits random, meaningless data onto the network. 2. In IEEE 802.3, a data packet whose length exceeds that prescribed in the standard.

JANET   Joint Academic Network. X.25 WAN connecting university and research institutions in the United Kingdom.

jitter   Analog communication line distortion caused by the variation of a signal from its reference timing positions. Jitter can cause data loss, particularly at high speeds.

JPEG   Joint Photographics Expert Group. A graphic file format that has standard adopted as a standard by the ITU-T and the ISO. JPEG is most often used to compress still images using discrete cosine transform (DCT) analysis.

jumper   Electrical switch consisting of a number of pins and a connector that can be attached to the pins in a variety of different ways. Different circuits are created by attaching the connector to different pins.

JUNET   Japan UNIX Network. Nationwide, noncommercial network in Japan, designed to promote communication between Japanese and other researchers.

JvNCnet   John von Neumann Computer Network. Regional network, owned and operated by Global Enterprise Services, Inc., composed of T1 and slower serial links providing midlevel networking services to sites in the Northeastern United States.

Karn's algorithm   Algorithm that improves round-trip time estimations by helping transport layer protocols distinguish between good and bad round-trip time samples.

KB   kilobyte.

Kb   kilobit.

KBps   kilobytes per second.

Kbps   kilobits per second.

keepalive interval   Period of time between each keepalive message sent by a network device.

keepalive message   Message sent by one network device to inform another network device that the virtual circuit between the two is still active.

Kerberos   A developing standard for authenticating network users. Kerberos offers two key benefits: it functions in a multivendor network and it does not transmit passwords over the network.

Kermit   Popular file-transfer and terminal-emulation program.

kilobit   Abbreviated Kb.

kilobits per second   Abbreviated Kbps.

kilobyte   Abbreviated KB.

kilobytes per second   Abbreviated KBps.

L2F Protocol   Layer 2 Forwarding Protocol. A protocol that supports the creation of secure virtual private dial-up networks over the Internet.

label swapping   Routing algorithm used by APPN in which each router that a message passes through on its way to its destination independently determines the best path to the next router.

LAN   local-area network. High-speed, low-error data network covering a relatively small geographic area (up to a few thousand meters). LANs connect workstations, peripherals, terminals, and other devices in a single building or other geographically limited area. LAN standards specify cabling and signaling at the Physical and Data Link layers of the OSI model. Ethernet, FDDI, and Token Ring are widely used LAN technologies. Compare with MAN and WAN.

LANE   LAN emulation. Technology that allows an ATM network to function as a LAN backbone. The ATM network must provide multicast and broadcast support, address mapping (MAC-to-ATM), SVC management, and a usable packet format. LANE also defines Ethernet and Token Ring ELANs. See also ELAN.

LAN Manager   Distributed NOS, developed by Microsoft, that supports a variety of protocols and platforms. See also NOS.

LAN Server   Server-based NOS developed by IBM and derived from LNM. See also LNM.

LAN switch   High-speed switch that forwards packets between data-link segments. Most LAN switches forward traffic based on MAC addresses. This variety of LAN switch is sometimes called a frame switch. LAN switches are often categorized according to the method they use to forward traffic: cut-through packet switching or store-and-forward packet switching. Multilayer switches are an intelligent subset of LAN switches. Compare with multilayer switch. See also cut-through packet switching and store and forward packet switching.

LAPB   Link Access Procedure, Balanced. Data Link layer protocol in the X.25 protocol stack. LAPB is a bit-oriented protocol derived from HDLC. See also HDLC and X.25.

LAPD   Link Access Procedure on the D channel. ISDN Data Link layer protocol for the D channel. LAPD was derived from the LAPB protocol and is designed primarily to satisfy the signaling requirements of ISDN basic access. Defined by ITU-T Recommendations Q.920 and Q.921.

LAPM   Link Access Procedure for Modems. ARQ used by modems implementing the V.42 protocol for error correction. See also ARQ and V.42.

laser   light amplification by stimulated emission of radiation. Analog transmission device in which a suitable active material is excited by an external stimulus to produce a narrow beam of coherent light that can be modulated into pulses to carry data. Networks based on laser technology are sometimes run over SONET.

LAT   local-area transport. A network virtual terminal protocol developed by Digital Equipment Corporation.

LATA   local access and transport area. Geographic telephone dialing area serviced by a single local telephone company. Calls within LATAs are called "local calls." There are well over 100 LATAs in the United States.

latency   1. Delay between the time a device requests access to a network and the time it is granted permission to transmit. 2. Delay between the time when a device receives a frame and the time that frame is forwarded out the destination port.

LCI   logical channel identifier. See VCN.

LCN   logical channel number. See VCN.

LCP   Link Control Protocol. A protocol that establishes, configures, and tests data-link connections for use by PPP. See also PPP.

LCV   line code violation. The occurrence of a bipolar violation (BPV) or excessive zeros (EXZ) error event.

leaf internetwork   In a star topology, an internetwork whose sole access to other internetworks in the star is through a core router.

leaky bucket   In ATM, a metaphor for the generic cell rate algorithm (GCRA), which is used for conformance checking of cell flows from a user or network. The hole in the bucket represents the sustained rate at which cells can be accommodated and the bucket depth represents the tolerance for cell bursts over a period of time. See also GCRA.

learning bridge   Bridge that performs MAC address learning to reduce traffic on the network. Learning bridges manage a database of MAC addresses and the interfaces associated with each address. See also MAC address learning.

leased line   Transmission line reserved by a communications carrier for the private use of a customer. A leased line is a type of dedicated line. See also dedicated line.

LE_ARP   LAN Emulation Address Resolution Protocol. A protocol that provides the ATM address that corresponds to a MAC address.

LEC 1. LAN Emulation Client. Entity in an end system that performs data forwarding, address resolution, and other control functions for a single ES within a single ELAN. A LEC also provides a standard LAN service interface to any higher-layer entity that interfaces to the LEC. Each LEC is identified by a unique ATM address, and is associated with one or more MAC addresses reachable through that ATM address. See also ELAN and LES. 2. local exchange carrier. Local or regional telephone company that owns and operates a telephone network and the customer lines that connect to it.

LECS LAN Emulation Configuration Server. Entity that assigns individual LANE clients to particular ELANs by directing them to the LES that corresponds to the ELAN. There is logically one LECS per administrative domain, and this serves all ELANs within that domain. See also ELAN.

LED light emitting diode. Semiconductor device that emits light produced by converting electrical energy. Status lights on hardware devices are typically LEDs.

LEN node low-entry networking node. In SNA, a PU 2.1 that supports LU protocols, but chose CP cannot communicate with other nodes. Because there is no CP-to-CP session between a LEN node and its NN, the LEN node must have a statically defined image of the APPN network.

LES LAN Emulation Server. Entity that implements the control function for a particular ELAN. There is only one logical LES per ELAN, and it is identified by a unique ATM address. See also ELAN.

Level 1 router Device that routes traffic within a single DECnet or OSI area.

Level 2 router Device that routes traffic between DECnet or OSI areas. All Level 2 routers must form a contiguous network.

LGN logical group node. The node that represents its peer group in the peer group's higher-level peer group. See also peer group.

limited resource link Resource defined by a device operator to remain active only when being used.

line 1. In SNA, a connection to the network. 2. See link.

line card Any I/O card that can be inserted in a modular chassis.

line code type One of a number of coding schemes used on serial lines to maintain data integrity and reliability. The line code type used is determined by the carrier service provider. See also AMI, B8ZS, and HBD3.

line conditioning Use of equipment on leased voice-grade channels to improve analog characteristics, thereby allowing higher transmission rates.

line driver Inexpensive amplifier and signal converter that conditions digital signals to ensure reliable transmissions over extended distances.

line of sight Characteristic of certain transmission systems such as laser, microwave, and infrared systems in which no obstructions in a direct path between transmitter and receiver can exist.

line turnaround Time required to change data transmission direction on a telephone line.

link   Network communications channel consisting of a circuit or transmission path and all related equipment between a sender and a receiver. Most often used to refer to a WAN connection. Sometimes referred to as a line or a transmission link.

link-state routing algorithm   Routing algorithm in which each router broadcasts or multicasts information regarding the cost of reaching each of its neighbors to all nodes in the internetwork. Link state algorithms create a consistent view of the network and are therefore not prone to routing loops, but they achieve this at the cost of relatively greater computational difficulty and more widespread traffic (compared with distance vector routing algorithms). Compare with distance vector routing algorithm. See also Dijkstra's algorithm.

LIS   Logical IP Subnet. A group of IP nodes (such as hosts and routers) that connect to a single ATM network and belong to the same IP subnet.

little-endian   Method of storing or transmitting data in which the least significant bit or byte is presented first. Compare with big-endian.

LLAP   LocalTalk Link Access Protocol. The link-level protocol that manages node-to-node delivery of data a LocalTalk environment. LLAP manages bus access, provides a node-addressing mechanism, and controls data transmission and reception, ensuring packet length and integrity.

LLC   Logical Link Control. Higher of the two Data Link layer sublayers defined by the IEEE. The LLC sublayer handles error control, flow control, framing, and MAC-sublayer addressing. The most prevalent LLC protocol is IEEE 802.2, which includes both connectionless and connection-oriented variants. See also Data Link layer and MAC.

LLC2   Logical Link Control, type 2. Connection-oriented OSI LLC-sublayer protocol. See also LLC.

LMI   Local Management Interface. Set of enhancements to the basic Frame Relay specification. LMI includes support for a keepalive mechanism, which verifies that data is flowing; a multicast mechanism, which provides the network server with its local DLCI and the multicast DLCI; global addressing, which gives DLCIs global rather than local significance in Frame Relay networks; and a status mechanism, which provides an on-going status report on the DLCIs known to the switch. Known as LMT in ANSI terminology.

LM/X   LAN Manager for UNIX. Monitors LAN devices in UNIX environments.

LNNI   LAN Emulation Network-to-Network Interface. Supports communication between the server components within a single ELAN. Phase 1 LANE protocols do not allow for the standard support of multiple LESs or BUSs within an ELAN. Phase 2 addresses these limitations.

LNM   LAN Network Manager. SRB and Token Ring management package provided by IBM. Typically running on a PC, it monitors SRB and Token Ring devices, and can pass alerts up to NetView.

load balancing   In routing, the ability of a router to distribute traffic over all its network ports that are the same distance from the destination address. Good load-balancing algorithms use both line speed and reliability information. Load balancing increases the utilization of network segments, thus increasing effective network bandwidth.

local acknowledgment   Method whereby an intermediate network node, such as a router, responds to acknowledgments for a remote end host. Use of local acknowledgments reduces network overhead and, therefore, the risk of time-outs. Also known as local termination.

local bridge   Bridge that directly interconnects networks in the same geographic area.

local explorer packet   Generated by an end system in an SRB network to find a host connected to the local ring. If the local explorer packet fails to find a local host, the end system produces either a spanning explorer packet or an all-routes explorer packet. See also all-routes explorer packet, explorer packet, and spanning explorer packet.

local loop   Line from the premises of a telephone subscriber to the telephone company CO.

LocalTalk   Apple Computer's proprietary baseband protocol that operates at the Data Link and Physical layers of the OSI reference model. LocalTalk uses CSMA/CD and supports transmissions at speeds of 230.4Kbps.

local traffic filtering   Process by which a bridge filters out (drops) frames whose source and destination MAC addresses are located on the same interface on the bridge, thus preventing unnecessary traffic from being forwarded across the bridge. Defined in the IEEE 802.1 standard. See also IEEE 802.1.

logical channel   Nondedicated, packet-switched communications path between two or more network nodes. Packet switching allows many logical channels to exist simultaneously on a single physical channel.

loop   Route where packets never reach their destination, but simply cycle repeatedly through a constant series of network nodes.

loopback test   Test in which signals are sent and then directed back toward their source from some point along the communications path. Loopback tests are often used to test network interface usability.

lossy   Characteristic of a network that is prone to lose packets when it becomes highly loaded.

LPD   line printer daemon. Protocol used to send print jobs between UNIX systems.

LSA   link-state advertisement. Broadcast packet used by link-state protocols that contains information about neighbors and path costs. LSAs are used by the receiving routers to maintain their routing tables. Sometimes called a link-state packet (LSP).

LSP   link-state packet. See LSA.

LU   logical unit. Primary component of SNA, an LU is an NAU that enables end users to communicate with each other and gain access to SNA network resources.

LU 6.2   Logical Unit 6.2. IN SNA, an LU that provides peer-to-peer communication between programs in a distributed computing environment. APPC runs on LU 6.2 devices. See also APPC.

LUNI   LAN Emulation User-to-Network Interface. The ATM Forum standard for LAN emulation on ATM networks. LUNI defines the interface between the LAN Emulation Client (LEC) and the LAN Emulation Server components. See also BUS, LES, and LECS.

MAC   Media Access Control. Lower of the two sublayers of the Data Link layer defined by the IEEE. The MAC sublayer handles access to shared media, such as whether token passing or contention will be used. See also Data Link layer and LLC.

MAC address   Standardized Data Link layer address that is required for every port or device that connects to a LAN. Other devices in the network use these addresses to locate specific ports in the network and to create and update routing tables and data structures. MAC addresses are 6 bytes long and are controlled by the IEEE. Also known as a hardware address, a MAC-layer address, or a physical address. Compare with network address.

MAC address learning   Service that characterizes a learning bridge, in which the source MAC address of each received packet is stored so that future packets destined for that address can be forwarded only to the bridge interface on which that address is located. Packets destined for unrecognized addresses are forwarded out every bridge interface. This scheme helps minimize traffic on the attached LANs. MAC address learning is defined in the IEEE 802.1 standard. See also learning bridge and MAC address.

MacIP   Network layer protocol that encapsulates IP packets in Datagram Delivery Protocol (DDP) packets for transmission over AppleTalk. MacIP also provides proxy ARP services.

MAN   metropolitan-area network. Network that spans a metropolitan area. Generally, a MAN spans a larger geographic area than a LAN, but a smaller geographic area than a WAN. Compare with LAN and WAN.

managed object   In network management, a network device that can be managed by a network management protocol.

management services   SNA functions distributed among network components to manage and control an SNA network.

Manchester encoding   Digital coding scheme, used by IEEE 802.3 and Ethernet, in which a mid-bit-time transition is used for clocking, and a 1is denoted by a high level during the first half of the bit time.

MAP   Manufacturing Automation Protocol. Network architecture created by General Motors to satisfy the specific needs of the factory floor. MAP specifies a token-passing LAN similar to IEEE 802.4. See also IEEE 802.4.

MARS   Multicast Address Resolution Server. A mechanism for supporting IP multicast. A MARS serves a group of nodes (known as a cluster); each node in the cluster is configured with the ATM address of the MARS. The MARS supports multicast through multicast messages of overlaid point-to-multipoint connections or through multicast servers.

MAU   media attachment unit. Device used in Ethernet and IEEE 802.3 networks that provides the interface between the AUI port of a station and the common medium of the Ethernet. The MAU, which can be built into a station or can be a separate device, performs Physical Layer functions including the conversion of digital data from the Ethernet interface, collision detection, and injection of bits onto the network. Sometimes referred to as a media access unit, also abbreviated MAU, or as a transceiver. In Token Ring, a MAU is known as a multistation access unit and is usually abbreviated MSAU to avoid confusion. See also AUI and MSAU.

maximum burst   Specifies the largest burst of data above the insured rate that will be allowed temporarily on an ATM PVC, but will not be dropped at the edge by the traffic policing function, even if it exceeds the maximum rate. This amount of traffic will be allowed only temporarily; on average, the traffic source needs to be within the maximum rate. Specified in bytes or cells. Compare with insured burst. See also maximum rate.

maximum rate   Maximum total data throughput allowed on a given virtual circuit, equal to the sum of the insured and uninsured traffic from the traffic source. The uninsured data might be dropped if the network becomes congested. The maximum rate, which cannot exceed the media rate, represents the highest data throughput the virtual circuit will ever deliver, measured in bits or cells per second. Compare with excess rate and insured rate. See also maximum burst.

MB   megabyte. 1,000,000 bytes.

Mb   megabit. 1,000,000 bits.

MBS   maximum burst size. In an ATM signaling message, burst tolerance is conveyed through the MBS, which is coded as a number of cells. The burst tolerance together with the SCR and the GCRA determine the MBS that may be transmitted at the peak rate and still be in conformance with the GCRA.

MBONE   multicast backbone. The multicast backbone of the Internet. MBONE is a virtual multicast network composed of multicast LANs and the point-to-point tunnels that interconnect them.

Mbps   megabits per second.

MCA   micro channel architecture. Bus interface commonly used in PCs and some UNIX workstations and servers.

MCDV   maximum cell delay variation. In an ATM network, the maximum two-point CDV objective across a link or node for the specified service category. One of four link metrics exchanged using PTSPs to determine the available resources of an ATM network. There is one MCDV value of each traffic class.

MCLR   maximum cell loss ratio. In an ATM network, the maximum ratio of cells that do not successfully transit a link or node compared with the total number of cells that arrive at the link or node. One of four link metrics exchanged using PTSPs to determine the available resources of an ATM network. The MCLR applies to cells in the CBR and VBR traffic classes whose CLP bit is set to zero. See also CBR, CLP, PTSP, and VBR.

MCR   minimum cell rate. Parameter defined by the ATM Forum for ATM traffic management. MCR is defined only for ABR transmissions, and specifies the minimum value for the ACR. See also ABR (available bit rate), ACR, and PCR.

MCTD   maximum cell transfer delay. In an ATM network, the sum of the MCDV and the fixed delay component across the link or node. One of four link metrics exchanged using PTSPs to determine the available resources of an ATM network. There is one MCTD value for each traffic class. See also MCDV and PTSP.

MD   Mediation Device. A device that provides protocol translation and concentration of telemetry information originating from multiple network elements and transport to an OSS. See also OSS.

MD5   Message Digest 5. Algorithm used for message authentication in SNMP v.2. MD5 verifies the integrity of the communication, authenticates the origin, and checks for timeliness. See also SNMP2.

media   Plural of medium. The various physical environments through which transmission signals pass. Common network media include twisted-pair, coaxial and fiber-optic cable, and the atmosphere (through which microwave, laser, and infrared transmission occurs). Sometimes called physical media.

media rate   Maximum traffic throughput for a particular media type.

megabit   Abbreviated Mb. Approximately 1,000,000 bits.

megabits per second   Abbreviated Mbps.

megabyte   Abbreviated MB. Approximately 1,000,000 bytes.

mesh   Network topology in which devices are organized in a manageable, segmented manner with many, often redundant, interconnections strategically placed between network nodes. See also full mesh and partial mesh.

message   Application layer (Layer 7) logical grouping of information, often composed of a number of lower-layer logical groupings such as packets. The terms datagram, frame, packet, and segment are also used to describe logical information groupings at various layers of the OSI reference model and in various technology circles.

message switching   Switching technique involving transmission of messages from node to node through a network. The message is stored at each node until such time as a forwarding path is available. Contrast with circuit switching and packet switching.

message unit   Unit of data processed by any network layer.

metasignaling   Process running at the ATM layer that manages signaling types and virtual circuits.

MHS   message handling system. ITU-T X.400 recommendations that provide message handling services for communications between distributed applications. NetWare MHS is a different (though similar) entity that also provides message-handling services. See also IFIP.

MIB   Management Information Base. Database of network management information that is used and maintained by a network management protocol such as SNMP or CMIP. The value of a MIB object can be changed or retrieved using SNMP or CMIP commands, usually through a GUI network management system. MIB objects are organized in a tree structure that includes public (standard) and private (proprietary) branches.

MIC   media interface connector. FDDI de facto standard connector.

MID   message identifier. In ATM, used to identify ATM cells that carry segments from the same higher-layer packet.

microcode   Translation layer between machine instructions and the elementary operations of a computer. Microcode is stored in ROM and allows the addition of new machine instructions without requiring that they be designed into electronic circuits when new instructions are needed.

microsegmentation   Division of a network into smaller segments, usually with the intention of increasing aggregate bandwidth to network devices.

microwave   Electromagnetic waves in the range 1 to 30GHz. Microwave-based networks are an evolving technology gaining favor due to high bandwidth and relatively low cost.

midsplit   Broadband cable system in which the available frequencies are split into two groups: one for transmission and one for reception.

MII Media Independent Interface. A standard specification for the interface between network controller chips and their associated media interface chip(s). The MII automatically senses 10 and 100 MHz Ethernet speeds.

MILNET Military Network. Unclassified portion of the DDN. Operated and maintained by the DISA. See also DDN and DISA.

MIME Multipurpose Internet Mail Extensions. An Internet messages, as defined by RFC 822, consists of two parts: a header and a body. MIME defines a set of five extensions to RFC 822: a content type header field, a content transfer encoding header field, a MIME version header field, an optional content ID header field, and and optional content descriptions header field. MIME has become the standard for attaching non-text files to e-mail messages in a way that allows the attachment to be received intact over a network.

MIP MultiChannel Interface Processor. Interface processor on the Cisco 7000 series routers that provides up to two channelized T1 or E1 connections via serial cables to a CSU. The two controllers on the MIP can each provide up to 24 1 or 30 E1 channel-groups, with each channel-group presented to the system as a serial interface that can be configured individually.

mips millions of instructions per second. Number of instructions executed by a processor per second.

MLP Multilink PPP. A method of splitting, recombining, and sequencing datagrams across multiple logical data links.

MMP Multichassis Multilink PPP. Extends MLP support across multiple routers and access servers. MMP enables multiple routers and access servers to operate as a single, large dial-up pool, with a single network address and ISDN access number. MMP correctly handles packet fragmenting and reassembly when a user connection is split between two physical access devices.

modem modulator-demodulator. Device that converts digital and analog signals. At the source, a modem converts digital signals to a form suitable for transmission over analog communication facilities. At the destination, the analog signals are returned to their digital form. Modems allow data to be transmitted over voice-grade telephone lines.

modem eliminator Device allowing connection of two DTE devices without modems.

modulation Process by which the characteristics of electrical signals are transformed to represent information. Types of modulation include AM, FM, and PAM. See also AM, FM, and PAM.

MOP Maintenance Operation Protocol. Digital Equipment Corporation protocol that provides a way to perform primitive maintenance operations on DECnet systems. For example, MOP can be used to download a system image to a diskless station.

Mosaic Public-domain WWW browser, developed at the National Center for Supercomputing Applications (NCSA). See also browser.

MOSPF Multicast OSPF. Intradomain multicast routing protocol used in OSPF networks. Extensions are applied to the base OSPF unicast protocol to support IP multicast routing.

MPEG Motion Picture Experts Group. A standard for compressing video. MPEG1 is a bit stream standard for compressed video and audio optimized to fit into a bandwidth of 1.5 Mbps. MPEG2 is intended for higher quality video-on-demand applications and runs at data rates between 4 and 9Mbps. MPEG4 is a low-bit-rate compression algorithm intended for 64Kbps connections.

MPOA Multiprotocol over ATM. An ATM Forum standardization effort specifying how existing and future network-layer protocols such as IP, IPv6, Appletalk, and IPX run over an ATM network with directly attached hosts, routers, and multilayer LAN switches.

MQI Message Queuing Interface. International standard API that provides functionality similar to that of the RPC interface. In contrast to RPC, MQI is implemented strictly at the Application layer. See also RPC.

MSAU multistation access unit. Wiring concentrator to which all end stations in a Token Ring network connect. The MSAU provides an interface between these devices and the Token Ring interface of a router. Sometimes abbreviated MAU.

MTU maximum transmission unit. Maximum packet size, in bytes, that a particular interface can handle.

mu-law North American companding standard used in conversion between analog and digital signals in PCM systems. Similar to the European alaw. See also a-law and companding.

multiaccess network Network that allows multiple devices to connect and communicate simultaneously.

multicast Single packets copied by the network and sent to a specific subset of network addresses. These addresses are specified in the destination address field. Compare with broadcast and unicast.

multicast address Single address that refers to multiple network devices. Synonymous with group address. Compare with broadcast address and unicast address. See also multicast.

multicast forward VCC A VCC set up by the BUS to the LEC as a leaf in a point-to-multipoint connection.

multicast group Dynamically determined group of IP hosts identified by a single IP multicast address.

multicast router Router used to send IGMP query messages on their attached local networks. Host members of a multicast group respond to a query by sending IGMP reports noting the multicast groups to which they belong. The multicast router takes responsibility for forwarding multicast datagrams from one multicast group to all other networks that have members in the group. See also IGMP.

multicast send VCC In an ATM network, a bi-directional point-to-point VCC set up by a LEC to a BUS. One of three data connections defined by Phase 1 LANE. Compare with control distribute VCC and control direct VCC.

multicast server Establishes a one-to-many connection to each device in a VLAN, thus establishing a broadcast domain for each VLAN segment. The multicast server forwards incoming broadcasts only to the multicast address that maps to the broadcast address.

multidrop line Communications line having multiple cable access points. Sometimes called a multipoint line.

multihomed host Host attached to multiple physical network segments in an OSI CLNS network.

multihoming   Addressing scheme in IS-IS routing that supports assignment of multiple area addresses.

multilayer switch   Switch that filters and forwards packets based on MAC addresses and network addresses. A subset of LAN switch. Compare with LAN switch.

multimode fiber   Optical fiber supporting propagation of multiple frequencies of light. See also single-mode fiber.

multiple domain network   SNA network with multiple SSCPs. See also SSCP.

multiplexing   Scheme that allows multiple logical signals to be transmitted simultaneously across a single physical channel. Compare with demultiplexing.

multivendor network   Network using equipment from more than one vendor. Multivendor networks pose many more compatibility problems than single-vendor networks. Compare with single-vendor network.

mux   A multiplexing device. A mux combines multiple signals for transmission over a single line. The signals are demultiplexed, or separated, at the receiving end.

NACS   NetWare Asynchronous Communication Services. Novell software that supports Novell's Asynchronous I/O (AIO) and NetWare Asynchronous Support Interface (NASI) programming interfaces. NACS promotes the sharing of communications resources such as modems, asynchronous hosts, and X.25 network services.

NADN   nearest active downstream neighbor. In Token Ring or IEEE 802.5 networks, the closest downstream network device from any given device that is still active.

Nagle's algorithm   Actually two separate congestion control algorithms that can be used in TCP-based networks. One algorithm reduces the sending window; the other limits small datagrams.

NAK   Negative acknowledgment. Response sent from a receiving device to a sending device indicating that the information received contained errors. Compare to acknowledgment.

name caching   Method by which remotely discovered host names are stored by a router for use in future packet-forwarding decisions to allow quick access.

name resolution   Generally, the process of associating a name with a network location.

name server   Server connected to a network that resolves network names into network addresses.

NAP   network access point. Location for interconnection of Internet service providers in the United States for the exchange of packets.

NARP   NBMA Address Resolution Protocol. A functional subset of NHRP that returns only the address mappings of nodes that are directly connection the NBMA network. Compare with NHRP.

NAT   Network Address Translation. A mechanism for reducing the need for globally unique IP addresses. NAT allows an organization with addresses that are not globally unique to connect to the Internet by translating those addresses into globally routable address space. Also known as Network Address Translator.

NAU   network addressable unit. SNA term for an addressable entity. Examples include LUs, PUs, and SSCPs. NAUs generally provide upper-level network services. Compare with path control network.

NAUN   nearest active upstream neighbor. In Token Ring or IEEE 802.5 networks, the closest upstream network device from any given device that is still active.

NBFCP   NetBIOS Frames Control Protocol.

NBMA   nonbroadcast multiaccess. Term describing a multiaccess network that either does not support broadcasting (such as X.25) or in which broadcasting is not feasible (for example, an SMDS broadcast group or an extended Ethernet that is too large). See also multiaccess network.

NBP   Name Binding Protocol. AppleTalk transport-level protocol that translates a character string name into the DDP address of the corresponding socket client. NBP enables AppleTalk protocols to understand user-defined zones and device names by providing and maintaining translation tables that map names to their corresponding socket addresses.

NBS   National Bureau of Standards. Organization that was part of the U.S. Department of Commerce. Now known as NIST. See also NIST.

NCIA   native client interface architecture. SNA applications-access architecture, developed by Cisco, that combines the full functionality of native SNA interfaces at both the host and client with the flexibility of leveraging TCP/IP backbones. NCIA encapsulates SNA traffic on a client PC or workstation, thereby providing direct TCP/IP access while preserving the native SNA interface at the end-user level. In many networks, this capability obviates the need for a standalone gateway and can provide flexible TCP/IP access while preserving the native SNA interface to the host.

NCP   1. Network Control Program. In SNA, a program that routes and controls the flow of data between a communications controller (in which it resides) and other network resources. 2. Network Control Protocol. A series of protocols for establishing and configuring different network layer protocols, such as for AppleTalk over PPP. See also PPP.

NDIS   network driver interface specification. Microsoft's specification for a generic, hardware- and protocol-independent device driver for NICs.

NE   network element. In OSS, a single piece of telecommunications equipment used to perform a function or service integral to the underlying network.

NEBS   Network Equipment Building Systems. In OSS, the Bellcore requirement for equipment deployed in a central office environment. Covers spatial, hardware and crafts person interface, thermal, fire resistance, handling and transportation, earthquake and vibration, airborne contaminants, grounding, acoustical noise, illumination, EMC and ESD requirements.

NEARNET   Regional network in New England (United States) that links Boston University, Harvard University, and MIT. Now part of BBN Planet. See also BBN Planet.

neighboring routers   In OSPF, two routers that have interfaces to a common network. On multiaccess networks, neighbors are dynamically discovered by the OSPF Hello protocol.

NET   network entity title. Network addresses, defined by the ISO network architecture, and used in CLNS-based networks.

NetBEUI   NetBIOS Extended User Interface. An enhanced version of the NetBIOS protocol used by network operating systems such as LAN Manager, LAN Server, Windows for Workgroups and Windows NT. It formalizes the transport frame that was never standardized in NetBIOS and adds additional functions. NetBEUI implements the OSI LLC2 protocol. See also LLC2 and OSI.

NetBIOS   Network Basic Input/Output System. API used by applications on an IBM LAN to request services from lower-level network processes. These services might include session establishment and termination, and information transfer.

NETscout   Cisco network management application that provides an easy-to-use GUI for monitoring RMON statistics and protocol analysis information. NETscout also provides extensive tools that simplify data collection, analysis, and reporting. These tools allow system administrators to monitor traffic, set thresholds, and capture data on any set of network traffic for any segment.

NetView   IBM network management architecture and related applications. NetView is a VTAM application used for managing mainframes in SNA networks. See also VTAM.

NetWare   Popular distributed NOS developed by Novell. Provides transparent remote file access and numerous other distributed network services.

network   Collection of computers, printers, routers, switches, and other devices that are able to communicate with each other over some transmission medium.

network address   Network layer address referring to a logical, rather than a physical, network device. Also called a protocol address. Compare with MAC address.

network administrator   Person responsible for the operation, maintenance, and management of a network. See also network operator.

network analyzer   Hardware or software device offering various network troubleshooting features, including protocol-specific packet decodes, specific preprogrammed troubleshooting tests, packet filtering, and packet transmission.

network interface   Boundary between a carrier network and a privately-owned installation.

Network layer   Layer 3 of the OSI reference model. This layer provides connectivity and path selection between two end systems. The Network layer is the layer at which routing occurs. Corresponds roughly with the Path Control layer of the SNA model. See also Application layer, Data Link layer, Physical layer, Presentation layer, Session layer, and Transport layer.

network management   Generic term used to describe systems or actions that help maintain, characterize, or troubleshoot a network.

Network Node Server   SNA NN that provides resource location and route selection services for ENs, LEN nodes, and LUs that are in its domain.

network number   Part of an IP address that specifies the network to which the host belongs.

network operator   Person who routinely monitors and controls a network, performing such tasks as reviewing and responding to traps, monitoring throughput, configuring new circuits, and resolving problems. See also network administrator.

NFS   Network File System. As commonly used, a distributed file system protocol suite developed by Sun Microsystems that allows remote file access across a network. In actuality, NFS is simply one protocol in the suite. NFS protocols include NFS, RPC, XDR (External Data Representation), and others. These protocols are part of a larger architecture that Sun refers to as ONC. See also ONC.

NHRP   Next Hop Resolution Protocol. Protocol used by routers to dynamically discover the MAC address of other routers and hosts connected to a NBMA network. These systems can then directly communicate without requiring traffic to use an intermediate hop, increasing performance in ATM, Frame Relay, SMDS, and X.25 environments.

NHS   Next Hop Server. A server defined by the NHRP protocol that maintains next-hop resolution cache tables containing the IP-to-ATM address mappings of associated nodes and nodes that are reachable through routers served by the NHS.

NIC   network interface card. Board that provides network communication capabilities to and from a computer system. Also called an adapter. See also AUI.

NIS   Network Information Service. Protocol developed by Sun Microsystems for the administration of network-wide databases. The service essentially uses two programs: one for finding a NIS server and one for accessing the NIS databases.

N-ISDN   Narrowband ISDN. Communication standards developed by the ITU-T for baseband networks. Based on 64Kbps B channels and 16- or 64Kbps D channels. Contrast with BISDN also BRI, ISDN, and PRI.

NIST   National Institute of Standards and Technology. Formerly the NBS, this U.S. government organization supports and catalogs a variety of standards. See also NBS.

NLM   NetWare Loadable Module. Individual program that can be loaded into memory and function as part of the NetWare NOS.

NLSP   NetWare Link Services Protocol. Link-state routing protocol based on IS-IS. See also IS-IS.

NMA   Network Management and Analysis. A Bellcore OSS providing alarm surveillance and performance monitoring of intelligent network elements.

NMP   Network Management Processor. Processor module on the Catalyst 5000 switch used to control and monitor the switch.

NMS   network management system. System responsible for managing at least part of a network. An NMS is generally a reasonably powerful and well-equipped computer such as an engineering workstation. NMSs communicate with agents to help keep track of network statistics and resources.

NMVT   network management vector transport. SNA message consisting of a series of vectors conveying network management specific information.

NN   network node. SNA intermediate node that provides connectivity, directory services, route selection, intermediate session routing, data transport, and network management services to LEN nodes and ENs. The NN contains a CP that manages the resources of both the NN itself and those of the ENs and LEN nodes in its domain. NNs provideintermediate routing services by implementing the APPN PU 2.1 extensions. Compare with EN. See also CP.

NNI   Network-to-Network Interface. ATM Forum standard that defines the interface between two ATM switches that are both located in a private network or are both located in a public network. The interface between a public switch and private one is defined by the UNI standard. Also, the standard interface between two Frame Relay switches meeting the same criteria. Compare with UNI.

NOC   Network Operations Center. Organization responsible for maintaining a network.

node   1. Endpoint of a network connection or a junction common to two or more lines in a network. Nodes can be processors, controllers, or workstations. Nodes, which vary in routing and other functional capabilities, can be interconnected by links, and serve as control points in the network. Node is sometimes used generically to refer to any entity that can access a network, and is frequently used interchangeably with device. See also host. 2. In SNA, the basic component of a network, and the point at which one or more functional units connect channels or data circuits.

noise   Undesirable communications channel signals.

nonextended network   An AppleTalk Phase 2 network that supports addressing of up to 253 nodes and only one zone.

nonseed router   In AppleTalk, a router that must first obtain, and then verify, its configuration with a seed router before it can begin operation. See also seed router.

non-stub area   Resource-intensive OSPF area that carries a default route, static routes, intra-area routes, interarea routes, and external routes. Nonstub areas are the only OSPF areas that can have virtual links configured across them, and are the only areas that can contain an ASBR. Compare with stub area. See also ASBR and OSPF.

Northwest Net   NSF-funded regional network serving the Northwestern United States, Alaska, Montana, and North Dakota. Northwest Net connects all major universities in the region as well as many leading industrial concerns.

NOS   network operating system. Generic term used to refer to what are really distributed file systems. Examples of NOSs include LAN Manager, NetWare, NFS, and VINES.

NREN   National Research and Education Network. Component of the HPCC program designed to ensure U.S. technical leadership in computer communications through research and development efforts in state-of-the-art telecommunications and networking technologies. See also HPCC.

NRM   Normal Response mode. HDLC mode for use on links with one primary station and one or more secondary stations. In this mode, secondary stations can transmit only if they first receive a poll from the primary station.

NRZ   nonreturn to zero. NRZ signals maintain constant voltage levels with no signal transitions (no return to a zero-voltage level) during a bit interval. Compare with NRZI.

NRZI   nonreturn to zero inverted. NRZI signals maintain constant voltage levels with no signal transitions (no return to a zero-voltage level), but interpret the presence of data at the beginning of a bit interval as a signal transition and the absence of data as no transition. Compare with NRZ.

NSAP   network service access point. Network addresses, as specified by ISO. An NSAP is the point at which OSI Network Service is made available to a Transport layer (Layer 4) entity.

NSF   National Science Foundation. U.S. government agency that funds scientific research in the United States. The now-defunct NSFNET was funded by the NSF. See also NSFNET.

NSFNET   National Science Foundation Network. Large network that was controlled by the NSF and provided networking services in support of education and research in the United States, from 1986 to 1995. NSFNET is no longer in service.

NTRI   NCP/Token Ring Interconnection. Function used by ACF/NCP to support Token Ring-attached SNA devices. NTRI also provides translation from Token Ring-attached SNA devices (PUs) to switched (dial-up) devices.

null modem   Small box or cable used to join computing devices directly, rather than over a network.

NVE   network-visible entity. A resource that is addressable through a network. Typically, an NVE is a socket client for a service available in a node.

NVRAM   nonvolatile RAM. RAM that retains its contents when a unit is powered off.

NYSERNet   Network in New York (United States) with a T1 backbone connecting NSF, many universities, and several commercial concerns.

OAM cell   Operation, Administration, and Maintenance cell. ATM Forum specification for cells used to monitor virtual circuits. OAM cells provide a virtual circuit-level loopback in which a router responds to the cells, demonstrating that the circuit is up, and the router is operational.

OAM&P   Operations Administration Maintenance and Provisioning.

OARnet   Ohio Academic Resources Network. Internet service provider that connects a number of U.S. sites, including the Ohio supercomputer center in Columbus, Ohio.

object instance   Network management term referring to an instance of an object type that has been bound to a value.

OC   Optical Carrier. Series of physical protocols (OC-1, OC-2, OC-3, and so on), defined for SONET optical signal transmissions. OC signal levels put STS frames onto multimode fiber-optic line at a variety of speeds. The base rate is 51.84Mbps (OC-1); each signal level thereafter operates at a speed divisible by that number (thus, OC-3 runs at 155.52Mbps). See also SONET, STS-1, and STS-3c.

ODA   Open Document Architecture. ISO standard that specifies how documents are represented and transmitted electronically. Formerly called Office Document Architecture.

ODI   Open Data-Link Interface. Novell specification providing a standardized interface for NICs (network interface cards) that allows multiple protocols to use a single NIC. See also NIC.

OIM   OSI Internet Management. Group tasked with specifying ways in which OSI network management protocols can be used to manage TCP/IP networks.

OIR   online insertion and removal. Feature that permits the addition, replacement, or removal of cards without interrupting the system power, entering console commands, or causing other software or interfaces to shut down. Sometimes called hot swapping or power-on servicing.

ONA   Open Network Architecture. SNA/IBM.

ONC   Open Network Computing. Distributed applications architecture designed by Sun Microsystems, currently controlled by a consortium led by Sun. The NFS protocols are part of ONC. See also NFS.

ones density   Scheme that allows a CSU/DSU to recover the data clock reliably. The CSU/DSU derives the data clock from the data that passes through it. In order to recover the clock, the CSU/DSU hardware must receive at least one 1 bit value for every 8 bits of data that pass through it. Also called pulse density.

open architecture   Architecture with which third-party developers can legally develop products and for which public domain specifications exist.

open circuit   Broken path along a transmission medium. Open circuits will usually prevent network communication.

OPS/INE   Operations Provisioning System/Intelligent Network Element. A Bellcore OSS that provides provisioning services for intelligent network elements. See also OSS.

OSI   Open System Interconnection. International standardization program created by ISO and ITU-T to develop standards for data networking that facilitate multivendor equipment interoperability.

OSINET   International association designed to promote OSI in vendor architectures.

OSI reference model   Open System Interconnection reference model. Network architectural model developed by ISO and ITU-T. The model consists of seven layers, each of which specifies particular network functions such as addressing, flow control, error control, encapsulation, and reliable message transfer. The lowest layer (the Physical layer) is closest to the media technology. The lower two layers are implemented in hardware and software, while the upper five layers are implemented only in software. The highest layer (the Application layer) is closest to the user. The OSI reference model is used universally as a method for teaching and understanding network functionality. Similar in some respects to SNA. See Application layer, Data Link layer, Network layer, Physical layer, Presentation layer, Session layer, and Transport layer.

OSPF   Open Shortest Path First. Link-state, hierarchical IGP routing algorithm proposed as a successor to RIP in the Internet community. OSPF features include least-cost routing, multipath routing, and load balancing. OSPF was derived from an early version of the ISIS protocol. See also Enhanced IGRP, IGP, IGRP, IS-IS, and IP.

OSS Operations Support System. A network management system supporting a specific management function, such as alarm surveillance and provisioning, in a carrier network. Many of these systems are large centralized systems running on mainframes or minicomputers. Common OSSs used within an RBOC include NMA, OPS/INE, and TIRKS.

OUI Organizational Unique Identifier. The three octets assigned by the IEEE in a block of 48-bit LAN addresses.

outframe Maximum number of outstanding frames allowed in an SNA PU 2 server at any time.

out-of-band signaling Transmission using frequencies or channels outside the frequencies or channels normally used for information transfer. Out-of-band signaling is often used for error reporting in situations in which in-band signaling can be affected by whatever problems the network might be experiencing. Contrast with in-band signaling.

packet Logical grouping of information that includes a header containing control information and (usually) user data. Packets are most often used to refer to Network layer units of data. The terms datagram, frame, message, and segment are also used to describe logical information groupings at various layers of the OSI reference model and in various technology circles. See also PDU.

packet switch WAN device that routes packets along the most efficient path and allows a communications channel to be shared by multiple connections. Formerly called an IMP. See also IMP.

packet switching Networking method in which nodes share bandwidth with each other by sending packets. Compare with circuit switching and message switching. See also PSN.

PAD packet assembler/disassembler. Device used to connect simple devices (like character-mode terminals) that do not support the full functionality of a particular protocol to a network. PADs buffer data and assemble and disassemble packets sent to such end devices.

PAM pulse amplitude modulation. Modulation scheme where the modulating wave is caused to modulate the amplitude of a pulse stream. Compare with AM and FM. See also modulation.

PAP Password Authentication Protocol. Authentication protocol that allows PPP peers to authenticate one another. The remote router attempting to connect to the local router is required to send an authentication request. Unlike CHAP, PAP passes the password and host name or username in the clear (unencrypted). PAP does not itself prevent unauthorized access, but merely identifies the remote end. The router or access server then determines if that user is allowed access. PAP is supported only on PPP lines. Compare with CHAP.

parallel channel Channel that uses bus and tag cables as a transmission medium. Compare with ESCON channel. See also bus and tag channel.

parallelism Indicates that multiple paths exist between two points in a network. These paths might be of equal or unequal cost. Parallelism is often a network design goal: if one path fails, there is redundancy in the network to ensure that an alternate path to the same point exists.

parallel transmission Method of data transmission in which the bits of a data character are transmitted simultaneously over a number of channels. Compare with serial transmission.

PARC   Palo Alto Research Center. Research and development center operated by XEROX. A number of widely-used technologies were originally conceived at PARC, including the first personal computers and LANs.

parity check   Process for checking the integrity of a character. A parity check involves appending a bit that makes the total number of binary 1 digits in a character or word (excluding the parity bit) either odd (for odd parity) or even (for even parity).

partial mesh   Term describing a network in which devices are organized in a mesh topology, with some network nodes organized in a full mesh, but with others that are only connected to one or two other nodes in the network. A partial mesh does not provide the level of redundancy of a full mesh topology, but is less expensive to implement. Partial mesh topologies are generally used in the peripheral networks that connect to a fully meshed backbone. See also full mesh and mesh.

Password Authentication Protocol   See PAP.

Path Control layer   Layer 3 in the SNA architectural model. This layer performs sequencing services related to proper data reassembly. The Path Control layer is also responsible for routing. Corresponds roughly with the Network layer of the OSI model. See also Data Flow Control layer, Data Link Control layer, Physical Control layer, Presentation Services layer, Transaction Services layer, and Transmission Control layer.

path control network   SNA concept that consists of lower-level components that control the routing and data flow through an SNA network and handle physical data transmission between SNA nodes. Compare with NAU.

path name   Full name of a DOS, Mac OS, or UNIX file or directory, including all directory and subdirectory names. Consecutive names in a path name are typically separated by a backslash (\) for DOS, a colon (for the Mac OS), or a forward slash (/) for the UNIX operating system.

payload   Portion of a cell, frame, or packet that contains upper-layer information (data).

PBX   private branch exchange. Digital or analog telephone switchboard located on the subscriber premises and used to connect private and public telephone networks.

PCI   protocol control information. Control information added to user data to comprise an OSI packet. The OSI equivalent of the term header. See also header.

PCM   pulse code modulation. Transmission of analog information in digital form through sampling and encoding the samples with a fixed number of bits.

PCR   peak cell rate. Parameter defined by the ATM Forum for ATM traffic management. In CBR transmissions, PCR determines how often data samples are sent. In ABR transmissions, PCR determines the maximum value of the ACR. See also ABR (available bit rate), ACR, and CBR.

PDN   public data network. Network operated either by a government (as in Europe) or by a private concern to provide computer communications to the public, usually for a fee. PDNs enable small organizations to create a WAN without all the equipment costs of long-distance circuits.

PDU   protocol data unit. OSI term for packet. See also BPDU and packet.

peak rate   Maximum rate, in kilobits per second, at which a virtual circuit can transmit.

peer-to-peer computing Peer-to-peer computing calls for each network device to run both client and server portions of an application. Also describes communication between implementations of the same OSI reference model layer in two different network devices. Compare with client/server computing.

peer group A collection of ATM nodes that share identical topological databases and exchange full link state information with each other. Peer groups are arranged hierarchically to prevent excessive PTSP traffic, so each peer group has a parent peer group.

performance management One of five categories of network management defined by ISO for management of OSI networks. Performance management subsystems are responsible for analyzing and controlling network performance including network throughput and error rates. See also accounting management, configuration management, fault management, and security management.

peripheral node In SNA, a node that uses local addresses and is therefore not affected by changes to network addresses. Peripheral nodes require boundary function assistance from an adjacent subarea node.

P/F poll/final bit. Bit in bit-synchronous Data Link layer protocols that indicates the function of a frame. If the frame is a command, a 1 in this bit indicates a poll. If the frame is a response, a 1 in this bit indicates that the current frame is the last frame in the response.

PGL Peer Group Leader. In ATM, a node in a peer group that performs the functions of the LGN. Peer group leaders exchange PTSPs with peer nodes in the parent peer group to inform those nodes of the peer group's attributes and reachability and to progagate information about the parent group and the parent group's parents to the nodes in the peer group.

PGP Pretty Good Privacy. Public-key encryption application that allows secure file and message exchanges. There is some controversy over the development and use of this application, in part due to U.S. national security concerns.

phase Location of a position on an alternating wave form.

phase shift Situation in which the relative position in time between the clock and data signals of a transmission becomes unsynchronized. In systems using long cables at higher transmission speeds, slight variances in cable construction, temperature, and other factors can cause a phase shift, resulting in high error rates.

PHY 1. physical sublayer. One of two sublayers of the FDDI Physical layer. See also PMD. 2. Physical layer. In ATM, the Physical layer provides for the transmission of cells over a physical medium that connects two ATM devices. The PHY is comprised of two sublayers: PMD and TC.

Physical Control layer Layer 1 in the SNA architectural model. This layer is responsible for the physical specifications for the physical links between end systems. Corresponds to the Physical layer of the OSI model. See also Data Flow Control layer, Data Link Control layer, Path Control layer, Presentation Services layer, Transaction Services layer, and Transmission Control layer.

Physical layer Layer 1 of the OSI reference model. The Physical layer defines the electrical, mechanical, procedural and functional specifications for activating, maintaining, and deactivating the physical link between end systems. Corresponds with the Physical Control layer in the SNA model. See also Application layer, Data Link layer, Network layer, Presentation layer, Session layer, and Transport layer.

PHYSNET   Physics Network. Group of many DECnet-based physics research networks, including HEPnet. See also HEPnet.

piggybacking   Process of carrying acknowledgments within a data packet to save network bandwidth.

PIM   Protocol Independent Multicast. Multicast routing architecture that allows the addition of IP multicast routing on existing IP networks. PIM is unicast routing protocol independent and can be operated in two modes: dense mode and sparse mode. See also PIM dense mode and PIM sparse mode.

PIM Dense mode   One of the two PIM operational modes. PIM Dense mode is data-driven and resembles typical multicast routing protocols. Packets are forwarded on all outgoing interfaces until pruning and truncation occurs. In Dense mode, receivers are densely populated, and it is assumed that the downstream networks want to receive and will probably use the datagrams that are forwarded to them. The cost of using Dense mode is its default flooding behavior. Sometimes called Dense mode PIM or PIM DM. Contrast with PIM Sparse mode. See also PIM.

PIM Sparse mode   One of the two PIM operational modes. PIM Sparse mode tries to constrain data distribution so that a minimal number of routers in the network receive it. Packets are sent only if they are explicitly requested at the RP (rendezvous point). In Sparse mode, receivers are widely distributed, and the assumption is that downstream networks will not necessarily use the datagrams that are sent to them. The cost of using Sparse mode is its reliance on the periodic refreshing of explicit join messages and its need for RPs. Sometimes called Sparse mode PIM or PIM SM. Contrast with PIM Dense mode. See also PIM and rendezvous point.

ping   packet internet groper. ICMP echo message and its reply. Often used in IP networks to test the reachability of a network device.

ping-ponging   Phrase used to describe the actions of a packet in a two-node routing loop.

PLCP   Physical layer convergence procedure. Specification that maps ATM cells into physical media, such as T3 or E3, and defines certain management information.

PLSP   PNNI Link State Packet.

plesiochronous transmission   Term describing digital signals that are sourced from different clocks of comparable accuracy and stability. Compare with asynchronous transmission, isochronous transmission, and synchronous transmission.

PLIM   Physical layer interface module.

PLP   Packet Level Protocol. Network layer protocol in the X.25 protocol stack. Sometimes called X.25 Level 3 or X.25 Protocol. See also X.25.

PLU   Primary LU. The LU that is initiating a session with another LU. See also LU.

PMD   physical medium dependent. Sublayer of the FDDI Physical layer that interfaces directly with the physical medium and performs the most basic bit transmission functions of the network. See also PHY.

PNNI 1. Private Network-Network Interface. ATM Forum specification for distributing topology information between switches and clusters of switches that is used to compute paths through the network. The specification is based on well-known link-state routing techniques and includes a mechanism for automatic configuration in networks in which the address structure reflects the topology. 2. Private Network Node Interface. ATM Forum specification for signaling to establish point-to-point and point-to-multipoint connections across an ATM network. The protocol is based on the ATM Forum's UNI specification with additional mechanisms for source routing, crankback, and alternate routing of call setup requests.

point-to-multipoint connection One of two fundamental connection types. In ATM, a point-to-multipoint connection is a unidirectional connection in which a single source end-system (known as a root node) connects to multiple destination end-systems (known as leaves). Compare with point-to-point connection.

point-to-point connection One of two fundamental connection types. In ATM, a point-to-point connection can be a unidirectional or bidirectional connection between two ATM end-systems. Compare with point-to-multipoint connection.

poison reverse updates Routing updates that explicitly indicate that a network or subnet is unreachable, rather than implying that a network is unreachable by not including it in updates. Poison reverse updates are sent to defeat large routing loops.

policy routing Routing scheme that forwards packets to specific interfaces based on user-configured policies. Such policies might specify that traffic sent from a particular network should be forwarded out one interface, while all other traffic should be forwarded out another interface.

polling Access method in which a primary network device inquires, in an orderly fashion, whether secondaries have data to transmit. The inquiry occurs in the form of a message to each secondary that gives the secondary the right to transmit.

POP 1. point of presence. In OSS, a physical location where an interexchange carrier has installed equipment to interconnect with an LEC (local exchange carrier). 2. Post Office Protocol. Protocol that client e-mail applications use to retrieve mail from a mail server.

port 1. Interface on an internetworking device (such as a router). 2. In IP terminology, an upper-layer process that receives information from lower layers. Ports are numbered, and each numbered port is associated with a specific process. For example, SMTP is associated with port 25. A port number is also known as a well-known address. 3. To rewrite software or microcode so that it will run on a different hardware platform or in a different software environment from that for which it was originally designed.

POST power-on self test. Set of hardware diagnostics that runs on a hardware device when that device is powered up.

POTS plain old telephone service. See PSTN.

power-on servicing Feature that allows faulty components to be diagnosed, removed, and replaced while the rest of the device continues to operate normally. Sometimes abbreviated POS. Sometimes called hot swapping. See also OIR.

PPP Point-to-Point Protocol. A successor to SLIP, PPP provides router-to-router and host-to-network connections over synchronous and asynchronous circuits. Whereas SLIP was designed to work with IP, PPP was designed to work with several Network layer protocols, such as IP, IPX, and ARA. PPP also has built-in security mechanisms, such as CHAP and PAP. PPP relies on two protocols: LCP and NCP. See also CHAP, PAP, and SLIP.

Presentation layer   Layer 6 of the OSI reference model. This layer ensures that information sent by the Application layer of one system will be readable by the Application layer of another. The Presentation layer is also concerned with the data structures used by programs and therefore negotiates data transfer syntax for the Application layer. Corresponds roughly with the Presentation Services layer of the SNA model. See also Application layer, Data Link layer, Network layer, Physical layer, Session layer, and Transport layer.

Presentation Services layer   Layer 6 of the SNA architectural model. This layer provides network resource management, session presentation services, and some application management. Corresponds roughly with the Presentation layer of the OSI model. See also Data Flow Control layer, Data Link Control layer, Path Control layer, Physical Control layer, Transaction Services layer, and Transmission Control layer.

PRI   Primary Rate Interface. ISDN interface to primary rate access. Primary rate access consists of a single 64Kbps D channel plus 23 (T1) or 30 (E1) B channels for voice or data. Compare to BRI. See also BISDN, ISDN, and N-ISDN.

primary ring   One of the two rings that make up an FDDI or CDDI ring. The primary ring is the default path for data transmissions. Compare with secondary ring.

primary station   In bit-synchronous Data Link layer protocols such as HDLC and SDLC, a station that controls the transmission activity of secondary stations and performs other management functions such as error control through polling or other means. Primary stations send commands to secondary stations and receive responses. Also called, simply, a primary. See also secondary station.

print server   Networked computer system that fields, manages, and executes (or sends for execution) print requests from other network devices.

priority queuing   Routing feature in which frames in an interface output queue are prioritized based on various characteristics such as packet size and interface type.

process switching   1. Operation that provides full route evaluation and per-packet load balancing across parallel WAN links. Involves the transmission of entire frames to the router CPU where they are repackaged for delivery to or from a WAN interface, with the router making a route selection for each packet. Process switching is the most resource-intensive switching operation that the CPU can perform. 2. Packet processing performed at process level speeds, without the use of a route cache. Contrast with fast switching.

PROM   programmable read-only memory. ROM that can be programmed using special equipment. PROMs can be programmed only once. Compare with EPROM.

propagation delay   Time required for data to travel over a network, from its source to its ultimate destination.

protocol   Formal description of a set of rules and conventions that govern how devices on a network exchange information.

protocol converter   Enables equipment with different data formats to communicate by translating the data transmission code of one device to the data transmission code of another device.

protocol stack   Set of related communications protocols that operate together and, as a group, address communication at some or all of the seven layers of the OSI reference model. Not every protocol stack covers each layer of the model, and often a single protocol in the stack will address a number of layers at once. TCP/IP is a typical protocol stack.

protocol translator   Network device or software that converts one protocol into another, similar, protocol.

proxy   Entity that, in the interest of efficiency, essentially stands in for another entity.

proxy ARP   proxy Address Resolution Protocol. Variation of the ARP protocol in which an intermediate device (for example, a router) sends an ARP response on behalf of an end node to the requesting host. Proxy ARP can lessen bandwidth use on slow-speed WAN links. See also ARP.

proxy explorer   Technique that minimizes exploding explorer packet traffic propagating through an SRB network by creating an explorer packet reply cache, the entries of which are reused when subsequent explorer packets need to find the same host.

proxy polling   Technique that alleviates the load across an SDLC network by allowing routers to act as proxies for primary and secondary nodes, thus keeping polling traffic off of the shared links. Proxy polling has been replaced by SDLC Transport. See SDLC Transport.

PSDN   packet-switched data network. See PSN.

PSE   packet switch exchange. Essentially, a switch. The term PSE is generally used in reference to a switch in an X.25 packet-switch. See also switch.

PSN   packet-switched network. Network that utilizes packet-switching technology for data transfer. Sometimes called a packet-switched data network (PSDN). See packet switching.

PSTN   Public Switched Telephone Network. General term referring to the variety of telephone networks and services in place worldwide. Sometimes called plain old telephone service (POTS).

PTI   payload type identifier. A 3-bit descriptor in the ATM cell header indicating the type of payload that the cell contains. Payload types include user and management cells; one combination indicates that the cell is the last cell of an AAL5 frame.

PTSE   PNNI topology state element. A collection of PINNI information that is flooded among all logical notes within a peer group. See also peer group and PNNI.

PTSP   PNNI topology state packet. A type of PNNI routing packet used to exchange reachability and resource information among ATM switches to ensure that a connection request is routed to the destination along a path that has a high probability of meeting the requested QOS. Typically, PTSPs include bidirectional information about the transit behavior of particular nodes (based on entry and exit ports) and current internal state.

PTT   Post, Telephone, and Telegraph. Government agency that provides telephone services. PTTs exist in most areas outside North America and provide both local and long-distance telephone services.

PU   physical unit. SNA component that manages and monitors the resources of a node, as requested by an SSCP. There is one PU per node.

PU 2   Physical Unit 2. SNA peripheral node that can support only DLUs that require services from a VTAM host and that are only capable of performing the secondary LU role in SNA sessions.

PU 2.1   Physical Unit type 2.1. SNA network node used for connecting peer nodes in a peer-oriented network. PU 2.1 sessions do not require that one node reside on VTAM. APPN is based upon PU 2.1 nodes, which can also be connected to a traditional hierarchical SNA network.

PU 4   Physical Unit 4. Component of an IBM FEP capable of full-duplex data transfer. Each such SNA device employs a separate data and control path into the transmit and receive buffers of the control program.

PU 5   Physical Unit 5. Component of an IBM mainframe or host computer that manages an SNA network. PU 5 nodes are involved in routing within the SNA Path Control layer.

PUP   PARC Universal Protocol. Protocol similar to IP developed at PARC.

PVC   permanent virtual circuit. Virtual circuit that is permanently established. PVCs save bandwidth associated with circuit establishment and tear down in situations where certain virtual circuits must exist all the time. Called a permanent virtual connection in ATM terminology. Compare with SVC. See also virtual circuit.

PVP   permanent virtual path. Virtual path that consists of PVCs. See also PVC and virtual path.

PVP tunneling   permanent virtual path tunneling. A method of linking two private ATM networks across the public network using a virtual path. The public network transparently trunks the entire collection of virtual channels in the virtual path between the two private networks.

Q.2931   ITU-T specification, based on Q.931, for establishing, maintaining, and clearing network connections at the B-ISDN user-network interface. The UNI 3.1 specification is based on Q.2931. See also Q.931 and UNI.

Q.920/Q.921   ITU-T specifications for the ISDN UNI Data Link layer. See also UNI.

Q.922A   ITU-T specification for Frame Relay encapsulation.

Q.931   ITU-T specification for signaling to establish, maintain, and clear ISDN network connections. See also Q.93B.

Q.93B   ITU-T specification signaling to establish, maintain, and clear BISDN network connections. An evolution of ITU-T recommendation Q.931. See also Q.931.

QLLC   Qualified Logical Link Control. Data Link layer protocol defined by IBM that allows SNA data to be transported across X.25 networks.

QOS   quality of service. Measure of performance for a transmission system that reflects its transmission quality and service availability.

QOS parameters   quality of service parameters. Parameters that control the amount of traffic the source in an ATM network sends over an SVC. If any switch along the path cannot accommodate the requested QOS parameters, the request is rejected, and a rejection message is forwarded back to the originator of the request.

quartet signaling   Signaling technique used in 100VG-AnyLAN networks that allows data transmission at 100Mbps over four pairs of UTP cabling at the same frequencies used in 10BaseT networks. See also 100VG-AnyLAN.

query   Message used to inquire about the value of some variable or set of variables.

queue   1. Generally, an ordered list of elements waiting to be processed. 2. In routing, a backlog of packets waiting to be forwarded over a router interface.

queuing delay   Amount of time that data must wait before it can be transmitted onto a statistically multi-plexed physical circuit.

queuing theory   Scientific principles governing the formation or lack of formation of congestion on a network or at an interface.

RACE   Research on Advanced Communications in Europe. Project sponsored by the European Community (EC) for the development of broadband networking capabilities.

RDI   remote defect identication. In ATM, when the physical layer detects loss of signal or cell synchronization, RDI cells are used to report a VPC/VCC failure. RDI cells are sent upstream by a VPC/VCC endpoint to notify the source VPC/VCC endpoint of the downstream failure.

RADIUS   A database for authenticating modem and ISDN connections and for tracking connection time.

RAM   random-access memory. Volatile memory that can be read and written by a microprocessor.

RARE   Réseaux Associés pour la Recherche Européenne. Association of European universities and research centers designed to promote an advanced telecommunications infrastructure in the European scientific community. RARE merged with EARN to form TERENA. See also EARN and TERENA.

RARP   Reverse Address Resolution Protocol. Protocol in the TCP/IP stack that provides a method for finding IP addresses based on MAC addresses. Compare with ARP.

rate queue   Value that is associated with one or more virtual circuits, and that defines the speed at which an individual virtual circuit will transmit data to the remote end. Each rate queue represents a portion of the overall bandwidth available on an ATM link. The combined bandwidth of all configured rate queues should not exceed the total bandwidth available.

RBHC   regional Bell holding company. One of seven regional telephone companies formed by the breakup of AT&T. RBHCs differ from RBOCs in that RBHCs cross state boundaries.

RBOC   regional Bell operating company. Seven regional telephone companies formed by the breakup of AT&T. RBOCs differ from RBHCs in that RBOCs do not cross state boundaries.

RCP   Remote Copy Protocol. Protocol that allows users to copy files to and from a file system residing on a remote host or server on the network. The RCP protocol uses TCP to ensure the reliable delivery of data.

RCP server   Router or other device that acts as a server for RCP. See also RCP.

reassembly   The putting back together of an IP datagram at the destination after it has been fragmented either at the source or at an intermediate node. See also fragmentation.

redirect   Part of the ICMP and ES-IS protocols that allows a router to tell a host that using another router would be more effective.

redirector   Software that intercepts requests for resources within a computer and analyzes them for remote access requirements. If remote access is required to satisfy the request, the redirector forms an RPC and sends the RPC to lower-layer protocol software for transmission through the network to the node that can satisfy the request.

redistribution   Allowing routing information discovered through one routing protocol to be distributed in the update messages of another routing protocol. Sometimes called route redistribution.

redundancy   1. In internetworking, the duplication of devices, services, or connections so that, in the event of a failure, the redundant devices, services, or connections can perform the work of those that failed. See also redundant system. 2. In telephony, the portion of the total information contained in a message that can be eliminated without loss of essential information or meaning.

redundant system   Computer, router, switch, or other computer system that contains two or more of each of the most important subsystems, such as two disk drives, two CPUs, or two power supplies.

relay   OSI terminology for a device that connects two or more networks or network systems. A Data Link layer (Layer 2) relay is a bridge; a Network layer (Layer 3) relay is a router. See also bridge and router.

reliability   Ratio of expected to received keepalives from a link. If the ratio is high, the line is reliable. Used as a routing metric.

reload   The event of a Cisco router rebooting, or the command that causes the router to reboot.

remote bridge   Bridge that connects physically disparate network segments via WAN links.

rendezvous point   Router specified in PIM sparse mode implementations to track membership in multicast groups and to forward messages to known multicast group addresses. See also PIM sparse mode.

repeater   Device that regenerates and propagates electrical signals between two network segments. See also segment.

RF   radio frequency. Generic term referring to frequencies that correspond to radio transmissions. Cable TV and broadband networks use RF technology.

RFC   Request for Comments. Document series used as the primary means for communicating information about the Internet. Some RFCs are designated by the IAB as Internet standards. Most RFCs document protocol specifications such as Telnet and FTP, but some are humorous or historical. RFCs are available online from numerous sources.

RFI   radio frequency interference. Radio frequencies that create noise that interferes with information being transmitted across unshielded copper cabling.

RHC   regional holding company.

RIF   Routing Information Field. Field in the IEEE 802.5 header that is used by a source-route bridge to determine through which Token Ring network segments a packet must transit. A RIF is made up of ring and bridge numbers as well as other information.

RII   Routing Information Identifier. Bit used by SRT bridges to distinguish between frames that should be transparently bridged and frames that should be passed to the SRB module for handling.

ring   Connection of two or more stations in a logically circular topology. Information is passed sequentially between active stations. Token Ring, FDDI, and CDDI are based on this topology.

ring group   Collection of Token Ring interfaces on one or more routers that is part of a one-bridge Token Ring network.

ring latency   Time required for a signal to propagate once around a ring in a Token Ring or IEEE 802.5 network.

ring monitor   Centralized management tool for Token Ring networks based on the IEEE 802.5 specification. See also active monitor and standby monitor.

ring topology   Network topology that consists of a series of repeaters connected to one another by unidirectional transmission links to form a single closed loop. Each station on the network connects to the network at a repeater. While logically a ring, ring topologies are most often organized in a closed-loop star. Compare with bus topology, star topology, and tree topology.

RIP   Routing Information Protocol. IGP supplied with UNIX BSD systems. The most common IGP in the Internet. RIP uses hop count as a routing metric. See also Enhanced IGRP, hop count, IGP, IGRP, and OSPF.

RJ connector   registered jack connector. Standard connectors originally used to connect telephone lines. RJ connectors are now used for telephone connections and for 10BaseT and other types of network connections. RJ-11, RJ-12, and RJ-45 are popular types of RJ connectors.

RJE   remote job entry. Application that is batch-oriented, as opposed to interactive. In RJE environments, jobs are submitted to a computing facility, and output is received later.

rlogin   remote login. Terminal emulation program, similar to Telnet, offered in most UNIX implementations.

RM   Resource Management. The management of critical resources in an ATM network. Two critical resources are buffer space and trunk bandwidth. Provisioning may be used to allocate network resources in order to separate traffic flows according to service characteristics.

RMON   Remote Monitoring. MIB agent specification described in RFC 1271 that defines functions for the remote monitoring of networked devices. The RMON specification provides numerous monitoring, problem detection, and reporting capabilities.

ROLC   Routing over Large Clouds. A working group in IETF created to analyse and propose solutions to problems that arise when performing IP routing over large, shared media networks such as SMDS, Frame Relay, X.25, and ATM.

ROM   read-only memory. Nonvolatile memory that can be read, but not written, by the microprocessor.

root account   Privileged account on UNIX systems used exclusively by network or system administrators.

root bridge   Exchanges topology information with designated bridges in a spanning-tree implementation in order to notify all other bridges in the network when topology changes are required. This prevents loops and provides a measure of defense against link failure.

ROSE   Remote Operations Service Element. OSI RPC mechanism used by various OSI network application protocols.

route   Path through an internetwork.

routed protocol   Protocol that can be routed by a router. A router must be able to interpret the logical internetwork as specified by that routed protocol. Examples of routed protocols include AppleTalk, DECnet, and IP.

route extension   In SNA, a path from the destination subarea node through peripheral equipment to a NAU.

route map   Method of controlling the redistribution of routes between routing domains.

route summarization   Consolidation of advertised addresses in OSPF and IS-IS. In OSPF, this causes a single summary route to be advertised to other areas by an area border router.

router   Network layer device that uses one or more metrics to determine the optimal path along which network traffic should be forwarded. Routers forward packets from one network to another based on Network layer information. Occasionally called a gateway (although this definition of gateway is becoming increasingly outdated). Compare with gateway. See also relay.

routing   Process of finding a path to a destination host. Routing is very complex in large networks because of the many potential intermediate destinations a packet might traverse before reaching its destination host.

routing domain   Group of end systems and intermediate systems operating under the same set of administrative rules. Within each routing domain is one or more areas, each uniquely identified by an area address.

routing metric   Method by which a routing algorithm determines that one route is better than another. This information is stored in routing tables. Metrics include bandwidth, communication cost, delay, hop count, load, MTU, path cost, and reliability. Sometimes referred to simply as a metric. See also cost.

routing protocol   Protocol that accomplishes routing through the implementation of a specific routing algorithm. Examples of routing protocols include IGRP, OSPF, and RIP.

routing table   Table stored in a router or some other internetworking device that keeps track of routes to particular network destinations and, in some cases, metrics associated with those routes.

routing update   Message sent from a router to indicate network reachability and associated cost information. Routing updates are typically sent at regular intervals and after a change in network topology. Compare with flash update.

RPC   remote-procedure call. Technological foundation of client-server computing. RPCs are procedure calls that are built or specified by clients and executed on servers, with the results returned over the network to the clients. See also client/server computing.

RPF   Reverse Path Forwarding. Multicasting technique in which a multicast datagram is forwarded out of all but the receiving interface if the receiving interface is one used to forward unicast datagrams to the source of the multicast datagram.

RR   relative rate. In ATM, one of the congestion feedback modes provided by ABR service. In RR mode, switches set a bit in forward and backward RM cells to indicate congestion. See also ABR.

RS-232   Popular Physical layer interface. Now known as EIA/TIA-232. See EIA/TIA-232.

RS-422   Balanced electrical implementation of EIA/TIA-449 for high-speed data transmission. Now referred to collectively with RS-423 as EIA-530. See also EIA-530 and RS-423.

RS-423   Unbalanced electrical implementation of EIA/TIA-449 for EIA/TIA-232 compatibility. Now referred to collectively with RS-422 as EIA-530. See also EIA-530 and RS-422.

RS-449   Popular Physical layer interface. Now known as EIA/TIA-449. See EIA/TIA-449.

RSH   Remote Shell Protocol. Protocol that allows a user to execute commands on a remote system without having to log in to the system. For example, RSH can be used to remotely examine the status of a number of access servers without connecting to each communication server, executing the command, and then disconnecting from the communication server.

RP   Route Processor. Processor module on the Cisco 7000 series routers that contains the CPU, system software, and most of the memory components that are used in the router. Sometimes called a supervisory processor.

RSP   Route/Switch Processor. Processor module used in the Cisco 7500 series routers that integrates the functions of the RP and the SP. See also RP and SP.

RSRB   remote source-route bridging. SRB over WAN links. See also SRB.

RSUP   Reliable SAP Update Protocol. Bandwidth-saving protocol developed by Cisco for propagating services information. RSUP allows routers to reliably send standard Novell SAP packets only when the routers detect a change in advertised services. RSUP can transport network information either in conjunction with or independently of the Enhanced IGRP routing function for IPX.

RSVP   Resource Reservation Protocol. A protocol that supports the reservation of resources across an IP network. Applications running on IP end systems can use RSVP to indicate to other nodes the nature (bandwidth, jitter, maximum burst, and so on) of the packet streams they wish to receive. RSVP depends on IPv6. See also IPv6.

RTCP   RTP Control Protocol. A protocol that monitors the QOS of an IPv6 RTP connection and conveys information about the on-going session. See also RTP (Real-Time Transport Protocol).

RTMP   Routing Table Maintenance Protocol. Apple Computer's proprietary routing protocol. RTMP establishes and maintains the routing information that is required to route datagrams from any source socket to any destination socket in an AppleTalk network. Using RTMP, routers dynamically maintain routing tables to reflect changes in topology. RTMP was derived from RIP. See also RIP (Routing Table Protocol).

RTP   1. Routing Table Protocol. VINES routing protocol based on RIP. Distributes network topology information and aids VINES servers in finding neighboring clients, servers, and routers. Uses delay as a routing metric. See also SRTP. 2. Rapid Transport Protocol. Provides pacing and error recovery for APPN data as it crosses the APPN network. With RTP, error recovery and flow control are done end-to-end rather than at every node. RTP prevents congestion rather than reacts to it. 3. Real-Time Transport Protocol. One of the IPv6 protocols. RTP is designed to provide end-to-end network transport functions for applications transmitting real-time data, such as audio, video, or simulation data, over multicast or unicast network services. RTP provides services such as payload type identification, sequence numbering, timestamping, and delivery monitoring to real-time applications.

RTS   Request to Send. EIA/TIA-232 control signal that requests a data transmission on a communications line.

RTSP   Real Time Streaming Protocol. Enables the controlled delivery of real-time data, such as audio and video. Sources of data can include both live data feeds, such live audio and video, and stored content, such as pre-recorded events. It is designed to work with established protocols, such as RTP and HTTP, to provide a complete solution for streaming media over the Internet.

RTT   round-trip time. Time required for a network communication to travel from the source to the destination and back. RTT includes the time required for the destination to process the message from the source and generate a reply. RTT is used by some routing algorithms to aid in calculating optimal routes.

RU   request/response unit. Request and response messages exchanged between NAUs in an SNA network.

run-time memory   Memory accessed while a program runs.

SAC   single-attached concentrator. FDDI or CDDI concentrator that connects to the network by being cascaded from the master port of another FDDI or CDDI concentrator.

sampling rate   Rate at which samples of a particular waveform amplitude are taken.

SAP   1. service access point. Field defined by the IEEE 802.2 specification that is part of an address specification. Thus, the destination plus the DSAP define the recipient of a packet. The same applies to the SSAP. See also DSAP and SSAP. 2. Service Advertisement Protocol. IPX protocol that provides a means of informing network clients, via routers and servers, of available network resources and services. See also IPX.

SAR   segmentation and reassembly. One of the two sublayers of the AAL CPCS, responsible for dividing (at the source) and reassembling (at the destination) the PDUs passed from the CS. The SAR sublayer takes the PDUs processed by the CS and, after dividing them into 48-byte pieces of payload data, passes them to the ATM layer for further processing. See also AAL, ATM layer, CPCS, CS, and SSCS.

SAS   1. single attachment station. Device attached only to the primary ring of an FDDI ring. Also known as a Class B station. Compare with DAS. See also FDDI. 2. statically assigned socket. A socket that is permanently reserved for use by a designated process. In an AppleTalk network, SASs are numbered 1 to 127; they are reserved for use by specific socket clients and for low-level built-in network services.

satellite communication   Use of orbiting satellites to relay data between multiple earth-based stations. Satellite communications offer high bandwidth and a cost that is not related to distance between earth stations, long propagation delays, or broadcast capability.

SBus   Bus technology used in Sun SPARC-based workstations and servers. The SBus specification has been adopted by the IEEE as a new bus standard.

SCR   sustainable cell rate. Parameter defined by the ATM Forum for ATM traffic management. For VBR connections, SCR determines the long-term average cell rate that can be transmitted. See also VBR.

SCTE   serial clock transmit external. Timing signal that DTE echoes to DCE to maintain clocking. SCTE is designed to compensate for clock phase shift on long cables. When the DCE device uses SCTE instead of its internal clock to sample data from the DTE, it is better able to sample the data without error even if there is a phase shift in the cable. See also phase shift.

SDH Synchronous Digital Hierarchy. European standard that defines a set of rate and format standards that are transmitted using optical signals over fiber. SDH is similar to SONET, with a basic SDH rate of 155.52Mbps, designated at STM-1. See also SONET and STM-1.

SDLC Synchronous Data Link Control. SNA Data Link layer communications protocol. SDLC is a bit-oriented, full-duplex serial protocol that has spawned numerous similar protocols, including HDLC and LAPB. See also HDLC and LAPB.

SDLC broadcast Feature that allows a Cisco router that receives an all-stations broadcast on a virtual multidrop line to propagate the broadcast to each SDLC line that is a member of the virtual multidrop line.

SDLC Transport Cisco router feature with which disparate environments can be integrated into a single, high-speed, enterprise-wide network. Native SDLC traffic can be passed through point-to-point serial links with other protocol traffic multiplexed over the same links. Cisco routers can also encapsulate SDLC frames inside IP datagrams for transport over arbitrary (non-SDLC) networks. Replaces proxy polling. See also proxy polling.

SDLLC SDLC Logical Link Control. Cisco IOS feature that performs translation between SDLC and IEEE 802.2 type 2.

SDSL single-line digital subscriber line. One of four DSL technologies. SDSL delivers 1.544Mbps both downstream and upstream over a single copper twisted pair. The use of a single twisted pair limits the operating range of SDSL to 10,000 feet. Compare with ADSL, HDSL, and VDSL.

SDSU SMDS DSU. DSU for access to SMDS via HSSIs and other serial interfaces.

SDU service data unit. Unit of information from an upper-layer protocol that defines a service request to a lower-layer protocol.

SEAL simple and efficient AAL. Scheme used by AAL5 in which the SAR sublayer segments CS PDUs without adding additional fields. See also AAL, AAL5, CS, and SAR.

secondary See secondary station.

secondary ring One of the two rings making up an FDDI or CDDI ring. The secondary ring is usually reserved for use in the event of a failure of the primary ring. Compare to primary ring.

secondary station In bit-synchronous Data Link layer protocols such as HDLC, a station that responds to commands from a primary station. Sometimes referred to simply as a secondary. See also primary station.

Section DCC Section Data Communications Channel. In OSS, a 192Kbps data communications channel embedded in the section overhead for OAM&P traffic between two SONET network elements. See also OAM&P and SONET.

security management One of five categories of network management defined by ISO for management of OSI networks. Security management subsystems are responsible for controlling access to network resources. See also accounting management, configuration management, fault management, and performance management.

seed router   A router in an AppleTalk network that has the network number or cable range built in to its port descriptor. The seed router defines the network number or cable range for other routers in that network segment and responds to configuration queries from nonseed routers on its connected AppleTalk network, allowing those routers to confirm or modify their configurations accordingly. Each AppleTalk network must have at least one seed router. See also nonseed router.

segment   1. Section of a network that is bounded by bridges, routers, or switches. 2. In a LAN using a bus topology, a segment is a continuous electrical circuit that is often connected to other such segments with repeaters. 3. Term used in the TCP specification to describe a single Transport layer unit of information. The terms datagram, frame, message, and packet are also used to describe logical information groupings at various layers of the OSI reference model and in various technology circles.

serial transmission   Method of data transmission in which the bits of a data character are transmitted sequentially over a single channel. Compare with parallel transmission.

server   Node or software program that provides services to clients. See also back end, client, and front end.

service point   Interface between non-SNA devices and NetView that sends alerts from equipment unknown to the SNA environment.

session   1. Related set of communications transactions between two or more network devices. 2. In SNA, a logical connection enabling two NAUs to communicate.

Session layer   Layer 5 of the OSI reference model. This layer establishes, manages, and terminates sessions between applications and manages data exchange between Presentation layer entities. Corresponds to the Data Flow Control layer of the SNA model. See also Application layer, Data Link layer, Network layer, Physical layer, Presentation layer, and Transport layer.

SF   Super Frame. Common framing type used on T1 circuits. SF consists of 12 frames of 192 bits each, with the 193rd bit providing error checking and other functions. SF has been superseded by ESF, but is still widely used. Also called D4 framing. See also ESF.

S-frame   Supervisory frame. One of three SDLC frame formats. See also I-frame and U-frame.

SGMP   Simple Gateway Monitoring Protocol. Network management protocol that was considered for Internet standardization and later evolved into SNMP. Documented in RFC 1028. See also SNMP.

shielded cable   Cable that has a layer of shielded insulation to reduce EMI.

shortest-path routing   Routing that minimizes distance or path cost through application of an algorithm.

signaling   Process of sending a transmission signal over a physical medium for purposes of communication.

signaling packet   Generated by an ATM-connected device that wants to establish a connection with another such device. The signaling packet contains the ATM NSAP address of the desired ATM endpoint, as well as any QOS parameters required for the connection. If the endpoint can support the desired QOS, it responds with an accept message, and the connection is opened. See also QOS.

silicon switching   Switching based on the SSE, which allows the processing of packets independent of the SSP (Silicon Switch Processor) system processor. Silicon switching provides high-speed, dedicated packet switching. See also SSE and SSP (Silicon Switch Processor).

simplex   Capability for transmission in only one direction between a sending station and a receiving station. Broadcast television is an example of a simplex technology. Compare with full duplex and half duplex.

single-mode fiber   Fiber-optic cabling with a narrow core that allows light to enter only at a single angle. Such cabling has higher bandwidth than multimode fiber, but requires a light source with a narrow spectral width (for example, a laser). Also called monomode fiber. See also multimode fiber.

single-vendor network   Network using equipment from only one vendor. Single-vendor networks rarely suffer compatibility problems. See also multivendor network.

SIP   SMDS Interface Protocol. Used in communications between CPE and SMDS network equipment. Allows the CPE to use SMDS service for high-speed WAN internetworking. Based on the IEEE 802.6 DQDB standard. See also DQDB.

sliding window flow control   Method of flow control in which a receiver gives transmitter permission to transmit data until a window is full. When the window is full, the transmitter must stop transmitting until the receiver advertises a larger window. TCP, other transport protocols, and several Data Link layer protocols use this method of flow control.

SLIP   Serial Line Internet Protocol. Standard protocol for point-to-point serial connections using a variation of TCP/IP. Predecessor of PPP. See also CSLIP and PPP.

slotted ring   LAN architecture based on a ring topology in which the ring is divided into slots that circulate continuously. Slots can be either empty or full, and transmissions must start at the beginning of a slot.

SMAC   source MAC. MAC address specified in the Source Address field of a packet. Compare with DMAC. See also MAC address.

SMB   Server Message Block. File-system protocol used in LAN Manager and similar NOSs to package data and exchange information with other systems.

SMDS   Switched Multimegabit Data Service. High-speed, packet-switched, datagram-based WAN networking technology offered by the telephone companies. See also CBDS.

SMI   Structure of Management Information. Document (RFC 1155) specifying rules used to define managed objects in the MIB. See also MIB.

SMRP   Simple Multicast Routing Protocol. Specialized multicast network protocol for routing multimedia data streams on enterprise networks. SMRP works in conjunction with multicast extensions to the AppleTalk protocol.

SMT   Station Management. ANSI FDDI specification that defines how ring stations are managed.

SMTP   Simple Mail Transfer Protocol. Internet protocol providing electronic mail services.

SNA Systems Network Architecture. Large, complex, feature-rich network architecture developed in the 1970s by IBM. Similar in some respects to the OSI reference model, but with a number of differences. SNA is essentially composed of seven layers. See Data Flow Control layer, Data Link Control layer, Path Control layer, Physical Control layer, Presentation Services layer, Transaction Services layer, and Transmission Control layer.

SNADS SNA Distribution Services. Consists of a set of SNA transaction programs that interconnect and cooperate to provide asynchronous distribution of information between end users. One of three SNA transaction services. See also DDM and DIA.

SNAP Subnetwork Access Protocol. Internet protocol that operates between a network entity in the subnetwork and a network entity in the end system. SNAP specifies a standard method of encapsulating IP datagrams and ARP messages on IEEE networks. The SNAP entity in the end system makes use of the services of the subnetwork and performs three key functions: data transfer, connection management, and QOS selection.

SNI 1. Subscriber Network Interface. Interface for SMDS-based networks that connects CPE and an SMDS switch. See also UNI. 2. SNA Network Interconnection. IBM gateway connecting multiple SNA networks.

SNMP Simple Network Management Protocol. Network management protocol used almost exclusively in TCP/IP networks. SNMP provides a means to monitor and control network devices, and to manage configurations, statistics collection, performance, and security. See also SGMP and SNMP2.

SNMP communities Authentication scheme that enables an intelligent network device to validate SNMP requests.

SNMP2 SNMP Version 2. Version 2 of the popular network management protocol. SNMP2 supports centralized as well as distributed network management strategies, and includes improvements in the SMI, protocol operations, management architecture, and security. See also SNMP.

SNP sequence number protection.

SNPA subnetwork point of attachment. A Data Link layer address (such as an Ethernet address, X.25 address, or Frame Relay DLCI address). SNPA addresses are used to configure a CLNS route for an interface.

socket 1. Software structure operating as a communications end point within a network device. 2. An addressable entity within a node connected to an AppleTalk network; sockets are owned by software processes known as socket clients. AppleTalk sockets are divided into two groups: SASs, which are reserved for clients such as AppleTalk core protocols, and DASs, which are assigned dynamically by DDP upon request from clients in the node. An AppleTalk socket is similar in concept to a TCP/IP port.

socket client A software process or function implemented in an AppleTalk network node.

socket listener Software provided by a socket client to receive datagrams addressed to the socket.

socket number An 8-bit number that identifies a socket. A maximum of 254 different socket numbers can be assigned in an AppleTalk node.

SONET Synchronous Optical Network. High-speed (up to 2.5Gbps) synchronous network specification developed by Bellcore and designed to run on optical fiber. STS-1 is the basic building block of SONET. Approved as an international standard in 1988. See also SDH, STS-1, and STS-3c.

source address Address of a network device that is sending data. See also destination address.

SP Switch Processor. Cisco 7000-series processor module that acts as the administrator for all CxBus activities. Sometimes called ciscoBus controller. See also CxBus.

span 1. Full-duplex digital transmission line between two digital facilities. 2. Switched Port Analyzer. Feature of the Catalyst 5000 switch that extends the monitoring abilities of existing network analyzers into a switched Ethernet environment. SPAN mirrors the traffic at one switched segment onto a predefined SPAN port. A network analyzer attached to the SPAN port can monitor traffic from any of the other Catalyst switched ports.

spanning explorer packet Follows a statically configured spanning tree when looking for paths in an SRB network. Also known as a limited-route explorer packet or a single-route explorer packet. See also all-routes explorer packet, explorer packet, and local explorer packet.

spanning tree Loop-free subset of a network topology. See also spanning-tree algorithm and Spanning Tree Protocol.

spanning-tree algorithm Algorithm used by the Spanning Tree Protocol to create a spanning tree. Sometimes abbreviated STA. See also spanning tree and Spanning Tree Protocol.

Spanning Tree Protocol Bridge protocol that utilizes the spanning tree algorithm, enabling a learning bridge to dynamically work around loops in a network topology by creating a spanning tree. Bridges exchange BPDU messages with other bridges to detect loops, and then remove the loops by shutting down selected bridge interfaces. Refers to both the IEEE 802.1 Spanning Tree Protocol standard and the earlier Digital Equipment Corporation Spanning Tree Protocol upon which it is based. The IEEE version supports bridge domains and allows the bridge to construct a loop-free topology across an extended LAN. The IEEE version is generally preferred over the Digital version. Sometimes abbreviated STP. See also BPDU, learning bridge, MAC address learning, spanning tree, and spanning tree algorithm.

speed matching Feature that provides sufficient buffering capability in a destination device to allow a high-speed source to transmit data at its maximum rate, even if the destination device is a lower-speed device.

SPF shortest path first algorithm. Routing algorithm that iterates on length of path to determine a shortest-path spanning tree. Commonly used in link-state routing algorithms. Sometimes called Dijkstra's algorithm. See also link-state routing algorithm.

SPID service profile identifier. Number that some service providers use to define the services to which an ISDN device subscribes. The ISDN device uses the SPID when accessing the switch that initializes the connection to a service provider.

split-horizon updates Routing technique in which information about routes is prevented from exiting the router interface through which that information was received. Split-horizon updates are useful in preventing routing loops.

spoofing   1. Scheme used by routers to cause a host to treat an interface as if it were up and supporting a session. The router spoofs replies to keepalive messages from the host in order to convince that host that the session still exists. Spoofing is useful in routing environments such as DDR, in which a circuit-switched link is taken down when there is no traffic to be sent across it in order to save toll charges. See also DDR. 2. The act of a packet illegally claiming to be from an address from which it was not actually sent. Spoofing is designed to foil network security mechanisms such as filters and access lists.

spooler   Application that manages requests or jobs submitted to it for execution. Spoolers process the submitted requests in an orderly fashion from a queue. A print spooler is a common example of a spooler.

SPP   Sequenced Packet Protocol. Provides reliable, connection-based, flow-controlled packet transmission on behalf of client processes. Part of the XNS protocol suite.

SPX   Sequenced Packet Exchange. Reliable, connection-oriented protocol that supplements the datagram service provided by Network layer (Layer 3) protocols. Novell derived this commonly used NetWare transport protocol from the SPP of the XNS protocol suite.

SQE   signal quality error. Transmission sent by a transceiver back to the controller to let the controller know whether the collision circuitry is functional. Also called heartbeat.

SRAM   Type of RAM that retains its contents for as long as power is supplied. SRAM does not require constant refreshing, like DRAM. Compare with DRAM.

SRB   source-route bridging. Method of bridging originated by IBM and popular in Token Ring networks. In a SRB network, the entire route to a destination is predetermined, in real time, prior to the sending of data to the destination. Contrast with transparent bridging.

SRT   source-route transparent bridging. IBM bridging scheme that merges the two most prevalent bridging strategies, SRB and transparent bridging. SRT employs both technologies in one device to satisfy the needs of all ENs. No translation between bridging protocols is necessary. Compare with SR/TLB.

SR/TLB   source-route translational bridging. Method of bridging where source-route stations can communicate with transparent bridge stations with the help of an intermediate bridge that translates between the two bridge protocols. Compare with SRT.

SRTP   Sequenced Routing Update Protocol. Protocol that assists VINES servers in finding neighboring clients, servers, and routers. See also RTP (Routing Table Protocol).

SS7   Signaling System 7. Standard CCS system used with BISDN and ISDN. Developed by Bellcore. See also CCS.

SSAP   source service access point. The SAP of the network node designated in the Source field of a packet. Compare to DSAP. See also SAP (service access point).

SSCP   system services control points. Focal points within an SNA network for managing network configuration, coordinating network operator and problem determination requests, and providing directory services and other session services for network end users.

SSCP-PU session   Session used by SNA to allow an SSCP to manage the resources of a node through the PU. SSCPs can send requests to, and receive replies from, individual nodes in order to control the network configuration.

SSCOP   Service Specific Connection Oriented Protocol. A data link protocol that guarantees delivery of ATM signaling packets.

SSCS   service specific convergence sublayer. One of the two sublayers of any AAL. SSCS, which is service dependent, offers assured data transmission. The SSCS can be null as well, in classical IP over ATM or LAN emulation implementations. See also AAL, ATM layer, CPCS, CS, and SAR.

SSE   silicon switching engine. Routing and switching mechanism that compares the Data Link or Network layer header of an incoming packet to a silicon-switching cache, determines the appropriate action (routing or bridging), and forwards the packet to the proper interface. The SSE is directly encoded in the hardware of the SSP (Silicon Switch Processor) of a Cisco 7000 series router. It can therefore perform switching independently of the system processor, making the execution of routing decisions much quicker than if they were encoded in software. See also silicon switching and SSP.

SSP   1. Switch-to-Switch Protocol. Protocol specified in the DLSw standard that routers use to establish DLSw connections, locate resources, forward data, and handle flow control and error recovery. See also DLSw. See also SSP in the Cisco Systems section. 2. Silicon Switch Processor. High-performance silicon switch for Cisco 7000 series routers that provides distributed processing and control for interface processors. The SSP leverages the high-speed switching and routing capabilities of the SSE to dramatically increase aggregate router performance, minimizing performance bottlenecks at the interface points between the router and a high-speed backbone. See also silicon switching and SSE.

standard   Set of rules or procedures that are either widely used or officially specified. See also de facto standard and de jure standard.

standby monitor   Device placed in standby mode on a Token Ring network in case an active monitor fails. See also active monitor and ring monitor.

StarLAN   CSMA/CD LAN, based on IEEE 802.3, developed by AT&T.

star topology   LAN topology in which end points on a network are connected to a common central switch by point-to-point links. A ring topology that is organized as a star implements a unidirectional closed-loop star, instead of point-to-point links. Compare with bus topology, ring topology, and tree topology.

startup range   A range of values (from 65280-65534) from which an AppleTalk node selects the network number part of its provisional address if it has no other number saved.

static route   Route that is explicitly configured and entered into the routing table. Static routes take precedence over routes chosen by dynamic routing protocols.

statistical multiplexing   Technique whereby information from multiple logical channels can be transmitted across a single physical channel. Statistical multiplexing dynamically allocates bandwidth only to active input channels, making better use of available bandwidth and allowing more devices to be connected than with other multiplexing techniques. Also referred to as statistical time-division multiplexing or stat mux. Compare with ATDM, FDM, and TDM.

STM-1 Synchronous Transport Module level 1. One of a number of SDH formats that specifies the frame structure for the 155.52Mbps lines used to carry ATM cells. See also SDH.

store and forward packet switching Packet-switching technique in which frames are completely processed before being forwarded out the appropriate port. This processing includes calculating the CRC and checking the destination address. In addition, frames must be temporarily stored until network resources (such as an unused link) are available to forward the message. Contrast with cut-through packet switching.

STP 1. shielded twisted-pair. Two-pair wiring medium used in a variety of network implementations. STP cabling has a layer of shielded insulation to reduce EMI. Compare with UTP. See also twisted pair. 2. See Spanning Tree Protocol.

STS-1 Synchronous Transport Signal level 1. Basic building block signal of SONET, operating at 51.84Mbps. Faster SONET rates are defined as STS-n, where n is a multiple of 51.84Mbps. See also SONET.

STS-3c Synchronous Transport Signal level 3, concatenated. SONET format that specifies the frame structure for the 155.52Mbps lines used to carry ATM cells. See also SONET.

stub area OSPF area that carries a default route, intra-area routes, and interarea routes, but does not carry external routes. Virtual links cannot be configured across a stub area, and they cannot contain an ASBR. Compare to non-stub area. See also ASBR and OSPF.

stub network Network that has only a single connection to a router.

STUN serial tunnel. Router feature allowing two SDLC- or HDLC-compliant devices to connect to one another through an arbitrary multiprotocol topology (using Cisco routers) rather than through a direct serial link.

subarea Portion of an SNA network that consists of a subarea node and any attached links and peripheral nodes.

subarea node SNA communication controller or host that handles complete network addresses.

subchannel In broadband terminology, a frequency-based subdivision creating a separate communications channel.

subinterface One of a number of virtual interfaces on a single physical interface.

subnet address Portion of an IP address that is specified as the subnetwork by the subnet mask. See also IP address, subnet mask, and subnetwork.

subnet mask 32-bit address mask used in IP to indicate the bits of an IP address that are being used for the subnet address. Sometimes referred to simply as mask. See also address mask and IP address.

subnetwork 1. In IP networks, a network sharing a particular subnet address. Subnetworks are networks arbitrarily segmented by a network administrator in order to provide a multilevel, hierarchical routing structure while shielding the subnetwork from the addressing complexity of attached networks. Sometimes called a subnet. See also IP address, subnet address, and subnet mask. 2. In OSI networks, a collection of ESs and ISs under the control of a single administrative domain and using a single network access protocol.

subvector   A data segment of a vector in an SNA message. A subvector consists of a length field, a key that describes the subvector type, and subvector specific data.

SURAnet   Southeastern Universities Research Association Network. Network connecting universities and other organizations in the Southeastern United States. SURAnet, originally funded by the NSF and a part of the NSFNET, is now part of BBN Planet. See also BBN Planet, NSF, and NSFNET.

SVC   switched virtual circuit. Virtual circuit that is dynamically established on demand and is torn down when transmission is complete. SVCs are used in situations where data transmission is sporadic. Called a switched virtual connection in ATM terminology. Compare with PVC.

switch   1. Network device that filters, forwards, and floods frames based on the destination address of each frame. The switch operates at the Data Link layer of the OSI model. 2. General term applied to an electronic or mechanical device that allows a connection to be established as necessary and terminated when there is no longer a session to support.

switched LAN   LAN implemented with LAN switches. See LAN switch.

synchronization   Establishment of common timing between sender and receiver.

synchronous transmission   Term describing digital signals that are transmitted with precise clocking. Such signals have the same frequency, with individual characters encapsulated in control bits (called start bits and stop bits) that designate the beginning and end of each character. Compare with asynchronous transmission, isochronous transmission, and plesiochronous transmission.

sysgen   system generation. Process of defining network resources in a network.

T1   Digital WAN carrier facility. T1 transmits DS-1-formatted data at 1.544 Mbps through the telephone-switching network, using AMI or B8ZS coding. Compare with E1. See also AMI, B8ZS, and DS-1.

T3   Digital WAN carrier facility. T3 transmits DS-3-formatted data at 44.736 Mbps through the telephone switching network. Compare with E3. See also DS-3.

TABS   Telemetry Asynchronous Block Serial. An AT&T polled point-to-point or multi-point communication protocol that supports moderate data transfer rates over intra-office wire pairs.

TAC   Terminal Access Controller. Internet host that accepts terminal connections from dial-up lines.

TACACS   Terminal Access Controller Access Control System. Authentication protocol, developed by the DDN community, that provides remote access authentication and related services, such as event logging. User passwords are administered in a central database rather than in individual routers, providing an easily scalable network security solution. See also TACACS+ in the Cisco Systems section.

TACACS+   Proprietary Cisco enhancement to TACACS. Provides additional support for authentication, authorization, and accounting. See also TACACS.

tag switching   A high-performance, packet-forwarding technology that integrates Network layer (Layer 3) routing and Data Link layer (Layer 2) switching and provides scalable, high-speed switching in the network core. Tag switching is based on the concept of label swapping, in which packets or cells are assigned short, fixed-length labels that tell switching nodes how data should be forwarded.

tagged traffic   ATM cells that have their CLP bit set to 1. If the network is congested, tagged traffic can be dropped to ensure delivery of higher-priority traffic. Sometimes called DE (discard eligible) traffic. See also CLP.

TARP   TID Address Resolution Protocol. In OSS, a protocol that resolves a TL-1 Terminal Identifier (TID) to a CLNP address (NSAP).

TAXI 4B/5B   Transparent Asynchronous Transmitter/Receiver Interface 4-byte/5-byte. Encoding scheme used for FDDI LANs as well as for ATM. Supports speeds of up to 100 Mbps over multimode fiber. TAXI is the chipset that generates 4B/5B encoding on multimode fiber. See also 4B/5B local fiber.

TBOS protocol   Telemetry Byte Oriented Serial protocol. A protocol that transmits alarm, status, and control points between NE and OSS. TBOS defines one physical interface for direct connection between the telemetry equipment and the monitored equipment.

TC   transmission convergence. A sublayer of the ATM Physical layer (PHY) that transforms the flow of cells into a steady flow of bits for transmission over the physical medium. When transmitting, the TC sublayer maps the cells into the frame format, generates the header error check (HEC), and sends idle cells when there is nothing to send. When receiving, the TC sublayer delineates individual cells in the received bit stream and uses HEC to detect and correct errors. See also HEC and PHY.

T-carrier   TDM transmission method usually referring to a line or cable carrying a DS-1 signal.

TCP   Transmission Control Protocol. Connection-oriented Transport layer protocol that provides reliable full-duplex data transmission. TCP is part of the TCP/IP protocol stack. See also TCP/IP.

TCP/IP   Transmission Control Protocol/Internet Protocol. Common name for the suite of protocols developed by the U.S. DoD in the 1970s to support the construction of worldwide internetworks. TCP and IP are the two best-known protocols in the suite. See also IP and TCP.

TCU   trunk coupling unit. In Token Ring networks, a physical device that enables a station to connect to the trunk cable.

TDM   time-division multiplexing. Technique in which information from multiple channels can be allocated bandwidth on a single wire based on preassigned time slots. Bandwidth is allocated to each channel regardless of whether the station has data to transmit. Compare with ATDM, FDM, and statistical multiplexing.

TDR   time domain reflectometer. Device capable of sending signals through a network medium to check cable continuity and other attributes. TDRs are used to find Physical layer network problems.

TEI   terminal endpoint identifier. A subfield in the LAPD address field that identifies a given TE device on an ISDN interface.

TE   terminal equipment. Any ISDN-compatible device that may be attached to the network, such as a telephone, fax, or a computer.

telco   Abbreviation for telephone company.

telecommunications   Term referring to communications (usually involving computer systems) over the telephone network.

telephony   Science of converting sound to electrical signals and transmitting it between widely removed points.

telex   Teletypewriter service allowing subscribers to send messages over the PSTN.

Telnet   Standard terminal emulation protocol in the TCP/IP protocol stack. Telnet is used for remote terminal connection, enabling users to log in to remote systems and use resources as if they were connected to a local system. Telnet is defined in RFC 854.

Tempest   U.S. military standard. Electronic products adhering to the Tempest specification are designed to withstand EMP. See also EMP.

TERENA   Trans-European Research and Education Networking Association. Organization that promotes information and telecommunications technologies development in Europe. Formed by the merging of EARN and RARE. See also EARN and RARE.

termid   SNA cluster controller identification. Termid is meaningful only for switched lines. Also called Xid.

terminal   Simple device at which data can be entered or retrieved from a network. Generally, terminals have a monitor and a keyboard, but no processor or local disk drive.

terminal adapter   Device used to connect ISDN BRI connections to existing interfaces such as EIA/TIA-232. Essentially, an ISDN modem.

terminal emulation   Network application in which a computer runs software that makes it appear to a remote host as a directly attached terminal.

terminal server   Communications processor that connects asynchronous devices such as terminals, printers, hosts, and modems to any LAN or WAN that uses TCP/IP, X.25, or LAT protocols. Terminal servers provide the internetwork intelligence that is not available in the connected devices.

terminator   Device that provides electrical resistance at the end of a transmission line to absorb signals on the line, thereby keeping them from bouncing back and being received again by network stations.

TFTP   Trivial File Transfer Protocol. Simplified version of FTP that allows files to be transferred from one computer to another over a network.

TH   transmission header. SNA header that is appended to the SNA basic information unit (BIU). The TH uses one of a number of available SNA header formats. See also FID0, FID1, FID2, FID3, and FID4.

THC over X.25   Feature providing TCP/IP header compression over X.25 links, for purposes of link efficiency.

THEnet   Texas Higher Education Network. Regional network comprising over 60 academic and research institutions in the Texas (United States) area.

Thinnet   Term used to define a thinner, less expensive version of the cable specified in the IEEE 802.3 10Base2 standard. Compare with Cheapernet. See also 10Base2, Ethernet, and IEEE 802.3.

throughput   Rate of information arriving at, and possibly passing through, a particular point in a network system.

TIA   Telecommunications Industry Association. Organization that develops standards relating to telecommunications technologies. Together, the TIA and the EIA have formalized standards, such as EIA/TIA-232, for the electrical characteristics of data transmission. See also EIA.

TIC   Token Ring interface coupler. Controller through which an FEP connects to a Token Ring.

TIRKS   Trunk Information Record Keeping System. A Bellcore OSS that provides record keeping for interoffice trunk facilities. See also OSS.

time-out   Event that occurs when one network device expects to hear from another network device within a specified period of time, but does not. The resulting time-out usually results in a retransmission of information or the dissolving of the session between the two devices.

TL-1   Transaction Language One. The Bellcore term for intelligent network elements.

TLAP   TokenTalk Link Access Protocol. The link-access protocol used in a TokenTalk network. TLAP is built on top of the standard Token Ring Data Link layer.

TMN   Telecommunication Management Network. The ITU-T generic model for transporting and processing OAM&P information for a telecommunications network. See also OAM&P.

TN3270   Terminal emulation software that allows a terminal to appear to an IBM host as a 3278 Model 2 terminal.

TNotify   Time Notify. Specifies how often SMT initiates neighbor notification broadcasts. See also SMT.

token   Frame that contains control information. Possession of the token allows a network device to transmit data onto the network. See also token passing.

token bus   LAN architecture using token passing access over a bus topology. This LAN architecture is the basis for the IEEE 802.4 LAN specification. See also IEEE 802.4.

token passing   Access method by which network devices access the physical medium in an orderly fashion based on possession of a small frame called a token. Contrast with circuit switching and contention. See also token.

Token Ring   Token-passing LAN developed and supported by IBM. Token Ring runs at 4 or 16Mbps over a ring topology. Similar to IEEE 802.5. See also IEEE 802.5, ring topology, and token passing.

TokenTalk   Apple Computer's data-link product that allows an AppleTalk network to be connected by Token Ring cables.

TOP   Technical Office Protocol. OSI-based architecture developed for office communications.

topology   Physical arrangement of network nodes and media within an enterprise networking structure.

TOS   type of service. See COS (class of service).

TP0   Transport Protocol Class 0. OSI connectionless transport protocol for use over reliable subnetworks. Defined by ISO 8073.

TP4   Transport Protocol Class 4. OSI connection-based transport protocol. Defined by ISO 8073.

TPD   A mechanism used by some ATM switches that allows the remaining cells supporting an AAL5 frame to be discarded when one or more cells of that AAL5 frame have been dropped. This avoids sending partial AAL5 frames through the ATM network when they will have to be retransmitted by the sender. Compare with EPD.

traffic management   Techniques for avoiding congestion and shaping and policing traffic, Allows links to operate at high levels of utilization by scaling back lower-priority, delay-tolerant traffic at the edge of the network when congestion begins to occur.

traffic policing   Process used to measure the actual traffic flow across a given connection and compare it to the total admissable traffic flow for that connection. Traffic outside of the agreed upon flow can be tagged (where the CLP bit is set to 1) and can be discarded en route if congestion develops. Traffic policing is used in ATM, Frame Relay, and other types of networks. Also know as admission control, permit processing, rate enforcement, and UPC (usage parameter control). See also tagged traffic.

traffic profile   Set of COS attribute values assigned to a given port on an ATM switch. The profile affects numerous parameters for data transmitted from the port including rate, cell drop eligibility, transmit priority, and inactivity timer. See also COS.

traffic shaping   Use of queues to limit surges that can congest a network. Data is buffered and then sent into the network in regulated amounts to ensure that the traffic will fit within the promised traffic envelope for the particular connection. Traffic shaping is used in ATM, Frame Relay, and other types of networks. Also known as metering, shaping, and smoothing.

trailer   Control information appended to data when encapsulating the data for network transmission. Compare with header.

transaction   Result-oriented unit of communication processing.

Transaction Services layer   Layer 7 in the SNA architectural model. Represents user application functions, such as spreadsheets, word-processing, or electronic mail, by which users interact with the network. Corresponds roughly with the Application layer of the OSI reference model. See also Data Flow Control layer, Data Link Control layer, Path Control layer, Physical Control layer, Presentation Services layer, and Transaction Services layer.

transit bridging   Bridging that uses encapsulation to send a frame between two similar networks over a dissimilar network.

translational bridging   Bridging between networks with dissimilar MAC sublayer protocols. MAC information is translated into the format of the destination network at the bridge. Contrast with encapsulation bridging.

Transmission Control layer   Layer 4 in the SNA architectural model. This layer is responsible for establishing, maintaining, and terminating SNA sessions, sequencing data messages, and controlling session level flow. Corresponds to theTransport layer of the OSI model. See also Data Flow Control layer, Data Link Control layer, Path Control layer, Physical Control layer, Presentation Services layer, and Transaction Services layer.

transmission group   In SNA routing, one or more parallel communications links treated as one communications facility.

TRANSPAC   Major packet data network run by France Telecom.

transparent bridging   Bridging scheme often used in Ethernet and IEEE 802.3 networks in which bridges pass frames along one hop at a time based on tables associating end nodes with bridge ports. Transparent bridging is so named because the presence of bridges is transparent to network end nodes. Contrast with SRB.

Transport layer   Layer 4 of the OSI reference model. This layer is responsible for reliable network communication between end nodes. The Transport layer provides mechanisms for the establishment, maintenance, and termination of virtual circuits, transport fault detection and recovery, and information flow control. Corresponds to the Transmission Control layer of the SNA model. See also Application layer, Data Link layer, Network layer, Physical Layer, Presentation layer, and Session layer.

trap   Message sent by an SNMP agent to an NMS, console, or terminal to indicate the occurrence of a significant event, such as a specifically defined condition or a threshold that has been reached. See also alarm and event.

tree topology   LAN topology similar to a bus topology, except that tree networks can contain branches with multiple nodes. Transmissions from a station propagate the length of the medium and are received by all other stations. Compare with bus topology, ring topology, and star topology.

TRIP   Token Ring Interface Processor. High-speed interface processor on the Cisco 7000 series routers. The TRIP provides two or four Token Ring ports for interconnection with IEEE 802.5 and IBM Token Ring media with ports independently set to speeds of either 4 or 16Mbps.

trunk   Physical and logical connection between two switches across which network traffic travels. A backbone is composed of a number of trunks.

TTL   Time to Live. Field in an IP header that indicates how long a packet is considered valid.

tunneling   Architecture that is designed to provide the services necessary to implement any standard point-to-point encapsulation scheme. See also encapsulation.

TUD   trunk up-down. Protocol used in ATM networks that monitors trunks and detects when one goes down or comes up. ATM switches send regular test messages from each trunk port to test trunk line quality. If a trunk misses a given number of these messages, TUD declares the trunk down. When a trunk comes back up, TUD recognizes that the trunk is up, declares the trunk up, and returns it to service. See also trunk.

TULIP   TCP and UDP over Lightweight IP. A proposed protocol for running TCP and UDP applications over ATM.

TUNIP   TCP and UDP over Nonexistent IP. A proposed protocol for running TCP and UPD applications over ATM.

TUV   German test agency that certifies products to European safety standards.

twisted pair   Relatively low-speed transmission medium consisting of two insulated wires arranged in a regular spiral pattern. The wires can be shielded or unshielded. Twisted pair is common in telephony applications and is increasingly common in data networks. See also STP and UTP.

TWS   two-way simultaneous. Mode that allows a router configured as a primary SDLC station to achieve better utilization of a full-duplex serial line. When TWS is enabled in a multidrop environment, the router can poll a secondary station and receive data from that station while it sends data to or receives data from a different secondary station on the same serialline.

Type 1 operation   IEEE 802.2 (LLC) connectionless operation.

Type 2 operation   IEEE 802.2 (LLC) connection-oriented operation.

UART   Universal Asynchronous Receiver/Transmitter. Integrated circuit, attached to the parallel bus of a computer, used for serial communications. The UART translates between serial and parallel signals, provides transmission clocking, and buffers data sent to or from the computer.

UB Net/One   Ungermann-Bass Net/One. Routing protocol, developed by UB Networks, that uses hello packets and a path-delay metric, with end nodes communicating using the XNS protocol. There are a number of differences between the manner in which Net/One uses the XNS protocol and the usage common among other XNS nodes.

UBR   unspecified bit rate. QOS class defined by the ATM Forum for ATM networks. UBR allows any amount of data up to a specified maximum to be sent across the network, but there are no guarantees in terms of cell loss rate and delay. Compare with ABR (available bit rate), CBR, and VBR.

UBR+   unspecified bit rate plus. A UBR service complemented by ATM switches that use intelligent packet discard mechanisms such as EPD or TPD. See also EPD and TPD.

UDP   User Datagram Protocol. Connectionless Transport layer protocol in the TCP/IP protocol stack. UDP is a simple protocol that exchanges datagrams without acknowledgments or guaranteed delivery, requiring that error processing and retransmission be handled by other protocols. UDP is defined in RFC 768.

U-frame   Unnumbered frame. One of three SDLC frame formats. See also I-frame and S-frame.

UL   Underwriters Laboratories. Independent agency within the United States that tests product safety.

ULP   upper-layer protocol. Protocol that operates at a higher layer in the OSI reference model, relative to other layers. ULP is sometimes used to refer to the next-highest protocol (relative to a particular protocol) in a protocol stack.

unbalanced configuration   HDLC configuration with one primary station and multiple secondary stations.

UNI   User-Network Interface. ATM Forum specification that defines an interoperability standard for the interface between ATM-based products (a router or an ATM switch) located in a private network and the ATM switches located within the public carrier networks. Also used to describe similar connections in Frame Relay networks. See also NNI, Q.920/Q.921, and SNI (Subscriber Network Interface).

unicast   Message sent to a single network destination. Compare with broadcast and multicast.

unicast address   Address specifying a single network device. Compare with broadcast address and multicast address. See also unicast.

uninsured traffic   Traffic within the excess rate (the difference between the insured rate and maximum rate) for an ATM VCC. This traffic can be dropped by the network if congestion occurs. See also CLP, insured rate, and maximum rate.

unipolar   Literally meaning one polarity, the fundamental electrical characteristic of internal signals in digital communications equipment. Contrast with bipolar.

unity gain   In broadband networks, the balance between signal loss and signal gain through amplifiers.

UNIX   Operating system developed in 1969 at Bell Laboratories. UNIX has gone through several iterations since its inception. These include UNIX 4.3 BSD (Berkeley Standard Distribution), developed at the University of California at Berkeley, and UNIX System V, Release 4.0, developed by AT&T.

unnumbered frames   HDLC frames used for various control and management purposes, including link startup and shutdown, and mode specification.

UPC   usage parameter control. See traffic policing.

URL   Universal Resource Locator. Standardized addressing scheme for accessing hypertext documents and other services using a WWW browser. See also browser.

USENET   Initiated in 1979, one of the oldest and largest cooperative networks, with over 10,000 hosts and a quarter of a million users. Its primary service is a distributed conferencing service called news.

UTC   Universal Time Coordinated. Time zone at zero degrees longitude. Formerly known as Greenwich Mean Time (GMT) and zulu time.

UTP   unshielded twisted-pair. Four-pair wire medium used in a variety of networks. UTP does not require the fixed spacing between connections that is necessary with coaxial-type connections. There are five types of UTP cabling commonly used: Category 1 cabling, Category 2 cabling, Category 3 cabling, Category 4 cabling, and Category 5 cabling. Compare with STP. See also EIA/TIA-586 and twisted pair.

UUCP   UNIX-to-UNIX Copy Program. Protocol stack used for point-to-point communication between UNIX systems.

uuencode   UNIX-to-UNIX encoding. A method of converting binary files to ASCII so that they can be sent over the Internet via e-mail. The name comes from its use by the UNIX operating system's uuencode command. See also uudecode.

uudecode   UNIX-to-UNIX decode. A method of decoding ASCII files that were encoded using uuencode. See uuencode.

V.24   ITU-T standard for a Physical layer interface between DTE and DCE. V.24 is essentially the same as the EIA/TIA-232 standard. See also EIA/TIA-232.

V.25bis   ITU-T specification describing procedures for call setup and tear down over the DTE-DCE interface in a PSDN.

V.32   ITU-T standard serial line protocol for bidirectional data transmissions at speeds of 4.8 or 9.6Kbps. See also V.32bis.

V.32bis   ITU-T standard that extends V.32 to speeds up to 14.4Kbps. See also V.32.

V.34   ITU-T standard that specifies a serial line protocol. V.34 offers improvements to the V.32 standard, including higher transmission rates (28.8Kbps) and enhanced data compression. Compare with V.32.

V.35   ITU-T standard describing a synchronous, Physical layer protocol used for communications between a network access device and a packet network. V.35 is most commonly used in the United States and in Europe, and is recommended for speeds up to 48Kbps.

V.42   ITU-T standard protocol for error correction using LAPM. See also LAPM.

VBR   variable bit rate. QOS class defined by the ATM Forum for ATM networks. VBR is subdivided into a real time (RT) class and non-real time (NRT) class. VBR (RT) is used for connections in which there is a fixed timing relationship between samples. VBR (NRT) is used for connections in which there is no fixed timing relationship between samples, but that still need a guaranteed QOS. Compare with ABR (available bit rate), CBR, and UBR.

VCC   virtual channel connection. Logical circuit, made up of VCLs, that carries data between two end points in an ATM network. Sometimes called a virtual circuit connection. See also VCI, VCL, and VPI.

VCI   virtual channel identifier. 16-bit field in the header of an ATM cell. The VCI, together with the VPI, is used to identify the next destination of a cell as it passes through a series of ATM switches on its way to its destination. ATM switches use the VPI/VCI fields to identify the next network VCL that a cell needs to transit on its way to its final destination. The function of the VCI is similar to that of the DLCI in Frame Relay. Compare to DLCI. See also VCL and VPI.

VCL   virtual channel link. Connection between two ATM devices. A VCC is made up of one or more VCLs. See also VCC.

VCN   virtual circuit number. 12-bit field in an X.25 PLP header that identifies an X.25 virtual circuit. Allows DCE to determine how to route a packet through the X.25 network. Sometimes called LCI (logical channel identifier) or LCN (logical channel number).

VDSL   very-high-data-rate digital subscriber line. One of four DSL technologies. VDSL delivers 13Mbps to 52Mbps downstream and 1.5Mbps to 2.3Mbps upstream over a single twisted copper pair. The operating range if VDSL is limited to 1,000 to 4,500 feet. Compare with ADSL, HDSL, and SDSL.

vector   Data segment of an SNA message. A vector consists of a length field, a key that describes the vector type, and vector-specific data.

VF   variance factor. One of three link attributes exchanged using PTSPs to determine the available resources of an ATM network. VF is a relative measure CRM normalized by the variance of the aggregate cell rate on the link.

VINES   Virtual Integrated Network Service. NOS developed and marketed by Banyan Systems.

VIP   1. Versatile Interface Processor. Interface card used in Cisco 7000 and Cisco 7500 series routers. The VIP provides multilayer switching and runs the Cisco IOS software. The most recent version of the VIP is VIP2. 2. virtual IP. Function that enables the creation of logically separated switched IP workgroups across the switch ports of a Catalyst 5000 running Virtual Networking Services software. See also Virtual Networking Services.

virtual circuit   Logical circuit created to ensure reliable communication between two network devices. A virtual circuit is defined by a VPI/VCI pair, and can be either permanent (a PVC) or switched (an SVC). Virtual circuits are used in Frame Relay and X.25. In ATM, a virtual circuit is called a virtual channel. Sometimes abbreviated VC. See also PVC, SVC, VCI, virtual route, and VPI.

virtual connection   In ATM, a connection between end users that has a defined route and endpoints. See also PVC and SVC.

virtualization   Process of implementing a network based on virtual network segments. Devices are connected to virtual segments independent of their physical location and their physical connection to the network.

Virtual Networking Services   Software on some Catalyst 5000 switches that enables multiple workgroups to be defined across switches and offers traffic segmentation and access control

virtual path   Logical grouping of virtual circuits that connect two sites. See also virtual circuit.

virtual ring   Entity in an SRB network that logically connects two or more physical rings together either locally or remotely. The concept of virtual rings can be expanded across router boundaries.

virtual route   In SNA, a logical connection between subarea nodes that is physically realized as a particular explicit route. SNA terminology for virtual circuit. See also virtual circuit.

virtual subnet   A logical grouping of devices that share a common layer-3 subnet.

VLAN   virtual LAN. Group of devices on one or more LANs that are configured (using management software) so that they can communicate as if they were attached to the same wire, when in fact they are located on a number of different LAN segments. Because VLANs are based on logical instead of physical connections, they are extremely flexible.

VLI   virtual LAN internetwork. Internetwork composed of VLANs.
See VLAN.

VLSM   variable-length subnet mask. Ability to specify a different subnet mask for the same network number on different subnets. VLSM can help optimize available address space.

VP   virtual path. One of two types of ATM circuits identified by a VPI. A virtual path is a bundle of virtual channels, all of which are switched transparently across an ATM network based on a common VPI. See also VPI.

VPC   virtual path connection. Grouping of VCCs that share one or more contiguous VPLs. See also VCC and VPL.

VPI   virtual path identifier. 8-bit field in the header of an ATM cell. The VPI, together with the VCI, is used to identify the next destination of a cell as it passes through a series of ATM switches on its way to its destination. ATM switches use the VPI/VCI fields to identify the next VCL that a cell needs to transit on its way to its final destination. The function of the VPI is similar to that of the DLCI in Frame Relay. Compare with DLCI. See also VCI and VCL.

VPL   virtual path link. Within a virtual path, a group of unidirectional VCLs with the same end points. Grouping VCLs into VPLs reduces the number of connections to be managed, thereby decreasing network control overhead and cost. A VPC is made up of one or more VPLs.

VT-n   Virtual Tributary level n. The SONET format for mapping a lower-rate signal into a SONET payload. For example, VT-1.5 is used to transport a DS-1 signal. See also DS-1 and SONET.

VTAM   virtual telecommunications access method. Set of programs that control communication between LUs. VTAM controls data transmission between channel-attached devices and performs routing functions. See also LU.

VTP   Virtual Terminal Protocol. ISO application for establishing a virtual terminal connection across a network.

WAIS   Wide Area Information Server. A distributed database protocol developed by Thinking Machines Corporation to search for information over a network. WAIS supports full-text databases, which allows an entire document to be searched for a match (as opposed to other technologies that only allow an index of key words to be searched).

WAN   wide-area network. Data communications network that serves users across a broad geographic area and often uses transmission devices provided by common carriers. Frame Relay, SMDS, and X.25 are examples of WANs. Compare with LAN and MAN.

watchdog packet   Used to ensure that a client is still connected to a NetWare server. If the server has not received a packet from a client for a certain period of time, it sends that client a series of watchdog packets. If the station fails to respond to a predefined number of watchdog packets, the server concludes that the station is no longer connected and clears the connection for that station.

watchdog spoofing   Subset of spoofing that refers specifically to a router acting for a NetWare client by sending watchdog packets to a NetWare server to keep the session between client and server active. See also spoofing.

watchdog timer   1. Hardware or software mechanism that is used to trigger an event or an escape from a process unless the timer is periodically reset. 2. In NetWare, a timer that indicates the maximum period of time that a server will wait for a client to respond to a watchdog packet. If the timer expires, the server sends another watchdog packet (up to a set maximum). See also watchdog packet.

waveform coding   Electrical techniques used to convey binary signals.

W-DCS   Wideband Digital Crossconnect System. A SONET DCS capable of crossconnecting DS-1 and VT1.5 signals. See also DCS, DS-1, SONET, and VT-n.

wildcard mask   32-bit quantity used in conjunction with an IP address to determine which bits in an IP address should be ignored when comparing that address with another IP address. A wildcard mask is specified when setting up access lists.

WinSock   Windows Socket Interface . A software interface that allows a wide variety of applications to use and share an Internet connection. WinSock is implemented as dynamic link library (DLL) with some supporting programs, such as a dialer program that initiates the connection.

wiring closet   Specially designed room used for wiring a data or voice network. Wiring closets serve as a central junction point for the wiring and wiring equipment that is used for interconnecting devices.

WISCNET   TCP/IP network in Wisconsin (United States) connecting University of Wisconsin campuses and a number of private colleges. Links are 56Kbps and T1.

workgroup   Collection of workstations and servers on a LAN that are designed to communicate and exchange data with one another.

WorkGroup Director   Cisco SNMP-based network-management software tool. Workgroup Director runs on UNIX workstations either as a standalone application or integrated with another SNMP-based network management platform, providing a seamless, powerful management system for Cisco workgroup products. See also SNMP.

workgroup switching   Method of switching that provides high-speed (100Mbps) transparent bridging between Ethernet networks and high-speed translational bridging between Ethernet and CDDI or FDDI.

wrap   Action taken by an FDDI or CDDI network to recover in the event of a failure. The stations on each side of the failure reconfigure themselves, creating a single logical ring out of the primary and secondary rings.

WWW   World Wide Web. Large network of Internet servers providing hypertext and other services to terminals running client applications such as a browser. See also browser.

X.121   ITU-T standard describing an addressing scheme used in X.25 networks. X.121 addresses are sometimes called IDNs (International Data Numbers).

X.21   ITU-T standard for serial communications over synchronous digital lines. The X.21 protocol is used primarily in Europe and Japan.

X.21bis   ITU-T standard that defines the Physical layer protocol for communication between DCE and DTE in an X.25 network. Virtually equivalent to EIA/TIA-232. See also EIA/TIA-232 and X.25.

X.25   ITU-T standard that defines how connections between DTE and DCE are maintained for remote terminal access and computer communications in PDNs. X.25 specifies LAPB, a Data Link layer protocol, and PLP, a Network layer protocol. Frame Relay has to some degree superseded X.25. See also Frame Relay, LAPB, and PLP.

X.28   ITU-T recommendation that defines the terminal-to-PAD interface in X.25 networks. See also PAD and X.25.

X.29 ITU-T recommendation that defines the form for control information in the terminal-to-PAD interface used in X.25 networks. See also PAD and X.25.

X.3 ITU-T recommendation that defines various PAD parameters used in X.25 networks. See also PAD and X.25.

X3T9.5 Number assigned to the ANSI Task Group of Accredited Standards Committee for their internal, working document describing FDDI.

X.400 ITU-T recommendation specifying a standard for electronic mail transfer.

X.500 ITU-T recommendation specifying a standard for distributed maintenance of files and directories.

X.75 ITU-T specification that defines the signalling system between two PDNs. X.75 is essentially an NNI. See also NNI.

XDMCP X Display Manager Control Protocol. Protocol used to communicate between X terminals and workstations running the UNIX operating system.

XID exchange identification. Request and response packets exchanged prior to a session between a router and a Token Ring host. If the parameters of the serial device contained in the XID packet do not match the configuration of the host, the session is dropped.

XNS Xerox Network Systems. Protocol suite originally designed by PARC. Many PC networking companies, such as 3Com, Banyan, Novell, and UB Networks used or currently use a variation of XNS as their primary transport protocol. See also X Window System.

XRemote Protocol developed specifically to optimize support for the X Window System over a serial communications link.

XStream Major public PSN in the United States operated by MCI. Formerly called TYMNET.

X terminal Terminal that allows a user simultaneous access to several different applications and resources in a multivendor environment through implementation of X Windows. See also X Window System.

X Window System Distributed, network-transparent, device-independent, multitasking windowing and graphics system originally developed by MIT for communication between X terminals and UNIX workstations. See also X terminal.

zero code suppression Line coding scheme used for transmission clocking. Zero line suppression substitutes a one in the seventh bit of a string of eight consecutive zeros. See also ones density.

ZIP Zone Information Protocol. AppleTalk Session layer protocol that maps network numbers to zone names. ZIP is used by NBP to determine which networks contain nodes that belong to a zone. See also ZIP storm and zone.

ZIP storm   Broadcast storm that occurs when a router running AppleTalk propagates a route for which it currently has no corresponding zone name. The route is then forwarded by downstream routers, and a ZIP storm ensues. See also ZIP.

zone   In AppleTalk, a logical group of network devices. See also ZIP.

zone multicast address   A data-link-dependent multicast address at which a node receives the NBP broadcasts directed to its zone. See also NBP.

Index

Note to the Reader: Throughout this index **boldfaced** page numbers indicate primary discussions of a topic. *Italicized* page numbers indicate illustrations.

C

E

I

M

O

W

CISCO® STUDY GUIDES
FROM NETWORK PRESS®

- Prepare for Cisco certification with the experts
- Full coverage of each exam objective
- Hands-on labs and hundreds of sample questions

ISBN 0-7821-2381-3
768 pp; 7½" x 9"; $49.99
Hardcover

ISBN 0-7821-2403-8
832 pp; 7½" x 9"; $49.99
Hardcover

ISBN 0-7821-2571-9
704 pp; 7½" x 9"; $49.99
Hardcover
Available April 1999

CCDA: Cisco Certified Design Associate Study Guide
ISBN: 0-7821-2534-4; 800 pp; 7½" x 9"
$49.99; Hardcover; CD
Available May 1999

CCNP: Cisco Internetwork Troubleshooting Study Guide
ISBN 0-7821-2536-0; 704 pp; 7½ x 9
$49.99; Hardcover; CD
Available May 1999

CCNP: Configuring, Monitoring, and Troubleshooting Dial-Up Services Study Guide
ISBN 0-7821-2544-1; 704 pp; 7½" x 9"
$49.99; Hardcover; CD
Available July 1999

SYBEX®
www.sybex.com

CCNP: Advanced Cisco Router Configuration

Exam #640-403 Objectives

OBJECTIVE	CHAPTER
1) Describe the key requirements of a scalable internetwork.	1, 2
2) Select a Cisco IOS feature as a solution for a given internetwork requirement.	1
3) Describe causes of network congestion.	1, 2
4) List solutions for controlling network congestion.	1, 2
5) Introduction to Managing Traffic and Access.	3
6) Configure IP standard access lists.	3
7) Limit virtual terminal access.	3
8) Configure IP extended access lists.	3
9) Verify access list operation.	3
10) Configure an alternative to using access lists.	3
11) Configure an IP helper address to manage broadcasts.	3
12) Describe IPX/SPX traffic management issues.	7, 8
13) Filter IPX traffic using IPX access lists.	7
14) Manage IPX/SPX traffic over WAN.	7, 8
15) Verify IPX/SPX filter operation.	7
16) Describe the need for queuing in a large network.	4
17) Describe weighted fair queuing operation.	4
18) Configure priority.	4
19) Configure custom queuing.	4
20) Verify queuing operation.	4
21) List the key information routers needed to route data.	5
22) Compare distance vector and link-state protocol operation.	6
23) Given an IP address, use VLSMs to extend the use of the IP address.	5
24) Given a network plan that includes IP addressing, explain if a route summarization is or is not possible.	5
25) Define private addressing and determine when it can be used.	5
26) Define network address translation and determine when it can be used.	5
27) Explain why OSPF is better than RIP in a large internetwork.	6
28) Explain how OSPF discovers, chooses, and maintains routes.	6
29) Configure OSPF for proper operation.	6
30) Verify OSPF operation.	6
31) Describe the issues with interconnecting multiple areas and how OSPF addresses.	6
32) Explain the differences between the possible types of areas, routers, and LSAs.	6
33) Configure a multiarea OSPF network.	6
34) Verify OSPF operation.	6
35) Describe Enhanced IGRP features and operation.	6

NOTE Exam objectives are subject to change at any time without prior notice and at Cisco's sole discretion. Please visit Cisco's Web site (http://www.cisco.com/warp/public/10/wwtraining/certprog/testing/exam_objective.htm) for the most current listing of exam objectives.